SOVIET LAW AFTER STALIN

Part III.   Soviet Institutions and the Administration of Law

LAW IN EASTERN EUROPE

A series of publications
issued by the
Documentation Office for East European Law
University of Leyden

General Editor
F. J. M. FELDBRUGGE

No. 20

SIJTHOFF & NOORDHOFF   1979
Alphen aan den Rijn   The Netherlands
Germantown, Maryland   USA

SOVIET LAW AFTER STALIN

Part III

Soviet Institutions and the Administration of Law

Edited by

DONALD. B. BARRY, F.J.M. FELDBRUGGE,
GEORGE GINSBURGS, and PETER B. MAGGS

SIJTHOFF & NOORDHOFF   1979
Alphen aan den Rijn   The Netherlands
Germantown, Maryland   USA

ISBN 90 286 0679 3

Library of Congress Catalog Card Number: LC 79-90672

Copyright © 1979 Sijthoff & Noordhoff International Publishers B.V.,
Alphen aan den Rijn, The Netherlands

Printed in The Netherlands

TABLE OF CONTENTS

TABLE OF ABBREVIATIONS

BNA	*Biulleten' Normativnykh Aktov Ministerstv i Vedomstv SSSR* [Bulletin of Normative Acts of the Ministries and Departments of the USSR]
BVS RSFSR	*Biulleten' Verkhovnogo Suda RSFSR* [Bulletin of the RSFSR Supreme Court]
BVS SSR	*Biulleten' Verkhovnogo Suda SSSR* [Bulletin of the USSR Supreme Court]
CC	Criminal Code
CCP	Code of Criminal Procedure
CDSP	*Current Digest of the Soviet Press*
CJA	Commission on Juvenile Affairs
CPSU	Communist Party of the Soviet Union
Ezhen. Sov. Iust.	*Ezhenedel'nik Sovietskoi Iustitsii* [The Weekly of Soviet Justice]
FPCL	Fundamental Principles of Criminal Law of the USSR and Union Republics
FPCLL	Fundamental Principles of Corrective Labor Law of the USSR and the Union Republics
FPCivL	Fundamental Principles of Civil Legislation of the USSR and Union Republics
FPCP	Fundamental Principles of Criminal Procedure of the USSR and Union Republics
FPLL	Fundamental Principles of Labor Legislation of the USSR and the Union Republics
FZMK	*Fabzavmestkom* [Factory, Plant, and Local Committee]
KZoT	*Kodeks Zakonov o Trude* [Code of Laws on Labor]
KTS	*Kommissiia po Trudovym Sporam* [Commission on Labor Disputes]
LG	*Literaturnaia Gazeta* [Literary Gazette]
NKT	*Narodnyi Komissariat Truda* [People's Commissariat of Labor]
PC	Production conference
PPO	Primary Party Organization
Pravovedenie	*Izvestiia Vysshikh Uchebnykh Zavedenii: Pravovedenie* [News of the Higher Educational Institutions: Legal Science]
SGiP	*Sovetskoe Gosudarstvo i Pravo* [Soviet State and Law]

SNK	*Sovet Narodnykh Komissarov* [Council of People's Commissars]
(S)TUO	(Soviet)Trade Union Organization
Sobr. Post RSFSR (or *SSSR*)	*Sobranie postanovlenii pravitel'stva RSFSR* (or *SSSR*) [Collected Decrees of the Government of the RSFSR (or USSR)]
Sobr. Uzak.	*Sobranie uzakonenii i rasporiazhenii rabochego i krest'ianskogo pravitel'stva RSFSR* [Collected Laws and Regulations of the Workers' and Peasants' [Government of the RSFSR]
Sobr. Zak. RSFSR	*Sobranie zakonov i rasporiazhenii raboche-krest'-ianskogo pravitel'stva RSFSR* [Collected Laws and Regulations of the Workers' and Peasants' Government of the RSFSR]
Sobr. Zak. SSSR	*Sobranie zakonov i rasporiazhenii raboche-krest'-ianskogo pravitel'stva SSSR* [Collected Laws and Regulations of the Workers' and Peasants' Government of the USSR]
Sots. Issled.	*Sotsiologicheskoe Issledovanie* [Sociological Research]
Sots. Zak.	*Sotsialisticheskaia Zakonnost'* [Socialist Legality]
Sov. Iust.	*Sovetskaia Iustitsiia* [Soviet Justice]
(U) TQH	(Unified) Tariff-Qualifications Handbook
UZ	*Uchenye Zapiski* [Scholarly Notes (followed by the name of the sponsoring institution)]
Ved. V.S. RSFSR	*Vedomosti Verkhovnogo Soveta RSFSR* [Gazette of the RSFSR Supreme Soviet]
Ved. V.S. SSSR	*Vedomosti Verkhovnogo Soveta SSSR* [Gazette of the USSR Supreme Soviet]
VLU (ser. obshch. nauk.)	*Vestnik Leningradskogo Universiteta, seriia obshchestvennykh nauk* [Herald of Leningrad University: Social Science Series]
VMU (pravo)	*Vestnik Moskovskogo Universiteta: Pravo* [Herald of Moscow University: Law]
VTsIK	(*Vserossiiskii*) *Tsentral'nyi Ispolnitel'nyi Komitet* [(All-Russian) Central Executive Committee]
VTsSPS	*Vsesoiuznyi Tsentral'nyi Soiuz Professional'nykh Soiuzov* [All-Union Central Council of Trade Unions]
ZSK	*Zhilishchnostroitel'nye kooperativy* [Housing Construction Cooperatives]

Participants and observers at the international conference "Soviet Institutions and the Administration of Law" commemorating the 25th anniversary of the Documentation Office for East European Law of the University of Leyden Faculty of Law

August 16-18, 1978 Leyden, The Netherlands

INTRODUCTION

This is the final part of a three-volume publication containing the results of extensive research on legal developments in the Soviet Union since the death of Stalin. The research has been conducted by a group of specialists from the United States, Canada, and several European countries under a grant from the Ford Foundation. The first volume was published in 1977 and the second volume in 1978.

All three volumes attempt to review broad sectors of Soviet law, albeit from different vantage points. The first volume (*The Citizen and the State in Contemporary Soviet Law*) concentrated on various legal aspects of the relationships between the individual and the Soviet state; in the second volume, social engineering was the key concept. *Soviet Institutions and the Administration of Law* is the title of the present volume.

The three themes do not stand for watertight compartments in which Soviet law may be divided. They are interrelated, and it would be therefore possible to transfer occasional studies from one volume to another without upsetting the general framework. Nonetheless, the accent in the present volume is on the people and the institutions which are primarily involved in making Soviet law work: the Procuracy, the Bar, jurisconsults, notaries, military courts, and others. The final study by Professor Sharlet goes into the most fundamental question of the overall role of the Communist Party in the administration of justice. Together, we believe that these three volumes cover recent developments in all the main areas of Soviet law.

The third meeting of the research group was planned to coincide with the 25th anniversary of the Documentation Office for East European Law of the University of Leyden Faculty of Law. It took place in the historic "Gravensteen" building of the Law Faculty on August 16-18, 1978. The meeting brought together the members of the original research group and an almost equal number of European specialists, many of whom contributed co-reports which have been incorporated in this volume. An Epilogue to the contents of the three volumes concludes this work.

The authors would like to thank the Ford Foundation, the University of Leyden, and the Leyden Faculty of Law for the financial support and hospitality which made the conference and the publication of this volume possible.

A photograph of the participants and observers in the August, 1978, conference appears on the page facing this introduction, and a list of conference participants and observers appears below:

Donald D. Barry, Lehigh University

René Beermann, Institute of Soviet and East European Studies, University of Glasgow

Ger P. van den Berg, Documentation Office for East European Law, University of Leyden Faculty of Law

William E. Butler, University College London, Faculty of Laws

G. Crespi Reghizzi, University of Pavia Faculty of Law

F. J. M. Feldbrugge, Documentation Office for East European Law, University of Leyden Faculty of Law

Felice Gaer, The Ford Foundation, New York City

George Ginsburgs, Rutgers University School of Law, Camden

John N. Hazard, Columbia University School of Law

William Jeffrey, Jr., University of Cincinnati College of Law

Erik H. de Jong, Documentation Office for East European Law, University of Leyden Faculty of Law

Peter H. Juviler, Barnard College, Columbia University

Michel Lesage, University of Paris I

Serge L. Levitsky, Documentation Office for East European Law, University of Leyden Faculty of Law

Leon Lipson, Yale Law School

Dietrich A. Loeber, University of Kiel

Yuri Luyri, The University of Western Ontario Faculty of Law

Peter B. Maggs, University of Illinois College of Law

A. R. Meijer, University of Leyden Faculty of Law

Boris Meissner, University of Cologne

Christopher Osakwe, Tulane University School of Law

Manfred Pieck, Creighton University School of Law

Leonid Polsky, New York City

Stanislaw Pomorski, Rutgers University School of Law, Camden

Bernard Rudden, Oriel College Oxford

Fr. C. Schroeder, University of Regensburg, Faculty of Law

Lothar Schultz, University of Gottingen

Cynthia Semmler, New York City

Robert Sharlet, Union College

William B. Simons, Documentation Office for East European Law, University of Leyden Faculty of Law

Gordon B. Smith, University of South Carolina

Henn-Jüri Uibopuu, University of Salzburg

Th. J. Vondracek, Documentation Office for East European Law, University of Leyden Faculty of Law

Zigurds L. Zile, University of Wisconsin-Madison, Law School

The Editors

THE DEVELOPMENT OF
SOVIET ADMINISTRATIVE PROCEDURE

Donald D. Barry*

1. Introduction

A paper by the author for Part II of *Soviet Law After Stalin* dealt with the judicial review of Soviet administrative acts.[1] This paper will take up the procedural aspects of administrative activity that precede possible court review. As in the previous paper, this study will concentrate mainly on the rights of citizens in their contacts with administrative authority, rather than on the aspects of administrative law that apply to the administration of the economy.

The analysis will proceed through the following stages. First, some historical background on the development of Soviet administrative procedure will be given, followed by a discussion of recent activity in connection with codifying Soviet administrative law and procedure. Then two major problems in Soviet administrative procedure will be examined. These are the process of adopting normative acts by administrative organs and the procedures for handling individual cases. The discussion of the latter will concentrate on the use of administrative hearings and the administrative appeal process. Because no general statutes have yet been adopted on either of these subjects, the discussion will largely involve the problems that exist in the present situation and the proposals for legislation offered by Soviet jurists.

2. Historical Background

Work on the development of Soviet administrative law began soon after the Bolshevik Revolution. Textbooks on the subject were produced as early as 1918, but they were, in general, little different from pre-revolutionary treatments of the subject and were not considered sufficiently steeped in Marxism-Leninism.[2] Work on an RSFSR Administrative Code was begun in 1923, and although it was never adopted, an Administrative Code of the

* The author would like to acknowledge his debt to Professor D. A. Loeber for help in finding several of the important documentary sources in this paper. Professor Henn-Jüri Uibopuu and Dr. G. P. van den Berg also gave useful advice and comments to the author.

Ukrainian SSR was adopted in 1927. In none of this work, however, was much attention devoted to administrative procedure.

In the "legal nihilism" that characterized the late 1920s and early 1930s, administrative law largely disappeared from view, both as an area of research and as a subject of training for law students. Its revival came in the late 1930s and early 1940s.[3] Even at this time, however, administrative procedure received scant attention from those writing on the subject.

The birth, so to speak, of administrative procedure as a separate area of consideration is generally traced to the late 1950s, particularly to the scholar G. I. Petrov, who in a 1958 article recommended the separate codification of administrative procedural law.[4] The details of proposals for such codification have varied over the years. Some writers recommend All-Union Principles of Administrative Law containing a section on procedure, with union republic codes on both administrative law and administrative procedure; others favor separate Principles of substantive law and procedure and separate union republic codes on both subjects; still others advocate including the procedural provisions within both the Principles and the codes on administrative law, or other schemes.[5] Whatever the codification arrangements put forward, however, it is clear that recognition of the importance of administrative procedure has now been generally accepted by Soviet legal writers. This is not to suggest that legislation on administrative procedure will come soon. Brezhnev, at the 25th Party Congress in February, 1976, said that the Politburo had instructed the competent organs to prepare recommendations for codification of administrative law, among other branches of law.[6] But it appears that the first aspect of administrative law to be codified will be administrative liability. A considerable amount of work on this subject has already been done. A draft of Principles of Legislation on Administrative Liability was prepared by the All-Union Scientific Research Institute on Soviet Legislation in 1965, and that institution devoted a whole publication to the subject the same year.[7] Such an act will be an important step in the codification of administrative law, and it will undoubtedly contain some provisions on procedure. But it is hardly the kind of comprehensive enactment on administrative procedure that many writers are calling for.

3. The Scope of Administrative Procedure

What would a comprehensive enactment on administrative procedure contain? This is open to question because of a series of disagreements about administrative procedure among Soviet lawyers. A review of these disagreements will clarify the matters at issue. As explained in the author's previous paper,[8] there is a disagreement among Soviet writers as to the breadth of the administrative process. Some hold that it only involves the procedure for applying measures of administrative compulsion, while others view it as embracing the totality of procedural rules by which administrative organs carry out their tasks. For reasons explained previously, this analysis will be based on the broader conception of the administrative process.

Another point of disagreement involves whether administrative procedure embraces both the arrangements for handling individual cases by administrative agencies and the processes by which administrators adopt rules of general application. In the United States and some other Western countries it includes both, while in those countries of Eastern Europe where administrative procedure has been codified, only the first of these functions is included.[9] In the Soviet Union the issue has not yet been resolved, and there are important scholars on both sides. Since the question of the procedure for the adoption of normative acts by administrative organs is an important one, we will follow those Soviet jurists who include it within administrative procedure.

The foremost proponent of this point of view is V. D. Sorokin, who has written the most extensive recent analysis of administrative procedure by a Soviet author. [10] Sorokin's opening statement in a recent article concisely summarizes his position:

> "The administrative process as a juridical category embraces not all state administration, but only the legal aspects of administrative activity: the adoption of normative acts of state administration and the application of the law. Therefore, it should not be reduced to law application activity, which is characteristic of the civil procedural and criminal procedural form. The administrative procedural form expresses, in addition, the law creation character of Soviet state administration. This finds expression in such a composite part of it [the administrative process] as the procedure [*proizvodstvo*] for the adoption of normative acts of state administration." [11]

We will examine below the recommendations of Sorokin and others concerning procedures for adopting normative acts. At this point, however, to answer the question raised at the beginning of this section, a comprehensive enactment on administrative procedure might cover—in addition to the procedure for adopting normative acts—the following categories of administrative proceedings:

1. The procedure on suggestions and petitions of citizens and appeals of socialist organizations.

2. The procedure in administrative law complaints and disputes.

3. The procedure on organizational matters in the state administrative apparatus.

4. The procedure in cases involving the awarding of incentives by state administrative bodies.

5. The procedure in cases involving the application of measures of compulsion.

3

These categories are suggested by Sorokin. [12] All involve the application of the law rather than law creation, and they have apparently met with little objection from other legal writers. [13] It may be, therefore, that comprehensive administrative procedure legislation will be subdivided along the above lines. In the analysis below, we will not deal with all of these categories but only with those in which an administrative hearing would be appropriate: the second category, on cases involving complaints and disputes, and the fifth category, on the application of measures of compulsion.

4. The Adoption of Normative Acts by Administrative Organs

Whether the procedure for adoption of normative acts by administrative organs is included within administrative procedural legislation, as favored by Sorokin, or is provided for in substantive administrative law codification, as advocated by some other Soviet writers, [14] there seems to be a general recognition that some sort of order must be brought to this process. The nature of the problem can be outlined as follows. Several kinds of organs in the Soviet state apparatus have the power to adopt normative acts that have the force of law. Limiting the discussion to all-union level organs, it will be necessary to discuss the USSR Supreme Soviet and its Presidium, the USSR Council of Ministers, and the ministries and state committees of the USSR Council of Ministers. The Supreme Soviet alone* has the power to adopt *zakony* (Article 108 of the 1977 Constitution), which we will refer to here as "statutes." The Presidium of the Supreme Soviet is empowered to enact "edicts" (*ukazy*) and "decrees" (*postanovleniia*) under Article 123 of the Constitution; it also may amend legislative acts currently in force, with subsequent ratification at the next meeting of the Supreme Soviet (Article 122). The edicts may contain normative provisions and are, in effect, transformed into statutes at a succeeding session of the Supreme Soviet. The Supreme Soviet and its Presidium are referred to as organs of state power (*vlast'*).

There are also organs of state administration, namely the Council of Ministers and its ministries and state committees, which are empowered to enact subordinate (*podzakonnye*) normative acts. The Council of Ministers may issue "decrees" (*postanovleniia*) and "resolutions" (*rasporiazheniia*) "on the basis of and in fulfillment of" statutes and other acts of the Supreme Soviet and its Presidium (Article 133). These decrees are typically normative in character, while the resolutions normally are not. Decrees of the Council of Ministers are much more numerous than statutes or edicts. Loeber has estimated that there is "one statute for every 50 edicts and 285 decrees." [15]

In the case of all of the organs so far discussed, the differences between

* For purposes of this discussion, we will ignore the provision in Article 108 of the 1977 USSR Constitution which also allows for the adoption of *zakony* by popular referendum.

4

the provisions in the old and new Constitutions are minimal. A somewhat more significant change was effected in the new Constitution with regard to the normative acts of ministries and state committees. Under the old Constitution (Article 73), ministries were empowered—"within the limits of their competence"—to issue "orders" (*prikazy*) and "instructions" (*instruktsii*) "on the basis of and in fulfillment of" statutes, as well as decrees and resolutions of the Council of Ministers. In the opinion of Nikolaeva, who has written the most complete recent analysis of normative acts at the ministry level, this constitutional language should have ruled out the adoption of anything but orders and instructions by ministries. [16] Yet, as she notes, under the General Statute on USSR Ministries (Article 17), adopted in 1967, a minister may also issue "directives" (*ukazaniia*) that are binding on union republic ministries of the same name and other organizations in the ministry's system. In addition, ministries are authorized under a variety of enactments to issue or affirm a number of other normative acts, including "circulars" (*tsirkuliary*), "letters" (*pis'ma*), "rules" (*pravila*), "charters" (*ustavy*), "statutes" (*polozheniia*), and many others. [17]

What is problematical about this multiplicity of names is that there is little rational basis for distinguishing many of these designations from each other. Even the distinction between the constitutionally-mandated "order" and "instruction" are not clear to legal specialists. [18]

One recommendation to improve the situation was that a constitutional change be enacted to broaden the number of acts a ministry may adopt. But in the new Constitution the problem was handled differently. Article 135 provides simply that ministries and state committees may issue "acts" (*akty*) within their areas of competence and on the basis of the enactments of the higher organs of state power and administration. This is a technical solution to the problem, since it makes legal the multiplicity of enactments on the books which have emanated from ministry-level organs. But it does not address the problem of the confusion of terminology.

To summarize regarding the adoption of normative acts, statutes are enacted by the Supreme Soviet, edicts by its Presidium, decrees by the Council of Ministers, and a variety of normative "acts" by ministries and state committees. If it were merely a matter of confusion of terminology with regard to administrative normative acts, the problem would be a relatively small one. But more important is the relationship, or lack of clear relationship, between these acts. Soviet jurists speak of a hierarchy of normative acts, and, technically speaking, there is one. Statutes are the highest level, next to the Constitution; Council of Ministers decrees are to be adopted "on the basis of and in fulfillment of" statutes; ministry-level acts are to be adopted "on the basis of and in fulfillment of" statutes and decrees. This hierarchy suggests an arrangement whereby a lower-level organ would only adopt a normative act within the framework of an already-existing normative act adopted by a higher-level organ. The purpose of the act by the lower-level organ would be to provide greater detail as to how the broad purposes of the higher-level act are to be carried out in practice.* But clearly this is not typically the way it works in Soviet law. As D. A. Loeber has put it: "Most matters may be regulated by both the organs of state power and by the agencies of state administration . . . they exercise a concurrent law-making jurisdiction. As long as the legislative bodies fail to make use of their powers . . . the Council of Ministers** is free to act." [19]

This arrangement sounds very much like the "inherent" (as opposed to the "delegated") power of administrative organs in France to adopt normative acts. As the American law professor Bernard Schwartz has put it: "The administration is invested with an inherent authority to promulgate rules with the force of law. This authority is something foreign to Anglo-American conceptions of executive power, for with us the administration possess only the rule-making authority delegated to it by the legislature . . . In the French system the administration is vested, in addition to the authority conferred upon it by legislature, with inherent rule-making powers that exist even in the absence of legislative delegation." [20] A statement of similar tone by a Soviet jurist about Soviet law reads as follows: ". . . it is impossible to understand subordinate legal acts [*podzakonnost'*] as the right of the Council Ministers to issue acts only on questions regulated by statute. The subordinate law-creation of the government involves all of its law-creation activity, as defined by the authority vested in the government by statute." [21]

But if this kind of arrangement works satisfactorily in France, it is clear that it is increasingly being called into question in the USSR by Soviet jurists themselves. For instance, N. S. Malein has recently spoken of substatutory acts "eclipsing" statutory law because of the vagueness of statutory provisions and the wide range of questions consequently covered by substatutory law. He also cites examples of statutory requirements that certain rules be adopted at the Council of Ministers level which have been improperly delegated to an individual ministry. He deplores the practice of "correcting" a statute by the adoption of substatutory act and urges the full operation of "the principle of hierarchy." [22]

What this line of argument suggests to the American specialist on the administrative process is that greater attention needs to be paid to the delegation of authority from higher to lower bodies. As indicated above, Soviet jurists define delegation narrowly, as "a temporary assignment by a higher

* This amounts to a restatement of a widely-held view on the nature of delegation of power from legislatures to administrative agencies in American law. But Soviet jurists hold to a stricter definition of delegation which makes it difficult to discuss the concept in the present context. The discussion will return to this question below.

** As Loeber indicates later in his discussion, this applies to the ministries as well. See p. 224 in his cited work (note 19).

6

organ to a lower organ of the right to affirm an act, the issuing of which is within and continues to be within the competence of the higher organ." [23] As such, delegation is seen as a rare phenomenon in Soviet law, and as often improper when it is used. [24]

But the concept of delegation is often employed more loosely in American law as "power to 'fill in the details' of legislative enactments." [25] And in England, where an immense amount of "delegated legislation" is adopted, the administrator "must always be able to show precise statutory authority" for rules adopted. Generally, an important act of Parliament will authorize the adoption of administrative regulations. [26] It is the lack of such a direct link between the statute and the substatutory act (and often between the Council of Ministers decree and the subordinate normative act) that seems to be a problem in Soviet law. There are, of course, some Soviet statutes which specifically grant rule-making powers to the Council of Ministers or to ministries; and there are some substatutory rules which cite the higher authority for their adoption. [27] But this is by no means a general practice. It is suggested by a Soviet jurist that it become a requirement. Under such an arrangement, she states,

> "it would be possible to establish quickly and easily on what basis and in fulfillment of what statute or decision of the government a given departmental normative act was issued, to define the precise relationship of this act to the act which serves as the basis for its adoption, to more fully elucidate the sense of the departmental act and to expose the completeness of the norm regulating the public relations in question, their interconnections and interdependence. It is proposed that this practice should be extended to the law-creation activity of all ministries and departments and be provided for in acts regulating the procedure for this activity." [28]

One of the problems with substatutory normative acts adopted by a ministry-level body is that they are not easily accessible to the general public. There is no general requirement that they be published. By contrast, statutes of the Supreme Soviet, edicts of its Presidium, and decrees of the Council of Ministers, so long as they are considered normative in character, are supposed to be published. [29] In addition to their publication in periodicals, some progress has been made in issuing multi-volume collections of statutes, some of which include decrees of the Council of Ministers. [30] But this activity has not involved normative acts of ministry-level bodies.

In 1975, however, an important Party-Government measure was adopted that held out some hope for a change in this situation. The joint decree of the Central Committee of the CPSU and the USSR Council of Ministers of June 25, 1975, "On Measures for Further Perfection of Economic Legislation" [31] ordered, among other things, that ministries and departments bring order to their collections of normative acts and publish lists of them. Certain ministry-level organizations such as *Gosplan* and the Ministry of Finance, which are authorized to issue normative acts whose provisions apply to other ministries and departments, were ordered to codify their normative acts by subject. A scientific information center was ordered established by the USSR Ministry of Justice and the All-Union Scientific Research Institute on Soviet Legislation to keep records on all normative acts and to organize an automated central information system on such acts. [32] In addition, the Ministry of Justice was ordered to adopt recommendations for use by other ministries and departments in preparing normative acts. In line with this latter charge, the Ministry of Justice adopted Methodological Rules for the Preparation of Drafts of Legislative Acts and Decisions of the Government of the USSR on July 9, 1976, and Recommendations for the Preparation of Normative Acts of Ministries and Departments of the USSR on October 16, 1975. [33] The latter document is too long to summarize completely, but among its provisions are the following: emphasis on the necessity to "bring order to normative acts issued previously and eliminate their great number (article 2); stress on the need for normative acts to correspond to existing legislation and other normative acts (article 4); a general description of procedures for drafting normative acts, including references to the need to determine who will participate in drafting in cases where, say, a decree is issued by two ministries (articles 10-15); suggestions on sources to consult in preparing drafts and on routine features of drafts (articles 16-29); emphasis on the need to indicate precisely which earlier normative acts lose force or are modified by the present act (article 25); suggestions on procedures for putting normative acts into force (articles 30-35); emphasis on the need to send copies of acts that are obligatory for other ministries and departments to such organizations and to the editors of the *Bulletin of Normative Acts of the Ministries and Departments of the USSR* for publication (article 35).

As follow-ups to this document, the USSR Ministry of Justice has issued a series of "Methodological Recommendations" to ministries and departments, industrial enterprises, and legal offices of local soviets on the work of the legal offices in these organizations, particularly on procedures for systematizing and keeping current the normative acts adopted by the institution in question. [34] These documents, like the "Recommendations on Preparation of Normative Acts by Ministries and Departments," are merely recommendations, however, and rather broad and general ones at that. They appear not to be obligatory for anyone. Moreover, their adoption at the ministry level—by the Ministry of Justice—will undoubtedly not carry the weight that similar enactments by the Council of Ministers or the Supreme Soviet would carry. Finally, the objective of these enactments, as of all of the orders in the 1975 Central Committee-Council of Ministers decree from which they emanated, seems to be to enhance the efficiency of administrative and economic organizations rather than to make normative acts more accessible to the public.

In connection with the 1975 Central Committee-Council of Ministers decree, a fifty-volume *Collection of Current Legislation of the USSR* was completed and published in very limited circulation. But this publication was also "intended for state organs" only, and, as Professor I. S. Samoshchenko noted recently in discussing it, "the level of legality in the life of a society depends on the completeness of obedience to laws not only by state organs and state officials, but also by its citizens." [35] Relying on Brezhnev's recommendation at the 25th Party Congress in 1976 that there be published a "code of laws of the Soviet state" which would "make our laws more available to all Soviet citizens," Samoshchenko discussed the possible ways that such a code might be issued. He argued that normative acts of ministries and departments "are often so closely connected" with statutes and Council of Ministers decrees that the latter are "difficult to understand and apply" without them. He indicated that including all such acts of ministries and departments in a code would be impossible, however, because of their great number, and suggested that some part of them, such as those having significance for two or more organizations and those affecting the rights of citizens, could be included in the code. And he mentioned the arrangement employed in the United States—a *US Code* of Congressional statutes and a separate *Code of Federal Regulations* for administrative agency rules—as a possible alternative solution. Samoshchenko's recommendation is one of the few to suggest a central, unified publication of important acts of ministries and departments rather than separate collections maintained by the ministries themselves. From the standpoint of public accessibility to the law, centralized publication is undoubtedly preferable. But at this point it does not appear that such an arrangement will soon come to pass.

Reference was made above to the *Bulletin of Normative Acts of the Ministries and Departments of the USSR*. This monthly periodical, published by the USSR Ministry of Justice, began in mid-1972. In the *Bulletin*, one can find the texts of some of the important normative acts adopted at the USSR ministry level. But the acts published follow no particular order, either chronological or by subject matter, so it in no sense amounts to a systematic publication. Nor does it seem to include all relevant normative acts. Moreover, some documents are excerpted rather than published in full, and most appendices to normative acts appear to be excluded. As helpful as the *Bulletin* is, therefore, as a source of administrative normative acts which were previously even more difficult to obtain, it doesn't go as far as some Soviet jurists suggest is desirable.

The discussion to this point has largely involved two matters: the establishing of closer links between higher acts of state power or administration and the normative acts adopted by ministries and departments; and the publication and public availability of such lower normative acts. But these are only two aspects of the general procedure for the adoption of such acts. Unfortunately, they are the only ones that have been very much discussed so far by Soviet writers. To round out the discussion, we will turn to the limited amount of further discussion of the problem that the author has found. Several authorities have noted that there is no general procedure for the adoption of normative administrative acts, and that this lack ought to be corrected, preferably in all-union principles and union republic codes of substantive administrative law or administrative procedure.

What should such enactments contain? Most of the writing on this subject up to now has been very brief, containing procedural recommendations in almost outline form, which would suggest that it will be a considerable time before any legislation is adopted. [36] The typical suggestion indicates that such procedures ought to be made up of several stages, including drafting, discussion of draft, issuance or adoption, notice to interested parties, publication, and a procedure for the act to go into force. Some writers recommend also a provision for appealing the issuing of such rules or for procuratorial protest of their issuance. In each of these stages, certain procedural steps would be required, *e.g.*, the participation of the legal department of the drafting agency or agencies to insure correspondence with existing law; the participation of certain parties in the drafting process (either "interested parties" or those designated by statute); a quorum present at the actual adoption of the rules; official notice, either through publication or by actual notice to certain designated parties; the designation of an effective date for the act to go into force. One of the typical elements in administrative rule-making in the United States is the opportunity for participation by interested members of the public. One Soviet author calls for what amounts to the closest Soviet equivalent, the participation of *obshchestvennost'* in discussing the proposed act. [37]

Sorokin notes that while no such procedures have been adopted at the all-union or republic level, "many" local organs have established equivalents. He discusses a procedure adopted by the executive committee of the Leningrad City Soviet in 1967 which contains many of the provisions mentioned above, as well as others. [38]

One of the novel proposals regarding the adoption by ministries of normative acts is that they be submitted to obligatory review and approval by either the Presidium of the Supreme Soviet or the Council of Ministers to ensure their conformity with higher acts. [39] Several writers have also suggested that the courts be allowed to declare inoperative administrative normative acts that conflict with higher law. In fact, it has been suggested that this capability already exists under Soviet law, but that it should be rearticulated in new legislation. [40]

The importance to Soviet law of adopting a uniform procedure for the issuance of administrative normative acts—which constitute such a great part of actual Soviet law—can hardly be exaggerated. In some ways, it is more

10

important than laying down legal procedures for administrative handling of individual cases, the matter to which the discussion now turns. As Sorokin put it recently, "in their concern about the proper procedure for regulating individual administrative acts, some authors ignore the incomparably great social significance of providing a proper procedure for adopting normative acts. If the possible imprecision of an individual administrative act violates the right or legal interest basically of only one subject, then the imprecision of a normative act potentially may violate the rights and interests of a significantly greater circle of subjects."[41]

5. Handling Individual Cases

As with the adoption of normative acts by administrative organs, there is no general procedural law governing the handling of individual cases by administrators. But greater structure is brought to the discussion of the latter problem because of the existence of certain models that commentators employ in the course of their analyses. These models are the administrative procedural legislation of the East European socialist states and several Soviet statutes of narrow application containing procedural provisions which might be adapted to a general administrative procedural enactment.

From time to time, East European scholars write on administrative procedure in Soviet law journals. In addition, some of their books are translated into Russian.[42] And Soviet authors make great use of East European examples in their analysis of Soviet administrative procedure.[43] Five East European states have adopted general laws on administrative procedure: Czechoslovakia in 1955, Yugoslavia in 1956, Hungary in 1957, Poland in 1960, and Bulgaria in 1970.[44] The pieces of Soviet legislation cited approvingly most often by Soviet commentators are: 1) the June 21, 1961, Edict of the Presidium of the USSR Supreme Soviet "On the Further Limitation of the Application of Fines Imposed by Administrative Procedure";[45] 2) the union republic statutes on the same subject;[46] 3) the union republic statutes on administrative commissions of the local soviets;[47] 4) the April 12, 1968, Edict of the USSR Supreme Soviet "On the Procedure for Considering Proposals, Applications, and Complaints of Citizens";[48] 5) and several other recent acts.[49]

The first three of the acts mentioned are closely interrelated. The 1961 edict on the limitation on administrative fines narrowed the range of bodies that could assess such fines. It also limited the power to legislate on fines to the highest organs of state power and administration at the USSR, union republic, and autonomous republic levels, thus removing the power to designate finable offenses at the ministry level and below. The edict provided that such fines shall be imposed by the administrative commissions of the local soviets and a number of other specifically-designated bodies. This led to a flurry of legislative activity at the union republic level to create or recreate systems of administrative commissions, as well as to adopt supplementary legislation on administrative fines.

The administrative commissions are composed of a chairman, a secretary, and a number of members, the total number varying from republic to republic. Giddings [50] describes the typical stages that a case before an administrative commission might go through as follows: 1) commission of the violation; 2) composition of the "protocol" or "act," the document describing the details of the violation; 3) consideration of the protocol and other relevant materials on the case; 4) the decision of the commission and the issuance of a "decree"; 5) appeal from the decree; 6) the possibility of procuratorial protest; 7) imposition of the administrative penalty. [51] Since Giddings has so fully covered these stages in her analysis, we will only comment briefly on several aspects of the process that are relevant to administrative procedure.

As detailed as the procedures for the operation of the administrative commission now are in comparison with the situation prior to the early 1960s, ambiguities and other problems remain. For instance, the exact status of the protocol, the basic official statement on the offense, is not clear, nor is it clear what the legal effect is of the "violator" (as he is known even prior to the decision of the administrative commission) signing the protocol. [52] Moreover, since the early 1960s, a number of types of offenses have been taken out of the jurisdiction of administrative commissions and given back to individual officials of the police and other organs. As a result, the number of cases heard by administrative commissions has fallen considerably, at least in some parts of the country. [53] As will be indicated, in those cases heard not by administrative commissions but by other officials, most of the normal procedural guarantees may be dispensed with.

Still, the creation of this legislation did amount to a step forward in this area of administrative procedure. The RSFSR Law on Administrative Commissions requires that cases must be heard within one month of the commission of the offense and within ten days of the receipt of the protocol. Administrative commission sessions are held in public and, as a rule, during non-working hours. The accused is informed of the session not less than three days in advance. He may participate in the case, familiarize himself with relevant documents and other materials, "give explanations concerning the substance of the offense, and submit petitions." Witnesses may be called, as well as representatives of state and social organizations, "in cases of necessity." When cases are heard before individual officials rather than administrative commissions, these provisions do not apply. Article 37 of the RSFSR Law on Administrative Commissions provides that, in such cases, imposition of a penalty may be effected at the time of the offense, and if the case is decided at a later date, the offender shall be notified "only when necessary to receive personal explanations from him."

The decree of the administrative commission, which is adopted by a simple majority, must contain precise personal data about the offender, as well as a description of the offense and the type of penalty assessed. The administrative commission may impose a warning or a fine of up to 50 rubles, and possibly other sanctions. [54] The decree may be appealed within ten days of its issuance to a higher administrative level or, in the case of a fine, to a people's court. [55]

The April 12, 1968, edict "On the Procedure for Considering Proposals, Applications, and Complaints of Citizens" is only the most recent in a long line of legislative acts on the subject. [56] Moreover, it has been followed by frequent discussion of the subject at high levels, including both the 24th and 25th CPSU Congresses and in a Central Committee decree following the 25th Congress, [57] all of which was overlaid by relevant new provisions in the 1977 USSR Constitution. Article 49 of the Constitution provides that a citizen "has the right to submit to state agencies and public organizations proposals on improving their activity and to criticize shortcomings in work." Officials are obliged to examine and give consideration to proposals and to make timely replies. Article 49 also prohibits persecution for criticism and states that persons who engage in such persecution "will be called to account." Article 58 gives citizens the right to file complaints against the actions of officials and state and public agencies. The article goes on to affirm that illegal actions of officials that infringe on the rights of citizens may be brought to court according to the procedure established by law.

All of this activity since 1968 connected with the edict on proposals, applications, and complaints would seem to suggest that the edict, by itself, is not having the desired effect of making Soviet bureaucrats more responsive to citizen complaints and opinions. Evidence of procuratorial supervision over the implementation of the edict supports this suspicion, [58] and some data appear to show that the mechanism is held in rather low esteem by some Soviet citizens. [59]

What Soviet jurists praise in the edict, however, has little to do with the effectiveness of the mechanism as a whole, but involves some of its specific procedural provisions. These provisions link up directly with the new constitutional guarantees just mentioned. Article 1 of the edict requires all state and social organizations to "provide the necessary conditions to effectuate the rights granted and guaranteed to USSR citizens to make proposals, applications, and complaints in writing or orally." Such organizations and their officials are required to resolve such appeal if within their legal powers, or to "send them within five days to the appropriate institution, notifying the applicant thereof," or, when the appeal is oral, indicating where the applicant should apply (Article 4). Officials are required "to hold office hours for citizens" on fixed days and at fixed hours at convenient times which are made known to citizens (Article 6).

Proposals (which relate to "questions of political, economic, or cultural life and to the improvement of legislation") and applications (which relate to "sociocultural, housing, and other questions in connection with effectuating rights granted to citizens") may be submitted directly to the level of the institution responsible for resolving the issue in question. Complaints (which "as a rule, are a form of reaction to facts of a violation of rights and interests of citizens protected by law") are submitted to the level directly above that at which the actions are being complained of. The edict specifically prohibits the sending of complaints to the officials directly involved (Article 5).

Officials are required to take all measures "to objectively resolve the issue," including demanding necessary documents and making on-site verification. They must render "reasoned decisions" and ensure their "timely and correct execution." When rejecting a proposal, application, or complaints, they must indicate the reasons. Such decisions must normally be rendered within one month, although a second month is allowed in more complicated applications or complaints, and an undesignated period of extra time is allowed for proposals. Decisions on applications and complaints may be appealed to a higher administrative level, and in certain instances complaints may be appealed to a people's court. [60] Finally, it is stated that violations of established procedures will entail disciplinary responsibility for guilty officials. Where such violations cause "material harm to state or social interests or to the rights and other interests of citizens protected by law," or where there is persecution of citizens by officials in connection with complaints or applications, criminal responsibility will ensue.

What the statutes just reviewed have in common is a set of procedural provisions considered sound and worthy of replication in the drafting of more general administrative procedural legislation. Taken together with the much more finished administrative procedural law in several East European countries, these provisions serve as the basis for proposals by a number of Soviet jurists for developing comprehensive legislative enactments.

It is fair to say that the basic aim of many of these proposals is to enhance the formality of administrative procedure, to require officials to conform to certain procedural steps in handling cases. Some of these steps occur in the early stages of an administrative proceeding, as, for instance, in the attempt by responsible officials to gather information concerning a possible administrative violation. Such an activity might involve the search of premises to look for home-brew equipment or for the illegal fruits of poaching, where the penalty for a violation might be an administrative fine. One jurist has recommended that such searches receive uniform regulation in administrative procedural law. He urges that such a search "be performed only in cases rigorously established by law and in accordance with a reasoned order of an official of an organ of state administration and with the sanction of a procurator." [61] Another possible early procedural step would be that of administrative detention. Jurists have recommended legislation giving a complete list of grounds, as well as a maximum time limit for such detention.[62] But many of the proposals involve a later stage in the process and have to do with the actual disposition of the case. Not all such cases would be decided on the basis of a hearing. Many would be handled by means of a more informal process, some even "on the spot." But the two foremost models in existing Soviet legislation, which were discussed above, are ones with proceedings akin to hearings, and among the most interesting recommendations by Soviet jurists are those that relate to the hearing process. It is on these proposals that we will concentrate.

On occasion Soviet commentators write of an "*otkrytoe zaslushivanie*," or a "*slushanie*" or the "*razbiratel'stvo dela*," and in the context it is clear that a hearing is what is meant,[63] even though the idea of a "hearing" as a formal stage in the administrative process does not seem to be uniformly recognized by Soviet jurists. When one examines recommendations by Soviet writers concerning desirable characteristics for an administrative procedure, however, it is clear that they often have in mind the rudiments of an administrative hearing of some kind, especially in cases involving the assessing of administrative penalties and cases involving complaints of citizens against some official act. With these considerations in mind, we will look at some of the recommendations recently put forward.

One of the first requirements of a hearing, according to the recommendations, would be "openness" (*glasnost*).[64] The law ought to contain "concrete manifestations of the principles of publicness and openness [*publichnost' i glasnost*] in the administrative process: the open hearing of the case with the summoning of the violator and all interested officials and representatives of the public." The writer of these lines, in fact, would like to see openness characterize the whole system of administrative procedure, including its less formal aspects. She explains that there exist procedural instructions as to how fines are to be assessed on the spot and how the police deal with petty hooliganism, minor traffic offenses, and the like. "But these [instructions] are not brought to the attention of citizens and they possess a kind of one-sided character, since they regulate only the activity of the official in question . . . In our view, such a situation hardly may be considered correct from the point of view of the procedural rights of citizens." But her main attention is directed at the hearing. She favors an "open and direct" review of the case with all sides present because, in her view, it strengthens legality and public faith in the process and has an educational effect on the participants, in addition to the fact that it produces the best result from a legal point of view.[65]

In terms of the timing of the hearing, two recommendations are relevant. First, it should be held at a convenient time for participants. Sorokin quotes favorably the provision of Hungarian law to the effect that the person testifying should "have the time to be present and his appearance before the administrative organ, if at all possible, will not interfere with his work." [66] Second, a basic principle of the process ought to be "speediness" (*bystrota*). In practice, what this should mean is the 30-day limit in the law on administrative commissions (including the 10-day limit from the time the protocol is drawn up) or the time-limit of one to two months provided for in several East European statutes. [67]

A key document in the hearing process is the protocol. It ought to be drawn up in the presence of the violator, in order to help acquaint him with the essential facts of the case from the standpoint of the official. Moreover, there ought to be a standard form for the protocol throughout the country, or at least in each republic, "to exclude local law-creation in the poor sense of the word." [68] In cases involving administrative penalties, Salishcheva would allow the citizen to introduce his own explanation and comments into the protocol. [69]

In connection with the hearing itself, the citizen ought to have the opportunity to familiarize himself with the materials of the case, "to be listened to in connection with additional explanation" on the case, to introduce new materials, to petition the officials to make further investigations, and to call witnesses. [70] With respect to familiarizing oneself with the materials of the case, Ivanov points out a divergence in two existing statutes. The RSFSR law on administrative hearings (Article 29) provides for this during the hearing, while the law on Commissions on the Affairs of Minors allows it to be done before the hearing. Ivanov recommends the latter arrangement as the general rule. [71]

Soviet jurists agree that there should be provisions obliging the official to conduct a fair and thorough hearing. In collegial bodies, a quorum should be present to hear the case and vote on the outcome. In important cases such as those involving administrative penalties, officials should have the right and obligation to demand from state or social organizations any relevant documents and to carry out further investigations. When officials improperly conduct proceedings, they should be subject to legal liability, either disciplinary or criminal. [72] Salishcheva would provide a special administrative appeal (in addition to the regular appeal, to be discussed below) in cases where a citizen complained of improper procedural acts during the hearing of a case, this appeal to be heard at a higher administrative level within no more than three days of the complaint. [73]

The provision in the statute "On the Procedures for Considering Proposals, Applications, and Complaints of Citizens"—which prevents the official whose behavior is the subject of the complaint from hearing the case—is recommended as a general principle. [74] Salishcheva believes that there ought to be a further guarantee against possible bias. She would allow a citizen to challenge the person conducting a proceeding and request his removal on such grounds

16

as family relationship to one of the parties, personal interest in the outcome, or having already reviewed the case in question. [75] One writer would go even further, removing citizen complaints completely from the jurisdiction of the governmental organization being complained of and turning such matters over to a special organ for the review and resolving of complaints. [76]

A common recommendation is that administrative proceedings be conducted in the language of the majority of the local population, with the providing of interpreters for those who don't know the language. [77]

The decree or order (*postanovlenie*), which represents the product of the hearing, is also a crucial document, and some fairly specific requirements regarding it are favored. The decree ought to indicate the legal basis for the decision, the norms applied, an assessment of the evidence, the specific kind and size of penalty, if any, the motivation for excusing from liability if this is the outcome, and other details. The law also should indicate the basis for voting (a simple majority is usually advocated) and a method of delivering the decree to the citizen within a specified time (*e.g.*, five days). [78] There is some difference of opinion as to whether the decree must be in the form of a written, reasoned opinion. It seems to be agreed, however, that at least in cases where judicial review is possible, there ought to be a written opinion. [79]

Finally, there seems to be agreement on the need for the general availability of administrative appeal to a higher level of the organization. This is simply not allowed in the case of some administrative acts, [80] and those statutes which specifically provide for such appeal, such as the 1968 RSFSR law providing for suspensions of driver's licenses for up to one year, [81] as well as the East European statutes which allow administrative appeals as a general rule, are praised by writers. While such an appeal is pending, it is recommended that as a general rule the execution of the administrative order be suspended. [82]

6. Concluding Remarks

In spite of the strong support for an expanded administrative appeal mechanism, however, it seems clear that the favored avenue of appeal among Soviet jurists is still judicial review. Even with a general system of administrative review, the capstone of the process for many cases based on administrative acts, in their view, ought to be an independent judgment by a court. [83] To some extent, at least, the new Soviet Constitution supports the position of those favoring broadened judicial review, and a number of prominent Soviet lawyers have devoted attention to this matter. [84] For instance, Professor A. Lunev recently urged that "all rights and freedoms designated in the Constitution should be protected by judicial procedure." He particularly singled out the need to provide for judicial review of the suspension of driver's licenses and of citizen complaints about construction projects and "any other actions, the carrying out of which would cause harm to the environment or pollute the atmosphere." [85]

N. S. Malein also invoked principles of the new Constitution in support of his call for extended judicial review. He pointed to the provision of Article 54 prohibiting arrest except on the basis of a court decision or with the sanction of a procurator. He noted that "measures limiting personal freedom" involving the involuntary commitment to an institution of a person judged to be mentally ill or an alcoholic, a drug addict or a juvenile, when that person has committed a socially dangerous act, may be taken only on the basis of a court order (Articles 58-63 of the RSFSR Criminal Code). Malein's suggestion is that this same requirement of a court order be extended to "cases of involuntary commitment to a psychiatric hospital of persons who have not committed" any crime. He noted that court proceedings are necessary to declare a person incompetent because of mental illness or feeble-mindedness (Article 15 of the RSFSR Civil Code) or of limited competence because of alcohol or drug abuse (Article 16 of the RSFSR Civil Code), and these procedures only involve the designation of a guardian or a curator. This amounts to, he says, "a limitation on the freedom to perform defined legal actions." Malein concludes that it is all the more necessary, therefore, to guarantee judicial control over the propriety of the involuntary commitment to psychiatric hospitals, since this involves a limitation "not just of civil law competence but also on individual freedom." [86]

Knowingly or not (and it seems clear that it must have been the former), Malein has thus raised an issue which constitutes one of the foremost complaints from the Soviet dissident community about state harassment of dissenters by incarceration in psychiatric hospitals. His proposal would bring involuntary commitment procedures under court control, impliedly because the administrative procedures presently in use have been abused. This, in microcosm, is the kind of general problem the authorities face in contemplating the adoption of general administrative procedural legislation: it can be employed (or attempted to be employed) not just for the purpose intended, but to correct any alleged wrong committed by an administrative official. Thus, when Soviet Jews desiring to emigrate request written explanations of the reasons for refusals of visa applications,[87] they are calling for an element of administrative procedure that, in the abstract at least, many Soviet administrative lawyers would support. And it may be this potentiality for unintended consequences which, in the end, prevents comprehensive administrative procedural legislation from being adopted. The cynic might respond that it makes little difference what the statute provides in cases of real political import; the authorities will act as they choose in such cases, whatever the statute says. But it would seem foolish to deliberately create this gap between legal provisions and actual practice by adopting a statute when the problem

18

could be avoided by not enacting any law at all. A Hungarian law professor, addressing a conference in Leningrad in 1975, said that "the necessity for an [administrative] procedural law arises when the state needs to politically and legally guarantee the rights of citizens." [88] It remains to be seen whether or not the Soviet state has reached that point of genuine commitment to this principle.

NOTES

1. "Administrative Justice and Judicial Review in Soviet Administrative Law," in Donald D. Barry, George Ginsburgs, and Peter B. Maggs, eds., *Soviet Law After Stalin, Part II, Social Engineering Through Law* (Alphen aan den Rijn, The Netherlands, 1978), pp. 241-269.

2. A. E. Lunev, "Sovetskaia Nauka Administrativnogo Prava za 60 Let" (The Soviet Science of Administrative Law for 60 Years), *SGiP*, 1977, No. 11, 61 and note 2, 61. Unless otherwise indicated, this discussion of the historical background is based on Lunev and the following sources: N. G. Salishcheva, *Grazhdanin i Administrativnaia Iurisdiktsiia v SSSR* (The Citizen and Administrative Jurisdiction in the USSR), (Moscow, 1970), pp. 131-134; V.D. Sorokin, *Administrativno-Protsessual'noe Pravo* (Administrative Procedural Law), (Moscow, 1972), pp. 216 *ff.*; M. G. Kirichenko and others, "Issledovanie Gosudarstvennogo, Administrativnogo i Finansovogo Prava" (Research on State, Administrative, and Finance Law), *Problemy Sovershenstvovaniia Sovetskogo Zakonodatel'stva* (Problems of Perfecting Soviet Legislation), No. 4, (Moscow, 1975), pp. 58-63.

3. Kirichenko and others, note 2, p. 59 and Robert Sharlet, "Stalinism and Soviet Legal Culture," in Robert C. Tucker (ed.), *Stalinism: Essays in Historical Interpretation* (New York, 1977), pp. 177-178.

4. G.I. Petrov, "Zadachi Kodifikatsii Sovetskogo Administrativnogo Prava" (The Tasks of Codification of Soviet Administrative Law), *SGiP*, 1958, No. 6, 21.

5. On the varieties of recommendations, see Salishcheva, note 2, pp. 131-137 and Sorokin, note 2, pp. 215-227.

6. *Izvestiia*, February 25, 1976, 9.

7. See Salishcheva, note 2, p. 141. The publication mentioned is *UZ* (VNIISZ), issue 5, (Moscow, 1965), devoted to "Problems of Perfecting the Legislation on Administrative Liability."

8. See above, note 1, p. 246.

9. V. A. Loriia, "Administrativno-Protsessual'naia Deiatel'nost' i Vidi Administrativnogo Proizvodstva," (Administrative-Procedural Activity and Types of Administrative Procedure), *SGiP*, 1978, No. 1, 19.

10. Sorokin, note 2. See also by Sorokin *Problemy Administrativnogo Protsessa* (Problems of the Administrative Process), (Moscow, 1968), and *Administrativno-Protsessual'nye Otnosheniia* (Administrative Procedural Relations), (Moscow, 1968).

11. V.D. Sorokin, "Proizvodstvo Po Priniatii Normativnykh Aktov Upravleniia" (The Procedure for the Adoption of Normative Acts of Administration), *Pravovedenie*, 1976, No. 2, 114.

12. Sorokin, note 2, pp. 227-237 and Sorokin, note 11, p. 114. Actually, these six categories comprise only the "special part" of Sorokin's proposed administrative procedural codification. He also offers a "general part" (note 2, pp. 227-230) centaining five more general categories of proposed norms.

13. Sorokin, note 11, 114.See also Loriia, note 9, for a somewhat similar list.

14. See, for instance, the views of A. P. Korenev as summarized in Sorokin, note 11, 115; also V. M. Manokhin (ed.), *Sovetskoe Administrativnoe Pravo* (Soviet Administrative Law), (Moscow, 1977), p. 196.

20

15. Dietrich A. Loeber, "Legal Rules 'For Internal Use Only'," *The International and Comparative Law Quarterly*, 19 (January, 1970), 76. See also W. E. Butler, "Sources of Soviet Law," *Current Legal Problems*, 28 (1975), 224.

16. M. N. Nikolaeva, *Normativnye Akty Ministerstv i Vedomstv* (Normative Acts of Ministeries and Departments), (Moscow, 1975), p. 62.

17. *Ibid.*, pp. 63-65. Nikolaeva gives the example of the Ministry of Merchant Shipping, which may issue "rules," "rules and additional conditions," "instructions," "statutes," "norms," "tariffs," and "rates of payment" in connection with its various functions. She states (p. 108) that there are "several tens of" such types of acts, while Butler (note 15, p. 224) states that there are "more than thirty denominations for enactments."

18. After a long discussion, Nikolaeva concludes that it is impossible to distinguish clearly between these two designations. Note 16, pp. 73-85, esp. pp. 84-85. For a discussion in English of these two terms, see F. J. M. Feldbrugge, (ed.), *Encyclopedia of Soviet Law* (Leyden, 1973), Vol 1, p. 424; also Butler note 15, pp. 224-230.

19. Dietrich A. Loeber, "Statutes (Polozheniia) of the Agencies of State Administration in the Soviet Union," in *Codification in the Communist World*, (organized by Donald D. Barry, F. J. M. Feldbrugge, and Dominik Lasok), (Leyden, 1975), pp. 223-224.

20. Bernard Schwartz, *French Administrative Law and the Common-Law World* (New York, 1954), pp. 89-90.

21. Nikolaeva, note 16, pp. 45-46, note 3.

22. N. S. Malein, "Tendentsii Razvitiia Grazhdanskogo Prava" (Tendencies in the Development of Civil Law), *SGiP*, 1978, No. 1, 45-47.

23. Nikolaeva, note 16, p. 36. See also A. F. Shebanov, "Nekotorye Voprosy Pravovoi Normy i Normativnykh Aktov v Sovetskom Obshchenarodnom Prave" (Several Questions about the Legal Norm and Normative Acts in Soviet All-People's Law), *SGiP*, 1964, No. 7, 106; B. M. Lazarev, "O Delegirovanii Polnomochii v Sfere Gosudarstvennogo Upravleniia" (On Delegation of Authority in the Sphere of State Administration), *SGiP*, 1965, No. 10, 27.

24. See, for instance, M. S. Studenikina, "O Sovershenstvovanii Sistemy Zakonodatel'stva ob Administrativnoi Otvetstvennosti" (On Perfecting the System of Legislation on Administrative Liability), *Problemy Sovershenstvovaniia Sovetskogo Zakonodatel'stva* (Problems of Perfecting Soviet Legislation), No. 3, (Moscow, 1975), pp. 23-24.

25. The quotation is from Sotirios A. Barber, *The Constitutional Delegation of Congressional Power* (Chicago, 1975), p. 7, and the internal quotation on filling in the details is from an often-quoted statement by Chief Justice John Marshall in an 1825 case, *Wayman* v. *Southard*, 10 Wheat. 1, 43: "The line has not been exactly drawn which separates those important subjects, which must be entirely regulated by the legislature itself, from those of less interest, in which a general provision may be made, and power given to those who are to act under such general provision, to fill up the details." The "non-delegation doctrine" is one of the most important and persistent issues in American administrative law. No attempt is made here to address the complexities of the issue. For a thorough but brief analysis of the issue, see the book by Barber referred to in this note.

26. Bernard Schwartz and H. W. R. Wade, *Legal Control of Government* (Oxford, 1972), pp. 96-97.

27. Examples of Supreme Soviet acts which grant lower organs power to make rules are the USSR Air Code of 1961, article 6, the USSR Customs Code of 1964, article 3, and the USSR Merchant Shipping Code of 1968, article 5. These acts are published in *Sbornik Zakonov SSSR i Ukazov Presidiuma Verkhovnogo Soveta SSSR, 1938-1975* (Collection of Statutes of the USSR and Edicts of the Presidium of the Supreme Soviet

of the USSR, 1938-1975), (Moscow, 1975), in 4 Volumes, Volume 1, pp. 385, 417, and 443, respectively. Council of Ministers decrees also sometimes grant rule-making power to ministries. An example of a lower-level rule citing higher authority would be the Methodological Recommendations of the Ministry of Justice cited below in note 34.

28. Nikolaeva, note 16, p. 35.

29. See the edict of the Presidium of the USSR Supreme Soviet of June 19, 1958, *Ved. V.S. SSRSR*, 1958, No. 14 and the decree of the USSR Council of Ministers of March 20, 1959, No. 293, *Sobr. Post. SSSR*, 1959, No. 6, item 37. Both of these acts are published in *Khoziaistvennoe Protsessual'noe Zakonodatel'stvo* (Economic Procedural Legislation), (Kiev, 1976), pp. 58 and 60.

30. The author has in mind, for instance, the four volume *Sbornik Zakonov SSSR* (see above, note 27) and the multi-volume *Sistematicheskoe Sobranie Zakonov RSFSR, Ukazov Prezidiuma Verkhovnogo Soveta RSFSR i Reshenii Pravitel'stva RSFSR* compiled between 1967 and 1971.

31. *Sobr. Post. SSSR*, 1975, No. 16, item 98.

32. Work being done on this Automated Information System for Legal Information—*ASPI*—is described in S. S. Moskvin, "Sistema Ucheta Normativnykh Aktov SSSR" (An Accounting System for Normative Acts of the USSR), *SGiP*, 1978, No. 3, 28.

33. The author has not been able to locate the first of these documents, and assumes that it may be unpublished. He has seen reference to it in several sources, including "Metodicheskie Rekomendatsii ob Organizatsii Raboty Iuridicheskogo Otdela Tsentral'nogo Apparata Ministerstva, Vedomstva SSSR" (Methodological Recommendations on the Organization of Work of the Legal Office of the Central Apparatus of a Ministry or Department of the USSR), affirmed by the Deputy Minister of Justice of the USSR, December 30, 1976, *BNA*, 1977, No. 6, 42. The latter document is published in *BNA*, 1976, No. 1, 44-48. Methodological Rules apparently similar to those adopted on the USSR level were adopted in the Estonian SSR in 1974. They are published in *Sovetskoe Pravo*, 1974, No. 3, 253-256. I am grateful to Dr. G. P. van den Berg and Professor D. A. Loeber for bringing these rules to my attention.

34. These Methodological Recommendations may be found in, *e.g.*, *BNA*, 1976, No. 5, 34; 1976, No. 7, 42; 1977, No. 2, 36; 1977, No. 6, 40; 1978, No. 1, 42.

35. I. S. Samoshchenko, "O Svode Zakonov Sovetskogo Gosudarstva" (On a Code of Laws of the Soviet State), *Problemy Sovershenstvovaniia Sovetskogo Zakonodatel'stva* (Problems of Perfecting Soviet Legislation), No. 8, (Moscow, 1977). The references in this paragraph are to pp. 3, 7, and 8.

36. The author is relying here largely on the following sources: Sorokin, note 2, pp. 152-153 and 230; Manokhin, note 14, pp. 194-198; A. P. Korenov, *Kodifikatsiia Sovetskogo Administrativnogo Prava* (The Codification of Soviet Administrative Law), (Moscow, 1970), pp. 70 *ff.*; V. I. Novoselov, *Zakonnost' Aktov Organov Upravleniia* (The Legality of Acts of Administrative Organs), (Moscow, 1968), pp.,68-83.

37. Korenev as cited in Sorokin, note 2, p. 231.

38. Sorokin, note 2, p. 152.

39. Studenikina, note 24, pp. 22-23. On a similar practice in the United States, see Harold H. Bruff and Ernest Gellhorn, "Congressional Control of Administrative Regulation: A Study of Legislative Vetoes," *Harvard Law Review*, 90 (May, 1977), 1369.

40. See Malein, note 22, 47; M. S. Studenikina, "Sudebnaia Praktika i Administrativnoe Pravo" (Judicial Practice and Administrative Law), in S. N. Bratus' (ed.), *Sudebnaia Praktika v Sovetskoi Pravovoi Sisteme* (Judicial Practice in the Soviet Legal System), (Moscow, 1975), p. 229; O. E. Leist, *Sanktsii v Sovetskom Prave* (Sanctions in Soviet Law), (Moscow, 1962), pp. 130-131.

41. V. D. Sorokin in P. E. Nedbailo and V. M. Gorsheneva (eds.), *Iuridicheskaia*

Protsessual'naia Forma (Juridical Procedural Form), (Moscow, 1976), p. 154.

42. See, *e.g.*, E. Staros'tsiak, "Instituty Administrativnogo Protsessa Evropeiskikh Sotsialisticheskikh Stran" (Principles of Administrative Process in the East European Socialist States), *SGiP*, 1964, No. 7, 122; S. Popovich, "Osnovnye Instituty Iugoslavskogo Administrativnogo Protsessa" (Basic Principles of Yugoslav Administrative Process), *SGiP*, 1966, No. 2, 118; and see the series of articles on "Law Creation in the USSR and the Hungarian People's Republic," which includes seven articles and some discussion of administrative procedure, *Pravovedenie*, 1976, No. 2, 104-124; P. Stainov and A. Angelov, *Administrativnoe Pravo Narodnoi Respubliki Bulgarii* (The Administrative Law of the People's Republic of Bulgaria), (Moscow, 1960).

43. See *e.g.*, Salishcheva, note 2, *passim.* and Sorokin, note 2, *passim.*, but especially Chapter 5, Part 5 on "The Administrative Process in the European Socialist States," pp. 173-184.

44. See *ibid.*, p. 173 *ff.*

45. *Ved. V.S. SSSR*, 1961, No. 35, item 368.

46. The RSFSR edict was adopted March 3, 1962. *Ved. V.S. RSFSR*, 1962, No. 9, item 121.

47. The RSFSR Statute was adopted March 30, 1962. *Ved. V.S. RSFSR*, No. 13, item 166. The enactments listed in notes 45 and 46 appear in English translation in *Soviet Statutes and Decisions* (hereinafter *SSD*), 5 (Fall, 1968), 18 and 29, respectively. A translation of the Statute on Administrative Commissions, as amended in 1965 and 1969, appears in *SSD*, 10 (Summer, 1974), 280.

48. *Ved. V.S. SSSR*, 1968, No. 17, item 144. An English translation may be found in *SSD*, 10 (Summer, 1974), 357.

49. Two of these are the edicts of the Presidium of the RSFSR Supreme Soviet of June 19, 1968, "On Increased Liability for Violation of Traffic Rules on Streets of Cities and Settled Areas and Highways and the Rules for the Use of the Means of Transport," *Ved. V.S. RSFSR*, 1968, No. 28, item 1009, and the Statute on Commissions on Affairs of Minors, affirmed by an edict of the Presidium of the USSR Supreme Soviet of June 3, 1967, *Ved. V.S. SSSR*, 1967, No. 23, item 536. Other acts in this category are suggested by V. A. Ivanov, "Sovershenstvovanie Garantii Prav Grazhdan v Administrativnom Protsesse" (The Perfection of Guarantees of the Rights of Citizens in the Administrative Process), *SGiP*, 1977, No. 2, 35 and note 17, 35.

50. Jane Giddings, "Administrative Commissions of the Local Soviets," *Review of Socialist Law*, 3 (1977), No. 1, 53-96. The discussion that follows relies heavily on Giddings' thorough analysis.

51. *Ibid.*, 65-66.

52. *Ibid.*, 68-69.

53. Salishcheva, note 2, pp. 80-81.

54. Giddings, note 50, pp. 74-75.

55. The right to appeal a fine to a people's court is provided in article 18 of the USSR Edict of June 21, 1961 (see above, note 45). Salishcheva (note 2, p. 112) states that in line with "the sense of" article 18 and the norms of the majority of union republic laws on the subject, the individual has a choice of either administrative review at a higher level or judicial review.

56. See generally V. V. Mal'kov, *Sovetskoe Zakonodatel'stvo O Zhalobakh i Zaiavleniiakh* (Soviet Legislation on Complaints and Applications), (Moscow, 1967), for background.

57. On Party and other enactments relevant to the edict, see P. Ia. Trubnikov, *Peresmotr Reshenii v Poriadke Sudebnogo Nadzora* (The Review of Decisions in Judicial Supervisory Proceedings), (Moscow, 1974), pp. 67-71; P. Skomorokhov, "Kuda Obratit'-

sia s Zhaloboi" (Whom to Turn To With a Complaint), *Chelovek i Zakon*, 1977, No. 1, 72; *Izvestiia*, February 9, 1977, 1.

58. See, *e.g., Sots. Zak.*, 1977, No. 9, 88.

59. See Barry, note 1, sources cited in note 55.

60. Mal'kov, note 56, p. 101 indicates that complaints concerning certain aspects of labor law, housing law, and several other areas of law are subject to judicial review.

61. Ivanov, note 49, p. 30.

62. See *ibid.* and Salishcheva, note 2, p. 149. Salishcheva would like to see the conditions for detention spelled out in a basic legislative act, "and not in an act that is hidden from the view of a wide circle of people" (p. 148).

63. These terms are used, for example, in *ibid*, pp. 151 and 153. Such a hearing may not approach the formality of a so-called trial-type hearing in American law, but one of the interesting recent developments in American administrative law is toward a more informal hearing. See Kenneth Culp Davis, *Administrative Law of the Seventies* (Rochester, NY, 1976), pp. 253-255 and 267-268 on the 1975 case of *Goss* v. *Lopez*.

64. See Sorokin, note 2, p. 142.

65. The quotations in this paragraph are from Salishcheva, note 2, pp. 151, 93, and 81.

66. Sorokin, note 2, p. 168.

67. *Ibid.*, pp. 142 and 168-169; Salishcheva, note 2, p. 96.

68. *Ibid.*, p. 147-148.

69. *Ibid.*, p. 150.

70. *Ibid.*

71. Ivanov, note 49, p. 31.

72. Sorokin, note 2, pp. 142 and 147; Salishcheva, note 2, pp. 150-151.

73. *Ibid.*, p. 150.

74. Sorokin, note 2, p. 156.

75. Salishcheva, note 2, p. 150.

76. D. M. Chechot, *Administrativnaia Iustitsiia* (Administrative Justice), (Leningrad, 1973), p. 63.

77. Sorokin, note 2, pp. 142 and 145; Salishcheva, note 2, p. 151.

78. *Ibid.*, pp. 153-155; Sorokin, note 2, p. 169.

79. See, *e.g.*, Chechot, note 76, p. 119; V. I. Remnev, "Povyshenie Effektivnost' Poriadka Rassmotreniia Obrashchenii Grazhdan" (Raising the Effectiveness of the Procedure for Reviewing Appeals of Citizens), *SGiP*, 1976, No. 12, 18.

80. Salishcheva, note 2, p. 111.

81. See above, note 49.

82. Salishcheva, note 2, p. 113.

83. For further discussion on this point, see Barry, note 1, text accompanying notes 51-61.

84. See *ibid.*, text accompanying notes 93-95.

85. A. Lunev, "Sovershenstvovanie Garantii Prav Lichnosti v Sfere Gosudarstvennogo Upravleniia" (Perfecting the Guarantees of the Rights of the Individual in the Sphere of State Administration), *Sov. Iust.*, 1978, No. 5, 20-21.

86. Malein, note 2, p. 43.

87. *The New York Times*, October 21, 1976, 13.

88. Professor P. Shmidt in V. F. Khokhlov, "Problemy Pravotvorchestva v Gosudarstvennom i Administrativnom Prave SSSR i Vengerskoi Narodnoi Respubliki" (The Problem of Law Creation in State and Administrative Law in the USSR and the Hungarian People's Republic), *Pravovedenie*, 1976, No. 2, 119.

THE INDIVIDUAL IN SOVIET ADMINISTRATIVE PROCEDURE

Henn-Jüri Uibopuu

1. Historical Approach

Russian legal tradition in general and the development of Russian administrative law in particular should be considered as background for the study and better understanding of both the attitude of Soviet administrative organs, based on contemporary Soviet administrative law, and the reactions thereto of the objects of Soviet administration—individuals. Bureaucratic organization of administration, with an obviously great degree of discretionary power, seems to be the heritage of centuries of arbitrary Tsarist administration. Equally, inaccessibility of the full body of normative acts, subconstitutional, and all the more, substatutory, subordinate law is in full conformity with Russian legal tradition. Even newer attempts to bring Soviet legislation into better order by compiling an annotated edition of valid legal norms, under the title of *Svod zakonov*, reminds one of similar attempts by Speranskii, with his *Svod zakonov Rossiiskoi Imperii* of the years 1826-1832 and the organizing and compiling of the *Polnoe Sobranie Zakonov*.

On the other hand, the *"nichevo-mentality"*—with its few or almost no objections to administrative discretion or shortcomings—is most significant for a vast majority of the Soviet population. This also can be regarded as a heritage from Tsarist times, and such a mentality, of course, makes possible the Soviet form of administrative practice, with such outstanding characteristics as the uncertainty of the *locus standi* of the individual in the administrative procedure. This special feature of Soviet administration, for example, can also be regarded as a result of the Soviet approach to human rights which involves an overevaluation of society (*obshchestvennost'*) in general, at the cost of both the individual human being and human dignity. The fact that the individual lacks legal remedies in almost all cases of administrative process demonstrates further the Tsarist influence.

2. The Equal Effects of Acts and Omissions of Administrative Bodies

A crucial point with regard to the treatment of individuals as objects of Soviet administration is the fact that their interests can not only be violated or challenged by acts of administrative bodies, but also by their refusal to act or by omission of action. Even if the administrative act in question did not comply with the application of the applicant, or did not meet his expectations, he might be in a better position to defend his interests than in the case when the administration declined to act, *e.g.* it failed to register a religious community. In case of a negative decision of the administration, the citizen would have at least informal remedies such as complaints to the Procuracy. If action was omitted, such remedies would be opened only in cases where time-limits were exceeded for the consideration of applications by administrative bodies. Such time-limits exist only very rarely. Professor Hazard reports that notarial acts or refusals to act may be appealed to a court, but he also states that this is an exception to general Soviet practice.

Effective protection of citizens against slow or lazy administration requires formation of a legal claim under administrative law to force action by administrative bodies, as in the case of Austrian law in the form of a *Säumnis-beschwerde* (objection against neglection of duties/default). But such a remedy would only then be effective when fixed time-limits for the consideration of applications do not only exist in internal administrative regulations, but also come to the knowledge of the applicant. To judge the legality of a refusal of an application or a refusal to act, the applicant must also be informed of the legal grounds which exist for rejection of applications. To demonstrate how sad the situation can become, one need only consider the degree of unawareness among the population of rights and remedies, including tactics and strategies, that might be employed by persons facing psychiatric administrative hearings which is evident from a reading of the report "Psychiatric Manual for Dissidents" which was allegedly written by Bukovskii and Gluzman and disseminated by *samizdat*.[1]

3. Impermissibility of Appeals from Administrative Acts

Acts of Superior State Organs

It should be pointed out that some administrative acts are not the subjects of appeal simply because they have been issued by superior state organs, and higher administrative bodies than these organs do not exist. Here, judicial review would be the only appropriate legal remedy for safeguarding the interests of the individual. The most prominent example of such administrative acts are the Decrees of the Presidium of the Supreme Soviet of the USSR on taking away the citizenship of Soviet dissidents. Based on Article 4 of the Soviet citizenship Law of 1938, citizens of the USSR are deprived of their citizenship for supposed ". . . actions discrediting the title of a citizen of the USSR . . ."[2]

As an act of the Supreme Organ of the USSR, such decrees could be understood to be final, but could still be subject to judicial review. Nevertheless, a Soviet author excludes acts of deprivation of citizenship from judicial settlement by regarding them as "implementations of competences of the Presidium of the Supreme Soviet."[3]

Explicit Lack of Jurisdiction of Courts

Judicial review could be explicitly excluded in certain cases. Professor Hazard reports a case where a change of the registered name of a child was claimed to be illegal by the divorced husband.[4] After the granting of the petition by the court of first instance, the claim was finally dismissed by the appeal court for lack of jurisdiction. The interests of the claimant were protected, however, because a proper agency to decide the case was actually named, the local Soviets' Department for Guardianship and Trusteeship. Although the opponents in this case were two individuals, an administrative act was at stake — namely, the registration of the change of the name of a child without the father's authorization.

Non-Justiciability of Administrative Acts because of their Political Character

Another crucial point is the non-justiciability of an administrative act because of its purely political character. This concept certainly exists in all legal orders, but the principle of *partiinost'*, partiality in the sense of communist ideology, considerably restricts the scope of administrative acts which do not touch upon politically sensitive questions. It is understandable that judicial review in the USSR is only permitted in very exceptional cases and not as a rule, since the life of an individual is almost always viewed as being subject to political considerations of the state. Admittedly, the question whether to deprive a person of his citizenship because of his misconduct is highly political, especially with regard to the stipulation of Article 59 (2) of the 1977 Soviet Constitution which refers to the honor and dignity of Soviet citizenship. Even the late H. Lauterpacht had recognized:

> "No State . . . depriving its nationals of their citizenship would have admitted that such measures would have been arbitrary. They were, in their view, dictated by the highest necessity of the State."[5]

So the sensitiveness of Soviet writers with regard to the justiciability of deprivation of citizenship issues might be understandable. But, could the political character of an issue curtail a person's procedural safeguards otherwise available? As far as deprivation of citizenship proceedings have come to the knowledge of western scholars, the individuals concerned were not even heard in these proceedings. If we take into account the fact that deprivation of citizenship is a serious value deprivation for the individual, it should be the case that the individual has at least some *locus standi* under Soviet administrative law.

Moreover, the USSR has committed herself internationally by ratification of both Human Rights Covenants of the UN. It could be thus argued that the due process clause of Article 4 of the Covenant on Civil and Political Rights must apply to Soviet administrative procedure, at least to the extent that the individual has at least a limited *locus standi* in such sensitive issues as those concerning deprivation of citizenship. This could be even more so for such administrative acts as the expulsion of Soviet citizens deprived of their citizenship. Since the deprivation of citizenship is covered by Soviet citizenship law, it may be regarded as legal in a positivistic sense. but expulsion has no legal justification in contemporary Soviet legislation, at least with regard to published statutes and statutory normative acts. (Expulsion as a measure of criminal punishment was provided for in Soviet criminal law up to the coming into force of the 1958 Fundamentals of Criminal Legislation of the USSR and the Union Republics). The only concept applicable here would be the expulsion of an alien who holds no valid residence permit. But, the otherwise legal deprivation of citizenship of a person for the sole purpose of making him an alien, and thus subject to expulsion, would certainly amount to an *abus de droit*, especially in view of an objective reading of Articles 2, 13, 14, 16, and 26 of the above-mentioned Covenant.

4. Administrative Discretion and Arbitrariness

Another factor which could lead to a restriction of rights of individuals in administrative proceedings is administrative discretion. This concerns both justiciability of administrative acts and permissibility of appeal. If discretion is understood in the sense that the administrative decision-maker has the right to choose between several legitimate decisions, the decision itself is still based on discretion and, thus, is not subject to appeal. In highly sophisticated legal systems, the individual concerned may challenge the legitimacy of the basis of the decision, but not the overall discretionary power of the administrative body. The affected individual should know the scope of discretion of the administrative body in order to defend his legitimate interests and rights. Above all, a body—preferably independent and impartial—should have the right to decide whether the concrete administrative act was in accordance with legal provisions and not in excess of discretionary power, thus amounting to arbitrariness or an abuse of power. Unfortunately, Soviet administrative law and practice offer very little information in this respect.

It is, however, true, that Article 58 of the 1977 Constitution gives USSR citizens the right to lodge complaints against actions of state officials, agencies, and public organizations. Such complaints must be examined within time-limits established by law. Appeals to courts against actions of officials, who have contravened the law or exceeded their powers and infringed the rights of citizens, may be appealed to a court, but only in a manner prescribed by law. Such a law, in fact, exists only with regard to a very limited number of enumerated administrative acts, for example, inaccuracies in the lists of voters or mistakes in the calculation of taxes and fixes. Only if such a law would enlarge the scope of administrative acts, subject to appeal or to judicial review, would this provision of the new Constitution become meaningful and improve the hitherto weak position of the individual in Soviet administrative proceedings.

NOTES

1. *Samizdat* Materials, *AS*/2055.
2. *Ved. V.S. SSSR*, 1978, No. 26, item 412 on O.Ia. Rabin.
3. S.V. Chernichenko, *Mezhdunarodnopravovye voprosy grazhdanstva* (Questions of Citizenship under International Law), (Moscow, 1968), pp. 80, 155.
4. *Sots. Zak.*, 1972, No. 8, 9.
5. *International Law and Human Rights*, (London, 1950), p. 432.

THE REFORM OF SOVIET MILITARY JUSTICE: 1953-1958*

George Ginsburgs

The apparatus of Soviet military justice emerged from the Second World War vastly enlarged in size and with its sphere of jurisdiction enormously expanded as a result of the many fresh responsibilities thrust upon it by martial exigencies. By the end of the hostilities, regular military tribunals operated in: independent brigades, divisions, fortified districts (*raion*), airbase districts, naval bases, defenses of the rear areas of fronts, corps, armies, fronts, fleets, independent armies, and military regions (*okrug*). This network was supplemented by an extensive system of military tribunals of the armed forces of the Ministry of Internal Affairs (*MVD*), railroads, water basins, and shipping lines. Organizational direction of the ensemble of military tribunals was exercised by three offices of the USSR Ministry of Justice: the Chief Administration of Military Tribunals of the Soviet Army, the Administration of Military Tribunals of the Naval Forces, and the Administration of Military Tribunals of the Armed Forces of the *NKVD* (*MVD*).[1]

The structure of the military procuracy kept pace with this growth. In addition to the peacetime inventory of military procuracies, a number of new branches were organized. The field armies were serviced by military procuracies of fronts to which were subordinated the military procuracies of armies and formations (regular, tank and air armies, independent tank and mechanized corps, cavalry corps, infantry divisions, artillery divisions, airborne brigades, etc.). The military procuracies of fronts also exercised operational control over the military procuracies of the armed forces of the *MVD* for the defense of the rear areas of the fronts and the military procuracies of the railroads of the armed forces of fronts. Military procuracies likewise functioned in civil defense fronts, in the strategic airforce, etc. In the rear zones, military procuracies were created in the military regions and put in charge of the military procuracies of garrisons, reserve infantry divisions and air brigades, airbase districts, training brigades, and so forth. The navy was staffed with military procuracies of fleets, flotillas, naval bases, naval defense districts, sectors, coastal defenses. Following the shift of railroad and water

---

* Western literature on Soviet military law is sparse. The principal works are still H.J. Berman, M. Kerner, *Soviet Military Law and Administration* (Cambridge, Mass., 1955), and N. Zorin, *Soviet Military Tribunals* (New York, 1954), (Research Program on the USSR, Mimeo ser. No. 50).

transport to military status, the transport procuracies underwent a similar conversion. In the first years of the war, a portion of the district and region procuracies situated in the zone behind the front line was placed on a military footing. They remained under the authority of the procuracy of the union republics, but performed their tasks in close contact with the military procuracy. In localities where, because of military action, no territorial procuracy existed, the military procuracy took over its assignments. At the head of the hierarchy of military procuracies stood the Chief Military Procuracy of the Red Army, the Chief Procuracy of the Navy, the Chief Military Procuracy of Railroad Transport (established in January, 1942) and the Chief Military Procuracy of Marine and River Transport (established in May, 1943). Meantime, the entire structure of military procuracies formed part of the single scheme of the USSR Procuracy and, hence, was officially presided over by the Procurator of the USSR.[2]

Coincidentally, the powers of the institutions of military justice increased at an equally rapid clip. Military tribunals now handled, for instance, cases involving crimes against the prescribed procedure for performance of service committed by rank and file and administrative-executive personnel of the militia, individuals who were members of extermination battalions, citizens serving in units of the home guard while on leave from production, persons drafted into local anti-aircraft defense units, workers on railroad and water transport, command and rank and file personnel of the militarized guard of enterprises and militarized fire-fighting units of the *NKVD* (*MVD*), and so on. Military tribunals were also entrusted with hearing cases pertaining to certain crimes by civilians, such as the dissemination in wartime of false rumors spreading alarm among the population, the divulgence of state secrets and loss of documents containing state secrets, etc. The decree of the Presidium of the USSR Supreme Soviet of June 22, 1941, on martial law[3] authorized military tribunals to try cases concerning all the most serious crimes committed by the civilian population, including state crimes, crimes covered by the Law of August 7, 1932, robbery, premeditated murder, forcible release from places of confinement or from custody, evasion from performance of universal military service, resistance to representatives of public authority, illicit purchase, sale, and storage of weapons, theft of weapons. Furthermore, military commanders had the right to transfer to the jurisdiction of the military tribunals cases featuring other crimes, if required by wartime circumstances: *e.g.*, speculation, malicious hooliganism, etc. Finally, in the zone behind the front, military tribunals often figured as the only courts and, in that event, were called upon to deal with the full assortment of criminal offenses.[4]

Again, the military procuracy's agenda duplicated the inflationary experience. The apparatus waged an unremitting struggle against infractions of military discipline and the combat strenght of the army and navy, against enemy agents, and other hostile elements, against panic mongers, cowards, deserters, plunderers of military property, disorganizers of the rear area and, in localities subject to martial law, also against crimes directed at defense, public order, and state security. The offices of the military procuracy exercised constant supervision over the strict observance of wartime laws, the resolutions of the State Committee of Defense and the USSR Council of People's Commissars, the orders of the higher military command, fought against tardy or poor quality delivery to the armed forces of weapons, battle gear, equipment, uniforms, and foodstuffs, ascertained the reasons and conditions prompting these and other violations of the law, and took steps to eliminate the factors causing the situation. Nor, we are told, did the military procurators neglect their job to protect the rights and lawful interests of the servicemen and their families, as well as of the military units and institutions. Jointly, the territorial and military procuracies exerted every effort to guarantee the maximum satisfaction of the needs of the front and maintain labor discipline in enterprises engaged in defense work. During the offensive operations of the Soviet Army, the military procuracies assumed a heavy duty load on the territory recaptured from the enemy and immediately after liberation fulfilled here the functions of the territorial procuracy. One of the most important tasks assigned to the branch was the investigation of Nazi war crimes committed in the formerly occupied areas, the arrest of the Germans guilty of these atrocities together with their native accomplices, and the prosecution of these cases in a series of special trials staged in the midst of the war.[5]

Both in terms of the circle of people and the range of social phenomena falling under its writ, then, the system of military justice manned a sprawling empire by the time World War II drew to a close. A certain amount of pruning of the offshoots of a period of relatively uncontrolled growth was inevitable. Just from a logistical standpoint, victory brought about mass demobilization and the decommissioning of various units automatically spelled the demise of the corresponding military tribunals.[6] In sheer numbers, the pyramid of military tribunals shrank in proportion to the decline in the size of the USSR's armed forces as the country moved to resume its usual lifestyle. The structure of the institutions of military justice, though, remained essentially unchanged and kept the shape it had gradually gained in the course of the war. A lone exception was the noticeable modification in the prevailing pattern effected in 1948 when, in connection with the repeal of martial law on railroad and water transport, the military tribunals of railroad and water transport were converted into normally functioning line and regional railroad transport courts and line water transport courts, and the activity of the respective transport collegia of the USSR Supreme Court was concurrently revived.[7]

The return of peacetime conditions also naturally meant some reduction in the swollen authority of the apparatus of military justice. Thus, the Plenum of the USSR Supreme Court in its resolution of September 28, 1945, already indicated that, in the localities where martial law had been revoked, the special exemptions established by the edict of June 22, 1941, could no longer apply. That measure, it will be recalled, had withdrawn from the jurisdiction of the ordinary courts and transferred to that of the military tribunals all cases involving crimes against the defense, public order, and state security perpetrated in areas placed under martial law. Similarly, the Plenum explained that, with the end of the war, the rationale for the Resolution of the USSR Council of Ministers of November 24, 1942—reclassifying malicious and repeated nonfulfillment of mandatory agricultural deliveries by collective farm households and single family holdings as a state crime for the duration of the war governed by the provisions of article 56[6] of the RSFSR Criminal Code—had lapsed. Henceforth, such acts were punished in accordance with the prescriptions of paras. 2 or 3 of article 61 of the RSFSR Criminal Code (featured in Chapter II on "Other Crimes against the System of Administration") and, as a consequence, these matters were consigned to the care of the people's courts.[8]

Once more, of course, the military procuracy followed suit. The need for militarized territorial and military transport procuracies now disappeared and they were reorganized into ordinary (territorial and transport) procuracies. On the basis of the Chief Military Procuracy of the Soviet Army and the Chief Procuracy of the Naval Forces, a single Chief Military Procuracy was created within the structure of the USSR Procuracy. Its local organs in the army and navy became the military procuracies of regions, fleets, formations, and garrisons.[9]

Soviet authors have a valid point, then, when they claim that, with the restoration of peace, several types of cases were removed from the jurisdiction of military tribunals and the job of hearing them fell to the lot of people's courts, oblast, krai, and transport courts.[10] Some truth also attaches to their statements that this period was marked by steady contraction of the sample of cases referred to military tribunals whose primary attention was instead focused on questions of struggling against violations of the law in the army and navy and on tasks connected with the strengthening of military discipline.[11] Yet, such accommodations notwithstanding, the record shows that until 1953 the apparatus of military justice essentially retained the organizational and procedural format forged in the thick of the war,[12] meaning that in physical size, the sweep of its official powers, the summary nature of much of its *modus operandi*, the system was still in business on a scale reminiscent of its wartime performance and had made few concessions to the fact that the nation had supposedly switched to peacetime routine.

In 1953, however, the first major step was finally taken to correct this abnormal situation. In line with the current downgrading of the role and power of the secret police, all corrective-labor institutions (corrective-labor camps and colonies) were transferred to the authority of the Ministry of Justice, the structure of which was accordingly supplemented with the Main Administration of Corrective-Labor Institutions (*GULAG*). [13] The military tribunals of divisions and corps were abolished, as well as the military tribunals of the *MVD* troops, and a single system of military judicial organs was created. [14] By a decree of the Presidium of the USSR Supreme Soviet of September 1, 1953, the dread Special Board of the Ministry of Internal Affairs—which had long enjoyed virtually unlimited extra-judicial powers of repression—was liquidated, [15] whereupon, it was said, "all categories of criminal cases came within the competence of judicial organs." [16] Some of the changes consummated by these secret enactments were confirmed indirectly by the contents of the decree of September 11, 1953, [17] which continued and amplified the liberalizing trend that had been gaining ground in the area of Soviet law and administration of justice ever since Stalin's demise and Beria's downfall.

On this occasion, the power of the military tribunals was drastically curtailed. Military tribunals lost their jurisdiction over crimes committed by members of the rank and file and administrative-executive personnel of the militia against the established procedure for performing service, service-connected crimes committed by the personnel of the militarized guard of industrial enterprises, railroad, water and air transport, and other departments, the militarized guard of corrective-labor camps (except the militarized guard of the first category), and crimes by civilians entailing disclosure of state secrets and loss of documents containing state secrets. These matters were turned over to oblast and krai courts, the Supreme Courts of autonomous and union republics, line transport and camp courts, correspondingly. In sum, military tribunals henceforth had the right to try all crimes committed by servicemen, as well as by reservists during their training periods, and crimes against the prescribed procedure for performing service committed by members of the operations personnel of the organs of the USSR Ministry of Internal Affairs and members of the command personnel of the Main Administration of Camps and Colonies of the USSR Ministry of Justice. Lastly, civilians could in the future be arraigned before military tribunals on charges of espionage alone (whether technically designated espionage or treason), with indictment before ordinary courts now mandatory for various other offenses previously handled by the military tribunals under the inordinately inflated powers conferred on them during Stalin's reign. [18]

The stock reason offered for closing down the military tribunals of divisions and corps, as well as naval formations (except independent flotillas), was the further reduction in the number of personnel of the Army and Navy. [19] The decision to curb the excessive jurisdiction of the military tribunals, especially with regard to civilians, presumably stemmed from the current desire of Stalin's successors to restore socialist legality and purge the operations, *inter alia*, of the military justice system of the abuses associated with the preceding regime. Indeed, Soviet authors tend to emphasize that, "having unmasked the criminal activity of Beria and his accomplices, the Party took determined steps to reinstate legality in all rungs of the governmental apparatus and, in particular, in the activity of the military tribunals." [20] The accent on military tribunals in this context would indicate a singular concern for the quality of their past performance in the sense of noticeable failure to observe the standards of "socialist legality," and the latest measures taken to prune the authority of the military tribunals in order to broaden the competence of the common courts, are explicitly credited with contributing to the enhancement of "socialist legality." [21]

The motives behind the move to dismantle the large inventory of judicial and quasi-judicial agencies run by the secret police are more varied and complex. Least enlightening of all is the occasional cryptic statement that the military tribunals of the *MVD* troops were abolished because the need for their existence had lapsed. [22] A much better explanation, once again, is the present leadership's strong interest in and commitment to the business of refurbishing the badly tarnished image of "socialist legality". Stripping the armed forces of the *MVD* of their own court system, and putting an end to "extra-judicial procedures for handling criminal cases" by vacating the Special Board went far toward vindicating the regime's pledge to breath new life into the concept of "socialist legality." [23]

Quite *à propos*, too, are the comments of one Soviet writer in discussing the record of the military procuracy during the Second World War to the effect that:

> "Supervision over adherence to legality in the course of investigation by the organs of state security of the cases assigned to them which fell within the jurisdiction of military tribunals, *i.e.*, cases involving counterrevolutionary crimes, occupied a significant place in the work of the military procurators. The military procurators were bound to make sure the accusation of any person of commission of these gravest crimes be proven and properly qualified, so that the parties guilty of their commission not escape punishment and innocent parties not find themselves in the dock. This responsible sector of work was attended to by many trained military procurators, who defended principled, Party positions. However, as is known, in the conditions of the cult of the personality, it is precisely here that occurred deviations from and violations of socialist legality which were corrected and wholly eliminated thanks to the steps taken by the Party." [24]

To the extent that the military establishment had been the principal victim of these wholesale "deviations and violations" and that the Soviet

36

Union's new ruling clique owed a heavy debt to the military hierarchy for its survival in the showdown with Beria and his henchmen, chances are the policy initiated in 1953 of demoting the secret police by slashing its status and power also evinced the wish of the military elite to take revenge on its former tormentor. Reasserting the authority of the regular tribunals over the *MVD*'s operations personnel was proof positive that the professional military men had gained the upper hand at this stage of the contest.

The campaign to promote "socialist legality" in the activities of the organs of military justice received an additional boost with the issuance of the decree of the Presidium of the USSR Supreme Soviet of August 14, 1954, which vested in the military tribunals of military regions and fleets the right to review the sentences of lower military tribunals and the late military tribunals of the *MVD* troops that had entered into force upon the protest of military procurators of regions and fleets and chairmen of the military tribunals of districts and fleets. The terms of this edict were next extended to the military tribunals of army groups by the decree of the Presidium of the USSR Supreme Soviet of December 25, 1956. The exercise by the military tribunals of regions, army groups, and fleets of these *nadzor* functions is said to have upgraded supervision over the judicial performance of the lower military tribunals and raised the efficacy of judicial supervision. [25] Or, to quote a second Soviet source, the reform "represented a serious measure aimed at further enhancing legality, increasing responsibility in the work of all the rungs of the military court system and improving the business of administering justice." Subsequent practice reportedly showed that the decision had been fully justified and confirmed that these revisions had been correct and necessary. [26]

The 1954 decree, which broadened the *nadzor* procedure within the structure of military tribunals, coincided with another federal edict which provided for the establishment of presidia in the Supreme Courts of autonomous and union republics, krai and oblast courts, and the courts of autonomous oblasts charged with exercising *nadzor* functions *vis-à-vis* the respective lower courts. In that sense, then, the changes now implemented within the military apparatus were part and parcel of the general movement for reform of the regular court hierarchy which happened to call for the overhaul and refinement of the special supervision mechanism. Whatever rationale underlay the regime's resolve to treat the reorganization of this particular institution as a high priority item in the case of the system of common courts thus applied equally where the branch of military tribunals was concerned.

However, in the latter instance, an ancillary consideration may have entered the picture and possibly influenced the outcome in favor of the solution that in the end was adopted. Indeed, an interesting point worth recalling here is the degree to which the official authorities had on earlier occasions relied on the *nadzor* technique to "police" the operations of the military court complex and how pleased they professed to be by the artifact's proven effectiveness as a device for controlling the quality of the system's performance. Suffice it to note, for example, that during the Second World War, major changes were introduced in the rules governing proceedings before military tribunals and drastic limitations imposed on the rights of the accused "due to the exigencies of wartime": the sentences of the military tribunals in localities declared to be under martial law were no longer subject to ordinary appeal, cases could be tried within 24 hours after the accused was handed the bill of indictment, and trials could be conducted in the absence of both procurator and defense counsel. [27]

Given this record, criticism surfaced even in Soviet quarters that, in the course of the last war, the military tribunals did not always strictly abide by the procedural norms fixed by law, that supervision over the judicial activities of the military tribunals had not been adequately maintained and that, as a result, the guarantee that a lawful and valid sentence would be pronounced was in some measure weakened. The absence of a right on the part of the accused to appeal the sentence was usually cited in support of this contention. Opponents of that view have branded these attitudes as "mistaken" and sought to refute them by insisting that the lack of opportunity to appeal was largely compensated for by the strengthening of judicial *nadzor* through enlargement of the category of court instances authorized to review sentences that had become final and of the circle of officials empowered to protest such sentences. To document this position, they refer to the terms of the decree issued shortly after the outbreak of the war, which extended the right to file protests against sentences rendered by military tribunals to the military procurators and chairmen of military tribunals of regions and fronts.

The move is described as having had "an exceptionally great significance" in that it enabled the military tribunals of fronts and fleets quickly and efficiently and in a substantive manner to correct on the spot any errors or violations of the law committed by the lower military tribunals. The importance of this review work done under adverse conditions, we are told, can hardly be overestimated, taking into account the fact that some of the cadres of lower military tribunals, especially reserve personnel summoned to active duty, did not have enough familiarity with the repertory of the organs of military justice and so made mistakes in handling cases involving military crimes as well as other matters. The military tribunals of fronts and fleets, at the behest of the corresponding military procurators and chairmen of the respective tribunals, took timely steps to rectify these errors. A substantial proportion of the sentences pronounced by the primary military tribunals was reexamined at the supervisory stage. Various methods were employed for ensuring the efficacy and completeness of this special auditing arrangement— from comprehensive monitoring of the court-martial record to spot-check inspections. [28]

In conclusion, what Soviet spokesmen today claim is that the performance of the military tribunals of fronts and fleets as organs of judicial *nadzor* fully proved its worth and that the job they did had not only been indispensable, but also highly effective. [29] The lavish praise heaped on the *nadzor* procedure in the context of the experience of World War II suggests that the technique strongly recommended itself to the regime already on these grounds alone— independently of its perceived current relevance to the task of raising the professional caliber of the regular court system. Thus, despite the apparent synchronization of the decisions to beef up the *nadzor* process in the apparatus of both the common courts and the military tribunals, the leadership might, for two good reasons, have been inclined to initiate that reform in the latter sector apart from any intent to pursue a similar course of action with regard to the main judicial branch. First, such conduct would fit the substance and style of valued precedent. Second, the *nadzor* as distinct from the appellate approach, possesses the marked advantage of responding solely to internal stimuli: the administrative hierarchy has total discretion on whether or not and when to set the mechanism in motion. By contrast, appeals emanate from individuals and the traffic does not lend itself as easily to official regulation. Putting the emphasis on the phenomenon of judicial supervision therefore allows the ruling elite to advertise its devotion to the cause of justice and yet simultaneously make sure that its own priorities are observed in this domain. A bid to promote the *nadzor* device, run as a state monopoly, at the expense of "private" appeal channels would be apt to achieve precisely this objective, while preserving the regime's popular credibility as a paladin of "socialist legality."

One should also mention here that the institutional format of *nadzor* operations in the apparatus of military tribunals differed from that in the ordinary courts: instead of resorting to the concept of presidia, special supervision in the military branch was effectuated in each case by a panel consisting of three members (professional judges) of the military tribunal.

The experiments just described date from the early post-Stalin years when the dominant theme on the agenda of the successor leadership was to cure the worst excesses associated with the preceding regime through a series of *ad hoc* adjustments in the practices inherited from the past affecting all areas of governmental activity, including the law. By 1955, however, the new ruling clique felt sufficiently secure to launch a more ambitious program of reform designed to produce major pieces of legislation articulating the political credo of the men now managing the nation's affairs. In the sphere of administration of justice, the shift to a more methodical schedule of reorganization occurs with the entry into force of the Regulation on Procuratorial Supervision in the USSR, confirmed by the edict of the Presidium of the USSR Supreme Soviet of May 24, 1955. [30] Its provisions related to the status of the military branch of the Procuracy, either as a constituent of the overall structure of the Procuracy or in a special complementary capacity.

Thus, the USSR Procurator General presided over the military procuracy along with the rest of the procuratorial machinery. The military procurators followed the same *modus operandi* as their civilian colleagues. The grant to the USSR Procurator General and his deputies of the right to lodge protests against judgments, decisions, rulings, and decrees of any court of the USSR that had become final meant that these officials exercised *nadzor* functions *vis-à-vis* the country's entire lot of military tribunals. The Chief Military Procurator was vested with *nadzor* powers specifically with regard to the whole cast of military tribunals, while the military procurators of military regions and fleets possessed such authority with respect to the judgments and decrees of lower military tribunals. Where the right of bringing *nadzor* protests to the attention of the Military Collegium of the USSR Supreme Court was concerned, the present solution consummated a significant innovation in comparison with the corresponding formula in the 1938 Law on the Organization of Courts in the USSR and the Union and Autonomous Republics. The latter had reserved that power for the USSR Procurator and the Chairman of the USSR Supreme Court (art. 16), and, as just mentioned, now it was extended to the Procurator General's deputies and the Chief Military Procurator. Furthermore, the USSR Procurator General and his deputies could suspend the execution of a protested judgment, decision, ruling, or decree of any court of the USSR prior to resolution of the case by medium of supervision, and this rule applied, of course, to the ensemble of military tribunals. On the other hand, the directive failed to indicate with which instance fulfilling judicial supervision a particular protest had to be filed. [31]

The Regulation also noted that the staff of the central Procuracy comprised a Chief Military Procuracy [32] headed by the Chief Military Procurator. Departments could be formed within the office of the Chief Military Procuracy. In the army and navy proper, the "local" procuratorial units consisted of the military procuracies of military regions, fleets, formations, and garrisons. To hold the post of military procurator, an individual had to be at least 25 years old.

The impact of the Regulation on existing legislation was spelled out by the edict of the Presidium of the USSR Supreme Soviet of July 13, 1955. [33] In reference to the military procuracy, the directive declared articles 11, 12, 13, 14, 14[1], 17, and 33 of the Regulation on military tribunals and the military procuracy of August 20, 1926, as subsequently amended, [34] forthwith abrogated. The 1926 law, although described by everybody as badly obsolete, still formed the statutory basis for the operations of the military procuracy. The adoption of the 1955 Regulation had the effect, as one Soviet author put it, of practically repealing Chapter I of its 1926 predecessor dealing with the military procuracy. [35]

Meanwhile, the process of gathering additional components of the Soviet Union's para-military establishment under the jurisdiction of the apparatus of

40

military tribunals continued. Thus, military tribunals began to handle cases involving crimes by persons drafted for service in the military-construction detachments of the USSR Ministry of Defense, the time spent on such work being counted toward the tour of active military duty. The decree of the Presidium of the USSR Supreme Soviet of September 5, 1955, specified that these individuals bore criminal responsibility on an equal footing with regular servicemen, and all cases stemming from crimes committed by them fell within the competence of military tribunals. As against that, cases involving crimes committed by persons performing service in the military-construction detachments of the USSR Ministry of Defense, but hired for the job and not assigned there by draft, were not subject to the authority of the military tribunals. [36]

The 20th Party Congress, held in February, 1956, represents a landmark in the political evolution of the USSR after Stalin. Khrushchev's use of that occasion to denounce Stalin's crimes affected every aspect of Soviet public life, including, of course, the legal sector. The renewed call for the elimination of all vestiges of the widespread abuses spawned by the "cult of the personality" from the repertory of the USSR's institutions of government coincided with a fresh pledge to restore respect for the norms of "socialist legality" in the activity of the Soviet state apparatus. Again, curiously enough, the Congress' decisions in this connection were rated as of "special importance to all organs of Soviet justice and, in particular, the military tribunals." [37] Without going into details as to why the latter should here have been singled out for such unique attention, the tone of the comment does manage to imply that the past record of the military tribunals required a greater amount of improvement to meet the current standards than apparently was true of the common courts.

The reticence about airing the pertinent facts concerning previous defects in the performance of this branch of the judiciary is very much in tune with the whole attitude of treating the topic as an essentially private matter and keeping the extramural discussion focused almost entirely on general propositions. Whether this phenomenon is a function of the extraordinary deference then owed to the military hierarchy, or bespeaks a sense that questions associated with the business of the military establishment ought to be spared the glare of public debate, or means that these issues are considered to be so narrowly specialized that they should be left largely to the care of the experts attending to the professional affairs of the vested interest group, with minimum popular intrusion into its domestic routine, is open to speculation. What is quite clear is the difference in style in how freely the former faults of the regular courts were now talked about and the multitude of proposals for suitable reforms this disclosure elicited compared with how little was said on both counts where the military tribunals were concerned, although, as the above evidence indicates, their conduct during the Stalinist era was no better and, indeed, was probably rather a bit worse than that of the plain courts.

The tenor of the Congress lent fresh impetus to the movement for the reorganization of various branches of the Soviet governmental structure. Tangible proof of the latest policy line in the judicial department was offered by the decision to abolish the USSR Ministry of Justice, announced in the Resolution of the Central Committee of the CPSU and the USSR Council of Ministers of May 30, 1956, [38] and formalized by the edict of the Presidium of the USSR Supreme Soviet of May 30, 1956. [39] The move put an end to the dual system of court administration previously in force in the USSR, whereby the federal Supreme Court exercised control over the judicial activities of subordinate courts and the USSR Ministry of Justice discharged the tasks connected with central direction of the logistics of court administration. The managerial powers of the USSR Ministry of Justice *vis-à-vis* the ordinary courts forthwith passed to the republican Ministries of Justice, but, since the military tribunals figured as federal courts and were exempt from republican oversight, the responsibility for providing organizational supervision over the operations of the national system of military tribunals was presently vested in the USSR Supreme Court. The consensus within the Soviet legal community at the time seemed to run heavily in favor of the liquidation of the USSR Ministry of Justice on grounds that the measure had a positive effect on the work of the regular judicial branch. Similarly optimistic views were voiced concerning the impact of the reform on the activity of the military tribunals which were expected to benefit substantially from the concentration of all supervisory functions in the Military Collegium of the USSR Supreme Court following the extinction of the Administration of Military Tribunals inside the USSR Ministry of Justice together with the demise of the parent body, [40] curing the "parallelism" that had hitherto hobbled the control mechanism. [41] Thus, according to one opinion, "the combination of organizational leadership and judicial superintendence on the part of the higher tribunals always created and creates today the possibility of steering the activity of the military tribunals in the direction of the most successful execution of the tasks awaiting them." [42]

Meanwhile, in a further attempt to restore faith in "socialist legality", the regime took the drastic step of reopening old cases in order, where necessary, to correct the record. Reportedly, "the judicial organs, including military tribunals, jointly with the organs of the procuracy and state security did a big job in rectifying violations of socialist legality that had been allowed to occur in the past." [43]

The departure of the federal Ministry of Justice from the scene meant that its stock of official duties had to be apportioned elsewhere. The ensuing process of redistribution resulted, *inter alia*, in a thorough overhaul of the status and *modus operandi* of the USSR Supreme Court. [44] The new Regulation on the USSR Supreme Court, confirmed by the law of February 12,

1957,[45] noted that the USSR Supreme Court was the highest judicial organ in the USSR and, in that capacity, maintained supervision over the judicial activity of the judicial organs of the USSR which, at this juncture, boiled down to the hierarchy of military tribunals. To that end, the structure of the USSR Supreme Court included a Military Collegium. Members of military tribunals of regions and fleets could be allowed, when necessary, to serve as reserve judges for the consideration of cases in the Military Collegium of the USSR Supreme Court.

The Military Collegium was charged with: 1) trying as a court of first instance criminal cases of exceptional importance assigned by law to its jurisdiction; 2) examining cassational appeals and protests against judgments of military tribunals of regions and fleets in instances provided by law; and, 3) examining as a function of judicial *nadzor* protests filed by the Chairman of the USSR Supreme Court, the USSR Procurator General, and their deputies, as well as protests filed by the Chairman of the Military Collegium of the USSR Supreme Court and the Chief Military Procurator against judgments and rulings of military tribunals of regions and fleets. The formulation contains several novel features. For example, whereas the Civil and Criminal Collegia of the USSR Supreme Court were now limited in the exercise of their *nadzor* rights *vis-à-vis* the republican Supreme Courts to certain specific instances involving judgments and decisions contrary to national legislation or violating the interests of other union republics, the Military Collegium was not so restricted. The explanation was that, because of the current concern for the authority of the republican Supreme Courts as the highest judicial organs of sovereign entities, their pronouncements were treated as final except in the two situations just mentioned where other rights were affected by their actions. Military tribunals, as courts of the USSR, did not enter into the republican judicial system. Hence, granting the federal Supreme Court the power to oversee all judgments, decisions, or rulings by lower military tribunals without reservation could not infringe on the sovereignty of the union republics and did not run counter to the prevailing policy of protecting the latter from undue intrusion by the central apparatus. [46]

Then, insofar as the Regulation expressly stipulated that the Military Collegium of the USSR Supreme Court was entitled to examine cassational appeals and protests against judgments of military tribunals of regions and fleets, the conclusion was drawn that its supervisory authority was confined to cases that had not met with correct solution in the military tribunals operating at that particular grade. If, by contrast, the case had been tried at the primary level (*i.e.*, the military tribunal at the rank of army, flotilla, military formation, or garrison) and had not been audited in appellate or *nadzor* procedure by the corresponding military tribunal on the rung of region or fleet, the Military Collegium was precluded from accepting the case for *nadzor* verification. Instead, the matter had to be returned to the proper military tribunal of region or fleet to be considered in *nadzor* proceedings initiated on the protest of the competent officials.[47] The picture one gets here is that the regime wanted to make sure that the traffic in the network of military tribunals flowed upward observing a strict sequential order, without jumping intermediate stages and generating logjams at the top.

Finally, the 1957 Regulation substantially expanded the circle of persons possessing the right to lodge protests on *nadzor* grounds before the Military Collegium of the USSR Supreme Court. The 1938 Law on Court Organization, it will be recalled, had vested that right in the USSR Procurator General and the Chairman of the USSR Supreme Court. The 1955 Statute on the Procuracy, as indicated earlier, had added the deputies of the USSR Procurator General and the Chief Military Procurator to the roster of individuals armed with such authority. The latest enactment further extended it to apply to the deputies of the Chairman of the USSR Supreme Court and the Chairman of the Military Collegium of the USSR Supreme Court.[48] Supervisory functions were thus assigned to a much larger group of people which, presumably, was intended to guarantee that in the future more effective use would be made of these powers.

Pursuant to the revised rules, the Collegia of the USSR Supreme Court hear cases as courts of first instance in the shape of a presiding judge—member of the USSR Supreme Court—and two people's assessors. Where the Military Collegium was concerned, the format represented a change from the past in that it dropped the old clause featuring an exemption permitting the Military Collegium, in instances specially sanctioned by the code of criminal procedure, to hear cases in the presence of three professional judges picked from among the members of the Collegium.[49] The norm prescribing mandatory participation of people's assessors in all trial proceedings was commonly assessed as a step toward strengthening democratic practices in the administration of justice and also helping raise the quality of judicial performance by supplying the trial court with fuller information on the conditions of army life, the personality of the accused, etc., and so enabling the tribunal to arrive at a fairer decision.[50] Cassational appeals and protests, as well as protests by way of judicial supervision, were to be considered by a panel of three members of the USSR Supreme Court. The judgments of the Military Collegium would be rendered in the name of the USSR.

The Chairman of the USSR Supreme Court was authorized to refer to the USSR Supreme Court, in accordance with the provisions of the current statute, protests against decisions, judgments, and rulings of the judicial Collegia of the USSR Supreme Court. He could preside at judicial sessions of the Collegia of the USSR Supreme Court during the consideration of any case and exercised general organizational direction of the work of these Collegia. In the absence of the Chairman, all his rights and responsibilities devolved on his deputy. Similarly, the chairmen of the Collegia of the USSR Supreme

Court were entrusted with the exercise of direction over the work of the respective Collegia; they presided at preparatory and judicial sessions of the Collegia, formed benches for judicial sessions of the Collegia from among the members of the respective Collegia and the complement of people's assessors, and reported to the Plenum of the USSR Supreme Court on the work of the Collegia. In additon, the Chairman of the Military Collegium was charged with the organizational direction of the entire lot of military tribunals.

The members, as well as the people's assessors, of the USSR Supreme Court could be relieved of their duties before the expiry of their term of office only by resolution of the USSR Supreme Soviet and, in the interval between sessions, by resolution of the Presidium of the USSR Supreme Soviet, with subsequent submission for approval by the USSR Supreme Soviet. The structure of the apparatus of the USSR Supreme Court was to be determined by the Presidium of the USSR Supreme Soviet. Following these instructions, on June 3, 1957, the federal Presidium adopted a decision on the Supreme Court's organizational table. [51] The staff of the Military Collegium was to consist of: 1) the Secretariat of the Military Collegium, with departmental status; 2) an organizational-inspectoral department; 3) a department for cadres; 4) a reception office (to which are routed appeals and protests related to cases concerning individuals sentenced by military tribunals), [52] with departmental status; and, 5) an administrative-executive department.

In short, the 1957 reform consummated some major changes in the design of the Soviet judiciary and, in the opinion of at least one Soviet author, the experience marked an important step in the way of implementation of the decisions of the 20th Party Congress regarding the further strengthening of "socialist legality." [53]

Initially, the successor regime seemed content to concentrate its attention on the task of institutional overhaul in seeking to eliminate perceived defects in the sphere of military justice. Other aspects of the agenda were ignored at the outset, and only after the events of the 20th Party Congress did the authorities proceed to back the various moves for structural reorganization with additional measures aimed at sustaining the pace of progress here. The political leadership now also addressed itself to the problem of operational priorities. Thus, pursuant to the current emphasis on "educational" approaches in lieu of the previous reliance on "repressive" techniques, the October 1957 Plenum of the CPSU Central Committee explained to the military courts "the imperativeness of continued strengthening of conscious discipline based not on fear, but on profound understanding by each serviceman of his patriotic duty." Much of the responsibility for putting these instructions into practice rested with the military tribunals which, in hearing cases, were henceforth expected to "uncover deficiencies that still occurred in the education of servicemen and not permit its substitution by methods of judicial repression." [54] The February 1958 session of the Plenum of the USSR Supreme

Court which heard a report by its Military Collegium sounded the same theme. While calling for the severe, yet fair, punishment of violators of military discipline, it cautioned the military tribunals to eschew unjustified sentencing of servicemen on purely formal grounds and urged them thoroughly and comprehensively to study the reasons and circumstances contributing to the commission of breaches of the law, raise the level of legal propaganda, and enhance the educational role of open court proceedings. [55]

A related issue was the professional quality of the personnel assigned to the system of military tribunals. Interestingly enough, this question had a broader import in that opinions favoring the recruitment of more competent individuals to man the regular judiciary likewise were commonplace at the time. The push for staffing the ordinary courts with judicial officials of better caliber in fact managed to score considerable gains, for, in apparent recognition of the validity of the implied criticism, the ranks of the judiciary were then reinforced with new cadres possessing superior training. [56] A parallel development may be observed in the military justice sector where, by 1958, thanks to steps recently taken, 97% of the military judges were said to have a higher legal education. If true, these figures are very impressive indeed, prompting a local verdict that the whole experiment had a positive effect on the work of the military tribunals. [57]

***

The picture just drawn of how the Soviet apparatus of military justice fared during the transitional period 1953-1958 looks sufficiently straightforward not to require any elaborate conclusions. Instead, let me make a few brief remarks concerning certain claims Soviet writers have advanced on behalf of that record and formulate one general observation occasioned by the manner in which the entire affair was handled.

First, we have the intriguing statement that "the Communist Party and the Soviet government always paid a lot of attention to the activity of the organs of military justice," as a result of which "the organization and procedure of their work was always precisely regulated by law." [58] Perhaps the Party and the government really did care, but the applicable law in this domain was in such sorry state by the late 1950s and had persisted that way for a long enough spell to make it obvious that the regime took very little notice of the utter confusion which reigned in this area. For decades, matters connected with the operation of the nation's system of military courts had been resolved in completely *ad hoc* fashion, with no evident concern for maintaining even a modicum of uniformity, symmetry, or clarity in the welter of normative prescriptions spawned almost at random.

Second, we are told that "the organs of military justice are staffed by highly qualified, politically mature cadres." [59] Although, as previously pointed out, the assertion fits the situation that emerged in 1958, the latter represented the climax of a concerted effort to rectify past practices and so amounts to a departure from, rather than a confirmation of, established precedent.

On the subject of style, the item worth bearing in mind is the degree to which the discussions about the pending reforms in the field of military justice were kept private. This phenomenon has already been alluded to and needs reemphasizing. In effect, compared to the proliferation of public proposals on how the regular judiciary should be restructured and heated debates revolving around the merits of the different recommendations, virtually nothing appeared in the standard legal publications to hint at what fate lay in store for its military counterpart. One logically assumes that a process of sifting alternative plans and suggestions did predate the enactment in December, 1958, of the new Regulation on Military Tribunals, but the tone, scope, and content of the research is a well-guarded secret. Several plausible explanations were offered earlier to account for this behavior, and the only reason for bringing up the topic once again is to stress the stark contrast in the procedures that the Soviet government chose to follow in apprising the nation of the changes it was thinking of introducing in the mechanisms of administration of civilian and military justice, respectively: the former were treated as a legitimate object of popular interest and the latter as a piece of intramural business best left to the decision of the departmental specialists. The distinction says something about the status of the military complex in the Soviet political scheme and sheds light on the kind of relationship which then existed between the local civilian and military elites. The cliché of the Party's pervasive authority was now at least inferentially belied by its plain willingness tacitly to acknowledge in some sense the autonomy of the military machine to determine the future shape of its own judicial branch.

NOTES

1. B.A. Galkin (ed.), *Organizatsiia suda i prokuratury v SSSR* (Organization of the Court and Procuracy in the USSR), (Moscow, 1967), p. 141.
2. A.G. Gornyi, G.M. Dolgopiatov, A.M. Medvedev, "Organizatsiia i deiatel'nost' sovetskoi voennoi prokuratury" (Organization and Activity of the Soviet Military Procuracy), in *Na strazhe sovetskikh zakonov* (Guarding Soviet Laws), (Moscow, 1972), pp. 369-370.
3. *Ved. V.S. SSSR*, 1941, No. 29; S.A. Golunskii (ed.), *Istoriia zakonodatel'stva SSSR i RSFSR po ugolovnomu protsessu i organizatsii suda i prokuratury 1917-1954gg., sbornik dokumentov* (History of the Legislation of the USSR and RSFSR on Criminal Procedure and the Organization of the Judiciary and the Procuracy, 1917-1954, Collection of Documents), (Moscow, 1955), pp. 581-582 (excerpts). An English translation of the decree may be found in H.J. Berman, M. Kerner (eds.), *Documents on Soviet Military Law and Administration* (Cambridge, Mass., 1958), pp. 133-135.
4. D.S. Karev, *Organizatsiia suda i prokuratury v SSSR* (Organization of the Judiciary and the Procuracy in the USSR), (Minsk, 1960), pp. 128-129; A.G. Gornyi *et al., op. cit.*, p. 367.
5. A.G. Gornyi *et al., op. cit.*, pp. 368, 370-371.
6. B.V. Borisoglebskii (ed.), *Nauchno-prakticheskii kommentarii k Polozheniiu o voennykh tribunalakh* (Scientific-Practical Commentary to the Regulation on Military Tribunals), (2nd rev. ed., Moscow, 1961), p. 67 (hereafter abbr. as *Kommentarii*). Cuts in the military justice branch for this reason have been common practice in the USSR. The same source notes, for instance, that "the Law on the new significant reduction in the Armed Forces of the USSR adopted by the Supreme Soviet of the USSR in January, 1960, had a substantive influence on the organization of military tribunals" (*ibid.*).
7. M.V. Kozhevnikov, *Istoriia sovetskogo suda 1917-1956 gody* (History of the Soviet Judiciary 1917-1956), (Moscow, 1957), pp. 347, 351.
8. *Ibid.*, pp. 346-347; *Sots. Zak.*, 1945, No. 10, 33-34.
9. A.G. Gornyi *et al., op. cit.*, p. 383.
10. D.S. Karev, *op. cit.*, p. 129.
11. G.I. Bushuev, "Voennye sudy" (Military Courts), in *Sud v SSSR* (The Judiciary in the USSR), (Moscow, 1977), p. 155.
12. B.A. Galkin (ed.), *op. cit.*, p. 141.
13. M.V. Kozhevnikov, *op. cit.*, p. 377. This source also mentions, however, that "soon after, the Ministry of Justice of the USSR was relieved of all these functions which exceeded the bounds of judicial administration."
14. D.S. Karev, *op. cit.*, p. 100; Ia.N. Umanskii, *Sovetskoe gosudarstvennoe pravo* (Soviet State Law), (Moscow, 1960), p. 337; S.S. Maksimov, "Osnovnye voprosy organizatsii i deiatel'nosti voennykh tribunalov" (Basic Questions of Organization and Activity of Military Tribunals), in S.A. Golunskii (ed.), *Vopros sudoproizvodstva i sudoustroistva v novom zakonodatel'stve Soiuza SSR* (Questions of Judicial Procedure and Court Organization in the New Legislation of the USSR), (Moscow, 1959), p. 416; B.A. Galkin (ed.), *op. cit.*, pp. 141-142, where one reads about the abolition of "military tribunals of divisions, corps, and naval formations (except independent flotillas)"; *Kommentarii*, p. 67.

15. M. Mikhailov, "Nekotorye voprosy sovetskoi konstitutsionnoi praktiki" (Certain Questions of Soviet Constitutional Practice), *SGiP*, 1956, No. 9, 15. The first Soviet reference to the liquidation of the Special Board appeared only in January, 1956. See the editorial "Za povyshenie roli pravovoi nauki v kodifikatsii sovetskogo zakonodatel'stva" (For Upgrading the Role of Legal Science in the Codification of Soviet Legislation), *SGiP*, 1956, No. 1, 3: ". . . as early as 1953, the Special Board under the Ministry of Internal Affairs of the USSR was abolished, with the transfer of all categories of criminal cases to the jurisdiction of the organs of the general judicial system." Since then, there have been many similar assertions, for instance, F.G. Tarasenko, *Voprosy organizatsii i deiatel'nosti sovetskikh sudov* (Questions of Organization and Activity of Soviet Courts), (Moscow, 1958), p. 13; R.A. Rudenko, "Zadachi dal'neishego ukrepleniia sotsialisticheskoi zakonnosti v svete reshenii XX s"ezda" (Tasks of Further Strengthening of Socialist Legality in the Light of the Decisions of the 20th Congress), *SGiP*, 1956, No. 3, 17; D.S. Karev, *op. cit.*, p. 100.

16. M.V. Kozhevnikov, *op. cit.*, p. 350.

17. For text, see *Sbornik zakonov SSSR i ukazov Prezidiuma Verkhovnogo Soveta SSSR (1938g.-noiabr 1958g.)* (Collection of Laws of the USSR and Edicts of the Presidium of the USSR Supreme Soviet (1938-November 1958), (Moscow, 1959), pp. 575-576; D.S. Karev (ed.), *Ugolovno-protsessual'noe zakonodatelstvo SSSR i Soiuznykh Respublik, sbornik* (Legislation on Criminal Procedure of the USSR and the Union Republics, Collection), (Moscow, 1957), p. 28.

18. A. Kostromin, M. Karyshev. "Voennye tribunaly v bor'be za sotsialisticheskuiu zakonnost'" (The Military Tribunals in the Struggle for Socialist Legality), *Sov. Iust.*, 1958, No. 12, 8.

19. *Kommentarii*, p. 67; S.S. Maksimov, *op. cit.*, p. 416.

20. N.V. Vasil'ev, V.N. Kudriavtsev, "O Zakone ob ugolovnoi otvetstvennosti za voinskie prestupleniia" (On the Law concerning Criminal Liability for Military Crimes), *SGiP*, 1959, No. 2, 90; P. Likhachev, "Sorokaletie voennykh tribunalov" (Fortieth Anniversary of Military Tribunals), *Sots. Zak.*, 1958, No. 12, 10; S.S. Maksimov, *op. cit.*, p. 416.

21. P. Likhachev, *loc. cit.*

22. *Kommentarii*, p. 67.

23. B.A. Galkin (ed.), *op. cit.*, pp. 141-142; S.S. Maksimov, *op. cit.*, p. 416; P. Likhachev, *loc. cit.*

24. A.G. Gornyi *et al.*, *op. cit.*, p. 372.

25. *Kommentarii*, pp. 53-54. Also, see P. Likhachev, *op. cit.*, 10.

26. S.S. Maksimov, *op. cit.*, p. 432.

27. A.G. Gornyi *et al.*, *op. cit.*, pp. 372-373; S.S. Maksimov, *op. cit.*, p. 433.

28. *Kommentarii*, p. 53; S.S. Maksimov, *op. cit.*, pp. 433-434.

29. A.G. Gornyi *et al.*, *op. cit.*, pp. 374-375; *Kommentarii*, p. 53; S.S. Maksimov, *op. cit.*, pp. 433-434.

30. *Ved. V.S.SSSR*, 1955, No. 9, item 222; *Materialy k izucheniiu kursa "Organizatsiia suda i prokuratury v SSSR"* (Materials for Study in the Course "Organization of the Judiciary and the Procuracy in the USSR"), (Moscow, 1960), pp. 133-144; A. Reigas (comp.), *Sbornik normativnykh aktov i instruktivnykh materialov k izucheniiu kursa "Organizatsiia suda i prokuratury v SSSR"* (Collection of Normative Acts and Instructional Materials for Study in the Course "Organization of the Judiciary and the Procuracy in the USSR"), (Riga, 1969), pp. 92-108.

31. *Kommentarii*, p. 55. The oversight was corrected by the Regulation on Military Tribunals, confirmed by the Law of December 25, 1958.

32. Confirmed by the Resolution of the Presidium of the USSR Supreme Soviet of

April 7, 1956, concerning the structure of the central apparatus of the USSR Procuracy. See *Ved. V.S. SSSR*, 1956, No. 8, item 186; A. Reigas (comp.), *op. cit.*, pp. 110-112; *Materialy* ..., pp. 145-146. See, also, the Order of the USSR General Procurator of April 10, 1956, No. 54, concerning the structure of the central apparatus of the USSR Procuracy and the procuracies of republics, krais, and oblasts. *Sovetskaia prokuratura, sbornik vazhneishikh dokumentov* (The Soviet Procuracy, Collection of the Principal Documents), (Moscow, 1972), pp. 294-296.

33. Text in *Sbornik*, pp. 598-599; *Sovetskaia prokuratura*, pp. 293-294.

34. *Sobr. Zak. SSSR*, 1926, No. 57, item 413; 1929, No. 13, item 106, and No. 70, item 655.

35. S.S. Maksimov, *op. cit.*, p. 402.

36. *Kommentarii*, p. 29.

37. S.S. Maksimov, *op. cit.*, p. 416.

38. *Izvestiia*, June 3. 1956.

39. *Ved. V.S. SSSR*, 1956, No. 12, item 250.

40. |M.V. Kozhevnikov, *op. cit*, pp. 380-381; P. Likhachev, *op. cit.*, 10.

41. B.A. Galkin (ed.), *op. cit.*, p. 142.

42. S.S. Maksimov, *op. cit.*, p. 434. Also, see V.V. Borisoglebskii, "Polozhenie o voennykh tribunalakh" (Regulation on Military Tribunals), *SGiP*, 1959, No. 2, 77.

43. P. Likhachev, *loc. cit.*

44. Generally, see D.D. Barry, "The USSR Supreme Court: Recent Developments," *Soviet Studies*, 1969, No. 4, 511-522.

45. *Ved. V.S. SSSR* , 1957, No. 4, items 84 and 85.

46. *Kommentarii* , pp. 51-52.

47. *Ibid.*, p. 52.

48. *Ibid.*, pp. 50-51.

49. Article 70 of the 1938 Law on Court Organization. The same rule, *mutatis mutandis*, applied to other military tribunals (art. 56). See, too, M. Subotskii, S. Orlovskii, L. Subotskii, V. Malkis, *Voennyi sud* (Military Court), (Moscow, 1926), p. 51.

50. *E.g.*, *Kommentarii*, pp. 12-13.

51. Text in A. Reigas (comp.), *op. cit.*, p. 16; *Materialy*. .., pp. 101-102.

52. *Organizatsiia suda i prokuratury v SSSR* (Organization of the Judiciary and the Procuracy in the USSR), (Moscow, 1961), p. 178.

53. P. Likhachev, *op. cit.* 10.

54. A. Kostromin, M. Karyshev, *op. cit.*, 9.

55. *Ibid.*

56. A.F. Gorkin, in *Vazhnyi etap v razvitii sovetskogo prava (Novoe obshchesoiuznoe zakonodatel'stvo v oblasti ugolovnogo prava, sudoustroistva i sudoproizvodstva)*, (Important Stage in the Development of Soviet Law (New All-Union Legislation in the Domain of Criminal Law, Court Organization, and Court Procedure)), (Moscow, 1960), p. 119.

57. P. Likhachev, *op. cit.*, 11. Note that, by contrast, the proportion of people's judges with a higher legal education was simultaneously raised to 55.4%, which, *inter alia*, shows the greater capacity of a specialized institution to mobilize its resources, coupled, of course, with the military establishment's unique ability to recruit necessary talent or funnel suitable people into desired slots.

58. B.S. Teterin, "Polozhenie o voennykh tribunalakh" (Regulation on Military Tribunals), in *Vazhnyi etap*, note 56 above, p. 95.

59. *Ibid.*

ARE MILITARY COURTS NECESSARY?

René Beermann

In this paper, I have decided to abstain from references to the existing military law of the USSR, and to consider the question of the necessity of military courts in general.

This is a natural question in the context of the general democratic rule that all are equal before the law (and in the courts of law); the privilege of a special professional court would appear *prima facie* a breach of a general overriding principle of justice, a principle which has been expressed in the 1977 Constitution (Basic Law) of the USSR, where Article 156 states "Justice in the USSR shall be carried out on the principle of equality of citizens before the law and the courts." Article 151 of the same Constitution, while *inter alia* setting up military tribunals for the Armed Forces, seems to contradict Article 156. Why is a group of people, and potentially the most dangerous at that, excluded from the general jurisdiction and provided with the privilege of its own legal institutions?

First, a retrospective introduction may be permitted in the form of a reference to Tsarist military justice and to one of the most famous lawyers of the early 20th century, O. O. Gruzenberg. One should note that Gruzenberg was a most conscientious and sensitive advocate. It was always a most excruciating experience for him to be defending counsel in a capital case. About his emotions, he writes in his memoirs:

> "You are like a schoolboy having to face examinations; you pray and intermingle your prayers with some magical, irrational guesses at the future. You are ashamed of such childish behaviour and yet you do it. You make guesses at the number of houses in the streets, the number of the next tramcar, and you hope that all will be well when you have guessed correctly."[1]

A young collegue once asked Gruzenberg to appeal in the Supreme Military Court the case of a Lieutenant Pirogov, condemned to die by the Priamur region Military District Court for conspiring to overthrow the Tsarist government, and, if necessary, to kill the Tsar. The other conspirators were civilians and received stiff sentences of penal servitude. The appeal, permitted only on formal grounds, contained arguments which seemed hardly sufficient to invalidate the decision and sentence of the trial court. One of the arguments was Pirogov's request to have the sentence quashed because he had been denied the services of a civilian counsel. Here, Gruzenberg was aware that—in the case of a member of the services being charged for offenses provided for and defined in the Military Penal Code—no civilian defense counsels were permitted in the military trial courts. The other grounds for the appeal were even less convincing than the first. The position of Gruzenberg as defense counsel was, in addition, aggravated because the records of the trial were unavailable for perusal before the hearing of the appeal. This meant that he would have to rely on the summary of the reporting judge. Luckily for Pirogov and Gruzenberg, the summary was read by the rapporteur with greater circumspection than usual at appeal hearings. The summary mentioned that Pirogov and the other conspirators were charged and sentenced for contraventions of art. 102, part 3, of the Criminal Code (*Ugolovnoe Ulozhenie*) *and* that Pirogov was also charged on the basis of arts. 110, 112 of v. XXIII of the Code of Military Laws. It was precisely the conjunction *and* (emphasis supplied), the Russian *i*, which struck Gruzenberg as somewhat odd, but therefore important, and which finally saved Pirogov's life.[2] Gruzenberg took the case and argued that because Pirogov (for reasons unknown to Gruzenberg) was charged not only for an offense according to the military criminal code but also for an offense under the civilian *Ugolovnoe Ulozhenie*, a civilian defense counsel, *i.e.* an advocate, should have been admitted. While the court was out to consider the appeal and counsel's arguments, some members of the procuracy came up to Gruzenberg and asked him if he was aware of whom he was fighting. Gruzenberg answered in the negative, because regrettably enough he had been unable to see the records. His colleagues informed him that it was the Tsar himself. It transpired that Pirogov had been charged and tried twice for the same offense. At his first trial, Pirogov had been charged exclusively on the basis of arts. 110 en 112 of the Militairy Code and sentenced to death "with the loss of all ranks, rights and privileges." The military commander of the Priamur army had commuted the death sentence to life imprisonment. The files had been seen by the Tsar, who had made a marginal note "*NAPRASNO*"—unnecessary.[3] The loyal judges put Pirogov on trial a second time for the same offense. Now Pirogov stood before the Military Court as a simple convict and no longer a lieutenant of the Russian Army. Therefore, the military judicial authorities, in order to be on the safe side, had added to the charges against Pirogov the article of the *Ugolovnoe Ulozhenie* (the article for which the civilian conspirators had been convicted and sentenced to life imprisonment and hard labor).

After a few hours of deliberation, with Gruzenberg's tension driving him almost to the point of insanity, the Supreme Military Court returned a verdict which quashed the sentence and returned the case to the Far East for a review of the case. At the retrial, Pirogov was again found guilty and sentenced to death. An appeal went to the Supreme Military Court for a second time. Now

Gruzenberg was aware of the circumstances and had a good knowledge of the minutes of the previous trials. His appeal was based on the *ne bis in idem* principle. In spite of the well-reasoned and valid arguments of the Military Procurator, Gruzenberg won the appeal. The Supreme Military Court decided to quash the third sentence, accepting the argument of the defense counsel that both the second and the third sentences of the trial court were gross violations of the *ne bis in idem* principle. Therefore, according to the Supreme Military Court, only the first commuted sentence was valid and the other two were gross violations of the law. Thus, Pirogov's life was saved in spite of the wishes of the Tsar.[4]

Now, in order to demonstrate the difference between the ethos of the pre-revolutionary Supreme Military Court and that of a civilian criminal college of the Supreme Court of the USSR, we will report a case that took place (almost half a century after Pirogov's trial) at the time of Nikita Sergeevich Khrushchev. On this occasion, a civilian court in Moscow tried not counter-revolutionaries or would-be assassins, but smugglers and speculators, among them two men by the name Rokotov and Faibishenko. The originally rather mild penalties for smuggling and speculating in currencies and precious metals were amended after the event in order to fit the case of a large scale offense, and the new, stiffer penalties—up to 15 years imprisonment—were now employed in the sentences.[4] This took place in spite of the rule that there is no retroactivity in criminal law. In the literature available on the trial, it is stated that the proceedings and sentences were reported by the Procurator General to Khrushchev, who (it is said) went into a state of outrage that at least five of the accused had not been sentenced to capital punishment. The Procurator's reply that there was no law which enabled the courts to do so was met by Khrushchev's shouts: "Why did they not tell me that there is no such law? If this is the case, we shall write and there will be such a law."[6] The desires of Nikita Sergeevich were met, and a second amendment was passed with the death penalty being made an alternative punishment for speculating in currencies, securities, and precious metals on a large scale or as a form of business.[7] The Supreme Court obliged by quashing the sentence of the trial court, and two of the accused, Rokotov and Faibishenko, were sentenced to death and shot after a retrial in the District Court of Moscow.

In his memoirs, Gruzenberg states that he preferred to defend appeals in the Supreme Military Court rather than under the jurisdiction of the Senate; cowardly and/or indolent Senators were usually chosen to hear appeals in political cases, and were inclined to go along with the directives received from above. The Supreme Military Court, however, lacked these "political virtues", but had instead, in the eyes of the administrative authorities, "judicial foibles." The judges of the Supreme Military Court, being senior officers, were trained throughout their whole lives and careers to shun cowardice and to exercise civilian as well as military courage in alle circumstances of life.

They belonged to a closely knit organisation, ruled by a strict ethical code and rules of discipline. Cowardice would have made them non-persons among their own colleagues. Gruzenberg provides ample proofs of instances where the Supreme Military Court quashed unjust and severe sentences of the lower military courts, whenever possible trying to act in accordance with their high ethical principles, and thus preventing the execution of innocent people.

It is, however, necessary to note that Nikita Sergeevich had, of course, his own ethical values and codes of rules and mores. For him, the principles obtained that profiteering and moneygrabbing, particularly if they took place on a large scale and as a business, were heinous offenses against the new revolutionary order and this justified capital punishment.

Some legal principles like *ne bis in idem* or no retrospective application of criminal laws were remnants and survivors of a defunct bourgeois-capitalist era, which seemed to him superfluous in a society approaching with great speed the advent of communism in the 1980s. It would be anybody's guess what decision a Military Division of the Supreme Court of the USSR would have taken. With its greater adherence to rules and ethical principles and as a corporate body enjoying greater cohesion and thus independence, it could have decided in favor of the prisoners. On the other hand, with its far greater politicization than was the case in the pre-revolutionary army, it could have decided in favor of the political demands of the day and against established legal and ethical principles.

However, there are reasons other than valor which induced the Supreme Military Court of pre-revolutionary Russia to leniency in the case of Pirogov and in other analogous cases. First, there is the feudal tradition of a justice administered by one's peers. Officers continued to be, in some ways, the descendents of the medieval knights. Knightly virtues and chivalry continued to play a vital part in their training and basic attitudes. Pirogov's life was spared, perhaps, because of a sense of corporate solidarity among his peers.

All laws are hypothetical statements of likely real events. They simplify and reduce the hypothetical events to the bare bones, to more or less rigorous definitions, in order to avoid particularism and pragmatism. (Here of course the Common Law has chosen a somewhat different path.)

Specific communities experience events and circumstances in their own specific ways, with their own specific emotions and assessments. A judge, almost subconsciously, will always apply and consider the specific views, beliefs, and habits which he has experienced from his very childhood and throughout his career. These views and beliefs will generate in him particular emotions. It seems to me that the English Common Law judge would be moved to act and to decide by a semi-bourgeois and semi-aristocratic tradition, which he quite naturally assumes to be the general one to be followed by all people. As a rule, it seems, labor problems and problems of tenant and landlord relations would be rather alien to him. Therefore, it is hardly surprising that alongside the military courts, which we tentatively termed survivors from the feudal period, new special "corporate" courts have emerged and are constantly proliferating. There are in Britain the labor tribunals, the landlord and tenant tribunals, and a wide variety of other special adjudicatory bodies.

The same has taken place since the revolution in the Soviet Union. Besides the people's courts and the higher echelons of Soviet justice, there are the military tribunals, *arbitrazh* for most economic disputes, the comrades' courts, the *skhody* of villages and other communities, the judicial functions of administrative authorities, and in labor disputes special procedures for the rank and file workers and employees and other procedures for members in specific, more responsible jobs, etc. I think that we are moving towards a period in which there well be an ever increasing number of special tribunals called upon to adjudicate in particular instances. The values that govern Crown Courts or Soviet judges are no longer applicable for alle conflict situations in real life, nor can they be used to experience the ethos of special groups.

Russia and the Soviet Union have experienced many upheavals, including a profound revolution with no rival in European history, and therefore their judicial system seems to Western opinion less acceptable and even unjust. Without attempting to make a value judgment, and without wanting to condone some events in their legal life which I personally cannot accept, I think that the reasons for their failure to satisfy a Westerner's sense of justice can be explained by the fact that the Soviet Union is still a society in flux, with rapidly changing scales of values.

The old rule of *pereat mundus fiat justitia* was possible only at a time when the judiciary represented a small but strong and influential ruling elite. Now there are many groups with their own key positions, who have all their own particular *mundi* and *justitiae*—their specific understanding and specific emotions as to the issues of equity and justice. Over and above that, there is still a quite different group which now quite openly proclaims that they "must have their cup of tea even if the *mundus* might perish." These nihilistic groups also have, of course, their own scale of values and their own emotional stimuli.

All this seems to indicate the tendency towards a greater democratization of legal forms and even legal systems. In other words, there is a shift towards a greater plurality of norm and value systems, where every group, or even specific interest of otherwise heterogeneous individuals, will want their special interests, i.e. values, to be heard. Here lies perhaps the answer to the question of whether military justice and military tribunals are necessary. Although they appear to be a survival of the past, they are pointing towards the future and towards a development that is by no means yet complete.

After all, the armed forces are a rather numerous and large *mundus*, with specific interests, specific requirements, and specific aberrations from the permitted and desirable behavior. As a *mundus*, it requires its own *justitia*. Unlike the more recent specific tribunals, it retains some survivals of its feudal past—*e.g.* the competence of the three instances of military tribunals (the garrison etc., the military district, and the Military College of the Supreme Soviet) have their jurisdiction fixed according to the gravity of the case, and also the rank of the defendant courts, so that full generals and higher officers are tried by the Military College of the Supreme Court of the USSR. Thus, the feudal principle that peers should be judged by peers still remains as a survival of the past.

Another peculiarity of the military tribunals is the institution of a specific branch of the Procuracy, headed by the Chief Military Procurator and his subordinate charges. Even here, the military is separated from the civilian jurisdiction and its accusatory and supervisory agency. It is interesting to note that the rehabilitation of the victims of the Stalin-Beria purges was entrusted to the military branch of the Procuracy.

It seems that Military courts function in a satisfactory way. There appear to be fewer appeals and supervisory protests before the Military College of the Supreme Court than in any other Colleges.[8] This seems to indicate that the decisions of the military tribunals satisfy all the people involved in their trials and that there were no serious controversies in respect of their decisions which would have merited appeals or protests to the Military College of the Supreme Courts or their publication in *Biulleten' Verkhovnogo Suda SSSR*.

In addition, I would like to mention the considerable efforts made by the military authorities to provide for an ethical education of their personnel by repeated publications of books on the subject.[9]

NOTES

1. O. O. Gruzenberg, *Vchera*, (Yesteryear), (Paris, 1938), chapter 11 "O poruchike Pirogove" (Concerning Lieutenant Pirogov), pp. 96-109.

2. *Ibid.*, pp. 101-102.

3. *Ibid.*, p. 103.

4. *Ibid.*, p. 108.

5. Faina Baazova, "Delo Rokotova" (The Case of Rokotov), in *Vremia i My* (The Times and Ourselves), No. 25, 173-196, and No. 26, 164-177.

6. *Op. cit.*, No. 26, 174.

7. Ukaz Prezidiuma Verkhovnogo Soveta SSSR "Ob usilenii otvetstvennosti za na-rushenie pravil o valiutnykh operatsiiakh" (On Strengthening the Liability for Violating the Rules on Monetary Transactions), *Ved.V.S. RSFSR*, 1961, No. 26, item 396. The first edict, which increased the penalties but did not provide for a capital penalty, and which was retrospectively applied against the defendants by a special order of the Presidum of the Supreme Soviet, was communicated to the court by a circular letter, which has never been published, *Vremia i My*, No. 26, *op.cit.*, 168-169.

8. *BVS SSSR*, 1976, No. 4, the last published decisions on pp. 39-41, after that– until at least No. 5 of 1978–no further decisions of the Military College of the Supreme Court have been reported.

9. A. V. Barabanshchikov, A. D. Glotochkin, N. F. Fedenko, V. V. Sheliag, *Problemy psikhologii voinskogo kollektiva* (Problems of the Psychology of the Military Collective), (Moscow, 1973); Colonel D. A. Volkogonov, *Etika sovetskogo ofitsera* (The Ethics of a Soviet Officer), (Moscow, 1973).

SOME TRENDS IN SOVIET CRIMINAL JUSTICE

Peter H. Juviler

All Soviet police, Procuracy (prosecution), courts, and correctional institutions work under central coordination, not fragmented into regional entities as non-federal agencies are in the US.[1] Unlike their American state and local counterparts, Soviet agencies of criminal justice form a single system, linked by unity of purpose and a high degree of operational integration. Thus, the Soviet criminal justice system can be re-directed after a change of leadership such as followed Stalin's demise in 1963. Also, a given leadership can promote new crime-prevention programs and campaigns nationwide—but subject of course to the inevitable bureaucratic inertia and local discretion inherent in large systems.

This chapter explores the basic changes in the purposes of Soviet criminal justice following Stalin's death. It goes on to review some important recent trends in the operation of the police and the judiciary, in corrections and the diversion of offenders from confinement, and in the place of criminal justice as a subsystem in a larger system of prevention. Overt de-Stalinization ended after Khrushchev. How did this affect criminal justice?

The main emphasis here is on criminal justice in non-political cases, some 99% of the total, because the repression of dissidents is much more common knowledge than is the day-to-day working of criminal justice in ordinary cases that are not connected with what the regime considers to be challenges to its ideological and political authority.

1. The Purposes of Criminal Justice

The authority for setting the purposes of criminal justice passed after Stalin from his personal clique to the "collective leadership" in which Nikita Khrushchev was preeminent from 1955 to 1964 and Leonid Brezhnev from 1964. The Party's well known authority as "guiding and directing force" of all public and state endeavors has been legally strengthened by enshrinement in the 1977 USSR Constitution.[2] Under the Party's authority, the purposes of criminal justice repression have been rearranged and new purposes added. Stalin's courts had convicted more ordinary criminals than courts today convict.[3] But thanks to the sentencing powers of the secret police under Stalin, "politicals" (persons convicted of "counterrevolutionary crimes") outnumbered ordinary criminals several times over. The prime functions of criminal justice were to repress "enemies of the people" and to recruit forced labor by the many millions.[4] Then followed the purpose of deterring ordinary crime.

Since Stalin, the repression of real or imagined opponents has diminished hundreds of times over. The present Soviet prisoner population of some 1.5 mln. in a population of 260 mln. (1978) is still large in world-wide comparisons.[5] But there are now 150 non-political prisoners convicted of common crimes, for every Soviet "prisoner of conscience" confined because of political, cultural, national, or religious dissent. The latter number about 10,000. The use of criminal justice repression is still intensive in the USSR, then, but its main target has shifted. Ordinary crime has become the central concern of the leadership.

As in other countries, Soviet lawmakers list as crimes those offenses considered the most serious threats to law and order.[8] For crimes, there are nearly a million convictions annually: 976,090 in 1976.[9] The reliability of this statistic is supported by the fact that its source cites numbers of convictions in 1976 (listed below) for various types of crimes that yield proportions close to those published in official Soviet sources (that omit total conviction figures because they are still censored state secrets). Of all criminal convictions "in recent years", according to published Soviet figures, between 14 and 19% (16% in 1976 says the unofficial source giving us the conviction figure for that year and cited hereinafter) are for "crimes against socialist property," the theft of which is the most politically troublesome and under-reported of all non-violent ordinary crimes. [10]

Fourteen to 16% of convictions (15.6% in 1976) are for crimes against personal property.

Crimes against persons (murder, rape, assault, infection with VD, homosexuality, criminal libel, etc.) accounted for about 15% of convictions "in recent years" (17% in 1976).

Hooliganism, the loosely defined crime against public order, frequently involving violence, brings the highest conviction total, about 20% "in recent years" (24.1% in 1976).

Convictions for traffic, drug, and other crimes injurious to health and safety hover around 13% (10% in 1976).

Seven or 8% of convictions have been for crimes largely peculiar to Soviet-type systems of socialized production and compulsory central state planning: economic crimes (4.5% in 1976) and crimes of misconduct in office (3.9% in 1976). These white collar crimes include the supervision of substandard production, false reporting on plan fulfillment ("eyewash"), the failure to meet certain kinds of delivery obligations, engaging in private enterprise, speculation, bribery, abuse of office. Convictions for such crimes barely skim the surface of an extensive non-underworld criminal subculture thriving among otherwise law-abiding and respected citizens.[11] It is a subculture of pilferage, black marketeering, "living on the left" by illegal sales of property and services, and various white collar crimes endemic in the Soviet economy of unequal but pervasive scarcities of consumer goods and consumer services.[12]

Convictions for "crimes against the administrative order" were about 4% in the late 1960s (3.9% in 1976). This category of crimes includes "the spreading of fabrications defaming the Soviet system" and "group activities which violate public order"—both politically oriented, repressive measures added in 1966 after the arrest and trial of writers Daniel and Siniavskii and the protest demonstrations in response. This category includes also passport violations (related mainly to the population control system of internal passports resurrected from tsarist times by Stalin in 1932 and kept ever since), and the growing item of environmental crimes.[13] Crimes against justice accounted for 1.4% of convictions in 1976.

Some of the 10,000 Soviet prisoners convicted of various forms of dissidence were convicted for crimes under the rubrics just listed. The rest were convicted of "state crimes," frequently, anti-Soviet agitation and propaganda. Now conviction for treason—a capital offense—threatens dissidents as a result of such convictions for treason as that of Anatolii Shcharanskii on July 14, 1978, when he was sentenced to three years in prison plus ten years in labor colonies of strict regime (see later, under *"Corrections"*). Criminal justice specialists are beginning to take up the task of dealing with a new form of defying authority: the commission of embezzlement and other crimes with the aid of computers.[14]

Prevention appeared alongside repression (punishment, deterrence, and isolation) as part of the general criminal justice purpose of "struggle with crime" in the middle 1950s. A candidate member of the Party Politburo (then Presidium) confirmed this in 1958: "Criminal repression is not the only or the chief way to fight crime . . . More important are preventive and educational measures which remove those factors contributing to the appearance of survivals of the past in people's minds."[15] Then and in the early 1960s, Khrushchev made it appear that "prevention and educational work" were mainly for social organizations and the duty of repression the chief task of a criminal justice system that would be left mainly the job of dealing with hard core criminals. Impatient even with the results of his own popularization of justice, Khrushchev greatly increased the repressive function of criminal justice in 1960-1961 by adding new crimes, raising penalties, and extending the death penalty to 16 more crimes, bringing the total to about 35 capital crimes.

After Khrushchev's fall, the then director of the Institute of State and Law noted that, whereas Stalinism overstressed administrative coercion, Soviet Law enforcement after him had over-emphasized "the role of the community in strengthening law and order" and underestimated "the role of the organs of state coercion" (*i.e.*, of criminal justice) "in educating the new man, in the struggle against survivals of the past." [16]

Practical suggestions on how to prevent crime became the main task of criminology when it revived after Stalin. He had seen no relevance of research for criminal justice; were not all the causes of crime removed under socialism? Now criminology was seen by Party and leading jurists alike as indispensable for effective criminal justice. [17] Prevention would have to become as broad as the causes: economic, ideological, cultural, educational psychological, and organizational, and lapses in security. [18]

The close link of Party and prevention is typified in many ways. For example, the writer of the views just cited picked them up from his criminologists in the Procuracy's Research Institute on the Causes and Prevention of Crime. He had been the deputy head of the Central Committee's Department of Administrative Organs (see below). His institute comes closest of any in the USSR to being a coordinating center for research on crime. The head of the *MVD* since its reappearance in 1966 has been N. A. Shchelokov, former Party *apparatchik* and associate of the secretary general of the Party. As stated alsewhere, *MVD* research programs on penology and long-range forecasting are also of prime criminological importance in the USSR. The *MVD* Academy has recently emerged as the coordinating center for all planning of the research connected with prospective new, broad-based drives against lawbreaking and other "anti-social manifestations." [19] Such a role for any repressive agency, let alone the *MVD*, would of course have been impossible during Stalin's last 20 years.

The Party has supported and promoted research in the *MVD*, Procuracy, law faculties, and elsewhere to help provide to those agencies, and to it as well, feedback of information on crime rates, trends, and forecasts of possible criminogenic processes like migration. Cooperation has grown between criminologists and criminal justice officials under Party aegis. [20] For the Party, crime research supports the purposes of criminal justice and, thereby, "the long-range purpose of the CPSU—to ensure the strict observation of socialist legality, the eradication of every violation of law and order, the liquidation of crime and the elimination of the causes giving rise to it." [21]

The Party line for criminologists turns a Marxist idea sideways, at least, if not on its head. This is the idea that socializing means of production will bring about the elimination of crime by ending the social conflicts causing crime. The line is that socialism, though superior to capitalism, though the only system under which the liquidation of crime can be seriously entertained, does not automatically bring about the withering away of crime. But, it is said, Soviet-type socialism eradicates criminogenic conflicts in society and provides the mechanisms of social and preventive planning, the preconditions for the success of a governmental drive to liquidate crime, as society moves toward its highest stage, communism.

62

This interpretation of Marxism gives the ideological impetus for accelerated crime research closely linked with preventive planning, [22] or, in the phraseology of the late 1970s, for "complex plans of social prohylaxis" (see below). Social prophylaxis means eliminating all "anti-social manifestations:" all violations of legal norms and law order, Party-approved moral norms and moral order—in sum, all violations of "social order." The Party-orchestrated quest for social order is presented as part of the larger move toward a more perfect "socialist way of life" in a "developed socialist society." [23]

This line—the possibility of liquidating crime in the USSR, the superiority of socialism to capitalism, the origins of crime in the USSR as alien "survivals"—is the price research must pay as it grapples for politically compatible middle-range theories of crime and struggles with the secrecy enveloping crime research and statistics and inhibiting full publication of results or even the unpublished sharing of results among experts. [24]

2. Enforcement and Judiciary

A post-Khrushchevian re-centralization of the criminal justice system ended the existing disparity between the toughening of criminal law on the one hand in the early 1960s, and the dismantling of central administrative control over enforcement and the judiciary, on the other. The same reorganization of 1966-1970 also allotted new functions to criminal justice agencies which reflected their broader purposes expressed in article 2 of the 1958 Fundamental Principles of Criminal Procedure (FPCP): to apprehend and punish criminals and "to promote the strengthening of socialist legality, the prevention and eradication of crime, the education of citizens in the spirit of undeviating obedience to Soviet laws and respect for the rules of socialist social relationships."

Khrushchev left two centralized agencies of criminal justice—the *KGB* and the Procuracy. His successors, impatient with social indiscipline and responsive to police demands for a freer hand, recreated the USSR *MVD* (abolished in 1962) and placed it over the republic ministries, with their name, Ministry for the Protection of Public Order. At the same time, the Party and government initiated an anti-hooliganism campaign, increasing punishment for that offense, giving the militia under the ministries for the protection of public order new powers to deal with hooliganism and drunkenness, and making drunkenness an aggravating factor in guilt. [25]

The ministries became *MVD*'s once again in 1968 as part of an order to modernize the *MVD* and improve recruitment by enfusing the militia with newly-recruited working activists in the Party and Komsomol. The *MVD* has become an extremely powerful ministry controlling cartography and firefighting, passports, the militia, internal security troops, places of confinement including the psychiatric prison hospitals, supervision of released convicts and parolees, persons banished and in exile, and conducting important research on crime and corrections, as part of its role in prevention, to which we shall return. How closely the Procuracy is, in fact, able to supervise the *MVD*'s operations and statistics remains an open question. [26]

Dissatisfied with the anti-hooliganism campaign of 1966, the regime by 1969 began a new campaign, against thieving and laxity in the economy and social disorder generally. Blame for the alleged drift and inefficiency of the courts fell partly on the abolition of the USSR Ministry of Justice in 1956 and its republic branches between 1956 and 1963. These ministries and the departments of justice of the regional and city Soviets reappeared in 1970. [27] Now the criminal justice system is back to its centralized Stalinist form with some exceptions. The *MVD* and *KGB* remain separate. Since their abolition in September, 1953, there have been no secret police tribunals; only a court may convict and sentence, according to article 7 of the FPCP and Article 160 of the new USSR Constitution. Under the new legislation, the Ministry of Justice regains responsibility for overseeing the courts and colleges of advocates and their local legal aid offices, for legislative drafting and legal research connected with it, control of the Notary and *ZAGS* (civil registration offices).

The ministry has new functions that reflect the preventive purposes of criminal justice: vastly expanded legal services to reduce illegalities and property losses in the economy, and a vastly expanded program of mass legal education (see below). [28]

Recentralization has left case flows basically unchanged. After the police have initiated a criminal case and interrogated a suspect, the case in many instances will go for a full pre-trial investigation conducted by investigators from the Procuracy, but also from the *KGB* and *MVD*. During this important stage, an accused may have the services of a defense lawyer only if a minor or if deemed incapable of conducting his or her own defense because of deafness, dumbness, blindness, or mental deficiency. For other adults, there is no right of defense until the late pre-trial stage, possibly many months after arraignment, when the pre-trial investigation is completed and the investigator presents findings and case material to the accused for perusal with the assistance of a defense lawyer, who will also help the accused to make procedural motions such as a request for further investigation. Requests to include wider rights to counsel in the 1958 criminal law reforms were turned down. Two decades later, it appeared that at high official level there was once again serious consideration of the possibility that the defense lawyer be admitted to the pre-trial investigations of all defendants, and even back to the initiation of a criminal case. [29]

When the supervising procurator approves the investigator's conclusion to indict, he sends the case to court. Once the court has accepted the case as ready for trial, and not to be sent back or dropped, a trial is held. Most cases are tried in the lower people's courts of a district or borough. More serious cases go to the second level, city courts or courts of provinces, national regions, territories, or the supreme courts of autonomous republics, or of Union republics without provincial subdivisions. Cases of exceptional importance are tried in supreme courts of the larger union republics or in the USSR Supreme Court (a great rarity).

There is one appeal from a sentence, to the next higher court. But a sentence already in legal force may be protested, the case re-opened for review upon the protest of the president and vice-presidents of the USSR Supreme Court, the USSR Procurator General and deputies, the procurators and supreme court presidents in the union republics (for rulings below the level of the presidiums of the supreme courts), presidents of the courts of the autonomous republics, provinces, territories, large cities, national regions, and by the procurators of those areas (against rulings at or below the level of the criminal benches of their courts). This presents the possibility of double jeopardy and increased sentences. Also, it presents the possibility of acquittal or reduction of penalty after the case is formally closed.

Trial courts consist of a professional judge elected by open ballot by public or workplace assemblies (people's court) or Soviets (higher courts) for five years and two people's assessors, lay judges, similarly elected for two and a half years. [30] Notice of the latter's equal right with the professional judge has moved up from the FPCP, article 9, into the 1977 USSR Constitution, Article 154. People's assessors take part in local extra-judicial efforts at crime prevention. But this writers' own observations and other sources indicate that the lay judges are usually passive in court and defer to the presiding judge. A recent quiz on the public's knowledge of the law seems to indicate that the respondents' knowledge of this practical situation of the living law of criminal justice, is accurate, even if this means they give the wrong answer when asked whether the opinion of people's assessors prevails when they both disagree with the judge on a verdict (legally it prevails, but in practice this has little meaning). The whole thing raises questions about what is correct legal knowledge. [31]

A new post in court is "consultant," resembling a law clerk, though not, apparently, attached to a specific judge. The budget line of one consultant for five judges was introduced in 1975 to help take some overload off judges' shoulders. Consultants help in research, advise on application of the law, keep court statistics, draw up reports on court work, conduct legal propaganda, help arrange the flow of court cases, receive and advise citizens. Much needed new court building is proceeding apace, and the replacement of antiquated longhand court journals by tape recordings of trial proceedings is just beginning. Meanwhile, the laboring and not necessarily accurate scribe-secretary remains the prevailing means keeping the record, [32] not counting possible hidden sensors. [33]

Defenders of the accused are usually lawyers (*advokaty* working in legal aid offices), though they do not have to be. [34] It is supposedly a boost to the prestige of Colleges of Advocates and their legal services that they now receive mention in the new USSR Constitution, Article 161. Such a boost in prestige and "authority" is sorely needed.

One gathers from informed sources inside and outside the USSR that the defense lawyers' official monthly salary rarely exceeds 250 rubles a month (as compared, say with the 400 rubles a professor receives). Hence the importance of "gifts" from the defendant and his family and of extras for publishing and other outside activity. Under the new rate scale of the Ministry of Justice's instructions in effect January 1, 1978, one may estimate that a defense lawyer will receive only about 77-80 rubles for conducting the defense in a relatively complicated case if it means three days' work after the pre-trial investigation, one day's visit to the defendant in his place of detention, and a three-day trial. [35] Moreover, the quality of Moscow lawyers (now numbering 1000-1200 in the Moscow College of Advocates) is said to have been declining in the last 25 years. [36]

Judges and prosecutors often see the defense lawyer not as a colleague at the bar, but as an "enemy," "as someone who is interfering with their work merely by insisting on complete observance of the law." The tension will mount during hard-pushed campaigns directed from above against certain crimes or in very touchy cases of particularly horrible violent crime when the local procuracy is hard-pressed to convict the perpetrator. Even then, an able and determined defense lawyer may sometimes win an acquittal over the heads of local Party and judicial authority by taking the case up on appeal or, that failing, by getting the case reviewed on protest by higher procuratorial or judicial instance, under the procedure already mentioned. I have heard graphic tales of such cases from emigré lawyers like Leonid Polsky and Yuri Luryi. Ida Kaminskaia and Lev Yudich, then working under the Moscow Collegium of Advocates, spent three years achieving the acquittal of two boys accused of murder and rape. During that time, the lawyers were "harried, victimized and subject to derision .. by the investigator and the court." During the trial they were not allowed to exercise their right to see the minors for fear they would "influence" them. The fact is, though, that the lawyers won acquittal. [37]

Given such judicial bias and the close supervision and interference of the Party in both political and ordinary criminal cases, as Robert Sharlet describes in his chapter and I touch on later, scholarly progress in reforming even the letter of criminal procedure is slow. Official consideration of the possibility of increasing rights for a defense lawyer was mentioned earlier. A step forward has been taken toward explicit presumption of innocence. It is implied in article 7 of the FPCP and in the similar but slightly stronger phrasing of Article 160 of the 1977 USSR Constitution: "Nobody may be found guilty of a crime, and also subjected to criminal punishment other than by sentence of court and in accordance with the law." But it has recently been made explicit in a major USSR Supreme Court directive to lower courts. The directive treats Article 160 as "the constitutional principle" of presumption of innocence and directs lower courts "strictly to observe the constitutional principle that the accused (defendant) shall be presumed innocent until proven guilty in a manner provided by law and affirmed by court sentence that has gone into legal force." Pushing their advantage, advocates of this reform will now try to have it incorporated in codes of criminal procedure. [38]

Presumption of innocence is unlikely to apply soon to political trials. There are never acquittals in these. Recent special targets of political justice have been persons prosecuted for criticizing the Soviet implementation of the 1975 Helsinki agreement as it touched on human rights, for nationalist self-assertion, non-conformist religious practices, and agitation for greater freedom of emigration. Anatolii Shcharanskii has engaged in at least three of these types of disapproved activities before his illegally long pre-trial confinement and his sentencing. As examples of the staged convictions of dissidents for allegedly ordinary crimes, one may cite the conviction, a month before Shcharanskii's, of two would-be emigrés for malicious hooliganism. Their acts were the crowd-stopping gestures of hanging sheets from their apartment balconies with signs reading: "Let Us Join Our Son in Israel," and "*KGB* Give Me My Visa." [39]

Soviet law and criminal justice express Party policy. It considers lawbreaking by ordinary citizens harmful to its development plans and a challenge to its authority. [40] The Party will permit its own lawbreaking in defense of that authority, especially in the trials of dissidents. [41]

The Party has many means of "guiding and directing" criminal justice. In fact, it takes a very close interest in the functioning of the police, Procuracy, and courts. It approves their purposes, as seen. It participates in their reorganization. The major steps just decribed to reorganize criminal justice after Khrushchev followed from joint Party-government resolutions. The Party monitors criminal justice through its local committees and primary party organizations and its departments of administrative organs in the *apparat* at the center, the republic, and regional-city level. [42] Approval of personnel appointments "on the basis of political and professional qualities" provides a "powerful lever of Party influence on criminal justice organs;" the texts keep this no secret. [43]

The Party wants more lawyers and the professionalization of criminal justice. [44] But the price of this supportive intervention is infringement on the legal principles of objectivity, presumption of innocence, and independence of the judges and people's assessors and their subordination only to law. The Party rejects the idea that criticism of local criminal justice practices violates judicial independence. For example, the Novgorod Province Committee of

67

the Party considered court sentencing of hooligans too light, and told the courts so. [45]

There is much non-official evidence that the Party organs also intervene in individual criminal cases, non-political as well as political. [46] For the first time, this writer has encountered published Soviet mention of Party intervention into individual cases by a text published under the imprimatur of the Higher Party School of the Central Committee. Building on Lenin's distinction between "inquiry" and "pressure", the text asserts that it is necessary and proper for Party organs "to demand of state organs the grounds for the correctness of their actions, impartially to verify all circumstances connected with an arrest, a conviction, etc. Such inquiries are widely used in the work of Party committees . . ." [47] Since this is checkup by political and not judicial agencies, it is hard to see how impartiality is possible. In any event, such "inquiries" directly violate judicial independence as interpreted by Soviet judges. [48] Party intervention at all levels and in individual cases too is, then, an inherent part of Soviet criminal justice.

The Colleges of Advocates operate not autonomously but under the political guidance of the Party Departments of Administrative Organs, the executive committees of the Soviets and the Department of Advocates of the USSR and republic ministries of justice. [49] The access of advocates as defense lawyers is limited not only overtly by the criminal code—normally after the completion of the pre-trial investigation, and at the trial stage if there is no pre-trial investigation—but also covertly, in two ways. First, advocates have no access to trials in the secret "special courts." [50] Second, lawyers may be extra-legally denied access to participate in particular cases, even non-political ones. Denial of the permit of access (*dopusk*) and possible disbarment follows conscientious defense of dissidents. [51]

When a Party committee's Department of Administrative Organs finds a case important to local Party interests, it may well decide verdict and sentence, even before trial. [52] Several years ago, Georgii Parkhomenko, still head of the Chief Pharmaceutical Administration of Moscow, was charged with serious abuse of office, theft and fraud, report padding, and receiving unearned bonuses thereby. Parkhomenko allegedly had conspired with subordinates to re-date over-age medicines, write them off the books, sell them to the unsuspecting public as fresh preparations, and pocket the proceeds for himself and his accomplices. Fridrikh Neznansky, the investigator in this case, now living in the US, came upon an article recently by Parkhomenko praising the supplying of medicines to Soviet citizens in comparison with distribution in the West. There, he said, only "affluent persons" can afford to buy essential medicines. True or not, this charge is ironic because of the ending of his case. The Department of Administrative Organs of the Moscow City Party Committee ordered the investigator and the Moscow City Procurator, his superior, to drop the case. Neznansky recalls the Procurator telling him that

"Party orders are law for the Procuracy, judges, and investigators." Besides, the Procurator whispered, Parkhomenko is the lover of Deputy Moscow Mayor Svetaeva. He supplies her and the Moscow City Party Committee with scarce medicines. [53]

Where such protectionism exists, will it be possible to invoke Article 58, the novelty of the 1977 Constitution, providing for citizen appeals and requests for compensation to the courts against the illegal acts of officials and organizations that violate their rights? Enabling law has been ordered to extend the present limited remedies against official abuse to reflect Article 58. This should provide for suits against criminal justice officials and agencies for false arrest, charges, and conviction. [54] But Party decisions would be decisive, given their "guiding and directing role."

3. Corrections

The convicted defendant faces 13 possible punishments: from censure, fines and restitution, corrective labor without confinement (usually a cut in pay) and the supplementary punishments of confiscation of property and stripping of rank, orders, and medals, to exile (to a specified location), banishment (from specified locations), and the death penalty (an "exceptional" but heavily used measure). [55] Confinement in correctional institutions, the most frequent punishment, follows about half of the convictions, [56] nearly half a million annually.

Minors 14 through 17 years old serve out sentences in separate educational labor colonies for juveniles. Juvenile corrections were drastically reformed after Stalin to separate out minors and give them more educational treatment. They remain differentiated. But there seems to be virtually no basic experimentation in juvenile criminal corrections such as the labor communes of Pogrebinskii and Makarenko in the 1920s and up to 1936-1937 when Stalin liquidated them. [57] Juveniles too young for criminal conviction or guilty of various non-criminal forms of lawbreaking go to another post-Stalin product— the special schools and special vocational schools run by ministries of education and receiving their charges from the *MVD* reception and distribution centers for minors and the Commissions on Juvenile Affairs, the hearing bodies and helping agencies for minors not under jurisdiction of the courts by reason of age or triviality of offense. [58] Special schools began to function in 1965.

Male adults serve out sentences in corrective labor colonies of ordinary regime, firm regime, strict regime, and special regime, and in prisons (divided internally into ordinary and special regime). The mildest of the MVD's seven regimes of confinement occurs in the semi-open "colony-settlements." They take parolees for a test period after long confinement, on their way back to freedom. Colony-settlements first appeared in 1963. [59]

69

The number of convicts in prisons and colonies as of January 1, 1977, was 1,612,378. [60]

From many leaks out of the underground, a picture emerges of harshness in corrections beginning in 1961-1962 after an interlude of liberalization. Regimes tightened even more in the early 1970s. Again and again one reads about cold, hunger, overwork, and terrible medical care in the camps. Because camp routine depends on secret *MVD* instructions on internal order and on the whims of correctional staffs, the Fundamental Principles of Corrective Labor Law of 1969 (FPCLL) and the corrective labor law codes of the republics give little hint of what a convict's conditions of confinement really are. Published writings extol the "humanism" of Soviet penal policy. [61]

But vague hints of trouble with correctional personnel appear occasionally in the official Soviet press, and a cautious mention of problems with colonies and prisons as places that really *correct*.

Signs of penologists' disillusionment with corrections as a way to reform criminals became unmistakable by the late 1960s. The trouble, wrote the penologists, was mainly one "inherent in deprivation of freedom as a means of criminal punishment." [62] This is what the experts say they found in colonies:

1. Labor training is inadequate. Only part of the colony population receives training in a useful skill. Some convicts spend too little time in confinement to learn. [63] Also, labor training—the ideological core of Soviet corrections—seems to take second place to use of the convict labor force in heavy, unskilled work.

2. Confinement means isolation from any normal, law-supporting social ties and functions an inmate had, leaving, research shows, only about 10% of normal social functions. [64] Reform is complicated even more because an inmate is confined closely with other inmates who may be hostile to the correctional staff, or hardened members of a still existing criminal counter-culture. Professional criminals, the *urki* and *vory v zakone*, are no longer permitted to rob and otherwise victimize other inmates at will as in Stalin's day. [65] Moreover, Soviet writings deny that organized crime in the form of powerful regional organizations exist in the USSR.

But we have alluded to networks of white collar corruption. This requires skilled organization. More to the point here, the same texts which deny the existence of organized crime describe the distinct criminal subculture touching on the fringes of respectable society with its distinctive code, esprit, and life style. [66] Theft, robbery, and the "sting" of the con game are the respectable employment in these circles. Their thieves' code and "romanticism" attract recruits among younger inmates in the colonies.

Bound together by a common "discipline," the professionals use terror against would-be defectors. How this revenge on defectors caught up with a

70

reformed criminal is depicted in Vasilii Shukshin's film, "Krasnaia Kalina," released in 1974 and considered representative by Soviet people with whom this writer discussed the film. The Soviet texts explain that terror within the camps prompted the parts of the USSR edict of May 5, 1961, making it a capital offense to terrorize inmates of prisons or labor colonies who have broken with their criminal past, to attack correctional personnel, to organize groups for that purpose, or to participate actively in such groups. [67] Some of this violence, it seems, hits not simply persons going straight, but *suki*, "bitches" or informers–cherished by administrations and hated by inmates the world over. [68]

Attitudes of inmates appear to contrast sharply within any one colony. Ten percent of the inmates in colonies of firm regime (for first offenders sentenced to more than three years' confinement), according to an *MVD* researcher's report, were "morally deteriorated," long-time "anti-social parasites" working nowhere, often in trouble with the authorities, a majority of them with records of violating the labor colony regime. Another 20% of the inmates in the firm regime colonies studied were persons with good records in and out of work before conviction. But the other 70% in between formed a "morally unstable" group. Presumably this large group provided potential members for informal groups alienated from the correctional staff and informal groups of outright crime-prone inmates. The contrast between inmate attitudes is even more striking in colonies of ordinary and strict regime. [69] A 24 year-old prisoner, Valerii, must be numbered among the incorrigibles. A letter of his appeared in *Literaturnaia Gazeta* of July 18, 1975, commenting on a previous article about the chase and capture of a band of payroll robbers. The police heroes capturing them had been alerted by the robbers' fire when they killed a young family man barring their way as they left with the loot. Valerii wrote that nobody in his right mind would stand up to a tommy gun. The robbers, he said, were only earning their living as the police were earning theirs. Valerii added that he had been twice convicted unjustly and that "after my release, I shall commit again what you call 'crimes' although you won't like it." [70]

3. Frustration is "typical for all prisoners" in Soviet correctional institutions. It grows out of "hopelessness, melancholy, a sense of being doomed." Frustration is worsened when callous or witless "upbringers" fail to notice prisoners' efforts to reform, and by sleeplessness, unjustified harshness, taunts and abuses of other prisoners, and an atmosphere of animosity, tension, and aggressiveness created when correctional personnel are nervous, rude, rough, or insulting. Frustration can prompt horrible acts of self-mutilation. [71]

4. Recidivists become even more dangerous and anti-social during their long sentences. Sentences lose deterrent effect for them. Evidence of punishment's failure to deter recidivist crime is that recidivists tend to commit new crimes soon after release. Forty-nine percent of one sample group of recidi-

vists committed another crime immediately after release, another 26.9% within their first year at liberty.

5. Prisoners become passive, institutionalized in confinement. Unused to a life of free choice and initiative, they tend to take the path of least resistance after release. Supervisory Commissions under local Soviets are supposed to follow up on and assist ex-convicts. But the task proves often beyond their resources.

6. Conditions outside, too, impede post-release adjustment. Families often have broken up. The ex-convicts have a hard time getting the militia to give them residence permits back where their families live. Enterprises are reluctant to hire the ex-convicts. Well earned or not, the distrust and hostility they encounter outside embitters them. After-release, support of and control over ex-convicts by agencies of criminal justice and the community are full of holes. It is relatively easy to slip back into the company of vagrants and thieves.

As a result of these and other problems, corrections tend to contribute to rather than to break the vicious cycle of correctional schooling to skills of crime rather than of lawful work, release into a ruined home life, local police agencies that diligently refuse residence permits to live with the family if it exists but that cannot effectively supervise ex-convicts, heavy drinking again, "friends" with criminal pasts, and a return to crime. [72]

The boldness, openness, imaginativeness, and idealism of Soviet penological research in the 1920s remains in the past. *MVD* officialdom and researchers confess that they have as yet no basis for recommending when punishment ceases to serve re-education and instead worsens character deformation, how to neutralize alienated and criminal group influences in places of confinement, how to develop and use correctional psychology. [73]

4. Diversion

"Prisons don't frighten and don't always correct . . . Suffice to say that a considerable portion of persons serving sentences in correctional institutions return there." This perception by a lieutenant general in the *MVD*, head of the *MVD* Academy, leaves the institutions unmoved for the present. [74]

It seems that, unable to budge the bureaucracy and inertia of the correctional world and conservatism wherever it may be, the penologists have been bringing about a modest series of measures bypassing conventional corrections and differentiating more *before* or *outside* confinement, even though it be impossible to differentiate more *within* places of confinement. Most of these measures so far appeared in edicts of February 8 and 15, 1977. The only significant change within the correctional system did not alter labor colonies. Rather, it diverted negligent criminals away from them.

Crimes due to negligence rather than intent have increased to account for 9% of convictions. Some penologists advocated regular punishment as a deterrent. Others argued that this would simply mean putting an increasing number of non-habitual criminals in among "carriers of anti-social views" in the colonies. The *MVD* gave them a chance in 1971-1975 to experiment with sending any but the most dangerously negligent of criminals to colony settlements specially set aside for them, apart from colony settlements for felons who have served long sentences and are moving back toward possible full freedom.

The results evidently satisfied the *MVD*. Part of the reform of February 8, 1977, provides that persons sentenced to up to five years for negligent crimes (and in some cases up to ten years) go to a new category of correctional institution—colony settlements for persons guilty of crimes by negligence. As for the rest of this category of offenders, they all go to colonies of ordinary regime despite the normal three-year limit on sentences of people going there [75]—a sure sign of problems with corrupting influences in the colonies, especially in the colonies of the three most rigorous regimes. Inmates of colony settlements lead an almost normal settlement life, without guards and barbed wire, and with their families where practical, but under *MVD* supervision, curfews, and permission to leave the settlement only under special conditions. [76]

Another target of reformers other than corrections for negligent criminals is a greater diversion away from criminal justice for persons labelled as criminally vagrant, but often not chronic vagrants at all, or sick old derelicts in need of care and a home. Preliminary research suggests that chronic vagrants are a small percentage of homeless persons detained by the militia, and that many of these persons are homeless because of the "ineffectiveness" of job placement (connected in part with refusals to hire them, especially if they have discrediting entries in the labor booklet); second, lack of housing and of residence permit; third, insufficient room in invalids' and old peoples' homes for the shelterless disabled and old people; fourth, lack of control over the subsequent behavior of vagrants after they are given work and a permanent place to live. [77]

The diversion from corrections after Khrushchev began with the edict of June 12, 1970, permitting the replacement of confinement or straight suspended sentences with a "suspended sentence with obligatory assignment to work" wherever sent by the *MVD* organs, in practice usually on distant construction sites. [78] The already-mentioned reform of February 8, 1977, adds the 1970 measure to the FPCL as article 44^2, while making it apply to more persons, that is, also to parolees. This procedure of assignment to obligatory labor has been used with some parolees without benefit of edicts since 1964. Parolees sent to assigned work live under closer *MVD* supervision than do parolees simply released back into the general population. Hence, virtually any prisoners can be paroled into this compulsory assignment program, including many persons previously ineligible for parole: persons guilty of serious state crimes, aggravated murder and rape, etc., as long as they have served up to three-fourths of their sentences and appear to be on the road to reform. [79]

The work-release program, say Soviet sources, is part of the "dying out of punishment . . . of humane tendencies in Soviet criminal legislation . . ." [80]

However humane or reformist their purpose, the work-release measures of 1970 and 1977 serve in fact to conscript forced labor, unskilled or semi-skilled, for heavy work in labor-short and remote areas to which it is difficult to attract free workers. According to one source, secret *MVD* figures list 495,711 persons working on construction sites under the edict of June 12, 1970—before the extension of its formal coverage to parolees. [81] Including the prisoners under confinement already mentioned, who work unless disabled, this means a total forced labor population of some two million in the Soviet economy.

Perhaps responding to unpublished directives, courts are not always judicious in their choices of whom to assign to work release. The RSFSR Supreme Court's survey of practices in the work release program shows sloppy work by the colony administrations and the supervisory commissions of the local Soviets, the volunteer bodies that keep in touch with correctional institutions and join in the screening for parole and the checkup on parolees. As an example, one colony and the local Supervisory Commission sent to the Volgograd Province Court a request to give work release parole to a malicious violator of colony regime who was in punitive solitary confinement at the time the materials on him went to court. The production line nature of parole hearings in court contributes to errors at the parole input end of the work release program. Sometimes courts process 30-40 cases a day and without representatives of the correctional institutions or the Procuracy. [82]

Problems appear to abound at places of obligatory work. There are delays in assigning to work and housing. Life is boring and boredom is not much relieved by what passes for political and educational work. Supervision is slack at times. So, under the noses of the *MVD*, people leave the site illegally, get drunk, and fall into lawbreaking and crime. When asked why they left their assigned administrative districts, a sample of respondents cited factors like homesickness, boring work, low wages, and bad health. [83]

5. Criminal Justice in a Larger System

Diversion from the labor colonies has taken potential prisoners not only out of the colonies into colony settlements or work release programs but also away from criminal punishment as the form of liability for crime. The 1977 reform has extended to more criminal suspects than before the possibility

74

that their cases will be terminated and transferred to comrades' courts at place of work or residence, to a CJA if a minor is involved, to a collective or individual for re-education, or to administrative proceedings in court with possibility of fine up to 50 rubles, arrest up to 15 days, or corrective labor at place of work for one or two months with a 20% loss of pay, where the suspects are charged with crimes involving punishment up to one year; *i.e.*, in the case of some 90 crimes listed in the RSFSR Criminal Code. [84]

The diversions touch juveniles also in a measure permitting courts to postpone execution of a criminal sentence for from six months to two years in cases where the minor faces a sentence of up to three years and his or her correction appears possible without isolation from society. The court may require that the minor go to work or school and that he or she be under the care of a collective or individual. It is up to the local CJA, together with the *MVD* organs, to ask the court to end the stay of execution of punishment because of violation of conditions of probation or to release from criminal punishment because the minor has reformed. [85]

The 1977 changes in the punishment of criminals by negligence, the widening range of work release and parole all open wider the legislative door to routes away from punishment in colonies. So do the measures expanding possibilities for dropping criminal cases involving misdemeanors (punishable by up to one year sentences) and for diverting minors from criminal punishment by stay of sentence. Some preliminary reports on results have been cited here. Much fuller reports are to be submitted to the USSR Supreme Soviet's Presidium by December 1, 1978, from the USSR Supreme Court, USSR Procuracy, USSR Ministry of Justice, and *MVD*. [86] The 1977 reforms test the judgment of criminal justice agencies and the thesis that prevention or other practical goals are better served by de-emphasizing punishment in colonies for situational or reforming criminals.

The last two measures discussed—for misdemeanants and minors—respond, it is said, to the decisions of the 25th Congress of 1976 that public participation in prevention be further stepped up. [87] Khrushchev's popularization came in for some slights later, as we saw. Yet his successors have carried farther than Khrushchev did the integration of criminal justice into a larger system of "complex means of the prophylaxis" of lawbreaking and other "anti-social manifestations."

Well established ways of linking criminal justice with the community agencies in prevention are being carried over from the 1960s and prodded periodically on, as always, unevenly and not always in the best interests of a fair trial, especially as regards visiting sessions of courts to workplaces and neighborhoods. Courts are supposed to ascertain the causes of crimes they deal with and to send special findings to the involved managements, and other agencies, for action. [88]

Their rejection of Khrushchev's emphasis on non-state crime prevention did not prevent his successors from later increasing non-state prevention and its linkages with state agencies of criminal justice.

First, they began a new program of legal propaganda, using the ministries of justice as administrative coordinators, and criminal justice personnel and lawyers as lecturers, writers on legal themes, and suppliers of legal aid. Instilling knowledge of and respect for the law has become an integral part of communist upbringing in general and vocational schools, extra-curricular clubs courses, and auxiliary police duties for youths, colleges, and the mass media. [89] A small format journal, "A Person and the Law," circulates monthly in 3,450,000 copies! Managerial and technical personnel take law courses in their refresher institutes. Universities and faculties of legal knowledge have multiplied. The proportion of trials in visiting session has risen from 1/10 to one out of 7 or 8.

The campaign appears to have three purposes: to help prevent lawbreaking and "strengthen socialist legality," to give citizens some rudimentary knowledge of their legal rights and obligations, and to act as a stopgap means of supplying a minimum expertise in the law until such time as the law schools can supply sufficient trained jurists. There is a basic ambivalence here between a beginning juridification of society—a growing knowledge of and application of the law, and the enveloping system of prevention and social control, heavy on obligations and discipline, lighter on rights. The success of the campaign for legal education researchers are finding hard to measure so far because of the vagueness of criteria of success and the many social factors such as working and living conditions and management practices that also affect attitudes and social discipline. [90]

Other possible influences come to mind: (1) the example set by officials themselves and the extent to which the Party and other agencies stretch or evade the law; (2) the extent to which the lessons in law teach facts of practical value to citizens about their rights to housing, about labor, family, and property law; [91] (3) the justness of justice itself: criminal justice influences attitudes toward the law by "its legality, well-foundedness, the fairness of court sentences, and by how much it avoids oversimplification, partiality, and reliance on appeals or protests to straighten out injustices in trials of first instance." [92] All this plus the historic legacy of alienation from legal culture among the populace leaves the question of the success of mass legal education an open one. Nevertheless, the program of mass legal education should be ranked as one of the important changes in the Soviet response to lawbreaking since Khrushchev's fall.

As a trend in prevention, though, legal education is overshadowed by the potentiality if not yet the actuality of recent new departures in drafting and implementing under Party direction—not simply campaigns against individual forms of lawbreaking, like drunkenness, but comprehensive "complex plans of social prophylaxis." Model plans eventually may emerge from the *MVD*

Academy and the Procuracy's Institute for Crime Study and Prevention, just made jointly responsible for presenting research proposals (plans for making plans!) to the Academy of Sciences. [93]

Meanwhile, local Party committees begin to exercise new authority for drafting and coordinating the fulfillment of "complex plans of social prophylaxis of lawbreaking and other anti-social phenomena."Characteristic of ideal plans are the integration of measures against specific offenses, the further involvement of public participation pursuant to Party and constitutional mandates [94] in the protection of law and order, and the integration of the plans into regional and enterprise social and economic plans. To help draft these first, pilot plans, the Party committees call in leaders of local government, criminal justice, the Komsomol, etc., and use as consultants experts from the research institutes of the Procuracy, the Ministry of Justice (The Research Institute on Soviet Legislation), the *MVD*, and the law faculties. The subject matter and eventual plan subdivisions at the drafting meetings are likely to cover adjoining topics like Protection of Socialist Property; Drunkenness, Parasitism, and Vagrancy; Preventing Lawbreaking and the Non-Supervision of Minors; The Dissemination of Legal Knowledge; and possibly, The Struggle with Hooliganism; Combatting Recidivist Crime; Enforcing Traffic Safety, plus prevention-oriented plans for housing, working conditions, social amenities, recreational facilities, etc. [95] Plans appear down to the level of the enterprise, under supervision of primary Party organizations and experimental entities under them, like volunteer, coordinating Councils of Social Prophylaxis.

The immediate purpose of all this effort by Party, criminal justice, and social organizations is to single out and deal with lawbreaking, *e.g.*, such as absenteeism, drunkenness, pilferage, loafing, before they lead to more serious offenses, and to increase the effectiveness of anti-crime campaigns. One consequence of this mobilization for discipline and conformity is an emphasis on the "workingplace collectives" as both scenes of trouble and as the basic means of social control and social pressure. During the discussion of the draft 1977 Constitution, a novelty—an article on workingplace collectives, to emphasize their political importance—was moved from Chapter II to Chapter I, Article 8. It mandated collectives to "strengthen labor discipline, instil the spirit of communist morality in their members, to be concerned with raising their political awareness, level of culture, and professional skills." Seemingly countless organizations (some 14 or so) like the trade unions, Komsomol, comrades' courts, people's guards detachments, councils to help the school and the family, various organizations for providing mentors and big brothers and sisters to erring young workers, People's Control, form out of or check on the collectives. [96] They are too numerous to list here, but linkages exist between these various agencies and agencies of criminal justice. [97]

Militiamen in residential microdistricts and their volunteer-staffed children's rooms answer not only to administrative superiors, but possibly to one of the now 20,000 "bases for the protection of public order," again, volunteer organizations, under the direction of a local Party leader.[98] In some regions, such bases keep registers of persons inclined to break the law, public drunkards and rowdies, ex-offenders back from confinement, alimony evaders, and other local deviants. Volunteers are assigned to keep in touch with such public nuisances, lawbreakers and potential criminals.

Despite reported successes, this elaborately orchestrated prevention faces a host of operative and economic difficulties. Here is but a sample.

Neither criminal justice agencies nor Party committees have enough personnel to call to account supervisors who prefer to ignore or whitewash disciplinary lapses rather than report them and penalize undisciplined workers as the law requires.

Agencies of criminal justice can do nothing about labor turnover, a big factor in social disorganization. Neither these agencies nor the Party have yet dealt effectively with managers who prefer to fire troublemakers rather than to try to reform them.

Amateur disciplinary code-making at the plant level brings violations of workers' rights, lacks guidelines.

Sometimes, criminal justice officials find themselves summoned to serve on Party bodies, like special commissions on cases of ex-offenders, which duplicate the work of their own agencies, or of local Soviet organizations on which they serve as volunteers.

Within the Party apparatus, economic branch Party departments neglect prevention to concentrate on economic matters, leaving coordination of prevention programs in the hands of the Departments of Administrative Organs. They lack the staff to see to the coordination of entire anti-lawbreaking campaigns. The staff they have as yet lacks legal training and, therefore, the qualifications effectively to influence criminal justice agencies and their primary Party organizations.

Plans for social prophylaxis do not assign individual responsibility frequently enough. As a result, the more organizations participate—and there are scores of them—the less anyone feels responsible for getting things done.

Rates of lawbreaking and crime are taken to be measures of the effectiveness of Party committee work and the work of criminal justice agencies. This is an open invitation to continue the time-honored practice of cover-up and report padding, as is already the case in the reporting of crimes.[99]

Many Party committees themselves have been involved in corruption and the cover up of corruption and thieving on high, to the point of stopping the prosecution of heinous felons.[100] Rot cannot be cut out with rotten tools.

Mobilizing collectives to sanction anti-social behavior costs much less than social investment in better living conditions, plant surroundings, transportation to work, housing, the reduction of other causes of job dissatisfaction like heavy and boring manual labor. Like all direct measures against crime and other deviance, the marshalling of grass root sanctions distracts attention away from the difficult improvements needed. [101]

It is as yet too early, and data are too secret for the outside observer to sort out appearances and intentions from results. The efforts of criminal justice, the Party, and social organizations to curb and eliminate crime surpass all previous ones. The preventive system within which criminal justice operates is vast, unprecedented in reach and elaboration. But the amateurs are overloaded and often unqualified, and the forces of criminal justice stretched thin. And what if this system actually worked as planned? What would life be like then in the collective and neighborhood?

6. Conclusions

Trends in the Soviet system of criminal justice present surprising contrasts. Repressiveness has been curbed greatly on the political side since Stalin, but only moderately in dealing with ordinary crime. Having reformed the criminal procedure, as it were begrudgingly, in the late 1950s, and liberalized punishment, the regimes of Khrushchev and his successors stalled further significant procedural reform—de-Stalinization or none—and treated serious felonies increasingly harshly in a climate of impatience that would be very familiar to the fellow citizens of this writer, a New Yorker. By giving the courts a monopoly of convicting and sentencing, and by eliminating the secret police "special boards," the regime curbed arbitrariness in criminal justice as a whole, but increased it in the regular courts—a situation compounded by the basic change for criminal justice. That basic change, the change in purpose, diluted the insulation and professionalism of criminal justice by the very nature of proceedings, like visiting sessions and massive prevention campaigns. The addition of prevention to the purpose of criminal justice appeared at first to threaten its very existence in 1959. Khrushchev soon relented on that and stiffened the criminal code. The re-emphasis on prevention in the 1970s puts enormous new burdens on criminal justice: legal education, discretion in the many new ways a suspect may be diverted out of the criminal justice flow into means of administrative or social influence; a preventive quest and emphasis in criminal procedure; much extra time to spend for many officials coaching, advising, lecturing, and directing amateurs.

The independence of the judiciary in ordinary criminal justice cases has appeared to suffer not only because of inherent intrusions, but because the Party center is trying to get local Party committees to find the time apart from their economic concerns to look to matters of social discipline, to plan ways to root out indiscipline all the way from petty lawbreaking to crime, arguing that social discipline, too, has great economic and political value. Both the influence of criminal justice professionals on the politicians' decisions in criminal policy and the influence of Party controls on the professionals have appeared greatly to increase under Khrushchev and his successors.

Trends in criminal justice lead, then, in two contradictory ways: to the juridification of society—a greater role and rule of law, and to the politicization of social controls in the sense of their mass mobilization to stamp in conformity and obedience to the law. One feels that the recent Party leaderships do not appreciate rule of law or legality as inherently good (where have we heard that before?) but, rather, as long as and in ways that enhance their authority, social stability, economic and community discipline. They are more inclined than Stalin was to listen to experts' advice on *how* to prevent lawbreaking, and to listen to the advise if it appears to have practical value and does not involve any number of pitfalls, including the breach of the incredible official secrecy veiling crime and corrections in the USSR.

Thus, the Party has permitted the insertion of a directive to the courts containing an explicit formulation of presumption of innocence. Elevated to a "constitutional principle," presumption of innocence may well appear also in the Fundamental Principle and the codes of criminal procedure as binding formally (if not in practice) on the other criminal justice agencies: the police, Procuracy, and criminal investigators. It appeared possible, also, by the late 1970s, that the right to defense counsel before, rather than after, the pre-trial investigation may be extended to all defendants (not just minors and the incapacitated).

Correctional institutions have seen the reform of juvenile labor colonies since Stalin and the addition of colony-settlements for adults. Otherwise, correctional reforms of the 1950s appear to have been undone. The most extensive change in criminal justice procedures for adults have been toward the diversion of lesser offenders away from labor colonies and the closer linking of the criminal justice system to a larger system of crime prevention. This trend includes recent measures of de-penalization, de-criminalization, the differentiation of flows among types of offenders, and what is on paper a large diversion away from correctional institutions. Witness also the new prevention programs in the 1970s: mass legal education and "complex programs of social prophylaxis," under activated Party direction.

As the USSR Minister of Internal Affairs summed up this trend, the approach to combatting crime means "while not relaxing severe measures against dangerous criminals, more widely to use punishment not involving confinement in correctional institutions," for example, various forms of conditional sentences and measures of administrative and social influence on those first committing crimes of little danger and capable of being reformed without isolation from society. The *MVD* itself initiated the practice of the new complex approach to prevention and research on long-range complex forecasting and programs, a situation inconceivable in Stalin's later years.

80

These trends are only that—trends. They may reverse or go farther. But the next breakthrough will occur when secrecy and political restraint decrease. Then we shall see whether the disadvantages of politicization and censorship for enforcement and corrections are inevitable concomitants of the centralized mobilization, goal setting, and integration that appear at times to allow for, as well as inhibit, rapid change in the Soviet criminal justice system.

NOTES

1. Richter H. Moore, Jr. *et al.* (eds.), *Readings in Criminal Justice* (Indianapolis, Ind., 1976), p. 5.
2. *Ved. V.S. SSSR*, 1977, No. 41, item 617, Article 6.
3. Peter H. Juviler, *Revolutionary Law and Order* (New York, 1976), p. 132.
4. Robert Conquest, *The Great Terror: Stalin's Purge of the Thirties* (New York, 1973); Juviler, note 3 above, pp. 58-65.
5. *Ibid.*, p. 106.
6. S. M. Krylov, "K voprosu o prirode antiobshchestvennykh proiavlenii i strategiia bor'by s pravonarusheniiami" (On the Nature of Anti-Social Manifestations and the Strategy of Struggle with Lawbreaking), *Sots. Issled.*, 1977, No. 3, 107.
7. Article 4, USSR Constitution, above note 2.
8. G. A. Zlobin *et al.*, "Sovetskaia ugolovnaia politika: differentsiatsiia otvetstvennosti" (Soviet Criminal Policy: Differentiation of Responsibility), *SGiP*, 1977, No. 9, 55; V. V. Korobeinikov, "Otvetstvennost' dolzhnostnykh lits za narusheniia postavok produktsii" (The Responsibility of Officials for Violations of Product Delivery), *SGiP*, 1977, No. 6, 79-87.
9. Fridrikh Neznansky, "New Information on Criminal Statistics," to be publ. in *Soviet Union*, citing information he received from the USSR *MVD*. See also the estimates of Valerii Chalidze in *Ugolovnaia Rosiia* (Criminal Russia), (New York, 1977), pp. 304-310.
10. The protection and punishment for the theft of socialist property are mandated in the USSR Constitution, Article 61, and a Decree of the Plenum of the USSR Supreme Court of February 3, 1978, "Novaia Konstitutsiia SSSR i zadachi dal'neishego sovershenstvovaniia sudebnoi deiatel'nosti" (The New USSR Constitution and the Further Improvement of Judicial Activity), *BVS SSSR,* 1978, No. 2, 9-10. Statistics are from *Kriminologiia* (Criminology), (Moscow, 3rd ed., 1976), pp. 120-121.
11. F. J. M. Feldbrugge (ed.), *Encyclopedia of Soviet Law* (2 vols.; Leyden, 1973), II, p. 478.
12. E. Bagaev and Iu. Solomonov, "Defitsit iz prokhodnoi" (Scarce Goods from the Back Alley), *Komsomolskaia pravda*, March 2, 2; Gregory Grossman, "The 'Second Economy' of the USSR," *Problems of Communism*, 1977, No. 5, 81-101; Chalidze, above note 9, pp. 230-303; Juviler, above note 3, pp. 153-155; Hedrick Smith, *The Russians* (New York, 1976), pp. 81-101.
13. S. S. Ostroumov, *Sovetskaia sudebnaia statistika* (Soviet Forensic Statistics), (Moscow, 1970), p. 248; T. A. Busheva, P. S. Dagel', "Ob"ekt ugolovno-pravovoi okhrany prirody," *SGiP*, 1977, No. 8, 77-83.
14. N. Belov, "Pravonarusheniia, sviazannye s ispol'zovaniem EVM" (Crimes Connected with Computer Use), *Problemy sovershenstvovaniia sovetskogo zakonodatel'stva* (Problems of Improving Soviet Legislation), *Trudy*, 1976, No. 5, 176-187.
15. D. S. Polianskii presenting law reforms December 25, 1958. *Zasedaniia Verkhovnogo Soveta SSSR. Piatogo sozyva. Vtoraia sessiia* (Sessions of the USSR Supreme Soviet. Fifth Convocation. Second Session), (Moscow, 1959), p. 487.
16. Juviler, above note 3, pp. 78, 82-84. Death penalty statistic is an estimate of Prof. Stanislaw Pomorski.

17. *Ibid.*, pp. 123-130, 143-148.

18. V. V. Klochkov, "Aktual'nye voprosy sovetskoi kriminologii" (Current Problems of Soviet Criminology), *SGiP*, 1977, No. 5, 39-47.

19. G. A. Tumanov, V. V. Sergeev, "Povyshenie effektivnosti bor'by s antisotsial'nymi iavleniiami–kompleksnaia obshchenarodnaia problema" (Increasing the Effectiveness of the Struggle against Anti-Social Occurrences Is a Complex National Problem), *Sots. Issled.*, 1977, No. 3, 123-130; Juviler, above note 3, pp. 160-162.

20. G. A. Avanesov, *Kriminologiia. Prognostika. Upravleniia* (Criminology. Forecasting. Control), (Gor'kii, 1975), pp. 36-43.

21. S. E. Zhilinskii, *Rol' KPSS v ukreplenii zakonnosti na sovremennom etape* (The Role of the CPSU in Strengthening Legality at the Present Stage), (Moscow, 1977), pp. 6, 94-101.

22. Avanesov, above note 20; Juviler, above note 3, pp. 158-166; N. A. Shchelokov, "Razvitie nauchnykh osnov ukrepleniia sotsialisticheskoi zakonnosti i pravoporiadka" (The Development of the Scientific Basis for Strengthening Socialist Legality and Law and Order), *SGiP*, 1977, No. 11, 29-36.

23. V. I. Nizhechek, "Sovetskoe pravo i razvitie sotsialisticheskogo obraza zhizni" (Soviet Law and the Development of the Socialist Way of Life), *SGiP*, 1978, No. 1, 23-30; A. V. Seregin, "Obshchestvennyi poriadok i obraz zhizni v usloviiakh razvitogo sotsializma" (Public Order and the Way of Life Under Conditions of Developed Socialism), *SGiP*, 1978, No. 4, 35-43: Preamble, USSR Constitution.

24. S. S. Ostroumov, A. S. Shliapochnikov, "Nekotorye problemy sotsial'nogo poznaniia antiobshchestvennogo povedeniia" (Some Problems of the Social Perception of Antisocial Behavior), *Sots. Issled.*, 1977, No. 3, 115-122; G. A. Zlobin, "O kharaktere i zadachakh moral'noi statistiki," *Vsesoiuznyi nauchno-issledovatel'skii institut sovetskogo zakonodatel'stva. Uchenie zapiski* (On the Nature and Purposes of Moral Statistics, All-Union Research Institute of Soviet Legislation. Research Notes), 1973, No. 28, 38; conversation with Prof. Louise Shelley.

25. Joint resolution of Party Central Committee, Presidium of USSR Supreme Soviet, and USSR Council of Ministers, July 23, 1966, summarized in *Pravda*, July 27, 1966, 1; edict of July 26, 1966, *Ved. V.S. SSSR*, 1966, No. 30, item 594.

26. Juviler, above note 3, pp. 103-104.

27. Resolution of the Party Central Committee and USSR Council of Ministers, July 30, 1970, *BVS SSSR*, 1970, No. 5, 3-4; *Ved. V.S. SSSR*, 1970, No. 36, item 361; N.V. Sheliutto, "Otdely iustitsii v sisteme oblastnykh (kraevykh) sovetov" (Department of Justice in Province (and Territory) Soviets), *Problemy sovershenstvovaniia sovetskogo zakonodatel'stva. Trudy*, 1976, No. 6, 91-98.

28. B. M. Dubrovinskii, "Organy iustitsii: razvitie funktsii, struktury, metodov upravleniia" (Organs of Justice: Development of Their Functions, Structure, Methods of Administration), *SGiP*, 1978, No. 4, 99-105.

29. The RSFSR Criminal Procedural Code and useful comment appear in *Kommentarii k ugolovnomu protsessual'nomu kodeksu RSFSR* (Commentary on the RSFSR Criminal Procedural Code), (Moscow, 1976). Changes in rights to defense lawyer subsequent to the 1958 reform are described in Juviler, above note 3, p. 117. Deputy Minister of Internal Affairs B. A. Viktorov introduced for discussion at the June, 1978, plenum of the USSR Supreme Court a proposal that defense lawyers be admitted as soon as the criminal case is initiated. *BVS SSSR*, 1978, No. 4, 5.

30. Juviler, above note 3, p. 75; USSR Constitution, Article 152. That people's assessors usually go along with professional judges on guilt and sentencing is discussed in M. I. Ponedelkov, *Uchastie narodnykh zasedatelei v rassmotrenii ugolovnykh del* (The Participation of People's Assessors in the Trying of Criminal Cases), (Moscow, 1978), pp. 62-66.

31. A. V. Mitskevich, "Issledovanie sostoianiia pravovogo vospitaniia trudiashchik-hsia" (An Investigation of the State of Legal Knowledge among the Working People), *Sots. Issled.*, 1976, No. 3, 109.

32. Z. Antioshko, L. Antonenko, "Ispol'zovanie zvukozapisi i mashinopisi v sude" (The Use of Tape Recording and Typewriting in Court), *Sots. Zak.*, 1978, No. 4, 64.

33. Conversations with Mr. Fridrikh Neznansky and Mr. Yuri Luryi.

34. FPCP, article 22, part 3.

35. Case fee estimated from "Instruktsiia ob uplate iuridicheskoi pomoshchi, okazy-vaemoi advokatami grazhdaninam, predpriiatiiam, uchrezhdeniiam i organizatsiiam, 4 avg. 1977" (Instructions on the Fees for Legal Assistance by Lawyers to Citizens, Enter-prises, Institutions, and Organizations, August 4, 1977), *Sots. Zak.*, 1978, No. 3, pp. 81-84. For comments on and a translation of this instruction by Robert Guttman, see *Review of Socialist Law*, 5 (1979), No. 2, 203-211. S. Natrushkin and I. Sukharev, "Oplata iuridicheskoi pomoshchi, okazyvaemoi advokatami," *Sots. Zak.*, 1978, No. 4, 31-36.

36. "Interview with D. I. Kaminskaia and K. M. Simis," *Radio Liberty Special Report*, January 11, 1978, pp. 15-16.

37. *Ibid.*, pp. 20-21; Conversations with Mr. Yuri Luryi and Mr. Leonid Polsky.

38. Decree of June 13, 1978, of the USSR Supreme Court, section 2, *BVS SSSR*, 1978, No. 4, 9; I. L. Petrukhin, "Prezumptsiia nevinovnosti—konstitutsionnyi printsip sovetskogo ugolovnogo protsessa" (Presumption of Innocence Is a Constitutional Prin-ciple of Soviet Criminal Procedure), *SGiP*, 1978, No. 12, 18-26; V. Savitskii, "Novyi etap v osushchestvlenii sotsialisticheskogo pravosudiia" (A New Stage in the Implementation of Socialist Justice), *Sov. Iust.*, 1978, No. 5, 7.

39. Vladimir Slepak got five years in exile for the first banner; Ida Nudel, four years for the other. "Soviet Sentences 2 Jewish Activists to Exile in Siberia," *The New York Times*, June 22, 1978, 2. Mariia Slepak later received a suspended sentence of three years exile, enabling her to join her husband.

40. Zhilinskii, above note 21, p. 9.

41. Interview, above note 36, p. 3; Aleksandr I. Solzhenitsyn, *The Gulag Archipela-go 1918-1956: An Experiment in Literary Investigation, V-VII* (New York, 1978), pp. 519-525; Juviler, above note 3, pp. 119, 229, note 279.

42. V. M. Semenov, *Sud i Pravosudie v SSSR* (The Court and Justice in the USSR), (Moscow, 1976), pp. 36-39; Zhilinskii, above note 21, pp. 4-9, 22-25, 103-104, 137-138; N. A. Shchelokov, "Sotsialisticheskii obraz zhizni i voprosy ukrepleniia pravoporiadka v usloviiakh razvitogo sotsializma" (The Socialist Way of Life and Questions of Strength-ening Law and Order under Conditions of Developed Socialism), *Sots. Issled.*, 1977, No. 3, 98.

43. Zhilinskii, above note 21, pp. 136-138.

44. Now 97% of judges have higher legal education. The number of law school graduates nearly doubled between 1970 and 1976, from 7900 to 14000. V. Terebilov, "Shest'desiat let vmeste so vsei stranoi" (Sixty Years Together with the Whole Country), *Sots. Zak.*, 1977, No. 10, 3-12.

45. Zhilinskii, above note 21, pp. 158-161.

46. See notes 49-53 below.

47. Zhilinskii, above note 21, p. 162.

48. S. Bannikov, "Sud: Shkola morala" (The Court: School of Morality), *LG*, Janu-ary 26, 1977, 12.

49. Fridrikh Neznansky, "Budet li osuzhden A. Shcharanskii? Iz zapisok byvshego sovetskogo sledovatelia" (Will A. Shcharanskii Be Convicted? From the Notebook of a Former Soviet Investigator), *Novoe Russkoe Slovo*, April 16, 1978, 3.

50. Yuri Luryi, "The Right to Counsel in Ordinary Criminal Cases in the USSR," Donald D. Barry, George Ginsburgs, and Peter B. Maggs (eds.), *Soviet Law after Stalin. Part I. The Citizen and the State in Contemporary Soviet Law* (Leyden, 1977), pp. 105-117.

51. Juviler, above note 3, p. 117.

52. Neznansky, above note 49.

53. Fridrikh Neznansky, "Iz zapisok byvshego sovetskogo sledovatelia: Lekarstvo ot tiur'my" (From the Notebook of a Former Soviet Investigator: Medicine against Prison), *Novoe Russkoe Slovo*, April 22, 1978, 2.

54. Savitskii, above note 38, p. 9; *Novaia Konstitutsiia . . .*, above note 10, p. 13; a USSR Supreme Soviet Presidium decree ordered a new law on such remedies by December 1980. *Ved. V.S. SSSR*, 1977, No. 51, item 764.

55. *Ugolovnyi kodeks RSFSR* (RSFSR Criminal Code), (Moscow 1975), articles 21, 23-27, 29-36.

56. Chalidze, above note 9, p. 309.

57. M. Pogrebinskii, *Fabrika liudei* (Making People), (Moscow, 1929); V. L. Shveitser, S. M. Shabalova (eds.), *Besprizornye v trudovykh kommunakh: praktika raboty s trudnymi det'mi* (Street Waifs in Labor Communes: Methods of Working with Difficult Children), (Moscow, 1926); A. S. Makarenko, *Sochineniia* (Works), (7 vols; Moscow, 1957); *e.g.*, Vol. I, *Pedagogicheskaia poema* (The Road to Life); James Bowen, *Soviet Education: Anton Makarenko and the Years of Experiment* (Madison, Wisc., 1965); Z. A. Astemirov, *Trudovaia koloniia dlia nesovershennoletnikh* (Labor Colony for Juveniles), (Moscow, 1969).

58. M. P. Evteev, V. A. Kirin (eds.), *Zakonodatel'stvo ob otvetstvennosti nesovershennoletnikh* (Legislation on the Liability of Juvenile Offenders), (Moscow, 1970); edict of February 15, 1977, on the duties and rights of inspections on juvenile affairs (*MVD*), juvenile reception and distribution centers (*MVD*), and special schools for preventing non-supervision and lawbreaking of children, *Ved. V.S. SSSR*, 1977, No. 8, item 138.

59. See Eraksin, below note 76.

60. Neznansky, above note 9.

61. A. E. Natashev, "Zakonnost' i gumanizm—osnova ispravleniia i perevospitaniia osuzhdennykh" (Legality and Humanism Are the Basis for Correcting and Re-Educating Convicts), *SGiP*, 1977, No. 3, 79-87; *Kommentarii k ispravitel'nomu trudovomu kodeksu RSFSR* (RSFSR Corrective Labor Code and Commentary), (Moscow, 1973). Compare that with sources cited in Juviler, above note 3, pp. 106-109; Yulia Voznesenskaia, "Life in a Transfer Prison," *Chronicle of Human Rights in the USSR*, 1977, No. 28, 36-40; F. J. M. Feldbrugge, "Soviet Corrective Labor Law" in Barry *et al.*, above note 50, pp. 33-69; Valery Chalidze, "A Propos the Application of Corrective Labor Law in the USSR," *ibid.*, pp. 71-76.

62. *Kriminologiia* (Criminology), (2nd ed.; Moscow, 1968), p. 322.

63. *Kriminologiia*, above note 10, p. 276.

64. I. V. Shmarov, "Preodolenie otritsatel'nykh posledstvii otbyvaniia ugolovnogo nakazaniia" (Overcoming the Negative Consequences of Criminal Punishment), *SGiP*, 1977, No. 2, 86-87.

65. Aleksandr Solzhenitsyn, *Arkhipelag Gulag*, I-II (Paris, 1973), pp. 501-509, 538-540, 552-555; *Sovetskaia Kriminologiia* (Soviet Criminology), (1st ed.; Moscow, 1966) p. 308.

66. *Kriminologiia*, above note 65, pp. 299-305; note 63, pp. 311-316; note 10, pp. 268-272.

67. *Ved. V.S. SSSR*, 1961, No. 19, item 207.

68. Chalidze, above note 9, and the three volumes of Solzhenitsyn's *Gulag Archipelago* are indispensable introductions to the language and lore of the criminal world and labor camps.

69. Shmarov, above note 64, pp. 85-86, 90. Judicial discretion to assign to any colony, except that of special (harshest) regime, dilutes whatever separation exists among prisoners of different degrees of incorrigibility. *Ved. V.S. SSSR*, 1977, No. 7, item 116; conversation with Fridrikh Neznansky.

70. O. Chaikovskaia, "Eto bylo v Rostove" (It Happened in Rostov), *LG*, July 18, 1973, 13; Valery U., "Pis'mo v redaktsiiu" (Letter to the Editor), *ibid*, April 3, 1975, 12.

71. A. D. Glomochkin and V. F. Pirozhkov, "Psikhicheskoe sostoianie cheloveka, lishennogo svobody" (The Mental State of a Person Deprived of Freedom), *Voprosy bor'by s prestupnost'iu* (Problems of Combatting Crime), 1972, No. 15, 100-104.

72. V. Andreev, "Rabota nabliudatel'nykh komissii po preduprezhdeniiu prestupnosti" (How Supervisory Commissions Prevent Crime), *Sots. Zak.*, 1977, No. 10, 37-39; *Kriminologiia*, above note 10, pp. 277-283.

73. Shchelokov, above note 42, p. 104; Tumanov and Sergeev, above note 19, p. 129; O. Shishov, "Istoriia nauki sovetskogo ispravitel'no-trudovogo prava" (The History of Soviet Corrective Labor Law) in V. N. Kudriavtsev (ed.), *Kriminologiia. Ispravitel'no-trudovoe pravo* (Moscow, 1977), pp. 69-109. I am indebted to Dr. Susan Heuman for this source.

74. Krylov, above note 6, p. 114. Seven-day emergency leaves and 5-day travel time were decreed in 1977. *Ved. V.S. SSSR*, 1977, No. 7, item 116.

75. *Ibid*.; on experiment, L. G. Krakhmal'nik, "Eksperimenty kak metod sovershenstvovaniia ispravitel'no-trudovogo zakonodatel'stva," *Problemy sovershenstvovaniia sovetskogo zakonodatelstva. Trudy*, 1977, No. 9, 119-131.

76. V. Eraksin, "Ispravitel'no-trudovye kolonii-poseleniia" (Corrective Labor Colony-Settlements), *Sots. Zak.*, 1977, No. 8, 40-42; Kh. B. Sheinin, "Tochno ispolniat' novoe zakonodatel'stvo o bor'be s prestupnost'iu" (Carry Out Precisely the New Legislation to Combat Crime), *SGiP*, 1977, No. 8, 90-98.

77. G. A. Zlobin, "Psikhicheskaia kharakteristika lits, zaderzhannykh za brodiazhnichestva" (The Mental Traits of Persons Detained for Vagrancy), *Problemy*, above note 75, 111-119.

78. Juviler, above note 3, pp. 92-94.

79. Edict of February 8, 1977, *Ved. V.S. SSSR*, 1977, No. 7, item 116, changing FPCLL (*Ved. V.S. SSSR*, 1969, No. 29, item 247 and 1973, No. 18, item 239). On procedures, surveillance, etc. see *ibid*., 1977, No. 7, item 118; Zlobin, above note 8, p. 55.

80. Iu. B. Mel'nikova, D. O. Khan Mogamedov, "Praktika primeneniia uslovnogo osuzhdeniia k lisheniiu svobody s ob'iazatel'nym privlecheniem osuzhdennogo k trudu" (Practice in Applying Suspended Sentences to Confinement with Obligatory Assignment to Work), *Voprosy bor'by s prestupnost'iu*, 1977, No. 27, 50.

81. Neznansky, above note 9.

82. V. Shubin on similar theme in *Sov. Iust.*, 1978, No. 6, 3-4.

83. *Ibid*., p. 5 and Mel'nikova and Khan Mogamedov, above note 80, p. 48.

84. *Ved. V.S. SSSR*, 1977, No. 7, item 116; *Ibid*., 1976, No. 49, item 713; Zlobin, above note 8, pp. 58-59.

85. The edict of February 15, 1977, adds Article 39^1 to FPCL (*Ved. V.S. SSSR*, 1959, No. 1, item 6). *Ved. V.S. SSSR*, 1977, No. 8, item 137.

86. *Ved. V.S. SSSR*, 1977, No. 51, item 75.

87. Zlobin, above note 8, pp. 55, 57; *BVS SSSR*, 1977, No. 2, pp. 7-9.

88. I. Albastov, "Rol' sudov i organov iustitsii v povyshenii effektivnosti profilaktiki pravonarushenii" (The Role of Courts and Organs of Justice in Raising the Effectiveness of the Prophylaxis of Crime), *Sov. Iust.*, 1978, No. 2, 6-7; S. Bannikov, "Zakon, obshchestvo, grazhdanin" (The Law, Society, the Citizen), *LG*, October 12, 1977, 11. Omitted here is mention of the greatly increased role of courts in prescribing compulsory cures for alcoholism and drug addiction, and venereal disease, as well as the role of the courts in committing persons to psychiatric hospitals. M. Maslov and A. Ovchinnikova, "Praktika naznacheniia prinuditel'nykh mer meditsinskogo kharaktera" (Court Practice in Committing to Compulsory Measures of a Medical Nature), *Sov. Iust.*, 1978, No. 7, 8-9; Juviler, above note 3, pp. 74-76, 89-90, 114-115.

89. *Ibid.*, pp. 94-98; Terebilov, above note 44. p. 8.

90. *Ibid.*, pp. 8-9; the issue of *Sov. Iust.*, 1978, No. 5, devoted to legal education, a novelty for that journal (to devote an issue to one theme); "Ukreplenie distsipliny i povyshenie sotsial'noi aktivnosti trudiashchikhsia–vazhnaia zadacha pravovogo vospitaniia" (Tightening Discipline and Increasing the Social Activeness of Workers Is an Important Task of Legal Education), *Sov. Iust.*, 1978, No. 2, 1-2, 5-6; A. Ia Sukharev, "Upravlenie pravovym vospitaniem trudiashchikhsia" (Administering the Legal Education of the Workers), *SGiP*, 1977, No. 11, 37-45, Mitskevich, above note 31, pp. 107-112.

91. *Ibid.*, p. 110.

92. Albastov, above note 88, p. 7.

93. Shchelokov, above note 42; Tumanov and Sergeev, above note 19.

94. "L. I. Brezhnev ob ukreplenii sovetskoi gosudarstvennosti i sotsialisticheskogo pravoporiadka" (L. I. Brezhnev on Strengthening the Soviet State System and Socialist Law and Order), *Sots. Zak.*, 1977, No. 9, 3-7; K. E. Igoshev, "Profilaktika prestuplenii: teoreticheskie i prakticheskie aspekty" (Theoretical and Practical Aspects of the Prophylaxis of Crime), *SGiP*, 1977, No. 6, 88-96; Constitution, Articles 61, 65.

95. M. Babin, "Organizatsionnaia rabota gorodskogo komiteta partii po preduprezhdeniiu pravonarushenii," *Sots. Zak.*, 1977, No. 10, 27-30; Zhilinskii, above note 21, pp. 58-59, 70-87, 96-97.

96. N. G. Kobets, "Sotsial'naia otvetstvennost' v sisteme preduprezhdeniia pravonarushenii na predpriatii" (Social Responsibility in the System of Prevention of Lawbreaking in the Enterprise), *SGiP*, 1978, No. 3, 88-95; Zhilinskii, above note 21, pp. 183-189; new edict on comrades' courts, *Ved. V.S. SSSR*, 1977, No. 7, item 121; on People's Control, one function of which is to refer possible cases of theft and economic crimes to the authorities, see B. M. Makarov, *Narodnyi kontrol'* (People's Control), (Moscow, 1975).

97. Juviler, above note 3, pp. 74-76.

98. Shchelokov, above note 42, p. 101; Zhilinskii, above note 21, pp. 201-202.

99. Iu. Melymuka, "Metody partiinogo rukovodstva pravokhranitel'nimi organami" (Methods of Party Guidance of Agencies of Criminal Justice), *Sots. Zak.*, 1977, No. 12, 23-25; S. E. Zhilinskii, "Vospitanie pravosoznaniia v rabochem kollektive (obshchee i osobennoe)" (Instilling Legal Knowledge in the Workplace Collective (General and Specific)), *SGiP*, 1978, No. 3, 12-21; Zhilinskii, above note 21, pp. 103-105.

100. *Ibid.*, pp. 72-78, 83-88; Juviler, above note 3, pp. 154-155.

101. I. A. Arabian, "Ustranenie prichin narusheniia trudovoi distsipliny" (Eliminating the Causes of the Violation of Labor Discipline), *SGiP*, 1978, No. 1, 124-127.

FURTHER TRENDS IN SOVIET CRIMINAL JUSTICE

Friedrich-Christian Schroeder

In my opinion, Professor Juviler has given us an excellent report, not limiting himself to trends in Soviet criminal justice, but giving a detailed picture of the actual situation. Although it is almost impossible to add to this report, perhaps Professor Juviler did not bring out clearly enough one tendency largely accentuated in present-day Soviet criminal justice: the demand for the *individualizatsiia nakazaniia*–differentiation of the sentence. This trend seems to me to be very important. It could be a key for research in the development of the Soviet criminal policy.

In my 1963 paper "The Development of Soviet Criminal Policy,"[1] I characterized Soviet criminal policy with the title of a well-known book on modern art as a "loss of the middle". Punishment in extremes has been typical for Soviet criminal justice through all of its periods. In the period immediately after the October Revolution, there was an abrupt bifurcation of criminal policy: merciless harshness against delinquents from circles of the formerly dominant classes combined with very far-reaching leniency for criminals from the class of workers and peasants. In order to allow for such sharp differentiation, the criminal code contained a wide spectrum of penalties with ample discretion for the judge. In addition, Soviet law very early adopted such modern features of criminal policy as conditional conviction and conditional release.

The more that socialism became established, the more this allowance for the proletarian criminal disappeared; indeed this allowance changed to moral indignation at the fact that crimes continued to be committed without the compulsion of capitalist conditions which disappointed the optimistic image of man under Marxism-Leninism. With the transition to socialism under Stalin, Soviet criminal policy therefore yielded to unqualified revenge and repression. While the criminal code of 1926 came to be described as the "criminal code without guilt and punishment", concepts of "guilt" and "punishment" were now reintroduced. For the purpose of effective deterrence, the penalty range was narrowly restricted. Previous special preventive institutions–such as conditional release and juvenile criminal law–either disappeared altogether or became obsolete like conditional conviction.

After the Second World War, this ruthless law of deterrence, far from

89

being dismantled, was actually extended for the protection of the new privileged class. Thus, the penalty for the theft of private property was upgraded in 1954 from imprisonment of up to 3 months to imprisonment from 5 to 6 years, in cases of recidivism from 6 to 10 years, and in cases of violence from 10 to 20 years—far harsher than in any capitalist country. Under the influence of this policy, penal camps in the Soviet Union rapidly filled; whole armies of prisoners were formed, estimated at between 5 and 15 million.

After Stalin's death and especially under Khrushchev, however, a new radical turn-around began. Besides categorically repudiating the Stalinist terror system, Khrushchev attempted to tackle anew the old Marxist thesis of the withering away of law and to achieve it through replacing compulsion with persuasion and state power with social organizations. On the basis of this concept, extensive possibilities were introduced for a retreat from deterrence and the ignominy of punishment in favor of education and rehabilitation. Thus, in place of penalties, reaction to criminality was widely given over to measures of social impact, such as *e.g.* transfer to a comrades' court or to surveillance by social organizations or workers' collectives. While these measures were mostly interpreted in the West as menacing symptoms of totalitarianism, in actuality they were much less radical in practice than at first blush.

Complaints increased that, because of the proverbial good naturedness of the Russian character and a certain solidarity against legal authority, the instructions of social law enforcement failed to attain their expected effectiveness and even led to a dubious dilution of the fight against criminality.

As a result of this, at the end of the Khrushchev period, the facilities of punishment in favor of the special prevention were restricted step-by-step and the old bifurcation of criminal policy came back, with the only difference being that now the differentiation took place not between the members of the different classes but between serious and petty offenders.

Since the end of the 1960's, however, Soviet criminal justice seems to have broken through this *circulus vitiosus*. Since then, *individualizatsiia nakazaniia* has become the main aim of criminal justice, and at present this is not limited to differentiation between extreme severity against serious criminals and leniency against petty offenders. Thus, the deficient social supervision of convicts under the new, stronger trend in the first period after Khrushchev had led to a systematic increase of prison sentencing. But to stop this development, a new form of conditional conviction was introduced in 1970, *viz.* conditional conviction with mandatory labor. This form of punishment has become very popular; it is used in about 12% of all sentences. In the spring of 1977, it was included in the federal fundamentals of criminal law. The same aim is contained in other parts of the 1977 legislation which provides for measures other than imprisonment for juveniles, release from punishment with administrative sanctions, and the establishment of special colony-settlements for persons who have committed crimes through negligence.[2] It is, however, interesting in that now the legislator himself tries to make the individualization of the punishment: the conditions, under which the reprieve from imprisonment and the other facilities are possible, are precisely prescribed in the law. Thus, the scope for the decisions of a single judge remains very narrow; the judge is considered, as he was during the Age of Enlightenment, as a simple automaton of the application of the law—*Subsumtionsautomat*.

As to particular areas of criminality, interest seems now to be focussed on economic crimes, especially the establishment of illegal private enterprises and the falsification of the reports on the fulfillment of the economic plan. For both kinds of crimes, the USSR Supreme Court issued guiding instructions during the last 2 years. In both cases, the main reason for the obvious increase in criminality seems to be the encouragement of the kolkhoz enterprise. Obviously, it is difficult to control all these enterprises of the collective farms. Thus, in the instruction on illegal private enterprises there was a special section which attempted to define the rights of the kolkhozes and to distinguish between legal enterprises of the kolkhozes and the illegal abuse of the legal form of a kolkhoz enterprise. The relevant section of the criminal code was enlarged; there was added the form of obscuring by collective form of enterprising. It is interesting to note, that this new regulation was adopted from Bulgarian law. It is not the first time that Soviet law adopted a regulation from the law of Bulgaria,[3] the old relations between these two systems of law seem to continue even now.

We find a similar situation in the field of falsification of the reports on the fulfillment of the economic plan. In a survey of court practice, given by the USSR Supreme Court in 1977, 10 cases of such falsifications were described; 4 of them took place within the enterprises of the kolkhozes. Incidentally, this offense can be committed only by the director of an enterprise and the chief bookkeeper, and therefore is to be considered as a typical form of white collar crime. In the above-mentioned survey, the USSR Supreme Court complained that the sentences for this crime were too low, which is another similarity to white collar crimes in the West.

If I were to try to give a summary of my observations on the subject "Trends in Soviet Criminal Justice", I would say, that, for the first time in the whole development of Soviet criminal justice, there is a trend toward avoiding the extremes, the radicalism, and toward striving for more normal, moderate justice—in short, a trend not to have trends any more.

NOTES

1. *Jahrbuch für Ostrecht*, IV (1963), No.2, 69-90.

2. For comments on this legislation, see *inter alia* F. J. M. Feldbrugge, "Correction Through Labor: New Criminal Legislation in the USSR," in *Review of Socialist Law*, 3 (1977), No. 3, 345-350; B. Schultze-Willebrand, "Ausbau des strafrechtlichen Sanktionensystems in der UdSSR," in *Jahrbuch für Ostrecht*, XVII (1976), No. 2, 61-76.

3. *Cf.* F.-C. Schroeder, "Verschärfung der 'Parasitenbekämpfung' in der DDR. Vergleich zu den übrigen sozialistischen Staaten," *Deutschland Archiv*, 1976, No. 8, 834-843.

CHARACTERISTICS OF SOVIET TAX AND BUDGETARY LAW

Peter B. Maggs

1. Introduction

The details of Soviet finance law have been extensively described in both English and Russian.[1] This paper will not try to compete with those published descriptions. Nor will the author, being a lawyer, encroach upon the ground traditionally belonging to economists in the analysis of taxation and budgeting. Rather, this paper will attempt to identify the characteristic legal features of Soviet finance law which distinguish it from the financial law of a capitalist country, such as the United States, and from the financial law of a typical developing country. The analysis will be limited to the Soviet domestic financial system.[2]

Within the spectrum of the world's systems of finance law, the Soviet system stands out in a number of respects. The tax system produces a large amount of revenue, both in absolute terms and relative to national income. Taxes actually collected are a very high percentage of those which the tax legislation says should be paid. Tax collection is accomplished with very little use of the civil or criminal courts. On the budgetary side, controls on expenditures have succeeded in preventing the inflation characteristic of the United States and many other industrialized countries. With some exceptions, the budgetary system works in the sense that expenditures are in fact made for the purposes for which they have been appropriated. The budgetary process is characterized by a high degree of centralization. However, this centralization is by no means total, and some decentralizing trends may be noted. An additional important development, with parallels in the United States, is that of transfer of budgetary agencies to a more businesslike profit-and-loss (*khozraschet*) system of management.

In many countries, the system of taxation and of allocation of budgetary measures is perceived as unjust by a high percentage of the citizenry. In the Soviet Union, even those dissidents who criticize many aspects of the legal system rarely raise serious objections to the system of taxes and budgeting. Some of the aspects of the system that created this perceived fairness will be examined.

2. Historical Background

Taxes and budgeting have not always functioned as smoothly in the Soviet Union as they seem to today. Pre-revolutionary Russia was the scene of power struggles between the Duma and the bureaucracy over the locus of fiscal power.[3] In the early years after the revolution, many peasants resisted taxes with armed violence, while the lack of revenues and of budgetary controls led to runaway inflation.

Major budgetary reform came with the start of economic planning in the late 1920s and early 1930s, with the establishment of the general outlines of the system in effect today.[4] The essence of the reform was to place most economic operations in the hands of state enterprises operating on a profit-and-loss basis. However, in the 1930s, many governmental units were still unable to cover their expenditures with their receipts, and an elaborate system of grants and subsidies was required. The system had begun to function smoothly by the late 1930s and met its greatest challenge—the financing of the Soviet was effort in the 1940s—extremely well. By the time of Stalin's death, the financial dislocations of the war period had been overcome, and the budgetary system was once again on a stable basis. Some highly unpopular tax policy measures were introduced by Khrushchev, but were reversed by his successors. Under Brezhnev, budgetary policy has been very cautious. Changes have been gradual, and have been aimed at the fine tuning of a system deemed generally satisfactory, rather than at major reform. Price reforms have placed most enterprises in a profit-making, tax-paying position. Only areas such as defense, health, education, and some public services remain organized as government agencies financed by budget appropriations.

3. Taxation

The revenue side of the budget will be considered first. Here three characteristics may be noted. First, the system runs with almost no litigation. Second, it is extremely effective in collecting taxes due under the law. Third, an extremely high percentage of the national income is collected in the form of taxes without creating a widespread perception of unfairness. How is this result—which would be the envy of bureaucrats and politicians in many other countries—achieved?

The key to the success of the process is clearly in the fact that most of the national income is produced by the socialized state enterprises and by the structure of rewards within those enterprises. In contrast to a capitalist enterprise, whose management is evaluated and rewarded, at least in theory, by the amount of income it produces for the stockholders *after* payment of taxes, the Soviet enterprise has traditionally rewarded its manager for its production of absolute quantities of goods and for gross profits before the government

94

takes its share. Thus, in many ways the Soviet enterprise manager can be as indifferent to the way in which his enterprise income is taken as government revenue as the manager of a capitalist firm is to the way in which stockholders spend their dividends.

Because of this lack of incentive to minimize taxes, and despite the rather broad freedom for constructive economic criticism in the Soviet Union, few voices can be heard calling directly for a lowering of taxes or for introduction of procedures for contesting tax assessments in court by state enterprises. If some of the more radical economic reforms which are sometimes suggested were implemented, if enterprises were given greater independence and were allowed to retain some portion of their net profits, one might expect the present system to come under serious pressures.

A second reason why the collection of taxes from state enterprises has been so successful has been the combination of rigidly formal definitions of payments due and of accounting standards uniformly imposed throughout the country. While in the United States, for instance, it is possible to litigate endless with the tax authorities over what are "ordinary and necessary" business expenses, in the Soviet Union we find extremely detailed guidelines in a variety of areas such as expense accounts, guidelines which simultaneously determine both permissible expenditures and allowable deductions from profits for tax purposes.

The existence of this rigid formalism should be a major aid to the Soviet government in the task now in progress of computerization of tax accounting and collection. While it is hard for a computer to decide if a business expense was necessary, it is easy for it to decide if a travel allowance exceeds a fixed per diem amount specified by administrative regulations. Thus during the 1980s, we may expect a substantial increase in the efficiency of the already very efficient system of tax collection from state enterprises, as modern methods of data processing are introduced. Because the present system is already very highly effective in producing the revenues required by law, this efficiency is more like to be reflected in a significant reduction of the staff required for tax enforcement than in a major increase in tax collections.

As will be seen in the discussion of the budget, another major reason for the success of Soviet tax collection is the fact that those levels of government responsible for the collection almost always are given a share of the revenues collected, providing a major incentive for efficiency in the collection process.

Popular acceptance of the system of taxes on state enterprises is greatly aided by the indirect nature of the taxation. In the United States, for instance, owners of stock in corporations are never happy paying taxes on corporate dividend, because they pay the taxes themselves. Even many types of excise taxes, such as sales tax, or gasoline tax, are frequently separately listed and assessed, and thus are brought separately to the attention of the customers. In the USSR, on the other hand, none of the taxes on the enterprise are really visible to the average citizen, and a number of the payments by enterprises which form important sources of state revenues do not even take the traditional forms of taxes.

The overwhelming majority of Soviet government revenues from state enterprises come from three basic sources: residual profits transferred to the state,[5] the turnover tax,[6] and payment for the use of enterprise assets.[7] The first two taxes took on their basic current form in the 1930s.[8] The third is the product of the economic reforms of the 1960s.

The turnover tax is levied at fixed rates for different types of goods.[9] In terms of administration, it has the advantage that the amount is easy to determine. The enterprise manager, under the incentive systems in effect, is interested in reporting the maximum amount of production and sales; however, this in turn leads to a maximization of the turnover tax.

The charge for the use of productive assets, introduced by the economic reforms of 1960s, again has the advantage of invisibility to the public. However, its nature is such as to create a type of tension for the manager not caused by the other taxes. In order to maximize production and profits, a manager would like to have as many productive assets as possible. This charge will tend to tempt the manager to understate the amount of his productive assets. Thus, a reform of considerable importance from the economic point of view has been achieved only at the expense of introducing some tension into the system of taxation.

The residual payment of profits to the government presents no such immediate problems. Even if profits could somehow be retained, rigid accounting controls and severe criminal penalties would make very difficult their diversion to other uses by management.

An entirely separate scheme is used for collection of taxes on collective farm income. The nature of farming operations and the seasonal timing of receipts are reflected in this legislation. [10]

Taxation on the individual in the Soviet Union is simplified greatly by the fact that the majority of employed persons work for state enterprises, institutions, and organizations. A simple payroll tax, collected at the source, thus can provide a convenient and effective, though not necessarily popular, means of tax enforcement. With respect to persons working in agriculture or in the extremely limited area of legal self-employment, the tax assessment and collection problem becomes much more difficult. For those engaged in illegal black-market operations, tax assessment and collection is virtually impossible.

Consider first those working for state-owned employers. The two major direct taxes they will pay are both based upon their wages or salary—the income tax, and the bachelor's and small family tax. [11] Thus, collection can be assured by the simple method of payroll deduction. Disputes over tax amounts are extremely unlikely, because the tax is assessed as a fixed percentage for various income brackets.

96

While ease of administration is a virtue of this type of tax, popularity is not. It is therefore by no means surprising that this was the tax which Khrushchev singled out for a promise of repeal. The failure of the regime in fact to succeed in repealing the income tax remains a continuing embarrassment for it. Successive legislation has removed income taxes from the very lowest wage levels. Presumably, the elimination of this most unpopular of Soviet taxes will remain a goal of the Soviet government. However, given the conflicting goal of balancing the state budget to avoid inflation, it remains to be seen how soon the promise made by Khrushchev can be fulfilled.

Collection of taxes and revenues from collective farms has been discussed above. With the transfer of collective farms to regular wage payments, the type of withholding scheme used in industry also became possible in agriculture. Much more difficult, however, is the fair assessment of taxes upon individual peasant household income from farming activities on plots allocated to the household by the collective farm. Here, the authorities have regarded as hopeless any attempt to allocate such income among family members, and as impossible the determination of money actually received for farm products sold and the cost of producing them. Rather, an approximation is made with an assessment based upon the size and fertility of the plot and the number of livestock. [12] This approach would appear to be a very realistic concession to the practical limits of enforceability of the law.

Under Khrushchev, the agricultural tax was increased and was used in a punitive manner, designed to force out the private farming activity of peasants. These extremely unpopular measures were rapidly reversed by his successors.

In certain limited areas of the Soviet economy, some types of self-employment are still allowed. These include, for instance, private practice by doctors, writing for royalties by authors, and certain private repair services. Many of these types of activities are ideologically suspect and are therefore taxed at very high rates. Others are considered ideologically acceptable—for instance, writing and inventing—and are in many instances freed from taxation or are taxed at low rates.

The combination of the high rate of taxation and the private nature of the activities make this area one of the most difficult for the Soviet tax collector. A number of legal measures have been adopted to simplify collection. The most effective of these is the requirement that fees be collected through a cashier employed by the state, with taxes withheld at the source. Thus, for instance, a doctor working in a medical center, which charges fees, will not receive the full charge for his services paid by the patient but will have taxes deducted by the medical center bookkeeping office. In the case of lawyers in legal consultation offices, a similar arrangement is used. The high taxation rates, and relatively low fee schedules, create severe temptations for those offering professional services through such an arrangement to demand under-the-table payments by their clients or patients. Such under-the-table payments, which appear to be widespread, of course escape taxation altogether.

Where self-employment involves income which does not pass through a state agency, taxation is done on the basis of a combination of self-assessment by the individual, and assessment on the basis of guidelines by the tax authorities, with judicial review available in case of a dispute. The mechanism of collection obviously is subject to all the drawbacks of similar mechanisms in capitalist countries. However, the Soviet authorities are blessed by the fact that they need rely upon this unsatisfactory mode of collection for only a miniscule proportion of their revenues.

Ideologically approved earnings, for instance those from author's royalties and inventor's remuneration, are typically not taxed at a high punitive rate. Since they are paid by the state, accounting for amounts paid and withholding of taxes present no serious problem. One interesting new development has been the imposition of relatively high tax rates upon royalties received from foreign publication of Soviet works.[13] Here, the requirement that royalties be channeled through the All-Union Agency on Author's Rights (*VAAP*) greatly eases the collection problems. The unpopularity of the high tax rate is probably mitigated by a number of factors. First, foreign royalties are essentially a windfall to Soviet authors, since few of them received any foreign royalties at all before the Soviet Union joined the Universal Copyright Convention in 1973. Second, the chance to receive some of the royalties in hard currency certificates with a real value much greater than their face value largely offsets the burden of the tax rate.[14] However, the inadequacy of compensation is implicitly recognized by other Soviet legislation, which provides a higher royalty rate for works specially commissioned for publication abroad. In such cases, the after-tax royalty is not a windfall—it must be high enough to provide an incentive to get the work written.

The most hopeless task for the Soviet tax collector is the taxation of profits from illegal private enterprise in the areas of manufacturing and trade. For obvious reasons, there are no published statistics on the proportion of income produced by such activity, but there is every reason to believe it is substantial. Unlike some countries, such as the United States, where income tax at times has been used at times as a weapon against illegal activity, while at other times those engaged in crime have been pressured to "launder" their illegal earnings and to pay taxes upon them, the Soviet Union seems not to use income taxation either as a weapon against crime or a source of revenue from crime.

One reason is that the appropriate remedies are lacking. The criminal code does not have an article punishing tax evasion, except in time of war. The penalties aimed directly at illegal private enterprise activity are severe; the authorities seem to regard their problem as being that of catching the criminals, not of taxing them.

In addition to taxes, there are a number of other methods whereby the Soviet government obtains funds from its citizenry to finance the budget. The most important are the issue of government bonds, the deposit of funds in savings banks, and the state lottery.

Under Stalin, state bonds were used essentially as a means of taxation. Each year there was a campaign for the sale of state bonds, and all workers who did not wish to be suspected of disloyalty to the state "voluntarily" bought a recommended quota of state bonds. Eventually, this obviously un-popular system became also unproductive of new revenues as payments on maturing bonds came to approach collections from newly-sold bonds. This quasi-compulsory sale of state bonds was abolished by Khrushchev, but at the same time he postponed redemption of outstanding bonds for many years. [15] On the one hand this was a welcome measure, but on the other it was a serious incursion upon the stability of property rights and the credibility of the government. Khrushchev's successors have not resorted to compulsory bond sales, and furthermore they have speeded up the schedule of bond repayments, so as to restore the fiscal respectability of the government.

In addition to these quasi-compulsory sales, there has always been, in addition, the possibility of voluntary purchase of state bonds or of voluntary deposit of money in savings accounts. Since Stalin's death, the rights of such voluntary purchasers have been fully protected—no Soviet citizen has lost a kopeck in a state savings bank, and the banking authorities have lobbied effectively to protect bank accounts from taxation and to limit possibilities of attachment of the accounts, so as to maintain the incentive for deposit.

The confidence of bank depositors is a fragile thing, as panics in many countries have shown. Only a long continued stable legal regime can encour-age citizens to keep the bulk of their free assets in banks. The Soviet Union by its conservative legal policy has been highly successful in this regard. However, it has gone beyond the mere offer of stability. Since bonds and deposits can earn up to 3% interest, and since this interest is not taxed and is perhaps greater than the annual rate of inflation, Soviet bank depositors have the possibility, almost unknown in other countries, of receiving real interest (after inflation and taxes) on their money. One can imagine that only in the direst of crises would the Soviet government make any major incursion upon the interests of depositors and bondholders—the investment in building up confidence has been too great.

4. Budgetary Law

The fundamental legal problems of a system of budgetary law concern the procedures for setting an overall limit on the budget, for allocating funds to competing interests within that limit, and for ensuring that funds allocated are spent as planned. [16] Whether expenditures are wise or foolish, whether money ends up being spent on guns or butter, is a question beyond the scope of this paper.

The first point to note about the Soviet budget is the way in which law and custom requires that it be balanced, a method which reduces but does not eliminate the possibilities of inflationary pressure. In theory, expenditures are limited to the total of revenues, plus increase in citizens' savings plus increases in foreign loans. While in fact, as foreign economic observers have clearly demonstrated, inflation could still very easily occur despite these restrictions, Soviet policy on total budget levels has been restrained, and inflation has been well-controlled, at least in comparison to a country such as the United States.

Allocation of budgetary sums among competing territorial governmental units remains largely a political question. However, the politics involved are increasingly being conducted within rather well-defined legal limits. With fewer and fewer exceptions, the budget of each geographical political subdivision—republic, region (*oblast'*), district (*raion*), and city is limited at the maximum to the amount of taxes collected within that region. [17]

However, only a few political subdivisions reach this maximum. Most are allocated percentages of each of the various types of taxes collected within their geographical area, with the percentages ranging from rather low amounts to a maximum of 100%. The most basic problem is one that seems to be an almost incurable feature of every budgetary institution—as the employee of a state institution and a participant in the budgetary process, the author of the present paper is intimately familiar with it.

This problem is described as follows by a Soviet author: [18]

> "The fact that the volume of the lower budget is determined proceeding from the needs for appropriations for financing planned measures, and insufficient assets are supplemented from an all-union fund (at the expense of transfers from all-union state taxes and incomes) leads sometimes to undesirable phenomena. This appears in a number of instances in the attempt to minimize the projection for the firm (own) receipts and to exaggerate the expenditures, so as to attain the maximum share of appropriations from the all-union fund of monetary assets . . .
>
> Such phenomena, of course, reduce the role and significance of the preliminary stage of development of lower-level budgets, to the extent that here a certain part of the efforts, time, and means are directed to the achievement of an 'easy' plan, insufficiently considering the internal reserves of an economy having the possibility of a supplementary mobilization of reserves."

The effort to counteract exaggerated demands has led to the use of a variety of types of budgetary guidelines. At the most general level, these specify the percentages of the various types of revenues that may be retained by a given budgetary unit. At the more specialized level, they set specific figures for specific types of expenditures, or even regulate these expenditures in detail.

Major decentralization of the legal right to control expenditure within budgetary categories came in with a 1955 decree. [19] The central all-union government, which had previously had the right to control some 20 different categories of budget expenditure, limited itself to the following four categories: (1) financing the national economy; (2) social and cultural measures; (3) supporting the agencies of administration of the union republics; (4) for wages.

Thus, the reform of the budgetary system to some extent parallels other aspects of the economic reform that followed Stalin's death, in the increase in the authority of local authorities by the reduction of the number of "plan indicators" dictated from above.

The use of guidelines extends throughout the system. A pressing problem in many countries is the control of the growth of public expenditures on hospital care. In the Soviet budgetary process, these are controlled by compulsory guidelines for budget preparation. Thus, for instance, numerous decrees establishes guidelines for expenditure for food, medicines, bandages, and supplies per hospital bed per year. [20]

The actual budgetary process is a complex one, with guidelines coming down from above while estimates move up from below. It is further complicated by the tendency mentioned above for lower levels to exaggerate their needs and to underestimate their resources. Foreign understanding of the process is further complicated by the fact that Soviet authors typically present only sketchy accounts of it and disagree among themselves as to exactly what steps take place when. The fact may be that, because of the largely political nature of the process, it does not really follow any very precise legal guidelines.

An important development of recent years has been the development of "control figures" to limit the discretion of governmental bodies below the *oblast'* level. The new process is described as working as follows by one Soviet commentator. [21]

First, a draft *oblast'* budget is prepared at the *oblast'* level.

Second, control figures are prepared to govern the general outlines of the lower level budgets.

Third, the districts and cities—the lower levels—form their budgets on the basis of the "control figures".

These drafts eventually move upward, becoming the basis for republic and all-union drafts. Then, after the all-union budget is approved in early December, the process moves downward, as each lower level sets its own budget within the general outlines set by the higher budget. The lower levels are not completely rigidly bound by the higher levels. Thus, for instance, the all-union budget indicates the expected levels of income from various sources for the individual republics. If the republics, after the all-union budget is adopted, in fact believe that more revenue can be collected, they may (and almost always do) provide for a balance of expenditures and revenues higher than that envisioned in the all-union budget. In other words, while the republics cannot change the proportion, say, of the turnover tax which is retained at the republic level, a republic can, by increasing production and sales beyond planned figures, in fact increase turnover tax receipts, and thus have more funds to allocate for various purposes. Thus, the system is structured so as to encourage maximum tax collection at each level, though collection difficulties do occasionally occur. [22]

Once the budget is finally approved on down to the lowest level of government (a process which may not be completed until sometime after the budget year has begun—necessitating interim operations on temporary guidelines), the next stage involves the carrying out of the budget. The various budgetary institutions are expected to carry out their planned tasks of educating children, treating the sick, cleaning the streets, etc., within the financial limits set by the budget.

Elaborate and uniform bookkeeping rules are designed to ensure that the higher authorities in fact have the capability of checking compliance by lower authorities with the budget. [23] Regular reports of expenditures, with detailed breakdown by standard category, are required from each budgetary institution. Disciplinary and possibly even criminal sanctions are available for failure to properly report.

Even if all services that are supposed to be rendered are rendered and all reports that are supposed to be submitted are submitted, there remains the possibility of embezzlement of funds or misuse of position. Reports of such happenings are often encountered in the Soviet press. Punishments seem to vary, depending upon the political situation, from none to the death penalty.

According to Soviet legislation, the purpose of the budget to is concentrate part of the national income and to direct it to "the planned development of industry, agriculture, transport, trade, and other branches of the national economy, to the raising of the material well-being and cultural level of working people, to the defense of the country, to the support of the agencies of state power and state administration."[24] In contrast, according to a recent Chinese publication,

> "The Soviet revisionist renegade clique is a bunch of arch-thieves who have stolen the state itself, and their gigantic bureaucratic machinery is the command headquarters for all criminals. . . . The Soviet bureaucrat-monopoly bourgeois lead a parasitic life of extravagance and

dissipation. They have no scruples about squandering the fruits of labour of the Soviet people. . . . The revisionists are furiously stepping up their arms expansion and war preparations in order to satisfy their needs in foreign aggression and aggrandizement and win world-wide hegemony." [25]

Whether one agrees with the Chinese or Soviet evaluations of the purposes for which the state collects and allocates its financial resources, it is clear that the Soviet financial system involves the sophisticated mobilization of legal instrumentalities for allowing those in charge of the country to carry out their plans.

NOTES

1. An extremely thorough account, though now out of date in some respects, may be found in D. Gallik, C. Jesina, and S. Rapawy, *The Soviet Financial System* (Washington, D.C., 1968); a standard Soviet text is V. V. Bescherevnykh and S. D. Tsypkin (eds.), *Sovetskoe finansovoe pravo* (Soviet Finance Law), (Moscow, 1974).

2. In the spring of 1978, the Soviet Union adopted new foreign tax legislation, *Ved. V.S. SSSR*, 1978, No. 20, item 313. This legislation is discussed in E. Maguire and D. D. Stein, "USSR: New Income Tax on Foreign Legal Entities and Individuals," *Tax Management International Journal*, September 1978, 3-10.

3. *Voprosy gosudarsvennogo khoziaistva i biudzhetnogo prava* (Questions of the State Economy and Budgetary Law), Vyp. I (St. Petersburg, 1907).

4. The history of Soviet financial law is discussed in R. W. Davies, *The Development of the Soviet Budgetary System* (Cambridge, 1958); V. V. Bescherevnykh, *Razvitie sovetskogo biudzhetnogo prava* (The Development of Soviet Budgetary Law), (Moscow, 1960); and F. Holzman, *Soviet Taxation* (Cambridge, Mass., 1955).

5. "O poriadke otchisleniia v biudzhet svobodnogo ostatka gosudarstvennykh predpriiatii i khoziaistvennykh organizatsii" (On the Procedure for Transfer to the Budget of the Free Remainder of the Profit of State Enterprises and Economic Organizations), Instruction of the Ministry of Finance of the USSR of June 30, 1972, *BNA*, 1973, No. 1, 12.

6. "Polozhenie o naloge s oborota" (Statute on the Turnover Tax), Decree of the Council of Ministers of the USSR, June 30, 1975, *Sobr. Post. SSSR*, 1975, No. 17, item 108.

7. "Instruktsiia o poriadke vzimaniia v biudzhet platy za proizvodstvennye osnovnye fondy . . ." (Instruction on the Procedure for Collection for the Budget of Payment for Production Assets), *Ekonomicheskaia gazeta*, 1967, No. 11, 11-13.

8. "O nalogovoi reforme" (On the Tax Reform), Decree of the Central Executive Committee and the Council of People's Commissars of the USSR, September 2, 1930, *Sobr. Zak. SSSR*, 1930, No. 46, item 476. "Polozhenie o naloge s oborota predpriiatii obobshchestvlennogo sektora" (Statute on the Turnover Tax for Enterprises of the Socialized Sector), *Sobr. Zak. SSSR*, 1930, No. 46, item 477.

9. For details of the operation of the turnover tax, see Bescherevnykh, *op. cit.*, and Holzman, *op. cit.*, and S. D. Tsypkin, *Dokhody gosudarstvennogo biudzheta SSSR; Pravovye voprosy* (Sources of Income of the State Budget of the USSR; Legal Questions), (Moscow, 1973).

10. "O podokhodnom naloge s kolkhozov" (On the Income Tax on Collective Farms), Edict of the Presidium of the Supreme Soviet of the USSR of April 10, 1965, *Ved. V.S. SSSR*, 1965, No. 15, item 206; "Ob izmenenii nekotorykh statei Ukaza Prezidiuma Verkhovnogo Soveta SSSR 'O podokhodnom naloge s kolkhozov' " (On Amending Certain Articles of the Edict of the Presidium of the Supreme Soviet of the USSR "On the Income Tax on Collective Farms"), Edict of the Presidium of the Supreme Soviet of the USSR of February 1, 1970, *Ved. V.S. SSSR*, 1970, No. 5, item 41. Other non-governmental organizations are taxed in accordance with an Edict of March 1, 1979, *Ved. V.S. SSSR*, 1979, No. 10, item 156, subject to the exemptions in *Sobr. Post. SSSR*, 1979, No. 7, item 40.

11. There have been frequent changes and amendments in the legislation on individual taxes. *Ved. V.S. SSSR*: 1953, No. 7; 1957, No. 28, item 656; 1960, No. 18, item 135; 1962, No. 39, item 401; 1967, No. 36, item 495; 1967, No. 39, item 521; 1970, No. 3, item 24; 1972, No. 52, item 518; 1971, No. 40, item 391; 1943, No. 17, 1947, No. 20; *Sobr. Post. SSSR*, 1972, No. 1, item 1.

12. M. I. Piskotin, *Nalogi s sel'skogo naseleniia; Pravovye voprosy* (Taxes on the Rural Population; Legal Questions), (Moscow, 1957).

13. Tax on royalties from abroad. *Ved. V.S. SSSR*, 1975, No. 21, item 338, No. 29, item 438.

14. D. A. Loeber, "The Second Currency in the Soviet Union: On the Use of Checks in 'Valuta-Rubles' by Soviet Citizens," unpublished paper.

15. "O gosudarstvennykh zaimakh, razmeshchaemykh po podpiske sredi trudiashchikhsia Sovetskogo Soiuza," Decree of the Central Committee of the CPSU and the Council of Ministers of the USSR of April 19, 1957, *Direktivy KPSS i Sovetskogo pravitel'stva po khoziaistvennym voprosam* (Directives of the CPSU and the Soviet Government on Economic Questions), (Moscow, 1958), vol. 4, p. 697.

16. For general discussions of the Soviet budget, see M. I. Piskotin, *Sovetskoe biudzhetnoe pravo; Osnovnye problemy* (Soviet Budgetary Law; Basic Problems), (Moscow, 1971) and Gallik, *op. cit.* The Soviet inflation rate is stated to be under 2% in *CIA Handbook of Economic Statistics* (Washington, D.C., 1978), p. 34.

17. For detailed analyses of the budgetary process at various levels of government, see B. B. Bescherevnykh, *Kompetentsiia Soiuza SSR v oblasti biudzheta* (The Competence of the Union of Soviet Socialist Republic in the Area of the Budget), (Moscow, 1976); N. A. Shirkevich, *Rol' biudzheta v razvitii ekonomiki i kul'tury soiuznykh respublik* (The Role of the Budget and the Development of the Economy and Culture of the Union Republics), (Moscow, 1972); Ia. N. Stepanov, E. A. Chernysheva, S. A. Vishniakov, *Sostavlenie i ispolnenie biudzheta raiona* (The Preparation and Execution of the Budget of a District), (Moscow, 1972); *Biudzhet poselkovogo Soveta* (The Budget of the Rural Soviet), (Moscow, 1970); N. I. Khimicheva, *Biudzhetnye prava oblastnykh (kraevykh) Sovetov deputatov trudiashchikhsia* (Budgetary Rights of Regional (and Provincial) Soviets of Working People's Deputies), (Moscow, 1968); M. I. Piskotin, *Biudzhetnye prava mestnykh sovetov deputatov trudiashchikhsia* (Budgetary Rights of Local Soviets of Working People's Deputies), (Moscow, 1961).

18. G. K. Shekhovtsov, *Svodnoe biudzhetnoe planirovanie* (Comprehensive Budget Planning), (Moscow, 1976), pp. 34-35.

19. Bescherevnykh, *op. cit.*, p. 147.

20. *E.g.,* "O povyshenii norm raskhodov na pitanie v bol'nitsakh i domakh rebenka, a takzhe norm raskhodov po priobretenie medikamentov v serdechno-sosudistykh i torakal'nykh otdeleniiakh bol'nits" (On Raising the Norms of Expenditures for Food in Hospitals and Children's Homes and also the Norms of Expenditures for Obtaining Drugs in Heart-Circulatory and Thoracic Departments of Hospitals), Decree of the Council of Ministers of the USSR of Nov. 10, 1971, *Sobr. Post. SSSR*, 1971, No. 19, item 142. "O rasshirenii prav rukovoditelei uchrezhdenii zdravookhraneniia, sostoiashchikh na gosudarstvennom biudzhete" (On Expanding the Rights of Heads of Health Institutions Supported by the State Budget), Decree of the Council of Ministers of the USSR, Dec. 3, 1976, No. 984. *Sobr. Post. SSSR*, 1977, No. 1, item 4.

21. Shekhovtsov, *op. cit.*

22. "V Kollegii Ministerstva finansov SSSR" (At the Board of the Ministry of Finances of the USSR), *Finansy SSSR*, 1972, No. 11, 94.

23. *Biudzhetnyi uchet. Sbornik normativnykh dokumentov* (Budgetary Accounting. A Collection of Normative Documents), (Moscow, 1975).

24. "O biudzhetnykh pravakh Soiuza SSR i soiuznykh respublik" (On the Budgetary Rights of the USSR and the Union Republics), *Ved. V.S. SSSR*, 1959, No. 44, item 22.

25. Wei Chi, *The Soviet Union Under the New Tsars* (Peking, 1978).

ON THE STATUS OF THE CPSU AND HIGHER STATE AGENCIES IN SOVIET FINANCIAL LAW

Dietrich André Loeber

Characteristic features in the taxation of (a) state enterprises operating on the basis of economic accountability (*khozraschet*) and (b) individuals have been discussed by Peter Maggs elsewhere in this volume. The present paper attempts to identify some additonal features which distinguish Soviet financial law from the financial systems of other countries. It deals with two problem areas not covered in the paper cited:

1) on the revenue side—taxation of social organizations; and

2) on the expenditure side—financing of budgetary institutions, *i.e.*, agencies not operating on *khozraschet*, but financed out of the state budget.

1. Taxation of the CPSU and Other Social Organizations

Social organizations (*obshchestvennye organizatsii*) are expressly distinguished from state organizations in Soviet law. This distinction is drawn in the Constitution[1] and in other statutes. It is also relevant in tax law.

The most outstanding social organization is the Communist Party of the Soviet Union (CPSU). It is considered to be "the guiding and directing force of Soviet society and the nucleus of its political system, of all state and social organizations."[2] Much has been written about the CPSU,[3] but less on its status in state law,[4] and little on its status in civil law[5] and international law.[6] I am not aware of any work on the status of the CPSU in tax law.

Other social organizations include:

1. the All-Union Leninist Communist Youth League (Komsomol);[7]
2. the trade unions;
3. unions of creative workers (*tvorcheskie soiuzy*) and their "Funds", such as the Writer's Union and the Literary Fund;
4. cooperatives, including consumer cooperatives and collective farms (*kolkhozy*);
5. the Novosti Press Agency (*APN*);[8]
6. the Copyright Agency of the USSR (*VAAP*);[9]
7. the Chamber of Trade and Industry of the USSR;[10]

8. colleges of advocates; [11]
9. voluntary associations, *e.g.*, in the field of culture, science, and sports.

Revenues of Social Organizations

Social organizations may have substantial property and income. This applies, *e.g.*, to the CPSU and the trade unions. The Party Rules provided: "The funds of the party and its organizations shall be composed of membership dues, revenues from party enterprises, and other receipts." [12] According to a study by Robert McNeal, the Party collects 250-840 million rubles annually in membership dues from its 15 million members. [13]

Although social organizations and their associations are juridical persons, [14] they do not, as a rule, engage in economic activities. This function is carried out by enterprises (*predpriiatiia*) of social organizations. This is also true of the CPSU which runs publishing houses. Two central Party publishing houses are "Pravda" and "Izdatel'stvo politicheskoi literatury" (*Politizdat*, Publishing house for political literature). [15] In the republics and at lower levels operate another 78 party publishing houses. They publish a total of 274 newspapers and 226 journals. Their business reaches considerable proportions. [16] One-third of Party revenues is from publishing. This share has been estimated by McNeal to amount to a sum between 120 and 420 million rubles a year. [17] The higher figure is equal to the profit from state publishing houses which enters the state budget annually (400 million rubles). [18]

Enterprises of the CPSU and other social organizations are part of the planning system. They are included in the classification scheme of *Gosplan* used for drafting the state economic plans. [19] Enterprises of social organizations are subject to taxation. Among the various types of taxes, the following will be considered here: income tax, tax on assets and profits, and turnover tax. [20]

Income Tax

Enterprises of social organizations are liable to pay income tax (*podokhodnyi nalog*). The obligation is based on an All-Union Statute of 1941. [21] Details are regulated in an Instruction of the Ministry of Finance of the USSR of 1961, [22] which presumably continues to be in effect. [23] The tax liability arises: (a) if the enterprise operates on the basis of economic accountability; (b) if it is subject to full bookkeeping reporting (*otchetnost'*); and (c) if it enjoys the right to distribute profits. [24] In such a case, the enterprise pays 35% of its balance-sheet profits in income tax. A privileged rate of 25% is set for enterprises of trade unions. [25]

The Ministry of Finance of the USSR has exempted, among others, enterprises of:

Party and Komsomol organizations (publishing houses, sanatoria, rest homes, etc.);

trade unions on profits received from sanatoria, rest homes, and other health and recreation establishments, as well as tourist resorts and other tourist-excursion establishments;

organizations of consumer cooperatives and of associations of the blind from income of newly-established enterprises during the first two years, provided they use 75 or more percent of local resources, *i.e.*, resources distributed outside the plan.

Exempted further are:

clubs, palaces of culture of social organizations on income from "club-type activities", such as dance classes against payment of a fee;

income of social organizations from the use of stadiums, swimming pools, and other sport facilities.

The tax exemption for Party publishing houses has its tradition. One earlier statute granting similar privileges dates from 1924. [27]

The proceeds of the income tax are assigned to the republican budgets. [28] The delimitation of revenues within the republic is determined by republican legislation. [29] The income tax plays an insignificant role among the overall revenues of the state budget of the USSR. It amounted to 0.6% (1,500 million rubles) in 1976.[30] Ninety percent of the income tax enters the budgets of local Soviets, [31] but its share in these budgets was only 1.4% (408 million rubles) in 1968. [32]

Tax on Assets and Profits

More than one-third of Soviet budget revenues derives from the profits of economic organizations. [33] The assessment takes various forms. The economic reforms of 1965 introduced three types: payment on assets, fixed payments, and payments of the free remainder of profits. Economic organizations operating under the old system are subject to withholdings on profits.

a) Payment on Assets

State enterprises are obliged to make payments on the basic (fixed) and working (current) assets assigned to them. The payments are determined as a percentage of the value of the assets. [34] For the majority of enterprises, they are set at 6%. [35] Details are regulated in an Instruction of the Ministry of Finance of the USSR. [36]

The obligation to make payments on assets applies to enterprises administering state property. Enterprises of social organizations use property of the parent institution, which is not state property but "socialist property." [37] Consequently, enterprises of social organizations are not subject to payment on assets.

b) Fixed Payments

Economic organizations which obtain a large profit as a result of "especially favorable natural and transportation conditions" are required to make "regular fixed (rent-like) payments" (*fiksirovannye* [*rentnye*] *platezhi*). [38] The law fails to identify the taxpayer. The Decree speaks of "enterprises", but the relevant regulation of the Ministry of Finances of the USSR uses the term "state enterprises."[39] The latter concept excludes enterprises of social organizations.

c) Free Remainder of Profit

The financial plan of an economic organization under the new system envisages payments on assets (to the treasury), payments into the incentive funds (adminstered by the enterprise in question), repayment of credits, financing of investments and other expenditures. Those economic organizations which have produced a "free remainder of profit" (*svobodnyi ostatok pribyli*) are obliged to remit a portion of it to the treasury (*biudzhet*). [40] The portion is set by the agency to which the enterprise is subordinated. It is fixed in the financial plan [41] and amounts to a "profit tax."

The profit tax is levied on "state enterprises and economic organizations." [42] The latter term includes social organizations. [43] The government of the USSR may grant exemptions. Some of them are listed in an Instruction of the Ministry of Finance of the USSR of 1972.[44] The exemptions are not identical with those given for the income tax. [45] Enterprises of Party organizations, trade unions, and cooperatives are not mentioned. Consequently, they have to remit a portion of their free profits to the budget.

The term "budget" is not defined in the regulations quoted. It can mean the "state budget" or the budget of the social organization in question. The latter alternative seems to be the more likely one, but no source can be cited to substantiate it. If this interpretation is correct, Party publishing houses, *e.g.*, would have to remit a portion of their free profit to the budget of the CPSU and not to the state budget of the Union. It would be in conformity with the general rule that the proceeds of the profit tax enter the budget of the agency to which the taxpayer is subordinated. [46]

d) Withholdings on Profits

Withholdings on profits (*otchisleniia ot pribyli*) are a form of profit tax levied on economic organizations which have not been transferred to the new economic system. The legal basis for this tax is a Statute of 1931 which identifies "state enterprises" as taxpayers. [47] The formulation excludes enterprises of social organizations. An Instruction of the Ministry of Finance of the USSR, however, also lists "economic organizations." [48] This description covers, as just mentioned, social organizations. [49] The extension makes sense, inasmuch as the amount of withholdings on profits is determined in the

110

financial plans of the enterprises. But the question is again whether the amount is earmarked for the state budget or whether it has to be paid into the budget of the social organization to which the enterprise belongs. The latter interpretation seems to be in line with general principles of Soviet financial law.

Turnover Tax

The turnover tax (*nalog s oborota*) provides a third of Soviet state revenues.[50] The tax obligation arises when a product passes from the producer to the consumer. The price of the product is used to compute the tax. In simplified terms, it can be said that the turnover tax amounts to the difference between the wholesale and retail price of a product. Thus, the turnover tax is ultimately borne by the customer.

The legal basis for the turnover tax is a Statute of 1975[51] and an Instruction of the Ministry of Finance of the USSR of the same year.[52] They supersede a Statute of 1930[53] which, however, still seems to be in effect.[54] Enterprises of social organizations are expressly mentioned among the subjects of the tax.[55] The obligation arises if the economic organization in question operates on the basis of economic accountability and if it has an independent balance and a checking account in the bank.[56]

The Statute provides for tax exemptions.[57] Additional exemptions may be granted by the Ministry of Finance of the USSR.[58] Enterprises of the CPSU or other social organizations are not listed among those exempted.[59] This means, *e.g.*, that Party publishing houses must pay the turnover tax. This is consistent with the treatment of "Voenizdat," the publishing house of the Ministry of Defense of the USSR. Voenizdat is not granted an exemption, although other organizations of the Ministry of Defense of the USSR enjoy the privilege.[60] Thus, the turnover tax is included in the sales price of books,[61] journals, and newspapers published by publishing houses of the CPSU and by Voenizdat.

Federal authorities decide at their discretion which portion of the sums collected as turnover tax are assigned for use by Union agencies and how much is left for the republics. This determination is made every year anew.[62] Practice shows that the Union claims the greater portion of the receipts from the turnover tax. In 1965 the share of the Union amounted to about 57%, leaving 43% to all 15 republics together.[63]

Some Observations

The tax status of enterprises reveals a considerable degree of differentiation. This is true on two levels. First, social and state organizations are treated differently. Secondly, within the body of social organizations some are more privileged than others. The differences are based on regulations issued by the Council of Ministers and by the Ministry of Finance of the USSR. It follows that administrative discretion is granted and used by governmental agencies in the making of tax law. A mechanism for judicial control is not available.

Another feature worthy of note is the sparsity of sources. Relevant regulations are not easily accessible to the outsider and those which have been published are not altogether explicit.

2. Financing of Budgetary Institutions

A certain portion of the budget is spent to finance "budgetary institutions", *i.e.*, agencies in the non-production sphere returning no income. [64] They are distinguished from "economic organizations" which operate in accordance with the plan, enjoy the rights of juridical persons, and are entrusted with the administration of specified funds of property (*obosoblennoe imushchestvo*). [65]

Financing of Social-Cultural Measures

Financing of budgetary institutions is a common phenomenon wherever governmental agencies exist. The Soviet case has some peculiar features, however. The reason is an economic one. The aim of "the fullest satisfaction of the growing material . . . needs of people" proclaimed in the Constitution [66] has not yet been achieved. The network of supplies and services available to the general population suffers from various deficiencies. This is stated, among others, in report on the results of the yearly economic plans. [67] To overcome existing difficulties, the general outlets available to the population are supplemented with special outlets. This practice goes back to the early years of the Soviet regime. Special facilities are organized at the place of work and are attached to a given enterprise, organization, or agency. Measures are taken to finance, *e.g.*:

(1) construction of cafeterias; cafeteria services; subsidies to improve meals and to reduce prices in the cafeterias;

(2) organization of service and repair shops (*predpriiatiia bytovogo obsluzhivaniia*) and other facilities for daily needs;

(3) construction of housing; [68]

(4) construction of kindergartens, clubs, rest homes, youth camps, sport facilities, and other objects for cultural and medical use; supply of equipment and means of transportation for the facilities; contributions towards the costs of passes (*putevki*) for the use of rest homes, etc.;

(5) financing of cultural and sport events organized by the labor collective in question. [69]

In addition, stores for consumer goods are set up within certain institutions. One example is the trade network within the Armed Forces, [70] an equivalent of the Army and Air Force Exchange Service (AAFES) in the

USA. Some agencies operate polyclinics, hospitals, and dispensaries under their jurisdiction.[71] The authorization to set up health institutions outside of the general system has been granted, *e.g.*, to the Academy of Sciences of the USSR.

The services offered as well as the recreation and entertainment facilities provided by the place of work represent, in many cases, important fringe benefits. They can significantly improve the living conditions of the staff.[72] It is this aspect of budget financing which will be the subject of the pages to follow.

Legal Regulations

The legal basis for financing special facilities differs for economic and budgetary organizations. Economic organizations administer a "Fund for social-cultural measures and housing construction."[73] It is financed from the profit of the organization. The sums allowed to be diverted into the Fund are fixed in the annual financial plan.[74] They reached a total of 1,894 million rubles for all industrial enterprises in 1976.[75]

Economic units enjoying the benefits of the "Fund" include economic organizations and their superior agencies which perform their functions "under conditions" *(na usloviiakh)* envisaged in the Statute on industrial associations.[76] Some ministries and departments of ministries conform to this definition. The social and cultural needs of the workers, as well as the "apparatus" of these agencies are satisfied from the Fund.[77]

Budgetary institutions, on the other hand, are assigned capital from the state budget to meet their social and cultural needs. The "budget classification" (art. 18) envisages expenditures for "improving social and personal services for workers in institutions in amounts set by the Council of Ministers of the USSR."[78] Regulations specifying the amounts have not been published. They can be presumed to serve as a basis for appropriations from the budget.[79] A guideline in this area has been formulated for USSR Ministries. They are under a duty to ensure "the improvement of housing, cultural, and everyday conditions for workers of . . . institutions of the system of the ministry, as well as the implementation of health measures."[80]

One narrow field is covered by a Decree of 1971. It deals with the provision of "special clothes and other industrial goods" for "state budgetary organizations." The Decree lists 70 "ministries and agencies of the USSR" entitled to receive such goods in accordance with the plan and in agreement with the Ministry of Trade of the USSR. The goods are envisaged for organizations subordinated to the said 70 ministries and agencies. The list includes not only state agencies, but also social organizations, such as the "Pravda" publishing house and the Novosti Press Agency.[81] Budgetary means are appropriated on the basis of the economic plan and in conformity with administrative directions of financial agencies addressed to the budgetary institution applying for the appropriation. [82] The plan and the directions vary with the status of the budgetary agency in question. The status is determined by the territorial level of subordination (all-union, republic, lower levels) and by the functional "system" to which the agency belongs, *e.g.*, economy, health, education, defense, administration, or Party work. It is not clear whether or not the appropriated means are paid into a "Fund." No "Fund for social-cultural measures and housing construction" exists for budgetary institutions. Perhaps its place is taken by the "Fund for the development of the agency (organization)" (*Fond razvitiia uchrezhdeniia [organizatsii]*). Soviet sources rarely mention the latter Fund [83] and fail to disclose the measures which may be financed out of the Fund. Whatever the instruments used are, the means appropriated can be spent only for the purpose defined in the appropriation. The local trade union committee is likely to have a say in the use of the assets.

Administrative Discretion

The procedure for drafting the estimates of individual budgetary institutions is established by the directing agency. The draft budget is called an estimate (*smeta*) and the procedure is termed "financing on the basis of estimates" (*finansirovanie v smetnom poriadke*). [84] Some budgetary institutions are entitled to generate and to use "special means", *i.e.*, non-budgetary means. [85]

The estimate is defended by the lower agency before the next higher one. After adjustments are made at each stage of the administrative hierarchy, aggregate estimates are drawn up comprising the corrected data of lower units. [86] In this process of consolidation, government agencies use their administrative discretion within the powers granted to them. A decisive role in determining the appropriations for social-cultural measures of higher agencies is played by the Ministry of Finance of the USSR. [87] The degree to which a budgetary institution is able to articulate and to defend its needs for social-cultural facilities will depend, to some degree, on its prestige and political weight.

Some observations

Summarizing, it appears that discretion is a characteristic feature of Soviet budgetary law. The quality of life of a number of members of Soviet society depends on the way government authorities exercise their administrative discretion in financing social-cultural facilities of budgetary institutions. This exercise of power is supervised by authorities on higher levels, but not in judicial proceedings.

Another feature is discreetness, *i.e.*, the effort to avoid publicity. Financing of social-cultural measures for budgetary institutions is treated as an internal matter of the government. It is not a matter of general knowledge. As a result, budgetary allocations are practiced without causing widespread feelings of unfairness among the population. In this respect, the system resembles the turnover tax and the taxes on enterprises. The latter are, as Peter Maggs correctly observed, not "really visible to the average citizen."

The fringe benefits available to the staff of higher agencies are of interest not only to the tax lawyer. They clearly have also economic, political, and social implications. The system of social-cultural measures reveals a pattern of societal differentiation. It is based not on classes but on categories created by administrative decisions in accordance with ministerial instructions.

NOTES

1. Constitution of 1977, Arts. 4, 6, 7, 9, 10, 48, 49, 51, 58, 100, 125, 162, 164. *Cf.* Program of the CPSU of 1961, Part 2, Chapter III 2.

2. Constitution of 1977, Art. 6.

3. For reference see, *e.g.*, Ts. Iampol'skaia, *Obshchestvennye organizatsii v SSSR* (Social Organizations in the USSR), (Moscow, 1972), pp. 60-61, 112-113 (English ed.: Moscow, 1975).

4. V. D. Sorokin, *Administrativno-protsessual'nye otnosheniia* (Administrative-procedural Relations), (Leningrad, 1968), pp. 33-35; G. I. Petrov, *Sovetskie administrativno-pravovye otnosheniia* (Soviet Relations under Administrative Law), (Leningrad, 1972), pp. 54-55; B. Meissner, "Die Rechtsstellung der KPdSU," *Jahrbuch für Ostrecht,* 2(1961) No. 2, 7-29; L. Revesz, "Legal Aspects of the Connection Between the Communist Party and the State in the Soviet Union and the People's Democracies," *The Review,* 3 (1961), No. 1, 34-67; K. Westen, *Die KPdSU und der Sowjetstaat* (Köln, 1968), 350 pp.

5. S. Braga, "Die Rechtsstellung der KPdSU ...", *Osteuropa-Recht,* 8 (1962), 13-15.

6. D. Frenzke, "Die KP-Chefs in den zwischenstaatlichen Verträgen ...," *Osteuropa-Recht,* 21 (1975), 178-203; B. Meissner, "Die Partei im sowjetischen Staats- und Völkerrecht," in *Recht im Dienst des Friedens, Festschrift für Eberhard Menzel* (Berlin, 1975), pp. 167-176; D. Schröder, "Supremacy of the CPSU Recognized in International Law?," *American Journal of International Law* 70 (1976), 322-327.

7. Constitution of 1977, Art. 7.

8. Established in 1961 (*Izvestiia*, March 23, 1961). The Charter of APN has not been published, but is available on file in: Yessenin-Volpin v. Novosti Press Agency. U.S. District Court, S.D., New York, January 23, 1978 (No. 77 Civ. 639), 443 *Fed. Suppl.* (1978), 849-857, also in *International Legal Materials,* 17 (1978), 720-725. APN runs a publishing house. On APN see, among others, P. I. Sedugin, "O prave sobstvennosti obshchestvennykh organizatsii" (On the Law of Property of Social Organizations), in *VNIISZ. Uchenye zapiski.* Vyp. 4 (1965), 57-58; P. Roth, *Osteuropa,* 29 (1979), 203-219.

9. Statute of 1973, Art. 1. English translation in *Soviet Statutes and Decisions,* 14 (1977-1978), 150-156.

10. Statute of 1967, Art. 1. Text in *Sbornik normativnykh materialov po voprosam vneshnei torgovli SSSR* (Collection of Normative Materials on Questions of Foreign Trade of the USSR), Vol. 1 (Moscow, 1970), pp. 539-548.

11. Constitution of 1977, Art. 161; Statute on the Institution of Advocates in the RSFSR of 1962, Art. 1. English translation (excerpts) in J. Hazard, W. Butler, P. Maggs, *The Soviet Legal System,* 3rd ed. (Dobbs Ferry, NY, 1977), pp. 77-78.

12. Rules of the CPSU of 1961. Art. 70, see also Art. 34. English translation in W. Butler, *The Soviet Legal System* (Dobbs Ferry, NY, 1978), pp. 361-377.

13. R. McNeal, "Paying for the Party," *Survey,* 22 (1976), No. 2, 58, 62-63.

14. Fundamentals of Civil Legislation of 1961, Art. 11. English translation in Butler, *supra* note 12, pp. 393-429.

15. V. A. Markus, *Organizatsiia i ekonomika izdatel'skogo dela* (Organization and

Economics of Publishing), 3rd ed. (Moscow, 1976), p. 40. "Pravda" publishing house publishes the newspaper *Pravda* (print run: more than nine million copies), five other newspapers and 28 journals: *Kul'tura, nauka, iskusstvo SSSR* (Culture, Science, Art of the USSR), (Moscow, 1965), p. 255; *Pechat' SSSR v 1971 godu* (The Press of the USSR in 1971), (Moscow, 1972), p. XXIV. On the status of the "Pravda" publishing house under administrative law, see Petrov, *supra* note 4, p. 35. On "Politizdat," see *O partiinoi i Sovetskoi pechati. Sbornik dokumentov* (On the Party and Soviet Press. Collection of documents), (Moscow, 1972), pp. 404, 602, 604-605. The Central Committee of the CPSU runs another publishing house: "Plakat."

16.   *Pechat's SSSR v 1970 godu* (The Press of the USSR in 1970), (Moscow, 1971), pp. XX, XXI; L. Revesz, *Kommentar zum Statut der KPdSU* (Bern, 1973), p. 859. The Publishing House for Newspapers and Journals of the Latvian Communist Party, *e.g.*, publishes 190 million copies of newspapers and journals annually. *Latvijas PSR Maza enciklopedija* (Small Encyclopedia of the Latvian SSR), Vol. 2 (Riga, 1968), p. 226.

17.   McNeal, *supra* note 13, 58, 62-63. These data can be compared with the profit from the publishing house "Sovetskii kompozitor" (Soviet Composer) which constitutes 20% of the revenues of the Union of Composers of the USSR: Iu.Ia. L'vovich, A. I. Tepsin, in *Tvorcheskie soiuzy v SSSR* (Creative Unions in the USSR), (Moscow, 1970), p. 138. *Cf.* Revesz, *supra* note 16, p. 859; and G. Walker, *Soviet Book Publishing Policy* (Cambridge, 1978), p. 25.

18.   The figure is quoted in: *Voprosy ideologicheskoi raboty KPSS. Sbornik* (Questions of Ideological Work of the CPSU. Collection.), (Moscow, 1972), p. 553.

19.   *Gosplan SSSR. Metodicheskie ukazaniia k razrabotke gosudarstvennykh planov razvitiia narodnogo khoziaistva SSSR* (Methodological Directives for the Drafting of State Plans of the Development of the National Economy of the USSR), (Moscow, 1974), pp. 701, 773. But the competence of the USSR State Committee on Matters of Publishing Houses does not extend to drafting plans for Party publishing houses and to coordinating the use of printing capacities of Party organizations. Statute of the USSR State Committee of 1973, art. 6, English translation in *Soviet Statutes and Decisions*, 14 (1977-1978), 132-146; Statute of the corresponding State Committee of the Estonian SSR of 1974, art. 5 No. 2, *Ved. V.S. Estonskoi SSR*, 1974, No. 24, item 214.

20.   Taxes on collective farms are discussed by P. Maggs in his paper.

21.   *Sobr. Post. SSSR*, 1941, No. 12, item 217. Art. 10 and 16 para. 2 were repealed by Decree of August 11, 1977, *Sobr. Post. SSSR*, 1977, No. 24, item 152, List item 69. *Note.* After the manuscript has been submitted for publication, the Statute of 1941 was replaced by an Edict of 1979, *Ved. V.S. SSSR*, 1979, No. 10, item 156, and a Decree of 1979, *Sobr. Post. SSSR*, 1979, No. 7, item 40. The two new acts do not introduce changes relevant in the present context.

22.   Instruction of April 21, 1961, No. 164. Text in *Sbornik postanovlenii, prikazov i instruktsii po finansovo-khoziaistvennym voprosam*, 1961, No. 7, pp. 1-5.

23.   The Instruction is quoted as a legal source in M. R. Azarkh, *Spravochnik po gosudarstvennym dokhodam* (Reference Book on State Revenues), 3rd ed. (Moscow, 1972), p. 77. The Instruction is summarized (without a reference to it) by A. S. Kupriianov, *Podokhodnyi nalog s pribyli* (Income Tax from Profits), (Moscow, 1973), pp. 15-21, and S. D. Tsypkin, in *Sovetskoe finansovoe pravo* (Soviet Financial Law), 2nd ed. (Moscow, 1974), pp. 252-254.

24.   Instruction, *supra* note 22, art. 2.

25.   Decree of November 4, 1974, *Sobr. Post. SSSR*, 1974, No. 24, item 144. It repeals an unpublished Decree of 1951 which apparently had set the rate of 25% used in the Instruction of 1961, *supra* note 22, art. 3. Before 1951, a system of differentiated tax rates between 30 and 70% of the profit was in effect. It was established in the Statute of 1941, *supra* note 21, art. 3.

26. Instruction of 1961, *supra* note 22, art. 22. The Instruction does not list enterprises of the Literary, Music, Architects' or Arts' Funds, although—according to a Soviet secondary source—they are exempted from "all types of taxes." L'vovich, in *Tvorcheskie soiuzy, supra* note 17, p. 126; L'vovich/Tsepin, *ibid.*, p. 134.

27. Decree of June 6, 1924, art. 1, reprinted in *Izdatel'skoe delo v SSSR 1923-1931* (Publishing in the USSR 1923-1931), (Moscow, 1978), pp. 31-32; *cf.* Decree approving Statute of 1941, *supra* note 21, art. 3 with list of repealed decrees.

28. Law on Budget Rights of 1959, art. 35. English translation in Butler, *supra* note 12, pp. 537-580. This provision was in conflict with the Statute of 1941, *supra* note 21, art. 16 before this article was repealed in 1977. Art. 16 provided, among others, that income tax paid by enterprises subordinated to federal agencies enters the union budget.

29. Law on Budget Rights of 1959, *supra* note 28, art. 38; M. I. Piskotin, *Sovetskoe biudzhetnoe pravo* (Soviet Budgetary Law), (Moscow, 1971), pp. 173, 179-180.

30. *TsSU SSSR. Narodnoe khoziaistvo SSSR za 60 let. Iubileinyi statisticheskii ezhegodnik* (National Economy of the USSR for 60 years. Jubilee Statistical Yearbook), (Moscow, 1977), pp. 652-653. The figures include income tax from the collective farms. The corresponding figure for 1965, but without income tax from collective farms, was 0.4% (388 million rubles): *Ministerstvo Finansov SSSR. Gosudarstvennyi biudzhet. Statisticheskii sbornik* (Ministry of Finance of the USSR. State Budget. Statistical Collection), (Moscow, 1966), pp. 10-11, 69-72; D. Gallik, C. Jesina and S. Rapawy, *The Soviet Financial System* (Washington DC, 1968), (US Dept. of Commerce. Foreign Demographic Analysis Division. International Population Statistics Reports, Series P-90, No. 23), Table 6-2 on pp. 87-88.

31. Tsypkin, *supra* note 23, p. 254.

32. *Mestnye biudzhety SSSR. Statisticheskii sbornik* (Local Budgets of the USSR. Statistical Collection), (Moscow, 1970), pp. 10, 12. The revenue from income tax reached 700 million rubles a year during 1971-1973, according to V. A. Evdokimov, *Kontrol' za ispolneniem gosudarstvennogo biudzheta SSSR* (Control over the Execution of the State Budget), (Moscow, 1974), p. 89. The figures quoted do not include income tax from collective farms.

33. In 1969: 34%. Figure from *Politicheskaia ekonomiia. Nagliadnoe posobie* (Political Economy. Visual Aid), No. 2 (Moscow, 1971), p. 98; *cf.* Gallik, *supra*, note 30, p. 103.

34. Decree No. 729 of October 3, 1965, art. 21. English translation (excerpts) in J. Hazard, L. Shapiro, P. Maggs, *Soviet Legal System*, 2nd ed. (Dobbs Ferry, NY, 1969), pp. 220-226, 246-253, 265-266. The Decree was amended in 1967 and 1971.

35. Tsypkin, *supra* note 23, p. 207; V. I. Kofman, in *Khoziaistvennoe pravo* (Economic Law), (Moscow, 1977), p. 149.

36. Instruction of March 12, 1973. Text in *BNA*, 1973, No. 10, 21-31. It replaces an Instruction of March 3, 1967.

37. Constitution, Art. 10. The right of possession, use, and disposition enjoyed by enterprises of social organizations may be called "operative administration" by analogy to the rights enjoyed by state enterprises over state property. See Sedugin, *supra* note 4; L'vovich, in *Tvorcheskie soiuzy, supra* note 17, p. 132; L'vovich/Tsepin, *ibid.*, pp. 139-140; A. I. Masliaev, *Pravo sobstvennosti profsoiuzov SSSR* (Right of Ownership of Trade Unions of the USSR), (Moscow, 1975), pp. 178-192; G. A. Kudriavtseva, in *Dobrovol'nye obshchestva* (Voluntary Associations), (Moscow, 1977), p. 335; *Cf.* Fundamentals of Civil Legislation of 1961, *supra* note 14, arts. 19, 24; RSFSR Civil Code of 1964, arts. 102-103.

38. Decree of October 4, 1965, *supra* note 34, art. 22.

39. Letter of the Ministry of Finance of the USSR of March 6, 1967, No. 69 as

118

summarized by Azarkh, *supra* note 23, pp. 233-236; Tsypkin, *supra* note 23, pp. 212-217; Gallik, *supra* note 30, p. 124.

40. Decree of October 4, 1965, *supra* note 34, art. 24. Tsypkin, *supra* note 23, pp. 217-218.

41. Instruction of June 30, 1972, art. 2. Text in *BNA*, 1973, No. 1, 12-26. Amended by Letter of October 10, 1975, *ibid.*, 1976, No. 4, 17-23.

42. Instruction, *supra* note 41, art. 1.

43. V.S. Iakushev in *Khoziaistvennoe pravo, supra* note 35, p. 158.

44. Instruction, *supra* note 41, art. 3.

45. *Supra* note 26.

46. The profit of the publishing house "Sovetskii kompozitor" (*cf. supra* note 18) is remitted to the Musical Fund. L'vovich/Tsepin in *Tvorcheskie soiuzy, supra* note 17, p. 138.

47. Statute of September 3, 1931, *Sobr. Zak. SSSR*, 1931, No. 57, item 357, with subsequent amendments. Excerpts reprinted in *Sbornik normativnykh aktov po sovetskomu finansovomu pravu* (Collection of Normative Acts on Soviet Financial Law), (Moscow, 1967), pp. 134-135.

48. Instruction of the Ministry of Finance of the USSR of August 26, 1958, reprinted in *Sbornik osnovnykh normativnykh aktov po sovetskomu finansovomu pravu* (Collection of Main Normative Acts on Soviet Financial Law), (Moscow, 1961), pp. 74-78.

49. Note 43. Tsypkin, *supra* note 23, p. 224, uses another description which also includes enterprises of social organizations. He lists "organizations which operate on the basis of economic accountability, have an independent balance and a checking account in a bank." Cf. Gallik, *supra* note 30, p. 113.

50. In 1969: 32%. Figure from *Politicheskaia ekonomika, supra* note 33, p. 98.

51. Statute of June 30, 1975, *Sobr. Post. SSSR*, 1975, No. 17, item 108.

52. Instruction of December 31, 1975, No. 123, in *BNA*, 1976, No. 9, 12-32.

53. Statute of September 2, 1930, *Sobr. Zak. SSSR*, 1930, No. 46, item 477, Excerpts reprinted in *Sbornik normativnych aktov, supra* note 48, pp. 132-133.

54. *Cf.* list of repealed norms attached to the Statute of 1975, *supra* note 51.

55. Statute of 1975, *supra* note 51, art. 2; Instruction of 1976, *supra* note 52, art. 2.

56. *Ibid. Cf.* Azarkh, *supra* note 23, pp. 87-88; Tsypkin, *supra* note 23, pp. 227-234; Gallik, *supra* note 30, pp. 88-103.

57. Statute of 1975, *supra* note 51, art. 27.

58. *Ibid.*, art. 28.

59. *Cf.* Instruction of 1975, *supra* note 52, art. 56-63.

60. *Ibid.*, art. 62.

61. Books were exempted from the turnover tax 1930-1936. See Decrees of 1930 and 1936 reprinted in L. G. Fogelevich, *Deistvuiushchee zakonodatel'stvo o pechati* (Legislation on Publishing in Effect), 3rd ed. (Moscow, 1931), p. 225 and 6th ed. (Moscow, 1937), p. 287.

62. Law on Budget Rights of 1959, *supra* note 28, arts. 29, 35; see Piskotin, *supra* note 29, pp. 172-173, 183.

63. *Gosudarstvennyi biudzhet, supra* note 30, pp. 14, 69-72, 95; Gallik, *supra* note 30, p. 100. No corresponding figures are reported in the statistical yearbook for 1976, *supra* note 30.

64. *Cf.* N., Kufakova, in *Sovetskoe finansovoe pravo, supra* note 23, pp. 319-320; Gallik, *supra* note 30, pp. 39-40.

65. Iakushev, *supra* note 43, pp. 153, 158, 179.

66. Constitution of 1977, Art. 15.

67. The report on the plan for 1973, *e.g.*, deplores that the "plan for the satisfaction of daily needs [*plan bytovogo obsluzhivaniia*] of the population has not been fulfilled. In a number of enterprises deficiencies . . . are removed slowly." Almost identical language is used to describe the results of the plan for 1972. Text in *Zabota partii i pravitel'stva o blage naroda. Sbornik dokumentov* (Party and Government Care for the Welfare of the People. Collection of Documents), (Moscow, 1974), pp. 730, 833.

68. *Cf. Gosplan SSSR, supra* note 19, p. 259. The construction of housing for the staff of organizations is financed "centrally" (*tsentralizovannye kapital'nye vlozheniia*) in accordance with plans for ministries and agencies to which the organizations are subordinated. The same applies to construction for cultural and daily needs. Details are regulated in a Decree of 1967, *Sobr. Post. SSSR*, 1967, No. 17, item 119 (see, in particular, art. 2 and the list of USSR ministries in Appendix 2).

69. *Cf. Gosplan SSSR, supra* note 19, p. 549; Methodical Directives of 1971, art. 43, in *Spravochnik normativnykh materialov dlia izdatel'skikh rabotnikov* (Handbook of Normative Materials for the Staff of Publishing Houses), (Moscow, 1977), pp. 32-40; *Voprosy profsoiuznoi raboty* (Questions of Trade Union Work), (Moscow, 1976), pp. 240-241.

, 70. The network is administered by *GUTMO* (*Glavnoe upravlenie torgovli Ministerstva oborony SSSR*) (Main Administration of Trade of the Ministry of Defense of the USSR). See *Gosplan SSSR, supra* note 19, pp. 493-495; Gallik, *supra* note 30, p. 101.

71. Fundamental Principles of Public Health Legislation of 1969, arts. 9, 46. English translation in Butler, *supra* note 12, pp. 621-637. See also *Gosplan SSSR, supra* note 19, pp. 554, 557.

72. *Cf.* M. Matthews, "Top Incomes in the USSR," *Survey*, 21 (1975), No. 3, 1-27; earlier version in *NATO. Directorate of Economic Affairs. Economic Aspects of Life in the USSR* (Brussels, 1975), pp. 131-154.

73. The "Fund" was created as part of the economic reform of 1965 on the basis of the Decree of October 4, 1965, *supra* note 34, arts. 5, 13, 15, 37. The estimate on the use of the Fund is approved jointly by the administration of the organization and the local trade union committee. See Fundamentals of Labor Legislation of 1970, art. 96, English translation in Butler, *supra* note 12, pp. 583-610; Labor Code of the RSFSR of 1971, art. 230; Statute on the Local Trade Union Committee of 1971, art. 5, 21, English translation in Butler, *supra* note 12, pp. 611-618. Social-cultural measures have to be distinguished from bonuses paid to individual workers and employees. On the bonus system in budgetary institutions, see N. I. Guseinov, "Osnovaniia dlia primeneniia pooshchrenii sluzhashchikh apparata gosdarstvennogo upravleniia" (Basis for the Application of Measures of Stimulation for Employees of the Apparatus of Government Agencies), *Problemy gosudarstva i prava*, 1974, No. 8, 150; *cf.* also his article, *ibid.*, 1971, No. 4, 114-121 and the sources quoted therein.

74. Details on the social-cultural Fund are regulated in the Basic Statutes on the Fund for 1976-1980, text in *BNA*, 1977, No. 8, 28-48; *Biulleten' Goskomtruda* (Bulletin of the State Committee of the Council of Ministers of the USSR for Labor and Social Questions), 1977, No. 4, 13-31. The measures which may be financed out of the Fund are listed in art. 36. See also the Basic Statutes on the Fund for 1971-1975, text in *Biulleten' Goskomtruda*, 1972, No. 8, 3-16; Statute on the Industrial Association of 1973, arts. 30-32, *Sobr. Post. SSSR*, 1973, No. 7, item 32; Statute on the Production Association of 1973, art. 39, English translation in Butler, *supra* note 12, pp. 135-168; Statute on the Enterprise of 1965, art. 14, English translation in *ibid.*, pp. 169-189. On planning of the Fund, see *Gosplan SSSR, supra* note 19, pp. 445, 449.

75. *Narodnoe khoziaistvo, supra* note 30, p. 649. *Cf.* p. 636 on the percentage of profits diverted into this and other funds of stimulation.

76. Decision (*reshenie*) of March 22, 1973, *BNA*, 1973, No. 7, 3-4.

77. V. V. Laptev, *Pravovaia organizatsiia khoziaistvennykh sistem* (Legal Organization of Economic Systems), (Moscow, 1978), pp. 134, 136; V. V. Laptev, *Pravovoe polozhenie promyshlennykh i proizvodstvennykh ob"edinenii* (Legal Status of Industrial and Production Associations), (Moscow, 1978), p. 109.

78. Directions (*ukazaniia*) on budget classification, no date. Text in *Bukhgalterskii uchet v biudzhetnykh uchrezhdeniiakh. Sbornik normativnykh dokumentov* (Bookkeeping Records in Budgetary Agencies. Collection of Normative Documents), (Moscow, 1965), pp. 79-85. The formulation is repeated in Evdokimov, *supra* note 32, p. 175; Gallik, *supra* note 30, p. 80; *cf.* N. A. Kufakova, *Pravovoe regulirovanie finansirovaniia biudzetnykh uchrezhdenii v SSSR* (Legal Regulation of Financing Budgetary Institutions in the USSR), (Moscow, 1955), Dissertation abstract, 13 pp.; V. A. Evdokimov, *Finansirovanie ministerstv i vedomstv* (Financing of Ministries and Agencies), (Moscow, 1962), p. 66.

79. A general basis for budgetary appropriations is the Law on Budget Rights of 1959, *supra* note 62, art. 15.

80. General Statute on USSR Ministries of 1967, art. 71, English translation in Butler, *supra* note 12, pp. 81-92.

81. *Sobr. Post. SSSR,* 1971, No. 8, item 69.

82. Piskotin, *supra* note 29, pp. 220-224; V. V. Bescherevnykh in *Sovetskoe finansovoe pravo, supra* note 23, pp. 146-147, 150-151; *Soviet Finance: Principles, Operations* (Moscow, 1975), pp. 222-224.

83. The Fund is mentioned, *e.g.*, in an Instruction of the Ministry of Finances of the USSR of 1973 on bookkeeping records (arts. 188, 190); text in *Biudzhetnyi uchet. Sbornik normativnykh dokumentov* (Budgetary Recording. Collection of Normative Documents), (Moscow, 1975), pp. 206-207. See also Instruction of the same Ministry of 1975 on annual bookkeeping reports (art. 5, 6, 12); text in *BNA*, 1976, No. 6, 8-29.

84. Piskotin, *supra* note 29, pp. 228-245; Gallik, *supra* note 30, pp. 35, 39, 41.

85. RSFSR Decree of July 28, 1967, *Sobr. Post. RSFSR*, 1967, No. 18-19, item 102, with further amendments; Instruction of the Ministry of Finance of the RSFSR of September 4, 1967, No. 01/673. For literature, see D. A. Bekerskaia, *Pravovoe regulirovanie spetsial'nykh sredstv biudzhetnykh uchrezhdenii* (Legal Regulation of Special Means of Budgetary Institutions), (Odessa, 1974), Dissertation abstract, 27 pp.; *Finansovo-kreditnyi slovar'* (Financial and Credit Encyclopedia), Vol. 2 (Moscow, 1964), pp. 366-367; Gallik, *supra* note 30, pp. 151-155, 218.

86. The process is ably described by Piskotin, *supra* note 29, pp. 230-239. See also Bescherevnykh, *supra* note 82, pp. 149-150, and the other sources cited in *supra* note 82.

87. *Cf.* Statute of the Ministry of Finance of the USSR of 1971, art. 6, *Sobr. Post. SSSR*, 1971, No. 4, item 28.

121

ADMINISTRATION OF SOCIALIST PROPERTY IN THE USSR: NEW TRENDS AND INSTITUTIONS*

Stanislaw Pomorski

The Soviet leadership solemnly declared the country to be at the era of "the scientific and technical revolution," to have passed from an "extensive" mode to an "intensive" mode of growth.[1] Efficiency and quality have been identified as the central goals in the current period, and accordingly the Tenth Five-Year Plan was labeled "the plan of efficiency and quality."[2]

> "Efficiency and quality [said Brezhnev addressing the Central Committee in October 1976] these two words have now become the motto of our entire economic activity."[3]

The fundamental economic policies aimed at these targets have called for concentration and specialization of production, adoption of technological novelty, as well as better cooperation between operational entities. The "scientific and technical revolution," its substantive goals and corresponding policies have generated substantial structural changes in the economic organization;[4] the changes have occurred primarily at the basic operational level. The old structure, with unitary production enterprises in industry and kolkhozes/sovkhozes in agriculture as primary operational links, has been found inadequate. New types of larger, specialized economic organizations have emerged and are gaining ground at the expense of traditional ones. One may perceive them as institutional responses or structural adjustments to the needs of "the scientific and technical revolution."[5] Naturally enough most of these developments, after some period of testing, have been translated into the language of law: some of them already surfaced in recent legislation, others are still awaiting legislative endorsement. The new Soviet Constitution of October 1977 clearly, if elliptically, affixed its imprimatur to some of these restructurings.[6]

In the present paper, I propose to deal with such institutional responses as have had a direct impact upon administration of socialist property. My major objective is to show what structural and institutional changes have been introduced in response to the new economic goals and related policies, and to

* Shirley Goldstein, a student at Rutgers University School of Law, has been very helpful in my research under a grant from the School.

123

discuss their legal aspects. I shall therefore adopt a perspective of the Soviet policy-makers, that is the authors of the responses. It is not my objective to address substantive questions, for example: whether and to what extent the current performance of kolkhozes and sovkhozes is a disaster; whether the proposed reform is an adequate response to these failures; the severity of labor pathology in the Soviet Union, and whether workers' participation in industrial management is a likely cure for these problems.

I do not aspire to even attempt to answer these questions. I have no ready prescription for the cure of various failures of Soviet agriculture and industry. I do not know whether workers' participation or agro-industrial integration will save the Soviet economy or socialist economies in general. These problems are clearly beyond the scope of the discussion. It is sufficient for my purposes to show that the Soviet leadership recognizes the need for institutional changes as a response to the needs of the scientific and technical revolution. I am satisfied that Soviet policy-makers do admit that the conspicuous failures of kolkhozes and sovkhozes require an overall organizational, structural reform and that such a reform is underway. I will focus only on such aspects of the changes as have exerted an impact upon the administration of socialist property, in particular on their legal implications.

1. The Restructuring of State Industry

1. On April 3, 1973, the Soviet leadership, after a substantial period of experimentation, announced a new major restructuring of state industry.[7] Two detailed statutes, the General Statute on the All-Union and Republican Industrial Association of March 2, 1973,[8] and the Statute on the Production Association (or Combine) of March 27, 1974 [9] provide a general legal framework for the reform and reflect its basic ideas. A new type of institution which has gained a position of foremost importance under the reformed system is the so-called association (ob"edinenie). A production association situated at the primary, bottom level of the new industrial organization has been perceived by the reformers as a principal type of operational entity. It was supposed to supersede a unitary enterprise. The most recent sources available report that as of the end of 1976, there were about 3,200 production associations in the country and that they contributed something close to 40% of the total industrial production. [10]

Since the economic, organizational, and legal aspects of the Soviet industrial and production associations (in industry) have been extensively discussed in the recent Western literature, there is no need to return to these issues at any length here. [11] It may be only of some interest to note that the 1977 Constitution mentions associations on an equal footing with enterprises, endorsing thereby their status as basic operational links of industrial organization (Art. 16, sec. 2). Whereas recent economic literature points out that production associations represent a higher level of socialization of production than unitary enterprises, the latter aspect is a step in the progressive transformation of socialist property into Communist property. [12]

2. Another institutional offspring of the new economic orientation is a scientific-production association (*nauchno-proizvodstvennoe ob"edinenie*), the type of organization specifically devised to promote technological innovation through organizational integration ("organic unity") under one roof of research and development with production. A scientific-production association is considered the newest among several "forms" of such integration. [13] Indeed, its origin is relatively recent. First, associations of this type were set up in 1967-1968. With clear encouragement from above, they grew in number. In 1977, the total number of scientific-production associations in the country reported was 128, and during the next 2-3 years from 200-250 more are expected to be established in the industrial organization alone. [14] At the end of 1975, the organizational and legal status of the scientific-production associations was established by special legislation. [15] The statute applies primarily to scientific-production associations in industry and, after appropriate adjustments, to similar associations in agriculture, transportation, and construction, as well as to "other branches of the national economy." [16] It follows that the scientific-production association is an economic organization of universal character, not merely an industrial organization. Indeed, some reports on the activities of the scientific-production associations in agriculture have been published. [17] Under the statute, the scientific-production association is "a unitary [*edinyi*] scientific-production and economic complex including scientific research, construction, design-construction, and technological organizations, plants (factories)" and other structural entities, depending on the tasks assigned to the association. [18] The scientific-production association has three distinctive features: 1) It is headed by a scientific-research or design organization, not by a production unit (as is always the case with the production associations); 2) Its major task is to turn up technical innovations corresponding to the highest modern standards. Accordingly, the performance of the association is not evaluated on the ground of standard quantitative indicators. [19] 3) Finally, the scientific-production association is responsible for the implementation of the full cycle of innovation; from initial research in the problem to its final technical solution and adoption in production. [20]

The scientific-production association functions as a corporate entity; it is set up upon the principle of economic accountability, holds state property assets in "operative management and use," and is a juridical person. [21] The structural component entities of the association do not enjoy economic or legal independence, nor do they have juridical personality. [22]

The emergence and growth of scientific-production associations, the role they are assigned, and the variety of organizational and legal issues of their structure and functioning certainly deserve a more detailed separate treatment.

3. The Soviet leadership recently put substantial emphasis on the participation of workers and employees in the management of the economy, especially at the level of operational entities (enterprises, production associations). The principle of participation of "labor collectives" in the discussion and resolution of state and public affairs in general and in management and administration of the enterprises, associations, etc., in particular has been written into the new Constitution. [23] If taken at its face value, the industrial democracy in the Soviet Union—management of state-owned corporations by the workers—would be nothing short of a profound revolutionary change. It would mean the most fundamental transformation in the administration of socialist property one can imagine; indeed, it would mean a break with the Soviet concept of socialization of the means of production. [24] Needless to say, nothing of this kind has happened or is intended by the Soviet rulers. Meaningful participation of workers in the economic management is irreconcilable with the fundamentals of the Soviet system, that is, total control of public life by the Party/state apparatus and strongly centralized economic decision-making. How, then, should the recently stepped up theory of workers' participation be explained? Should it be dismissed as a propaganda trick, perhaps predominantly for foreign consumption?

There is no doubt that propaganda goals, not without an eye on foreign lands, have played a role. But mere propaganda purposes, so it seems, do not account for all essential aspects of the story. I propose also to consider the following hypothesis:

The Soviet system is currently experiencing severe problems with its labor force. Labor resources have basically been exhausted; many jobs stay vacant with no one willing to fill them. Perspectives are rather gloomy; the demographic situation of the country has been identified as serious. [25]

The demoralization of the active labor force is high; people are not interested in their work, the moods of apathy, indifference, and alienation from the production process prevail. The pathology of labor is pervasive; too many people change jobs far too often, absenteeism and drunkenness on the job are appalling, "labor discipline" is in shambles. [26] There are serious problems with women's labor; reconciliation of women's responsibilities as mothers and wives has proved their full-time employment impossible. The current needs of the country press for their retention as full-time employees, yet on the other hand, the demographic situation suggests strongly that this would be a very short-sighted solution.

The trade unions and other mass-organizations, perceived as extensions of the Party/state apparatus, have no appeal to the labor force. The appearance

126

of independent, spontaneously created labor unions is very telling in this regard. [27] Now, from the perspective of those running the system, the labor problems could not have occurred at a worse time. The transition to the "intensive" mode requires well trained, well disciplined, sober, and interested laborers. All those qualities are in extremely short supply. [28] The USSR is not alone with these problems; other socialist countries have experienced problems of comparable magnitude. In Poland, for example, the Party/state leadership turned in despair to the Catholic hierarchy for help: [29] tell the proletariat that good Christians should work honestly. The Soviet leadership has no one to turn to, no one is independent from the Party/state who could speak with moral authority. What is to be done, then? One obvious option is to activate the theme of workers' participation in order to involve the labor force more extensively in decision-making. It is possible that such a step will make workers more job-satisfied and will bring them closer to the managerial goals without serious jeopardy to total control by the state apparatus. Industrial democracy has promoted such hopes in the past in other lands. [30]

4. Finally, I would like to point out the processes of "concentration and specialization of agricultural production" and their consequences for the administration of socialist property. I decided to focus on this set of issues in a somewhat more detailed fashion in the second part of this paper having in mind the following factors:

1) the importance attributed to them by the Soviet leadership;

2) their far-reaching legal consequences for the system of socialist ownership; and

3) the close interrelations between the processes and socio-economic changes prophesied by the doctrine of "full Communism."

2. Concentration and Specialization of Agricultural Production

Conspicuous and chronic failures of Soviet agriculture at last convinced the leadership to pour substantial resources into its modernization. Brezhnev, in the speech already quoted in this paper, told the Central Committee,

> "at the present time, there is not a more pressing task than elevation of the agricultural sector of our economy to the most modern level." [31]

Capital investments in agriculture have recently increased very substantially. [32] The leadership has shown some concern about improvement of alarmingly poor living conditions of collective farmers. At the same time, it was decided that extraeconomic coercion, keeping kolkhozniks forcibly on their farms should be discontinued. [33] The present organizational structure was found grossly inadequate as a framework for modern agriculture. Hence, the decision to create larger production entities capable of running select lines of

127

production, lending themselves to mechanization, and capable of absorbing modern technology and employing trained personnel.

The policy, stated already at the XXIV Party Congress, was made one of the major themes at the next CPSU Congress. [34] The basic Party document on the subject labels it as "specialization and concentration of agricultural production on the basis of interfarm cooperation and agro-industrial integration." [35] The simplest organizational solution may seem to be quick amalgamation of kolkhozes and turning them into large state farms. This avenue, followed with some caution with respect to some weak kolkhozes, has been flatly rejected as a general method of reform.[36] Probably, the leadership wanted to avoid serious disruptions of agricultural production likely to be caused by a rapid reorganization. A country as deeply troubled by food shortages as the Soviet Union can hardly afford risky experimentation with agriculture. Another danger to be avoided was transformation of the reform into a game of appearances. Such was, for example, a substantial part of the experience with the parallel reform of the industrial structure. [37] Therefore, a more cautious course of action was chosen: a gradual building up of large agricultural or agro-industrial organizations and complexes on the basis of cooperation and integration of existing entities (kolkhozes, sovkhozes, industrial enterprises, etc.). [38] Since interfarm cooperation and agro-industrial integration involve state as well as kolkhoz organizations, one of the natural outcomes of the processes is the emergence of state-kolkhozes joint enterprises as well as of complexes (ob"edineniia) which include kolkhozes as well as state corporations. That is how a current economic policy of "concentration and specialization of agricultural production" results in "the drawing together" (sblizhenie) of state and collective farm ownership. The policy has materialized in a variety of new types of economic organizations, only some of which have received up to now legislative recognition. A review and a typology of these organizations will be presented a little later. Close interrelations between the processes of "specialization and concentration of production" and sblizhenie of the two principal forms of socialist ownership have been emphasized on many occasions. [39] Such seems to be the current pragmatic policy dimension of the "drawing together" of state and collective farm ownership. Its practical importance put it high on the agenda of the Soviet leadership and, to some extent, explains the writing of the doctrine into the new Constitution. Article 12 section 3 of the Charter [40] may be read as a very concise policy statement: the first part of the sentence seems to warn the apparatus against outright abolition of kolkhozes, the second part in highly abstract language summarizes the policy of "interfarm cooperation and agro-industrial integration." The very fact of the inclusion of the policy statement in the Constitution endorses once again previously articulated views of the leadership that while the policy is deemed of fundamental importance, its implementation is perceived as a long-range operation.

128

"The drawing together doctrine" has also another, ideological dimension with strong affinity to the eschatology of "full Communism." This aspect of the doctrine may be traced back at least to Stalin's *Economic Problems of Socialism in the USSR*. [41] It was one of the highlights of the 1961 Party Program. [42] The "drawing together" allegedly consists of gradual elevation of collective-farm/cooperative ownership to the level of "all-people's," that is state ownership [43] with ultimate transformation of the former into the latter. [44] A development of group ownership to ever higher stages of socialization, its gradual convergence and ultimate merger with state ownership, mark progressive changes in the economic infrastructure of socialist society in its evolution toward Communism. In this fashion, the narrow limits of group ownership are being overcome and all-people's ownership will come to dominate indivisibly first in the form of state ownership, which in turn will be transformed into Communist ownership. This is a necessary precondition for the eradication of commodity exchange, as well as for eradication of differences between town and countryside, between the agricultural and the industrial, fundamental distinctive features of the economy of full Communism. [45] The steadily growing homogeneity of socialist ownership corresponds well with, indeed, underlies the parallel changes in the social structure characteristic for developed socialism. [46] The "eschatological" dimension of the "drawing together" constitutional provision fits well together with some of the provisions of Chapter 3 of the Constitution ("Social Development and Culture"), notably with Articles 19 and 22, as a part of the "full Communism" package. The convergence of the two forms of socialist ownership doctrine is instrumental in demonstrating a further progress toward "the supreme goal." Its political utility obviously consists in legitimation of the political power of the CPSU.

A policy of "interfarm cooperation and agro-industrial integration" may have its practical justification, and, if effectively implemented, may be fruitful. It is impossible to judge economic effectiveness of this endeavor at this point. Self-congratulatory reports by local Party executives must not, of course, be taken at their face value. [47] Presenting the transformation of collective-farm/cooperative ownership into state ownership as a profound change in the economic infrastructure is, however, nothing short of a gross distortion. Given full control of the Party/state apparatus over collective farms and cooperatives, one can say that there is no substantive, *i.e.*, economic, difference between the two principal forms of socialist ownership. In terms of effective control, the Soviet state "owns" kolkhozes on an equal footing with state farms or state enterprises. Judging from this perspective, we can say that the Soviet system of socialist ownership already complies in full with the etatist model. By the same token, any reshifting of property between socialist sectors of the economy is, in practical terms, an in-house state operation. The proposed transformation will simply adjust the rules

129

pertaining to legal ownership to correspond fully with the economic reality. The claim that the transformation will bring about a higher degree of socialization of the means of production is of doubtful validity. As long as society has no effective disposition over the means of production, as long as the *de facto* disposition is in the hands of an established group holding state power, the system fails to meet Marxian criteria of socialization. [48] In this regard, the "drawing together" process changes nothing.

The claimed evolution in the direction of ever-higher stages of socialization of the means of production is strongly contradicted by the recent policies concerning personal property in general and subsidiary households in particular.

The 1977 Constitution, [49] consistently with the well-established Party line of the current leadership, [50] elevates the *rank* of the subsidiary household, broadens its social basis, dispels any doubt about its legitimacy and viability, and calls upon the Party/state apparatus to render affirmative aid to its further development. The policy, if consistently implemented, should bring about a further enlargement of an already substantial private sector of the Soviet economy, a sector based upon admittedly non-socialist ownership of the means of production. [51]

While the policy of "interfarm cooperation and agro-industrial integration" and a related process of "drawing together" have had no impact upon the model and social essence of socialist ownership in the USSR, they have brought about substantial *institutional* changes in the administration of socialist property. The policy has materialized in a variety of new types of economic organizations, only some of which have to date received legislative recognition.

Classification of these new organizations into clear-cut categories is not a simple task, since the whole structure is still in a formative period. [52] Up to now, only one major type of the several organizations under discussion has received comprehensive legislative treatment. [53] With this qualification in mind, I will outline a rough typology of the new organizations. [54]

I. Institutions of "Interfarm Cooperation."

Two basic types of organizations may be distinguished in this area: an interfarm enterprise (organization) and an agricultural production association. [55]

A. Interfarm Enterprises.

Interfarm enterprises are probably the most numerous among the new economic organizations of Soviet agriculture. As early as 1974, all of the collective farms and about half of the state farms participated in interfarm enterprises. [56] The origins of this type of organization can be traced back to the 1950s. [57] Up to the present time, they are the only ones which have been given a comprehensive legislative treatment. [58] One may distinguish the following characteristics of an interfarm enterprise:

1. It is set up by participating farms (kolkhozes, sovkhozes, and other organizations) which combine their efforts as shareholders in pursuit of one specific aspect of their activity. Shareholders are unaffected with regard to the remaining aspects of their affairs, retaining both their economic and their legal independence. [59] Thus, interfarm enterprises have been set up to run particular lines of agricultural production (*e.g.*, cattle or poultry breeding), or to process the agricultural production of shareholders or to service the participating farms (*e.g.*, interfarm construction enterprises). [60]

2. The interfarm enterprise is set up on the principal of *khozraschet*, holds property assets contributed by the participating farms in operative management, and has juridical personality. [61] If shareholders include collective farms only, property assets of the enterprise are co-owned by participating kolkhozes proportionately to the contributions made. [62] Soviet commentators hastened to point out that in this way, "interkolkhoz ownership" is created, representing a higher degree of socialization, however still within a general category of collective-farm/cooperative ownership. [63] In case of an interfarm enterprise set up by state farms and kolkhozes, the property of the enterprise is co-owned by the state and participating collective farms. [64] This has been acclaimed as a definite manifestation of *sblizhenie* of the two forms of socialist ownership. Some writers even claimed that mixed state-kolkhoz ownership should be legislatively recognized as a new, independent "form" of socialist ownership. [65] The draftsmen of the Constitution stopped short of such recognition. It should be noted that interfarm organizations have often been used as a façade for illegal entrepreneurial activities, highly profitable for the operators. [66]

B. Agricultural Production Associations (APA).
Their legal status and organization have not yet been legislatively settled. A long list of legal issues connected with this type of amalgamation awaits resolution. [67] An agricultural production association integrates basic economic activities of the participating farms. Therefore, the degree of integration is higher than in cases of interfarm enterprises, which involve cooperation on one aspect of their activities only, and not necessarily the basic one. A higher degree of integration requires a centralized management. The association may include farms which preserve their legal personality, farms which do not have legal personality, and may include both kinds of organizations. The latter two types of APA would have their own distinct legal personality. The association may consist of state farms solely, the collective farms only, or both types of organizations. In cases where an association includes only state farms with

distinct legal personalities, it is virtually impossible to distinguish it from a trust of sovkhozes. [68] Kolkhozes participating in APAs always preserve their legal personalities and remain owners of their assets. Nevertheless, it is claimed, a certain amount of *sblizhenie* is accomplished since:

1. In APAs where only collective farms are amalgamated, the production processes transcend the narrow limits of individual collective farms and reach a higher stage of socialization. Certain productive functions are centralized at the level of the associations, as a whole; participating kolkhozes contribute to the centralized funds, thereby combining their property assets.

2. Analogous processes occurring in APAs, which include collective farms and state organizations, contribute more directly to the "drawing together" of group and state ownership. An agricultural production association may include industrial operations as well, but its basic activity is always oriented toward agricultural production. [69]

II. Institutions of Agro-industrial Integration.

The two basic types of organizations that have developed in this area are: an agro-industrial enterprise and an agro-industrial association (AIA).

A. An Agro-industrial Enterprise (AIE).

The most common AIE in current practice is the *sovkhoz-zavod* (there are also *kolkhozy-zavody*). Characteristic for *sovkhozy-zavody* is a very high level of integration of the agricultural and the industrial line of production, as well as high profitability of both. *Sovkhozy-zavody* have uniform balance sheets, make payments to the budget, and create uniform funds of economic stimulation for both sectors of production. *Sovkhozy-zavody* have become particularly popular in grape-growing and wine production. [70]

B. An Agro-industrial Association (AIA).

Comprehensive legislation on agro-industrial associations is still pending. AIAs always include farms as well as industrial enterprises, and may also include other organizations (for example, research laboratories, transportation enterprises, etc.). The agricultural and the industrial sectors should be fairly balanced; it has been pointed out that for AIAs, both kinds of economic activity are considered basic. [71] Therefore, the difference between APAs, including some industrial enterprises, and AIAs is in the degree of the development of the industrial basis. Component parts of the AIA may or may not have juridical personalities; there exist some AIAs which include member organizations of both kinds. It is felt that the forthcoming legislation should not resolve the issue of legal independence of member organizations in any absolute way. The question should be resolved on a case-by-case basis by the organizations concerned on the basis of considerations of expediency. AIAs which include state organizations and kolkhozes are still few in number. In all such cases, collective farms preserve their legal personality. A much more popular method of kolkhoz-state agro-industrial integration are stable *contractual* links between collective farms and state AIAs. This development is considered preferable since *sblizhenie* should be implemented gradually, on the basis of growing specialization of kolkhozes. [72]

NOTES

1. L. I. Brezhnev, "Otchet Tsentral'nogo Komiteta KPSS i ocherednye zadachi Partii v oblasti vnutrennei i vneshnei politiki" (Report of the Central Committee of the CPSU and Current Tasks of the Party in the Area of Internal and Foreign Policy), in *Materialy XXV s"ezda KPSS* (Materials of the XXV Congress of the CPSU), (Moscow, 1976), pp. 44, 47. An "extensive" mode of economic growth means growth based upon increases in the labor force and the capital stock; an "intensive" mode means growth resulting from improved technology leading to higher productivity. D. Yergin, "Politics and Soviet-American Trade: The Three Questions," *Foreign Affairs*, April 1977, 521.

2. Brezhnev, note 1, p. 44.

3. L. I. Brezhnev, *Voprosy upravleniia ekonomikoi razvitogo sotsialisticheskogo obshchestva* (Problems of the Management of the Economy of the Developed Socialist Society), (Moscow, 1976), p. 581.

4. Brezhnev, note 1, p. 44, for a further discussion see: M. I. Piskotin (ed.), *Gosudarstvennoe upravlenie v SSSR v usloviakh nauchno-tekhnicheskoi revoliutsii* (State Management in the USSR under Conditions of the Scientific and Technical Revolution), (Moscow, 1978), particularly pp. 316-359; L. M. Gatovskii *et al.* (eds.), *Ekonomika razvitogo sotsialisticheskogo obshchestva* (Economy of the Developed Socialist Society), (Moscow, 1977), pp. 126-193.

5. L. M. Dashevskaia, "Pravovye formy agropromyshlennoi integratsii na sovremennom etape" (Legal Forms of Agro-industrial Integration at the Current Stage), *SGiP*, 1978, No. 4, 60; Gatovskii, note 4, p. 180.

6. Compare *Konstitutsiia (Osnovnoi Zakon) Soiuza Sovetskikh Sotsialisticheskikh Respublik*, October 7, 1977, *Ved. V.S. SSSR*, 1977, No. 41, item 617, Arts. 12, section 3, 16 section 2 (hereafter, the Constitution).

7. See the Resolution of the CC of the CPSU and the Council of Ministers of the USSR of March 2, 1973, "On Some Measures for the Further Improvement of Industrial Management", *Sobr. Post. SSSR*, 1973, No. 7, item 31.

8. *Sobr. Post. SSSR*, 1973, No. 7, item 32.

9. *Sobr. Post. SSSR*, 1974, No. 8, item 38.

10. *Narodnoe Khoziaistvo SSSR za 60 let* (National Economy of the USSR in 60 Years), (Moscow, 1977), p. 170. The source actually reports the total number of "production and scientific-production associations" as 3,312; given that the number of scientific-production associations in industry is estimated to be about 100, the substraction of the first figure from the second brings about 3,200 production associations.

11. C. Gorlin, "Industrial Reorganization: The Associations" in *Soviet Economy in a New Perspective*. A Compendium of Papers submitted to the Joint Economic Committee, Congress of the U.S. (Washington, DC, 1976), 162-188; by the same writer, "The Soviet Economic Associations," *Soviet Studies*, XXVI (1974), No. 1; A. Nove, *The Soviet Economic System* (London, 1977), 79-84; S. Pomorski, "The Soviet Economic Associations; Some Problems of Legal Status and Organization after the 1973 Reform," *Review of SocialistLaw*, 2 (1976), No. 3, 129-172. See also A. Bilinsky, "Wirtschaftsvereinigungen in der UdSSR und in Bulgarien" (Economic Associations in the USSR and Bulgaria), *Jahrbuch für Ostrecht*, 13 (1972), No. 2.

12. Gatovskii, note 4, pp. 180-181.

13. K. I. Taksir, *Nauchno-proizvodstvennye ob"edineniia'* (Scientific-Production Associations), (Moscow, 1977), p. 13.

14. *Id.*, pp. 36, 159.

15. Decree of the Council of Ministers of the USSR "On the Approval of the Statute on the Scientific-Production Association," December 30, 1975, *Sobr. Post. SSSR*, 1976, No. 2, item 13; The Statute on the Scientific-Production Association, *id.*

16. The Decree of December 30, 1975, note 15, section 3.

17. Taksir, note 13, pp. 61-70.

18. The Statute, note 15, sec. 1.

19. See the Decree, note 15, section 4; V. F. Maslov (ed.), *Pravovye formy nauchno-tekhnicheskogo sotrudnichestva* (Legal Forms of Scientific-technical Cooperation), Khar'kov, 1976), p. 22.

20. Taksir, note 13, p. 14.

21. The Statute, note 15, section 2.

22. *Id.*, section 1.

23. The Constitution, Article 8. From recent political literature, see M. M. Diatlova, *Deiatel'nost' KPSS po razvitiiu aktivnosti rabochikh v upravlenii proizvodstvom v period razvitogo sotsializma* (Activity of the CPSU in the Area of the Development of Workers' Participation in the Production Management in the Period of Developed Socialism), (Leningrad, 1977). From recent legal writings, see V. T. Prokhorov, *Uchastie trudiash-chikhsia v upravlenii proizvodstvom. Pravovye formy* (Participation of Workers in the Production Management. Legal Forms), (Moscow, 1977); S. A. Ivanov, R. Z. Livshits, "Konstitutsiia SSSR i voprosy trudovogo prava" (Constitution of the USSR and Problems of Labor Law), *SGiP*, 1978, No. 4, 14-24; O. P. Sidorova, M. A. Svistunova, "Povyshenie effektivnosti uchastiia trudiashchikhsia v upravlenii" (Increase of the Effectiveness of Workers Participation in Management), *SGiP*, 1976, No. 3, 69-74; V. A. Maslennikov, "Sotsial'no-pravovaia priroda uchastiia trudiashchikhsia v upravlenii proizvodstvom" (Social and Legal Nature of Workers' Participation in the Production Management), *SGiP*, 1973, No. 6, 37-42; A. I. Tsepin, "Pravo rabochikh i sluzhashchikh na uchastie v upravlenii proizvodstvom" (The Right of Workers and Employees to Participate in the Production Management), *SGiP*, 1973, No. 12, 71-78.

24. The Soviet concept of socialization has almost from the very beginning of the Soviet state corresponded with the etatist model. "In the etatist model socialization *boils down* to transfer of the means of production to the ownership of the socialist state." W. Brus, *Socialist Ownership and Political Systems* (London-Boston, 1975), p. 33.

25. E. L. Manevich, "Manpower-Shortage and Reserves," *Ekonomika i Organizatsiia Promyshlennogo Proizvodstva*, No. 2, March-April 1978, as abstracted in *CDSP*, 30 (1978), No. 16, 4-5, 23; "Two Troublesome Demographic Problems," *CDSP*, 29 (1977), No. 11.

26. See, for example, a random selection from the Soviet newspapers: S. Sheverdin, "Sobriety," *Zhurnalist*, 1977, No. 3, in *CDSP*, 29 (1977), No. 12, 15ff; V. Neiman, "How Can Labor Turnover Be Reduced? ,"*Ekonomicheskaia Gazeta*, No. 32, August 1973, in *CDSP*, 25 (1973), No. 6, 21; A. E. Kotlyar *et al.*, "How to Keep Young Cadres in Their Jobs," *Ek. i. Org. Prom. Proizv.*, July-August 1977, in *CDSP*, 29 (1977), No. 34, 1 ff.; G. M. Podorov, "Experience in Sociological Research on Labor Discipline at Gorkii Province Enterprises," *Sotsiologicheskie Issledovaniia,* October-December 1976, in CDSP, 29 (1977), No. 8, 17 ff.

27. "Disgruntled Workers in Soviet Decide to Form Unofficial Union," *The New York Times*, January 27, 1978; "Dissident Unionists in Moscow Pledge Continuing Struggle," *The New York Times*, February 28, 1978.

28. Compare a monologue of one of the acting persons in the excellent *Svetloe budushchee* (The Bright Future) by A. Zinovev (Paris, 1978), p. 217:

> "Before we resolved crude tasks. . . . Now it is different. Mechanisms of our life have become too complex . . . Our little tasks require now, honesty, conscientious, interested labor, mastery, economy, care. And where to find them? We produce, in abundance, irresponsibility, eyewash, *pokhazukha, khaltura*, mismanagement and thoughtlessness."

29. D. Morawski, "Korespondencja z Rzymu" (A Dispatch from Rome), *Kultura* (Paris), 1978, No. 6, 69.

30. M. Hirszowicz, "Industrial Democracy, Self-Management and Social Control of Production" in L. Kolakowski and S. Hampshire (eds.), *The Socialist Idea. A Reappraisal* (New York, 1974), p. 196.

31. Brezhnev, note 3, p. 577.

32. *Id.*, pp. 577, 585; *Narodnoe khoziaistvo SSSR za 60 let*, note 10, p. 297; V. B. Ostrovskii, *Novyi etap v razvitii kolkhoznogo stroia* (A New Stage in the Development of the Kolkhoz System), (Moscow, 1977), pp. 19-29.

33. *Sobr. Post. SSSR*, 1974, No. 19, item 109.

34. Brezhnev, note 1, p. 52.

35. Decree of the Central Committee of the CPSU, May 28, 1976, "On Further Development of the Specialization and Concentration of Agricultural Production on the Basis of Interfarm Cooperation and Agro-Industrial Integration" in *Resheniia Partii i pravitel'stva po khoziaistvennym voprosam* (Decisions of the Party and Government on Economic Problems), Vol. 11 (Moscow, 1977), pp. 317-330. The policy has recently been vigorously confirmed by the Soviet leadership at the plenary session of the Central Committee of the CPSU in July 1978. See L. I. Brezhnev, *O dal'neishem razvitii sel'skogo khoziaistva SSSR* (On Further Development of Agriculture of the USSR), (Moscow, 1978), pp. 33-36; Decree of the Central Committee of the CPSU, July 4, 1978, *id.*, pp. 47-48. Brezhnev reported that at present "more than 8,000 interfarm and agro-industrial enterprises and associations are operating in the country." *Id.*, p. 34.

36. Decree of May 28, 1976, preceeding note, p. 326.

37. Pomorski, note 11 above, p. 159.

38. Decree, note 35, pp. 320-322.

39. See Decree of May 28, 1976, note 35, pp. 320, 323; V. F. Semenov, "Vzaimodeistvie protsessa kontsentratsii proizvodstva i razvitiia sotsialisticheskoi sobstvennosti" (Mutual Influence of the Processes of the Concentration of Production and Development of Socialist Ownership) in V. F. Semenov (ed.), *Sotsialisticheskaia sobstvennost' i sovershenstvovanie form obshchestvennoi organizatsii proizvodstva* (Socialist Ownership and Improvement of the Forms of Social Organization of Production), (Kazan', 1974), pp. 55, 60; Iu. K. Tolstoi, "Konstitutsiia SSSR i pravo sobstvennosti" (The Constitution of the USSR and the Right of Ownership), *SGiP*, 1978, No. 7, 14-15.

40. The provision reads, "The state promotes the development of collective-farm/cooperative ownership and its drawing together with state ownership."

41. J. V. Stalin, "Economic Problems of Socialism in the USSR," in J. V. Stalin, *Sochineniia* (Works), Vol. III (Stanford, 1967), . 220. See also A. F. Shebanov, "O roli sovetskogo prava v osushchestvlenii perekhoda ot sotsializma k kommunizmu" (On the Role of Soviet Law in the Implementation of the Transition from Socialism to Communism), *SGiP*, 1953, No. 5, 48.

42. Programma KPSS (Program of CPSU) in *XXII s"ezd KPSS. Stenograficheskii otchet.* (XXII Congress of the CPSU. Stenographic Report), Vol. III (Moscow, 1962), pp. 285-290.

43. A. N. Kosygin, "Osnovnye napravleniia razvitiia narodnogo khoziaistva SSSR na 1976-1980 gody" (Fundamental Directions of the Development of National Economy USSR in 1976-1980), in *Materialy XXV s"ezda KPSS*, note 1, p. 146.

44. Programma KPSS, note 42, pp. 285, 290-291.

45. Programma KPSS, note 42, pp. 285, 295; M. Kozyr', "Sotsialisticheskaia sobstvennost' v perekhodnyi k kommunizmu period" (Socialist Ownership in the Period of Transition to Communism), *Sov. Iust.*, 1961, No. 21, 4-6; Ie. A. Vladimirskii, I. P. Pavlova, *Lichnaia sobstvennost' kak ekonomicheskoe otnoshenie* (Personal Ownership as an Economic Relation), (Leningrad, 1977), 33; L. V. Nikiforov, "Problemy razvitiia, sblizheniia i sozdaniia uslovii dlia sliianiia dvukh form sotsialististicheskoi sobstvennosti" (Problems of Development, Drawing Together and Creation of Conditions for Merger of the Two Forms of Socialist Ownership) in V. F. Semenov (ed.), *Sotsialisticheskaia sobstvennost' i sovershenstvovaniie form obshchestvennoi organizatsii proizvodstva* (Socialist Ownership and Perfection of Forms of Social Organization of Production), (Kazan', 1974), p. 100.

46. Programma KPSS, note 42, p. 284; Decree of May 28, 1976, note 35, p. 320.

47. See, for example, an article by A. Ievlev, Secretary of Voronezh Province Party Committee, "Mezhkhoziaistvennaia kooperatsiia: problemy partiinogo rukovodstva" (Interfarm Cooperation: Problems of Party Leadership), *Kommunist*, 1977, No. 4, 36-47; I. Bodyul, First Secretary of the Moldavian CP Central Committee, "Interfarm Cooperation and the Development of Socialist Property," *CDSP*, 30 (1978), No. 37, 17.

48. Brus, note 24, p. 17.

49. The Constitution, Article 13, section 2.

50. L. I. Brezhnev, "Otchetnyi doklad TsK KPSS XXIV S"ezdu Kommunisticheskoi Partii Sovetskogo Soiuza" (Report of CC CPSU to XXIV Congress of the Communist Party of the Soviet Union), in *XXIV s"ezd KPSS. Stenograficheskii otchet* (XXIV Congress of the CPSU. Stenographic Report), (Moscow, 1971), p. 74 and in particular his speech at the plenary session of the CC CPSU, October 25, 1976, in L. I. Brezhnev, note 3, 578. See also Resolution of the CC CPSU, October 27, 1964, "On Removal of Unjustified Limitations on the Personal Subsidiary Household of Kolkhozniks, Workers and Employees," in *Resheniia Partii i pravitel'stva po khoziaistvennym voprosam* (Decisions of The Party and the Government on the Economic Problems), Vol. 5 (Moscow, 1968), p. 517.

51. For a further discussion on subsidiary households under the new Soviet Constitution, see G. Ginsburgs and S. Pomorski, "A Profile of the 1977 Soviet Constitution," in F. J. M. Feldbrugge (ed.), *The Constitutions of the USSR and the Union Republics: Analyses, Texts, Reports* (Alphen aan den Rijn, The Netherlands, 1979), pp. 27*ff*. For a most comprehensive discussion of subsidiary households, see K. E. Wadekin, *The Private Sector in Soviet Agriculture* (Berkeley, Calif., 1973).

52. Dashevskaia, note 5, 61; Z. S. Belaeva, "Pravovye aspekty uchastiia kolkhozov v mezhkhoziaistvennykh predpriiatiiakh i ob"edineniiakh" (Legal Aspects of the Participation of Kolkhozes in Interfarm Enterprises and Associations), *SGiP*, 1976, No 7, 53; Editorial, "Novyi etap v razvitii sel'skogo khoziaistva SSSR i iuridicheskaia nauka" (A New Stage in the Development of the Agriculture of the USSR and Juridical Science), *SGiP*, 1977, No. 1, 3 ff. See also M. I. Kozyr' *et al.* (eds.), *Pravovoe polozhenie agrarno-promyshlennykh predpriiatii i ob"edinenii* (Legal Status of Agro-Industrial Enterprises and Associations), (Kishinev, 1974), pp. 79-101.

53. Decree of the Council of Ministers of the USSR, April 14, 1977, "On the Approval of the General Statute on the Interfarm Enterprise (Organization) in Agriculture," Sobr. Post. SSSR, 1977, No. 13, item 80; "General Statute on the Interfarm Enterprise (Organization) in Agriculture," *id.*

54. In this regard, I rely heavily on a typology suggested in Dashevskaia's article, note 5.

55. Dashevskaia, note 5, p. 61.

56. Belaeva, note 52, p. 54.

57. M. I. Kozyr', "Aktual'nye problemy kolkhoznoi sobstvennosti na sovremennom etape" (Current Problems of Kolkhoz Ownership on the Contemporary Stage of Development), *SGiP*, 1959, No. 8, 60. The issue of the "drawing together" of the two forms of socialist property sub specie "full Communism" theme was strongly emphasized in this context. *Id.*

58. The General Statute, note 53.

59. Dashevskaia, note 5, p. 62.

60. The General Statute, note 53; Dashevskaia, note 5, p. 62.

61. The General Statute, note 53.

62. The General Statute, note 53.

63. Kozyr' *et al.* (eds.), note 52, 96, Belaeva, note 52, p. 55.

64. The General Statute, note 53.

65. Kozyr' *et al.* (eds.), note 52, p. 97; V. B. Kozlov, "Konstitutsiia SSSR i problemy razvitiia agrarno-pravovykh nauk" (The Constitution of the USSR and Problems of Development of Agro-Legal Sciences), *SGiP*, 1978, No. 4, 144.

66. "Rassmotrenie ugolovnykh del o chastnopredprinimatel'skoi deiatel'nosti i kommercheskom posrednichestve (Obzor sudebnoi praktiki)" (Consideration of Criminal Cases On Private Entrepreneurial Activity and Activity as Commercial Middleman (An Examination of Judicial Practice)), *BVS SSSR*, 1977, No. 2, 25-32.

67. Editorial, note 52.

68. Dashevskaia, note 5, p. 63. The legal status and organization of a trust of sovkhozes is governed by the Statute on the Trust of Sovkhozes, October 20, 1975, *Sobr. Post. SSSR*, 1975, No. 21, item 145.

69. Dashevskaia, note 5, p. 63. For a further discussion of the differences between interfarm enterprises, APA's and agro-industrial associations, comp. Belaeva, note 52, pp. 54 ff.

70. Dashevskaia, note 5, pp. 64-65.

71. *Id.*, p. 64.

72. *Id.*, pp. 66-67.

138

COMMENTS ON THE ADMINISTRATION
OF SOCIALIST PROPERTY IN THE USSR

Leonid Polsky

In his article appearing elsewhere in this volume, Professor Pomorski has given us some interesting ideas regarding the decades of the formation of the current situation in the fundamental areas of the economy of the Soviet Union; namely, in the area of industy, scientific-research investigations, and agricultural production.

From my point of view, the primary value of this research is that it provides us with a deep analysis of the basic flaws in these leading sectors of the economy and uncovers the causes which have given birth to them.

In connection with this, it seems to me to be completely logical that in his research, Professor Pomorski has shown, in chronological order, which legal measures the Soviet Party and government leadership have carried out to eliminate these flaws and the difficult obstacles that must be overcome on this path.

Permit me to express my own point of view concerning the basic theses of this research, by using actual examples from the life of Soviet society as illustrations.

In the area of industry, beginning in 1959 periodic reforms have been carried out which concentrated enterprises into associations (*ob"edineniia*) according to their specialization. In 1975 in the Soviet Union, scientific-industrial associations began to be established, the purpose of which was to significantly shorten the road from a discovery to its introduction in industrial enterprises.

For the past twenty years in the Soviet Union, there has been propaganda about raising the level of activity of workers in the administration of the enterprise. It was with this in mind that, at the end of the 1950s, permanently-functioning industrial conferences were created in all industrial enterprises under the leadership of the enterprise, with the direct participation of the workers of the enterprise.

From this, it can be seen that the Party and governmental leadership of the Soviet Union has—for the past twenty years—been quite concerned about the unhealthy situation in industry and, with the goal of improving it, has made an entire series of changes and reforms. But all of these changes and reforms in industry have not given and are not giving rise to any perceptible positive results, since in enterprises in the Soviet Union the principle of the material incentives (*material'naia zainteresovannost'*) of the workers—who are serving these enterprises and creating resources with their labor—is entirely ignored. Frequently, this factor results in something like "quiet strikes" at large enterprises.

In support of this, I refer to one very clear example. In the enterprises of the Soviet Union, the situation exists where a worker, who is paid for piece-work, together with his industrial assignment receives an order where the type of work, which he is to perform, is reflected in the time-work norm of output and compensation therefor, established by *Gosstandart.* In Moscow, there is one of the largest enterprises in the country—the First State Ball-bearing Factory where a several-thousand strong collective of workers is employed. As in every state industrial enterprise, this factory has a strictly established wage fund, which it may not exceed.

While on the piece-work system, naturally, the workers try to produce as much as is possible so as to most rationally utilize and maximally fulfill working time and thereby to earn more. However, when the time has come to compute the earnings of workers, in order not to exceed the limits of the wage fund, established for the factory, the rates for what had already been produced were reduced on all the orders to the workers. All of the workers refused to receive their salaries and to sign a receipt, although they remained on the job and the factory continued to function normally. Keeping in mind that near to this factory there are also several other large enterprises, such as the Automobile Factory Named after Likhachev and others, and also not wanting this to be a victory for the workers, the minister, to whom this factory was subordinate, immediately ordered the recalculation of the workers' salaries in accordance with the rates established in the orders.

The continual ignoring of the principle of material incentives for the workers creates an entire series of problems which are difficult to resolve and which impede the development of industry. The workers have ceased to value their own work, and this has led to serious fluctuations and insufficient levels of manpower in enterprises. As a result of this, there is often a very low level of labor discipline in enterprises, which gives rise to mass alcoholism, especially during the time of payment of advances and salaries.

There then arises another question: why in a society, which announces to the whole world that it is the most humane, the most highly organized, that it is based upon the highest principles of communist morality, why are there so many unrestrained alcoholics in this society and where is the source of this mass alcoholism which encompasses almost all levels of the Soviet society? From my point of view, it is necessary to seek the reason in the social structure of society in which such abnormal tendencies occur. Only that person can thoughtlessly fill himself with alcohol who does this as a type of protest against the injustice and hypocrisy which he sees day-in-and-day-out in the society in which he lives.

All of these factors certainly do not promote the raising of productivity and the improvement of the quality of what is produced; on the contrary, they retard these processes.

In the field of agricultural production, the situation is even more gloomy than in industry. Since the 1930s, an unsolved problem has stood before the Party and government leadership of the Soviet Union—how, and more important with what to feed the 250 million people of the country and how to provide industry with raw materials for the production of necessary consumer goods. As is well known, at the end of the 1920s, in the years of Stalin's rule, after the extermination of millions of the best toilers of the countryside, there were created—under the aegis of the liquidation of the kulaks as a class—the so-called social-cooperative agricultural enterprises, the *kolkhozy*, and parallel with that the state agricultural enterprises, the *sovkhozy*.

In the primary stages of their creation, both the *kolkhozy* and the *sovkhozy* were on a small scale, and naturally, they were not very productive, which resulted in the lack of products of primary and daily necessity. As in industry, the Soviet Party and government leadership has for decades been seeking new ways and possibilities for improvement and raising of productivity in the field of agricultural production. With this as the goal, a campaign was begun at the end of the 1950s to unite the *kolkhozy* in one huge agricultural enterprise and to provide it with the latest agricultural technology. It was believed that this measure would stimulate the raising of productivity of agricultural production. However, this time they had still not studied the important factors which were impeding the development of agriculture; namely, the principle of material incentives, the raising of the level of agrarian know-how in agricultural production, and allowing the *kolkhozy* the right to conduct their own affairs so that they themselves could resolve questions of which agricultural crops grow best on the land worked by them. Clearly the result is a farcical picture, side-by-side with the disastrous situations for the populace in questions of the supply of foodstuffs. In fact, paragraph 4 of Article 12 of the 1977 USSR Constitution proclaims the duty of *kolkhozy* and other land users (referring to the *sovkhozy*) to efficiently utilize the land, to treat it with care, and to increase its productiveness. But this constitutional provision is a bluff, an absolute fiction. Having proclaimed this duty of the *kolkhozy* and *sovkhozy* in the Constitution, it is imperative to first of all allow the leadership of the agricultural enterprises the opportunity to practically exercise this duty in real terms. But, in fact, a tragic comedy results in just this area. The leaders of the *kolkhozy* and *sovkhozy* do not have the right to independently resolve questions such as which crops they may plant on the lands which they work, taking into account the nature of the area being cultivated and the data for this purpose from agrarian science. The planning organizations in *Gosplan* and in the Ministry of Agriculture dictate to the *kolkhozy* and *sovkhozy* which crops they must plant on the land being worked by them and, what is more, the harvest they must bring in. And all of this is done without taking into account the nature of the areas being cultivated by these agricultural enterprises and the yearly conditions, which are certainly not immaterial for the harvest. So, it turns out that the land, on which peas can grow well, is planted with grain, and where grain can grow well, peas are planted.

What are the results of this? Even in favorable climatic conditions, there is neither a harvest of grain nor of peas. But under present conditions, the Soviet leadership does not worry, for they have discovered the maxim that the richest country in the world is America, which will always sell them grain at a favorable price and in unlimited quantities.

An analogous and just as bleak situation also ensues with regard to the productiveness of livestock, located in *kolkhozy* and *sovkhozy*, and all of this represents the links in one chain.

For decades, as the result of the improper utilization of arable land, the *kolkhozy* and *sovkhozy* are not in a position to solve the feed problem for livestock, and this is the basic cause of the constant lack of diary products in the country. The situation is no better with regard to agricultural technology. Expensive combines, tractors, and other agricultural machinery—after their seasonal use lasting several months—stand out in the *kolkhozy* and *sovkhozy* in the dust and dirt and are covered with a thick coating of rust. When the time comes to use them again, they have to be dragged out into the fields where it is not even possible to make one out of ten work, since they have all fallen into ruin.

In this gloomy picture, the current situation in agriculture has been presented where, if not every, then almost every leader of an agricultural enterprise cites the reason that if it was acceptable to our grandparents, then who are we to complain; if idiotic plans are established at the center, not taking into account the realistic possibilities for their fulfillment, then we are given silently the moral right to report back to the center about the labor successes of the *kolkhozy* and *sovkhozy* in gathering large harvests when they are not there—*i.e.*, given the moral right to lie and commit eyewash.

PROCURATORIAL CAMPAIGNS
AGAINST CRIME

Gordon B. Smith

A prominent and enduring characteristic of the Soviet press is the publicizing of cases of various forms of anti-social activity and drawing public and Party attention to safeguarding Soviet society from them. Cases frequently focus on hooliganism, alcoholism, theft from factories and shops, and parasitism. Although presumably spontaneously generated by letters from readers, Party officials, or local law enforcement officials, cases dealing with one particular social ill tend to glut the popular and scholarly press for a period of time, suggesting the presence of a well-orchestrated campaign. Campaigns against crime have long been recognized in Soviet law. However, no attempt has been made to analyse these campaigns either to chart their frequency and subject matter or to examine how they are organized and implemented. This paper seeks to undertake both questions. We will begin by differentiating various types of campaigns against crime and then analyze the anatomy of the campaigns. Finally, we will chart the frequency of campaigns and their subjects over the last thirty years, looking for recurring patterns and possible links to larger issues dominating the political scene.

Campaigns, as referred to in this paper, are the coordinated efforts of several law enforcement related agencies and institutions to reduce the incidence of certain types of crime. Campaigns are sometimes associated with extensive press coverage; however, the crucial element for our discussion will be actual law enforcement efforts. Although press coverage may augment procuratorial campaigns by enhancing their deterrent effect, it is not a necessary ingredient of the procuratorial campaigns against crime that we analyze here.

The present research draws on several data sources, in addition to the secondary literature of Soviet legal scholars. We analyzed 496 cases of general supervision published in the Procuracy's journal, *Sotsialisticheskaia Zakonnost'* from 1955 through 1976 to provide a detailed picture of the subjects of procuratorial action concerning campaigns against crime and to point out changes over time. In addition, survey data collected from procurators by the scholars at the Laboratory for the Study of Procuratorial Supervision of the Juridical Faculty of Leningrad State University were analyzed. Finally, consultations were conducted with several Soviet legal scholars and practicing procurators to obtain their responses to questions not covered in the literature.

Campaigns against crime in the Soviet Union can first be differentiated by the level at which they are initiated. A major policy pronouncement by a Party leader or the enactment of a new decree by the Presidium of the Supreme Soviet might well be associated with a general nation-wide campaign. On the other hand, local procuracies on their own initiative frequently undertake campaigns against illegal activity in their regions. While initiated locally, these campaigns are, of course, carried out within general limits set by central decision-makers and supported by them.

In addition, we can differentiate campaigns against crime by the frequency of their occurrence. In the past, campaigns against some types of crimes have occurred only once or sporadically. Other campaigns show a relatively consistent cyclical pattern. We will begin our analysis of campaigns against crime by examining nationwide campaigns, looking in detail at three particular campaigns.

1. Crime in the National Spotlight

In the last twenty years, three major national campaigns against crime deserve particular attention because of their intensity. The first was the campaign against the illegal imposition of administrative fines following the enactment of a decree of the Presidium of the Supreme Soviet on June 21, 1961. The second was the campaign surrounding the drafting of new laws on alcoholism and hooliganism in 1966. Lastly, we will examine a major shift in the focus of campaigns against crime resulting from economic difficulties encountered during the mid-1960s.

Campaign Against the Illegal Imposition of Fines

Legislation establishing various Soviet administrative organs after the death of Stalin incorporated a vast array of administrative powers to fine and punish. By the early 1960s, these multiple grants of authority had resulted in a considerable degree of inequality and confusion. There were almost 5,000 administrative commissions in the Soviet Union handling a heavy load of cases—totalling more than 400,000 per year.[1]

The number of new legislative acts incorporating fining powers also was proliferating rapidly. In 1960 in Moscow *oblast'*, twelve new acts incorporating the power to issue fines were passed by executive committees of local Soviets.[2] In Ordzhonikidze in the Ossetian ASSR, the number of new fining provisions passed in 1959-1960 totalled 34.[3]

Seeking to standardize the complex web of normative acts establishing the power to impose administrative fines, the Presidium of the Supreme Soviet of the USSR on June 21, 1961, enacted a decree, "On the Further Limitation of

Application of Fines Imposed by Administrative Procedure."[4] The decree established limits on the size of administrative fines of up to 50 rubles for officials and up to 10 rubles for citizens. For especially serious administrative violations, fines may be increased to 100 rubles for officials and 50 rubles for citizens. The decree also established that the authority to generate laws incorporating the power to fine rests solely with higher political and administrative organs. The effect of the decree, therefore, was to abolish or amend many normative acts which included fining powers. Table 1 presents figures for eight republics, showing the number of acts losing force or being amended as a result of the decree.

As a result of the decree, the number of instances in which local Soviets or their administrative commissions can impose fines was decreased by two to three times.[5] The decree was interpreted as a clear signal to procurators to begin a nationwide campaign to insure compliance with the legislative provisions. In Figure 1, we analyze the fluctuations in the number of published cases of procuratorial action directed against the illegal imposition of administrative fines.

We see a clear and dramatic increase in the number of published cases of procuratorial actions concerned with the illegal imposition of administrative fines in 1963-1964. In 1963-1964, procurators directed more than 45% of their protests and representations against cases of the illegal imposition of administrative fines. The lag-time from the promulgation of the decree in June 1961 to the peak of procuratorial activity reflected in the published cases in 1963-1964 is attributed to the time it takes to initiate action based on the new decree, compounded by publishing delays.

Table 1. *Normative Acts Incorporating Fining Powers Abolished or Amended by the Decree of the Presidium of the Supreme Soviet of June 21, 1961.*

Republic	Abolished	Amended	Total
Belorussia	53	14	67
RSFSR	35	11	46
Tadzhik	28	8	36
Kirgiz	22	8	30
Uzbek	20	9	29
Kazakh	18	10	28
Turkmen	19	4	23
Georgia	12	8	20
Total	207	72	279

Source: M. S. Studenikina, *Zakonodatel'stvo ob administrativnoi otvetstvennosti i problemy ego kodifikatsii* (Legislation on Administrative Responsibility and Problems of its Codification), (Unpublished candidate dissertation, All-Union Scientific-Research Institute on Soviet Legislation, Moscow, 1968), pp. 39-40.

145

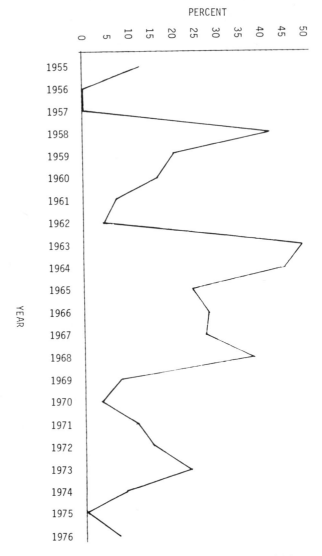

Figure 1. *Procuratorial Actions Against the Illegal Imposition of Administrative Fines, 1955-1976. (Percent of total procuratorial actions for each year).*

Since 1963, the percentage of published procuratorial actions against the illegal imposition of administrative fines has peaked every five years. This may be a random pattern or an indication of the recurring desire to police administrative abuses. It also may be significant that the actions giving rise to this cyclical pattern seem to occur during the first or second year of the five-year planning period.

146

The effect of the standardization of administrative fining powers was to considerably reduce the number of cases of imposition of administrative fines reviewed by the courts. In the period 1957 to 1961, the number of such cases appearing in the courts each year ranged from 730,000 to 797,000.[6] However, after the 1961 decree, administrative fine cases before the courts declined by more than 80 times—to 9,000 to 11,000 per year from 1965-1968.[7]

In looking at the legislation since 1961, in no republic is there a normative act of a ministry or department which independently establishes the power to impose a fine for the violation of an administrative rule. This power lies principally with the Council of Ministers of the USSR or the republic councils of ministers, but in practice is frequently delegated to republic ministries acting in the name of the councils of ministers.[8] For example, fines for the violation of trade rules are usually established by the republic ministries of trade, acting in conjunction with the republic councils of ministers.

The 1961 decree is a vivid example of the use of a procuratorial and press campaign to inform administrators, procurators, and citizens of new national legislation. The relatively infrequent occurrence of fine-related cases since 1964 would suggest that this campaign was quite successful.

Campaign Against Hooliganism

Alcoholism and hooliganism have long plagued Russian rulers. In the first months of World War I with the pressing demands to mobilize for war, the Tsarist regime instituted prohibition with notoriously counterproductive results. In 1922, the new Soviet government in an attempt to cut down on instances of public drunkenness and other public disturbances introduced a new article in the criminal codes on "hooliganism."[9]

Despite their longevity, no consensus has been reached as to the best methods for counteracting these social problems. Professor Solomon has analyzed the vacillation between preventive strategies and punative strategies from the post-Stalin liberalization through the enactment of new legislation on alcoholism and hooliganism in 1966-1967.[10] The debate between the hard-liners headed by V. S. Tikunov, Minister for the Defense of the Social Order (*MOOP*), and the soft-liners represented by Professor A. A. Gertsenzon, of the Procuracy Institute, and G. Z. Anashkin, head of the criminal division of the USSR Supreme Court, came to a head in the spring of 1966. As the hard-liners assumed the position of dominance, the foundations began to be laid for a massive campaign to coincide with the anticipated new legislation. In late May, an extensive press campaign was initiated against hooliganism. *Izvestiia* published a series of letters, commentaries, and articles on the dangers of hooliganism and the need for public vigilance. It is perhaps significant that only one of the articles was attributed to a scholar, while the vast majority were submitted by interested citizens, journalists, and officials.

A draft hooliganism law was completed by a subcommission of the Commission on Legislative Suggestions of the Supreme Soviet in late June or early July 1966. The legislation envisaged both procedural and substantive changes. The chief of police or his deputy were given authority to impose fines of 10 to 30 rubles for petty hooliganism without a court hearing. [11] In addition, the decree incorporated new provisions allowing the courts and police chiefs considerable discretion in transferring cases to comrades' courts or social organizations, devising and supervising corrective labor, and extending sentences up to 30 days. Minimum terms for petty hooliganism were increased and new punishments were established for hooliganism and malicious hooliganism. Most notable was the new provision that intoxication may constitute an aggravating circumstance in the consideration of crimes. As a consequence, a murder resulting from a domestic argument committed while under the influence of alcohol might be given a more severe sentence than a premeditated murder committed for mercenary reasons.

On July 23, 1966, three days before the announcement of the new legislation, a public campaign began with full force. A trial of a man accused of hooliganism in Riazan' was broadcast live over national television. [12] Predictably, newspapers, local administrative and Party officials, and television stations received a flood of letters from viewers demanding a hard-line on hooliganism. On July 26, the new legislation was introduced amid statements that it had been demanded by the public.

In the public campaign which followed, hooliganism dominated feature articles in the major newspapers and popular journals. Party organizations, workers' collectives, and trade unions met to discuss the new legislation. The capstone of the campaign was a televized press conference including prominent officials of the Procuracy, *MOOP*, Supreme Court and correspondents for *Pravda, Izvestiia, Trud, Sovetskaia Rossiia, Krokodil*, and *Smena*, and the state radio and television networks. [13] Criminologists played a relatively small role in the campaign, mostly limited to writing scholarly articles on the legal finepoints of the new law.

Procuratorial Supervision and Economic Violations

The most striking development in procuratorial supervision over the period since 1955 has been the increase of procuratorial attention to economic violations since 1968. Economic violations constituted only a marginal subject of procuratorial activity until 1969. During the period 1955-1968, procurators primarily concerned themselves with redressing grievances of individual citizens against administrative agencies—*e.g.* illegal firings and other labor violations and the illegal imposition of fines by administrative bodies. This redress function in many ways resembled that of the Swedish ombudsman and led several western observers to consider it the "Soviet ombudsman." [14]

However, the change in emphasis which occurred in 1968-1969 represents a clear departure from this redress function. From 1969 to the present, the

148

Procuracy has concerned itself much more intensively with actions which detrimentally affect state economic interests and not the interests of individual citizens. The most plausible explanation for this shift lies in economic developments in the mid-1960s.

In late September 1965, Premier Kosygin signalled the end of the lengthy Liberman debates by announcing a series of economic reforms. The reforms were prompted by a deceleration in the rate of economic advance since 1958. During the period 1958-1966, the economic growth rate of the USSR slipped from 8.5% to 6.8%. [15] Furthermore, it had become clear that the unusually demanding targets of the Seventh Five-Year Plan would not be met. The 1965 reforms recentralized economic management after Khrushchev, restoring the ministries and "branch" system of administration. In addition, the reforms incorporated sales and profits of enterprises as indicators of performance, reducing the number of centrally-set indices. By the end of 1968, more than 26,000 industrial plants—producing three-quarters of the total industrial output of the Soviet Union—had been converted to the new system. [16] The greater autonomy for enterprise managers was expected to result in more efficient use of labor and equipment. It also necessitated better supervision and control of economic violations in industrial enterprises and state farms.

The shift in emphasis of procuratorial action also parallels the debate during the mid-1960s over the "scientific-technical revolution." Robert Miller states that the thrust of the economic reforms of 1965 was to attack the increasing problems of stagnation and inefficiency by long-term qualitative improvements in the technological level of administration and performance evaluation. [17] A flurry of articles appeared in Party and technical journals on information processing, automatic control theory, information theory, and mathematical modeling as appropriate tools for economic administration. [18] Some proponents of cybernetics and administrative behavioral science identified the Procuracy as a major control/feedback mechanism in Soviet administration and the Soviet economy. [19]

Given the two-year lag-time for publication, we would not expect to see these economic and administrative concerns reflected in cases of procuratorial supervision published in legal journals until 1968 or 1969. This is precisely when we find the shift of procuratorial action from issues primarily affecting individual aggrieved citizens to economic violations which damage the State's economic interests. (See Table 2).

With the completion of the Eighth Five-Year Plan in 1970, procuratorial action on economic violations appears to have tapered off until 1974. However, the target figures of the Ninth Five-Year were uncommonly high. Thus, in 1974 and 1975 an intensive campaign was mounted leading up to the termination of the plan period on December 31, 1975.

This shift in emphasis of procuratorial attention since 1968 may indicate at least three major developments. First, it is an indication that the Soviet

Table 2. *Economic Violations, 1955-1976 (in percent).*

	1955	1958	1959	1960	1961	1962	1963	1964	1965	1966
Economic	0.0	8.3	20.0	0.0	6.3	13.0	8.0	6.5	5.9	15.2
Non-Economic	100.0	91.7	80.0	100.0	93.7	87.0	92.0	93.5	94.1	84.8

	1967	1968	1969	1970	1971	1972	1973	1974	1975	1976
Economic	7.7	10.3	48.4	43.3	30.8	24.2	27.3	50.0	73.9	58.8
Non-Economic	92.3	89.7	51.6	56.7	69.2	75.8	72.7	50.0	26.1	41.2

leadership, confronted with serious economic difficulties, has felt compelled to reorient the energies of one of its most highly centralized and powerful control organizations—the Procuracy.

Second, the fact of this shift means that Soviet citizens aggrieved by administrative actions must look to other mechanisms for relief. The 1977 USSR Constitution provides two clues as to what those mechanisms will be. Article 58 broadens the jurisdiction of the courts to review citizens' complaints against state administration. The Constitution also places a heavy stress on participatory rights and citizen involvement in the policy-making process in local governmental bodies.

Finally, this general shift in procuratorial activity is congruent with the general conservative nature of the Brezhnev regime and its continual preoccupation with economic performance—what George Breslauer refers to as a "conservative restoration." [20]

2. Cyclical Trends

Whereas the three campaigns we have examined so far were isolated instances, prompted by new legislative enactments or major policy reorientations, other procuratorial campaigns appear much more frequently and regularly. Longitudinal analysis of procuratorial supervision of several economic violations reveals some interesting cyclical patterns of investigation and prosecution. During the last two five-year plans, three economic violations (theft from state enterprises and collective farms, improper maintenance of state property, and production of defective or substandard goods) have dominated procuratorial activity during the third and fourth years of the plans. (See Figures 2, 3, 4, and 5.) Theft is especially the focus during the fourth year of the plan. The increase in procuratorial activity is undoubtedly aimed at discouraging factory managers from taking shortcuts that would hurt produc-

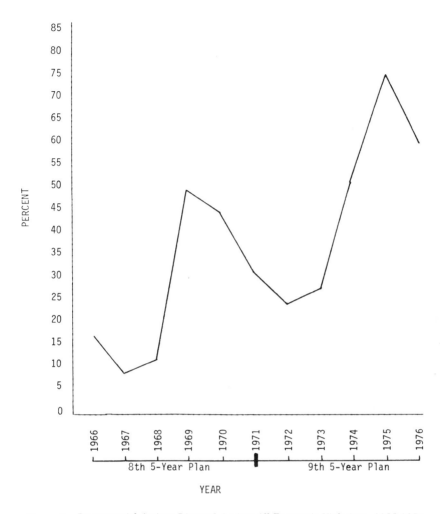

PERCENT

YEAR

Figure 2. *Procuratorial Actions Directed Against All Economic Violations. 1955-1976 (in percent).*

tion. For example, in the construction industry, managers frequently attempt to fulfill the plan at any cost. In the Kazakh republic in 1973, only 48% of all new housing received good evaluations upon inspection. [21] According to two procurators in the Kazakh republic, an extremely widespread cause of low quality construction is "storming." More than 35% of all housing starts were begun in the last quarter of the plan year. Of these, 70% were begun in the last week of December. [22] "Storming" often results in the exploitation of workers and even job-related accidents.

Procuratorial attention typically shifts to padding and altering planning

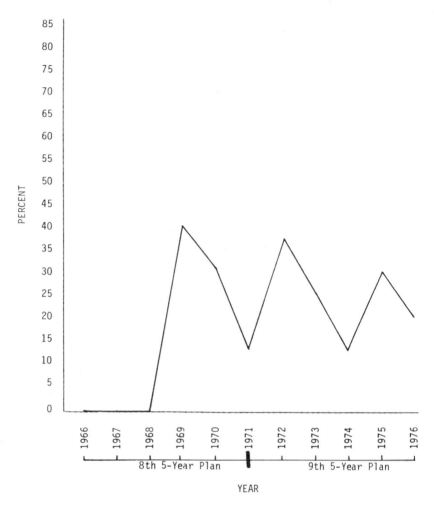

Figure 3. *Procuratorial Actions Directed Against Theft of State Property, 1955-1976 (in percent).*

records and accounts during the final year of the plan—the year during which production figures on plan-fulfillment are reported to central authorities. (See Figure 6.)

What we seem to be witnessing, then, is a regular pattern of ebb and flow of procuratorial activity governed by the economic plan. The intensity of procuratorial campaigns might also serve as a barometer of difficulties that are being experienced in the economy in general, and various sectors of the economy in particular. The overall trend of procuratorial supervision since 1968 has been associated clearly with the planning period. In the first two

152

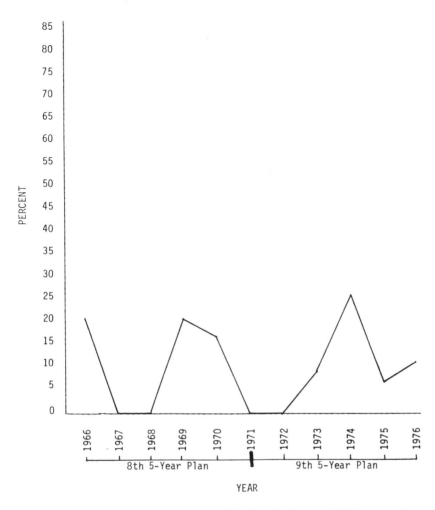

Figure 4. *Procuratorial Actions Directed Against the Improper Maintenance of State Property, 1955-1976 (in percent).*

years of the plan, procurators supervise a wide array of violations–labor, housing as well as economic. But as the pressures to fulfill production quotas rise in the fourth year, procurators institute campaigns against theft and other economic violations which might threaten production. During the final year of the plan, particular attention is given to padding and falsification of reporting records.

The accelerated pace of procuratorial activity toward the end of the plan might also suggest that the Procuracy is engaged in some "storming" of its own in order to fulfill its quota of investigations.

153

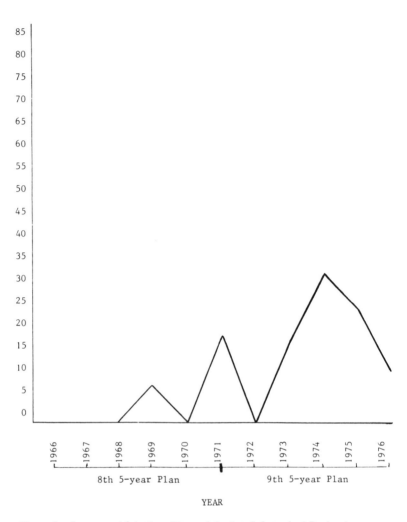

Figure 5. *Procuratorial Actions Directed Against Substandard Production, 1955-1976 (in percent).*

3. The Formulation of Campaigns

Ideally, campaigns represent an integrated, total approach to combatting crime, incorporating investigation, prosecution, follow-up supervision, and preventive measures. We will discuss each phase of the campaign in turn, citing examples to illustrate Soviet juridical practice.

Procurators rely principally upon two methods to uncover violations. [23] First, article 14 of the Statute on the Procuracy empowers procurators to receive and review citizens' complaints. [24] Most protests are prompted by

154

Figure 6. *Procuratorial Actions Directed Against Padding and Altering Accounting Records, 1955-1976 (in percent).*

information from the press, citizens' complaints, or "signals" received by procurators during the course of their contact with *oblast'* and regional organizations, Soviets, auditing departments, tax offices and safety inspectorates, or attendance at meetings of worker collectives. [25]

Second, procurators conduct periodic investigations of administrative organizations, agricultural and industrial enterprises, and social organizations to: (1) check the legality of their orders, instructions, and decisions, and (2) check the extent to which they are executing fully laws and decrees already in effect. Article 11 of the Statute on the Procuracy gives procurators

155

the right to obtain documents and evidence pertaining to citizens' complaints and suspected violations. [26]

In a survey of procurators in 1972, 70% of the respondents indicated that complex investigations are useful in uncovering illegal activity. [27] However, research of V. I. Shind in the Latvian SSR shows that investigations and inspections are of little effect when no signal of violations has been received. For example in Khmel'nitskii *raion*, 122 of 125 fruitless investigations were undertaken without having received signals of violations. Similarly in Anikadiaiskii *raion*, 58 of 59 fruitless investigations occurred when no signal had been received. [28] Shind recommends that procurators organize investigations or inspections only after they received signals of violations of laws. [29]

Research findings also help procurators in combatting crime by pinpointing the causes of crime and the types of people most likely to become offenders. For example, a study conducted by the Procuracy of Staroruskii *raion* found that one-third of all juvenile offenders come from broken homes. [30] The procurators of Shchuchinskii *raion* on their own initiative investigated juvenile crime in eight villages in the region. [31] They concluded that the majority of juvenile offenders were neither working nor enrolled in school. Consequently, subsequent anti-crime campaigns in the region focused on putting unemployed youths to work. Since 1971, the L'vov city Procuracy has kept city-wide statistics on crime, studying the dynamics and character of violations. The study concluded that the incidence of juvenile crime increased markedly during vacations and the summer months. [32] The researchers recommended summer work projects for students.

Criminological research also helps direct the efforts of the police, *druzhina*, and other organs of social order. The L'vov study found that the majority of violations, especially alcohol-related crime, occurs in non-work time. Consequently, organs of public order in L'vov concentrate their efforts on housing complexes during non-working hours. To provide further assistance, 40 regional support stations were established in L'vov in 1975, manned with *druzhinniki*. As a result, the crime rate dropped by 9% in one year. [33]

In general, we see a marked increase in the number of procuratorial investigations in recent years. Figures for the RSFSR indicate that procurators conducted 123,934 investigations in 1970; 173,508 in 1971 (an increase of 40%); 192,089 in 1972 (an increase of 55% over 1970). [34]

Walter Gellhorn noted in 1966 that procuratorial investigations tend to concentrate on administrative commissions where citizens are most likely to be directly affected by official decisions. [35] In 1959, Berezovskaia called for special attention by investigators to the legality of commissions that impose fines and other administrative penalties. [36] However, figures of the RSFSR Procuracy for 1972 indicate that the most frequent object of procuratorial investigations are industrial enterprises and social organizations, rather than administrative commissions. See Table 3.

Table 3. *Objects of Procuratorial Investigations in the RSFSR in 1972.*

Enterprises and social organizations	130,964
Kolkhozy	42,078
Raion and city organs of administration	25,642
Agricultural and rural soviets	22,077
Raion and city executive committees	9,692
Krai, oblast', and autonomous republic administrative organs	2,641
All-union and republic ministries	870
Krai, oblast' and autonomous republic executive committees of soviets	211
Total	234,175*

* In several cases, there were multiple objects of investigations. This accounts for the disparity between the figures in Table 3 and the aggregate figures presented previously.
Source: L. A. Nikolaeva, *Teoreticheskie i prakticheskie problemy obespecheniia zakon-nosti v sovetskom gosudartsvennom upravlenii organami prokuratury i suda* (Theoretical and Practical Problems in Insuring the Legality of Soviet State Administration by Organs of the Procuracy and the Court), (Unpublished doctoral dissertation, Leningrad State University, 1974), p. 181.

According to several Soviet sources, the effectiveness of investigations of crime is heightened when procurators construct yearly schedules or plans for investigation. [37] Most procuratorial offices organize their investigatory activity in relation to quartely and annual plans, in addition to the five-year plans. However, a study conducted by the Institute of the Procuracy recommends more frequent investigation of important economic enterprises and factories and state organs having control/supervisory powers. [38] Every quarter, procurators receive reports from state inspection agencies, the Ministry of Trade of each republic, *Gosstandart*, the Central Statistical Administration of each republic, and *Gosabitrazh*. [39]

The researchers recommend *kolkhozy* be inspected once or twice every three to five months; administrative commissions, offices of the State Automobile Inspection, and other organs with fining powers once or twice a quarter; and schools, nurseries, day-care centers, post offices, and savings banks once a year. [40]

Frequently campaigns against crime continue for two or three years. For example, in August 1976 the bureau of the Rostov *obkom*, without any apparent consultation with the Procuracy, initiated a three-year anti-crime campaign. [41]

The duration of campaigns is extended frequently by follow-up investigations and public education programs. For instance, when the Dzerzhinskii District Party committee uncovered extensive violations of labor discipline in

157

local factories, a campaign was initiated to punish guilty workers. The campaign was followed by periodic investigations, and lectures in legal topics relating to work discipline were presented at local factories by local procurators.

Periodic inspection campaigns are particularly common in the agricultural sector. V. Kuznetsov, procurator in Moscow *oblast'*, presents an image of contemporary procurators strongly reminiscent of the accounts of the role rural procurators played in supervising harvests during the collectivization campaigns in the late 1920s. He reports that every year during harvest, the *raion* procuracies coordinate their supervision of state and collective farms with the organs of the people's control, the State Agricultural-Technical Inspection, and trade unions to insure that the grain is properly handled and technical safety standards are being met. [42]

Complex investigations present procurators with significant organizational and coordination problems. A single complex investigation against petty theft from factories by employees might require the participation of the Procuracy, police, courts, Ministry of Trade of the republic, factory managers, comrades' courts, trade unions, councils on prophylaxis, primary Party organizations, and possibly commissions on minors, Komsomol organizations, fire inspection, technical safety inspection, and *Gosstandart*. Coordination problems are multiplied when complex investigations are organized during a campaign against crime. For example, the three-year anti-crime campaign in Rostov *oblast'*, cited earlier, necessitated the coordination of more than 3,000 *druzhina*, 230 Komsomol organizations, 5,000 comrades' courts, 500 support points (*opornye punkty*), and 2,000 councils on prophylaxis. [43] In fact the single greatest stumbling block to the effectiveness of campaigns against crime might well be the problem of organization and coordination.

Many crimes occurring in the industrial sector require specialized, technical expertise to uncover. Increasingly in recent years, procurators are turning for assistance to technical inspection agencies, *Gosstandart*, and engineers and scientists affiliated with scientific-research institutes. When conducting investigations in enterprises and firms, procurators may enlist the aid of jurisconsults in those enterprises. Until the late 1920s, it was quite common for jurisconsults to send signals to procurators concerning violations in their organizations. However, a resolution of the Council of People's Commissars of the RSFSR in 1927 established responsibility of jurisconsults for violations in their enterprises and organs. [44] The decree created an incentive to quietly correct any violations and, at all costs, hide them from the Procuracy.

Of 243 *raion* procurators surveyed in 1972, 44.4% use the legal services of jurisconsults in enterprises and organizations. [45] Of those responding affirmatively, over half include the jurisconsults in investigations of legal violations and approximately one-fourth consult with jurisconsults concerning measures to prevent legal violations. [46]

158

When conducting investigations into economic-financial activities in enterprises and firms, 64.3% of the surveyed procurators claimed to use materials of control-auditing organs, while 35.7% demand documents and records directly from the enterprises and firms in question. [47] More than one-half of the procurators engage specialists in these investigations.

In other words, procurators are more likely to enlist the support of persons outside of the organs they are investigating than jurisconsults affiliated with those organs. Some procurators have criticized jurisconsults for allying themselves with the organs with which they are associated, thus obstructing procuratorial investigations. [48]

The Party's role in campaigns against crime appears to be in providing overall impetus and supervision. Most campaigns and complex investigations are initiated at the local level. [49] City and regional Party committees oversee the formulation of annual and five-year plans for procuratorial investigation, frequently in response to resolutions of Party Congresses or Plenums of the Central Committee.

The degree of local or regional Party pressure on the Procuracy and other law enforcement agencies varies from locale to locale. Some regions have a reputation for having a harder Party line than other regions. But some degree of influence is evidenced virtually in every administrative jurisdiction in the USSR. A former senior investigator in the Moscow Procuracy reports that Party officials do not hesitate to contact procuratorial officials to recommend action on economic crimes.

Upon conclusion of an investigation, procurators frequently report their findings to Party and state organs. In a survey of 180 procurators, 42.3% reported that they frequently send copies of representations resulting from campaigns and complex investigations to Party organs. [50] More than one-quarter of the respondents send copies of representations to superior administrative organs, 21% to executive committees of local Soviets, and 8.6% to trade union councils. Only 2.8% of the procurators surveyed did not feel that issuing multiple representations was expedient.

Having uncovered violations, the procurator may recommend corrective action or the initiation of criminal, administrative, or disciplinary proceedings. Criminal charges are initiated when the procurator encounters a violation of the criminal codes. He transfers the case to the Department of Investigations and Prosecution, and it eventually goes to the people's court. Disciplinary punishments may be imposed by administrative organs, economic enterprises, and social organizations to sanction their own members. Finally, administrative punishments may be imposed only by special bodies invested with those powers (*e.g.* the police, inspectorates, and game wardens).

Corrective relief frequently is sought in those cases in which someone has suffered material damages as a result of an illegal administrative action. For instance, procuratorial protests against the illegal firing of workers usually direct enterprises to reinstate workers and pay back wages. Corrective relief is frequently employed also when personal property has been illegally seized.

Soviet law also recognizes material responsibility of citizens, officials, and corporate bodies. In contrast to corrective relief, material responsibility is more symbolic than corrective in that it does not attempt to compensate for specific damages. Measures of material responsibility are imposed apart from administrative, disciplinary, or criminal punishments. The procurator merely poses the question of material responsibility, while guilt of the person or institution and the imposition of a fine or other punishment is determined by the court. In practice, material responsibility has been used to strengthen penalties for official negligence concerning technical safety and anti-pollution regulations.

Procurators may also recommend that cases be transferred to comrades' courts or commissions on minors for disposition. However, the transfer of cases to comrades' courts occurs relatively infrequently. For example, in 1968 in L'vov *oblast'*, comrades' courts heard 15,292 cases. Of these, only 517 (3.4%) were directed to them by procurators. [51] Similarly, in Khmel'nitskii *oblast'*, 394 of 15,282 (2.6%) cases were transferred to comrades' courts by procurators. [52]

Essential to most campaigns against crime in the economic and administrative sectors are follow-up investigations and inspections to check on compliance. For example, the city procuracy in Kokchetav in the Kazakh republic in 1976 conducted a campaign against theft of state property from enterprises and observance of technical safety regulations. Procurators inspected 23 enterprises and construction sites. The Procuracy issued representations directed at the violations they uncovered and recommended disciplinary punishments and criminal prosecution for several managers. After a short period of time, inspections were repeated at the same enterprises and continued periodically for more than a year. [53]

In our survey of 180 procurators, 77% actively check up on the measures which officials claim to be implementing in response to representations. Approximately 40% rely on special follow-up investigations, 24% rely on periodic, planned inspections, 12% check informally by contacting the official who receive the original representation, and 23% do not check at all. [54]

Not only do campaigns aim at detection and prosecution of violators, but they also seek to draw attention to violations and stimulate preventive action. The press campaigns which accompany most procuratorial campaigns against crime are intended to inform citizens, officials, procurators, and managers, and encourage them to be vigilant in preventing violations. According to S. G. Berezovskaia and K. F. Skvortsov of the Institute of the Procuracy, cases are carefully selected for publication in *Sotsialisticheskaia Zakonnost'* in order to present cases that are either typical, or in some cases indicative of

160

violations which have not heretofore been adequately handled by procurators. [55]

Similar to the role of the press in educating the public to violations, procurators frequently present reports and lectures to sessions of Soviets, trade union councils, social organizations, and worker collectives. According to a study by V. T. Mikhailov and V. I. Shind of the Institute of the Procuracy, 20% of the working time of procurators in departments of general supervision is devoted to public information activities. [56] The number of reports to local Soviets by procurators has increased significantly in recent years, from approximately 10,000 in 1968 to 19,000 in 1969, 22,377 in 1971, and 25,290 in 1972. [57] The number of reports of procurators to enterprises, institutions, social organizations, and worker collectives is also quite high. For instance, in 1969 there were more than 25,000 such reports and 28,000 in 1970. [58] In addition, in 1969 procurators gave more than 200,000 public lectures and authored more than 27,000 articles in newspapers and popular journals. [59] Compared with 1961, procuratorial reports to worker collectives in 1970 had increased 16 times. [60] Social assistants have been especially active in this area, presenting more than 20,000 reports to Soviets in 1970. All these efforts are designed to raise the level of citizen awareness of legal violations.

Two specific institutions merit special attention for their work in preventing violations in factories, enterprises, shops, and collective and state farms. They are the Councils of Prophylaxis and the People's Control. In most enterprises and factories, Councils of Prophylaxis exist to assist procurators, Party officials, and factory managers in detecting violations and recommending measures to prevent them. These councils function, in essence, as committees subordinate to the primary Party organizations. The members of the Councils of Prophylaxis are Party members who volunteer their time. The councils report regularly to the local Party cell and the *raikom* on conditions that may lead to violations of labor discipline in factories and enterprises.

Similar in function to the Councils of Prophylaxis are the local organs of the People's Control. Established soon after the revolution in 1917 under the direction of the All-Russian Council of Workers' Control, these bodies are charged with checking the fulfillment of state plans, labor productivity, reduction of administrative costs, and maintenance of state property. The Council of Workers' Control was reorganized in 1919 into the People's Commissariat for State Control of the RSFSR. Today, the name has been changed to the Committee of the People's Control and it is subordinate to the USSR Council of Ministers. There are people's control committees in all geographic regions, and each factory, collective and state farm, and social organization. In order to fulfill their responsibilities, organs of the people's control have the right to carry out raids of factories and enterprises and to inspect documents and question officials. In addition, they have the power to censure persons responsible for violations and may transfer cases to the comrades' courts or the Procuracy.

4. The Role of Campaigns in Soviet Judicial Administration

Campaigns against crime assume a central position in the Soviet system of criminal justice. In actuality, campaigns serve four separate functions: (1) to uncover, punish and, by example, prevent violations; (2) to communicate new policies or laws to officials and the public; (3) to inform Party and state officials of the state of legality in a region; and (4) to provide an outlet for ritualistic participation in government.

The most obvious function of campaigns against crime is the creation of a disincentive for managers or other officials to take shortcuts. The shift in emphasis of procuratorial activity in the mid-1960s from grievance cases to economic violations was just such an example.

While the uncovering and punishing of violators is a central function of the Procuracy, there has been some sensitivity to the fact that inspections can result in procuratorial interference in the operation of factories, enterprises, and collective and state farms. An order of the Procurator-General in 1964 specifically addressed this danger and warned procurators to limit the scope of their supervision to legal, as opposed to economic, managerial, or administrative questions. [62]

As we have seen in relation to the campaigns against the imposition of administrative fines in 1961-1962, campaigns also may be used to publicize and inform procurators, comrades' courts, Party officials, and judges of how to handle cases relating to new laws or policies.

Campaigns also communicate to officials, and the public, issues which trouble the political leadership. The periodic campaigns against hooliganism and alcoholism are not intended so much to apprehend and prosecute alcoholics, as to raise public and official concern over the issue of alcoholism and other forms of anti-social (and uneconomic) behavior.

Campaigns serve a useful function in informing Party and state officials of the extent of various violations in the Soviet Union. Anyone who has attempted to conduct research in the area of Soviet law is aware of the serious difficulties in obtaining accurate statistical data. For the most part, crime statistics are classified and unavailable to Western scholars. Our Soviet counterparts do not have it much easier, however, when they attempt to assess the level of crime in their society. Boris Polikarpovich Kochetov, chief of the Department of General Supervision of the Leningrad Procuracy, explained that he frequently organizes procuratorial campaigns against particular types of violations or particular sectors of the economy just to discover as he puts it, "the state of legality." [63] Thus, procuratorial supervision not only attempts to punish and deter violations, it also functions as a barometer of "the state of legality." Presumably, the information acquired by these campaigns is filtered to higher levels and used to redirect procuratorial practices and Party policy nationwide.

Finally, campaigns against crime provide an opportunity for the regime to mobilize Party, state, and industrial officials, as well as average workers in support of general societal goals. Campaigns give substantive duties to Soviet "transmission belt" organizations, such as the Komsomol, trade-unions, and *druzhiny*, integrating them into the process of policy implementation and supervision. The ritualistic function of campaigns is especially evident in the area of economic crimes, which have resulted in much popular preventive activity within factories. Hooliganism and parasitism have also prompted considerable public involvement, not only in factories, but also in housing blocks, neighborhoods, and social organizations.

A final question of campaigns against crime in the Soviet Union is the effect they have on legality and procedural due process. Theoretically, campaigns could result in a higher standard of legality by encouraging the more efficient enforcement of rules. However, as Pomorski maintains, campaigns may also result in the abandonment of rules for the sake of expediency. [64] "Anti-crime campaigns ... tend to blur the line between administration, governed by considerations of expediency, and adjudication, governed by impersonal, general rules." [65] The degree to which campaigns result in a retreat from due process may well depend on the level and degree of Party involvement in the campaign. There is little doubt that the anti-parasite campaigns of the early 1960s were instituted at the initiative of the highest Party elite. Those campaigns were notorious for producing summary justice. On the other hand, the rather routine, cyclical campaigns against economic violations are instituted and coordinated locally and are general much less "politicized."

At present, there is not enough empirical data to verify or refute the broad claim that campaigns against crime in the Soviet Union deliver "political justice." What is clear in all campaigns is that procurators and other juridical cadres have very little discretion in selectively enforcing laws which fall within the purview of the campaign.

Emerging from the above analysis of campaigns is the central role the Procuracy plays in coordinating the administration of justice in the USSR. Procurators occupy a crucial linkage point between the Party and the rest of the law enforcement and judicial apparatus. That position entails both political dangers and political opportunities. During a campaign, the dangers may well outweigh the opportunities. But it is to the credit of the Procuracy that campaigns against crime during the Brezhnev era have been less frequent, less politicized, and more routinized than those of previous regimes.

NOTES

1. B. B. Khangel'dyev, "Osobennosti kodifikatsii sovetskogo administrativnogo prava v sovremennyi period" (Features of the Codification of Contemporary Soviet Administrative Law), in *Materialy konferentsii po itogam nauchno-issledovatel'skoi raboty* (Materials of a Conference on the Results of Scientific Research Work), (Sverdlovsk, 1968), p. 11.

2. R. F. Vasil'ev, "Nekotorye voprosy suzheniia sfery administrativnogo prinuzhdeniia," (Several Questions on Reducing the Sphere of Administrative Coercion), *VMU (pravo)*, 1965, No. 4, 66-74.

3. *Ibid.*

4. Decree of the Presidium of the Supreme Soviet of the USSR of June 21, 1961, "O dal'neishem ogranichenii primeneniia shtrafov, nalagaemykh v administrativnom poriadke" (On the Further Limitation of Application of Fines, Imposed by Administrative Procedure), *Ved. V.S. SSSR*, 1961, No. 35, item 368.

5. M. S. Studenikina, *Zakonodatel'stvo ob administrativnoi otvetstvennosti i problemy ego kodifikatsii.* (Legislation on Administrative Responsibility and Problems of its Codification), (Unpublished candidate dissertation, All-Union Scientific-Research Institute on Soviet Legislation, Moscow, 1968), p. 46.

6. D. M. Chechot, *Administrativnaia iustitsiia* (Administrative Justice), (Leningrad, 1973), p. 82.

7. *Ibid.*

8. Studenikina, *op. cit.*, p. 48.

9. *Ugolovnyi kodeks RSFSR*, article 206, cited in Peter H. Solomon, Jr., *Soviet Criminologists and Criminal Policy* (New York, 1978), p. 81.

10. *Ibid.*, pp. 81-90.

11. *Ibid.*, p. 88.

12. N. V. Zhogin, *Bor'ba s khuliganstvom—delo vsekh i kazhdogo* (Fight Against Hooliganism—A Concern of Each and Everyone), (Moscow, 1967), pp. 7-9.

13. "Press-konferentsiia tsentral'nogo televideniia Prokuratury SSSR i Verkhovnogo Suda SSSR" (A Press Conference of the Central Television Network by the Procuracy of the USSR and the Supreme Court of the USSR), *Sots. Zak.*, 1966, No. 11.

14. For example, see Walter Gellhorn, *Ombudsmen and Others* (Cambridge, 1967), pp. 336-371; and Darrell P. Hammer, *USSR: The Politics of Oligarchy* (Hillsdale, Ill., 1974), p. 347.

15. These figures were calculated by Professors Moorsteen and Powell at the Yale University Economic Growth Center and cited in *The Economist*, June 8, 1968, 42.

16. Cited in Karl W. Ryavec, "Soviet Industrial Managers, Their Supervisors and the Economic Reform: A Study of an Attempt at Planned Behavioral Change," *Soviet Studies*, October 1969, 220.

17. Robert F. Miller, "The Scientific-Technical Revolution and the Soviet Administrative Debate," in Paul Cocks, *et al.* (eds.), *The Dynamics of Soviet Politics* (Cambridge, Mass., 1976), pp. 137-155.

18. For example, "Obzor otklikov na materialy k teme 'Nauchnoe rukovodstvo sotsial'nymi protsessami' " (Survey of Responses on Materials on the Theme "The Scientific Management of Social Processes"), *Kommunist* (Communist), 1965, No. 17, 62;

V. G. Afanasev, "Nauchnoe rukovodstvo sotsial'nymi protsessami" (The Scientific Management of Social Processes), *Kommunist* (Communist), 1965, No. 14, 58-73; and B. A. Chagin, *Subektivnyi faktor: struktura i zakonomernosti* (The Subjective Factor: Structure and Conformity with the Law), (Moscow, 1968).

19. For example, V. T. Kvitkin, "Voprosy sootnosheniia sudebnogo kontrolia s drugimi vidami kontrolia i nadzora" (Questions of the Correlation of Court Control with Other Forms of Control and Supervision), *VMU (pravo)*, 1968, No. 1, 54-61; and K. F. Skvortsov, "K postroeniiu modeli prestupnogo povedeniia" (Toward the Construction of a Model of Criminal Behavior), in *Voprosy ugolovnogo prava, ugolovnogo protsessa i kriminologii* (Questions of Criminal Law, Criminal Process and Criminology), (Dushanbe, 1966), pp. 158-166.

20. George Breslauer, "Khrushchev Reconsidered," *Problems of Communism*, March 1976, 66-71.

21. V. Kim and L. Ivanov, "Nadzor za ispolneniem zakonov ob otvetstvennosti za nedobrokachestvennoe stroitel'stvo" (Supervision of Execution of Laws on Accountability for Substandard Construction), *Sots. Zak.*, 1975, No. 5, 35-38.

22. *Ibid.*

23. Two other means of uncovering administrative violations are used much less frequently. At one time, procuratorial offices required that all administrative regulations, instructions, decisions, and orders be forwarded to the procurator for obligatory review. However, this practice swamped procuratorial offices in a flood of paperwork and was discontinued in the mid-1960s. Presently, procurators selectively monitor these documents. Procurators also occasionally review administrative violations brought to light during the course of investigations by people's courts or comrades' courts.

24. Statute on Procuratorial Supervision in the USSR, May 24, 1955, article 14, *Ved. V.S. SSSR*, 1955, No. 9, item 222.

25. Procuratorial contact with these organizations is quite extensive and constant. For instance, *raion* and city procurators in Kiev, Khmel'nitskii, Dnepropetrovsk, and Ternopol' *oblasti* in 1967 and 1968 participated in 70 to 75% of all executive committee sessions of Soviets. Iu. S. Shemshuchenko, *Obespechenie zakonnosti v deiatel'nosti mestnykh organov sovetskogo gosudarstvennogo upravleniia sredstvami prokurorskogo nadzora* (Insuring the Legality in the Actions of Local Organs of Soviet State Administration by Means of Procuratorial Supervision), (Unpublished candidate dissertation, Institute of State and Law, Ukrainian Academy of Sciences, Kiev, 1969), p. 195. Kochetov claims that this figure is low. In Leningrad, procurators participate in every executive committee session and almost every session of administrative commissions. Consultation with B. P. Kochetov, chief of the Department of General Supervision, Leningrad *prokuratura*, April 26, 1976.

26. Statute on Procuratorial Supervision in the USSR, *op. cit.*, article 11.

27. Data provided by the Laboratory for the Study of Procuratorial Supervision, Juridical Faculty, Leningrad State University.

28. V. I. Shind, "O sovershenstvovanii zakonodatel'stva o prokurorskom nadzore v SSSR" (On the Perfection of Legislation on Procuratorial Supervision in the USSR), in N. V. Zhogin (ed.), *Sovershenstvovanie prokurorskogo nadzora v SSSR* (The Perfection of Procuratorial Supervision in the USSR), (Moscow, 1973), p. 134.

29. However, Iu S. Shemshuchenko presents evidence showing that signals are not necessary for successful procuratorial action. Of a sample of 150 illegal decisions of local executive committees of Soviets in the Ukraine, only 52 (34.7%) were protested as a result of receiving a signal. Iu. S. Shemshuchenko, *op. cit.*, p. 167. The conflict of Shemshuckenko's and Shind's data may be explained in part by the fact that signals of violations play a much more important role in uncovering violations in enterprises and social organizations, with whom procurators do not maintain constant contact. By con-

trast, local procurators actively monitor the decisions of local executive committees, thus obviating the need for the receipt of signals.

30. "Kompleksnoe planirovanie i edinstvo deistvii v bor'be s narusheniiami zakona" (Complex Planning and the Unity of Actions in the Fight With Legal Violations), *Sots. Zak.*, 1977, No. 10, 44-47.

31. U. Seitov, "Organizatsiia raboty po preduprezhdeniiu prestuplenii nesovershennoletnykh" (Organization of the Work on the Prevention of Juvenile Crime), *Sots. Zak.*, 1977, No. 12, 26-28.

32. I. Sadovskii, "Planirovanie bor'by s prestupnost'iu" (Planning Campaigns Against Crime), *Sots. Zak.*, 1977, No. 10, 34-36.

33. *Ibid.*

34. L. A. Nikolaeva, *Teoreticheskie i prakticheskie problemy obespecheniia zakonnosti v sovetskom gosudarstvennom upravlenii organami prokuratury i suda* (Theoretical and Practical Problems in Insuring the Legality of Soviet State Administration by the Organs of the Procuracy and the Court), (Unpublished doctoral dissertation, Leningrad State University, 1974), p. 181. The rapid increase of investigations is corroborated by S. G. Berezovskaia and T. L. Markelov in "Nadzor za zakonnost'iu aktov organov upravleniia" (Supervision of the Legality of Acts of Administrative Organs), *Sots. Zak.*, 1974, No. 12, 18. At the *oblast'* level, procuratorial investigations frequently number 200 to 300 annually. See Iu,. S. Shemshuchenko, *op. cit.*, p. 182.

35. Gellhorn, *op. cit.*, p. 358.

36. S. G. Berezovskaia, *Prokurorskii nadzor za zakonnost'iu pravovykh aktov organov upravleniia v SSSR* (Procuratorial Supervision of the Legality of Legal Acts of Organs of Administration in the USSR), (Moscow, 1959), pp. 52-53.

37. For example, see I. Ivanov, "Preduprezhdenie pravonarushenii—vazhnaia zabota partiinykh i obshchestvennykh organizatsii" (Prevention of Legal Violations—The Important Task of Party and Social Organizations), *Sots. Zak.*, 1977, No. 9, 28-32; A. Shchelochinin, "Za vypusk nedobrokachestvennoi produktsii—k otvetstvennosti" (For the Production of Substandard Production—To Accountability), *Sots. Zak.*, 1977, No. 7, 16-19; A. Narozhnyi, "Organizatsiia prokurorskoi proverki ispolneniia zakonov o trude na predpriiatii" (Organization of Procuratorial Investigations of the Execution of Laws on Labor in Enterprises), *Sots. Zak.*, 1977, No. 6, 46-47; and A. D. Berenzon, V. G. Melkumov, *Rabota prokurora po obshchemu nadzoru* (The Work of the Procurator Concerning General Supervision), (Moscow, 1974), p. 27.

38. Berenzon and Melkumov, *Ibid.*

39. Shchelochinin, *op. cit.*, pp. 16-19.

40. Berenzon and Melkuvom, *op. cit.*, p. 27.

41. Ivanov, *op. cit.*, pp. 28-32.

42. V. Kuznetsov, "Effektivnost' obshchenadzornoi raboty" (The Effectiveness of General Supervision Work), *Sots. Zak.*, 1977, No. 3, 12-14.

43. Ivanov, *op. cit.*, pp. 28-32.

44. Resolution of the Council of People's Commissars of the RSFSR, "Ob iuriskonsul'takh gosudarstvennykh uchrezhdenii i predpriiatii i kooperativnykh organizatsii i o nadzore za ikh deiatel'nost'iu" (On Jurisconsults in State Enterprises and Establishments and Cooperative Organizations and on the Supervision of Their Activity), March 30, 1927, *Sobr. Zak. RSFSR*, No. 36, item 238; also available in *Sovetskaia prokuratura: sbornik vazhneishikh dokumentov* (The Soviet Procuracy: Collection of the Most Important Documents), (Moscow, 1972), pp. 174-175.

45. Data provided by the Laboratory for the Study of Procuratorial Supervision, Juridical Faculty, Leningrad State University.

46. *Ibid.*

47. *Ibid.*

48. For example, see V. G. Rozenfeld, *Prokurorskii nadzor za sobliudeniem zakonnosti dolzhnostnykh lits predpriiatii* (Procuratorial Supervision of Observance of the Legality of Officials in Enterprises), (Voronezh, 1973), pp. 49-51.

49. Narozhnyi, *op. cit.*, pp. 46-47.

50. Survey data provided by the Laboratory for the Study of Procuratorial Supervision, Juridical Faculty, Leningrad State University.

51. I. V. Mart'ianov, *Prokurorskii nadzor—sposob obespecheniia zakonnosti v rabote organizatsii obshchestvennoi samodeiatel'nosti* (Procuratorial Supervision—A Method of Insuring Legality in the Work of Organizations by Social Independent Action), (L'vov, 1973), p. 64.

52. *Ibid.*

53. Seitov, *op. cit.*, pp. 26-28.

54. Survey data provided by the Laboratory for the Study of Procuratorial Supervision, Juridical Faculty, Leningrad State University.

55. Consultation with S. G. Berezovskaia and K. F. Skvortsov, Institute of the Procuracy of the USSR, November 26, 1975.

56. Cited in S. G. Berezovskaia, "Glasnost' v deiatel'nosti sovetskoi prokuratury" (Publicity in the Activity of the Soviet Procuracy), in Zhogin, *op. cit.*, p. 117.

57. The figures for 1969 come from G. S. Murashin, *Organy prokuratury v mekhanizme sovetskogo gosudarstva* (Organs of the Procuracy in the Mechanism of the Soviet State), (Kiev, 1972), p. 108. The figures for other years come from Berezovskaia, *ibid.*, p. 122.

58. Murashin, *ibid.*, and V. K. Zvirbul', *Diatel'nost' prokuratury po preduprezhdeniiu prestupnosti* (Activity of the Procuracy in the Prevention of Crime), (Moscow, 1971), p. 162.

59. Murashin, *ibid.*

60. Zvirbul', *op. cit.*, p. 162.

61. Nikolaeva, *op. cit.*, p. 121.

62. Order of the Procurator-General of the USSR, No. 55, of July 4, 1964, "O merakh uluchsheniia raboty organov prokuratury po obshchemu nadzoru" (On Measures for Improving the Work of Organs of the Procuracy Concerning General Supervision), cited in Berenzon and Melkumov, *op. cit.*, p. 33.

63. Consultation with B. P. Kochetov, chief of the Department of General Supervision, Leningrad Procurary, April 26, 1976.

64. S. Pomorski, "Criminal Law Protection of Socialist Property in the USSR," in D. Barry, G. Ginsburgs, P. Maggs (eds.), *Soviet Law After Stalin, Part I, The Citizen and The State in Contemporary Soviet Law* (Leyden, 1977), p. 235.

65. *Ibid.*

JURISCONSULTS IN THE
SOVIET ECONOMY

Yuri Luryi*

According to the definition in *Black's Law Dictionary* and *Webster's New Collegiate Dictionary*[1], a jurisconsult is a person versed in international and public law. Such a definition, however, is very far from conforming with the reality of the activity of the tens of thousands of Soviet jurisconsults. The overwhelming majority of jurisconsults in the Soviet Union have nothing to do with international law. As a rule, they also have no knowledge of public law, inasmuch as this term is considered by Soviet jurists to pertain to bourgeois law.

Soviet jurisconsults are lawyers who work in industrial enterprises, agriculture, construction organizations, cultural institutions, in scientific-research or design institutes, in the organs of administrative management, or many of the other enterprises, institutions, and organizations which characterize Soviet society.

Apparently there is no English equivalent for this term, nor a translation which covers the range of its meaning in Russian. The term is not synonymous with In-House Counsel, Legal Adviser, Law Officer, or Corporate Solicitor. It is no accident that Donald D. Barry and Harold Berman,[2] Earl Johnson,[3] Jane Giddings,[4] and Samuel Kucherov[5] in their works on the Soviet legal system/profession preferred to retain the Soviet term jurisconsult, without attempting to translate it into English. The compilers of *Black's Law, Webster's,* and other such dictionaries would be well advised to follow their example and append to their definition of jurisconsult an additional entry: "Jurisconsult in the Soviet Union."

In this study, I propose to give an account of the work of the Soviet jurisconsult. Primary attention shall be given to a consideration of those peculiarities which distinguish his work from that of Western jurists who are attached to industrial and commercial companies. In addition, an attempt shall be made to explicate the changes in the position of the Soviet jurisconsult in the post-Stalinist period and especially in the 1970s.

* I am grateful to Professor Bernard Rudden for the many valuable remarks and suggestions he made at the August 1978 Conference at the University of Leyden.

1. A Short History

Jurisconsults before the Revolution

The profession of jurisconsults is encountered even in the pre-revolutionary period. Legal sections and the posts of jurisconsults had been established in the government ministeries and even in the central departments of the ministeries. They existed, for example, in the Ministry of Finance and in the Administration for the Construction of Railways. The post of jurisconsults similarly was attached to the chancellery of the "Ober-Procuror" of the Holy Synod, and to the Chief of Police who was the head of the "Third Section personally in the hands of his Majesty's Chancellery,"[6] in charge of matters of state security. The latter circumstance provoked Iablonsky, a member of the Kharkov Judicial Chamber, to comment: "I cannot understand it, it is impossible to understand it! A jurisconsult attached to the Third Section? It is the same to say, "Priests attached to a whorehouse".[7] We should note that this remark attests not only to the skeptical attitude of the observer towards the Third Section, but also to the esteem in which the profession of jurisconsult was held.

The responsibilities of the jurisconsult included the examination of legal questions, as they arose, as well as the conduct of cases of litigation in the capacity of state's attorney. The decisions of the jurisconsult did not have to conform with those of the Minister or the head of the Department.[8] In contrast to his present day Soviet colleagues, pre-revolutionary jurisconsults were, as a rule, members of the Bar and were able to combine their work for the Ministry or the Department with the conduct of private cases in their capacity as barristers. In certain instances, their work as jurisconsults provided them with their principal, chief and stable earnings. The famous Russian jurist, A. F. Koni, recounted that after the acquittal of Vera Zasulich (who had attempted to assassinate the Governor of Petersburg and Chief of the City Police, F. F. Trepov), the Junior Assistant Prosecutor of the Petersburg Regional Court, S. A. Andreevskii, was dismissed for refusing to act as prosecutor in the case. Immediately after his dismissal, Andreevskii entered into the Bar.

A. F. Koni noted that, although Andreevskii was somewhat embarrassed in the short run due to his lack of practical experience, with Koni's help he succeeded in obtaining a post as jurisconsult with an International Bank. This position provided Andreevskii "with a sufficiently stable material position."[9]

Jurisconsults after the Revolution

In the first years following the establishment of Soviet power, jurisconsults practically ceased to exist. Nationalized enterprises, having become state property, lost their autonomy. They lost their budgets (internal financing), and thereby ceased to have any economic independence. In a word, they

169

ceased to be juridical persons. Their need for legal services also vanished. The fundamental legal order for Soviet economic organizations became their planned tasks (*promfinplan*), which had the force of law.

Legal workers/jurisconsults, like the law itself, were declared to pertain to bourgeois society. On the basis of Marx, the most eminent theoreticians of the period of War Communism, Bukharin, Stuchka, Reisner, and Goikhbarg, proclaimed the imminent withering away of proletarian law and the state in Russia. Altough their principal printed works were only published a number of years after the Revolution, their theoretical conceptions had been put into practice almost immediately. This had not been difficult to accomplish since all of these men occupied positions either in the Party or the Government. This meant that their ideas were not only based on the power of authority, but also on the authority of power.

The introduction of the New Economic Policy inevitably entailed the development of civil law. The first Soviet Civil Code was instituted in 1922. In Stuchka's own words, this Code was taken almost entirely and verbatim from the best examples of Western Civil legislation. [10] Government economic enterprises acquired a certain autonomy. They began to operate on the basis of their own budgets, and gained definite, although limited, rights of disposition, in addition to those of use and possession. They obtained the right to enter into contractual relations, to plead cases before the courts, and to respond to charges in the courts themselves. In short, Soviet enterprises came to possess all the requisites of the status of juridical persons. The formal reinstatement of the concept of the judicial person as a subject of law came with the introduction of article 13 of the Civil Code of the RSFSR in 1922.

It could be said that the reestablishment of private capitalist relations in the country provoked the genuine burgeoning of civil law. The necessity for legal services arose both in the government and in private economic organizations. To meet this need, the first Soviet jurisconsults came into being.

The functions performed by Soviet jurisconsults in the first years of their activity differed very little from those of their pre-revolutionary predecessors. They performed the ordinary tasks associated with such professional workers—providing legal information and advice, formulating agreements or giving them a legal appraisal, drawing up various necessary legal documents, (orders, claims, suits, etc.), and representing the interests of their enterprises in court or before *arbitrazh*. Jurisconsults were subordinated to the manager of the enterprise and bore the same disciplinary responsibility as other white collar workers.

In 1922 the Moscow Soviet, at the request of the Moscow Bar (College of Defenders), passed a resolution "On the recognition of the permissibility of the joint holding of the title of member of the Bar and the maintenance of a position in a government institution or enterprise." [11] The right to such a joint position, however, appears not to have been automatic, but, in conformance with the decision of the Regional Court, required separate applications in each case. Petitions had to be submitted both from the Presidium of the Bar and the corresponding government institution. [12] The right of a member of the Bar to act as a jurisconsult did not extend to enterprises in the private sector. Even a single instance of aid to a private enterprise was considered a reprehensible act. Members of the Bar who were also communists were usually prohibited from appearing in court on the side of "bourgeois elements" in their disputes with government of cooperative organizations or with their workers. [13] The defense of such enterprises was associated with considerable risk, even to non-party members. The Presidium of the Moscow College of Defenders disbarred a member of the College, D. M. Nechaev, in 1923 as a result of his having "taken upon himself functions incompatible with his membership in the College." Nechaev had acted as a mediator in a conflict between the manager of the enterprise Reshetnikov and Company and the workers at that enterprise. Nechaev was the representative of the firm at the sessions of the Rates and Disputes Commission—the organ which permanently functioned on the basis of the labor legislation at that time. [14] His second sin consisted of the fact that he questioned the legality of the workers' claim that they had the right to remove icons from the factory premises. Nechaev adjudged this action to have been a willful seizure of property which did not belong to the workers. This in spite of the fact that the Chairman of the Factory Trade Union Committee was involved in the incident. Nechaev maintained that the establishment by the People's Commissariat of Justice of the RSFSR of a prohibition against the hanging of icons "in government and other public social premises" did not apply to privately-owned factory premises. He therefore determined the worker's action to have been arbitrary. The Presidium of the College found that Nechaev "had deviated from his direct duty and had acted exclusively as the servant of the bourgeoisie for money." It is interesting that the Moscow Regional Soviet manifested greater indulgence towards Nechaev than did his colleagues and softened the punishment, limiting his indefinite exclusion to a period of a single year. [15]

It does not necessarily follow, however, that the reader should consider that staff jurisconsults, who were not members of the Bar, could be overlooked. They all belonged to what were known as *spetsy*. This term was applied to all people who had acquired a university education before the Revolution and who did not belong to either the category of worker or peasant. These individuals were necessarily tolerated by the new power as a result of their skills, but were treated with suspicion. The Senior Assistant of the Procurator of the RSFSR, N. Krylenko, reported in June 1924 that many of the staff of the local Procuracy were interested in knowing the methods by which the work of jurisconsults attached to Soviet institutions were to be "regulated." He indicated two possibilities: 1) the centralization of the management of jurisconsults in the executive committees of the Provincial Soviets of Worker-Peasants and Red Army Deputies; 2) the convocation of periodic conferences of jurisconsults with the participation and under the supervision of the procurators. [16] Six months later, Krylenko was compelled to come out against the excessively energetic attempts of the procurators to subordinate the jurisconsults to themselves. He recommended to the procurators that they "should not be carried away" in sending their instructions directly to jurisconsults, bypassing their superiors, as the immediate direction of jurisconsults should remain with their supervisors. Krylenko also warned the procurators against various "exceptional measures, such as the institution of various examinations, demands for dismissals, etc.", emphasizing once again the value of conferences in which the procurators could participate, and through which they could exercise supervision. [17]

These jurisconsults who were attached to enterprises in the field of heavy industry attempted to free themselves from the procurator's wardship tutelage. On June 27, 1925, the Supreme Economic Council issued a statute concerning jurisconsults in government enterprises which were subordinated to it, and also ratified a statute on the Bureau of Jurisconsults which was to be attached to the All-Union, Republican, and Provincial Departments of the Supreme Economic Council. [18] These Bureaus were called upon to coordinate the work of jurisconsults and to convene various conferences. The participation of the procurators in such conferences was not mentioned, however. The responsibilities of jurisconsults were clearly delimited within a legal framework by these statutes: the imposition of administration functions on jurisconsults was not to be tolerated (article 4); their conclusion on legal questions were to be considered as opinions and would not be binding on the management of the enterprise; jurisconsults would only be held responsible for the legal aspects of the contracts concluded by the enterprise, not for their economic advisability nor for the choice of parties in the concluded agreement (article 5); the responsibilities of the jurisconsults did not include overseeing the fulfillment of the requirements of agreements nor the settling of accounts resulting from these agreements (article 8).

The reaction of the procurators was not long in coming. In the Spring of 1926, the People's Commissar of Justice and the Procurator of the Republic, Kurskii, communicated a special circulating letter to all regional, district, and provincial procurators and judges. This circular, in turn, dealt with the question of the establishment of "the fullest possible supervision over the activity of jurisconsults" and demanded the urgent despatch of the necessary information for the drafting of new legislation. [19] Within a year, the work was completed.

The first legislative act defining the activity of jurisconsults, their tasks, and responsibilities, "On Jurisconsults in Government Institutions, Enterprises, and Cooperative Organizations, and on the Supervision of their Activity," was issued by the Council of People's Commissars of the RSFSR on

March 30, 1927.[20] It would be inappropriate to suggest that this legislation entrusted jurisconsults with any new duties.

The restrictions imposed by the statute, rather than the duties enumerated, constituted a departure from previous practice. As a result of this legislation: 1) Only people who had not been deprived of suffrage could act as jurisconsults (to be a "deprivee" (*lishenets*), it was sufficient not to have a "worker-peasant lineage"); 2) Jurisconsults were prohibited from working for private enterprises; 3) Jurisconsults were prohibited from defending the interests of private persons or private enterprises against government or cooperative organizations; 4) Jurisconsults were prohibited, as a rule, from performing administrative functions in enterprises in which they acted as jurisconsults.

The question of supervision or "control" over the jurisconsults was also resolved by this Statute. General supervision over jurisconsults was placed in the hands of the procurators at the republican and district levels. In order to implement this control, "conferences" (*soveshchaniia*) were instituted and attached to the provincial procurator's office. All local jurisconsults as well as representatives of the courts and members of arbitration and land commissions were to be included in these conferences. These "conferences" attached to the procurator's office proved to be shortlived instruments for exercising control. The wave of terror which commenced in the last years of the 1920s and characterized the 1930s brought with it newer and more terrible conferences: "The Special Conferences (*soveshchaniia*) attached to the People's Commissariat for Internal Affairs"—otherwise known as the *troiki*. Few remember the original conferences.

The role and importance of jurisconsults grew with the development of economic law. The credit reforms of the 1930s, the expanded use of *khozraschet*, the institution of state *arbitrazh* for the resolution of disputes between economic organizations, and the establishment of special procedures for the consideration of economic disputes; all promoted this development.

The issuance in 1926 of the second Criminal Code of the RSFSR, in which the criminal liability for crimes committed by officials was increased dramatically in comparison with the 1922 Code, resulted in jurisconsults expanding their functions. They were no longer considered merely the defenders of the enterprises' interests, but also as useful advisers to the managers themselves, safeguarding them from dangerous mistakes and consequent personal liability.

Unexpected Alternatives

Jurisconsults were confronted with a choice in 1939, either to act as jurisconsults or as lawyers. The new statutes of that year concerning the Bar rescinded those provisions which had previously enabled lawyers to be members of the Bar and staff jurisconsults at the same time.[21] Although in the Statute on the Advocacy, among other tasks, the provision of legal aid to enterprises, institutions, and other organizations, on the basis of contracts between organizations and legal offices was permitted, the permanent attachment of a lawyer to any single organization was forbidden. This was considered as a "concealed pluralism." The army of jurisconsults not only decreased, but the quality of those remaining worsened. Many talented jurisconsults preferred to give up their work in order to remain at the Bar. On the other hand, those who left the Bar remaining as jurisconsults did not establish any alternative organizational entity. The severing of their connection with the Bar was reflected in a decline in the quality of the work performed by these jurisconsults. Within the Bar, lawyers had the opportunity to perfect their skills, take various courses, study new legislation and its application, and discuss complex cases encountered in their work. This constant and useful aid was forfeited by staff jurisconsults.

The number of enterprises served by the Bar, however, did not increase. Many managers of organizations were not interested in working with a number of different lawyers, preferring to have the same lawyer attached to their organization. As a result, a significant number of enterprises remained without jurisconsults. The act, which in its conception was intended to be "anti-lawyers," turned out to be anti-economic and produced complaints from both sides.

The situation changed at the beginning of 1941 when *Narkomiust* permitted the attachment of lawyers to enterprises and other organizations. The price schedule on various aspects of jurisconsults' work was maintained, but responsibility for the "imposition of control over the provision of legal aid services to institutions, enterprises, and organizations" by the colleges was entrusted to regional directorates of justice. [22] The existence of two independent groups of jurisconsults in the USSR dates from this period. One group consists of those on staff, the other of lawyers who serve by agreement with the legal consultation office of enterprises which do not have the post of jurisconsult on their staff schedules.

Each of these groups differs from the other both in their merits and their shortcomings. It was noted above that the lawyer-jurisconsults benefitted from the opportunity to improve their knowledge and exchange experiences. To this should be added their lesser dependence on the management of the organization being services. It would be a mistake to underestimate the significance of this fact. Let us recall the condition of the period. Beginning in the latter half of the 1930s, an additional feature of the Stalin cult became apparent, the mania of the cult of the mini-*vozhd'*. Such individuals personnally managed organizations of various sizes and in diverse areas of activity. The majority of the most talented managers of the nation's economy from the People's Commissars/Ministers and Heads of the Central Directorates or Trusts down to the directors of plants and the shop superintendants were eliminated by the terror of the 1930s. They were replaced in their posts by people who, for the most part, had been promoted from below as a result of their active "exposure of enemies of the people" at meetings, or by having distinguished themselves in their cooperation with the organs of the *NKVD*, whether hidden or direct, secret or open. It must have been supposed that their irreproachable worker-peasant lineage and political "scent" were sufficient compensation for their lack of knowledge and experience. They perceived the dictatorial methods of direction from above as the only correct method of direction within the organizations under their own supervision. Rudeness, demands that subordinates unquestioningly submit to any order, servile relations towards their own bosses on the one hand while maintaining a satrapy in relation to their underlings (especially the white collar workers) on the other, created a completely peculiar social climate in all spheres of activity, including the economic. The epoch of the "voluntary" (Khrushchev had a particular weakness for this term) decision ruled.

The inspection of the results of economic activity became more perfunctory and formalized. In particular, the least attention was addressed to those losses or unproductive expenditures of enterprises which were exonerated by the decision of a court or an arbitration tribunal. The fact of the imposition of a monetary fine or the refusal of compensation for losses to an enterprise had no significance and did not establish guilt so far as it was connected with the decision of government organs—either judicial or arbitrational. Consequently, *arbitrazh* tribunals and courts were overloaded with cases of unsubstantiated claims or, on the other hand, with demands which the respondents should have clearly satisfied without the necessity for the institution of proceedings. The single aim behind the creation of such cases was to obtain a decision of an arbitration tribunal or court which could be used in seeking indulgence with regard to inspections or the annual accounts of the firm's economic activity.

Under these circumstances, the jurisconsults on the staff of enterprises were compelled to fulfill the will of their chiefs without a murmur and to be prepared to take any position in the case, irrespective of their professional advice and independent of whether or not it coincided with the interests of the organization or the economy of the country as a whole. The only valid considerations were was it in any way welcome to the manager and did it threaten the jurisconsults' jobs.

The lawyer-jurisconsults were less dependent on the management of the enterprise than were their staff colleagues. This was due to the fact that they were subordinated to their own superiors, the presidium of the Bar and the managers of the consultation offices, from whom they could expect understanding and support. Additionally, this lack of dependence can be attributed to the fact that the manager of the enterprises could not generally discharge a lawyer-jurisconsult. They could, however, cancel contracts with the consultation office or request the services of a different lawyer. Such a repudiation of the services of a particular lawyer would not constitute a serious trauma. He would retain his basic work in the college, and if needed, it would not generally be difficult for him to find work with a different organization. The most significant advantages of having a jurisconsult on the staff of the organization would be his constant presence on the premises, and his thorough knowledge of all aspects of the organization.

One remaining distinction between the two types of jurisconsult is worthy of notice. Jurisconsults on the staff of enterprises or organizations frequently took on work of the greatest diversity, having no relation to their area of specialization. To refuse to have done so would have been risky. At the same time, lawyer-jurisconsults were able to evade participation in such work since they were hired on the basis of contracts which clearly defined and enumerated their duties. On the other hand, lawyer-jurisconsults were compelled, besides rendering legal services to organizations, to allocate a considerable amount of time to legal consultation and propaganda. This peculiarity, it is true, was not simply connected with their activity as jurisconsults. In the struggle for survival, in their constant efforts to demonstrate the usefulness of the Bar even in the conditions of the state at the dictatorship of the proletariat, to prove that the Bar went hand-in-hand with all the builders of socialism, lawyers from the very first days of their existence under Soviet conditions had placed upon their shoulders the fulfillment, without pay, of a number of services which the government customarily provides or finances. As a result, jurisconsult-lawyers were required to deliver lectures and talks in enterprises and other public places, to provide members of trade union organizations, comrades' courts, and other social organizations with consultations, and to render legal advice to the workers within the enterprises they served concerning personal matters unrelated to their work. These jurisconsults were required to provide their superiors with a monthly account of such public work. Lack of demand was not considered sufficient justification for a poor record. Jurisconsults were required to search for audiences and to display initiative in organizing lectures. In my experience, approximately sixteen lectures a month was considered appropriate. The text of the lectures had to be elaborated and approved by the Bar before their delivery. A few standard themes included: "Lenin and Stalin on socialist legality;" "Socialist property—sacred and inviolable;" "On the rules of behavior in socialist society." It is interesting to note here that since the beginning of the 1970s, the Party leadership have involved in this "enlightening" activity court workers, procurators, and militia. In my opinion, the way in which these lectures were presented rendered them a poor surrogate for legal education. [23] As before, this was necessary and strictly controlled work. In the post-Stalinist period, the themes were scarcely changed, despite the fact that, in the lecture "on socialist legality," Lenin was left without the company of his successor Stalin. Staff jurisconsults were not exempted from legal propaganda duties as well. We shall see below that, as of 1972, this became part of their professional responsibilities.

Jurisconsults under Khrushchev

The activity of jurisconsults attracted the attention of the state authorities again in the post-Stalinist period. On June 8, 1959, the Council of Ministers of the Ukraine ratified "A Model Statute on Jurisconsults in State Organizations." On March 29, 1963, the Council of Ministers of the RSFSR issued "A Model Statute on Legal (Contractual-Legal) Departments, Head (Senior) Jurisconsults, Jurisconsults of Enterprises, Institutions and Organizations."[24] Analogous statutes were issued in the same period in a number of other union republics.

The new and generally applicable situation was the tendency to include jurisconsults in the struggle against what were termed "localistic manifestations." The idea was to induce jurisconsults to defend only those interests of their enterprises which correspond with the general interest of the state. Jurisconsults were directed to refuse to take cases to court or *arbitrazh* in which their organizations position was "not founded on the law." The obligation was imposed on the jurisconsult to report any violations of the law which occurred in their organizations to higher authorities, if his immediate superior had not taken steps to eliminate the violation. In order to accomplish this goal, jurisconsults were granted a somewhat more independent status. Firstly, jurisconsults were subordinated to a single authority, the manager of the enterprise. Secondly, the hiring, transfer, or firing of a jurisconsult could only be accomplished with the agreement of higher organizations. The first of these innovations was clearly necessary. Jurisconsults, as a rule, had formerly been subordinated not to their immediate superiors, but to the firm's chief accountant or to one of the managers of a variety of sections of the enterprise (financial, personnel, or supply and sale). This practice had limited the independence of the jurisconsult and his ability to interfere in the work of the enterprise's many subdivisions.

According to the Soviet statistics cited by Barry and Berman, there were 20,309 jurisconsults in the USSR in 1959. My own estimate would be somewhat higher. First, one must take into account the large number of hidden jurisconsults who officially occupy other positions. This phenomenon occurs when the personnel schedule for the enterprise does not include the position of a jurist, despite the clear necessity for legal services. Secondly, in the 1950s in a number of cities in the RSSR, artels of disabled jurisconsults were organized. These artels concluded contracts for legal services with various enterprises on the same bases as the legal consultation offices of the Bar. The artels, in contrast to the latter, did not have the right to represent the interests of citizens in either civil or criminal proceedings, with the exception of tort cases involving work-related suits.

It cannot be said that the new status of jurisconsults introduced any essential changes in their work. Jurisconsults, as before, preferred not to mar their relations with their own managers, upon whom in the final analysis their fate resided, continuing to serve their "masters" and not the state as a whole. Experience demonstrated that the manager of an enterprise who was dissatisfied with this overly zealous legal adviser found little difficulty in procuring the necessary permission from higher authorities to dismiss him.

A system by means of which the work of jurisconsults could be regularly checked and through which their work would be brought into conformity with the new demands placed upon them had yet to be developed. Such a system was created later.

2. The Soviet Jurisconsult Today

The Reasons for the New Changes

The difficulties experienced in the Soviet economy in the first post-war decade could easily be attributed to the problems arising from and connected with the wartime devastation and reconstruction. The performance of the economy in the second postwar decade, however, was scarcely more remarkable. Although an analysis of the Soviet economy is not the subject of this work, there is a direct connection between the economic situation and the increased interest in the work of jurisconsults which unexpectedly arose in the Soviet Union in the 1970s.

The decentralization of the system of organization of the Soviet economy introduced under Khrushchev was countermanded after his fall and was replaced by a system of strict centralization. The results were not much better, and the difficulties were scarcely alleviated. In 1965 the Central Committee of the CPSU and the Council of Ministers of the USSR jointly issued a Statute "On the Improvement of Planning and the Strengthening of Economic Stimulation in Industrial Production," but the chaos in the planning system remained. From time to time, the Central Statistical Board of the USSR placed reports in the newspaper about unusual industrial successes, and comparisons of the achievements of the 1960s with 1913. However, in practice these achievements were little noted. In the early 1970s, a rumor circulated to the effect that Brezhnev stated at a session of the Politburo that if all the metal which the economic reports claimed had been produced, actually existed, and not simply on paper, that the country would not be faced with a deficit, but a surplus, of metal.

In 1961 the Central Committee and the Council of Ministers issued a resolution "On Measures for the Prevention of Criminal Deception of the State and for the Strengthening of Control over Authentic Accounts of Plan

Fulfillment and Liabilities." Sixteen years later the same alarming call was being issued for the "strengthening of the struggle against false reports." [25] This phenomenon, as before, testified to the epidemic character of the problem. For instance, the Deputy Chairman of the Supreme Court of the USSR, V. Kulikov, reported that in 1971 in the reports of the construction contractors of only two of the many ministeries fictitious work to the sum of 24.5 million rubles was discovered. [26] In my own observations, the amount of false reporting uncovered by the multitudinous control organizations comprises an insignificant part of this universal practice. The situation was not changed in the 1960s with the introduction of the new legislation—All-Union Fundamental Principles and the republican codes despite the fact that they were well harmonized.

The serious continuing shortfalls in industry as compared with the West (except perhaps in military areas) and the systematic insufficiencies in agricultural production in the USSR are facts which are just as well known as is the low standard of living of the overwhelming majority of the population.

It was necessary to offer a new and more sophisticated explanation of the continuing causes of economic stagnation which official propoganda continually referred to as "temporary difficulties." This was not easily accomplished. References to wartime devastation had become obsolete. References to the tenacious "survivals of capitalism in the consciousness of certain individuals" had been so overworked as to become meaningless. The few attempts at complex sociological analyses which were initiated were cut short by the ruling ideologues who considered certain of their conclusions as dangerous heresies infringing upon the inviolable dogmas of Soviet Marxism. [27] The root of all evil, finally, and the source of all economic misfortune, was discovered to be the low level of legal culture characterizing the country. This "discovery" pertained equally to the legal illiteracy of the population (the mobilization of all jurists to propagandize Soviet law finds its origin here) and to the unsatisfactory state of legal work in the Soviet economy. This new explanation was distinguished by at least two merits. Firstly, it was based on observable facts: the level of legal culture in the USSR is extraordinarily low. Secondly, it enabled the leadership to deflect attention from more of the serious causes imminent within the economic system itself or bound up with the quality of the management of the nation's economy. During the 1970s, the Central Committee of the CPSU and the Council of Ministers of the USSR, both jointly and separately, issued a number of statutes devoted to the problems of legal work in the country.

On December 23, 1970, the Central Committee of the CPSU and the Council of Ministers of the USSR adopted a statute "On the Improvement of Legal Work in the People's Economy." [28] The provisions of this statute produced dramatic changes in the jurisconsults' conditions of work.

New Requirements

The preamble of the statute, in conformity with traditional practice, dealt with the achievements in legal work, but the authors moved quickly to the consideration of its deficiencies. The most significant ones were: "Legal workers in the ministries, administrations, enterprises, and (state) organizations have been insufficiently involved in the working out and effectuating of measures directed at the observance of planning and contractual discipline, strengthening economic accountability [*khozraschet*], as well as combating embezzlement, the issuance of poor quality products, non-production losses, violations of economic, labor, housing and other legislation, and the norms of Soviet and collective farm democracy. Up until the present time, there has not been sufficient work on the systematization of economic legislation."

The disarray in the corpus of Soviet economic legislation was truly disturbing. The Minister of Justice of the RSFSR, V. Blinov, reported that in 1977 in his republic alone there were "no fewer than forty thousand all-union and republican legislative acts in force; additionally, there were hundreds of thousands of administrative orders, ministerial and departmental instructions, state *arbitrazh* (decisions and) explanations, and other sources of legal norms." The Minister of Justice of the USSR, V. Terebilov stated that throughout the sixty years of the existence of Soviet power, approximately four hundred thousand legislative (normative) acts were issued. [29] It is certainly clear that, if the Justice Minister of the USSR has enumerated legislative acts in the hundreds of thousands, that the number of instructions, orders, and clarifications must be measured in the millions. The work of bringing this enormous mass of legal documentation into order and harmony was imposed on the Ministers of Justice of the USSR and the fifteen union republics. "Administrations for the Systematization of Legislation and the Preparation of Amendments" were especially created to achieve this goal within each of these ministries. These bodies have not only to deal with the enormous quantity of legislation, but its quality as well.

Four and a half years after the issuance of the above-mentioned statute, the Central Committee of the CPSU and the Council of Ministers of the USSR stated that the nation's economic legislation still suffered from a number of defects: many are mutually contradictory, "uncoordinated," or outdated, while, on the other hand, significant economic problems are not regulated by any laws at all. [30] The problems involved in improving Soviet economic legislation are not among the duties of jurisconsults, however, and are not properly the concern of this work.

It is more interesting for us to consider the reasons behind the imposition on jurisconsults of functions which more properly belong to the police (the struggle against embezzlement), the Procuracy (the struggle against the violation of the law), technical management (the struggle against the issuance of poor quality goods), or plan-economic services (the working out and effectu-

180

ating of measures for the observance of planning and contractual discipline). Why must jurisconsults now struggle with their colleagues within their own organizations and advise the Soviets even when they have not been consulted, instead of conducting their routine work of combating the opponents of their enterprises and proffering advice in response to enquiries? The official answer to this query states that the improvement of the nations's economic activity directly depends upon the improvement of legal work, on "the strengthening of its action on social production, and the increased observance of socialist legality in economic relations." The defense of the rights and interests of the enterprise within which the jurisconsult works are given last place in the statute.

Concrete measures for the improvement of legal work were included in this legislation. We will briefly analyze those which directly relate to the activity of jurisconsults.

a) The "Fundamental Tasks of Legal Workers" cited above were later included in the Statute on Jurisconsults and Legal Sections adopted in 1972 by the Council of Ministers of the USSR. This statute will be analyzed below.

b) It was decided to "strengthen the staff of jurisconsults with well-qualified workers who had demonstrated initiative." For this purpose, it was proposed that the network of law schools, in particular, be expanded and that law faculties with a specialization in the field of legal work in the "People's Economy" be organized. It was additionally recommended that all jurisconsults be released "from the fulfillment of non-pertinent functions".

c) The most substantial provision, however, reflected the decision to impose "the methodical leadership of legal work in the economy" on the Ministries of Justice. In all of the Ministries of Justice of the USSR and the union republics, and in all the provincial departments of justice, new sections on legal work in the economy were established. Their functions were not limited to questions of methodical guidance, however. They were also to exercise control over the work of jurisconsults by means of spot checks, to examine the cases which they handled in the courts or *arbitrazh*, to request reports on their work, and so on. These examinations, as a rule, involved a thorough audit of all aspects of the jurisconsults' work and the subsequent preparation of recommendations about possible means of improvement. Such recommendations were obligatory, and dealt not only with questions of method, but also advice to management. This advice could include proposals to discipline an insufficiently industrious jurisconsult, or to dismiss one who was incompetent. Such a case occurred at the "Red Vyborg" plant. The head of the Department of Justice of the city of Leningrad, B. Zhegulin, noted in his article that the legal service at the "Red Vyborg" had been "reinforced." [31] The term "reinforced" in Soviet phraselogy is equivalent to the word "dismissed," the only difference being that the use of the latter requires the specific mention of the individual displaced.

On the whole, the appearance of a new network of control was beneficial to Soviet legal work in general, and to jurisconsults in particular. For the first time since the 1920s, jurisconsults were able to take courses and improve their professional qualifications. They were able once again to consult and seek advice concerning complex legal problems which transcended their personal experience and knowledge. Finally, jurisconsults acquired not only controllers, but defenders in the organs of the Ministry of Justice. Where the legal opinion of the jurisconsult, or his too active interference in the affairs of the organization provoked the anger of a boss who was unaccustomed to discussing his "voluntary" decisions, the jurisconsult could rely on the support of the independent and authoritative organs of the ministry.

One can state without fear of exaggeration that the imposition on the Ministry of Justice of the duty to supervise and guide the work of jurisconsults was a radical and useful measure.

New Concerns

We will confine ourselves (in this section) to a treatment of those aspects of the work of the Soviet jurisconsult which distinguish the Soviet jurisconsult from his Western counterparts. These duties were established on the basis of the "General Statute on the Legal Section (or Office), Chief (or Senior) Jurisconsult, and Jurisconsult of a Ministry, Department, Executive Committee of a Soviet of Working People's Deputies, or Enterprise, Organization or Institution," which was adopted by the Council of Ministers of the USSR on June 22, 1972. [32]

The Statute is constructed in the following manner. The basic tasks which pertain to all jurisconsults are laid down first. These, it should be noted, had already been established in 1970 on the basis of the joint resolution of the Central Committee of the CPSU and the Council of Ministers of the USSR, the text of which was almost identical with the Statute. Only one new task was included in this section: "to propagandize Soviet legislation."

Organizational questions are considered second. In order to increase the independence of jurisconsults, the right to dismiss these workers, even with the permission of superior authorities, was removed. This was a substantial departure from past practice. The Statute provided that jurisconsults were to be both appointed and dismissed only by higher organizations (within the ministries) or the central departments' chief of the department personally. Regardless of this change, jurisconsults continued to be subordinated, as before, to their managers.

The Statute made a higher legal education a requisite for the job of jurisconsult, and emphasized that this provision could be waived only "in exceptional circumstances." The extent to which "exceptional circumstances" were the rule can be deduced from the following figures. In 1976 the head of the personnel department of the Ministry of Justice of the USSR, M. P. Vyshinskii, stated that 65% of the jurists attached to the *Tsentrosoiuz* (the All-Union Society of Consumers' Cooperatives, which was comprised of 64 million members, more than 370,000 trade enterprises, more than 25,000 industrial enterprises and shops, and with an annual commodity turnover which is valued in excess of 60 million rubles) had neither higher (university) nor middle level (secondary school) legal educations. Vyshinskii added that "such a situation can be observed in other fields of the economy as well." [33]

The "General Statute" provides that "in questions relating to the methods utilized in the conduct of legal work, jurisconsults were to be guided by the directives of the legal sections of superior organizations." This is an example of the lack of "linkage" or internal conformity within Soviet legislation. The earlier Joint Resolution of the Central Committee and the Council of Ministers had established that guidance in matters of legal methods pertaining to economic work would be provided by the Ministry of Justice and its lower organs. The ministry and its organs were to examine the legal work of all organizations and provide recommendations for its improvement. It goes without saying that it was precisely these recommendations concerning methods which ruled jurisconsults in the first instance. In addition to *ad hoc* concrete recommendations, the Ministry of Justice of the USSR worked out and issued general "Recommendations on the Methods of Organization of Work in Legal Services . . ." for various different types of enterprises. These "Recommendations" undoubtedly bore the force of law, a fact which is attested to by their publication in *The Bulletin of Normative Acts of Ministries and Departments of the USSR,* [34] and not in one of the standard legal journals.*

The specific duties of jurisconsults were enumerated further in the statute. The list of rights and limitations on the competence of jurisconsults, and

---

* By the way, this is not the only defect in legislative techniques which was noted during the preparation of this article. For example, in the new "tariff" (schedule of prices) for lawyers' services,[35] alternative methods of payment were provided for contracts concluded for legal assistance between legal consultation offices and enterprises. Payment may be based on a retainer (*i.e*, a previously determined amount may be paid on a weekly or monthly basis, regardless of the work performed) or on the basis of particular fees for specific jobs (article 39). The legislation specifies that those contracts which call for payment on a retainer basis "*must be concluded between the head of the legal office and the manager of the enterprise. . .*" (article 40). And what of those contracts which call for "piece work" payments? Who concludes them? Would it not be the same person? In all contracts, the same parties are involved. Actually, the parties are the legal office, which is represented by its head, and the particular organization, represented by its empowered staff. These individuals only certify the conclusion of the contract with their signatures. Legally, the contract is concluded between the two legal persons—the legal office and the particular organization. This should have been formulated more precisely, without the ambiguities which only raise superfluous questions.

questions referring to the duties of all such legal workers, employed in organizations ranging from enterprises to ministries, were laid down in the conclusion.

The duties set out arose out of the "fundamental tasks" cited above. They were presented in three variants; 1) for jurisconsults employed in ministries and main departments; 2) for jurisconsults employed by the executive committees of provincial, city, and district soviets; and 3) for jurisconsults employed in enterprises, institutions, and public organizations. We will confine ourselves in this study to the consideration of those duties which were imposed on jurisconsults working in economic organizations.

The First Fundamental Task:

> "On the Strengthening of Socialist Legality in the Activity of the Ministries, Departments, Enterprises, Organizations and Institutions in which Jurisconsults Work."

In order to accomplish this, the jurisconsult was required, in particular: a) as before, to check on the conformability of the drafts of orders, instructions, regulations, and other documents of a legal character presented for the signature of the director with the appropriate legislation, and to visa (endorse with his stamp) them, thereby authenticating with his signature their legal validity, as well as his own responsibility in case of error. In the enterprises where I worked, I found that in the course of a single duty, twenty such documents would cross my desk. These, however, were small organizations (a furniture factory, a printing house, a film studio, and a design institute, among others).

In cases where the draft was incompatible with the legislation in force, the jurisconsult was obliged not to visa it, to prepare an opinion as to the reasons why the document did not conform with the legislation, and to propose an alternative variant which would achieve the same ends in an appropriate manner. In cases where the director signed the draft despite the jurisconsult's findings, the latter was obligated to report this to the superior organization. In this way, the director of the enterprise was placed in a position in which he was forced in all cases to check with the jurisconsult concerning his actions, even when he considered it unnecessary. Although the resolution was dedicated to jurisconsults, it imposed definite responsibilities on the directors of organizations as well.

b) To exert systematic control over all orders and other acts issued by the heads of structural subdivisions (shops, sections, services, etc.), and to take measures for the cancellation or alteration of acts which were in violation of the legislation.

c) To prepare, together with other subdivisions, recommendations for modifications in current activities or the repeal of orders and other legal provi-

184

sions, issued in the organization during its entire existence, but which have lost force.

d) To participate in the preparation of drafts of all new normative documents worked out by their enterprises, as well as in the preparation of conclusions as a response on the drafts of those documents dealing with the enterprise sent to their enterprise for such a response.

The absence of a visa on a document which did not correspond with the law was insufficient to save the jurisconsult from responsibility. Unless the jurisconsult complied with all of the measures outlined above for the elimination of legal violations, he bore responsibility for those violations "right alongside with the director." The Procurator of the Frunzenskii District of Moscow, while checking the legality of the legal documents issued by the Administration of the Moscow Telephone Network, disclosed a great number of violations of the law. Explanations for these violations were demanded and obtained in the first instance, not from the director, but the jurisconsult. [36] The authors of this report, Party and Procuracy workers, stated sadly that even in 1976, jurisconsults in a number of Moscow enterprises are still removed from their responsibilities to examine the drafts of legal documents, not demanding them to be visaed. There are also jurisconsults who consider themselves to be "the confidential agents of the administration."

The Second Fundamental Task:

> "The active utilization of legal measures for the strengthening of economic accounting, in the struggle against mismanagement, and for the improvement of economical indices of the work in enterprises, public organizations, and institutions."

For the fulfillment of this task, the jurisconsult was required, in part, a) to organize, together with the other white collar workers in his enterprise, work regarding the conclusion of economic agreements with other organizations (supply contracts, contracts concerning construction, etc.), to participate in the preparation of draft contracts, and, finally, to visa them.

In conformity with the above cited "Recommendations on Method . . ." of the Ministry of Justice of the USSR, the jurisconsult in line with this aim had, first of all, to occupy himself with a profound analysis of the practice of the conclusion and fulfillment of the economic contracts of the past year. He had, for instance, "to clarify and, to a certain extent, rationalize the structure of contractual connections established by enterprises which had the possibility for expansion into direct and enduring economic links." He also had to study the evidence pertaining to penalties for the violation of contractual responsibilities; this included those which had been paid by the enterprise, received by them, and those which had not yet been received by them, but had been accorded to them. Having studied all the insufficiencies of

185

contractual work for the past year, the jurisconsult had to present the manager of his enterprise with necessary proposals for their elimination. However, the jurisconsult and his superiors still found insurmountable barriers before them.

It has been established that the enterprises' structure of contractual relations was not made in the most efficient manner possible. Instead of direct connections between buyers and suppliers, these relations are complicated by the quantity of sections involved. Frequently the jurisconsult, as well as his superiors, can only lend a hand. In most cases, this kind of structure is strenghtened by imperative acts (orders, laws) or is dependent on the discretion/judgment of supply and marketing organizations. Such organizations are the indispensable yet frequently superfluous link (participant) in the system of contractual ties. According to the evidence of N. I. Klein,[37] more than 80% of the surveyed staff of enterprises in both light and heavy industry supported the conclusion of contracts directly with the purchaser, without the participation of intermediate functions. However, under the existing system of a centralized planned economy, it is hard to believe that the situation will be ameliorated despite the efforts demanded from jurisconsults. This was cautiously stated in Klein's interesting study in the following manner, "the causes which hinder the improvement of the system can be found, as a rule, in the economy. There are also a number of other causes, such as the social or psychological. Among these it is possible to find the purely legal ones . . ."

In the journal *Sovetskaia Iustitsiia* (Soviet Justice), one can often find examples presented of how to strengthen *khozraschet* and improve the economic accounts of the enterprise by legal methods. The example produced below was presented at a seminar in Moscow at the "School for Advanced Experience (*Shkola Peredovogo Opyta*) in the Utilization of Legal Remedies for Increasing the Effectiveness of Industry and the Improvement of the Quality of Production" in the textile industry. Jurisconsults employed in the textile industry attended this seminar from all over the country.

A silk producer had systematically obtained its dyes in 200-liter containers. The supplier required that the silk company return the containers, but the railroad administration refused to allocate the space to ship the empties. The nonreturn of the containers resulted in thousands of rubles of fines. Although the management of the silk enterprise was resigned to the situation as a necessary evil, the head of the legal section, Mrs. T. Iuganova, began to search for an alternative. Having ascertained that it was impossible to persuade the railroad administration to transport the cans or the dye supplier to forego compensation, she instituted a search by the workers of the supply service of her enterprise for an organization which could use the boxes. Such an organization was duly discovered, but its requirements demanded a container with a smaller volume. Once the silk enterprise insisted that the dye supplier utilize smaller containers, the dyes began to be delivered in the 75-liter containers needed by their final user.

The solution to the problem was eminently reasonable; what is unclear, however, is where the *legal* issue arises in this matter. It is likewise unclear why the economist, supply department, financial workers, and the manager of the enterprise had to await the initiative of the jurisconsult for a resolution of the problem. Although the issue was not overly complex, and the solution could have easily been discovered at an earlier date, the problem was allowed to persist because it did not fall within the particular competence of any particular department or individual within the enterprise. The matter, strictly speaking, should not have become the responsibility of the jurisconsult until it became necessary to compel the dye supplier to change the containers it used. It would have been natural to expect that this story would include an account of the jurisconsult's arguments before the *arbitrazh* or the legal conclusions presented. The author of this instructive example, however, concluded the account with the phrase "and it was achieved." Since nothing more is available, it can only be assumed that the dye supplier readily agreed to the change in containers and that the further involvement of the jurisconsult was not required. Why then was this example presented at a seminar for jurisconsults at the School for Advanced Experience? The purpose behind this narrative was to illustrate the work of the jurisconsult of the new type: "Today's jurisconsult in the enterprise is not merely a jurist, versed in legislation, knowledgeable of methods of contract formulation, and capable of defending the interests of his enterprise before the courts or *arbitrazh*. Today's jurisconsult is an erudite man, familiar with the law, economics, and the production processes utilized in the enterprise where he works. It is even better when he additionally is aware of the requirements of the enterprises which supply his own." [38]

If we recall, however, that two-thirds of the jurisconsults in the USSR do not have any legal eduction, the picture presented above pales. This ideal picture is significant for, although it does not describe the actual situation at present, it does reveal the desired direction for future development. A different author has stated, "Today's industry requires not only a consultant on legal questions, but a lawyer-economist, a lawyer-production manager who is distinctly aware of how his work will effect the volume of production sold, the profit realized, the costs of production, the liquidation of indebtedness, and the elimination of nonproductive expenses." [39] How should the jurisconsult apply his broadened knowledge in practice to effectively influence by legal means the enterprise within which he works?

"In order to evaluate the contribution of legal services to the enterprise's economy, let us mentally follow the course of events initiated by any contractual obligation. Let us suppose that [the contract calls for the production of] a sophisticated electronic device. As such, the device must be prepared in accordance with a specified plan. The necessary documents to procure the requisite materials would have to be obtained. It would be necessary to conclude innumerable contracts for the supply of tens and sometimes hundreds of diverse materials, metals, plastics, optics, glasses, dyes, and electrical wires. One would also have to obtain a great number of complex articles: various transistors, resistors ... and many others. The jurist would have to watch over the precise fulfillment of contractual obligations by suppliers, after all the debts had been paid he would have to check that all materials and semi-processed articles were delivered to the plant on time, watch over their proper reception and storage, and the organization of their proper registration and accounts. He would have to see that contractual relations with the client were registered in time, he would also have to see that all necessary claims were made, and that all those [filed against the enterprise] were examined and acted upon. And any number of non-planned and unexpected things could arise in the course of production! Either the construction of the device would have to be changed, or new materials would be needed, or an error in calculations had been made. This was a new field of work for the jurisconsult. Finally, the device was prepared and sent to the shipping department. It was necessary, in conformity with the contract, to ship and to receive payment from the other party within time-limits. Additionally, it was necessary to keep precise accounts of the enterprises costs of production of the device and the extent to which there was a profit. If some accident had occurred, it was necessary to have an investigation into its causes, [it was necessary to determine] how to avoid fines, what were the losses to be, would it be possible to compensate for them, who was responsible, what could be submitted to the *arbitrazh*?" [The author concludes:] "In general, the jurist has numerous concerns in all the stages of production—from the reception of the order to the sale of the finished product."

The Third Fundamental Task:

"Provision for the safety of socialist property by legal means, the improvement of the quality of the output of production, [the fulfillment] of obligations imposed concerning supplies, [and the fulfillment of] agreements for capital construction, as well as other contracts."

In order to fulfill this task, the jurisconsult is obliged in particular to do the following:

a) To take an active part in checking on the fulfillment of agreements, and unswervingly to seek the imposition of sanctions on those organizations

188

which fail to fulfill their conctractual obligations. To watch over the fulfillment of agreements within his own enterprise.

Experience has demonstrated that the attempt to recover fines or have other sanctions imposed for nonfulfillment (or the improper fulfillment) of contracts can be dangerous for both parties, and is an extremely delicate operation. Enterprise managers are aware that their plans can sometimes prove to be impossible to fulfill, since they surpass the capabilities of their plants. The recognition of this possibility can lead the plant manager to forego a suit for nonfulfillment, since the default today by his partner may be his own tomorrow. This practice (known as "mutual amnestying") is still popular today.

A few examples of the kinds of difficulties which produce this practice may be in order. The jurisconsult and the manager of a food enterprise complained in a letter that, in spite of the fact that once a plan is confirmed superior authorities are not entitled to alter it,

> "their production output plans were frequently changed. The enterprise then suffers losses as a result of the superior organs assigning the delivery of final products which the enterprise could not produce, either due to a shortage of materials or the kind of technical equipment available, etc. This can lead to a situation where the malfunctioning of an assembly line station within the enterprise can result in the imposition of a fine on the enterprise for the delivery of insufficient quantities . . ." [40]

The initiation of cases at *arbitrazh* for the delivery of poor quality goods may result in disproportionately severe penalties against the manager of an enterprise, including criminal liability. (Article 152 of the Criminal Code of the RSFSR). Consequently, many managers of enterprises in the Soviet economy prefer to avoid suits before the *arbitrazh*.

The prevalence of "mutual amnestying" compelled the state to institute new measures to combat the practice. State *arbitrazh* organs received a directive which empowered them to institute proceedings and impose fines on their own initiative. The organs of the Procuracy began to charge the managers of enterprises with both material and criminal liability more energetically than before. The coordination of the activity of the Procuracy and the *arbitrazh* on the one hand, and the various control organizations (the State Standards Committees, Construction Inspectorates, Control Departments of the Ministry of Finance, etc.) on the other were reinforced. These organizations began to inform each other more often about violations they uncovered which came under the competence of different authorities, or about areas which warranted investigations.

Nevertheless, jurisconsults continued to be blamed for "not checking on the fulfillment of agreements," and for being insufficiently active in submitting suits for the recovery of fines which were still outstanding. "The exaction of sanctions is the duty of the parties to a contract. Reciprocal amnestying does not promote the strengthening of state discipline", stated V. Rvachaev, N. Baskakov, and many others.[41] At first glance, such complaints could give the impression that the inertia of jurisconsults was leading to a situation where organs of the *arbitrazh* were left without work. This, however, would be incorrect. According to the report of the Chief of the RSFSR *Arbitrazh*, N. Sapozhnikov, the total number of cases of contractual violations reported in the republic in 1974 was 375,000. The total of fines and forfeits recovered totalled 295 million rubles. In 6400 cases where the plaintiff had not requested that a fine be extracted for the violation of the agreement, *arbitrazh* on its own initiative recovered fines totalling 2 million rubles. On the basis of the reports of the control organizations and banks, as well as information published in the newspapers, the state *arbitrazh* of the republic instituted two and a half thousand cases on their own initiative and recovered fines totalling 9.2 million rubles in the same year.[42] In the process of researching these cases, the "*causes* for these violations of state discipline" were clarified. As one might expect, the crux of the matter was not the state of legal work in the economy, but "objective causes." The analysis of these causes was not the subject of Sapozhnikov's article, but he nevertheless mentioned a number of them: the lack of productive potential, the labor force, raw materials. The author states "and others;" it would be closer to the truth to say: "and many others."

N. I. Klein, cited above, conducted a sociological research study into the causes of the extremely low incidence of suits for the recovery of fines for violations in the area of the planning system and contractual economic relations pertaining to supply. According to her data, which were based on the years 1971 and 1972, the percentage of cases submitted for the exaction of fines which arose out of delays in the despatch of goods or delays in the distribution of the necessary documents for funded materials procurement were only 0.07% of the total number of cases considered by the state *arbitrazh*. Whereas, in 74% of the cases submitted to the *arbitrazh* in which the plaintiff sought that the supplier be compelled to conclude an agreement, the supplier had avoided the conclusion of the agreement on the basis of various mistakes of the planning organizations.

N. I. Klein based her analysis on 505 replies received from the managers of enterprises and institutions, jurisconsults, and the heads of supply and sale departments within various enterprises. Workers from a great number of different branches of the economy were embraced in this study: light and heavy industry, trade, and enterprises and institutions subordinated to the Chief Committee for Supply (*Glavsnab*). According to Ms. Klein, the results of the analysis of the survey confirmed the supposition that the extreme unpopularity of the laws of fines is the result of two factors: 1) the fact that the

sanctions established as norms by the legislation are considered incommen-
surate with the nature and the content of the relations which they seek to
protect; and 2) the lack of interest evidenced by enterprises in utilizing the
norms of material liability. One way or the other, the medicine was not
working.

b) The jurisconsult is also obliged to oversee the observance of the rules
of procedure for the reception and registration of articles and goods. This
involves checking that the products received are of the appropriate number
and quality, and that they were shipped in accordance with the rules in
effect. Here is an example of the manner in which this recommendation has
been put into effect: in the textile industry, "it has become a rigid rule that
the staff can only open packages, containers, and boxes of raw materials,
equipment, and materials in the presence of special commissions, *in which the
jurisconsults are included*. Legal workers are similarly included on inventory
commissions," whose work consists of checking that those items entered on
the books of the enterprise are physically present on the premises.

c) The jurisconsult must ascertain that any deletion of items from the
enterprises registry lists are legitimate, *i.e.* that only those items are written
off which are in reality lost, irreparably broken, or worn out. He is responsible for ascertaining the causes of the damage and the individual(s) responsible
for the damages. This involves the determination of willfull damage or accident. In most cases, this is an exceptionally difficult problem to solve, and
the more suspicious the story, the more impeccable are the documents
which attest to its veracity.

The jurisconsult has greater opportunities for success in his role of safeguarding enterprise property through crime prevention. One aspect of this
work involves the elaboration of contracts which specify the full personal
financial liability of the particular employee for damages to property and
equipment. (According to labor legislation, there may be limited or full liability for damages caused to state or social property by employees.) The process
of concluding such a contract permits the jurisconsult to inquire into the
conditions under which the materials—which the employee will be required to
store and handle—are preserved, and the suitability for the job. For a time,
such innovations seemed effective in safeguarding state property. The jurisconsult at the state farm "Sladkovskii" [43] introduced, for example, a system
whereby new parts for trucks, tractors, combines, and other agricultural
machinery were only made available to farm workers upon the presentation
of the defective part which was to be replaced. This worked until a system
was devised to circumvent it.

A more complex problem is the extent to which the jurisconsult is able to
ensure the quality of the produced output by legal means. Here, they are
often limited from taking actions against those guilty of producing poor

quality goods by the difficulty of ascertaining who are culprits, if many employees produced the same materials. In many cases, the battle for the production of quality output is beyond the limited means possessed by the jurisconsult. The Procurator of the USSR sent a representation to the Minister of the Chemical Industry of the USSR "concerning the liquidation of violations which give rise to the output of nonstandard or poor quality goods from industrial enterprises." [44] It was pointed out in this representation that the control departments of *Gosstandart* had excluded from the accounts, filed by chemical enterprises, 3.2 million rubles worth of production in 1975 as a result of its poor quality. In the first half of 1976 alone, this figure had risen to 4 million rubles. Although the representation dealt only with particular examples, they provide us with a general picture of the problem. A number of plants, which had been officially recognized as the best enterprises in their fields, were discovered to have issued massive quantities of nonstandard goods; they were awarded the "challenge red banner" and the highest monetary prizes. In one example, the head of the complex of chemical fertilizer enterprises allowed these enterprises to ship the product in bulk rather than in individual boxes, a procedure which he was aware would worsen the quality of the product. There is no evidence that the situation in the chemical industry is exceptional.

In 1972 a disaster occurred in Minsk, the capital of Belorussia. The shop of the television factory was demolished as a result of an explosion. This shop manufactured cabinets for television sets. More than a hundred people were killed and many more were injured. The Supreme Court of the USSR was the court of first instance in the case. The manager of the enterprise, and the members and director of the design institute were charged in the criminal case. The case was described in the volume *Supreme Court of the USSR*, which is published in both Russian and English. [45] The author of the description was the judge who presided over the trial. The explosion was set off by an accumulation of dust in excess of safety limits (every kind of dust has its own limit of concentration, beyond which the dust becomes explosive). The description of the technical details of the case missed one significant point— the shop was newly built, and had only recently been approved for use by a government commission. In preparing for the case, I discovered the "Act of Approval for Use" issued by this commission; the signatures were all those of officials of high rank. In the Act, it was stated that all of the sanding/grinding machines (the main sources of the dust) and the corresponding exhaust ventilation system "were tested and functioned normally." However, during the course of the investigation, it was established that the ventilation system had not been installed. The members of the so-called government satisfaction commission had consciously attested with their signatures to a lie (there was no jurisconsult on the commission).

"The output of the enterprise was the only concern of the manager," concluded the author of the description. But were they the only ones? During the preparation of the case, I became acquainted with the state of affairs in a number of similar factories in the Leningrad area. In every case without exception, I observed the same or similar deviations from the safety norms. When the equipment was installed, all the safety precautions were followed to avoid the danger of fire, but not explosion, in regards to the types of motors and ventilators utilized.

All of this became quite well known. The opinions of the most authoritative technical experts already had been available after the disaster, both to the departments of the Central Committee and to all those ministries in which woodworking factories and shops existed. Nothing changed. It is difficult to imagine that a jurisconsult could rectify such a situation by recourse to legal means.

The Ministry of Justice of the USSR organized numerous schools throughout the country to further the legal education of managers and specialists working in the economic system. Several programs were devised, the level and nature of which would depend upon the particular audience and their specializations. [46] Whether this measure will prove effective, and whether it will inculcate not only a knowledge of the law but respect and conformity with its provisions only the future will show.

The Fourth Fundamental Task:

> "The defense of the rights and legal interests of the enterprise, organization, institution, and citizenry."

The fulfillment of this task is routine and common to jurisconsults in all systems. It requires, therefore, little supplementary explanation.

There may be some question as to the inclusion of the citizenry among those whose rights and legal interests the jurisconsult of an organization is required to defend. This does not oblige the jurisconsult to act as an official defense counsel for the workers employed by his institution or organization. In our opinion, this task refers to the citizens, first of all, in terms of their labor rights. This interpretation is supported by the report of V. Blinov, the Minister of Justice of the RSFSR, who stated that in 1976 the courts of the Kemerovo Province granted "about half of all suits seeking reinstatements at work." The examination of these cases revealed that "in every second [case, the employee] had been dismissed unlawfully." [47] It is necessary to take into consideration two factors here. Firstly, the example provided by V. Blinov concerning Kemerovo Province is not an exceptional one, but speaks of the general situation. According to the data presented by V. I. Chudnov, 60% of all employees who had been fired in the RSFSR in 1966 were reinstated by the courts. In 1967 this figure dropped slightly to 58.5%. In 1968 the courts ruled in favor of the complaints in 75% of the cases alleging illegal deductions

193

by management and other organizations from employees' salaries. [48]

In the majority of the cases in which the court found in favor of the complainant, the suits involved mostly ordinary industrial workers, office men, junior technicians, and ordinary engineers. The total number of such cases, and mentioned percentages as well, would undoubtedly have been even higher were it not for the exclusion by special legislation of wide groups of senior employees (including foremen in the industry) from recourse to the courts in cases of dismissals and other infringements on their labor rights. [49]

Secondly, the jurisconsult must be involved in every stage of the dismissed process. It is his duty to weigh all the legal pros and cons of the contemplated dismissal. Dismissals of these employees who are eligible for court protection are only undertaken with the agreement of the trade union committee. It is also the duty of the jurisconsult to present the reasons for the dismissal to the trade union when the request for their agreement is presented. Unlawful dismissals have a number of adverse results. Firstly, the courts compel the enterprise to pay compensation to the employee for the period during which he was without work. Such dismissals additionally result in damage to the labor force and adversely affect the productivity of the enterprise.

The prevention of unlawful dismissals is the direct obligation of the jurisconsult. It can not be said, however, that they perform this function very successfully. One of the roots of this failure may be the different approach taken by jurisconsults to those intersts of employer and employees which appear conflicting on the surface but which are similar in fact. This is, perhaps, why the jurisconsult is now required to protect the interests not only of their enterprise or organization, but also those of their workers and the citizenry at large.

The Soviet jurisconsult—in contrast to his colleagues in Canada or the United States—is not required to be a member of the Bar in order to take cases before the courts. If, however, the jurisconsult is not a member as a result of having been disbarred, he is not eligible to handle cases in court. This restriction is contained in Article 60 of the current RSFSR Code of Civil Procedure, and had been included in the previous code as well.

Fifth Fundamental Task:

"Propaganda [concerning] Soviet legislation."

Up until the issuance of the Statute on Jurisconsults in 1972, the jurisconsult was only sporadically involved in propagandizing the legal system. This meant that he fulfilled this function only from time-to-time in response to particular Party campaigns or in the course of fulfilling trade union duties. Upon the introduction of the 1972 Statute, the delivery of lectures and reports, working in special organizations of *agitpunkt* or social law consultation offices, (*obshchestvennaia iuridicheskaia konsul'tatsiia*) and constant availability for

194

consultations with workers and employees of the enterprise or organization, as well as with the multitudinous social organizations (trade unions committees, comrades' courts, people's control organizations, etc.) became the normal daytime consuming duties of every Soviet jurisconsult. This work is not limited to working hours, and is considered to be conducted on "social principles," that is without charge.

It has already been noted that the Soviet authorities evaluate the importance of this legal propaganda work quite highly. It is viewed as "an important means of Communist education, of furthering the strengthening of socialist legality and the socialist order, and ensuring state and labor discipline." [50] New forms for this work are continually researched. Jurisconsults write columns in local newspapers and deliver lectures on Soviet law, both on radio and television. A new magazine has been issued entitled, *Chelovek i Zakon* (Man and the Law), with the goal of popularizing this issue.

The Deputy Ministry of Heavy Machine Construction of the USSR, G. Sotnikov, reported that the centers of legal propaganda and legal aid for the workers of the enterprises of this ministry were the "social" legal consultation offices mentioned earlier. [51] Those who come to these offices are free from any obligation to pay. The state is also free from any expense, since the jurisconsults have been "freed" from the opportunity to charge a fee for their service. Approximately 18,000 such consultation offices were established in the USSR in 1977. "People's Universities (or Faculties) of Legal Knowledge" have also become increasingly popular. These function on the same financial principles as the consultation offices. By 1977, close to 3,500 such universities or faculties had been established. An additional statistic which attests to the order of magnitude of the work we have been discussing is the aggregate of number of lectures delivered on the issue by the Soviet legal profession in 1976—more than one and a half million. [52] No small portion of this work was performed by jurisconsults.

Rural jurisconsults carry an especially heavy work load. Generally these jurisconsults are members of "Interfarm Legal Groups" which were created to provide legal services to the state or collective farms of one or more districts. These farms are widely dispersed over great areas. Jurisconsults are not provided with their own means of transportation and are therefore compelled to wait on the movements of others. "One is forced to waste a considerable amount of valuable time waiting for an automobile travelling in the same direction," complained V. Degtiarenko, a senior inter-state farm jurisconsult. [53] Additionally, each rural jurisconsult is compelled to serve ten to twenty collective or state farms, despite the fact that the established norm is not more than six. [54] This occasionally results in curious consequences. Having discovered a violation of the law the jurisconsult, reports this to the Procuracy, the people's control committee, or the executive committee of the district soviet. Time and distance frequently prevent the jurisconsult from speaking with all of the affected managers of state or collective farms. Thus, the enterprise which pays for the jurisconsult's services is the last to be informed of the shortcomings and errors in his work which require rectification forthwith.

We have described only a part of the work the jurisconsult is called upon to fulfill in the Soviet economy. It remains for us to discuss the question of personnel and their training. Before we turn to this issue, however, it is useful to note an additional area of activity in which the jurisconsult's time is spent rather unproductively. This concerns the drawing up of reports, plans or accounts. The local administrations of the Ministries of Justice do not have a sufficient number of employees to enable them to gain concrete information concerning the state of affairs in all the enterprises of a province or a large city. Yet the ministry is responsible for the state of legal work in all those enterprises, it is obligated to become informed of the conditions pertaining there and to present their superiors with an account of all the various aspects of the jurisconsults' work. In order to fulfill this obligation, the ministry requires the jurisconsults to compile all kinds of reports on their work. The same or similar reports must also be prepared by the jurisconsult and submitted to the legal sections of their superior organization.

According to the Chairman of the Council on the Methodology of Legal Work in the Economy, which is attached to the Department of Justice in L'vov Province, those who read these reports are able to gain an impression of the "actual volume of work," and "how it affects the enterprises' economic indicators, (and) the strengthening of socialist legality." In any case, these reports can assist these administrators in their efforts to work out a "system of indicators of the effectiveness of the influence of legal services on the economy of the enterprise, the strengthening of legality, and the raising of the legal consciousness of the workers collective." [55]

Once one of the jurisconsults has finished with his reports, he must turn to the drafting of his plans. The preparation of various plans is considered almost the major factor in ensuring the success of the jurisconsults' work; "practice has demonstrated that the most important condition in the organization of legal services in the economy is skillful planning." There is no rest for the jurisconsult. They must prepare various plans: working plans, perspective plans, and complex plans, according to the jurisconsult N. Sibulatov. [56] Some are drafted to cover as much as two or three years. On the other hand, "every jurisconsult in a group prepares perspective plans of work for a year, current plans for each quarter, and working plans for each month and week." It goes without saying that "during the fulfillment of these and other measures, the references, observations, acts, and other documents" are also drafted.

196

3. The Problem of Personnel

According to V. Terebilov, the Minister of Justice of the USSR, there were 29,000 jurisconsults in the Soviet Union in 1971, 1,500 of whom were employed in the agricultural sector. By 1976 the total number had increased to 50,000, with 7,000 employed in the agricultural economy. The Minister has stated that within the next 8-10 years, the number of jurisconsults must be doubled in order to reach the optimal correlation of one jurisconsult for every 2,000 blue and white collar workers. [57] At first glance, the achievement of this goal seems entirely within the realm of possibility. In 1976 there were 104.3 million blue and white collar workers in the USSR. [58] The optimal proportion called for 52,000 jurisconsults, whereas in actual fact there were 43,000. This shortfall is aggravated by two factors. Firstly, more than half of the jurisconsults currently practising, as was noted above, do not have any advanced legal education. Secondly, the vast majority of legal workers are concentrated in the large cities (for the most part in Moscow, Leningrad, and in the capitals of the union republics) where the standard of living has always been considerably better than in the remaining sections of the country.

A large party of decentralized industry is in real need of the services of jurisconsults. For example, in the Donetsk Province not all, not even some of the largest, economic organizations have their own legal service. There are only eight jurisconsults employed in 88 enterprises engaged in repairs and other services which employ 40,000 workers. [59] The Deputy Minister of Justice of Uzbekistan reported an "acute shortage of jurists in the people's economy." [60] The situation in the agricultural sector of the economy is certainly no better, if not worse. It is in this sector especially that instances of the arbitrary appropriation of the rights of collective farms or other economic entities by district organizations frequently occur. Similarly, instances of the deception of the management of collective farms by workers in industrial organizations are not uncommon. The USSR Minister of Agriculture recognized in 1967 that the state of legal service in the agricultural sector was deficient, and issued an order establishing staff legal services in all links (*zven'ia*) of agricultural enterprises. "But the process or organizing staff services turned out to be complex and is still far from having been completed," commented the Deputy Minister of Justice of the RSFSR, A. Grun, five years after the order's issuance. [61] Only 10% of the state farms in Azerbaidzhan are served by jurists, according to the report of Deputy Minister of Justice of that republic, M. Aliev. [62] Out of the many thousands of collective farms of that republic, only 13 have the services of a jurisconsult available to them. In the 136 collective farms which have the position of jurisconsult on their staff schedules, these posts are occupied by economists, veterinarians, and agronomists. According to the data supplied by the Ministry of Justice of the USSR, 70% of the nation's state farms are provided with legal services by the interfarm legal groups. [63] The high percentage attests more to the power of statistics than it does to the healthy state of legal services in the USSR. "In our trust, for instance, the staff of the legal group was composed of three individuals, and the jurisconsult was able to visit each collective farm only once every two weeks. For this such groups are needed?"—bitterly questioned the leader of one such group, I. Billeris. [64]

In the efforts to improve this situations, a great deal of hope has been placed on planning on the one hand, and an increase in the number of Faculties of Law preparing jurisconsults on the other.

Education

In 1976 there were forty Faculties of Law and four Institutes of Law in the Soviet Union. Despite the students' thorough general theoretical training, there was a general feeling that they lacked sufficient practical knowledge. "The graduates were well-prepared in matters of theory, but when they were required to apply their knowledge in practice, it showed as a lack of skill in their work. The preparation of specialists of a broad type is not justified in practice," stated E. Kogan, the Khabarovsk State Arbitrator. [65] Even more strongly negative opinions were expressed by the heads of the legal departments of the ministries when they were questioned by a legal journal: "The graduates of the Faculties of Law and Legal Institutes have not received the necessary knowledge and skills to work as jurisconsults in enterprises or the organs of economic administration. This is particularly (due to the fact that) the law schools do not devote intensive study to economic legislation, the fundamentals of the economy, or to the organization of the work of the legal service." [66] In recent years, this situation has improved. New courses in the field of economic law have been introduced, and in a number of faculties, the opportunity for specialization in the fields of industrial and agricultural economics were made available to senior students.

The Saratov Legal Institute opened the country's first "Faculty of Legal Service in the People's Economy" in 1976. The Director of the Institute, the Dean, and the Professors of the newly-established Faculty described this system for the preparation of the future "jurist-economist" in the following terms: "First of all, [we] ensure that the basic socio-political knowledge necessary to every Soviet jurist is provided." [67] Since the curriculum must be approved by the USSR Ministry of Secondary and Post-Secondary Special Education, it necessarily includes courses on the History of the CPSU, Marxist-Leninist Philosophy, Scientific Communism, Political Economy, History of Soviet State and Law, History of State and Law in Foreign Countries, Marxist Theory of State and Law, etc. General educational courses are also provided: Logic, Foreign Languages, Physical Education. These courses are set out in the "Model Plan" of every Faculty of Law or Law Institute. The future jurisconsult is additionally taught courses in the following fields: a)

198

Legal Principles of the Regulation of Economic Activity; b) Legal Regulation of Economic Links; c) the Adjudication of Economic Disputes in the USSR. After a thirty-year interruption, legal-economic education has been resumed.

The number of graduating jurists has increased from year to year: approximately 13,000 in 1975 and 14,000 in 1976, in contrast with 8,000 in 1970. The Deputy to the Chief of the Personnel Department of the Ministry of Justice of the USSR reported that, in 1976, "the plan for the distribution of recently graduated specialists" was fulfilled by the ministries of all union republics, excepting only Tadzhikistan. [69] Here we have, however, such peculiarities of statistics and planning that this is not an occasion for patting oneself on the back, or, as Russians say, "for beating the kettledrum."

Planning

The Senior Jurisconsult of the Ministry of Light Industry of Uzbekistan complained of a shortage of jurisconsults. She cited eleven enterprises in which there was not a single jurist. She further noted that the legal institutes were not producing specialists in this area. She stated that she considered one of the causes of this situation to be "mismanagement on the part of the republic's planning organs." [69] Her letter was published in the January 1977 issue of the journal *Sotsialisticheskaia Zakonnost'* (Socialist Legality). It was clarified in the February issue that this mismanagement had occurred within the ministry itself: it had submitted a claim to *Gosplan* for two jurisconsults per year, which was clearly insufficient at the time. [70] It seems likely, however, that even this meager request had not been met.

The example produced above is by no means exceptional. Only half of the 104 ministries and main departments of the USSR submitted claims for jurisconsults during the period of the ninth five-year plan (1971-1975). These claims generally called for one-two jurisconsults per year, a figure which by no means reflects the actual need for legal workers. The total number of requested new jurisconsults varies between 1100 and 1700 specialists a year, for all branches of the economy: industrial, agricultural, and administrative. This number, however, cannot keep up even with the increasing numbers of legal positions which open year and much less compensate for the three to five thousand vacancies which result yearly from the retirement of senior members of the profession. But even those claims which were submitted by half of the ministries and departments were granted in only 60-70% of the cases "on average." These statistics were taken from an article by the head of the Personnel Department of the Ministry of Justice of the USSR, M. P. Vyshinskii. [71] He determined that the number of new jurisconsult graduates must reach nine or ten thousand each year if the nation's needs were to be met by 1980.

What are the causes of this unfortunate situation? We will attempt to describe a few of them, but our examination will be far from exhaustive.

1) A particular phenomenon has been observed in the Soviet Union for the last several decades which merits study by social-psychologists and sociologists. It can conditionally be termed "the phenomenon of widespread concealed disobedience." It is widespread in that it can be observed at all levels of Soviet society, it is concealed in that it is always accompanied by hearty assurances of immediate fulfillment. The vast number of instances of non-fulfillment of statutes, laws, and even the imperatives of common sense are difficult to explain on the basis of either the complexities of the task or a misunderstanding of the requirements. It is difficult to imagine, for example, that fully one half of the heads of ministries and main departments of the USSR were unable to understand or fulfill the directive of Central Committee of the CPSU and the USSR Council of Ministers concerning the implementation of measures which would ensure the provision of legal services to all of their enterprises.

2) Attempts to implement the existing legislation on the mandatory distribution of university graduates to areas selected by special "Commissions for Personnel Distribution" [72] encountered several unforeseen obstacles. Firstly, only graduates of the universities' general day-course divisions were required to obey the commissions' decisions. Graduates of the evening or correspondence divisions were not covered by the legislation, despite the fact that there were several times the number of students enrolled in the latter divisions than there were enrolled in the day programs. A definite dynamic can be discerned in this disproportion. In 1952, 40% of all graduates had obtained their degrees in the evening or correspondence divisions. In 1955 this percentage had risen to more than 50% of the 7,396 total. By 1975 the correlation had stabilized at roughly 1:3, only 30% of the total number of graduates therefore came under the jurisdiction of the Commissions of Personnel Distribution. This percentage has remained stable since 1975, and has proved very difficult to alter. This primarily is the result of certain economic and political factors. It is impossible to increase the enrollment in the day division, while it is dangerous to restrict the opportunities of students to receive higher education in the evening and correspondence divisions which furnish the country with the bulk of its specialists-jurists.

Additional difficulties were provoked by the large numbers of students who dropped out of their programs. According to our figures, 18-20,000 jurists should have received their diplomas in 1975, but in actual fact only 12,891 did so. (This calculation was based on the fact that 78,900 students were recorded as enrolled in juridical faculties and institutes in 1974 and that the general educational term is four years.)

The first Deputy to the Minister of Justice of the USSR, A. Sukharev, who provided the above cited data, [73] stated that the students' social and national composition lay at the basis of this complex problem. Firstly, "The strata of worker and collective farm youth was very small," and secondly, the strata composed of "persons having the basic nationality" was very small.

As far as the first assertion is concerned, this only confirms the well-established fact that the state of (so-called) developed socialism has not been able to avoid social stratification and further, that self-reproduction occurs within the strata. [74]

The second assertion, which divides the citizens of the country into aliens and those who form part of the basic nationalities, is reminiscent of the legislation of the pre-1917 period, which was based on the principles of Great Power chauvinism. Similar statements can be found even in the post-revolutionary writings of especially active anti-Semites, but their incorporation into the report of a highly-placed staff member of the Central Committee of the CPSU bespeaks a lamentable link between the spiritual outlook of pre- and post-revolutionary Russian chauvinists.

One way or the other, if A. Sukharev is unable to perceive any other causes of this problem, necessarily he is also unable to discern any methods of alleviating it. This is certainly a sad state of affairs. History has demonstrated that recourse to racist or anti-Semitic (as a particular kind of racism) policies has in no instance provided positive results, not in the Soviet Union nor in any other part of the world.

3) The second possible reason for the low number of jurisconsults is the unpopularity of the profession with the young graduates of legal faculties. The majority of jurisconsults with whom I was acquainted in the Leningrad region worked in this field only because they were not qualified to enter the Bar. Many jurisconsults transfer to other specialist positions within the enterprises where they have been employed (becoming financial managers, economists, personnel staff, etc.), once they have accumulated sufficient expertise.

4) The low wage schedule offered jurisconsults is not an insignificant factor in this development. The most experienced jurisconsults generally maintained a number of posts with different enterprises. One of these was considered their permanent position, while the others were "pluralisms." The introduction of more stringent legislation prohibiting the maintenance of pluralisms limited the possibilities of many jurisconsults (criminal cases were instituted against a number of offenders). A sizeable number of jurisconsults moved to the *advokatura* as a result. This shift was observed throughout the 1970s, despite the fact their wages were somewhat increased. Nevertheless, they still receive less pay than judges, procurators, and senior lawyers. R. Nizovskii and I. Rogal have provided data on the incomes of rural jurisconsults-

sults. [75] These vary from 90 to 140 rubles a month for ordinary jurisconsults, and from 110 to 190 rubles a month for senior jurisconsults who are heads of inter-farm legal groups.

Are jurisconsults able to meet the demands with which they are confronted at the present time—as the representative of the law checking on conformity with legislation; as the controller who protects the true interests of the state against his own employer; as economist, detective, engineer, lecturer, and teacher? I have grave doubts on this matter. Will they be able to fulfill all of these duties in the future? Possibly. But the real issue lies in a different direction. Will the future university-educated, multi-faceted guardian of the much-suffering Soviet economy be able to improve substantially its state? Apparently, there is no panacea short of radical changes in the political and economic systems. And it will not provoke a great deal of surprise when a new and joint Party and government decree is issued in a few years describing the new and different causes for the contemporary difficulties of the Soviet economy. As Saul Bellow so aptly put it, "a great deal of intelligence can be invested in ignorance when the need for illusion is deep."

NOTES

1. *Black's Law Dictionary*, rev. 4th Edition, (St. Paul, Minn., 1968), p. 991; *Webster's New Collegiate Dictionary*, (Springfield, Mass., 1977), p. 628.

2. Donald D. Barry, Harold J. Berman, "The Soviet Legal Profession," in *Harvard Law Review*, 82 (1968), No. 1, 17-20.

3. Earl L. Johnson, *An Introduction to the Soviet Legal System* (London, 1969), p. 241.

4. Jane Giddings, "The Jurisconsults in the USSR," *Review of Socialist Law*, 1975, No. 3, 171-211.

5. Samuel Kucherov, *The Organs of Soviet Administration of Justice: Their History and Operation* (Leyden, 1970), pp. 572-574.

6. The "Third Section personally in the hands of His Majesty's Chancellery," which dealt with state security affairs, was instituted in 1826 and ceased in 1880.

7. A. F. Koni, *Sobranie Sochinenii* (Collected Works), vol. 5, (Moscow, 1968), p. 5.

8. See, for example, *Entsiklopedicheskii Slovar'* (Encyclopaedic Dictionary), vol. 41, (St. Petersburg, 1904), p. 419.

9. A. F. Koni, *op. cit.*, p. 171. The italics here and after are mine.

10. P. Stuchka, *Revoliutsionnaia Rol' Sovetskogo Prava* (Revolutionary Role of Soviet Law), (Moscow, 1931), p. 168.

11. *Otchet Prezidiuma Moskovskoi Gubernskoi Kollegii Zashchitnikov za pervoe polugodie s 8 oktiabria 1922 goda po 1 aprelia 1923 goda* (Semiannual Report of the Moscow Province Bar from October 8, 1922 to April 1, 1923), (Moscow, 1923), p. 9.

12. "Polozhenie o Kollegiiakh zashchitnikov, utv. NKIu RSFSR" (Statute on the Colleges of Defenders adopted July 5, 1922), quoted from E. S. Rivlin, *Sovetskaia Advokatura* (Soviet Bar), (Moscow, 1926), pp. 26, 27.

13. See, for example, A.Ia. Sukharev (ed.), *Rol' i zadachi sovetskoi Advokatury pod red. A.Ia. Sukhareva* (The Role and the Tasks of the Soviet Bar), (Moscow, 1972), p. 18.

14. See RSFSR Labor Code 1922, Chapter 14, section 174.

15. Cited in note 11, *Otchet*, pp. 64-68.

16. Circular letter No. 89 from June 13, 1924, published in *Ezhen. Sov. Iust.*, 1924, No. 25, 594.

17. Circular letter No. 3 from January 3, 1925 published in *Ezhen. Sov. Iust.*, 1925, No. 1.

18. *Sbornik Dekretov, Postanovlenii, Rasporiazhenii i Prikazov po Narodnomu Khoziaistvu* (Collection of Decrees, Statutes, Instructions and Orders in the Soviet Economy), July (pp. 18, 19) and August (pp. 22, 23), (Moscow, 1925).

19. *Ezhen. Sov. Iust.*, 1926, No. 13, 416.

20. See Statute of the RSFSR Council of Ministers, March 30, 1927, in *Sobr. Uzak.*, 1927, No. 36, item 238.

21. Statute on the Advokatura of the USSR, adopted by the USSR Council of Ministers, August 16, 1939, *Sobr. Post. SSSR*, 1939, No. 49, item 394.

22. Order of the *NKIu SSSR* (Ministry of Justice of the USSR), No. 18, January 24, 1942, see *Sovetskaia Advokatura* (Soviet Bar), (Moscow, 1942), p. 20.

23. See Joint Decree of the Central Committee of CPSU and USSR Council of Ministers of July 30, 1970, "On measures for improvement of the work of the court and

procuratorial organs" in *KPPS v rezoliutsiiakh i resheniiakh s"ezdov, konferentsii i plenumov TsK* (CPSU in the Resolutions and Decisions of Congresses, Conferences and Plenary Sessions of the Central Committee), Vol. 10, (Moscow, 1972), pp. 298-303.

24. *Sobr. Post. Ukr.SSR*, 1953; *Sobr. Post. RSFSR*, 1963, No. 7, item 44.

25. See, for example, the articles of the USSR Supreme Court judge, G. Eliseev, "Usilit' Bor'bu s Pripiskami" (Reinforce the Struggle against False Additions [to the Account Reports]), *Sots. Zak.*, 1977, No. 6, 12; or of the Deputy of the Procurator of Estonian SSR, A. Gretsy, "Za obman gosudarstva–k otvetu" (To Call to Account for the Deception of the State), *Sots. Zak.*, 1977, No. 2, 8.

26. V. Kulikov, "Iskazhenie otchetnykh dannykh–protivogosudarstvennoe deianie" (Falsification of Account Information is an Anti-state Action), *Sots. Zak.*, 1973, No. 5, 10.

27. Regarding this subject at length, see Victor Zaslavsky, "Contemporary Sociology in the Soviet Union," *Social Research*, 44 (Summer 1977), No. 2, 330-353.

28. *Op. cit.*, note 23, pp. 317-322. An imcomplete text of this reslolution (of 15 September 1970) can be found in *KPSS o formirovanii novogo cheloveka. Sbornik dokumentov i materialov (1965-1976)* (The CPSU on the Formation of the New Man. Collection of Documents and Materials (1965-1976), (Moscow, 1976), pp. 116-120.

29. V. Blinov, "Ekonomika i pravo" (Economy and Law), *Izvestiia*, January 28, 1977. V. Terebilov said this in his speech at the session of the USSR Supreme Soviet at October 1977 (Quoted from *Sots. Zak.*, 1977, No. 11, 7).

30. See Joint Decree of Central Committee of CPSU and USSR Council of Ministers, June 25, 1975, "On Measures for the Further Perfection of Economic Legislation," quoted from *Sots. Zak.*, 1975, No. 9, 3-6.

31. B. Zhegulin, "Iuridicheskoi sluzhbe–nashe vnimanie i zabotu" (Our Attention and Concern to the Legal Service), *Khoziaistvo i pravo* (Economy and Law), 1977, No. 10, 71.

32. See *Sobr. Post. SSSR*, 1972, No. 13, item 70.

33. M. P. Vyshinskii, "Sovershenstvovanie khoziaistvennogo zakonodatel'stva i voprosy podgotovki iuridicheskikh kadrov" (The Perfection of Economic Legislation and the Problems of the Preparation of the Legal Personnel), *SGiP*, 1977, No. 6, 60. See English condensed text in *CDSP*, 29 (1977), No. 30.

34. "Metodicheskie rekomendatsii" (Methods Recommendations) in *BNA*, 1976, No. 5, 34-48, and No. 7, 42-48.

35. Instruction on the Payment for the Legal Service Rendered by Advocates to Citizens, Enterprises, Institutions, and Organizations, approved by the USSR Minister of Justice, August 4, 1977, *Sots. Zak.*, 1978, No. 3, 81-84. For comments on and a translation of this instruction by Robert Guttman, see *Review of Socialist Law* 5 (1979), No. 2, 203-211.

36. E. Kubankov, staff member of the Moscow City Committee of CPSU, and Iu. Orlov, head of the General Supervision Division of the Moscow City Procurator's Office, "Preduprezhdenie narushenii zakonnosti v pravovykh aktakh organov upravleniia i khoziaistvovaniia" (Prevention of Violations of Legality in the Legal Acts Issued by the Organs of Administration and Economic Management), *Sots.Zak.*, 1977, No. 5, p. 30.

37. N. I. Klein, *Organizatsiia dogovorno-pravovykh sviazei* (Organization of Legal-Contractual Links), (Moscow, 1976), pp. 135-189.

38. See, for example, V. Strelkov, "Iuridicheskaia sluzhba i ekonomika" (Legal Service and Economics), *Sov. Iust.*, 1978, No. 7, 16.

39. V. I. Chudnov, *Polpredy zakona. O rabote iuriskonsul'tov* (Empowered Representatives of Law. On the Work of Jurisc100sults), (Moscow, 1977), pp. 22-23.

40. V. Groshev and I. Skibo, "Ispol'zovanie pravovykh sredstv dlia uluchsheniia kho-

ziaistvennoi deiatel'nosti" (The Use of Legal Remedies for the Improvement of Economic Activity), *Sots. Zak.*, 1976, No. 7, 74. Regarding rights of enterprises and higher organs to draft and to change previously approved plans, see Statute of the USSR Council of Ministers adopted October 4, 1965 in *Sobr. Post. SSSR*, 1965, Nos. 19-20, item 155.

41. V. Rvachev, N. Baskakov, "Metodicheskoe rukovodstvo deiatel'nost'iu iuridicheskikh sluzhb" (Methods Guidance in Legal Service Activities), *Sots. Zak.*, 1976, No. 1, 70. See also I. Sukharev, "Advokat i khoziaistvennyi dogovor" (The Advocate and the Economic Contract), *Khoziaistvo i Pravo* (Economy and Law), 1977, No. 9, 69; A. Vaksnin'sh, "Juristy otrasli v interesakh proizvodstva" (Jurisconsults and the Interests of the Branch of Industry), *Khoziaistvo i Pravo*, 1977, No. 12, 55; N. Sapozhnikov, "Gosudarstvennyi arbitrazh i ukreplenie distsipliny v khoziaistvennykh otnosheniiakh (State *Arbitrazh* and the Strengthening of Discipline in Economic Relations), *Sots. Zak.*, 1975, No. 11, 5.

42. N. Sapozhnikov, *op. cit.*, 37.

43. V. Strelkov, *op. cit.*, 17.

44. See *Sots. Zak.*, 1977, No. 1, 87-88.

45. L. N. Smirnov, V. V. Kulikov, B. S. Nikiforov (eds.), *Verkhovnyi Sud SSSR* (Supreme Court of the USSR), (Moscow, 1974).

46. See, for example, "V kollegii ministerstva iustitsii SSSR" (In the College of the USSR Ministry of Justice), *Sots. Zak.*, 1977, No. 2, 86.

47. V. Blinov, *op. cit.*, note 29.

48. V. I. Chudnov, *Iuridicheskaia sluzhba predpriiatiia v sovremennykh usloviiakh* (Legal Service of the Enterprise in Contemporary Conditions), (Moscow, 1970), p. 33.

49. See RSFSR Labor Code, art. 220.

50. V. I. Chudnov, *op. cit.*, note 48, p. 67.

51. G. Sotnikov, "Pravovaia rabota v otrasli promyshlennosti i puti ee sovershenstvovaniia" (Legal Work in the Branch of Industry and Ways for its Improvement), *Sots. Zak.*, 1973, No. 8, 13.

52. V. I. Terebilov, "Shest'desiat let vmeste so svoei stranoi" (Sixty Years Along With One's Own Country), *Sots. Zak.*, 1977, No. 10, 9.

53. V. Degtiarenko, "Iuridicheskaia pomoshch' sovkhozam" (Legal Assistance to State Farms), *Sots. Zak.*, 1976, No. 2, 40.

54. This quota was established by the order of the USSR Minister of Agriculture No. 408, November 19, 1973. See R. Nizovskii and I. Rogal', "Mezhkhoziaistvennye iuridicheskie gruppy v sel'skikh raionakh" (Interfarm Legal groups in Rural Regions), *Sots. Zak.*, 1975, No. 8, 19-22.

55. A. Poliakova, "Organizatsiia raboty iuridicheskoi sluzhby" (Organization of Legal Service Work), *Sots. Zak.*, 1973, No. 10, 70.

56. N. Sibulatov, "Mezhkolkhoznaia iuridicheskaia gruppa" (The Intercollective Farm Legal Group), *Khoziaistvo i Pravo* (Economy and Law), 1977, No. 6, 62.

57. V. Terebilov, *op. cit.*, 3-12.

58. *Ezhegodnik Bol'shoi Sovetskoi Entsiklopedii* (Year Book of the Great Soviet Encyclopedia), (Moscow, 1977), p. 71.

59. V. Rvachev, N. Baskakov, *op. cit.*, 69.

60. See *Sots. Zak.*, 1977, No. 2, 39.

61. *Op. cit.*, note 13, p. 71.

62. M. Aliev, "Pravovaia sluzhba v kolkhozakh i sovkhozakh Azerbaidzhana" (Legal Service in the Collective Farms and in the State Farms of Azerbaidzhan), *Sots. Zak.*, 1973, No. 12, 9.

63. R. Nizovskii and I. Rogal', *op cit.*, note 54, 20.

64. V. Billeris, "Iuridicheskaia sluzhba v sel'skom khoziaistve Zaporozhskoi oblasti" (Legal Service in the Agriculture of the Zaporozh'e Province), *Sots. Zak.*, 1976, No. 11, 70.

65. *Sots. Zak.*, 1973, No. 12, 55.

66. *Sots. Zak.*, 1973, No. 10, 44.

67. *Khoziaistvo i Pravo* (Economy and Law), 1977, No. 8, 59-63.

68. *Sots. Zak.*, 1977, No. 8, 88.

69. R. Khoroshikhina, "Ispol'zovanie pravovykh sredstv dlia uluchsheniia kachestva produktsii" (The Use of Legal Remedies for the Improvement of the Quality of Production), *Sots. Zak.*, 1977, No. 1, 71.

70. *Sots. Zak.*, 1977, No. 2, 39.

71. Cited *supra* in note 33; the article of M. P. Vyshinskii was also published in *Sots. Zak.*, 1976, No. 11, 21-26, which is unusual practice in cases when the authors are not top rulers.

72. Statute on mandatory appointments for "junior specialists" graduated from universities and colleges, issued by the USSR Minister of Higher Education on March 18, 1968, was published in the *Biulleten' Ministerstva Vysshego i Srednego Spetsial'nogo Obrazovaniia SSSR* (Bulletin of the USSR Ministry of Higher and Secondary Special Education), 1968, No. 6.

73. A. Sukharev, "Nasushchnye problemy podgotovki kadrov" (Pressing Problems in the Preparation of [Legal] Cadres), *Sots. Zak.*, 1974, No. 2, 3-8.

74. See, in this regard, V. Zaslavsky, Y. Luryi, "The Passport System in the USSR and Changes in Soviet Society" to be published in a forthcoming issue of *Soviet Union*, Special Issue on Soviet Legal Policy, 1979.

75. R. Nizovskii, I. Rogal', *op. cit.*, 22.

SOVIET ADVOKATURA TWENTY-FIVE YEARS AFTER STALIN

Zigurds L. Zile

1. Introduction

Broadly defined, the Soviet legal profession comprises people who perform specialized law-related mental work which, although differentiated, has been deemed sufficiently alike to "constitute interest-group activity by persons acting in their professional capacity."[1] Soviet statistical compilations refer to them as "juridical personnel [*iuridicheskii personal*]."[2] This essay, however, focuses on only one sector of the profession–the *advokatura*. The term *advokatura* describes the aggregate of colleges of advocates (*kollegii advokatov*), those purportedly "voluntary social organizations"[3] that draw their clientele from the public at large. The *advokatura*, therefore, can be roughly approximated to the private practising bar in polities of the Western type. The practitioners, who are members of the colleges or "bar associations," are known as advocates (*advokaty*).

The passing of Stalin and the subsequent declarations at the 20th Party Congress in 1956 about the political past and future had a noticeable positive impact on law and the role of the advocates in the Soviet system. Both the political ideology and the political behavior of those in power became relatively stable and more predictable. The moderation of the crisis mentality and the concomitant easing of the heavy hand of decades of reactive, impulsive, and capricious rule improved the climate for the creation and normative regularization of people's expectations. This revivified "legality" reduced, to some extent, the subservience of the advocates to the state and politics and the timidity with which they had all too often interceded in behalf of their clients. Vigorous defense in ordinary criminal cases and representation in civil matters not only became respectable but were held out as the advocates' essential responsibilities. In the rhetoric of the first post-Stalin decade, the exercise of these responsibilities, far from doing harm to the administration of Soviet justice, could only benefit it.[4] A change in mood came first; discussion and implementation of a statutory reform followed. During the early 1960s, all union republics enacted statutes on the *advokatura* under the authority of article 13 of the Principles of Court Organization of the USSR and the Union and Autonomous Republics. This effectively accomplished the

207

transfer of the regulation of the *advokatura* from the federal[5] to republic levels for some time to come.

The course of the reform itself and the organizational structures and operational principles it consolidated have been amply described and commented on in non-Soviet literature;[6] there is no need to rehash them. Instead, this essay looks at the situation of the *advokatura* from a vantage point some fifteen years after the reform and twenty-five years after Stalin. It focuses, above all, on the operational sphere of the *advokatura* as distinguished from the adjacent sectors of the profession and on the specific characteristics of the advocates' position and work that thus far have supposedly set them apart from other practitioners of law. It also tries to identify and assess the trends in the demand for and the modes of delivery of legal services and the staffing and distribution of legal professionals that may drastically affect the status of the *advokatura* as a distinct and distinctly important component of the Soviet legal profession.

2. Size and Distribution of the Advokatura

The members of the other sectors of the Soviet legal profession have heretofore been distinguishable from advocates mainly by their status as staff employees of their clients. As a general rule, members of the colleges of advocates may not serve in the employ of institutions (agencies), organizations, and enterprises. Exceptions have been allowed for members pursuing pedagogical or scholarly work (RSFSR Stat., art. 37) and, in some republics, in cases in which an advocate's practice does not amount to what would be regarded as a full workload. Conversely, the Soviet bar purports to be integrated—"only a person who is a member of a college of advocates may engage in the practice of legal advocacy [*advokatskoi deiatel'nost'iu*]" (RSFSR Stat., art. 4). But the attempted distinguishing principle has not entirely protected the advocates' turf from encroachments. Moreover, further encroachments are probable. While the advocates have no apparent reason to feel professionally threatened by judges, procurators, investigators, notaries, and academic lawyers, the balance between the respective spheres of the advocates and the staff or house counsel (*iuriskonsul'ty*) of governmental bodies, institutions, social organizations, and, above all, economic entities may be a matter of concern to the *advokatura*. To the extent that a growing number of institutional clients are hiring staff attorneys, general and special retainers of advocates are likely to become less common, with negative effect on the operational sphere of the *advokatura*. And, finally, the lawful representation by lay persons also impinges upon the *advokatura*'s supposed monopoly on "private" practice, with potentially the same negative effect.

The *advokatura* is neither the largest sector of the Soviet legal profession, nor is it large in absolute terms. As is often the case, the available official

208

Soviet compilations of statistics give no direct and precise answer as to its size. But we believe that the data we have permit reasonably accurate approximations.

The reports of the most recent all-union census yield the following 1970 figures for juridical personnel: [7]

	Total at the beginning of 1970	1970 total in % of the figure for the beginning of 1959	Employed in state administration, credit and insurance institutions, and Party, komsomol, trade union, and other social organizations (a)
USSR	108,720	138	78,716
RSFSR	63,116	134	45,376
Ukrainian SSR	19,188	140	13,021
Belorussian SSR	3,237	136	2,283
Uzbek SSR	3,374	143	2,666
Kazakh SSR	5,607	167	4,296
Georgian SSR	2,851	131	2,395
Azerbaidzhan SSR	1,688	127	1,404
Lithuanian SSR	1,869	178	1,377
Moldavian SSR	1,348	183	936
Latvian SSR	1,452	134	1,079
Kirghiz SSR	1,142	141	901
Tadzhik SSR	910	134	688
Armenian SSR	1,178	186	951
Turkmen SSR	758	120	629
Estonian SSR	1,002	147	714

(a) *Note:* The figures in this column are from tables titled "Distribution of Population by Occupation in the Several Branches of the National Economy." Besides "State Administration, etc.," the tables list eight other branches. However, only five ("Industry," "Construction," "Transportation and Communications," "Trade, Catering, Provisioning, Procurement, and Supply," and "Education, Cultural Affairs, Arts, Sciences, and Scientific Services") give data on juridical personnel. The remaining three ("Agriculture," "Housing and Communal and Everyday Services," and "Health, Physical Training, and Social Services") give none. The tables on six republics (Azerbaidzhan, Kirghiz, Tadzhik, Armenian, Turkmen, and Estonian) do not include the category of juridical personnel in any of the eight branches which, as a minimum, represent house counsel in economic enterprises, law teachers, and some legal scholars. The ninth category ("State Administration, etc.") is a catch-all. Inferentially, it lumps together judges, procurators, investigators, notaries, and some governmental staff counsel. But it is not clear whether, for instance, lawyers on the staffs of industrial ministries are counted under "Industry" or "State Administration, etc." Unfortunately for us, the latter rubric also embraces the *advokatura* without a hint as to how the members of this rather significant "social organization" could be sifted out.

There is a discrepancy between the total figure of juridical personnel and the sum of the figures broken down by branches. Thus, the USSR total is 108,720, while the sum of the branch figures for the USSR as a whole comes to only 105,947 (Industry – 12,980, Construction–2,397, Transportation and Communications–1,702, Trade, etc.–8,341, Education, etc.–1,811, and State Administration, etc.–78,716). The difference of 2,773 probably represents the personnel in the three branches averaging less than a thousand per branch and not reported. We do believe, therefore, that any estimate of the number of house counsel in economic enterprises should take this figure into account. The resulting figure of 30,004 house counsel is, then, very close to the roughly contemporaneous estimate by Barry and Berman.[8]

In 1939 there were approximately 8,000 advocates or about 4 per 100,000 of population in the USSR. The entire juridical personnel numbered 62,000 or 32 per 100,000.[9] Over the next two decades, the numbers of both juridical personnel, in general, and advocates, in particular, grew faster than the Soviet population. War losses suffered by the population at large were not reflected in the regime's ability and willingness to refill the law-related positions. The 1959 figures for juridical personnel stood at 78,711 [10] and 38, respectively, in a population of 208,800,000;[11] for the advocates–at 12,828 [12] and 6. Clearly, the improvement in the ratio of advocates to the population was more pronounced. The average annual increment was about 835 for the juridical personnel as a whole and 240 for the *advokatura*. The situation changed during the next eleven years immediately preceding the 1970 census. Juridical personnel grew at a yearly average of 2,728 to reach, as we saw above, 108,720 and a ratio of 45/100,000 by the beginning of 1970. By contrast, the size of the *advokatura* remained virtually unchanged at 13,000 in 1967,[13] and we have no reason to think the figure appreciably changed over the remaining two or three years. Thus, the number of advocates, we surmise, did not exceed 13,500 in 1970, which meant a slightly worsened ratio of 5.6/100,000.

The size of the *advokatura* can also be expressed as a percent of the total juridical personnel. It was about 12% (13,500 ÷ 108,720) in the USSR in 1970. At the same time, the percent of house counsel employed by economic enterprises was already about two-and-a-half times higher. It should be noted that the corresponding percent for the RSFSR was also about 12 (7,500 ÷ 63,116).[14] The same ratio obtained in Belorussia (390 ÷ 3,237).[15] One should not, however, assume the general applicability of the coefficient of .12. The exceptionally high ratios of juridical personnel per 100,000 of population in republics such as Estonia (70), Latvia (slightly more than 61), Georgia (slightly less than 61), and Lithuania (60) may be explained in terms of the presence of a relatively large *advokatura* in each of them. Presumably, the legal staffs of the judiciary, procuracy, and other state organs are roughly proportional to the republic population. Unless the number of house counsel is inordinately high in any of them, advocates may conceivably make up from

25 to 35% or even a larger share of juridical personnel in these "juridically strong" republics. In the Ukrainian republic where there were 41 juridical personnel per 100,000 inhabitants, advocates constituted 17% (3,340 ÷ 19,188) of the juridical personnel. [16]

On December 23, 1970, the Central Committee of the CPSU and the Council of Ministers of the USSR issued a joint decree "On Improving Legal Work in the National Economy." [17] It was, above all, a clarion call to mobilize the forces of law in support of the increasingly complex economy. The recent improvements had fallen short of the actual needs. A general USSR statute on house counsel of June 22, 1972, [18] and a federal ministerial instruction on legal services to farms of January 3, 1973,[19] were direct outgrowths of this call. Both were concerned mainly with the creation, filling, and functions of positions of staff legal counsel. It should come as no surprise, therefore, if most of the numerical increase in the Soviet juridical personnel since 1970 has come about through additions to the ranks of staff counsel rather than advocates.

Within a period of just seven years (*i.e.*, up to the beginning of 1977), juridical personnel in the USSR expanded by one-third to 145,000. [20] If the *Advokatura* has held its relative position, its present size is in the vicinity of 17,000, *i.e.*, 12% of the total. Data from the RSFSR suggest this might be so. In December of 1974, the Minister of Justice of the RSFSR, Blinov, cited the figure of 9,000.[21] It is further corroborated by an article written in early 1976, according to which the number of advocates in the RSFSR had increased by almost 1,500 since 1970. [22] Again, assuming that the growth of the juridical personnel of the RSFSR had kept pace with that of the USSR as a whole, there would have been about 78,000 of them by the end of 1974, including between 9,000 and 9,500 advocates (78,000 x .12). An RSFSR figure of 10,000 on January 1, 1977, is a reasonable approximation. On the basis of these estimated figures, the ratio of advocates to 100,000 population was approximately 6.6 for the USSR (up 1 since 1970) and 7.4 for the RSFSR (up 1.6 since 1970), as of the beginning of 1977. [23] The ratios for the four small republics named earlier might well be twice as high or better.

While the aggregate numerical relationships within the legal profession of the RSFSR appear to be closely reflected in the statistics at the federal level because of the republic's size, the same relationships do not necessarily obtain within the constituent parts of the RSFSR. Just as some of the other republics either rise above or drop below the country's averages, so do parts of the RSFSR with reference to the republic's averages. The membership of the *advokatura* is unevenly distributed and, here and there, the unevenness seems less a function of a variable need for legal services than of the advocates' particular preferences for working and living environments. While there has been a great need for legal assistance in rural areas, most law graduates are urbanites and prefer to remain in cities. [24] In 1975, 950 advocates belonged to the Moscow city college of advocates, for 12.7 advocates per 100,000 residents. At the other end of the vast republic, in Krasnoiarsk territory, each 100,000 inhabitants had to share about 4.4 advocates. [25] In Kostroma region, one half of the advocates are in the city, giving it a ratio of 10, while the other half serve the rest of the region where the ratio is 4.6. Nearly 80% of the advocates in Astrakhan region live in the regional center. [26] Minister Blinov wrote: "Unfortunately, the staff sizes of some legal consultation offices are formed without analyzing or calculating the volume of work. Thus, in Altai territory about one-third of the lawyers live in the city of Barnaul, while there are none at all in 16 districts." [27] There have been improvements in this respect over the last decade, however. Not so long ago, the situation was worse. In 1967 the roughly 7,000 advocates of the RSFSR were working at approximately 250 legal consultation offices with up to 50-60 members each. [28] There were about as many cities with a population of 50,000 or more in the RSFSR at the time. [29] Today the "law firms" are smaller, there are more of them, and they are, comparatively speaking, better distributed. For example, in 1975 the 200 advocates of Krasnoiarsk territory were working at 62 consultation offices. [30] The practice of extending the consultation office by means of consultation desks or points (*konsul'tatsionnye punkty*) strategically located within concentrations of potential clients—at local government buildings, factories, palaces of culture, etc., [31] has further eased access to the advocates' services. Complementary figures suggest that the distribution of advocates in the RSFSR may have been worse than in, at least, a few other republics. At the end of 1971, the 3,340 Ukrainian advocates reportedly staffed 624 legal consultation offices. [32] The 390 Belorussian advocates in 1972 were organized into 105 such offices, 56 of which were staffed by only one advocate. [33]

In sum, by the beginning of the 1970s, the Soviet *advokatura* found itself numerically eclipsed by another practitioner sector of the legal profession—the house counsel. Moreover, while public pronouncements repeatedly stressed the role of the *advokatura* in strengthening socialist legality under the contemporary conditions, the policy-makers' actions did not indicate that the ranks of the *advokatura* itself would be substantially augmented and re-equipped to meet the rising demand for legal services at all levels of the society. Despite the advocates' historical and present image and their long recognized powers and responsibilities as the hired counsellors and defenders of "the laws and the legal interests of citizens, enterprises, institutions, organizations and collective farms" (RSFSR Stat., art. 2), the opportunities presented by the elevation of law and lawyers seemed to be passing them by.

The Soviet legal literature has not lacked articles urging the raising of the advocates' role and the quality of their work in the changing legal climate. Nor has it failed to endlessly report figures purporting to demonstrate how the advocates were rising to the challenge and fulfilling and overfulfilling their production plan. Much of this genre, however, originates within the *advokatura* itself or the ministries of justice within the republics which exercise the "overall direction of the colleges of advocates ... and control over their activities" (RSFSR Stat., art. 5), not a disinterested authorship. It is our impression that various options for the delivery of legal services are being considered at the highest levels of policy-making and implementation. We must not assume that there is a deep commitment to the organizational uniqueness of the *advokatura* [34] at those levels; instead, one might expect it to be regarded as a means to an end, along with other means. For example, all-union economic ministries under pressure to improve legal work within their jurisdictions might have to and, indeed, prefer to employ their own staff counsel. Despite instances of misallocation of personnel and workloads, the *advokatura* has no discernible surplus resources to meet the allegedly massive demand for legal services by economic entities. In addition, the delivery of legal services by a staff counsel on the payroll of enterprises under a ministry's control would assure the competent ministries of better control over the way the legal services are delivered. Too much independence and assertiveness that legalism fosters are feared by a system that refuses to share power. [35] House counsel can be organized by branches and trained and controlled accordingly. By contrast, a single organization unifying all advocates (or, for that matter, all house counsel or, even worse, all legal practitioners or juridical personnel) might be seen as too influential a group for the Soviet system to tolerate.

It is for this latter reason, above all, that the *advokatura* cannot be accused of having let a magnificent opportunity slip by. Analogies from Western-type polities of the bar yielding vast segments of modern law practice (administrative law, taxation, estate planning, etc.) to emerging groups of other professionals by reason of tradition or inertia are inapposite. It would have been unthinkable for the Soviet advocates openly to agitate against the further expansion of existing groups and the creation of new rival groups of legal practitioners and thereby admit of a monopoly interest. And as long as the allocation of resources is centrally determined, a professional group located at the periphery of the system can do virtually nothing on its own initiative to expand its size and penetrate new fields of activity when an opportunity seemingly presents itself. This is not to say that the advocates' professional interests could not be or were not articulated at some stage of policy-making. [36]

Article 161, paragraph 1 of the new 1977 USSR Constitution declares that "there are colleges of advocates to provide legal assistance to citizens and organizations." This is at once reassuring and ambiguous. The paragraph only refers to "citizens and organizations." On the one hand, "organization" can be read as a generic term covering all kinds of legal entities. On the other hand, such usage is unconventional in the context of legal services. Thus, the

RSFSR Statute on the *Advokatura* invariably defines its clientele as "citizens, enterprises, institutions, organizations, and collective farms" (arts. 1, 2, 3). The legislation on house counsel likewise lists and thereby implicitly distinguishes between the last four types of entities.[37] So do the Principles of Court Organization of the USSR and the Union and Autonomous Republics (art. 13) and the Law on Court Organization of the RSFSR (art. 23). In fact, the Constitution itself distinguishes between "organizations" and the other types of entities (*e.g.*, Arts. 105, 146, 164). If the choice of terms in Article 161 is deliberate, the *advokatura* has no guaranteed role in serving economic entities. The Constitution would have, by implication, assigned this sector of legal services to counsel paid and directly controlled by agencies of the state. Under the principle of federal supremacy, republic statutes—notwithstanding the second paragraph of Article 161—would be powerless to define the *advokatura*'s sphere of operation as extending beyond these limits. The Constitution recognizes another competitor of the *advokatura* less ambiguously. Article 162 states: "Representatives of social organizations and labor collectives are permitted to participate in court proceedings in civil and criminal cases." We take this article to mean that certain guarantees of representation contained in such provisions as article 44, paragraph 3 of the RSFSR Code of Civil Procedure, and article 47, paragraph 4 of the RSFSR Code of Criminal Procedure, as well as article 250 of the RSFSR Code of Criminal Procedure are now secured by the Constitution.

3. Advocates' Work in Relation to Other Forms of the Practice of Law

Soviet advocates do very much the same things their counterparts in other polities do in the discharge of their professional functions and responsibilities, even though each may give a different emphasis to aspects of their work and adopt their own style. Article 1 of the RSFSR Statute on the *Advokatura* mandates the colleges of advocates "to provide defense counsel at preliminary investigations and in court; to act as representatives in civil cases in court and before *arbitrazh*; and to render any other legal assistance required." Article 3 expresses "other legal assistance" essentially as counselling and drafting. Finally, article 30 obligates each advocate "actively to participate in propaganda for Soviet law."

In this section, we shall survey these modes of the advocate's practice and attempt, as much as practicable, to describe their extent, competition from other practitioners, and the future outlook from the perspective of the *advokatura*. While we would prefer to give data on the volume of each type of practice in the appropriate subsection, we have chosen to abstract whatever we have on the four principal categories in the introductory pages. The reason for this is again the need for extrapolation from incomplete data, some of

214

which indicate interdependencies between the categories. By displaying and explaining our computations at the outset, we will avoid repeating essentially the same matter in each subsection.

We found the most complete and concise statement of the volume of advocates' work by category in a 1975 issue of *Sovetskaia Iustitsiia*:

> "It suffices to point out that during the previous year [1974] alone, the advocates of the Russian Federation gave citizens advice and counsel on legal questions in more than two million instances, prepared 600 thousand applications [*zaiavlenii*] and petitions of grievance [*zhalob*], took part in the preliminary investigation of every fourth criminal case, and handled about 70 percent of the criminal and a large number of the civil cases in courts." [38]

Since the data for the last three items are not sufficiently revealing, we will attempt to make them more meaningful with the help of other fragments of relevant information. The fact that some of our data are from different years, come from small samples, or are given as rough approximations makes the process cumbersome and indirect and the results less reliable than one might wish.

A decade or so ago, the college of advocates of the Dagestan ASSR lamented that its members appeared in only 3 to 4% of the civil cases tried by the courts of Dagestan in 1967. This represented a mere 420 civil trials. [39] Consequently, there were altogether 12,000 (420 ÷ .035) civil trials in Dagestan that year. The population of Dagestan was about 1,300,000 in 1967, about 34% of it urban. The corresponding figures for the RSFSR as a whole were 127,000,000 and 54%. [40] There was, on the average, one civil trial per every 108 inhabitants of Dagestan. Applying double that ratio (*i.e.*, 1/54) to the RSFSR to compensate for Dagestan's relative backwardness and thus, presumably, the much lower rate of civil litigation, we obtain 2,352,000 civil trials in 1967. The figure adjusted to the population of 1974 (132,900,000) [41] is 2,461,000. According to Barry and Berman, "civil matters ... make up about 85 percent of all cases in Soviet courts." [42] Proceeding on this assumption, we postulate a total of 2,895,000 (2,461,000 ÷ .85) court cases in the RSFSR in 1974. The difference of 434,000 (2,895,000-2,461,000) is to be attributed to criminal litigation. We can now restate the workload of the 9,000 advocates of the RSFSR in 1974:

Counselling and legal advice	2,000,000+
Preparation of applications and petitions	600,000
Preliminary investigation (434,000 x .25)	108,500
Criminal trials (434,000 x .70)	303,000
Civil trials (2,461,000 x .06 (the coefficient of .06 is from the late 1960s) [43]	147,700

One more inferential leap yields the estimate of the more current 1977 workload of the 17,000 advocates of the entire USSR. For the purposes of this computation, we are varying only the population figure, while keeping the other assumptions and relationships constant. The population of the USSR on January 1, 1977, was 1.94 times that of the RSFSR three years back. Applying this coefficient to the 1974 figures for the RSFSR, we get the following for the USSR in 1977:

Counselling and legal advice	3,880,000+
Preparation of applications and petitions	1,164,000
Preliminary investigation	210,500
Criminal trials	588,000
Civil trials	286,500

or altogether 6,129,000 instances of legal services rendered. The total number of 840,000 (588,000 ÷ .70) criminal trials for the USSR arrived at by this method is quite close to Juviler's estimate of 900,000 convictions per year but more decidedly below the 1,000,000 calculated by Chalidze. [44] One final cautionary remark. Nothing in the data we have used to construct this composite suggests that "civil trials" includes appearances before *arbitrazh*. This could be another fairly significant category of work. We are also unsure as to how the work content of advocates retained as virtual house counsel by enterprises, collective farms, and other entities is reflected in the statistics as far as itemization of practice is concerned.

Criminal Investigations and Trials

The threat to the advocate's criminal practice from lay people, though resting on unimpeachable revolutionary precedent, [45] seems largely theoretical some sixty years later. The Fundamental Principles of Criminal Procedure of the USSR and the Union Republics still provide that "representatives of trade unions and other social organizations, and other persons to whom such right is given by legislation of union republics, shall be permitted to serve as defense counsel" (art. 22). The RSFSR Code of Criminal Procedure extends this right to "close relatives and statutory representatives of the accused, as well as other persons," subject to "ruling of the court or decree of the judge" (art. 47). But the people listed in this paragraph of the RSFSR Code cannot participate at the stage of preliminary investigation [46] and are barely mentioned in the current Soviet legal literature. Presumably, no lay takeover will come from these quarters.

The competitive capabilities of organization representatives are a different matter. They are likely to be either a house counsel of the accused's enterprise (apparently, acting on behalf of the trade union in order to qualify under a strict reading of the statute) or a staff member of his or her trade union's legal service. As a class, they may be as qualified as advocates, albeit perhaps with less direct experience in criminal trials. They enjoy the same rights as advocates at all stages of a criminal proceeding and act in their own name. [47] Nonetheless, the competition does not seem acute for the time being. We have gained the impression from the available material that, whenever a criminal defendant is assisted by a defense counsel, that counsel is an advocate rather than a lawyer from another sector of the legal profession.

But even in the absence of overt rivalry, the advocates are not assured of a fixed domain. The need for advocates in criminal practice can be expected to vary directly with criminality in the country and the level of procedural rights of criminal suspects and defendants. The more serious the crime problem, the more prosecutions and opportunities for the participation of advocates. Conversely, the greater the strides toward extirpation of crime, the smaller the arena for the criminal defense practitioner. By the same token, a return to the early ideal of procedural simplicity would either obviate or drastically reduce the need for skilled professional analysts of alternative rules and mechanisms, evaluators of evidence, negotiators, and oratorical persuaders. By contrast, a growing perception of the criminal process as essentially adversary is apt to lead to procedural formality and complexity and open still further opportunities for advocates in criminal practice.

According to undisclosed statistics, crime in the Soviet Union has been decreasing since as far back as one cares to remember. [48] Yet the lawyers' work seems never done in this area. Mokichev, Rector of the All-Union Correspondence Institute of Law, and Dobrovolskii, a member of the RSFSR Supreme Court deny there is a contradiction:

> "The family of one of our mutual acquaintances was holding an important conference. Their son, a young worker, intended to enter a higher school. But which one? The son's choice was law school.
>
> 'But is it worthwhile?' the father said. 'Crime is declining in our country, and so the demand for jurists will, too. Wouldn't it be better to consider some other, more promising, specialty?'
>
> One frequently hears opinions such as that above. They have their origin mainly in the fact that at one time an alleged 'over-production' of lawyers was discovered, and some higher and all secondary educational institutions specializing in law were closed.
>
> Crime is actually on the decline in our country. This is a natural phenomenon, since the social causes that drive people to crime are being eliminated in the socialist society.
>
> However, the final liquidation of crime is still a task that will take many years of stubborn labor, not only by jurists, needless to say, but also by all Party and Soviet agencies and the broad public." [49]

Procedural formality also remains relatively stable. The 1977 Constitution of the USSR restates the accused's right to defense (Art. 158). A new Arti-

217

cle 160 elevates the varying contents of criminal law and procedure to the constitutional level by providing that "[n]o one can be adjudged guilty of commission of a crime and subjected to criminal punishment other than by verdict of court and in accordance with the statute." The 1958 Principles of Criminal Procedure initially defined the procedural right to counsel during the preliminary investigation fairly narrowly. Since then, the right has served as a sort of an impoundment of potential demand for advocates' services from which subsequent reform measures expanding the right to counsel have judiciously released small quantities of that demand. [50] There was, however, a limited retreat in 1972. [51] The right to counsel at the trial stage is quite liberally defined in law, and the highest courts have, on the whole, rendered decisions favoring the full exercise of what the statute has given in more general terms. Striking examples are the *Case of Karapetian* [52] and the *Case of Rudomenko.* [53]

The advocates are, at present, excluded from participation at any stage in cases within the competency of the so-called "special" procurator's office and "special" courts. These "special" institutions have jurisdiction over matters involving employees in security-classified enterprises and institutions. According to Luryi's most revealing article, "[A] limited number of defense counsel already form part of the legal staff of these institutions, so regular advocates are not allowed to participate in the cases. Unlike regular defense counsel, these staff lawyers are paid fixed salaries by the government." [54] In view of the Soviet penchant for wrapping many aspects of their country's life in secrecy, this field of criminal practice might be substantial but vary in size from time to time. It also serves, in a manner of speaking, as a reminder and example of the possibility of dispensing criminal justice, including legal defense, in a tightly controlled society entirely by persons on the state payroll and with the investigator, prosecutor, judge, and defender functioning in a closed world and very likely as a close-knit group. The ostensibly illegal practice of clearances for counsel in political trials does not seem to reduce the total responsibility of the advocates for criminal defense, but merely removes it from the hands of some and concentrates it in those of preferred ones. [55]

Advocates are also active at the supervisory stage of criminal practice. A significant percentage of protests against criminal judgments that have gone into effect lodged by procurators and the presidents of the cassational courts are in response to petitions prepared by advocates.[55a]

Civil Claims and Trials in Courts and in the Organs of Arbitrazh
Just as the dying out of crime is in the Soviet ideological future, so is the disappearance of disputes between all persons, natural and juristic, over their respective rights and duties. Should this occur, a line of advocates' work as we know it today would also be lost. This is not a short-run prospect, however.

For the time being, there are considerably more such disputes in the Soviet Union than the advocates either can or care to handle. We rely on the First Deputy Minister of Justice of the USSR, Sukharev, to elucidate the underlying dialectic for us:

"As the material well-being of the population grows, the problems of protecting the citizens' [individual, property, and other] rights acquire an ever greater significance. Of course, the number of civil disputes in courts is dropping. This expresses, above all, the solicitude of the state about meeting ever more adequately the material needs of the people, the growth of citizens' legal and general culture, and the rise of their consciousness. Many conflicts are successfully resolved through societal channels. One can confidently state that the process of curtailment of disputes in courts will repeat itself in other categories of cases, too. However, the character and significance of the interests that law protects will, obviously, not only undergo a change but also become more complex. Therefore, advocates should pay more attention to participation in civil litigation and show concern, in every way, for ensuring legality in labor, housing, marital-family, copyright and other cases affecting the rights and the individual and property interests of citizens and of state and social institutions and organizations." [56]

Like the Principles of Criminal Procedure, the Principles of Civil Procedure of the USSR and the Union Republics also provide for both professional and lay representation in court (art. 28). Article 44 of the RSFSR Code of Civil Procedure lists six categories of lay representation—four kinds of organization representatives and two others. One of the latter categories is quite narrow. A person involved in an occurrence or transaction with another may authorize the other (if adult and not under guardianship) to represent the interests of both. The remaining category is a catch-all comprising "persons which the court hearing the case has admitted to representation in the case." Article 47, however, disqualifies, besides minors and individuals under guardianship, persons excluded from a college of advocates and certain legal professionals, namely, judges, procurators, and investigators. Since the admission is by ruling of the court, one must not assume that article 44 guarantees that any person not disqualified under article 47 will be able to act as a representative. [57] Again, these provisions merely permit occasional lay representation in suitable cases and should not be taken as an example of burgeoning practice by non-advocates or, indeed, non-lawyers. We have seen nothing in the Soviet legal literature even intimating that this is a common phenomenon.

Authorized agents of trade unions might be the most important class of professionals and paraprofessionals delivering legal services in areas ordinarily associated with the advocates' civil trial practice. It is noteworthy that the services of the union counsel are not limited to union members, but can

219

extend to all workers and employees of the entity within which the union local operates. Moreover, the services of the legal consultation offices of trade unions may also reach the members' families, pensioners, and students. In addition, other organizations properly empowered by statute, charter, or bylaws may represent their members in civil court. At present, this possibility seems to be confined to the area of intellectual property. The All-Union Copyright Agency (*VAAP*) is, we are told, the only organization (other than colleges of advocates or trade unions) authorized by statute, charter, or by-laws to render representation in court to persons other than its members. [58] Finally, the house counsel of state institutions, enterprises, collective farms, and other cooperative and social organizations may appear in court on behalf of their employers.

As our survey of the advocates' workload shows, the recent experience does not speak well of the role of the *advokatura* in civil litigation. Some figures sound downright alarming. As we reported earlier, only 5 to 6% of civil cases were tried with the participation of advocates in the RSFSR in the late 1960s. [59] This being an average figure, the rate in areas served by some consultation offices of the *advokatura* has been even lower and sinking. [60] We shall recall that the figure for the Dagestan ASSR was a mere 3 to 4%. [61]

We have been unable to ascertain whether the parties to most of the cases tried without the assistance of advocates enjoy other professional legal counsel or appear *pro se*. We do have evidence, however, that the advocates have not been displaced from civil litigation against their will, but have stayed away despite opportunity, [62] possibly for lack of incentive.

While advocates may shun the mass of civil trials and possibly the antecedent claims work involving the everyday concerns of individuals, they seem to be less reluctant to take the cases of economic entities. But it is precisely here that they encounter the state policy of expanding the delivery of legal services in house. The more-or-less-free-lancing advocate and the lawyer-employee (*i.e.*, the house counsel) have coexisted from virtually the very beginning of the Soviet rule. However, the work of the house counsel received little attention until the economic reforms of the 1960s. [63] Reorientation of the Soviet economy on profit-motivated decisions at the level of operating units breathed new life into the law of contract and put an accent on their legal rights and duties. Relatively easily comprehended economic costs attached to the failure to vindicate one's legal rights or perform one's legal duties. A contemporary *Izvestiia* editorial commented: "The economic reform has made managers keep track of every ruble of profit and loss with great exactitude, and it is also making them take a new look at legal services at their enterprises. ... In present-day conditions, knowledge of law is inseparable from knowledge of concrete economics." [64]

If rigorously pursued, the new staffing policy could have preempted a vast sector of legal practice. After all, in 1969 only one in every ten industrial, transportation, construction, trade, and other enterprises and organizations had one or more house counsel. [65] But the *advokatura* was not about to renounce this promising yet heretofore neglected territory. Armed with unquestioned powers to render legal assistance to anyone, including the economic entities of the state, and a decades-long professional tradition of sorts, some colleges of advocates began hustling even before the rousing decree of 1970. They stressed the benefits of letting advocates fan out into the economy rather than hiring house counsel. The variety and complexity of the legal problems facing an enterprise were too formidable for a single staff person to master, the advocates contended; *advokatura*'s consultation offices being collectives could designate just the right specialist for each set of problems. In other words, a retainer of a consultation office of advocates put the enterprise into more competent and reliable hands. Simultaneously, they warned individual advocates not to overreach themselves by trying to serve more than two enterprises, to avoid an absentee's loss of sensitivity to the operational peculiarities of each client entity. [66]

By now, every aspect of the economic life has come to be seen as shot-through with authoritatively proclaimed and binding rules. Control through strict adherence to rules purportedly aims to displace expediency and improvisation in day-to-day activities. As a concomitant the lawyer is, all of a sudden, being thrust into the role of a generalist who must be everywhere, watch and see everything, work with everyone, and know and understand it all. [67] But even though the USSR Ministry of Justice has outfitted the advocates with a model retainer contract[68] to enable them better to respond to the challenge of the economy, it remains to be seen if the *advokatura* will actually claim and be assured of a significant permanent role for itself in serving the economic entities of the state.

The larger enterprises, as one might have surmised, have been the first to hire house counsel. This has not occurred to the same degree in the smaller enterprises, of which only a small percentage have filled a legal staff position. The staffing of certain types of institutions is even worse. In Saratov region, for example, there are only two legal counsel for 1,700 public health institutions. [69] It is mostly in the small local enterprises that advocates find their "company" clients. [70] On the occasion of its fiftieth anniversary in 1972, the Soviet *advokatura* served some 16,000 industrial clients. [71] In 1974, the advocates of the RSFSR had retainers from 9,000 enterprises and institutions without counsel of their own. [72] But all is not well with advocates' services. They do almost exclusively what they are best at—claims' work and trials. They rarely show up at the client enterprises and neglect most of the items on the idealized plant lawyer's agenda. [73] In the earlier phase of their re-awakened interest in working with enterprises, the consultation offices of the colleges of advocates might have resembled little roving bands of miracle workers. They would get a retainer from an enterprise, discover that the latter was surrounded by obligors in default, present claims to or, if need be, serve summons on each of them, and *voilà* the entity was thousands, even tens of thousands of rubles richer; all for a small fee. Measuring the success of the advocates' services in terms of monetary recoveries for their institutional clients was usual. [74] An illusion of a universally favorable balance of payments was created. This was possible because legal assistance was rare. The obligees of the successful claimant/plaintiff perhaps were unaware of or did not care about *its* defaults and did not pursue legal remedies. That is to say, we cannot assume that the advocates managed invariably to secure retainers from the good guys; yet wherever they stepped in, they somehow got a bundle for the client. A 1976 news item out of Moscow indirectly exposed the fallaciousness of attempts to justify legal services solely by the sums of contract damages, forfeits, or fines they bring in. It seems that while an advocate on retainer was doing *his* thing at the plant, the plant lost in fines alone 43,000 rubles in 1973, 21,000 in 1974, and 36,000 in 1975 on successful claims against it. The report intimated that a full-time counsel might have prevented this from happening. [75] Thus, the 120,000,000 rubles which the advocates of the RSFSR allegedly recovered for their client economic entities in 1975 [76] might not conceivably have enriched any one of them. But good sense aside, a recent issue of *Sovetskaia Iustitsiia* still reported a kind of Siberian advocates' olympiad with barratry as the main event. [77] It occurs to us that the reason for the work on contract claims and suits should rather be found in goals such as proper internalization of costs or encouragement of responsible interstitial planning and management at the periphery. [78]

The current impossibility of giving every small enterprise a staff counsel, in combination with widespread criticism of the performance of advocates in the industry, had led to the suggestion of another alternative—legal services bureaus for enterprises. They themselves would be state enterprises under the control of an appropriate soviet. Their lawyers would be state employees on a fixed salary. They would differ from house counsel in that the employer would not be their client. Just as the consultation offices of colleges of advocates (and herein lies a threat to the *advokatura*), they would contract with institutional clients to provide legal services. [79]

Assuming that litigation constitutes a large share of the advocates' work in enterprises, we still have no inkling regarding the weight of their effort in the total volume of litigation by enterprises. This would not show up in the statistics on civil cases we cited earlier. The overwhelming majority of actions brought by enterprises is before the *gosarbitrazh*. Unfortunately, the statistics do not separately report the civil cases brought in the two fora. [80]

While the preceding leaves us a bit uncertain about the present importance of advocates' services to industrial enterprises, Soviet commentators friendly to the *advokatura* think of them as doing a great job. Until quite recently, they used to contrast the advocates' performance in industry with the situation of legal services to collective and state farms where deficiencies were glaring. [81]

At first, there were no agricultural staff lawyers directly to serve the farms. Thus, farms seemed to provide a new clientele for the *advokatura*, and its members were stepping in. While advocates were serving only 500 collective farms (out of approximately 44,000) in 1960, by 1967 their services were reaching 2,400 collective and 1,460 state farms [82] (out of the combined number of some 48,600 farms, or still slightly less than 8%).[83] The distribution of services was uneven, however. In Kaluga region, for instance, advocates were working with only four out of 159 state farms. [84] But, if we are to believe the figures and chance to put the correct interpretation on them, there was a drastic shift towards services by various categories of staff counsel within the span of a few years. Even as the Decree of December 23, 1970, was being prepared, there were 1,500 such lawyers working exclusively in agriculture, most of them doing legal work directly for the farms. [85] The decree noted the continuing inadequacy of legal services in the agricultural sector and mandated the USSR Ministry of Agriculture and the union republic councils of ministers to work out concrete measures to overcome the problem (sec. 4). The response was almost instantaneous and seemingly effective. Within weeks, the ministry issued an implementing order. [86] By the beginning of 1972, the number of lawyers was up by almost a thousand— 2,400. Of the 47,000 collective and state farms 760—or 1.6%—had house counsel. In addition, inter-farm legal groups employed 1,200 lawyers serving over 16,000 farms, or 34% of the total. Thus, more than 35% of all farms were regularly receiving legal services by these devices. The remainder of the lawyers were on the staffs of regional (or territorial) agricultural administrations, ministries of agriculture of autonomous republics, and trusts (aggregates) of state farms. Since they have not been included in the 35-percent figure, their services to farms were either negligible or extended only to farms already served by other lawyers. In the three Baltic republics, all or virtually all farms were provided with legal services. [87] By the end of 1975, allegedly 80% of the farms were receiving legal services. The number of lawyers in agriculture or "rural lawyers [*sel'skie iuristy*]," as they are ordinarily referred to, had risen to 6,000; 3,000 of them were associated with inter-farm legal groups. [88] Allowing for a rise in the number of lawyers on the staffs of the agencies at the intermediate level of agricultural administration, say, from 440 in 1972 [2,400 − (760 + 1,200)] to somewhere between 500 to 700 in 1975, the remaining 2,300 to 2,500 lawyers must have been farm house counsel. Thus, still only 5% of the farms had in-house legal help.

Expansion of these forms of legal services to farms is likewise commonly justified by citing monetary recoveries. "In 1974, rural lawyers helped farms recover 114,200,000 rubles in the Russian Federation, 93,500,000 rubles in the Ukrainian Republic and 14,000,000 rubles in the Kazakh Republic. The total figure for the whole country was around 300,000,000. . . . [L]egal counsel in the Russian Republic Ministry of Agriculture recovered over 1,500,000 rubles in forfeitures alone for collective farms from organizations of the Farm Machinery Association for violations of contractual obligations." [89] And we read that among the Estonian inter-farm groups, "the economic effect per group member is 12,000 rubles per year."[90] But it is deemed "efficient"[91] to seek the services of legal specialists to farms for other reasons as well. The point has very properly been made that collecting money on the obligations of others should go hand-in-hand with preventing one's own liability. An individual farm might, naturally, regard money paid out unnecessarily as money wasted. Yet neither enforcement nor prevention of liability is costless. And a cost-benefit analysis becomes exceedingly complex as one moves beyond the fundamental insight that resources allocated to one activity or concern cannot be devoted to another, that an oppurtunity taken is another opportunity foregone. Experientially, determined enforcement of every claim may spoil "useful" relations in the future. [92] One's own meticulous compliance with legal duties carries with it inconvenience, if not disruption of the whole operation. Consequently, the now fashionable and ostensibly single-minded pursuit of legalism in the agricultural as well as non-agricultural sectors of the economy might eventually be perceived as not cost-justified. This would not necessarily lead to the decline in the importance of the law-trained professional in the Soviet economy. However, his or her role might rather be that of a general problem-solver or trouble-shooter (qualities already discernible in Soviet lawyers, in general, and the *advokatura*, in particular) than of a mere technician skilled mainly in deciphering turgid texts, filling forms, and exhorting others to obey the law.

In any event, a triumph of such legalism through mass-produced lawyers is not imminent. Despite the recent promotional policies, the Soviet countryside, for one, is not saturated with lawyers. To merely state that 80% of all farms are receiving legal services is to say nothing about the adequacy of those services. Again, citation of striking examples of what some lawyers have done tells nothing about what they and the rest have neglected. In 1972, each lawyer associated with an inter-farm legal group, the principal supplier of direct legal services, served on the average 13.3 farms. The other data we have cited above indicate that the corresponding figure for 1975 was about 12. "Many legal consultants now [in 1975] 'tour' 20 or more collective farms and state farms, which significantly impairs their performance." [93] There are wide deviations from the mean. "In one district there is one lawyer for every five or six farms (as there should be), but in another, one for every 20 to 25 farms. Unfortunately, the same situation is true of state farms; almost 150 farms are served by five lawyers (?!)" [94] The USSR Ministry of Agriculture may have exceeded its implementing ability by ordering extension of legal services to all collective and state farms during the 10th Five-Year Plan

224

(1976-1980). According to the ministry's plan, farms which have a considerable amount of legal work could have their own lawyers; the rest would get the services they need from sufficiently large lawyers' groups, each member of which would serve no more than six or seven farms. [95] If we assume that the combined number of collective and state farms will continue to decrease at the low post-1965 rate because of the occasional amalgamation of the smaller units, there will be about 46,400 farms in 1980. [96] And if we further assume that, in view of the scarcity of trained legal personnel, only 500 more farms will rate their own house counsel, Soviet agriculture will need about 4,000 more lawyers to meet the stated goals: [46,400 − (2,000 + 500)] ÷ 7 ≅ 6,270; 6,270-3,000 = 3,270; 3,270 + 500 = 3,770. If attrition in the number of rural lawyers is taken into account, the figure of 3,770 may have to be enlarged by a few hundred. Our calculation on the basis of the scattered data is corroborated by Sukharev, USSR First Deputy Minister of Justice, who wrote in 1974: "According to the Ministry of Agriculture, the branch already needs an additional 4,000 jurists." [97] It goes without saying that the Ministry of Agriculture has to rely on other state agencies for the supply of the requisite number of people with the essential legal skills. [98] The day, evening, and extension divisions of the Soviet law schools are graduating about 5,000 persons annually. [99]

What, then, of the role of advocates in the agricultural sector since 1967, the last year for which we cited some figures? Retainer contracts with the consultation offices of the colleges of advocates are still expressly recognized as the third mode of servicing the farms. [100] In 1973 the USSR Ministry of Justice approved a model contract for legal services by advocates at collective farms. [101] Yet none of the above sources of our figures or commentary on the developments in rural legal services gives the slightest hint of the volume, the effect, and the prospects of the contribution of advocates. However, another source asserts that while the so-called rural lawyers were serving 16,760 collective and state farms, advocates were rendering services on a regular basis to an additional 8,000 collective farms and 3,000 state farms by 1972. [102] Since in 1974, 4,000 collective and state farms in the RSFSR were utilizing the services of advocates, [103] we can reasonably infer that the number of farms served by advocates countrywide had not appreciably declined by 1975, *i.e.*, the other year for which we had figures on the delivery of legal services in agriculture. These facts put the previously cited figures into a somewhat different light. With 10,000 added to the "serviced" list in each of the two years, we get 26,760 (760 + 16,000 + 10,000) or almost 57% of the total (26,760 ÷ 47,100) in 1972, and 47,680 ((47,100 x .80) + 10,000) or more than the total of 47,100 farms! Consequently, if all these figures are to be trusted and if there was no duplication of legal services (*i.e.*, no farm was the recipient of more than one form of legal service), all Soviet farms were getting some qualified legal assistance by 1975. At a republic-wide advocates' convention in Ul'ianovsk early in 1977, First Deputy Minister of Justice of the RSFSR, Mishenin, stated: "As of now, not every college [of advocates] has taken measures with a view to expanding and improving juridical servicing of enterprises and organizations, in particular collective farms and state farms where juridical services have not been set up for the time being." [104] If his statement means what it seems to say, it implies at least three things: that advocates generally do not duplicate services, *i.e.*, they do not, as a rule, serve farms that are already being served through other channels; that the farms which are presently served by advocates could stand expansion of and improvement in these services; and that as the rural lawyers expand their services to farms, the advocates will be displaced from this sector of practice. If and when the advocates are displaced from enterprises and farms, they may find ordinary civil claims and trials more attractive practice. Even if the number of such cases were gradually to decrease, the presently low level of advocates' involvement in them implies a reserve source of practice and sustenance.

Counselling and Drafting: Herein of Administrative Practice

Our description of the advocates' work with institutional clients was mainly about civil claims and trials. But client counselling—both to help prevent legal problems from arising and to aid in responding to existing problems— and preparation of legal documents for every occasion were implicit in the story. Clients such as enterprises and collective farms, typically, have simultaneous needs more numerous and diverse than those of any individual seeking the advocate's assistance. In discussing the advocate's work on institutional retainers, we felt it useful to refer to all aspects thereof in the same place, lest a misimpression of retainers-for-litigation-only was created. The present section is about counselling, drafting, and like matters in general, but with an emphasis on service to individuals.

This aspect of advocates' work most frequently concerns questions arising out of legal relations regulated by civil, family, labor, and administrative law. A large number of matters involves housing, partition of property, inheritance, child support, divorce, dismissals from work and transfers to other work, wages, and pensions. Although counselling sometimes can be broadly advisory or informational, the clients, as a rule, bring up matters that are real and pressing. The advocate's advice is supposed to be directed at elucidation of the rights and duties of the clients with a view to establishing the simplest and most noncontentious way of resolving the client's problem. Ideally, the advocate attempts to achieve voluntary compliance with law. Soviet commentators recognize that the quality of counselling at this stage will have much to do with the client's decision to commence an action or, conversely, to defend one in court if brought by the other party. The advocate's correct appraisal of a claim or a defense as weak is apt to prevent unnecessary

226

litigation, just as the right advice regarding the client's conduct in the face of a difficulty is likely to ward off complications before litigation is even considered by anybody involved. [105]

Counselling is mainly conducted at the legal consultation offices—the "law firms." But recently, as we mentioned earlier, the consultation offices in many localities have been supplemented by a network of consultation desks or points easing the physical access to legal services. [106] In the late 1960s, for instance, about 18 advocates were attached to the Leningrad city soviet to be on call for consultations with deputies of the USSR and RSFSR Supreme Soviets and the Leningrad city soviet. [107] Sometimes, advocates are also informally attached to comrades' courts for purposes of consultation. [108] Finally, counselling by telephone has been experimented with. [109]

Much counselling is provided as uncompensated social services. [110] Moreover, we have no evidence that this is done only either in the absence of paid business or as overtime work. We are not clear regarding the impact this has on the earnings of the advocates and their colleges or on the quality of the advice. We have seen Soviet commentary complain about a viewpoint among advocates according to which counselling is secondary and not decisively important. [111] A connection between compensation and the quality of advocates' services has also been recognized. [112] The statistics in the area of counselling are notoriously unreliable and, consequently, it is well nigh impossible to judge what passes for and is counted as a reportable instance of legal advice. [113]

Preparation of miscellaneous documents and petitions other than judicial-procedural papers is another important function of advocates. It is inextricably connected with client counselling; that is to say, counselling is a necessary prior step. Among the more common documents are contracts of sale, gift or loan of personal property, wills, powers of attorney, etc.

Most petitions are addressed to administrative authorities which raises the question of the advocate's role in the Soviet administrative process. Since the internal life of the Soviet Union is heavily administered by the state, Soviet citizens must frequently interact with the administrative bureaucracy to secure various permits and other benefits or to resist the imposition of administrative forfeitures. There is a great unmet need for legal services in the administrative process and, in principle, a vast opportunity for the *advokatura* to extend its services. The process is essentially adversary, especially that of administrative commissions, and calls for skills with respect to which the advocates still seem to possess a comparative advantage. However, the advocates have not got into it to any great extent for reasons which are not entirely clear.

The RSFSR Statute on the *Advokatura* does not mention the possibility of advocates' appearing before administrative tribunals or agencies. Indeed, there was resistance to this notion during the preparation of the statute. Dean

Karev argued that advocates should not appear before administrative authorities, but should concern themselves only with juridical questions; a contrary practice, he maintained, would "turn the lawyer into a [professional] intercessor." Even though advocates had, in fact, been appearing before certain administrative tribunals, some Soviet writers insisted that the statute not mention this point, lest it achieve unwarranted emphasis. At the same time, the statutes of the Estonian, Kazakh, Tadzhik, and Uzbek republics provided for representation before administrative authorities. [114] The new Constitution of the USSR acknowledges the citizens' "right to file complaints against the actions of officials and state and public agencies" and provides for their examination "according to the procedure ... established by law" (Art. 58). The administrative procedure legislation presently under consideration may resolve the question of legal representation. There is some support for the "formalization" of the administrative process along the lines of an adjudicatory model. It would provide "for the opportunity to call in a lawyer" and ensure "that the investigation and the evaluation of evidence take place in the proper sequence." [115] A recent administrative law text explains that the participation of defense counsel in an administrative proceeding is not presupposed because the proceeding is relatively uncomplicated and there is no procurator to maintain the state's claim of forfeiture. But there is nothing, it continues, "to exclude the possibility of the participation of both defense counsel and the procurator in administrative proceedings which examine more complex administrative offenses, and this should be stated in the statute." [116] Division Five of the 1977 federal fee schedule is titled "Fees for Handling Civil and Administrative Matters;" Section 27 sets the fees in administrative cases. [117]

Even in the area of counselling and drafting and, by implication, in the administrative process, competing legal services are in evidence. An example is the purportedly successful experiment with a factory-based consultation service at Uralelektrotiazhmash in Sverdlovsk since 1964. The fifteen-member consultation service includes staff lawyers of the factory, president of the district people's court, assistant district procurator, chief of the section of plant safety, and deputy chief of the section of labor and wages. The group receives clients twice a week between 4 and 6 p.m. "The workers and employees of the plant now turn for counselling not to administrative organs (courts and the procuracy) but get advice on any legal question right at the plant.'[118] The report does not mention the role of advocates either individually or as a group at all.

Advocates' work with persons given suspended sentences and on probation (*shefstvo advokatov nad uslovno osuzhdennymi*) is a peculiar form of counselling, partaking more of the function of a social worker than that of a lawyer. According to one view, this is the advocate's personal responsibility more than his or her social obligation as a professional with relevant special skills. "The advocate, having established the inexpediency of his client's isolation from the society before the court, cannot be indifferent toward his future fate. . . . By systematically keeping an eye on [*kontroliruia*] the former defendants and maintaining an interest in the affairs of their wards, the advocates strive to make sure that many former offenders take the path to reform." [119] We did not spot any discussion of the criminal advocates' enthusiasm for this sideline and their possible reluctance to press for conditional sentences when the prospect for after-hours social work seems unattractive.

Legal Propaganda

The advocates are expected to be propagandists of Soviet law in whatever they do—in criminal cases, civil trials, administrative proceedings, and at counselling and drafting sessions. The client must, in every instance, be instructed and enlightened as well as helped in his or her legal rights and interests. [120] In addition, they have an obligation to affirmatively reach out to the masses and explain to them how to stay in line and how to claim what the state has allowed them. [121] "Each advice the advocate gives is individualized propaganda of the rules of Soviet law and facilitates dissemination of legal knowledge among the working people." [122]

The RSFSR Statute on the *Advokatura* enjoins the advocates "actively to participate in propaganda for Soviet law" (art. 30).

The advocates' achievements in legal propaganda are likewise quantified for purposes of statistical reporting. Thus, in 1967 alone the advocates of the RSFSR read at least 100,000 popular lectures and reports on strengthening the public order in the country. [123] In 1970 they presented already 130,000 lectures and reports explaining the decisions of the Party and the government regarding measures for strengthening the public order in the country. [124] One could legitimately wonder if this tempestuous rate of growth could be indefinitely sustained or whether, as in track and field, the limits of human strength and endurance were about to be reached. The figure for 1975 was sobering: the number of reports, lectures, *and* discussions in 1975 increased over the 1974 count by a pitiful 3,500, and that for the USSR as a whole! [125]

Since in a socialist society (of the Soviet type) propaganda is everybody's business and since in this enterprise fervor may weigh more than substantive competence, the advocates might be in for a stiff competition in this department as well. Yet the ample availability of captive audiences offers broad professional vistas to the future graduates of Soviet law schools who have chosen and been admitted to the ranks of the *advokatura* and remain compelled to accept this as a necessary aspect of their professional life.

229

4. Conclusion

The present drive to expand and upgrade the delivery of legal services in the Soviet Union has neither significantly added to the importance and functions of the *advokatura* nor swelled its ranks. In fact, we have witnessed an apparent decline of the *advokatura*'s size and role relative to other sectors of the legal profession. This might be but a temporary setback, however. Certainly, we do not mean to imply that the *advokatura* is marked for extinction. It suffices to point to Article 161 of the 1977 USSR Constitution and Article 173 of the 1978 RSFSR Constitution which consecrate the *advokatura* as a constitutional institution. But, perhaps more importantly, foreseeable changes in the perceptions of law may cause all Soviet legal practitioners and particularly advocates to gain more influence in the Soviet decision-making process. The currently propagandized strict observance of law as a panacea is likely to yield to a view that frankly recognizes that clashes between diverse interests are unavoidable even in "a society of a new type" and that law can, at best, provide a matrix within which these interests are assessed and adjusted. Should that occur, the processes of the administration of law and justice will, of necessity, become more adversary with an attendant demand for professionals skilled in the general art of advocacy and not necessarily steeped in the technical regulations of the economic ministries. That might lead to the consolidation of the *advokatura*'s position as the trial bar of the Soviet Union with fewer of its present adjunct functions. Moreover, as the complex interconnections of problems are more readily recognized, a need for a class of general problem analyzers and solvers might arise. If the legal profession either takes on or be called to the performance of this task, the *advokatura* might serve as the model of legal practitioners most suitable to this task, mainly by reason of its tradition of "general practice."

This speculative prognosis is not a mere transfer of the American experience. The Soviet legal process has become more adversary over the years and the cessation of this trend should not be assumed. It has affected lawmaking and administration to some extent, but has been most evident in the courts. Advocates have, by and large, preferred trial practice, particularly criminal trials which represent the most adversary form of litigation. Soviet legal literature is already reporting the use of legal counsel as general problem-solvers in enterprises, even though some of the problems reportedly propounded to them until now seem hardly to challenge the "legal mind." [126] Professor Alekseev assures the entering law students of a bright future for the legal profession—even under full communism, after state and law "as political phenomena" have withered away. "There's every reason to believe," he writes, "that a developed communist society retains public activity connected with normative regulation. This activity will be one of great social significance and will demand from the specialists, evidently no less than now, profound knowledge, training in skills and mastery of all the subtleties of regulation." [127]

As for the immediate future, one can expect a shift back to federal control over the *advokatura*. The second paragraph of Article 161 of the USSR Constitution, added after the publication of the draft version, states that "the organization of and procedure for the activity of the *advokatura* are defined by USSR and union republic legislation." This is not, of course, a source of new federal power. Prior federal jurisdiction was indicated by the USSR Constitution of 1936 (Art. 14(u)), the Principles of Court Organization of the USSR and the Union and Autonomous Republics (art. 13), the Statute on the USSR Ministry of Justice (art. 6(r)), [128] and the ministerial order of December 25, 1972. [129] The federal fee schedule adopted two months before the 1977 Constitution and in force since January 1, 1978, [130] was the last significant exercise of the pre-existing jurisdiction. The added constitutional language, however, presages more encompassing lawmaking at the federal level. [131] It is rumored that a general all-union statute on the *advokatura* will appear in the spring of 1979 and an RSFSR enactment will follow a half-a-year or so later. [132] But as far as we have been able to determine, the reports on the implementation of the Constitution published in the open press have set no timetable specifically for such legislation. [133]

NOTES

1. D. D. Barry & H. J. Berman, "Soviet Legal Profession," *Harvard Law Review*, 82 (1968), 7; D. D. Barry & H. J. Berman, "The Jurists," in G. Skilling *et al.* (eds.), *Interest Groups in Communist Politics*, (Princeton, NJ, 1971), p. 291.

2. *Itogi Vsesoiuznoi perepisi naseleniia 1970 goda–Tom VI: Raspredelenie naseleniia SSSR i soiuznykh respublik po zaniatiiam* (Results of the All-Union Population Census of 1970–Volume VI: Distribution of the Population of the USSR and the Union Republics by Occupation), (Moscow, 1973), *passim* (hereinafter cited as *Itogi*).

3. Statute on the *Advokatura* of the RSFSR of July 25, 1962, art. 1, *Sov. Iust.*, 1962, No. 15-16, 31 (hereinafter cited as RSFSR Stat.), transl. in L. M. Friedman & Z. L. Zile, "Soviet Legal Profession: Recent Developments in Law and Practice," *Wisconsin Law Review*, 1964, 32-77.

4. M. S. Strogovich, "O zashchitnike i o zashchititel'noi rechi" (On the Defense Counsel and the Defense Speech), in M. S. Strogovich (ed.), *Zashchititel'nye rechi sovetskikh advokatov* (Soviet Advocates' Defense Speeches), (Moscow, 1956), pp. 5-7; T. E. Neishtadt, *Sovetskii advokat* (The Soviet Advocate), Moscow, 1958), pp. 3-6; Y. Zaitsev & A. Poltorak, *The Soviet Bar* (Moscow, 1959), pp. 5-6.

5. The former federal or all-union law was the Statute on the *Advokatura* of the USSR of August 16, 1939, *Sobr. Post. SSSR*, 1939, No. 49, item 394.

6. *E.g.*, L. M. Friedman & Z. L. Zile, note 3 above; H. J. Berman & J. W. Spindler, *Soviet Criminal Law and Procedure: The RSFSR Codes*, 2d ed., (Cambridge, Mass., 1972), pp. 106-112.

7. *Itogi*, pp. 14-447.

8. D. D. Barry & H. J. Berman, "The Jurists," note 1 above, p. 306.

9. *Narodnoe khoziaistvo SSSR za 60 let: Iubileinyi statisticheskii ezhegodnik* (The National Economy of the USSR After 60 Years: Anniversary Statistical Yearbook), (Moscow, 1977), p. 7 (hereinafter cited as *1977 Nar. khoz. SSSR*); D. D. Barry & H. J. Berman, "The Jurists," note 1 above, p. 304.

10. *Itogi*, p. 22.

11. *1977 Nar. khoz. SSSR*, p. 7.

12. D. D. Barry & H. J. Berman, "The Jurists," note 1 above, p. 304.

13. *Ibid.*, p. 305n.

14. It has been reported that there were about 7,200 advocates in the RSFSR in 1968. *Ibid.* A figure of 7,500 two years later is probably a good approximation.

15. The figure of 390 is from I. I. Martinovich, *Advokatura v BSSR* (The *Advokatura* in the Belorussian SSR), (Minsk, 1973), as reported by Professor William E. Butler who commented on the draft of this paper at the International Conference on the Occasion of the 25th Anniversary of the Documentation Office of East European Law, University of Leyden, 16-18 August 1978 (hereinafter cited as Professor Butler's comments).

16. The population figure is from *Narodnoe khoziaistvo Ukrainskoi SSR: Iubileinyi statisticheskii ezhegodnik* (The National Economy of the Ukrainian SSR: Anniversary Statistical Yearbook), (Kiev, 1977), p. 9. The figure of 3,340 is from V. I. Zaichuk, "Organizatsiia i deiatel'nost' advokatury Ukrainskoi SSR" (The Organization and Activities of the *Advokatura* of the Ukrainian SSR), in A. Ia. Sukharev (ed.), *Rol' i zadachi*

sovetskoi advokatury (The Role and Tasks of the Soviet *Advokatura*), (Moscow, 1972), pp. 85*ff.*, as reported in Professor Butler's comments.

17. *Sobr. Post. SSSR*, 1971, No. 1, item 1, transl. in *Soviet Statutes and Decisions*, 10 (1973), No. 1, 59 (hereinafter cited as *SSD*).

18. *Biulleten' Normativnykh Aktov*, 1973, No. 3, 3 (hereinafter cited as *BNA*), transl. in *SSD*, 1973, No. 1, 70.

19. *BNA*, 1973, No. 4, 39, transl. in *SSD*, 10 (1973), No. 1, 81.

20. *1977 Nar. khoz. SSSR*, p. 475.

21. *Pravda*, Dec. 15, 1974, 3, transl. in *CDSP*, 26 (1975), No. 50, 5.

22. I. Mishenin, "Povyshat' professional'noe masterstvo advokatov" (To Raise the Advocates' Professional Skills), *Sov. Iust.*, 1976, No. 13, 1.

23. The population figures for the USSR are from *1977 Nar. khoz. SSSR*, 7; for the RSFSR–from *Narodnoe khoziaistvo RSFSR za 60 let: Statisticheskii ezhegodnik* (The National Economy of the RSFSR: Statistical Yearbook), (Moscow, 1977), p. 5.

24. P. Voskoboinikov, "Podbor i vospitanie molodykh advokatov" (Recruitment and Training of Junior Advocates), *Sov. Iust.*, 1974, No. 16, 23.

25. A. Kogan, "Advokatura i otdel iustitsii" (The *Advokatura* and the Judicial Department), *Sov. Iust.*, 1975, No. 13, 16.

26. Note 21 above. The population figures are from *1977 Nar. khoz. RSFSR*, pp. 6, 12, 13.

27. Note 21 above.

28. I. K. Kukarskii, "Razvitie sovetskoi advokatury, ee deiatel'nost' i zadachi na sovremennom etape" (Development of the Soviet *Advokatura* and Its Activities and Tasks at the Contemporary Stage) in A. A. Kruglov (ed.), *Sovetskaia advokatura: Zadachi i deiatel'nost'* (The Soviet *Advokatura*: Its Tasks and Activities), (Moscow, 1968), p. 25 (hereinafter cited as *Sovetskaia advokatura*).

29. *1977 Nar. khoz. RSFSR*, pp. 10-15.

30. A. Kogan, note 25 above.

31. See, *e.g.*, I. N. Batakov, "Konsul'tatsionnaia rabota–vazhnyi uchastok deiatel'nosti advokatury" (Counselling–An Important Part of the Activities of the *Advokatura*) in *Sovetskaia advokatura*, pp. 70-72; K. N. Apraksin *et al.* (eds.), *Advokatura v SSSR* (*Advokatura* in the USSR), (Moscow, 1971), p. 52 (hereinafter cited as *Advokatura*); S. Markova, "Organizatsiia konsul'tatsionnoi raboty advokatov" (Organization of Counselling by Advocates), *Sov. Iust.*, 1973, No. 14, 20.

32. V. I. Zaichuk, note 16 above, as reported in Professor Butler's comments.

33. I. I. Martinovich, note 15 above, as reported in Professor Butler's comments.

34. For a sympathetic appraisal of the distinctiveness of the *advokatura*, see Iu. I. Stetsovskii, "Iuridicheskaia priroda sovetskikh kollegii advokatov," *SGiP*, 1976, No. 8, transl. as "The Legal Standing of Soviet Collegia of Attorneys" in *Soviet Law and Government*, 15 (1977), No. 4, 28 (hereinafter cited as *SL&G*).

35. On the delicate balance between state guidance and organizational autonomy, see Iu. I. Stetsovskii, *SGiP*, 1973, No. 10, transl. as "Ways of Improving State Guidance of Advocates" in *SL&G*, 13 (1972), No. 1, p. 93, and V. Raudsalu, "Rukovodstvo deiatel'nost'iu advokatury" (Guidance of the *Advokatura's* Activities), *Sots. Zak.*, 1974, No. 11, 18.

36. *Cf.* D. D Barry & H. J. Berman, "The Jurists," note 1 above, pp. 316-321.

37. Indeed, the title of the Statute reads: "On the Legal Section (or Office), Chief (or Senior) Jurisconsult, and Jurisconsult of a Ministry, Department, Executive Committee of Soviet of Working People's Deputies, Enterprises, Organizations, or Institutions."

38. S. Natruskin, "Povyshat' kachestvo professional'noi deiatel'nosti advokatov" (To Raise the Quality of Advocates' Professional Activities), *Sov. Iust.*, 1975, No. 12, 6.

39. S. Temirova, "Nekotorye voprosy raboty advokata po grazhdanskim delam" (Some Questions Regarding Advocate's Work in Civil Cases) in *Sovetskaia advokatura*, p. 76.

40. *1977 Nar. khoz. SSSR*, pp. 42-45.

41. *1977 Nar. khoz. RSFSR*, p. 5.

42. D. D. Barry & H. J. Berman, "The Jurists," note 1 above, p. 301.

43. I. K. Kukarskii, note 28 above, pp. 20-21.

44. P. H. Juviler, *Revolutionary Law and Order: Politics and Social Change in the USSR* (New York, 1976), p. 131; V. Chalidze, *Criminal Russia: Crime in the Soviet Union* (New York, 1977), p. 201.

45. See Decree of December 5 (November 22), 1917, "On the Judiciary (No. 1)," *Sobr. Uzak.*, 1917, No. 4, item 50.

46. A. K. Orlov (ed.), *Kommentarii k Ugolovno-protsessual'nomu kodeksu RSFSR* (A Commentary on the RSFSR Code of Criminal Procedure), (Moscow, 1976), p. 71.

47. *Ibid.*, p. 71 The organization representative we are talking about is not to be confused with the "social defense counsel (*obshchestvennyi zashchitnik*)" who intercedes in the name of the collective of the accused. See H. J. Berman & J. W. Spindler, note 6 above, pp. 69-70.

48. *Cf.* P. H. Juviler, note 44 above, pp. 130-131; V. Chalidze note 44 above, pp. 197-199.

49. *Pravda*, Apr. 16, 1969, 3, transl. in *CDSP*, 21 (1969), No. 16, 20.

50. See, *e.g.*, J. N. Hazard, "Expansion of the Right to A Defense Attorney under Soviet Law," in International Commission of Jurists, *The Review*, 1971, No. 6, 17.

51. H. J. Berman & J. W. Spindler, note 6 above, p. 85.

52. Plenum of the USSR Supreme Court, June 27, 1966, *BVS SSSR*, 1966, No. 4, 26.

53. Criminal Division of the RSFSR Supreme Court, October 22, 1976, *BVS RSFSR*, 1977, No. 1, 9.

54. Y. Luryi, "The Right to Counsel in Ordinary Criminal Cases in the USSR" in D. D. Barry, G. Ginsburgs, & P. B. Maggs (eds.), *Soviet Law After Stalin, Part I, The Citizen and the State in Contemporary Soviet Law* (Leyden, 1977), pp. 105-107.

55. Y. Luryi, "The Role of Defence Counsel in Political Trials in the USSR," *Manitoba Law Journal*, 7 (1977), 307.

55a. *Advokatura*, p. 129; I. K. Kukarskii, "Uchastie advokatury v ukreplenii zakonnosti" (Participation of the *Advokatura* in the Strengthening of Legality), *SGiP*, 1968, No. 9, 72.

56. A. Ia. Sukharev, "Piatidesiatiletie sovetskoi advokatury" (The Fiftieth Anniversary of the Soviet *Advokatura*), *SGiP*, 1972, No. 5, 15.

57. R. F. Kallistratova *et al.* (eds.), *Kommentarii k GPK RSFSR* (A Commentary on the Civil Code of Procedure of the RSFSR), (Moscow, 1976), p. 87.

58. *Ibid.*, pp. 85-87.

59. See note 43 above and accompanying text.

60. V. Semiannikov & I. Sukharev, "Organizatsiia raboty iuridicheskikh konsul'tatsii" (Organization of the Work of Legal Consultation Offices), *Sov. Iust.*, 1976, No. 8, 19.

61. Text above, p. 17.

62. See, *e.g.*, I. K. Kukarskii, note 28 above, pp. 20-21; S. Temirova, note 39 above, p. 76; V. Semiannikov & I. Sukharev, note 60 above, p. 19.

63. J. Giddings, "The Jurisconsult in the USSR," *Review of Socialist Law*, 1 (1975), 171-180.

64. *Izvestiia*, Jan 9, 1970, 1, transl. in *CDSP*, 22 (1970), No. 2, 17.
65. Note 49 above.
66. I. K. Kukarskii, note 28 above, p. 22.
67. *Cf.* Decree of the USSR Ministry of Justice, August 31, 1973, "Methods Instructions Concerning the Work of Advocates in Rendering Legal Assistance to Enterprises, Institutions and Organizations (Except Collective Farms)," *BNA*, 1974, No. 1, 43, transl. in *SSD*, 10 (1974), No. 4, 370.
68. Decree of the USSR Ministry of Justice, December 8, 1972, "Model Contract Regarding Legal Services at Enterprises, Institutions, and Organizations (Except Collective Farms) By Legal Consultation Offices of Colleges of Advocates," *BNA*, 1973, No. 5, 47, transl. in *SSD*, 10 (1973), No. 1, 56.
69. *Izvestiia*, Jan. 28, 1977, 2, transl. in *CDSP*, 29, No. 4, 16.
70. "V Ministerstve iustitsii SSSR: V Kollegii" (In the USSR Ministry of Justice: Before the Board), *Sots. Zak.*, 1978, No. 6, 86.
71. *Izvestiia*, May 19, 1972, 3, transl. in *CDSP*, 24 (1972), No. 20, 24; A. Ia. Sukharev, note 56 above, p. 16.
72. Note 21 above.
73. See note 67 above and accompanying text.
74. *E.g.*, "Vystupleniia v preniiakh" (Statements during Discussions) in *Sovetskaia advokatura*, pp. 134-135.
75. *Izvestiia*, Sept. 9, 1976, 2, transl. in *CDSP*, 28 (1976), No. 36, 20.
76. I. Mishenin, note 22 above, p. 2.
77. V. Stuchkov, "Sorevnuiutsia advokaty dal'nego vostoka" (The Advocates of the Far East Are Competing), *Sov. Iust.*, 1978, No. 6, 19.
78. See, *e.g., Advokatura*, p. 60.
79. Note 75 above.
80. *Cf.* A. Kogan, note 25 above, p. 16.
81. *E.g., Advokatura*, p. 64.
82. I. K. Kukarskii, note 28 above, p. 22.
83. The farm figures are from *Narodnoe khoziaistvo SSSR v 1967 g.* (The National Economy of the USSR in 1967), (Moscow, 1968), p. 325 and *1977 Nar. khoz. SSSR*, p. 269.
84. I. K. Kukarskii, note 28 above, p. 23.
85. G. Petrov, "Sel'skie iuristy," *Sots. Zak.*, 1972, No. 6, 3, transl. as "Rural Lawyers" in *SL&G*, 11 (1973), No. 4, 375, 377.
86. *Ibid.*, p. 375.
87. *Ibid.*, pp. 376-377.
88. *Pravda*, Dec. 24, 1975, 3, transl. in *CDSP*, 27 (1976), No. 51, 12; L. Florent'ev, "Pravovuiu rabotu v sel'skom kozhiaistve–na uroven' sovremennykh zadach," *Sov. Iust.*, 1976, No. 10, 3, transl. as "Improve Legal Work in Agriculture to Meet Present Day Needs" in *CDSP*, 28 (1976), No. 37, 16.
89. *Izvestiia*, Feb. 10, 1976, 5, transl. in *CDSP*, 28 (1976), No. 6, 22.
90. *Pravda*, Dec. 24, 1975, 3, transl. in *CDSP*, 27 (1976), No. 51, 12.
91. See, *e.g., Izvestiia*, Oct. 24, 1974, transl. as V. Komov & A. Ilyichev, "Efficiency Factor of the Rural Lawyer" in *CDSP*, 26 (1974), No. 43, 19.
92. *Cf. ibid.*
93. *Pravda*, Oct. 7, 1975, 3, transl. in *CDSP*, 27 (1975), No. 40, 23.
94. Note 91 above; see also, note 90 above.
95. Notes 93, 90, and 89 above.
96. *Cf. 1977 Nar. khoz. SSSR*, p. 269.
97. A. Sukharev, "Nasushchnye problemy podgotovki iuridicheskikh kadrov," *Sots.*

Zak., 1974, No. 2, 3, transl. as "Key Problems of Training Legal Cadres" in *CDSP*, 26 (1974), No. 26, 9.

98. *Cf.* notes 93 and 88 above.

99. L. K. Suvorov, "Problemy sovershenstvovaniia iuridicheskogo obrazovaniia v SSSR" (Problems of Perfecting Juridical Education in the USSR), *Pravovedenie*, 1977, No. 1, 7.

100. Note 90 above.

101. Decree of the USSR Ministry of Justice, August 31, 1973, "Model Contract Regarding Legal Services at Collective Farms by Colleges of Advocates," *BNA*, 1974, No. 1, 38, transl. in *SSD*, 10 (1974), No. 4, 365.

102. A. Ia. Sukharev, note 56 above, p. 16.

103. Note 21 above.

104. V. Volkova, "Obsuzhdaiutsia puti sovershenstvovaniia deiatel'nosti advoka- tury" (Ways of Perfecting the Activities of the *Advokatura* Are Being Considered), *Sov. Iust.*, 1977, No. 13, 30.

105. I. N. Batakov, note 31 above, pp. 65, 68, 69; S. Markova, note 31 above, p. 19; *Advokatura*, pp. 53-54.

106. I. N. Batakov, note 31 above, pp. 70-71; *Advokatura*, p. 52.

107. I. N. Batakov, note 31 above, pp. 71-72; D. A. Teregulov, "Sovetskii advokat— obshchestvennyi deiatel' " (The Soviet Advocate–A Public Functionary) in *Sovetskaia advokatura*, p. 117.

108. D. A. Teregulov, note 107 above, p. 118.

109. S. Markova, note 31 above, p. 20.

110. L. M. Friedman & Z. L. Zile, note 3 above, p. 46; I. N. Batakov, note 31 above, p. 65; D. A. Teregulov, note 107 above, p. 117; Iu. Bobrova, "Konsul'tatsionnaia rabota advokatov" (Counselling by Advocates), *Sov. Iust.*, 1978, No. 12, 15.

111. I. N. Batakov, note 31 above, p. 65.

112. Note 74 above, p. 135.

113. I. N. Batakov, note 31 above, p. 73.

114. L. M. Friedman & Z. L. Zile, note 3 above, p. 43.

115. *Pravda*, Dec. 28, 1977, 3, transl. in *CDSP*, 29 (1978), No. 52, 12, 19.

116. O. M. Iakuba, *Sovetskoe administrativnoe pravo: Obshchaia chast'* (Soviet Ad- ministrative Law: General Part), (Kiev, 1975), pp. 191-192.

117. Decree of the USSR Minister of Justice, August 4, 1977, "Instruction on the Fees for Legal Services Rendered by Advocates to Citizens, Enterprises, Institutions and Organizations," *Sots. Zak.*, 1978, No. 3, 81. For comments on and a translations of this instruction by Robert Guttman, see *Review of Socialist Law*, 5 (1979), No. 2, 203-211.

118. G. Noskov, "Obshchestvennye formy pravovogo vospitaniia trudiashchikhsia" (Societal Forms of Legal Services for the Working People), *Sov. Iust.*, 1973, No. 8, 6.

119. *Advokatura*, p. 220.

120. *Cf. Advokatura*, p. 55.

121. I. Brodskii, "Pravovaia propaganda na promyshlennykh predpriiatiiakh" (Legal Propaganda at Industrial Enterprises), *Sov. Iust.*, 1973, No. 14, 18.

122. Iu. Bobrova, note 110 above, p. 15.

123. I. K. Kukarskii, note 28 above, p. 12.

124. *Advokatura*, p. 206n.

125. V. I. Semiannikov & I. Sukharev, note 60 above, p. 20.

126. V. Strelkov, "Iuridicheskaia sluzhba i ekonomika" (Juridical Services and the Economy), *Sov. Iust.*, 1978, No. 7, 16-17.

127. S. S. Alekseev, *Vvedenie v iuridicheskuiu spetsial'nost'* (Introduction to the Ju- ridical Specialty), (Moscow, 1976), p. 91.

128. Decree of March 21, 1972, "Statute on the Ministry of Justice of the USSR," *Sobr. Post. SSSR*, 1972, No. 6, item 32, transl. in *SSD*, 10 (1973), No. 1, 6.

129. Order of USSR Ministry of Justice of December 25, 1972, "On Improving the Direction of the Activity of Colleges of Advocates," *BNA*, 1973, No. 6, 44, transl. in *SSD*, 10 (1973), No. 1, 48.

130. The RSFSR repealed its 1966 fee schedule effective January 1, 1978, Decree of December 30, 1977, "On Declaring the RSFSR Council of Ministers' Decree of February 14, 1966, No. 155, without Effect," *Sobr. Post. RSFSR*, 1978, No. 2, item 20.

131. *Cf.* M. Fincke, "Das Justizverfassungsrecht," *Osteuropa Recht*, 24 (1978), No. 1/2, 113.

132. Professor Butler's comments.

133. See, *e.g.*, Law of October 7, 1977, "On the Procedure for Putting the Constitution (Basic Law) of the USSR Into Effect," *BVS SSSR*, 1977, No. 6, 36; Decree of December 30, 1977, "On Organizing the Work of Aligning the Legislative Acts of the USSR and the Decisions of the Government of the USSR with the USSR Constitution," *Sobr. Post. SSSR*, 1978, No. 2, item 8; Decree No. 1 of the Plenum of the USSR Supreme Court of February 3, 1978, "The New USSR Constitution, and the Tasks in Further Perfecting the Judicial Function," *BVS SSSR*, 1978, No. 2, 9; Decree of January 30, 1978, "On Measures to Carry Out the USSR Council of Minister's Decree of December 30, 1977, No. 1135. 'On Organizing the Work of Aligning the Legislative Acts of the USSR and the Decisions of the Government of the USSR with the USSR Constitution,' " *Sobr. Post. RSFSR*, 1978, No. 4, item 34, "V Ministerstve iustitsii SSSR: V Kollegii" (In the USSR Ministry of Justice: Before the Board), *Sots. Zak.*, 1978, No. 2, 82; "Zadachi sovershenstvovaniia zakonodatel'stva v svete novoi Konstitutsii SSSR" (The Tasks of Perfecting Legislation in Light of the New USSR Constitution), *Sots. Zak.*, 1978, No. 7, 3.

SOME REFLECTIONS ON THE SOVIET ADVOKATURA: ITS SITUATION AND PROSPECTS

William E. Butler

It is somewhat startling how little we know of the Soviet advocate, that species of Soviet jurist who seems most proximate in function to the western private pratitioner. We seem disposed to look upon him as a component of a group in Soviet society called jurists, which may be classified as both an interest-group and a profession, and to credit him with a role in restoring socialist legality in the post-Stalin era; yet, paradoxically, we are not even sure how many advocates there are in the Soviet Union.

Rather than looking back at the past 15 years to assess the impact of the reforms of the early 1960s on the *advokatura*, I should like to suggest that we are in fact on the eve of a new reform in response to both the kinds of legal services now being expanded in the USSR, which Professor Zile discusses, and to other concerns, some new and some not. In March 1979, we can expect a new legislative act on the *advokatura* in the USSR, which will restore a measure of all-union direction of the advocates presaged in the 1972 Statute on the USSR Ministry of Justice and in the second paragraph of Article 161 of the USSR Constitution, *added after the draft was published*. And the new Instruction Concerning Payment for Legal Assistance Rendered by Advocated to Citizens, Enterprises, Institutions, and Organizations, confirmed 4 August 1977, it should be noted, is an all-union document.[1] A new RSFSR enactment on the *advokatura* is anticipated for September 1979. So manifestly one of the concerns with regard to the *advokatura* in recent years has been to reintroduce a greater uniformity of regulation, which now will be sought through the all-union/union republic pattern of legislation. Obviously, we will want to look again at the pattern of the 1939 legislation.

A second concern, which may or may not find direct expression in the forthcoming legislation, has been the composition of the *advokatura*. Data from two union republics is illustrative and will complement Professor Zile's extrapolations about the number of advocates. At the end of 1971 in the Ukrainian SSR, some 3,340 advocates reportedly staffed 624 legal consultative offices. Of these, 95% had a higher legal education (five individuals were *kandidat iuridicheskikh nauk* and one held a doctorate) and 63% were members of the Communist Party.[2]

The data from Belorussia is more interesting because it shows something of a trend. On January 1, 1971, there were 390 advocates in Belorussia, up from 349 in 1967. Of the 390 advocates, 55% (215) were members of the Communist Party; 90% (351) had a higher legal education; 54% (214) had at least ten years work experience as an advocate; 41% (160) were of Belorussian nationality; and 39% (155) were women.[3] Most persons became members of the Belorussian *advokatura* at an advanced stage of their career, usually after experience in the procuracy or the courts. In 1967 nearly 79% of the Belorussian advocates were age 40 or above and only 6% below age 30. An effort to recruit younger members reduced the 79% figure to 70% by 1972. The Belorussian advocates in 1972 were organized into 105 legal consultation offices, 56 of which were staffed by only *one* advocate.

A third concern, which I suspect will be to some extent reflected in the new legislation, has been the formation in some union republics—if not all—of various councils and commissions attached to the *advokatura* which have the purpose of shaping, guiding, or streamlining its operation. These are little-known, but in all likelihood of considerable significance for an understanding of how the advocates administer their affairs. I have in mind such bodies as the "Social Councils for Affairs of Advocates," an advisory organ composed of representatives from local soviets, trade unions, komsomol, and academic institutions, and empowered to discuss matters relating to the advocates, make proposals to improve their work, participate in drafting normative acts, and the like; or the Methods Councils, to which experienced advocates and other leading legal personnel are appointed to deal with verifying the quality of legal work; and the "certification commissions", composed of advocates, court personnel, procurators, and representatives from local soviets and trade unions, which recertify at periodic intervals the qualifications of advocates.

A fourth concern, perhaps related to the first, is whether the relationship of the state to the *advokatura* will be modified under the new legislation. The balance between state responsibility for generally supervising the affairs of the *advokatura*, chiefly through the USSR Ministry of Justice, and the *advokatura* as a voluntary social organization is a delicate one, a balance which raises the question of why the *advokatura* continues to exist. Is it not an anachronism to perpetuate a segment of the legal profession who commands a fee (regulated, to be sure) directly from his client for services rendered? The answer, I think, must be negative because the advocate performs certain functions which can not readily be assumed by other categories of Soviet jurist or the layman.

Zile's thesis that the present drive to expand and upgrade legal services in the national economy will not significantly add to the importance of the *advokatura* is, I suspect, well-founded, although this drive has certainly added to the advocate's functions, on Zile's own evidence. But the advocate's role in advising national economic units is essentially a stop-gap one until sufficient

240

jurisconsults have been produced to give full-time legal services to state enterprises, institutions, collective farms, local soviets, etc. Thereafter, the advocate in all likelihood will service only smaller entities whose operations do not require a full-time or substantially shared resident jurisconsult.

But I would caution against portraying this as a competitive or conflict situation for the *advokatura*. The advocates have expanded their activities in this direction because they have been instructed to do so and because institutions have been instructed or persuaded to avail themselves of legal services. Instead of being an assertive branch of the profession, seeking to extend areas in which their expertise and services may be utilized, the record suggests that on the whole the advocates have not behaved in this manner. I am reinforced in this impression by an account Martinovich gives of the attitude of Belorussian advocates toward involvement in preliminary investigations. When criminal procedure reforms were introduced in the early 1960s allowing advocates to be involved in the preliminary investigations in certain instances, there was a general reluctance on the part of the advocates to participate. A survey of attitudes made by the Minsk College of Advocates in 1963 ultimately led to the Belorussian College of Advocates being requested to write to the Procurator of the BSSR, asking the latter to instruct his investigators on the right of advocates to take part; to seek from the BSSR Supreme Court an explanation to lower courts on the payment of fees for an advocate's participation in the preliminary investigation; and to insist upon monthly reports from each legal consultation office regarding such participation. By the early 1970s, although the situation had improved, it was still felt that many advocates still did not fully use rights available to them under the code of criminal procedure and were not fully conversant with the methods and tactics of effective representation at this stage of a criminal proceeding.[4]

Yet, in a criminal proceeding structured as the Soviet model is, the advocate is the only individual acting for the person under investigation or accused who is not salaried by the state (and even this distinction disappears if legal aid is involved). Among the arguments for retaining the *advokatura* as a non-state body, surely this must have great weight, for otherwise it seems to me the checks and balances devised to ascertain the objective truth would be irretrievably weighted against the individual and be seen to be a Kafkaesque parody. If the advocate's functions are to expand, I would have thought that the areas to watch were: earlier and more extensive involvement in the preliminary investigation which many Soviet jurists favor; participation in administrative proceedings, and a higher level of representation in civil cases. Legislation on administrative offenses also is anticipated in 1979-1980 and may contain innovations in this respect which many Soviet jurists have urged and which in some union republics have been tried to a limited extent. But if we are to see the advocate performing an enhanced role, it will be in these areas where he has traditionally acted rather than, I think, assuming legal functions permanently in the economic domain.

Finally, it will be interesting to see whether the new era brings to fruition proposals to create special law courses or diplomas for advocates which would inculcate forensic skills needed in the court room or clinical skills in interviewing or dealing with clients.[5] This kind of development assuredly would contribute to the distinctiveness of the advocate as a member of the Soviet legal profession; perhaps the recent dialogue on the ethical conduct of the advocate has enhanced the self-awareness of the advocates.[6]

NOTES

1. The Instruction is translated in William E. Butler, *Collected Legislation of the USSR and Constituent Union Republics*, (Dobbs Ferry, NY, 1979-); and with introductory comments by Robert Guttman, see *Review of Socialist Law*, 5 (1979), No. 2, 203-211.

2. V. I. Zaichuk, "Organizatsiia i deiatel'nost' advokatury Ukrainskoi SSR" (The Organization and Activity of the Bar of the Ukrainian SSR), in A. Ia. Sukharev (ed.), *Rol' i zadachi sovetskoi advokatury* (The Role and Tasks of the Soviet Bar), (Moscow, 1972), pp. 85*ff.*

3. I. I. Martinovich, *Advokatura v BSSR* (The Bar in the Belorussian SSR), (Minsk, 1973).

4. *Ibid.*

5. See *Izvestiia*, May 18, 1972.

6. As a postcript to this comment, it should be noted that as of September 1979, the new USSR legislation of the *advokatura* had not appeared, one of the few acts which has not met the legislative plan approved by the USSR Supreme Soviet. The draft enactment has been under preparation since late 1976 pursuant to a decree of the Presidium of the USSR Supreme Soviet of December 20, 1976, and obviously has an interdepartmental life of its own.

HUMBLE GUARDIANS OF ROUTINES
(NOTARIES AND ZAGS)

John N. Hazard*

1. Introduction

A Soviet critic of foreign approaches to the study of Soviet Law has told Westerners that they should focus on routine application of law rather than social breakdown evidenced by procuratorial protests and court decisions.[1] In his view, the role of law in Soviet society is seen better in the order it keeps than the disorder it punishes. If this be so, there are no institutions more worthy of examination than those humble guardians of routines, the State Notaries and the Civil Registration Bureaus (*ZAGS*), for they participate daily in holding social relationships to standardized patterns. No citizen, no matter how lowly, can escape their attention. Literally, they follow every one's footsteps from the cradle to the grave.

Yet, their function is not wholly routine, not wholly colorless. During the more than 60 years of Soviet history, they have had their moments of high political importance. One need only recall the Communist Party's bitter struggle with religious domination of the family, exercised during the Imperial period by ecclesiastical authorities through their monopoly over vital statistics. The newly organized *ZAGS* were the formal instruments of this struggle as they took over the recording functions.[2]

ZAGS came to the fore again in 1944 to implement government policy as it swung away from recognition of factual marriage and divorce to require registration in the interest of a strengthened family. Even today, *ZAGS* has a vital role to play in fashioning the new Soviet man. The registration of births has been characterized as a lay substitute for the politically abhorrent baptism, and its marriage registration has been reformed from a dry registration of the fact to a festive ceremonial in a "marriage palace," conducted with many of the trimmings of an ecclesiastical wedding, including the strains of a taped recording of Wagner's wedding march from Lohengrin when the bridal couple enters and the Mendelssohn march as they leave.[3] A deputy of the local soviet, sometimes dressed for the occasion with a red ribbon across her

* Research has been aided by Roger Morie of the Columbia University Law School under a grant from the School.

chest, stands beside the recording clerk of *ZAGS* to admonish the couple to lead a model socialist married life in terms reminiscent of admonitions used formerly by ecclesiastical authorities concerned with preservation of a holy union of man and wife.[4]

For the Notaries, their functions have been no less meaningful politically. Although no Notarial Office survived the revolution when the Tsarist Notarial Offices were "municipalized" and local soviets administered decedents' possessions, some city soviets soon established, as staff bureaus, Notarial Departments under a "People's Notary." These departments were ordered liquidated by the People's Commissariat of Justice of the RSFSR in December, 1918, and their functions were distributed where appropriate among the departments of communal affairs, social security, legal affairs, and *ZAGS*.[5] Thus, the State Notary passed from the scene as a legal entity, not to be revived until the introduction of the New Economic Policy.[6]

Like the Procuracy, which was brought into existence at the same time to watch over and punish any wily bourgeois who might be tempted to misuse his newly established right to produce goods to trade, the new Notaries were conceived as "dikes" to hold back what was feared to be a likely bourgeois flood. Their task was to oversee the NEPmen's commercial life and to prevent forbidden steps. They were, therefore, "preventive" rather than "punitive" institutions. They were to stop the impermissible before it occurred. Thus, they were to spare the Procuracy and the courts the need to intervene after the fact to restore the balance between bourgeois and worker.

On federation, the federal government followed its practice of establishing fundamental principles by enacting fundamentals on Notarial Offices, and the republics followed suit, bringing their legislation up to date as the circumstances required.[7]

While the days of the NEP are long since gone, the Notaries are still admonished to be vigilant, as is evident from the reports on current activities, for Soviet society still includes citizens who show little hesitation in attempting to turn an illegal penny. Notaries remain the watchdogs of what marketplace still functions, notably in overseeing the legality of personal property transactions. No sale of a dwelling, a motor car, or a motorcycle is to occur without their imprimatur.[8]

Both institutions operate, of course, under the supervision of higher authority. Since restoration of the Ministry of Justice of the USSR in 1970, there has been created within the Ministry a Department (*otdel'*) for the Notariat and *ZAGS*. Each institution under the Department functions under Fundamental Principles applicable to it. Those currently applicable to *ZAGS* are dated June 2, 1969,[9] and those applicable to Notaries are dated July 19, 1973.[10]

Republic legislation in each of the fifteen union republics has developed in great detail the USSR's fundamental principles. That of the RSFSR on Notaries is dated August 2, 1974, to become effective November 1, 1974. [11] That for *ZAGS* is dated June 19, 1974. [12] For both of the institutions, the enabling legislation is not enough to determine their place in the Soviet legal system, for in both cases the codes of law, and most notably the Family and Civil Codes, and in some cases even the Criminal Codes of the various union republics, need to be read to define the roles they play. [13] In the case of the Notaries, the complexity of their work is evidenced by the requirement of the new Statute that they have higher legal education, a requirement not yet legally stated for judges, although *de facto* the full-time professional judges are today almost all graduates of law faculties. To the legal education requirement there is an exception for persons who have had three years' experience in the offices of advocates, notaries, or legal advisers to state enterprises (generally classed in Soviet parlance as "jurists"). For the officials of the *ZAGS*, no such requirement of legal education has been established.

2. Notaries

Although there were in 1973 more than 2,500 State Notarial Offices in the USSR, said to be "touching the interests of over 30 million Soviet citizens," [14] not all communities are served by these institutions. Editors of the Journal of the RSFSR Ministry of Justice, *Sovetskaia Iustitsiia*, have reported that no Notarial Office exists in about 50% of the counties (*raiony*) of the RSFSR and of the cities subordinate to province (*oblast'* and *krai*) soviets or to the autonomous republics having no provincial subdivisions. [15]

For communities without Notaries, the executive committee of the county or city soviet is authorized to perform the Notarial functions, and this authority is extended also to executive committees of village soviets as designated by legislation of the union republic concerned, although in such cases the number of functions to be performed is reduced to twelve from the twenty conferred upon the Notarial Offices themselves. This devolution of authority to local soviets is said to have been authorized in the interest of the population's convenience by saving citizens the time and expenditure necessary to travel to a center where a Notarial Office exists. To assist Soviet citizens who may be outside the USSR, the Soviet Consuls are authorized to perform Notarial functions.

A Senior Notary is named by the Ministry of Justice of the union or autonomous republic in which he serves, and lower-level Notaries are named by the heads of departments of justice of provincial soviets. No one of them may be employed elsewhere in state offices, economic enterprises, or organizations, although as an exception, a Notary may be permitted to teach or to engage in research. Notaries enter upon their careers on graduation from a Faculty of Law, after appointment by the Personnel Distribution Committee of the Ministry of Justice of the republic where the Faculty is located. Appointments are made under the standard procedures established for the Committees, which means that prospective law graduates file a statement of preference as to career and place of work. Appointments are made in consideration of this statement of preferences and also the needs of the various services. Like appointees to any of the various services, Notaries must serve a minimum of three years at the post to which they are appointed, after which they are free to withdraw from the service or request reassignment. Salary levels are said to be comparable throughout the beginning ranks of the various services, whether judicial, procuratorial, investigative, or notarial. This means that Notaries' salaries are unrelated to the volume of services performed in one or another Notarial Office, in distinction from salaries of members of the Bar, who receive payments indexed to the fees they bring to their communal consultation offices. The career is said to attract primarily those law graduates who want to avoid the demanding tasks of judges, procurators, and investigators, and who prefer routines, standard hours, and a minimum of nervous tension.

Notarial Offices are instructed to preserve the secrecy of what they do, which means that no citizen not directly concerned in the transaction may obtain information on it. Nevertheless, the agencies of justice, the courts, the procurators, the investigators, and the police (*doznanie*) are authorized to request information which they deem necessary to the performance of their duties, and, indeed, the Notary is obligated to inform the procurator of any illegal activity he discovers in performing his duties. Curiously, one commentator on the USSR Law of 1973 says that the law puts an end to a practice conducted by the police (*doznanie*) of obtaining information from Notaries to facilitate their efforts to discover crime.[16] She notes also that the republics are not allowed in their enabling statutes to enlarge the list of agencies having access to Notarial records, giving the impression by making this comment that she believes the police are completely excluded from "snooping". A reading of both the USSR and RSFSR statutes fails to support this conclusion, for the police is listed along with the court, the Procuracy, and the investigating organs as authorized to ask for information on notarial activity and for documents required by them for criminal or civil cases in process (USSR Law, art. 7). Perhaps her elation at the exclusion of the police is justified by the requirement of the Statute that the information relate to a criminal or civil case in process, which might mean that "snooping" through Notarial records to see what might be turned up in the process is now not included among authorized practices.

Notarial acts, or refusal to act, may be appealed to a court, in an exception to usual Soviet procedure which generally excludes from judicial practice what a common lawyer would call a writ of *mandamus*. Not only may a court declare a concrete Notarial act illegal, but it may require a Notary to perform a Notarial act which he or she has refused to perform. This type of judicial intervention seems, however, to have been exceptional, as reports on Notarial practice appearing in the journal *Sovetskaia Iustitsiia* suggest that Notaries look to the Ministry of Justice of their republic for guidance in cases of doubt, and perform in accordance with instructions from the Ministry. Some of these references will be reviewed later in this paper.

One court case merits attention, however, for it illustrates the extent to which control over the Notariat may be applied by a court.[17] A Senior Notary refused to certify a contract granting the use in perpetuity of a plot of land for the construction of a private dwelling in a city on the ground that the contract violated the RSFSR Decree of September 3, 1963. The citizen appealed to the city people's court, arguing that he had extreme need of living space. The trial court ordered the Notary to certify the contract, but was reversed by the presidium of the provincial court on the ground that allocation of plots of land for use was prohibited by the 1963 decree in cities of over 100,000 population, and this city was of such a size. Therefore, the allocation—having occurred after the effective date of the decree—was illegal, and the trial court had no right to require the Notary to certify the contract.

A senior consultant of the department of Notaries and *ZAGS* has reported the frequency of various types of activities of Notaries. Her conclusion is that the most frequent certifications are of signature on documents concerning inheritance, the ownership of dwellings, and family legal relationships.[18] Those concerning inheritance had to do with acceptance of inheritance, issuance of certificates of right to inheritance, the taking of measures to protect decedent's estates, consent of heirs to include in the certificate of the right to inherit heirs deprived of the opportunity to present evidence of their relation to the decedent, rejection of inheritance, etc. Those concerning dwellings had to do with the consent of a spouse to alienate a dwelling acquired after registration of a marriage and constituting the communal property of the spouses, release by one who is joint owner of a dwelling of his priority right to purchase it, and consent of adult members of a collective farm household (*dvor*) to alienate a house located in a village. Those having to do with family relationships had to do with consent to divorce, naming of guardians, documents concerning adoption and paternity, amending a birth certificate of a child born out of wedlock after his parents marry, and declaration by parents of consent to the marriage of their minor child.

Somewhat rarer certifications of signatures occur when documents are presented to reformulate rights of an heir to a motorcycle or automobile, to confirm the fact that a citizen had been a member of a partizan brigade during World War II, to confirm the fact that persons worked together in the same office, to withdraw a power of attorney previously given, to consent to division of a plot of land assigned to construct a dwelling on a section of the original plot, to consent to an exchange of living space, and to sublet premises.

Some hint as to the type of requests Notaries receive for certification of signatures on documents to which they may not attach their seals is given by the consultant's list of prohibited acts. These are: a release by a spouse on entering marriage of her right to live in the space allotted to her husband (violates Civil Code RSFSR, art. 201); a document setting forth the substance of an agreement, such as an agreement to make a gift, unless the donor is prevented by physical incapacity, illness, or for other reasons from execution of the document. In such a case, and to avoid any possibility of misrepresentation, the signature of the person signing for the incapacitated donor can be certified by a Notary, by an official of the place were the donor works, or by the housing administration of his or her place of habitation, or, finally, by an official of a hospital where the donor is being treated (Civil Code RSFSR, art. 44). Exclusion of a Notary from an agreement made by a person of full capacity is because the law requires no notarization of such agreements, only that they be in written form.

The likelihood that influence may be brought to bear upon Notaries to perform illegal acts or to refrain from acting was recognized by the 1965 Statute, for the first time. Reports had been published for some time of illegal certification of sales of dwellings on speculative terms, suggesting that something had caused the Notary to fail to perform his duty to scrutinize documents brought to him for certification. Perhaps in response to these reports, the 1965 Statute provided that Notaries are independent and responsible only to the law. This provision, which is identical to the USSR Constitutional provision relating to judges, is interpreted similarly by two commentators on the 1965 Statute, for they say that the Notary alone decides what he shall do or not do, and interested parties have no recourse except an appeal to the people's court, whose decision is binding both upon the Notary and those appealing. The provision was hailed as helping the Notary to struggle with illegalities committed by state offices, organizations, state officials, and collectives when he discovered them in the course of his work.[19] The 1973 USSR Statute does not repeat the stricture on interference, perhaps because it is currently presumed, but this question remains to be examined. Not only is the provision omitted from the USSR Statute of 1973, but it does not appear in the RSFSR Statute of 1974 either.

Some suggestion of the extent to which Notaries chastize officials of state agencies, enterprises, housing departments, and nursing homes is to be found in an account of a study made by the notarial department of the RSFSR Supreme Court (before its notarial supervisory functions were returned to the Ministry of Justice of the Republic).[20] Its study showed that in the relatively distant Komi Autonomous Republic, the Notary had made representations to many state agencies which had refused to give certificates of work or residence to citizens requiring these to obtain wages, savings bank deposits, stipends, or state grants in aid, while other agencies had made illegal demands for documents certified by a Notary. Meetings were held with officials making such demands, as the result of which their illegal demands for documents dropped by 35% in one year. This latter work of the Notaries was hailed as protecting citizens from constantly mounting demands for papers from the bureaucracy.

The same study found that Notaries continued to discover wide violation by local soviets of regulations relating to assignment of plots of land for perpetual use in constructing a private dwelling. When the contrasts of assignment were presented to the Notaries for notarial certification, it was learned that soviets had permitted construction of a dwelling exceeding permitted norms or architectural limitations. Some had even permitted assignment of plots when the assignee intended to build only for sale. Some enterprises which had made loans to employees to permit them to build a dwelling had failed to include in the contract a clause prohibiting alienation of the dwelling, and builders had taken advantage of the omission to attempt to sell the dwelling and require the purchaser to assume the debt. Some sellers of dwellings were found on verification of the contract of sale to have been able to sell because a local soviet had assigned them space in public housing in violation of the regulation permitting allocation of public housing only to persons owning no private dwelling. One can imagine that such intervention by Notaries into the work of the soviets can have caused ill feeling.

Not all Notaries have taken care to follow up on references to malfeasors when errors are found in their work. This becomes evident from the remark of the two commentators on the 1965 Statute cited earlier. They found that Notaries file with the offenders laconic reports of facts drawing no conclusions and failing to state the problem they have discovered with clarity; that no request for a reply is placed in the report; and that once the report has been sent, the Notaries give it no further thought. Notaries and officials of local soviets performing notarial fuctions are admonished to give serious attention to their communications and to follow-ups, and to inform the responsible officials once again if they think the measures taken to rectify the situation inadequate.

As examples of effective Notarial intervention the commentators cite two cases in the city of Ufa. In one, the Notary after reviewing the work of the bureaucrat informed the executive committee of the Lenin borough soviet of the city that the forms being used for the allocation of plots in perpetuity to applicants did not conform to the requirements of the order of January 1, 1964. Another borough soviet's executive committee was informed of violations of law committed by the communal department of the borough soviet in allotting small plots. In both situations, the executive committees concerned examined the Notary's complaints and took measures to eradicate the illegalities.

Notaries have been praised even for intervening in cases not included within their list of functions. Thus, the commentators praise the Senior Notary of the city of Petropavlovsk in Kamchatka for noting violations of regulations establishing procedures to be followed in the distribution of dwelling space. The Notary sent complaints to the provincial committee of the watchdog agency, People's Control, to the executive committee, and to the managements of enterprises and organizations authorized to distribute dwelling space in public and enterprise housing. Measures were taken after review of the complaints to conform procedures to law. To this the commentators say, "This activity must be considered correct."

Violations of labor law have also been noted by Notaries reviewing hiring practices in their jurisdiction, and also in examining practices in matters concerning communal services (*bytovyie voprosy*). Again, the Notarial function has been to take measures to ascertain that such illegalities are eradicated.

From this recital of types of Notarial intervention to assure adherence to law by the state bureaucracy, it is evident that Notaries must have access to a law library sufficient to their needs. This fact is noted by the commentators, and they even indicate what sources are to be included in a minimum library for the Notarial office. The items listed are:

> Fundamental Principles of Civil Law of the USSR and the Union Republics, Fundamental Principles of Civil Procedure of the USSR and of the Union Republics.
>
> Codes of Law: Civil, Civil Procedure, Marriage and Family, Criminal, and also Compendia of Normative Acts concerning Civil Law, these being Compendia for Housing, Inheritance, and other branches of law.
>
> The Collections of Decrees and Orders of the Governments of the USSR and of the relevant union republic, and as a separate publication, the Order of the Council of Ministers of the union republic approving the list of documents on which levy of execution may occur without contest on the basis of the signature of the Notary without more.

This library is declared inadequate to decide all matters coming before a Notary, and the commentators recommend that the minimal library be augmented to include the Notary's Reference Book (*Spravochnik*), textbooks in Civil Law, Family Law, and Civil Procedure. The Notary is advised to subscribe to three journals: *Sovetskaia Iustitsiia* (for publication of Notarial practice, as well as instructions of higher supervisory authority), *Sotsialisticheskaia Zakonnost'* (for publication of materials necessary to resolution of questions concerning Civil Law), and the USSR and RSFSR Supreme Court Reporters (*Biulleteni*), as well as the Reporter for the union republic in which the Notary functions.

Notaries have several other functions established by the Statute on Notaries, in addition to those relating to attestation of documents concerning legal transactions, and the distribution of decedents' estates. Generally, these have to do with attestation of a fact not in dispute; these being attestation of the fact that a given person is alive; that a person lives in a given place; that he or she is the person whose photograph appears on the document; that a document was presented on a given date, protesting non-payment of a bill of exchange, or protesting the facts of a collision at sea as presented by the captain of the vessel concerned.

Additionally, the Notary certifies to the accuracy of a translation; accepts documents for safekeeping, including money and money equivalents. Further, the Notary accepts from citizens and institutions for transmission by mail communications which the sender wishes to be able to prove as having been despatched. The Notary is not a Savings Bank, so deposits of money or money equivalents are received only when the depositor wishes them transmitted to another in payment of a debt. Once in the hands of the Notary, the deposit may not be returned to the depositor without the creditor's consent.

Finally, a Notary is authorized to take measures to preserve for later examination by a court or administrative office evidence which seems to an interested party likely to be unavailable at the time of the court or administrative hearing. This evidence is not only documentary and material; it may also be the testimony of witnesses whose presence is unlikely at the trial because of grave illness or death or absence in remote regions of the USSR or abroad. Curiously, this type of work is not included in the 1974 Statute of the RSFSR, as item 20 in art. 14, is in the same form as it appeared in the RSFSR Statute of 1965, art. 3 item 13, and art. 66. Presumably, the absence of such an authorization in the federal Statute is because some of the republics have traditionally refused to grant this authority to a Notary, preferring to leave it to a court, even when suit concerning the evidence has not yet been filed with the court. [22]

The respective roles of Notaries and courts has generally been defined so as to place on the Notaries the task of establishing facts that are not contested, and upon the court the task of determining facts that are contested. Thus, a dispute over the persons who may be included among a circle of heirs goes before a court for resolution, while a Notary can establish only those heirs about whom no one raises question. Likewise, a dispute as to what has happened to a missing person whom a party wishes declared dead goes to a court for resolution.

The Notary's right to take testimony from a witness unable to attend a court or administrative hearing could raise in some minds the issue of fairness. That may by the reason why four republics forbid the practice. The Notary is not authorized, as is the Soviet judge, to take an active part in questioning a witness, nor would attorneys be present, representing other interested parties, to cross examine. To be sure, Soviet practice, like that of most Romanist systems, places less emphasis upon cross examination than do the common law systems, but it is practice within what is said to be an adversarial system in spite of its inquisitorial features, and uncontested testimony can raise doubts. Perhaps the Russian draftsmen had in mind the rule of evidence that judges are expected to search for "absolute truth" and in doing so they may hear whatever they wish. There is no jury to be confused by what is presented. Even common lawyers would not object to the preservation of the testimony of a dying witness, for the hearsay rule of the common law provides an exception for dying declarations, but the preservation of testimony of living persons in good health could be considered another matter. Whatever the considerations, it is evident that most of the union republics are prepared to add this duty to those authorized by the federal statute as within a Notary's functions.

Reports of Notarial practice in the pages of *Sovetskaia Iustitsiia* provide some insight into the wide variety of problems met by Notaries for the solution of which they sense the need for advice. The reports also indicate how much the Notaries need to be conversant with the law. A sampling suggests that Notaries are cautious, asking the Ministry of Justice for guidance on frequent occasions. Most of the reports indicate this practice, although a few arise because citizens think themselves wronged by what the Notary has done or refused to do. Because the Ministry's decisions on error are few, it may be appropriate to begin the survey with these decisions.

Cases in which Notaries acted in violation of law all concerned inheritance problems. A minor under the age of 18 requested certification of his will by the Notary, but his request was refused on the ground that he was under the age of eighteen and not authorized to make a will. He argued that he was married under special dispensation of the executive committee of the local soviet, as permitted by law, and that as a married man, he was qualified to make a will. The Notary was informed that the RSFSR Civil Code permitted execution of a will by a married minor, and certification was his right. [23]

Another Notary refused to enquire of a Savings Bank whether the decedent had a Savings Account at the time of his death. The heir was directed to make the enquiry himself. The RSFSR's Ministry of Justice's Notarial Office declared that this was error. Under the Notarial Statute, Notaries are required to make the request on behalf of heirs when they present evidence of death and other documents proving their rights as heirs. [24]

A Notary who certified a will signed by both spouses was informed by the legal department of the provincial soviet's executive committee that a single last will and testament may not be certified if signed by two persons, even when both spouses request certification. [25]

Finally, a general comment was issued to all Notaries based on a review of their activities to inform them that they had been failing to perform their duties when they refused to certify the signatures of heirs seeking to qualify for inheritance after the expiration of the six-month period established for presentation of a claim as heir, if the heir within the six-month period in-

254

formed the Notary at the place where the estate was administered that the inheritance was accepted. In short, the decisive moment for representing oneself as heir was at the time of the request whether the inheritance would be accepted or rejected, and not the date when the formal document claiming inheritance was filed. [26]

The cases in which Notaries have asked for advice on applicable law are more numerous than those where action was taken in violation of law. A sampling will indicate the type of practice and the extent to which the law is unknown to Notaries.

In the first a sister of a decedent, killed in an accident together with the beneficiary who had been named the beneficiary under an insurance contract, sought to recover the insured sum as heir at law. She petitioned the Notary to issue her a certificate of the right to inherit, but he was in doubt as to what to do and sought advice. The response was a citation to the Rules for Joint Life Insurance confirmed by the USSR Ministry of Finance providing that unless the contract provides otherwise, the insured sum shall be paid in such cases of simultaneous death of the insured and the beneficiary to the heirs at law, and the Notarial certificate should issue. [27]

Two requests had to do with the rights of an adopted child to inheritance from the estate of a natural parent. In one case, the natural parent had died before adoption. In the other, the natural parent had died after adoption. The response was quotation of RSFSR Civil Code, art. 532 to the effect that an adopted person and their descendants shall not inherit from a natural parent, his other blood relatives in direct line, as well as his blood brothers and sisters. Thus, in the case of death before adoption, there would be inheritance, but not so in the case of death after adoption. In the latter case, the adopted child had argued that he deserved special consideration since his step-father who had adopted him (presumably the step-father had been the second husband of the child's mother) had gone off to the war and never returned to the family so that he had given the step-son no upbringing, a fact that had been recognized by a court in dismissing the step-father's suit many years after departure for maintenance, because of disability, from the step-son. This extenuating circumstance was indicated as without influence on the rule of the code. [28]

Two inheritance claims were presented to Notaries by members of collective farm households (*dvor*) to whom the usual inheritance rules applicable to urban households do not apply, since they continue to live in community as of old. In the first, a member of the household sought a certificate from the Notary which would permit him to reregister a motorcycle registered in the name of a deceased member of the household so that it might be registered in his name. The Notary was advised that such a certificate might be given only if the executive committee of the village soviet certified that the claimant was a member of a collective farm household, and a declaration of all members of

255

the household consenting to reregistration in the claimant's name was presented, and, finally, that the motorcycle is in the common ownership of the household. [29] Presumably, this procedure preserved the common ownership of the motorcycle but permitted a single member to use it as registrant.

The second collective farm household case was a request as to what agency must give its consent to alienation of part of a household dwelling, if the household had among its members minor children. The Ministry of Justice's department informed the Notary that in accordance with various cited laws consent from the local soviet's agency for trusteeship and guardianship was necessary if the property was valued at not more than 100 rubles, while if it had a greater value, the consent of the entire executive committee of the county (*raion*) soviet was required. [30]

Similar confusion as to the agency that must approve a sale of a part of a private dwelling to be reconstructed for non-residential purposes arose. The Ministry of Justice's Notarial Department advised the Notary that the question of non-residential construction is to be decided by the communal economy department of the executive committee of the soviet concerned, or by the office of chief architect if there is one, but in no case is the consent of the entire executive of the soviet required. [31]

Evidently, determination of the agency authorized to approve sales is a continuing problem, for there is yet another case where a Notary asked who must approve the alienation of a dwelling located on land whose use is allotted to a collective or state farm in perpetuity. The response was that notarial certification of the sale of such a dwelling may be executed only if the applicant presents a resolution of the general meeting of members, if the usage of land is that of a collective farm, or of the management of a state farm, if its land use is in issue. If no such decision is produced, the Notary may certify a sale only for the purpose of demolition of the dwelling, [32] presumably to use the building materials elsewhere.

There seems to be no feeling among some dwelling owners that they will be unable to obtain Notarial certification on contracts of lease when illegalities are involved. In one case, a dwelling owner appeared at the Notary's office with a request that he certify the lease of the dwelling. On investigation, the Notary discovered that the dwelling had been constructed without permission of the local soviet. The Notary was informed by the Ministry of Justice's Notarial Bureau that a dwelling constructed without permission cannot be an object of a property interest, and the citizen who has constructed it has no right to dispose of it by lease or sale. Contracts purporting to do so shall not be certified. [33]

A good many requests from Notaries to the Ministry of Justice seem to concern indecision as to what type of property is included in an estate and, therefore, subject to inheritance. Thus, a Notary asked what to do about a tort judgment not yet paid to the victim before his death. The Ministry of

Justice declared that a judgment delivered by a people's court, prior to the death of the victim, for damages resulting from an accident is part of the decedent's estate and may be the subject of a certificate of inheritance. [34]

Likewise, a pension question was raised. Here, the Ministry of Justice informed the Notary that the unreceived portion of a pension does not pass by inheritance to heirs, and no certificate of inheritance may issue on this. The money must be paid over directly to dependents in the decedent's family unable to work. A USSR Council of Ministers decision of 1972 was cited as authority. [35]

When a monetary sum owing a decedent because of an unused holiday was put in issue, the Ministry told the Notary that this, like wages not paid the decedent before death, was inheritable, and a certificate should be issued. [36]

Certification of copies of academic diplomas has presented Notaries with questions on which they seek advice. In one case, the applicant presented a diploma signed by the president of the State Examining Committee functioning at the time of issuance but not at the moment of completion of study. The Ministry of Justice, citing an Instruction of the USSR Ministry of Higher and Specialized Education, informed the Notary that the president of the Examining Committee functioning at the time of issuing the document should sign, and duplicates of such a document might be certified. [37]

A graduate fared less well in another case where the diploma had been signed not by the rector of the agricultural institute but by other officials. The Ministry informed the Notary that a diploma signed in any other way than that authorized by the Instruction previously cited was invalid and copies cannot be certified by a Notary. The Notary was told to suggest to the applicant that he return his diploma to the institution and ask for an exchange. [38]

Finally, when a diploma holder called at the Notary's Office to obtain certification of copies of his certificate of completion of a two-year clinical internship, the Notary thought it necessary to ask the Ministry of Justice who might sign such a document legally. The Ministry cited in reply a number of orders of various ministries conducting such programs through institutes subordinate to each, and the specific form established by the Ministry of Public Health for programs of the type completed by the applicant was indicated. [39]

This chronicle indicating how difficult it may be for a Notary to know the appropriate law, and how necessary it is for him to be informed of such a law before he even certifies that a copy is like the original, may be brought to an end with two cases concerning the appropriate tax for services performed by a Notary, and one having to do with right to keep a document presented to him for certification until he has had an opportunity to check on its legality.

The two tax cases were highly specialized. In one, the applicant sought to register a contract of sale of a garage belonging to him as a private owner. The response cannot but remind lawyers everywhere of the complexity of tax statutes, for the Ministry of Justice referred the Notary to RSFSR Ministry of Finance explanation No. 03327 of July 22, 1976, instructing that on certification of documents of sales of garages belonging to private citizens, the tax should be levied under point 1 "b" of paragraph 40 of the USSR Ministry of Finance's Instruction No. 71 of April 4, 1972, "On State Duty," and if this were done, it would be learned that the tax was to be in the amount of 3% of the sale price, but not less than 5 rubles. [40]

In the other tax case, Notaries asked for an interpretation of an RSFSR Ministry of Finance letter releasing certain categories of citizens from payment of the State Tax on devolution of estates. The Ministry of Justice obliged by stating in detail which categories of citizens qualified under the exemption and which did not, but it would have taken a lawyer fully conversant with all of the regulations to follow the explanation. [41]

The final case selected for comment in this sequence is that of a request from Notaries as to whether they must give to an applicant a receipt for a document which is being held for verification because of doubts as to its veracity, or until more information about it has been obtained. The RSFSR's Ministry of Justice's Notarial Department responded that such a receipt must be given, with indication of its designation, its number, and how and when it was given to the Notary. [42]

Notaries established in newly-developing remote regions are expected to bear the heavy burden of starting the new community on the path of socialist legality. It is reported that along the totally undeveloped road bed of the new Baikal-Amur Railroad in Eastern Siberia, they have been called upon to help local soviets get started, and to organize collective farms. [43] As the agencies directed to see to the future rather than to clean up the violations of the past, they have greater roles to play in the establishment of new communities than the courts. This role has been illustrated also with data from the distant Udmurt Autonomous Republic. [44]

3. ZAGS

In contrast to Notaries, the registration clerks of the *ZAGS* have far narrower functions, and their knowledge of law need not extend beyond the statute which creates them and the Family Code of the republic where they function. None of these clerks is required to have a legal education as are the Notaries. Thus, clerks at *ZAGS* are simply civil servants, serving under the standard regulations for the civil service, which means that they are recruited and paid in accordance with civil service regulations concerning requirements of applicants for jobs, and paid according to the wage scale established for the grade to which they are appointed.

Although *ZAGS* clerks are trained only to perform the bureaucratic function of registration, the duty placed upon them of attempting to mediate quarrels of couples appearing with a request that a dissolution of marriage be registered suggests that they could do with some knowledge of psychology and marriage counselling as well. Also, the duty they now bear of organizing registration of births and marriages to give them the ceremonial aura of politically abhorrent baptism and religious marriage—for centuries the festive occasions in the life of villages and even of urban communities—suggests that they would do well to seek advice from those who are dramatically inclined on the art of conducting impressive ceremonies.

As has been indicated earlier, their role as registrars of marriages and births was of vital importance in 1917 when the Bolsheviks decided to strike a decisive blow at ecclesiastical institutions by depriving them of their right to register vital statistics and marriages and to transfer these duties to the newly created offices of *ZAGS*. Further, in 1944, their task was to overcome, if possible, the lax relationships between men and women who since 1926 had not been required to declare to any official their desire to be recognized as married or separated after the breakdown of marriage. Again, the transfer to *ZAGS* of the obligation to record all marriages from which consequences were to flow was the major step taken by policy makers to stabilize a family structure which had deteriorated so much during the war that juvenile crime had mounted.

The 1944 decree had significant impact upon children, for it reestablished a status for those born out of wedlock which, although not called "illegitimacy" nevertheless carried with it such social opprobrium that a nickname was developed for such offspring. They became the "*procherk*" children, because their birth certificate bore a line drawn through the blank space for "father". [45] Further, such children had no rights of maintenance or inheritance from their father nor even to bear his surname and patronymic. They carried the surname only of their mother and whatever patronymic she chose to contribute to the child's sense of dignity.

The situation of compulsory registration was not to last as it related to children, although it is still today necessary to establish legal relationships of husband and wife. With the advent of the post-Stalin Fundamental Principles of Legislation on Marriage and the Family on June 27, 1968, [46] children born out of wedlock recovered some of their lost status under the law prior to 1944. Their parents were authorized to go before *ZAGS* with a request that the father's paternity be recorded in the registry (art. 6). It mattered not whether the parents were maintaining a joint household or the child had been born of a casual relationship. Once the record was made, the child had all rights against a father that he or she would have had against him had there been a recorded marriage, *i.e.*, rights of upbringing, maintenance, and inheritance, and the mother and father had full parental rights and duties with respect to the child, even though as between themselves there was no marriage relationship. The *ZAGS* is, however, no more than a recording bureau in

259

this instance. The registrar hears only the statement of the parents; he or she makes no investigation of the facts. If there is a dispute as to parentage, it is for a court to determine the facts, not *ZAGS*.

The same limitation on function applies also under the 1968 Fundamental Principles with regard to dissolution of marriage. If the two spouses appear with a request that dissolution be registered, *ZAGS* may make the entry, although it is required to attempt to reconcile the parties. Reports indicate that it has been successful in some districts, as for example Kaluga City where 136 couples out of 321 filing for divorce are reported to have been reconciled. [47] If there is a contest, or if there are children under the age of majority (18 years), *ZAGS* has no authority to register a divorce until a court decree has been obtained and delivered to it.

Because of mounting divorce rates, *ZAGS* has also been given by its statute the duty to impress upon persons wishing to register marriage the seriousness of their decision. By current Family Law, a waiting period between one and three months may be established by *ZAGS* depending upon its evaluation of the situation before the marriage will be registered. Some *ZAGS* are said to have reduced the waiting period in exceptional circumstances to three days, a period which has been sharply criticized as defeating the purpose of the law. [48]

Surnames are important to individuals, and *ZAGS* as the keeper of records of names, although not the agency that makes the change, has come in for litigation. In a suit in Estonia, a divorced husband found that his former wife had obtained a change in the surname of their child to the name of her new husband. This change, authorized by the Tallin City Soviet, was registered by *ZAGS*. In the suit, the father sought to restore to the child his own name since his consent had not been obtained to the change. The trial court granted his petition, but the suit was dismissed on appeal for lack of jurisdiction in a court. The proper agency to determine the surname of a child if the parents are in disagreement is the local soviet's department for guardianship and trusteeship. [49]

Court decisions depriving parents of their parental rights over a child have sometimes been followed by a request filed with *ZAGS* by the parent concerned to have his or her name expunged from the birth record. In response to a request for guidance filed with the Ministry of Justice, the response was received that deprivation of parental rights has no impact upon the record of birth. The duty to maintain the child continues, so that the record of parentage must be preserved, and sometimes rights are restored when the conditions which gave rise to the deprivation have been removed. [50]

ZAGS' registrations provide not only records of the status of one or another individual. Their individual entries, when aggregated, provide statistical data for policy makers in ministries, soviets, and the Communist Party.

Increases or decreases in birth rates, marriages, or divorces are tabulated,[51] and provide the basis for measures designed to stimulate population growth, to strengthen the family currently weakened by a high rate of divorce, or to plan the construction of schools. Records of *ZAGS* provide a supplement to the periodical census which occurs only at long intervals. *ZAGS* is critical in determining which individuals have reached the age of military service, which individual is not permitted to marry because a prior marriage has not been dissolved, which man or woman qualifies for retirement and old age pensions, and who qualifies as an heir at law to a decedent estate. The Notary issues the inheritance certificate, but family relationship is proved by the records at *ZAGS*.

4. Conclusion

From the record, both the Notaries and the recording clerks of *ZAGS* are seen to have gained importance among Soviet legal institutions justifying more attention than is usually accorded them both within the USSR and among Sovietologists abroad. Indeed, one cannot conceive of a complex modern society such as that developed in the USSR without the record keeping performed by *ZAGS*. And the Notaries also perform a vital role in regulating what is left of market relationships. So long as personal property incentives are relied upon to stimulate production and so long as state resources are inadequate to provide government-financed housing for all, the Notaries will remain important as agencies of supervision and prevention of illegality.

Of course the Notary's role could be played, as is the case in common law jurisdictions, by probate courts as far as inheritance is concerned. Their role as supervisors and watchdogs over individuals bent on turning an illegal penny could be tapered off as private ownership of dwellings is phased out. Yet, given the Romanist foundations of Soviet inheritance law, and the reaffirmation of the right to own private dwellings in the 1977 Constitution of the USSR, it seems unlikely that diminution of their current functions can be expected.

Were personal property in dwellings, bank accounts, and articles of personal consumption, currently guaranteed by Article 13 of the 1977 Constitution, to be terminated in some new constitution designed to signal the end of ·"developed socialism," and the advent of what might be called the "threshold to communism," much of the Notary's work would vanish, but some would still be required. Some one would still have to certify the identity of individuals signing documents required in the administration of things, and documents presented for certification of copies might still require a check on conformity to regulations. This would not mean that the Notary as such would be needed. Perhaps the work of the Notaries and of *ZAGS* could be merged in a single office of records. Both institutions are already supervised by a single department of the USSR Ministry of Justice, and this signifies official appreciation of the fact that their work is not unrelated.

Officers of such a new record bureau could be educated in such aspects of regulations concerning family relationships as were necessary to record vital statistics, and the provisions of the current education law on the execution of academic diplomas could be simplified and easily made known to those who had to inspect them, whether recording officers or some one within the Ministry of Education. A combination of record keeping and certification in the same office would make it possible to administer the function uniformly throughout the entire country, for executive committees of local soviets could be authorized to establish departments for the purpose, and there would be no need to draw distinctions between populated places where Notarial Offices could be established and those where the executive committee of the local soviet had to perform the Notarial function.

Finally, there would remain for allocation to some other office the function currently performed by Notaries along the Baikal-Amur Railroad and remote autonomous republics. The Ministry of Justice would seem to be a logical center for the direction of such a program of vulgarization of regulatory measures. Already, it is directed to educate in legal procedures, and it would seem reasonable to extend this function to include what the Notaries are now said to be doing for want of some other agency specifically trained for the purpose.

Whatever institutions were given the functions remaining after those of *ZAGS* and the Notaries were combined in a single agency would probably continue to be used for political purposes, for every Soviet institution, no matter how humble, is charged with furthering the development of the "good society" and the new Soviet man. These critically important functions will remain even when the state has withered away, but the institutions need not take the form which has become traditional during the years leading up to "developed socialism."

NOTES

1. Dr. V. Toumanov of the Institute of State and Law of the USSR Academy of Sciences made this comment in Budapest during a 1969 conference of the International Association of Legal Science discussing teaching and research in comparative law. His brief summary report of the Conference did not include in full his observation made on the floor of the Conference. See V. T., "Mezhdunarodnaia konferentsiia po sravni-tel'nomu pravovedeniiu" (The International Conference of Comparative Jurisprudence), *SGiP*, 1970, No. 1, 141.

2. Decrees on divorce and marriage of December 18-19, 1917, refer to *ZAGS* as the recording agency. Curiously, the words creating *ZAGS* appear only in the second decree. For texts, see *Sobr. Uzak.*, 1917, No. 10, item 152, and *id.*, No. 11, item 160.

3. Ceremony was prescribed by Council of People's Commissars' decree of June 8, 1946; executive committees of provincial and city soviets being required to provide *ZAGS* with well-appointed quarters with waiting rooms, and a separate room for registration of marriages and births. *Sobr. Post. RSFSR*, 1946, No. 3, item 8; also published in *Sistematicheskoe Sobranie Zakonov RSFSR, ukazov prezidiuma verkhovnogo soveta RSFSR i reshenii pravitel'stva RSFSR*, (Systematic Collection of Laws of the RSFSR, Edicts of the Presidium of the Supreme Soviet of the RSFSR, and Resolutions of the Government of the RSFSR), Vol. 13, (Moscow, 1967), p. 646. A second effort to improve the ceremony was made by decree of the presidium of the RSFSR Supreme Soviet of June 15, 1960, instructing district soviet executive committees to supervise *ZAGS* and to raise the culture of their work. *Ved. V.S. RSFSR*, 1960, No. 23, item 352. Also published in *Sistematicheskoe Sobranie, op. cit.*, p. 649. The RSFSR Council of Ministers, by decree in 1964, ordered local soviets to see that *ZAGS* conducted registrations in a festive way to displace religious cermonies. *Sobr. Post. RSFSR*, 1964, No. 3, item 22, also published in *Sistematicheskoe Sobranie, op. cit.*, p. 651. The marriage of the Greek heiress, Christine Onassis, to a Soviet citizen on August 1, 1978, attracted wide attention to the festive ceremony conducted by *ZAGS* in accordance with these decrees. The *ZAGS* official is reported to have told the bridegroom, "Wherever you live, do not forget your Soviet motherland." The music followed the standard pattern with the Mendelssohn wedding march played by a string ensemble as the couple departed. See Craig R. Whitney, "Miss Onassis Weds and Espouses Simple Life," *New York Times*, August 2, 1978, 1 and 10. Later, the bride was reported to have been doubtful about the wisdom of the marriage, caused in part "by the ceremony itself." See Nicholas Gage, "Miss Onassis Now Called Unsure on Rejoining Husband in Soviet Union," *New York Times*, August 9, 1978. 1. Later, she evidently overcame the doubt and rejoined her husband.

4. A Soviet academician has argued that deputies of soviets have not yet countered the priest, mullah, or pastor in conducting the registration ritual because the attending deputy does not know the parties intimately, and will not continue to counsel them as they mature. He proposes creation of a deputies' commission to accept responsibility for the family lives of the electorate. See Iu. V. Bromlee, *LG*, August 31, 1977, 12. Eng. transl. in *CDSP*, 29 (1977), No. 35, 15-16. Continuing reports in the Soviet press indicate that in Central Asia religious tradition lingers in Komsomol weddings. See *Turkmenskaia Iskra*, May 11, 1978, 2.

5. The history of the early years is set forth in M. G. Avdiukov, *Notariat v SSSR*

(The Notary's Office in the USSR), (Moscow, 1974), pp. 14-20. Avdiukov states that as early as February, 1919, only three months after liquidation of Notarial departments in local soviets, the People's Commissariat of Justice of the RSFSR ordered reconstitution of Notarial chairs in *guberniia* departments of justice and in *uezd* people's courts when need was felt for them. No statute defined their competence, but in fact they certified copies of documents and signatures.

6. Decree of October 4, 1922. *Sobr. Uzak.*, 1922, No. 63, item 807. Even before this Statute recreating the Notaries, a decree of the RSFSR Council of People's Commissars regulating contracts between state organizations and private persons required that they be controlled by compulsory notarial verification to be accepted as valid. *Sobr. Uzak.*, 1921, No. 60, items 410 and 417 (amended, No. 69, item 549). To perform this function, Notarial chairs were established in all departments of justice of *guberniia* soviets and in the bureaus of justice of the *uezd* soviets under the authorization of February 1919, referred to by Avdiukov, *op. cit.* note 4.

7. The first federal action was enactment of Fundamental Principles of Court Structures of the USSR and of the Union Republics of July 15, 1924. *Sobr. Zak. SSSR*, 1924, No. 23, item 201 (art. 18 concerns Notaries). This first action was followed by enactment of a federal statute, entitled Fundamental Principles of Organization of the State Notariat, signed by both the Central Executive Committee and Council of People's Commissars of the USSR on May 24, 1926. *Sobr. Zak.. SSSR*, 1926, No. 35, item 252. Republic legislation was then enacted to conform to the federal statute. For the RSFSR, see law of October 4, 1926, *Sobr. Uzak.*, 1926, No. 74, item 576. Amended forms of the Statute were adopted on July 20, 1930, *Sobr. Uzak.*, No. 38, item 476; December 31, 1947, *id.*, 1947, item 980; and September 30, 1965, *Ved. V.S. RSFSR*, 1965, No. 40, item 991.

8. Although originally patterned upon the model of Western European legal institutions of the same name, rather than upon the model of the Anglo-American common law systems, they are no longer comparable to the Notarial Offices of some Western countries because of the extraordinary growth of Notarial functions in the complex "post-industrial" capitalist systems of the West. For a stimulating comparison of notaries in socialist and contemporary capitalist systems of Europe, see G. Crespi Reghizzi, "Il Notariato sovietico (Evoluzione, principi e reforma 30 settiembre 1965)," published in *Revista del Notariate (Rassegna di diritto e practica notarile)*, 21 (Settiembre-Octobre 1967), No. 5, 556-610.

9. *Sobr. Post. SSSR*, 1969, No. 16, item 85. Excerpts reprinted in Iu. M. Gusev, *Registratsiia aktov grazhdanskogo sootnosheniia: Sbornik ofitsial'nykh materialov* (Registration of Legal Documents concerning Civil Relationships: A Collection of Official Materials), (Moscow, 1974), pp. 253 and 282.

10. *Ved. V.S. SSSR*, 1973, No. 30, item 393. Reprinted in P. I. Sedugin, I. A. Belyk, *O gosudarstvennom notariate* (On the State Notary), (Moscow, 1974), pp. 99-118. For Eng. transl., see W. E. Butler, *The Soviet Legal System: Legislation and Documentation* (Dobbs Ferry, N.Y. 1978), pp. 263-273.

11. *Sov. Iust.*, 1974, No. 18, 3-15.

12. *Sobr. Post. RSFSR*, 1974, No. 17, item 94, For Eng. transl., see W. E. Butler, *op. cit.*, note 10, pp. 275-278.

13. The relevant provisions of codes are included in M. S. Makarov, *Spravochnik gosudarstvennogo notariata: Sbornik ofitsial'nykh materialov* (Reference Book of the State Notary: Collection of Official Materials), (Moscow, 2nd ed., 1972).

14. See P. I. Sediukhin and I. A. Belyk, *op. cit.*, note 10, p. 6, citing *Pravda*, July 20, 1973.

15. See editorial, *Sov.Iust.*, 1974, No. 18, 1.

16. L. F. Lesnitskaia, "Zakon o gosudarstvennom notariate" (The Law on the State Notary), *SGiP*, No. 12, 53, 54.

17. *In re Kudriavtsev, BVS RSFSR*, 1967, No. 2, 14.

18. R. Vinogradova, "Zasvidetel'stvovanie gosudarstvennymi kontorami podlinnosti podpisi na dokumentakh" (Authentification by State Offices of Signatures on Documents), *Sov. Iust.*, 1973, No. 21, 15-16.

19. K. S. Iudel'son and A. K. Kats, *Nauchno-prakticheskii kommentarii k polozheniiu o gosudarstvennom notariate* (A Scientific-Practical Commentary to the Statute on the State Notary), (Moscow, 1970), p. 19.

20. "Iz praktiki raboty notarialnykh kontor" (From the Practice of the Work of Notarial Offices), *Sov. Iust.*, 1966, No. 24, 13-14. No. 24, 13-14.

21. Iudel'son and Kats, *op. cit.*, note 19, p. 23.

22. When the RSFSR Statute of 1965 was in force, granting to the Notary the authority to preserve evidence, the Codes of Civil Procedure of Belorussia, Lithuania, Ukraine, and Uzbekistan reserved the function to a court. See Iudel'son and Kats, *op. cit.*, note 19, p. 158.

23. *Sov. Iust.*, 1973, No. 16, back cover.

24. *Sov. Iust.*, 1976, No. 13, 34.

25. *Sov. Iust.*, 1976, No. 8, 32.

26. *Sov. Iust.*, 1965, No. 5, back cover.

27. *Sov. Iust.*, 1970, No. 18, 32.

28. *Sov. Iust.*, 1974, No. 5, 34.

29. *Sov. Iust.*, 1968, No. 16, 69.

30. *Sov. Iust.*, 1977, No. 20, 34.

31. *Sov. Iust.*, 1977, No. 5, 34.

32. *Sov. Iust.*, 1977, No. 20, 34.

33. *Sov. Iust.*, 1976, No. 18, 33.

34. *Sov. Iust.*, 1977, No. 4, 33.

35. *Sov. Iust.*, 1977, No. 9, 33.

36. *Ibid.*

37. *Sov. Iust.*, 1976, No. 5, 34.

38. *Sov. Iust.*, 1977, No. 7, 35.

39. *Sov. Iust.*, 1977, No. 18, 33.

40. *Sov. Iust.*, 1977, No. 4, 33.

41. *Sov. Iust.*, 1977, No. 18, 33.

42. *Sov. Iust.*, 1977, No. 20, 34.

43. See A. Stepanova, "Deiatel'nosti gosudarstvennykh notarialnykh kontor v zone BAM i rukovodstvo im" (The Activities of State Notarial Offices in the Zone of the Baikal-Amur Railway and Guidance to Them), *Sov. Iust.*, 1977, No. 8, 9.

44. See V. Zorina, "Organizatsiia rabotoi starshego konsul'tanta po notariatu" (Organization of the Work of Senior Consultation in a Notarial Office), *Sov. Iust.*, 1977, No. 11, 13.

45. See Peter H. Juviler, "Whom the State has Joined: Conjugal Ties in Soviet Law" in D. Barry, G. Ginsburgs, P. Maggs (eds.), *Soviet Law After Stalin, Part I, The Citizen and the State in Contemporary Soviet Law* (Leyden, 1977), p. 139.

46. *Ved. V.S. SSSR*, 1968, No. 27, item 241.

47. Iu. Gusev, "Luchshii otdel zagsa" (A Better Department of *ZAGS*), *Sov. Iust.*, 1976, No. 13, 23.

48. B. Stolbov, "Applying the Legislation on Marriage and the Family," *Soviet Law and Government*, 12 (Summer 1973), 77.

49. Meilakh vs. *ZAGS* and Freidina, *Sots. Zak.*, 1972, No. 8, 91.

50. From the Practice of *ZAGS, Sov. Iust.*, 1973, No. 8, back cover.

51. See V. Pervedentsev, "Marriage and the Family," *Soviet Law and Government*, 13, (February 1974), No. 2, 79; translated from *Zhurnalist,* 1974, No. I.

SOVIET TRADE UNION ORGANIZATIONS IN LEGAL AND HISTORICAL PERSPECTIVES

Christopher Osakwe

1. Introduction: The Origin and Nature of Soviet Trade Union Organizations–STUO's

Western debate as to whether or not STUO's are in fact what they claim to be, *i.e.* labor unions, is almost as old as the Soviet republic itself.[1] The reasons for such Western apprehension about the nature of STUO's are obvious. The immediate predecessors of the STUO's–the Russian trade union organizations (RTUO's)–were created at the instigation of the Russian Communist Party (Bolshevik) and they functioned as an ally of the latter. From their inception, the RTUO's repudiated the "philosophy of pure wage consciousness" as the sole basis of their operations and instead adopted the policy of political activism. Believing, like any true Marxist organization, that there cannot be a revolutionary movement without a revolutionary theory, they adopted Marxism-Leninism as their political ideology. To the leaders of these trade unions, the economic power of the working class flows only from the barrel of the political gun. As such, to them workers' economic struggle was not an end in itself, but only the bridesmaid of a political revolution. In short, they looked upon workers' solidarity as an instrument with which to "bury" the capitalists, first in Soviet Russia, and later on in all the other countries where capitalism reigned supreme. This strategy ceased to be functionally useful after 1917. Thus, right from the creation of the Soviet state STUO's operated as a subservient instrument of the Soviet government and the Communist Party of the Soviet Union. Between 1917 and 1920, they were operationally integrated into the system of the Peoples' Commissariat of Labor (*NKT*). Membership in the unions was soon made compulsory for all workers. They performed functions that were essentially governmental in nature. Key positions within the unions were concentrated in the hands of Party members. They soon abandoned the "principle of professionalism" as the basis for organizing workers and instead adopted the so-called "production principle".

All of these features of STUO's prompted traditionalist Western commentators to assert that what the Soviet Union called "*professional'nye soiuzy*" (trade unions) were not labor unions in the traditional meaning of that term.

267

To such Westerners, a labor union is "a continuous association of wage earners for the purpose of maintaining and improving the conditions of their working lives".[2] To them, STUO's were anything but labor unions.

For a long period of time, Western governments also took the uncompromising position that STUO's were not trade unions and should not be treated as such in those international organizations where trade union representation was an issue. This was the case when the Soviet Union sought to include representatives of STUO's in its official delegation to International Labor Organization (ILO) general conference as required under the Constitution of ILO.[3]

In response to such Western attitude towards STUO's, the apologists[4] of the Soviet system steadfastly assert that what they have are in fact trade union organizations (TUO's), but that they are TUO's of a new type. These Soviet commentators maintain that Western nations do not have a monopoly over the definition of what constitutes a TUO. In their view, the Soviet Union just happens to have TUO's that are qualitatively different from their Western counterparts, but that this does not make a STUO less of a labor union.

Rather than waste precious time attempting to deny or defend the existence of labor unions in the USSR, we propose in this study to attempt to explain the social, economic, political, and historical reasons for the differences between STUO's and Western TUO's. We believe that STUO's can best be analyzed and understood against the following background.[5]

First, it must be borne in mind that the entire Soviet society operates under the unchallenged leadership of the CPSU which is the acknowledged brain, mind, and conscience of the Soviet people. Soviet social, economic, and political developmental policies are first worked out within the framework of the CPSU.[5a] Thereafter, they filter down to the respective agencies of government for execution. STUO's in their activities do not and cannot lay claims to any special immunity to this universal Party control.

Secondly, one should remember that the Soviet economy is centrally[6] planned and tightly controlled from above. This factor in turn conditions all labor relations in the Soviet society. State economic plans are worked out at the highest levels of government under the inevitable control of the CPSU. The economic plans not only establish production targets for the various industries and enterprises, but also they include wage scales for the workers. This, of course, does not mean that Soviet workers do not have any input into the determination of wages or into the preparation of economic plans.[7] Workers' views on these matters are generally made known to the State Committee on Questions of Labor and Wages[8] attached to the USSR Council of Ministers and to *Gosplan* (State Planning Committee) through the All-Union Central Council of Trade Unions (*VTsSPS*) and the Central Committees of the respective national TUO's.

Thirdly, it is important to remember that under the general Soviet program for the construction of communism, the Soviet government plans to gradually transfer all of its present functions to the various mass (social) organizations.[9] STUO's are readily the most representative of all existing Soviet social organizations. For this reason, STUO's are increasingly being asked to take over functions[10] which, in a traditional Western society, are virtually non-delegable to non-governmental organizations.

Fourthly, it is worth noting that the labor-management relationship in the Soviet Union is not an antagonistic one.[11] Soviet workers are, at least in theory, the owners of the means of production and distribution. This means that they are the collective owners of the factories, enterprises, or institutions where they work. The director of the enterprise is just another worker who happens to be in white collars. The highest administrators in any enterprise, including the director and the chief engineer, are themselves members of the cell organization of the TUO. Both the cell organization of the TUO and the management of the enterprise operate under the shadow of the CPSU.

This is not to suggest however, that the relationship between labor and management in the Soviet Union is frictionless. Disputes generally arise within the Soviet production processes. When this happens, STUO's will expectedly come out to defend the interests of the workers. But even though disputes are inevitable between labor and management in the Soviet Union, the fact still remains that the economic postures of labor and management are not mutually antagonistic. A chairman of a factory-plant and local committee of the TUO (*FZMK*) at a Soviet heavy equipment plant was reported to have made the following remark to an American researcher:

> "Whether there is a dispute [between labor and management] depends on the director. A clever director never has a dispute with the workers. If he can convince us, the committee accepts his opinion. But his plant committee is able to settle questions itself; it has no need for outside help."[12]

Fifthly, the reader should bear in mind that the position of the Soviet enterprise director is quite different from that of his Western counterpart. For one thing, his responsibility is to the state and not to a board of directors. The cell organization of the TUO exercises both *de facto* and *de jure* control over his actions, even though in the long run he (the director) alone is responsible for the failures of the enterprise. He is not only a member of the cell organization of the TUO, but chances are that he is also a member of the *FZMK* which is supposed to act as a check on his actions. His primary concern is not to maximize the profits margin of his enterprise, but rather to fulfill the state economic plan allotment for his enterprise.

Sixthly, it may be recalled that most of the social and economic aspirations of the Western TUO's have since been secured for the Soviet worker through Soviet social legislations. These include: freedom from unemployment;[13] the right to disability benefits;[14] guaranteed annual vacation with pay;[15] generous maternity leave and payment of other maternity benefits;[16] the right to belong or not to belong to a TUO;[17] the right to participate in the management of the enterprise where one works;[18] the right not to be fired from one's job unless upon statutorily defined grounds and, in certain instances, only with the consent of the *FZMK*; the right to old age pension benefits;[19] exemption of workers from direct contributions towards their social insurance and retirement funds;[20] an effective voice in the preparation and adoption of laws which affect labor and labor relations;[21] equal protection of all workers under law regardless of their sex, race, religious beliefs, or national origin.[22] Soviet commentators feel that any TUO that operates in a system where all of these workers' rights are already provided for by law must, of necessity, depart from the traditional *modus operandi* for TUO's.

From considering all of the above factors, one gets the following composite picture of the nature of STUO's. First, they are voluntary, social, non-Party organizations which unite wage earners and salaried employees of all occupations; secondly, the grouping of workers into the respective TUO's does not preserve the traditional lines between the respective professions. Rather, workers are organized based on the industry or group of related industries where they work; thirdly, STUO's operate in close collaboration with and under the control of the CPSU; fourthly, despite this overriding control from the CPSU, STUO's enjoy at least some semblance of operational autonomy from overt intervention by Party organs; fifthly, STUO's are continuously expanding their role as the Leninist "school of communism"; sixthly, the essential task of STUO's consists in the mobilization of the masses for the creation of the material and technical base for communism, in the struggle for the further stengthening of the economic power and defensive might of the Soviet state, in the organization of a steady growth of the material welfare and cultural education of the working people, as well as in the protection of the rights and legal interests of the workers.

STUO's maintain an autonomous existence because the CPSU wants them to. The CPSU is unquestionably dominant over the labor-management relationship in the Soviet Union, but it is certainly not omnipotent. The CPSU needs STUO's and uses them as a conduit to get to the millions of workers, most of whom are not members of the Party. In many ways, STUO's act a listening post for the CPSU—they monitor workers' sentiments at the grass roots level and transmit them to the CPSU. This master-servant relationship between the CPSU and STUO's was ably captured in the following passage by a leading American student of the Soviet trade union scene:

> "At the top, the union central committees and the Central Council of Trade Unions, led by trusted communists, function as agents of the

Communist Party and the state, more like sections in a governmental department of labor than as independent trade union centers. The national union bodies are not independent organizations expressing the will of their members. Their rights were given them by the party, not derived from the power of the working class. At anytime their work is oriented to the current instructions from the Party. But they also have the duty and right to speak in the name of the workers before governmental bodies. National officers of the unions are communists first and union leaders second."[23]

In this study, we propose to develop each of the major points made in the foregoing paragraphs. Before we go any further, it should be pointed out that our purpose is not to analyze substantive Soviet labor law.[24] Rather, the narrow purpose is to examine STUO's as a vehicle for the administration of Soviet labor laws and other related social legislations.[25] Where issues of substantive labor laws are inextricably interwoven with the particular topic under discussion, the former would be given only a fleeting treatment in the footnotes. Other components of this study include: an analysis of the working relationship between STUO's, the CPSU, and the Soviet government; a discussion of the organization, structure, and juridical status of STUO's; and a systematization of the functions of STUO's. The concluding section of the study will look at STUO's in terms of their past, present, and future functions.

2. The Relationship between STUO's, the CPSU, and the Soviet Government

Soviet society is conceived as an integrated whole, as a complex unity. Within this society, all of man's activities are intended to serve the ultimate goal, i.e. the construction of communism. Failure on the part of any segment of the Soviet society to plug into this central nerve system of the Soviet body politic would be tantamount to camouflaged counterrevolution. In this sense, no conscious activity on the part of any Soviet citizen or Soviet organization can afford to be politically neutral.

As if to stress this point a Soviet commentator aptly noted:

"In the USSR none of the mass [social] organizations exists in isolation; they all plug into the system of political organization of the Soviet society. Their activities represent a mutually-connected and mutually-instigated process, which reflects the deeply democratic character of the socialist state ... It follows, therefore, that life itself demands of STUO's cooperation with all the other social organizations."[26]

271

As a result of this social, economic, political, cultural, and scientific integration of the Soviet state, the administration of the Soviet society consists of one vertical chain of command which culminates in the CPSU at the apex. This leadership network incorporates all the three organizational hierarchies in the Soviet Union, *i.e.* governmental (state), political (Party), and social. These three hierarchies of authority however do not operate in total isolation. Thus, it is not uncommon for the same person to hold offices in two or more of these sectors. Such interlocking leadership arrangement[27] ensures better harmonization of the operation of the three hierarchies of Soviet power.

STUO's in Lenin's words "stand, if one may say so, between the CPSU and the state authority".[28] STUO's are therefore, neither a functional subdivision of the CPSU nor a branch of the Soviet government. They are autonomous, social organizations which are very conveniently situated between the CPSU and the state authority. STUO's look up to the CPSU for guidance and leadership in all of their activities. At the same time, the CPSU relies upon STUO's for on-the-spot implementation of its general directives in those areas that fall within the jurisdiction of STUO's. At the recently concluded 16th Congress of STUO's, the General Secretary of the Central Committee of the CPSU, L. I. Brezhnev, offered the following words of support to STUO's. He told the delegates to the Congress:

> "I assure you, comrades, that all justifiable demands made by the TUO's to the economic planners as well as to the administrators of enterprises shall be unconditionally supported by the Party. But note my emphasis on the word 'justifiable'."[29]

On its part, STUO leadership feels that there are no noteworthy differences between the interests of the CPSU and those of STUO's. These union leaders believe that the CPSU has the best interest of the Soviet workers at heart and therefore they urge STUO's to accept and carry out the programs of the CPSU as if it were their very own.[30] In short, these trade union bosses have come to accept the fact that the leadership of the CPSU always was, is, and will forever be a source of inspiration and strength for them.

In addition to these subjective factors, there are historical reasons why the national officers of STUO's have come to accept the leadership role of the CPSU. Whereas TUO'S in the West sprang up before political parties were even organized, the reverse is true in Russia. Here, TUO's emerged after and at the instigation of the Communist Party of Russia.[31] Right from the inception of the Russian TUO's, Lenin urged that "there must be a close unity between the Party of the working class and the trade unions of workers which must operate under the leadership of the Party".[32]

The fact that the STUO leadership has internalized the idea of the leadership of the CPSU into the constitutional framework of the STUO's is evidenced by the following provision of the Preamble to the Charter of STUO's:

"The struggle for a successful implementation of the Program of the CPSU constitutes the essence of all the activities of STUO's . . STUO's carry out their function under the leadership of the CPSU—the organizing and leading force in the Soviet society ... STUO's rally all workers, collective farmers, and civil servants around the CPSU, mobilize them in the struggle for the construction of communism." [33]

The CPSU exercises its leadership role in the following major ways: [34] first, it promulgates the general plan for the development of the Soviet society; and secondly, it articulates the correct line of political, economic, and social development of the Soviet state.

The fact that STUO's are autonomous in the performance of their functions, however, does not mean that they are immune from CPSU influence. Such influence is exerted in STUO's through those CPSU members who are also members of STUO's. At its 8th Congress in 1919 the CPSU, for example, obligated its members to join STUO's [35] so that they may carry out CPSU policies within the ranks of STUO's. The CPSU has since lifted [36] such formal obligation which it had imposed on its members, [37] but the spirit of the 8th CPSU Congress resolution has since become a tradition in the Soviet Union where virtually all CPSU members, on a voluntary basis, [38] are members of the respective TUO's. Not satisfied with merely urging its members to join STUO's, the CPSU goes even further to encourage its members to actively participate in the activities of STUO's and particularly to compete with non-CPSU members for offices within the respective national TUO's. [39] Finally, the CPSU seeks to actively involve STUO members who are not CPSU members in the various educational activities of the CPSU. In short, STUO's serve as a conduit between the elitist CPSU and the estimated 113.5 million members of STUO's. [40]

The relationship between STUO leadership and the Soviet Government is equally cordial. [41] STUO leaders, for reasons already discussed in the foregoing paragraphs, do not view the Soviet government with any antagonism. They strongly believe that the Soviet Government has the best interest of workers at heart. The fact that both the Soviet government and STUO's operate under the shadow of the CPSU is a guarantee to the STUO bosses that the Soviet government will not work against the interest of workers.

As a "school of administration and economic management", STUO's are gradually schooling their members in the art of government, and it is hoped that by the time the Soviet society attains full communism the Soviet government will have handed over to STUO's all of its present functions in the areas of labor and labor relations. Having done this, the Soviet government will wither away and take its rightful place in the museum of antiquity along with the bronze axe.

3. The Organization, Structure, and Juridical Status of STUO's

In this section of our study, we propose to discuss three interrelated issues, i.e. the coordination of the activities of STUO's at the national level, the internal structure of each of the national TUO's, and the legal status of TUO's.

3.1. The Organization of STUO's

We have already mentioned that STUO's group workers not according to their professional callings, but rather according to the production principle. [42] This means that in the Soviet Union there are different national TUO's for each of the major industries or group of related industries. For example, there is a separate TUO for workers in the metallurgical industry, a TUO for workers in the textile and light industries, etc. Generally, these TUO's include all persons who work in the particular industry, including blue collar workers, engineers and technicians, civil servants, as well as the cleaners and security service personnel.

Such an arrangement, according to its proponents, has numerous advantages: it promotes unity among the various professionals within the given industry; it facilitates the conduct of socialist competition among the various enterprises within the same industry or among different but related industries; it allows for better participation of the workers in the decision-making processes within the enterprise where they work. Within this system, individual professionals may still organize themselves into trade union groups and factory committees in order to pursue their narrow professional interests.

As of 1972 there were twenty-five [43] national TUO's in the USSR. Of this number, 14 unions represented workers in the various areas of industrial and agricultural economy: 5 unions represented construction workers, transport workers, and communications workers; 6 unions represented workers in the spheres of health services, cultural services, state institutions, and the service industry. As of 1972, it was estimated that 97.4% [44] of all Soviet workers were members of TUO's. In certain TUO's, the percentage of worker' representation was much higher. For example, the TUO of workers in the medical industry, the coal industry, textile industries, and educational institutions represented 98.9% of all workers in those respective industries. Thus, it could be said that virtually all Soviet workers, including industrial workers, agricultural workers, [45] intellectual workers, and civil servants, are members of the respective TUO's. [46]

All TUO's operate according to the principle of democratic centralism. [47] This means that: all organs of the TUO's are elected [48] by and accountable to the members of the organization; all decisions of the respective organs must conform with the provisions of the Charter of STUO's and must comply with the general decisions handed down by the central organs of STUO's; all decisions of all the organs of the TUO's shall be adopted by a majority vote. It also means that the inferior organs of the TUO's are subordinated to the superior organs and as such must adhere to the decisions of the latter. The principle of democratic centralism also incorporates the concepts of: collective leadership; democratic elections [49] with secret ballot, except in those instances where special exceptions are made; and open criticism and discussion of past work of the current office holders as a prelude to holding any new elections. In short, it ensures wide participation of the rank and file of the union membership in the conduct of the affairs of the TUO's.

Once admitted to membership in the union, [50] a worker enjoys all the rights [51] and privileges of membership. These include: the right to vote and to be elected to union office; the right to be a delegate to any trade union conference or congress; and the right to freely express one's views at all meetings of the union. Once a decision has been made by a majority, however, the dissenting members are required to succumb to the wish of the majority. The rights of a member also include: the right to constructively criticize, publicly or privately, any officer of the union without fear of reprisal; the right to make suggestions to any organ of the TUO, including the *VTsSPS*, on any matter within the jurisdiction of the TUO. Under a special arrangement between the TUO's and the colleges of advocates, members of the TUO's receive free legal assistance from the participating colleges of advocates on all questions of law ranging from disputes over the terms of their individual work contracts, wages, social security and pension benefits, patent rights, etc. Members of the TUO's enjoy free access to all sporting and cultural facilities operated by the TUO. Finally, union members enjoy preferential treatment in the payment of certain social insurance benefits.

Alongside these rights, a member of a TUO also assumes certain concomitant obligations. [52] His duties include the following: the duty to perform, conscientiously and honorably, his tasks at the production unit; to preserve and protect socialist property; to observe rules of state and labor discipline; to strive to improve his level of ideological, political, and cultural education; to participate actively in socialist competitions; to exercise caution in the handling of working tools; and to economize the resources of the production unit. A member of the TUO also has a duty to work to strengthen international peace among nations; to help combat any manifestations of anti-social behavior by his fellow workers; and to live by the rule of socialist communal living. In short, a member of the TUO should constantly strive to be an exemplary worker in all respects.

3.2. *The Internal Structure of STUO's*

Since all of the twenty-five national TUO's have practically the same internal structure, the description which follows applies, *mutatis mutandis*, to all of them.

The primary unit of a TUO is the cell organization [53] which exists at the level of the enterprise, institution, or factory. All members of the TUO who work at an enterprise, institution, or factory are *ipso facto* members of the cell organization. The highest organ of the cell organization is the general meeting of its members. [54] In addition to the general meeting, the cell organization also establishes the following elected organs: *FZMK*; [55] shop committees (in production enterprises or factories) or bureaus (in non-production institutions). [56] At the regional level, [57] the various cell organizations may come together to form a Regional Committee of the TUO's and endow such a committee with the powers of an *FZMK*. [58] The lowest level of a cell organization is the professional group. [59]

All the twenty-five national TUO's in the Soviet Union come together to form a sort of national umbrella organization. This all-union federation of STUO's has the following organs: Congress of STUO's; [60] and the *VTsSPS*. [61] Each of the respective twenty-five national TUO's culminates in the following national organs: Congress of individual TUO's; [62] and a Central Committee of the individual TUO. [63] There are also organs of the TUO's at the level of the region, national area, and city. These intermediate organs coordinate the activities of the various cell organizations within their respective territorial limits. Cooperation among the various trade union organs develop along vertical as well as horizontal lines.

3.3. The Juridical Status of STUO's

The TUO, like all the other lawfully constituted social organizations [64] in the USSR, is a legal person.[65] This means that: it may sue and be sued[65a] as an entity; that it may own, acquire, and dispose of property in its own name; that it has its own constituent instrument (the Charter) which establishes its internal organs, competence, the terms of membership, as well as the procedure for the admission and expulsion of members; and that it has an independent accounting system. [66]

The juridical status of the TUO is expressly recognized in art. 61 of the Charter of STUO's. Under art. 62 of the Charter, each national TUO shall have its own charter. The Charter of a TUO, once adopted, becomes immediately operational and, as such, does not need to be registered with a state agency in order to take effect. [67]

Art. 102 of the RSFSR Civil Code provides that trade union organizations shall have the right to possess, use, and dispose of all such property (including realty and personalty) which belongs to them. The right of the TUO to possess, use, and dispose of property, however, is not absolute. [68] The TUO may own only such property which is consistent with the purpose of the organization. [69] In keeping with this principle, the TUO may own only such items that are necessary for the furtherance of its charter goals. These include:[70] sanatoria, prophylactoria, rest homes, health resorts, tourist camps, stadiums, swimming pools, gymnasiums, libraries and reading rooms, as well as buildings, including residential buildings.

STUO's also own, as of right, all such property that is under the operational control of all of their subsidiary institutions, including: the trade union printing press, hotels, automobile depots, repair shops, supply depots, factories for the manufacture of sporting goods and tourist equipments, factories for the manufacture and repair of furniture for rest homes, eating places, etc.

Art. 59 of the Charter of STUO's provides that the funds and property of a TUO shall be administered by the elected organs of the respective TUO's. Such organs shall also be responsible for preserving and protecting such trade union property from misuse. Next to the Soviet government, the STUO's are perhaps the second largest owners and operational controllers of socialist property in the Soviet Union today. [71]

4. The Functions of STUO's as a "School of Communism"

The functions [72] of STUO's may be fully understood only when viewed from a historical perspective. Prior to 1917, the Russian TUO's functioned as a "school of socialism". Since 1917, however, the functions of STUO's may be summarized in one phrase—"school of communism", *i.e.* a training ground for the new Soviet communist worker.

The term "school" was first used by Karl Marx and Friedrich Engels to refer to TUO's in general. [73] That term has since been received into Soviet usage and was popularized by V. I. Lenin in his works on the goals of STUO's. [74] In the views of Marx and Engels, TUO's under conditions of capitalism represented a major training ground (school) for class solidarity, a platform for workers' struggle against the bourgeoisie for their social, economic, and political rights, a form of struggle for socialism. In other words, according to Marx and Engels, the social mission of TUO's in a capitalist system is to transform the capitalist economic relationships into socialist, hence the term "school of socialism". The Russian (pre-1917) TUO's served as such a "school of socialism".

With the triumph of the Bolshevik socialist revolution in Russia, the proletariat class, in Soviet official pronouncements, ceased to be the oppressed class and instead became the ruling class. This led to a radical change in the social mission of STUO's. Henceforth, they became the "school of communism".

Under the general heading of "school of communism", the STUO's perform the following combination of functions: a "school of administration and economic management"; a platform for the exercise of the workers' right of legislative initiative; a mechanism for protecting the legal rights and interests of workers; administrator of state social insurance and pension benefits; administrator of sanatoria, prophylactoria, holiday resorts, and health resorts;

277

co-administrator of housing for workers; a "school for cultural education of workers"; a promoter and organizer of sports and tourism inside the USSR; and finally, as an instrument of Soviet foreign policy. What follows is a detailed discussion of each of these major official functions of STUO's.

4.1. STUO's as "a School of Administration and Economic Management"

One of the functions contemplated for STUO's by Lenin was that of "school for administration and economic management". In this capacity, STUO's were to provide the workers with an unprecedented opportunity to participate actively in the administration of certain governmental social services, as well as in the management of the national economy. Through the medium of STUO's, the Soviet workers exercise the following rights and privileges: the right to oversee the proper implementation of labor legislation relating to the rules and norms of work; the right to participate in the preparation and implementation of state economic plans; the right to participate in decisions relating to the distribution and expenditure of material and financial resources of the state; as well as the opportunity to participate in the management of the production processes.

The right of STUO's to participate in the preparation and adoption of state economic plans is provided for in the Fundamental Principles of Labor Legislation (FPLL) of the USSR and the Union Republics of 1970. [75] The adoption of the five-year state economic plan generally begins with the adoption of a five-year plan by each production unit. The *FZMK* takes an active part in the preparation of this production unit five-year plan. Before the final plan is drawn up, the draft plan shall be circulated among and fully discussed by the workers at the plant. As a result of such participation at the grass roots level, it is contemplated that the interests of the workers would be fully reflected in the plan.

Once the five-year plan has been adopted by the production unit, it is sent to the appropriate union-republican ministry or to the higher planning agency. At this level, the corresponding organs of STUO's are assured an equally active participation in the reformulation of the five-year plan. The draft economic plan for the entire USSR is then discussed by the *VTsSPS* with an eye toward making sure that the interests of the workers are adequately reflected in the plan. All suggestions and recommendations for modifications in the plan made by the *VTsSPS* are submitted to the Central Committee of the CPSU, to the Council of Ministers of the USSR, and to *Gosplan* which are responsible for making the final decision on the five-year economic plan.

Alongside the adoption of the state economic development plan, each enterprise adopts its own plan for the social development of the workers. The purpose of this social development plan is to formulate a general program for meeting the material and cultural needs of the workers. These plans contain measures aimed at improving working conditions, workers' wages, workers'

278

living standards and living conditions, cultural and social services, facilities for physical exercises for workers and members of their families, etc. Like in the case of the preparation and adoption of the economic plans, the STUO's take an active part in the preparation and adoption of these ancillary workers' social development plans. The final plan is generally adopted jointly by the director of the enterprise, the local CPSU committee, the local committee of the Young Communist League, and the *FZMK*. Since these five-year social development plans call for the expenditure of funds, they are generally integrated into the general economic plan for the period covered.

Another major role of STUO's as a school for administration and economic management is their participation in the formulation and adoption of wage policy. Art. 96 of the FPLL provides that in establishing working conditions as well as workers' wages, the management of any enterprise, industry, or institution shall either consult with or act jointly with the respective TUO's.

Wages in the USSR are far from equal for all workers. [76] Rather, they are graduated in order to reflect such variables as: level of qualification of the worker, the complex nature of the job performed, the benefits of the job performed to the national economy or to society at large. For a large portion of workers engaged in the national economy, wages are based upon the Unified Tariff-Qualifications Handbook (UTQH). This Handbook is prepared and adopted by the State Committee of the USSR Council of Ministers on Labor and Social Questions, acting jointly with the *VTsSPS*. In addition to the UTQH, there are other Tariff-Qualifications Handbooks (TQH) for certain individual industries. These TQH's are also prepared and adopted jointly by the *VTsSPS* and the State Committee on Labor and Social Questions.

Operating on the basis of these UTQH and TQH's, the management of an individual enterprise, industry, or institution, upon consultation with the *FZMK*, ranks workers for purposes of determining their wages. In determining workers' wages, discrimination based on sex, age, race, or national origin is categorically prohibited by law. [77] In the final analysis, a worker's wage—as determined by either the UTQH or the applicable TQH—shall not be less than the minimum wage established by state law. [78] Workers' wages shall be reviewed periodically by the management, acting in conjunction with the *FZMK*.

In addition to their regular wages, Soviet workers, as a form of material incentive, are also paid bonuses for abnormally good job performance. Each enterprise maintains a special fund from which such bonuses are to be paid to deserving workers. The management also collaborates with the *FZMK* in dispensing these special funds.

In short, the *FZMK* actively participates in all stages of governmental activities connected with workers' wages, *i.e.* in the preparation and adoption of both the UTQH and TQH's; in the matching of individual workers with the established scales in the Handbooks by the local management of industries,

279

factories, and enterprises; in the periodic review of workers' wages; in the tarification of new professions; in the dispensing of bonuses to deserving workers; etc. On a much higher level of governmental wage policy, the *VTsSPS*, from time to time, joins with the Central Committee of the CPSU and the Council of Ministers of the USSR to issue decrees on major issues of workers' wages.

In addition to the above forms of workers' participation in the administration and economic management of the enterprise, the production conferences (PC's) afford Soviet workers yet another avenue of participation in managerial decision-making. The PC's[79] are permanently functioning production meetings with elected members and officers. Such agencies are established in all plants which employ more than 100 persons. Membership in the PC includes: direct representatives of the workers, representatives of the *FZMK*, the local committee of the CPSU, the local committee of the *Komsomol*, the management, the Society of Inventors, and the Scientific-Technical Society. Workers' representatives to these conferences are elected at a general meeting of the cell organization of the TUO for the same term as that of the members of the *FZMK*. The PC in turn elects an executive committee which is charged with the following responsibilities: the selection of the preparation of topics to be studied by the conference; the agenda for the regular meetings of the conference; and the advertisement of the schedules of meetings of the conference among the workers. Decisions of the PC are reached by a majority vote. Two-thirds of the entire membership constitutes a quorum at any meeting of the PC. The management shall provide all secretarial services to the PC.

In order to involve more workers in the activities of the PC's, all parties agree to give the workers a majority representation in the conference. But membership in the executive committee of the PC is generally weighed in favor of experts, engineers, skilled technicians, inventors, etc. The work of the PC is directed by the *FZMK* and the shop committees. The management shall execute the decisions of the PC. However, if the management disagrees with the decision of the PC, it may take the case to the *FZMK* or to the shop committee or, if necessary, to a higher organ of the TUO or of the management.

The PC's often study major questions and make recommendations to the management. Questions which are known to have been studied by the PC's in the past include the following: periodic reorganization of a shop or of a production line; mechanization of certain processes; modernization of equipment; improvement of services; supply of materials and tools; how to eliminate bottlenecks in the production processes; reasons for non-fulfillment of production standards or plan; and the director's annual report or draft economic plans. Recent studies show that the workers use the production conferences not just as a vehicle to advise the management but, in fact, to demand changes from the management. In a spirit of cooperation, the directors generally accept the decisions of the PC's as binding upon the management.

It appears to this writer, however, that the law is fuzzy on the exact jurisdiction of these PC's. Their work seems to overlap with those of the *FZMK*, the shop committees, and the numerous labor-management commissions which exist within the production processes. Whatever the shortcomings regarding the jurisdiction of the PC's might be, one thing is clear, however, *i.e.* the PC's appear to be an effective mechanism for securing workers' input into managerial decisions at the level of the plant, factory, or enterprise. [80]

4.2. *STUO's as a Platform for the Exercise of Workers' Right of Legislative Initiative*

Perhaps the most governmental of all the official functions of STUO's is the exercise of their right to initiate and participate in the preparation and drafting of major social legislations which directly affect labor and labor relations. Art. 113 of the 1977 USSR Constitution provides that all social (mass) organizations, including STUO's, have the right of legislative initiative and that such right may be exercised through their national (central) organs. This concentrated constitutional right is further crystallized in art. 96 of the FPLL which provides that the right of STUO's to propose legislation before the USSR Supreme Soviet shall be exercised through the *VTsSPS*. A similar provision is contained in art. 226 of *KZoT*-RSFSR. [81] In the past, STUO's have put this right to frequent use, and there is no reason to believe that they will cease to do so in the future.

It is generally agreed that the highest organ of state power in the USSR (the USSR Supreme Soviet) and the highest organs of state power in the union republics (the supreme soviets of the respective union republics) will not adopt any legislation dealing with labor without prior consultation with the *VTsSPS* or with the Central Committees of the various national TUO's. Some of the union republics, including the RSFSR, have laws which obligate all governmental agencies to work actively with the TUO's before adopting or implementing rules or regulations affecting the interests of workers. The 1961 CPSU Program specifically provides that STUO's shall be granted the right of legislative initiative. The 1963 Charter of STUO's as amended, also acknowledges this right of STUO's. [82] Two Soviet researchers bluntly assert that there has never been an instance in which a statute or government regulation affecting labor was adopted over the objection of the *VTsSPS*. [83]

The *VTsSPS* and the Central Committees of the respective national TUO's exercise this right of legislative initiative in a combination of the following ways: they take part in the preparation and consideration of all governmental decisions affecting labor in the USSR; they participate in the preparation of *Gosplan* proposals for submission to the Council of Ministers of the USSR; they send their own proposals directly to the Council of Ministers or suggest changes to be made in the proposals submitted by *Gosplan*; they issue binding interpretations as well as implementing regulations regarding questions of labor law and social insurance law; they establish rules for the safety inspections carried out by regional and local unions. [84]

Pursuant to this authority, the *VTsSPS* has drafted or participated in the drafting of major legislations dealing with labor in the USSR. For example, the 1974 decree "On the Procedure for the Settlement of Labor Disputes" [85] and the 1958 decree "On the Rights of the FZMK" [86] were drafted by the *VTsSPS* and subsequently approved by the Presidium of the USSR Supreme Soviet. The draft of the current FPLL was also prepared by the *VTsSPS* and was thereafter adopted by the Presidium of the USSR Supreme Soviet.

The *VTsSPS* has also joined with the Central Committee of the CPSU and the Council of Ministers of the USSR in issuing decrees on labor and social insurance matters. Examples of such joint decrees include: the 1973 decree "On the Permanently Functioning Production Conferences"; [87] the 1962 decree "On Improving Safety Protection in Enterprises"; [88] the 1956 Minimum Wage Law; the 1958 decree "On the Shift to the Shorter Work Day", and the decree "On Revision of Wages in the Heavy Industry".

Furthermore, the *VTsSPS* collaborates with the State Committee of the USSR Council of Ministers on Labor and Social Questions in adopting major decisions in the area of wages, manpower training, resourceful utilization of workers' time, as well as workers' rest, etc. Examples of such joint decisions include: the decree "On the Adoption of the Model Regulation Relating to the Granting of Bonus to Industrial Workers Who are Transferred to a New System of Planning and Economic Stimulation"; the decree "On the Procedure for the Conclusion of Collective Bargaining Agreements"; etc.

One example of the many binding interpretative rules and implementing regulations issued by the *VTsSPS* is the decree "Regarding the Adoption of the Regulation Relating to the Investigation and Recording of Industrial Accidents". Furthermore, whenever the respective Soviet ministries and departments of government propose to adopt special rules on work safety or on sanitary working conditions, they are required to consult both with the *VTsSPS* and with the central organs of the appropriate national TUO's.

What all of this means is that the STUO's are granted an official standing within the legislative processes. They may propose new legislation whenever one is needed. They may comment on draft laws which are initiated by government agencies. In all of these activities, they have been assured of the full backing of the Central Committee of the CPSU, so long as their demands are not unreasonable. Unlike in the past when instructions issued by STUO's in the area of labor and labor relations had to await implementation through the issuance of an executive order by the Council of Peoples' Commissariats, today the interpretative rulings and implementing rules issued by the *VTsSPS* are self-executing. Thus, what is formally termed a right of legislative initiative is gradually turning into a right to engage in quasi-legislative activities.

4.3. STUO's as a Mechanism for Protecting the Legal Rights and Interests of Soviet Workers

The third and perhaps most traditional function of STUO's is that they serve as a mechanism for protecting the legal rights and interests of Soviet workers. As an integral part of this function, STUO leadership constantly seeks to improve the living and working conditions of trade union members.

Under the Soviet economic system, this otherwise traditional function of labor unions has taken on a new meaning. Since the Soviet state, as the principal employer in the Soviet Union, supposedly, does not have an interest which is antagonistic to that of the workers, since the CPSU claims to give top priority to the protection of the interests of all Soviet workers, it follows that STUO's do not have a monopoly over the task of protecting the legal interests and rights of Soviet workers. Thus, the first major difference between the protection-of-rights-of-workers functions of STUO's and the equivalent function by a Western TUO lies in the fact that the STUO's, it is officially claimed, do not operate from a position of isolation and antagonism *vis-à-vis* the employer.

The second difference between the performance of the protective function by both STUO's and any Western TUO lies in the methods used by both organizations. On this latter question a leading Soviet commentator notes:

> "Our TUO's in their struggle to protect the interests of the working class have gone outside of the traditional concept of the "protective" functions [of trade unions], to the extent that the class of economic exploiters has long been liquidated in our society. For the purpose of achieving this protective function, our TUO's have at their disposal extensive legal rights and practical possibilities ranging from various social forms and methods of pressure to various methods of governmental-legal coercion, *e.g.* the right of a technical inspector[89] appointed by STUO's to issue orders which are binding upon the administration in the area of labor law violations."[90]

Finally, it is worth mentioning that if one were to believe the official Soviet position on this matter, the opinion of the *FZMK* is, as a matter of general practice, sought before any appointments are made to an administrative position within the enterprise. The granting of such consultative status to STUO's within the administrative appointive process affords the *FZMK* yet another method of controlling the actions of the administration.

STUO's perform their protective functions through a combination of the following methods: [91] participation in the formulation of all governmental policies directed at improving workers' wages, as well as at material and moral incentives to workers;[92] and oversight over the proper implementation and observance of labor legislations relating to work safety, labor standards, and working conditions. [93]

Also, as part of this protective functions, STUO's monitor the actions of the management to make sure that the latter observes state norms relating to working hours [94] and vacations. [95] STUO leadership sees to it that the Soviet citizen's constitutionally protected right to work is not violated. [96] It is the TUO that sees to it that a Soviet worker is not unlawfully fired from his job. As a general principle of Soviet labor law, the administration may not fire a Soviet worker, at its own initiative without first receiving the advice and consent of the *FZMK*. [97] Soviet law [98] requires that before firing any worker at its own initiative, the administration must furnish to the *FZMK* in writing the reasons for the proposed firing. The *FZMK*, at a meeting in which the defendant, as well as no less than two-thirds of its general membership must be present, shall examine the petition of the administration for probable cause. If the *FZMK* finds that the reasons given by the administration are insufficient to support such an extreme measure, it shall withhold its consent. The decision by the *FZMK* not to permit such firing is binding upon the administration. It is also final and not reviewable by any higher authority.

On the other hand, if the *FZMK* gives its consent to fire the defendant worker, the latter may, within one month from the time a decision is taken to fire him, appeal the decision to the court. If the worker prevails in court, the judge is granted substantial discretion under Soviet law in fashioning the remedy in each case. [99]

STUO's also protect the rights of workers against: unlawful transfers either from one location to another or from one job to another; violations of work regime or rules on rest periods; unlawful withholding of portions of a worker's wages; violations of laws governing woman [100] and child labor; [101] etc.

Depending on the nature of the violation, the TUO may resort to any of the following procedures to defend the interest of the aggrieved workers: initiation of a case before the Committee for the Resolution of Labor Conflicts; discussion of the actions of the administration at a meeting of the *FZMK*; bring to the attention of the administration instances of noted violations of worker's rights; pursuant to art. 20 of the FPLL, the *FZMK* may initiate the procedure for the removal of the administrator who persistently violates norms of Soviet labor law or breaches the terms of collective bargaining agreements or is guilty of bureaucratism and unnecessary red tape. [102]

Soviet commentators hasten to point out that despite the fact that there are no antagonistic differences between the positions of the management and labor in the Soviet Union, there is still a need to maintain a mechanism for resolving disputes between Soviet labor and management. Such occasional disputes, one is told, are generally caused by factors which are quite different

284

from those which cause disputes between capitalist labor and management. For example, two Soviet commentators[103] suggest three reasons for labor disputes in the Soviet society: the first reason is lack of knowledge of labor legislation on the part of both the managers and the workers; the second reason is attributed to "survivals of the past" in the consciousness of individuals;[104] the third reason is what the Soviet commentators call "a wrong conception of the state's interest by directors".[105] Whether or not one agrees with these canned reasons for labor disputes in the Soviet Union, the fact is that disputes do exist and what follows below is an examination of the mechanism for resolving such conflicts.

Procedure for the Settlement of Labor Disputes [106]

From the point of view of settlement procedures, Soviet law draws a distinction between two sets of labor disputes: those concerned with establishing new conditions of work, and those disputes arising from the contentious application of labor laws, regulations, interpretative rules, or collective bargaining agreements. The first type of disputes (these are generally disputes between the *FZMK* and the management) is regarded as "*neiskovye*", *i.e.* non-actionable in a court of law. These disputes are settled essentially within the framework of intra-industry procedures. [107] The second type of disputes, *i.e.* the "*iskovye*" (actionable) disputes, are handled within the framework of the *Kommissiia po Trudovym Sporam* (Commission on Labor Disputes— *KTS*), the *FZMK*, and the regular (Peoples') courts. [108] What follows is a description of this latter procedure. [109] As will be demonstrated below, STUO's are given a major role in this matter. [110]

The first organ that handles such disputes is the *KTS* which is established in every factory, enterprise, or institution. The Commission consists of an equal number of representatives of the administration and of the *FZMK*. [111] The chairmanship of the Commission, as well as the position of Secretary of the Commission, rotates from one session to another between representatives of the *FZMK* and the administration.

The *KTS* has jurisdiction[112] over disputes arising from the following matters:[113] fulfillment of work norms by workers; conditions of work designed to facilitate the fulfillment of work norms by workers; transfer of workers to another job; application of the established systems of wages; computation of wages for overtime work; production standards and premiums; dispensation of special work uniforms and special work diet; withholding of determined percentage from workers' pay for causing material damage to the property of the enterprise; etc. The *KTS* also has primary jurisdiction over all disputes arising from the application of labor laws, collective bargaining agreements, and individual employment contracts;[114] the implementation of rules of discipline at the enterprise, *e.g.* right to vacation and free days; disciplinary penalties; discharge without the consent of the *FZMK*; etc. In other words, the *KTS* has primary jurisdiction over all labor disputes, with the exception of those which are reserved to the exclusive jurisdiction of the courts or other organs. [115]

When a worker files a petition with the *KTS*, a hearing shall be scheduled within five days of the receipt of such petition.[116] He has a right to be present at such a hearing, which is open to the members of the particular enterprise, factory, or institution. The general practice is to hold the hearing during non-working hours, in order to afford to all interested persons the opportunity to attend.

All decisions of the *KTS* shall be reached through the agreement by the representatives of the *FZMK* and the management. [117] If the administration withholds its consent or if the *KTS* substantially rejects the claims of the worker, the worker shall have the right to take his case to the next step, [118] *i.e.* to the *FZMK*, which in turn must hold a hearing on the petition within seven days of its filing. [119] The *FZMK* has the power to either affirm, overrule, or amend the decision of the *KTS*.

All decisions of the *KTS* or *FZMK* are subject to enforcement by the administration within ten days from the time they were rendered. [120] If the administration fails or refuses to implement the said decision within the established period of time, the *FZMK* shall issue the prevailing worker with an *udostoverenie* (a judgment order) to be presented to a court bailiff (*sudebnyi ispolnitel*) who shall immediately enforce the judgment as if it were the judgment of a court. [121]

In those situations where the worker disagrees with the decision of the *KTS* or the *FZMK*, as well as in those cases where the law does not grant primary jurisdiction to the *KTS*, the worker may take his case directly to the peoples' court for adjudication. [122] However, since the decision of the *KTS* requires the agreement of the representatives of management sitting on the Commission, once such consent has been duly given, the management would be estopped from either retracting the consent so given or challenging the decision so reached. Thus, in practice, it could be said that the management does not have the right to appeal a decision of the *KTS*. By contrast, since the decision of the *FZMK* does not require the consent of the management, it follows that if the management feels that the decision of the *FZMK* is contrary to law, it may appeal it to the peoples' court. [123]

Decisions of the peoples' court are appealable by both parties to a higher court in accordance with established court procedures. At any stage in the pre-court proceedings, *i.e.* at the level of the *KTS* or the *FZMK*, the procurator may intervene on his own initiative and appeal the case to the peoples' court if he feels that it is necessary to protect the interests of either the worker or the state. During the court proceedings, the *FZMK* may, if it so decides, send its representative to court to appear in the name of the workers as an *amicus curiae*.

In addition to the formalities discussed in the foregoing paragraphs, Soviet law relating to the procedure for the settlement of employee-management disputes contains the following miscellaneous provisions: the right of an aggrieved worker or employee to seek settlement of his dispute with the administration is not subject to any statute of limitation; [124] an employee who seeks to challenge an unlawful firing in the peoples' court must do so within one month from the time he is notified of the decision to fire him; [125] an aggrieved worker or employee who takes his labor dispute to the peoples' court shall be exempted from paying any court costs;[126] if the organ handling the labor dispute reaches the conclusion that an employee has been unlawfully fired or transferred to another job, it shall order his reinstatement to his original position, [127] as well as order that such worker be paid half wages for the time of the forced idleness or the difference between the pay at his original job and the pay at the new job to which he was unlawfully transferred. [128]

The Perennial Question: The Right of STUO's to Organize Labor Strikes

Conspicuously absent from the list of methods that the STUO's may use in seeking to protect the interests of workers are traditional methods such as peaceful strikes, picketing, and boycotts, including secondary boycotts. Whereas to most Westerners the utmost test of industrial democracy is the right of the workers to strike, to the Soviet legal mind the strike is the weapon of the industrial jungle. It is the position of STUO leadership that Soviet workers do not need the collective work stoppage method in order to effectively defend their interests.

The argument is made that in the Soviet Union strike action is economically and socially unnecessary. One is told that in a society where the state owns the means of production and distribution, where the workers effectively participate in the administration and economic management of the production and distribution processes, where the CPSU is an effective protector and guarantor of the interests of the working masses, the workers would be striking against themselves if they should resort to strike actions.

Strikes, according to the apologists of the Soviet system, presuppose an antagonism of interests between the striking workers and the employers. To resort to strikes where there is no such antagonistic polarization of the parties would be meaningless, self-defeating, and counter productive. In the words of a Soviet commentator, "... in a state where the means of production and distribution have been socialized, there is neither a basis nor a reason for strike actions. That for which the working class in a capitalist society is persistently struggling, has long become a reality for the Soviet worker as well as for the workers of the other socialist countries." [129]

Soviet official position on this question was released for the record in

1959 in response to an investigation into Soviet trade union practices by the Committee on Freedom of Association of the International Labor Office. [130] In that statement, the Soviet government stated:

> "A collective stoppage of work is not, and never has been, regarded as absenteeism, and Soviet law does not provide, nor has it ever provided, for any penalties to be imposed for a collective stoppage of work, where called by workers in support of their demands.
>
> There is no reason for surprise at the absence of strikes in the Soviet Union, because the workers have every possibility of obtaining satisfaction in other ways—through production meetings and through the governmental and legislative authorities whose membership consists of workers' representatives." [131]

Contemporary Soviet law seems to differentiate between workers' strikes and workers' absenteeism. The former is a collective, conspiratorial, intentional stoppage of work by employees. It includes stoppage by reason of the expiration of a collective bargaining agreement and any concerted slow-down or other concerted interruption of operations by workers. The latter is a non-conspiratorial failure, for whatever reason, of individual workers to show up for work. Workers' strikes under Soviet law are arguably violations of Soviet criminal law. [132] On the other hand, absenteeism, if malicious or recurrent, may be sanctionable administratively. It is not a crime, however. Despite the restriction on the right of workers to strike, there have been reports of illegal strikes in the Soviet Union. [133]

The Rights Enjoyed by the FZMK *within the Production Unit*

The *FZMK*, as an elected organ of the TUO at the level of the production unit, enjoys a wide range of rights. The status of the *FZMK* today is governed by the 1971 Law on the *FZMK*, [134] which was adopted by the *VTsSPS* on September 27, 1971, and given effect of law by a decree of the Presidium of the USSR Supreme Soviet. The Law provides that the *FZMK* is the organ that shall represent the interests of workers and civil servants at any given enterprise, plant, factory, or institution.

Pursuant to this Law, the management of any given plant or enterprise is required to consult with the *FZMK* before promulgating any policy, rule, or regulation. Some of these regulations shall be adopted by the management either after consultation with the *FZMK* or with prior notification of the *FZMK* or in conjunction with the *FZMK*. It is the *FZMK* which, in the name of the workers, shall negotiate all collective bargaining agreements with the management. Should the management violate the terms of a collective bargaining agreement or show tendencies toward bureaucratism or unnecessary red tape, the *FZMK*, acting through the regional organ of the TUO, has the

288

right to petition a higher management organ with a request to either fire or transfer the offending manager from the plant.

In other words, the *FZMK* serves as the vehicle for carrying out the workers' watchdog function over the activities of the management.

The Collective Bargaining Agreement: Its Contents and the Procedure for Its Conclusion [135]

Soviet commentators hasten to point out that collective bargaining agreements serve two diametrically opposed functions in both the capitalist and the socialist economic systems. In the words of Professor Smirnov, under capitalism "collective bargaining agreement serves as a form of class struggle by the workers for their rights and against the oppression of the monopolies, whereas under socialism the same collective bargaining agreement is one of the major ways of getting the workers involved in the management of the enterprise, as well as in the development of their constructive activism". [136]

In the USSR, collective bargaining agreements are concluded within the framework of each enterprise or, as the case may be, within the framework of a large production complex. Negotiation and conclusion of a collective bargaining agreement on behalf of the workers is entrusted to the *FZMK*. [137] By law, the provisions of the collective bargaining agreement apply to all workers at the given enterprise, regardless of their membership of the local trade union organization. [138]

In all enterprises that have an independent accounting system and enjoy the status of a juridical person, the duration of a collective bargaining agreement is generally one year. [139] By law, a new collective bargaining agreement must be concluded no later than February of each year. The general practice in most large enterprises is to conclude collective bargaining agreements at the same time that they are preparing their annual production plans.

The proper parties to the collective bargaining agreement are the *FZMK* and the management. A typical collective bargaining agreement contains the following provisions: [140] the general provisions (which include, among other things, a general clause on working conditions, workers' wages, material incentives, work safety, working hours, and rest periods); the obligations of the parties (regarding the fulfillment of production plans, acquisition of modern technology, increase in labor productivity, improvement in the quality of products, reduction in the costs of production, expansion of the system of socialist competition among workers); social services (which include the general provisions on workers' social insurance, improvement in the housing and living conditions of workers, improvement in workers' food services, development of networks of educational and cultural facilities for workers, improvement in the economic education of the workers, etc.). As a general rule of Soviet labor law, any provision of the collective bargaining agreement which is in violation of law is deemed to be null and void *ab initio*. [141]

Before the agreement is signed, the *FZMK* shall present a draft to the workers for their full discussion of each section thereof. [142] Upon conclusion of these procedures, the final agreement shall be signed by the chairman of the *FZMK* and the director of the enterprise on behalf of the respective parties. A final copy of the agreement shall be printed and copies thereof shall be posted at conspicuous locations throughout the factory or enterprise.

Technically speaking, the terms of the collective bargaining agreement are binding on the parties. In practice, however, whereas the obligations of the management are legally enforceable, those of the *FZMK* have "only a moral and political character, subject to social influences". [143] In other words, what might seem at first glance to be a bilateral contract at law is, in fact, a unilateral assumption of non-reciprocal obligations by the management. [144] It is the responsibility of the *FZMK* and the management, however, to secure compliance with the terms of this agreement. [145]

From everything that has been said so far, it should not be inferred that the TUO's run the Soviet enterprise all by themselves, or that the manager of a Soviet plant is relieved of all personal responsibility for the operation of the plant. Rather, the true picture is one of cooperation between the STUO leadership and the management. The plant manager is still the unquestionable governor of the plant, but he is subject to control from below, *i.e.* by the trade union bosses. Art. 97 of the FPLL merely speaks of the workers' participatory control over the production processes, but not of any complete displacement of the plant manager. In the final analysis, it is the plant manager who shall be held to personal liability for the failures of the enterprise.

It should be noted, however, that despite the phenomenal expansion in recent years of the power of STUO's, a recent study of working conditions in the Soviet Union still suggests that the TUO's are not the effective protector of the interests of workers which they appear to be. Commenting on why Soviet workers want to flee USSR, Robin Wright noted:

> "Trade unions are of little help in tackling the nation's [labor] problems. Unionism as developed in the U.S. is nonexistent in the Soviet Union. The main purpose of official unions here is to persuade employees to stay on the job, not to improve working conditions ... The dissident workers complained that their union leaders always sided with management, that individuals who protested against corruption, unfair norms and bad working conditions were often fired. These individuals found it impossible to gain redress in the courts or through Communist Party channels." [146]

All we can say is that the discrepancy between the theories of Soviet labor law as described in this section of our study and the practical realities of the working conditions of Soviet workers as articulated in the passage quoted above is symptomatic of Soviet law in general. To any seasoned student of

Soviet law, it is common knowledge that the "law on paper" is disquietingly different from the "law in action". But to conclude from this fact that the effectiveness of STUO's as a vehicle for promoting the interests of Soviet workers has not witnessed any quantitative improvements since the founding of the TUO's would be tantamount to intellectual dishonesty. Even though the present Soviet trade union leadership continues to demonstrate strong loyalty to the CPSU and subservience to the Soviet government, the inescapable fact of contemporary Soviet labor relations is that the traditional antagonism between labor and management has been considerably blunted, and that STUO's are slowly but surely assuming a more meaningful role as protectors of the interests of Soviet workers.

4.4. STUO's as Administrator of the State Social Insurance and Pension Benefits

The USSR Constitution guarantees to all Soviet citizens the right to material support during old age, as well as during loss of work capability either due to illness or due to work related accident. [147] One vehicle for the implementation of this constitutional right is the state social insurance system. Despite the generous coverage of this social insurance policy, it is worth noting that the insured workers are not required to pay any premiums whatsoever. [148]

The present Soviet social insurance system [149] covers the following benefits [150] to workers: pension benefits; [151] disability benefits payable to workers as a result of job-related injuries; maternity benefits; burial payments; and payments to dependents who lose their breadwinners, even where such death is not job-related.[152] Social insurance funds also are used to provide Soviet workers with the following services: treatment at a sanatorium, health resort, or prophylactorium; health diet to those who need it; state-subsidized rest at a rest home, holiday resort, or tourist camp; as well as various services to the children of workers.

During the early years of Soviet power, the STUO's collaborated with the *NKT* in the administration of the state social insurance system. But as of 1933, the Soviet government fully entrusted to the STUO's full responsibility for the administration of the system. Also at the beginning, the social insurance system covered only workers and civil servants. But since the 1964 reforms, the system has been expanded to cover virtually every Soviet citizen, *i.e.* wage earners, salaried employees, collective farm workers,[153] as well as the chairman, engineers, and other hired specialists who work for the collective farms. Funding for the system is exclusively derived from the following contributions: allocation from the state budget; payments by enterprises, collective farms, and social organizations. [154]

Mechanism for the Administration of the State Social Insurance System

As already mentioned above, the administration of the state social security system in the USSR is entrusted to the STUO's acting through the *VTsSPS*. At the level of the production units, direct responsibility for administering the social insurance system is entrusted to the *FZMK*. In its capacity as the local administrator and overseer of compliance with the social insurance laws, the *FZMK* performs the following functions: recommends the payment of social insurance benefits to deserving persons; dispenses tickets to the various sanatoria, prophylactoria, health resorts, holiday resorts, and sporting camps; checks on the organization of health services for compliance with the law; participates in the determination of workers' qualification for pensions benefits; checks to see that the enterprise makes its timely and proper contribution towards the social insurance fund; and, where necessary, it issues binding orders to the management to make payments to deserving workers.

In order to make sure that the management does not use the social insurance fund for an undesignated purpose, [155] Soviet law provides that all expenditures from such fund shall be authorized only by the appropriate organ of the TUO. To carry out its functions properly, the *FZMK* relies upon the preparatory work done by its special committee—the Committee of Social Security.

The Role of STUO's as Administrator of Soviet Pension Benefits

The qualification for, as well as the amount of pension benefits, is generally determined by the state organs of social insurance. However, the state commission that ultimately makes the final decision on these matters, by operation of law, includes representatives of the STUO's. Should the need arise to establish a medical-work commission of experts in order to determine the degree of injury suffered by a petitioner for pension benefits, law requires that a representative of the STUO must be included in such a commission. In order to enable it to properly perform its functions of oversight over the administration of the pension funds, the *FZMK* establishes a special committee—Committee on Pension Matters.

4.5. STUO's as Administrator of Sanatoria, Prophylactoria, Holiday, and Health Resorts

In one of its earliest decrees—*Dekret o Domakh Otdykha* (Decree on Rest Homes) of 1919—the Soviet government committed itself to the principle that rest homes and holiday resorts should be run for the benefit of the workers and by the workers' TUO's. Following that tradition, STUO's today have under their control a network of over 1000 sanatoria, prophylactoria, and rest homes. This entire holiday and health resort industry is funded by appropriation from the state social insurance system. It is estimated that 20% of all tickets issued to the sanatoria and about 100% of the tickets issued to the rest homes are free of all charges to their recipients. The other portion of the tickets is subsidized by the social insurance system to the tune of 70% of their face value.

The application for a *"putevka"*, *i.e.* a ticket which grants a worker the right of occupancy in a designated resort, goes first to the *FZMK* Commission on Social Insurance for a preliminary determination. If approved by the Commission, the recommendation goes to the *FZMK* wich makes the final determination on the question. As a matter of policy the FZMK, in issuing these *putevki*, gives priority to requests from the following persons: heroes of socialist labor; invalids of World War II; single mothers; blood donors; and minors. Because of the special medical regime provided by the sanatoria and the prophylactoria, any worker who wishes to undergo treatment at any one of these health resorts shall accompany his petition with a recommendation from a physician. These petitions are processed in the same manner as those for the rest homes. Tickets to these health resorts are either free of all charges to their recipients or subsidized by the social insurance system to the tune of 70% of their face value.

In addition to the above resorts in which the worker and his family may spend a relatively long period of time, STUO's also set up what they call *zagorodnye bazy otdykha* (sururban weekend resorts) to which workers may retreat for a short period of 1-2 days for rest and leisure. The *FZMK* encourages each enterprise to set up such weekend resorts for its workers. Generally, these bases are equipped not only with modestly furnished accommodation, but also with sporting facilities, libraries, first-aid stations, and where possible, beaches and marinas. These weekend resorts are also operated by the *FZMK*.

STUO's devote special attention to the important question of the organized rest and education for the children of workers. With the active participation of the STUO's, the Soviet Union operates a massive network of kindergartens and day care centers for the education of pre-school workers' children. Parents who leave their children in such day care centers pay only 15-25% of the actual costs of their maintenance. The rest of the costs is subsidized by the state from its general social welfare funds. According to one Soviet commentator, a major goal of this pre-school education of workers' children is, "in a simplified form, but without oversimplification or primitivism, to explain to these pre-school youngsters the ideas of communism and the way to construct communism in our country, to inculcate into them the esteemed duty of all citizens before the fatherland and before the people, to prepare each of the pupils for socially useful work". [156]

For the children of school age, the STUO organizes a network of young pioneers' camps throughout the country. These holiday camps are organized by the trade union committees in cooperation with the local councils for children of first through eighth grades, *i.e.* from age 7-15 years. In order to go to one of these camps, the children are issued with a trade union *"putevka"*, which enables them to spend 26 days during the summer and 12 days during the winter at these camps. The parents of these children pay less than one-third of the actual costs of the children's upkeep of these camps. For the older children, the TUO's organize special holiday camps which are run on the same principle as the young pioneers camp as described above.

4.6. STUO's as Co-administrator of Housing for Workers

Generally speaking, housing in the USSR [157] is under the ownership and/ or operational control of various agencies. These include: [158] the local city councils; individual state enterprises and institutions; cooperative organizations, especially the construction-cooperative organizations; the various social organizations, including the TUO's; and individual citizens. A great bulk of Soviet housing stock, however, is owned by the state and placed under the operational control of the local councils and the state enterprises.

In the area of administration of state-owned houses, the TUO's play a major role. The participation of TUO's in this matter is in two stages: First, they have a substantial impact on the determination of the housing needs of individual workers and in the keeping of the records of the housing needs of workers; secondly, they collaborate with the respective governmental agencies in the dispensing of available housing to workers.

The initial determination of the housing needs of workers begins at the level of the plant, factory, enterprise, or institution, *i.e.* at the place of work. Workers are asked to file in their housing needs either with the *FZMK* or with the management of the enterprise. Thereafter the *FZMK*, operating through its Committee on Housing and Housing Conditions, conducts a preliminary investigation into the housing needs of the applicant and makes its recommendation on the application. A unified record of persons wanting housing, indicating the order of priority among such applicants, is drawn up jointly by the *FZMK* and the management.

In some situations, the record of the housing needs of workers may be maintained at the place of residence, in which case, by the executive committee of the local city council. This is done primarily in relation to those applicants who work at enterprises that do not have their own housing stock and do not engage in the construction of housing for workers. But even in these latter instances, the workers are also required to file their requests for housing at their regular place of work. After the routine preliminary investigation and determination of the applicant's housing needs by the *FZMK* Committee on Housing and Living Conditions, the *FZMK* and the management of the enterprise reach a joint decision on the application and send it to the executive committee of the local city council. Final decision both on the eligibility of the applicant and on the order in which housing shall be made available to competing applicants shall be made by the executive committee of the local city council in consultation with the representatives of the TUO's. For the worker, inclusion in this waiting list is a very critical stage in his search for adequate housing.

The second level of TUO involvement in the administration of state-owned housing is at the time the worker takes actual possession of the allotted housing. According to a provision of the Statute on the Rights of the *FZMK*, a decision to transfer possession of any space in a house constructed with the funds of a state enterprise or institution shall require a joint order (authorization) of the *FZMK* and the management. Notice of such decision shall be duly communicated to the executive committee of the local city council purely for informational purpose. On the other hand, if the space being allotted is in a house which was constructed with the funds of the state or of a social organization, a joint decision of the *FZMK* and the management regarding the allotment of such space shall be forwarded to the executive committee of the local council for its ratification. Acting through its representative in the Committee on Housing, the TUO directly participates in the allocation of houses within the housing stock of the local city councils. In all of the above cases, priority in the allotment of housing shall be given to those workers and civil servants who fulfill their working norms, observe work discipline, and conscientiously perform their assigned tasks. The determination of the *FZMK* in this regard could be and often is crucial.

The participatory role of the TUO's in the administration of state housing does not end with the taking of possession of the living space by the worker. The TUO is also actively involved in the day-to-day administration of the occupied houses. In order to follow up on the living conditions in these houses, the *FZMK* organizes the tenants into house committees. In those houses which are under the operational control of a state enterprise or institution, the house committees shall function under the direction of the *FZMK*. The house committees serve as listening posts for the *FZMK* in the respective houses. They report their findings, *e.g.* the need for repair, the need to install certain equipment, violations of health and sanitary standards by individual tenants, etc., to the *FZMK* for action. The oversight activities of the *FZMK* are particularly accentuated in the administration of the so-called young workers dormitories. Here the so-called social organ of self-government, which is responsible for running the place, operates under the direct control of the *FZMK*.

One other form through which the TUO's influence the fulfillment of the housing needs of Soviet workers is its encouragement of the formation by workers of housing-construction cooperatives *(zhilishchnostroitel'nye kooperativy–ZSK)*. In those locations where housing shortage is very acute, the *FZMK* directs its Committee on Housing to help individual workers who wish to form a ZSK. Both the management of the enterprise and the *FZMK* help the ZSK at the following stages in the realization of their goal: in their effort to secure an adequate plot on which to build their condominium; in drawing up their construction plan; and in securing mortgage from the state bank. The mortgage generally covers 60% of the estimated costs of the construction and is repayable in 10-15 years. In certain instances, with the active intervention of the *FZMK*, the bank mortgage could go up to 70% of the cost of construction. Of course, the lot on which the condominium is constructed belongs to the state and by law it cannot be an object of any commercial transaction. The land is transferred to the cooperative organization free of all charges and for an unlimited time.

For the same reason that they aid workers' cooperative to build their own condominium, *i.e.* to help reduce housing shortage in the USSR, the TUO's also render needed assistance to individual citizens who wish to construct their own houses. Any such individual shall send in his application for mortgage loan to his place of work. The application is examined at a regular meeting of the *FZMK*. Upon approval by the *FZMK*, the latter joins with the management in supporting the application to the state bank. Failure to receive such joint backing by the *FZMK* and the management could be fatal to the mortgage application.

What all of this means is that a Soviet worker can hardly receive housing in the Soviet Union today without the blessing of the TUO's. It makes no difference whether the worker receives his apartment in a building owned and/or operated by the city council, by individual enterprises or institutions, or by a TUO. From the moment that he files his application for housing, through the time that he actually takes possession of such housing, and throughout his occupancy of the apartment, he is at the mercy of the TUO's. In those instances where the house or apartment is owned either by individual citizens or by cooperative organizations, the favorable intervention of the TUO could be of great assistance to such persons or groups. This makes the STUO's a force to be reckoned with in the administration of all Soviet housing stock, regardless of their form of ownership.

4.7. STUO's as a "School for Cultural Education of Workers"

The proponents of Soviet communism strongly believe that it is impossible to attain communism without an adequate ideological, political, and cultural reeducation of the masses. Communism, to them, is not just a state of supreme material wealth, but also a society in which the new man shall be both ideologically stable, politically conscious, and culturally enlightened. At its 24th Congress, the CPSU noted that " ... without a higher degree of culture, education, social consciousness of the masses, and inner maturity of the masses, communism is unattainable, just as much as it is unattainable without an adequate material-technical basis." [159] The Program of the CPSU expresses the need for such cultural reeducation of the workers even more eloquently. It states: "Communism is a highly organized society of free and conscientious workers in which social self-administration shall prevail, where work for the interest of society shall become not only a necessity of life, but also a cognitive necessity, where each worker shall utilize his efforts unselfishly for the good of the people." [160] Obviously, if the Soviet Union is to attain this goal, it must give a high priority to the revolutionary transformation of the workers.

STUO's are working in tandem with all the other hierarchies of Soviet authority to attain this goal, *i.e.* the creation of the new cultured Soviet man whose attributes shall include: a Marxist-Leninist outlook on life, a deep sense of Soviet patriotism, an inner conviction in the merits of internationalism and friendship among nations, a communist attitude towards work and towards social property, and a high degree of individual discipline and organization. One of the many forms through which the TUO's hope to inculcate a new communist work ethic in the workers is through the organization of socialist competitions among the workers. The primary purpose of such socialist competition is to raise the level of productivity and to instill in the workers a new attitude towards work. Soviet commentators are quick to point out that, contrary to the expectations of most Western observers, socialism does not seek to kill all forms of competition. Rather, socialism—one is told—not only encourages competition among the workers, but, more importantly, it democratizes and humanizes competition.

In defense of socialist competition, one Soviet commentator notes: "Judged by its very functions, socialist competition stands in direct contrast to capitalist competition. The latter, by its very nature, is founded upon private property and the principle of the exploitation of man by man. Capitalist competition is a form of struggle by the monopolies for more profits, for markets, and for cheap labor." [161] In short, capitalist competition, one is told, has a built-in tendency to dehumanize the individual workers and all the other participating competitors.

Back in 1929, the Central Committee of the CPSU adopted a Decree "On Socialist Competition in Factories and Enterprises" which, among other things, provided that socialist competitions must be organized and conducted by the TUO's, not by the management. Ever since then, the organization of socialist competitions among workers has grown into one of the major functions of the STUO's. The four general principles of socialist competition are: publicity (*i.e.* openness in the adoption and fulfillment of the set goals of the competitive efforts); comparison of the results; [162] the possibility that the experience of the winners can be copied and followed by other workers and workers' collectives; and fraternal mutual assistance among the competitors.

The winners of such competition shall receive either moral or monetary rewards, or both. The moral rewards take many forms [163] including: decoration with a medal; conferment of the title of "Hero of Socialist Labor"; issuance of a certificate of merit, or a letter of thanks to be jointly signed by the *FZMK* Chairman and the plant director; entry of the name of the winner into the Honor List (*Kniga Pocheta*); etc. As an added incentive, Soviet law confers other privileges[164] on exemplary workers.

A second device used by the TUO's to instill communist work ethics in the workers is the so-called "brigade of communist labor". These are units of workers whose members pledge "To Learn to Work and Live by Communist Principles". Members of such brigades engage in self-education and self-criticism. Each member of the brigade watches over the personal morals, the work habits, and life styles of all the other members. Outstanding members of these brigades are designated as "*udarniki Kommunisticheskogo truda*" (shock workers of communist labor). An *udarnik* is supposed to embody all the exemplary qualities of a communist worker—moral purity, conscientious attitude toward work, as well as towards one's social obligations, and unwavering conviction in the ideals of communism. In essence, the brigade of communist labor is a sort of study group where, through peer pressure, each member cleanses himself of his decadent attitude toward work and social obligations. All brigades of communist labor are created at the instigation of and operate under the direction of the TUO's—the great cultural educator of all Soviet workers.

A third method of cultural education of the workers is the organization of a series of public lectures on current issues of communist upbringing. These well publicized lectures are held everywhere: in factories and in construction sites, in the state and collective farms, in enterprises, in workers' dormitories, in residential homes, etc. It is estimated that each year STUO's in conjunction with the *Znanie* Society organizes over 11 million public lectures, talks, and informal discussions throughout the USSR.

In addition to these public lectures, the committees of the *FZMK* organize continuing seminars for the workers at their respective enterprises. The seminar topics cover such issues as: the general principles of Marxism-Leninism, the socio-political development of the Soviet society, the life of Lenin, etc. STUO's organize a special series of public lectures under the general headings of "Peoples Universities" and "Schools of Communist Labor". In 1972 the Secretariat of the *VTsSPS* adopted a two-year program of study for the "School of Communist Labor" series. As part of its cultural educational network, the STUO's operate—at various locations throughout the USSR— such things as trade union clubs,[165] red corners,[166] libraries,[167] houses of culture, movie houses, etc. The STUO's also publish their own newspapers[168] and journals. Finally, they sponsor special programs on the radio and television networks.

A fourth form of cultural education among the workers is through the effective use of the comrades' courts. Charges arising from violations of work discipline, as well as from other minor anti-social conduct by individual workers, are handled by the comrades' courts which are set up at the level of the

298

enterprises and institutions and are directed and controlled by the *FZMK*. The comrades' court sees its function as essentially educational. Persons who are found guilty of the charges against them may be subject to any one or a combination of the following sanctions: he may be ordered to publicly apologize to his fellow workers or to any individually aggrieved co-worker; he may be subjected to a social censure with or without publication of such censure in a local newspaper; he may be ordered to pay a fine; the comrades' court may recommend to the administration to transfer the worker to a different, less-desirable job or to demote him in rank. Throughout the proceedings before the comrades' court, the stress is on making the defendant worker realize his mistake. If he persists in comporting himself in a manner that is unbecoming of a socialist worker, he may face more serious charges before a regular court of law.

4.8. STUO's as a Promoter and Organizer of Sports and Tourism inside the USSR

Operating under the principle that a Soviet worker, in order to possess a healthy mind, must also possess a healthy body, the STUO's organize various sporting activities for their members. In collaboration with the State Committee on Physical Education and Sports of the USSR Council of Ministers, and with the Central Committee of the *Komsomol*, the *VTsSPS* directs all sporting activities in the USSR.

On March 1, 1977, the Soviet Union instituted an all-union physical education program under the general name of "*Gotov k Trudu i Oborone SSSR*" (Ready to Work and Defend the USSR–GTO). This program plans physical education programs for all citizens from the age of 10 to 60 years. Based upon age groups, the programs are broken down into five sections as reflected by their respective headings: "*Smelye i Lovkie*" (Bold and Agile)–for persons between the ages of 10-13 yrs; "*Sportivnaia Smena*" (The Sporting Shift)–for persons between the age of 14-15 yrs; "*Sila i Muzhestvo*" (Strength and Boldness)–for persons between the ages of 16 and 18 years; "*Fizicheskoe Sovershenstvo*" (Physical Perfection)–for women between the ages of 19 and 34 years and for men between the ages of 19 and 39 years; "*Bodrost i Zdorovie*" (Cheerfulness and Health) for women from age 35 to 55 and for men between the ages of 40 and 60 years. The STUO's orchestrate the organization of Soviet workers into various voluntary sporting associations (*dobrovol'nye sportivnye obshchestva–DSO's*) the best known of which are: "*Spartak*", "*Lokomotiv*", and "*Burevestnik*".

As part of their physical education program, the STUO's have won for the workers the right to take a few minutes off from work in order to engage in on-the-job physical exercises. These exercises are popularly referred to as "*piatiminutka bodrosti*" (five minutes of cheerfulness) or "*proizvodstvennaia gimnastika*" (work gymnastics). The form of on-the-job exercises is tailored to meet the needs of the workers at individual plants, depending on the type of work they perform.

The culminating point in Soviet domestic sporting activities is the trade union sponsored *Spartakiad* of the USSR which is held once every four years—one in the summer and the other in the winter. In addition to the *Spartakiad* of the USSR, there is also the all-union trade union sporting festival which is held once every five years.

In order to permit workers to take full advantage of these organizational efforts, the STUO's use their own funds to construct throughout the territory of the USSR a network of sporting facilities which are open to the general public. These include: stadiums, gymnasiums, swimming pools, skating rinks, skiing facilities, special forest reserves for hunting, and closed waters for fishing, tennis courts, volleyball and basketball courts, etc. Members of the *DSO's* not only have free access to these facilities, but they also have free use of the requisite equipments for the individual games, *e.g.* tennis balls, tennis rackets, soccer balls, volley balls, basket balls, etc. The STUO's also are granted the right of operational control over the construction of those sporting facilities which are financed by funds from either the local city councils or from the various state institutions, enterprises, and plants.

In addition to organizing various sporting activities among the workers, the STUO's also promote internal tourism among their members. The STUO's regard tourism as a form of active rest. The direction of tourism and tourist expeditions in the USSR is concentrated in the hands of the STUO's. The organ charged with coordinating all such activities is the Central Council on Tourism and Excursions which is attached to the *VTsSPS*. This Council has its branches in the union republics, in the regions, and in the autonomous areas.

Through the medium of domestic tourism, according to one Soviet commentator, STUO's seek not only to keep the bodies of Soviet workers physically tuned up, but also to expose Soviet citizens to the unique beauty of the Soviet country-side, to instill in them love for the socialist fatherland, and dedication to the revolutionary and combatant tradition of the Soviet people.[169] Thus, even sports and tourism, in the context of Soviet reality, are not without an ideological content and STUO's accordingly use them as a form of political education of the workers.

4.9. *STUO's as an Instrument of Soviet Foreign Policy*

According to their Charter, the STUO's consider themselves to be an integral part of the international trade union movement.[170] They fully subscribe to the principle of proletarian internationalism, and all their activities on the international scene are conducted under the general slogan of "Proletarians of All Countries, Unite".

At the first Congress of the STUO's in 1918, the TUO's resolved to dedicate themselves to the cause of international proletarian struggle. In 1921 the STUO's were instrumental in setting up the Red International of TUO's—the Profintern—a trade union movement which brought together the national trade union organizations of over 40 different countries. The Profintern was ultimately dismantled in 1937.

Between the years 1939 and 1945, the STUO's were instrumental in forming various international trade union committees which were designed to further friendship among nations. Examples of these were the Anglo-Soviet Trade Union Committee, the Franco-Soviet Trade Union Committee, etc. Throughout all of these foreign contacts, the STUO's have sought to further the international workers' struggle against imperialism. Working relationship between the STUO's and the various Western TUO's is mainly carried out on a bilateral level. The STUO's have been known to maintain contacts with Western TUO's, regardless of whether or not the latter belonged to the WFTU, the ICFTU, or the World Confederation of Labor. The STUO's, however, are more closely allied with the WFTU of which they were a co-founder in 1945. By the same token, the STUO's maintain contacts with members of the International Confederation of Arab Trade Union Organizations and the All-African Federation of Trade Union Organizations.

In addition to maintaining working relationships with foreign trade union organizations, [171] the STUO's also organize international conferences on various topics of interest to the working class of the world. One example of such conferences was the 1971 International Trade Union Conference on Social Insurance which was held in Moscow at the initiative of the *VTsSPS*. It was estimated that over 127 foreign TUO's representing 90 countries were in attendance at this Conference. [172]

The STUO's maintain special contacts with the national TUO's in the other socialist countries, specially with the TUO's of the member countries of Comecon. With the latter, the STUO's regularly exchange cultural visits, hold periodic consultations on matters of mutual interest, and organize international conferences. As a part of the trilateral Soviet delegation to the ILO, the STUO's take an active part in the work of the ILO and this includes participation in the preparation and discussion of various ILO conventions, declarations, and other international acts dealing with labor and related matters.

The full impact of STUO's on the conduct of Soviet foreign policy may be better appreciated when one realizes: that all Soviet citizens who work at Soviet embassies, foreign trade missions, consulates, and diplomatic missions abroad are invariably members of one STUO or another; that all Soviet correspondents who are based abroad are invariably members of one STUO or another; that all Soviet exchange students who are studying abroad are card-carrying members of one STUO or another; that cell organizations of STUO's are organized and function in most Soviet embassies, diplomatic missions, foreign trade missions, and consulates abroad. It will be hard to find a more influential Soviet foreign policy actor than a Soviet ambassador in a foreign country who doubles up as a CPSU member and TUO activist. It will be difficult for such a Soviet ambassador to refuse to carry out instructions from the *VTsSPS* in Moscow asking him to cultivate and maintain contacts with leaders of local TUO's on behalf of the STUO's.

5. Some Conclusions: STUO's in Historical Perspective

According to the teachings of Marxism-Leninism, TUO's are an historical phenomenon. This means that the evolution of the TUO is attributable to identifiable historical events in the course of the socio-economic development of the human society; that the historical mission of TUO's is bound to change in direct relationship with any revolutionary re-ordering of economic relationships in society. Unlike the state, however, the TUO's will not wither away as society approaches communism.

According to this thinking, the essence of all TUO activities in a pre-socialist society is to prepare the worker for socialism, *i.e.* to act as a "school for socialism". By contrast, the primary function of a TUO in a socialist economy is to prepare the workers for communism, *i.e.* to act as a "school for communism". Within this order of things, it is expected that TUO's—as an element of the superstructure—would in turn act as a catalyst to transform the socio-economic basis which determined their form and existence in the first place.

Historical materialists tell us that TUO's are, historically speaking, the product of the era of industrial capitalism; that under capitalism the organization of workers into trade unions was an historical necessity; that this necessity was precipitated by the concentration of capital in the hands of the capitalists, a fact which in turn led to a further aggravation of the conflicts between the interests of the workers and the capitalists; that in order to defend themselves against the more organized class of capitalists, the workers had to organize themselves into labor unions. In short, one is told that the TUO emerged as a form of economic (class) struggle, *i.e.* as a vehicle for promoting the economic interests of workers. [173]

Karl Marx urged workers in a capitalist economy to rise above mere economic struggle and to expand the activities of their TUO's to include political struggle as well. In order to do this, they would need to ally themselves with a progressive political party, *i.e.* a revolutionary party of workers. Thus, according to Karl Marx, a TUO cannot afford to take a neutral position *vis-à-vis* the proletariat political party. In effect, such neutrality would be tantamount to a camouflaged counterrevolutionary step. The ideal trade union organization, therefore, is that which is welded to a proletarian political party and not that which, like the American Federation of Labor, is dedicated to "a philosophy of wage consciousness". [174] Soviet TUO's heeded this advice and have since

302

their inception allied themselves with the CPSU, the vanguard of the Soviet working class.

Soviet law, also an element of the superstructure, has played an effective role in shaping the changing roles of the STUO's throughout the years. As the socio-economic and political functions of the STUO's changed, so did Soviet laws regarding the activities of the TUO's. Soviet legal historians generally recognize seven phases [175] in the development of Soviet legislations dealing with TUO's.

The *first* phase covers the period from 1917 to 1922. During this period, the STUO's operated virtually as an agency of the *NKT* which was charged with the responsibility of coordinating all governmental functions in the area of labor and labor relations. The 1918 *KZoT*-RSFSR tacitly recognized this fact and, as such, did not bother to delineate the jurisdiction of the STUO's from that of the *NKT*. Certain provisions of the General Statute on Tariffs [176] later expanded the powers of the STUO's, but in doing so they failed to draw a line between the jurisdiction of the *NKT* and the STUO's. One could hardly speak of an "independent" TUO in Russia at this time.

The *second* phase of Soviet labor legislation (1922-1933) began with a call from the 11th Congress of the CPSU to the Soviet government urging the latter to devote more attention to the affairs of STUO's. Beginning in 1921, the Soviet government resolved to delineate the jurisdiction of the STUO's from those of governmental agencies working in the same areas. This new Soviet government commitment culminated in the adoption of arts. 151-167 of the 1922 *KZoT*-RSFSR which clarified the jurisdiction of the STUO's but also conceded to the *NKT* a dominant role in matters relating to labor and labor relations. The second phase therefore ended with a minor step in the direction of removing the TUO's from the domination of the *NKT*.

The process which began toward the end of the second phase continued into the *third* (1933-1955). The latter stage witnessed a substantial expansion in the jurisdiction of STUO's in labor matters. At its 16th Congress, the CPSU called for a transfer of major responsibility over the administration of the social insurance program to the STUO's. Pursuant to this call by the Party, the Central Executive Committee of the USSR, acting in conjunction with the Council of People's Commissars of the USSR and the *VTsSPS*, adopted, on June 23, 1933, a statute "On the Merger of the *NKT* of the USSR with the *VTsSPS*". [177] This statute liquidated the *NKT* and transferred all of its functions to the *VTsSPS*, including its functions in the area of social insurance administration.

Pursuant to a Law of August 21, 1934, [178] all orders issued by the *VTsSPS* in exercise of its authority in the area of the administration of labor laws were to be put into legal force by implementing orders to be issued by the Council of Peoples' Commissariats of the USSR. To say the least, such a procedure was not only clumsy, but also complicated. But the message was clear—the Soviet government wished to transfer more responsibilities to the STUO's in the field of labor and labor relations.

The *fourth* legislative stage covers the period from 1955 to 1958. During this period, it became clear that the *VTsSPS* as well as the Central Committees of the national TUO's neither possessed the expertise nor had the aptitude to deal with wage matters which were recently transferred to their jurisdiction. This resulted in general dissatisfaction with the administration of wage policy. To remedy this situation, the Soviet Union in 1955 established a State Committee on Labor and Wages which was to be attached to the USSR Council of Ministers. This newly formed State Committee assumed primary responsibility for administering wage policy. Further clarification of the jurisdiction of the *VTsSPS* and the State Committee was accomplished by the adoption of the FPLL of 1958.

The *fifth* phase (1958-1965) witnessed the implementation of the Resolution of the 1957 Plenum of the Central Committee of the CPSU "On the Working of the STUO's". This Resolution called for the expansion of the powers of the *FZMK* in the area of economic management and in the administration of the enterprise. Pursuant to this Resolution, the Presidium of the USSR Supreme Soviet on July 15, 1958, adopted a new "Statute on the Rights of the *FZMK*", which vastly expanded the authority of the *FZMK* in these two areas. Thereafter, the Council of Ministers of the USSR, acting in conjunction with the *VTsSPS*, adopted on July 9, 1958, a new Statute *"O Proizvodstvennom Soveshchanii na Promyshlennom Predpriiatii, Stroike i Sovkhoze"* [179] (On the Production Conference in Industrial Enterprises, Construction Sites, and State Farms). This law transformed the production conferences into one of the major forms of worker participation in the management of the enterprise. At this point, the STUO's were clearly beginning to merge as a dominant force in the administration of Soviet labor laws and other related social legislations.

The *sixth* stage covers the period from 1965 to 1970. The first major law adopted during this phase was the joint Statute of the Central Committee of the CPSU and the Council of Ministers of the USSR of October 4, 1965, "On How to Improve Economic Planning and Strengthen the Economic Stimulation within the Sphere of Industrial Production". [180] Pursuant to this law, the *VTsSPS* was brought into the process for the preparation and adoption of economic stimulation plans. A second act which was adopted during this period [181] substantially expanded the functions of the union republican organs of the TUO's especially in the areas of labor and wages. Furthermore, a new 1965 Statute "On the Socialist State Production Enterprise" [182] substantially expanded the powers of the *FZMK* both in the area of management of the enterprise as well as in the regulation of labor relations as a whole. By the end of the sixth stage, the STUO's were fully in control of things. But this

304

was not the end of the expansion of their powers. The growth continues into the seventh stage.

The *seventh* stage began in 1970 with the adoption of the new FPLL.[183] Following the adoption of this federal law, the Presidium of the USSR Supreme Soviet promulgated a new Statute "On the Rights of the *FZMK*".[184] This was followed by the adoption of a new labor code (*KZoT*) by the respective union republics. All of these post-1970 laws have continued the trend in the direction of expanding the powers of the STUO's. It is expected that the adoption of a new USSR Constitution in 1977 will trigger a new wave of legislative reforms aimed at a further expansion of the functions of the STUO's as administrators of Soviet socialism.

Looking back to 1917, one cannot help but notice the growth in the powers of STUO's. They started as an inconsequential appendage of the *NKT*. Today they have grown into an all-union conglomerate which, by US analogy, performs all or some of the functions presently allotted to the following US departments and administrative agencies: the US Department of Labor; the National Labor Relations Board; the Department of Health, Education, and Welfare; the Department of Housing and Urban Development; the Civil Service Commission; and the Occupational Safety and Health Administration. In addition to performing the functions of the above-named governmental agencies and departments, STUO's also subsume all of the functions of the American TUO's. Whether or not an organization such as the STUO qualifies to be called a labor union is up to the reader to decide.

It is expected that the 73-year old alliance (1905-1978) between the STUO's and the dominant political party, *i.e.* the Bolshevik Party and the CPSU, will continue to mature until and into communism. If everything goes according to the schedule for the withering away of the Soviet state, one would expect to see a further expansion in the role of the STUO's and a concomitant abdication of responsibilities by the Soviet government in the areas of labor law and labor relations. A knowledgeable Soviet commentator notes: "As the Soviet society advances towards communism, the TUO's will progressively assume responsibility for more of those functions which traditionally were performed by State agencies."[185] Whether or not this full transition will take place in our lifetime is a matter for idle speculation.

In the final analysis, the true role of STUO's is in the eye of the beholder: to some observers, they are merely dignified lackeys of the CPSU; to others, they are partners with the CPSU and the Soviet government in the administration of Soviet labor laws and related social legislations. Whatever the case may be, the inescapable fact is that the STUO's are increasingly becoming a major force in the maintenance of labor peace in the Soviet Union. It will be unrealistic to expect all 113.5 million members of the labor unions to agree with the positions taken by the union leadership on all questions of labor

305

relations. Whether or not the recognition of workers' right to strike is an irreducible element of industrial democracy is highly debatable. One's position on the above questions notwithstanding, one can clearly expect that—at the present rate of development—the STUO's will eventually become the best protector of the interest of Soviet workers. Today, any discussion of the administration of Soviet law would be incomplete without a mention of the expanding role of the STUO's as the managers of the Soviet labor scene.

NOTES

1. In 1920 the International Labor Organization (ILO) suggested to the Soviet Government to grant access to an Investigative Committee of the ILO to study the trade union situation inside Russia. As was expected, the request was flatly rejected by the Soviet Government. See *Official Bulletin of the International Labor Office*, 1 (1923), 490, 502, as cited in C. Osakwe, *The Participation Of The Soviet Union In Universal International Organizations*, (Leyden, 1972) at footnote 48 on p. 96 (hereafter cited as: C. Osakwe, *Soviet Participation*).

In 1927 the ILO published a most unfavorable report on the trade union situation inside Russia. See International Labor Office, *The Trade Union Movement in Soviet Russia*, (Geneva, 1927). For a general review of Soviet Government attitude towards ILO between 1919 and 1934, see C. Osakwe, *id.*, pp. 63-70.

2. See, Sidney Webb and Beatrice Webb, *The History of Trade Unionism*, (London, 1920). A traditional definition of a labor union may be found in the National Labor Relations Act of the United States. Section 2, para. 5 of this Act defines a labor organization as "any organization of any kind, or any agency or employee representation committee or plan, in which employees participate and which exists for the purpose in whole or in part, of dealing with employers concerning grievances, labor disputes, wages, rates of pay, hours of employment, or conditions of work". See National Labor Relations Act, Sect. 2, para. 5, 49 Stat. 449 (1935), as amended by 61 Stat. 136 (1947), 65 Stat. 601 (1951), 72 Stat. 945 (1958), 73 Stat. 541 (1959), 88 Stat. 395 (1974); 29 USC 151-169.

3. At the initiation of the USSR Government, the ILO in 1959 sent a special mission to survey the trade union situation inside the Soviet Union. The ILO Mission focussed its study on three questions: whether the workers in the USSR were free to join trade unions; whether they were free to set up any trade unions they felt like setting up; and whether the trade unions were completely independent of all forms of government control. The report of the Mission was published by the ILO. See ILO, *The Trade Union Situation in the USSR*, (Geneva, 1960). For a general discussion of some of the related problems that surrounded Soviet participation in the ILO at this time, see C. Osakwe, *Soviet Participation, supra* note 1, pp. 52-100.

4. What follows is this author's condensation of the prevailing Soviet doctrine on the nature of Soviet trade union organizations. For a representative Soviet view on this subject, see N. G. Aleksandrov, S. S. Karinskii, G. K. Moskalenko, V. I. Nikitinskii, V. I. Smoliarchuk and N. L. Tumanova (eds.), *Trudovoe pravo – entsiklopedicheskii slovar'* (Encyclopedia of Labor Law), (Moscow, 1969), pp. 404-407 (hereafter to be cited as: N. G. Aleksandrov *et al.*, *Encyclopedia of Labor Law*); S. N. Bratus', N. V. Zhogin, P. V. Kovanov, V. I. Terebilov, N. L. Tumanov and V. M. Chkhikvadze (eds.), *Entsiklopedicheskii slovar' pravovykh znanii–Sovetskoe pravo* (Encyclopedia of Soviet Law), (Moscow, 1965), pp. 391-392 (hereafter to be cited as, S. N. Bratus' *et al.*, *Encyclopedia of Soviet Law*).

5. The six general principles discussed below are extracted from the prevailing Soviet doctrine on the nature and essence of labor relations in the Soviet socialist society. For a sampling of Soviet view on this subject, see L. Ia. Gintsburg, *Sotsialisticheskoe trudovoe pravootnoshenie* (The Legal Aspects of Socialist Labor Relations), (Moscow, 1977).

There is no doubt that there are Soviet writers, both inside and outside the Soviet Union, who hold a minority or dissenting view on these issues. The extrapolation of these dominant principles of Soviet doctrine does not represent either a judgmental endorsement or condemnation of these views by the author.

5a. The dominant role of the CPSU within the Soviet socialist society is enshrined in Art. 6 of the 1977 USSR Constitution, which provides: "The Communist Party, armed with Marxism-Leninism, determines the general perspectives of the development of society and the course of the domestic and foreign policy of the USSR, directs the great constructive work of the Soviet people, and imparts a planned, systematic and theoretically substantiated character to their struggle for the victory of communism" (Art. 6, para. 2). Art. 6, para. 1 of the 1977 Constitution also describes the CPSU as "the leading and guiding force of Soviet society and the nucleus of its political system, of all state organizations and public organizations."

6. The principle of central economic planning as the basis of the development of Soviet economy was given constitutional recognition in Art. 16, para. 2 of the 1977 USSR Constitution.

7. As a general recognition of the principle of "input from below" into the preparation of the central economic plans in the USSR, Art. 16, para. 2 of the 1977 USSR Constitution provides that the state economic plans shall take "due account of the sectoral and territorial principles and by combining centralized direction with the managerial independence and initiative of individual and amalgamated enterprises and other organizations". The STUO's play an active part in the formation of economic plans at the level of the enterprise. For an indepth discussion of the workers' role in this regard, see Section 4.1. of this study.

8. The former State Committee on Questions of Labor and Wages has now been renamed "State Committee on Labor and Social Questions".

9. The 1961 Program of the CPSU defines communism as ". . . a classless social system . . . consisting of socially conscious working people in which public self-government will be established." It is contemplated that as society advances toward communism, the state will progressively wither away and consequently will transfer all of its present functions to the social organizations, including the STUO's.

10. For a detailed discussion of some of the functions that are presently being performed by STUO's, see Section 4 of this study.

11. To a great extent, the absence of antagonism between labor and management in the USSR is the result of the fact that the leadership of the STUO's seems to have pledged full support both to the CPSU and to the Soviet government. It is conceivable, however, that there may be some disagreement between the position of the STUO leadership and that of the rank and file of the unions. To the outside observer, there is no reliable way of determining the extent of such rank and file disagreement with the leadership of the STUO's. All that can be said here is that it is virtually impossible that, in the course of human relationships, there could be perfect harmony between the leaders and the ordinary members of the STUO's on the critical issues of the relationship of the STUO's with the CPSU, the Soviet government, or with the enterprise management. In this study, our reference to the position of the STUO's, unless if otherwise qualified, is a reference to the official position of the leadership of the trade unions.

12. E. C. Brown, *Soviet Trade Unions and Labor Relations*, (Cambridge, Mass., 1966), at p. 181. (Hereafter cited as: Brown, *Soviet Trade Unions*).

13. Art. 40 of the (1977) USSR Constitution recognizes the right of all Soviet citizens to work, *i.e.* the right to receive guaranteed work and remuneration for one's work in accordance with its quality and quantity. See Art. 40, Constitution of USSR, *Ved. V. S. SSSR*, 1977, No. 41, item 617. Hereafter all references to the USSR Constitution, unless otherwise stated, are to the current (1977) Constitution.

308

14. Art. 43 of the USSR Constitution.

15. Art. 66 of *Kodeks zakonov o trude*-RSFSR (Labor Code of RSFSR). Hereafter cited as *KZoT*-RSFSR. For the legislative history of this Code, see note 81 below.

16. Arts. 165-169, *KZoT*-RSFSR.

17. Art. 51 of the USSR Constitution recognizes workers' freedom of association. This includes the right to belong or not to belong to a TUO. This provision of Art. 51 of the USSR Constitution has been received into art. 225 of *KZoT*-RSFSR. The right of Soviet workers to organize into trade unions entails a reciprocal obligation on the part of the employer not to restrain, interfere, or coerce employees in the exercise of this right. The employer is obliged not to engage in any other unfair labor practices that might directly or indirectly vitiate the right of workers to self organize, to form, join, or assist trade union organizations.

18. This right is exercised through the mechanism of the TUO's. See the detailed discussion of the participation of STUO's in economic management and in the administration of enterprises in Section 4.1. of this study. The right of Soviet workers to participate in management is specifically recognized in art. 226, *KZoT*-RSFSR.

19. Art. 43 of the USSR Constitution.

20. See art. 237, *KZoT*-RSFSR.

21. See the discussion in Section 4.2. of this study.

22. See the equal protection clause (Art. 34) of the USSR Constitution. For a general discussion of the equal protection clause of the USSR Constitution see, C. Osakwe, "Equal Protection Under Soviet Constitutional System." *Netherlands Studies in Comparative Law*, 2 (1975), 159-211.

23. Brown, *Soviet Trade Unions, supra* note 12, pp. 319-320.

24. For a general discussion of substantive Soviet Labor Law see R. Livshitz and V. Nikitinsky, *An Outline of Soviet Labor Law* (Moscow, 1977); R. Conquest, *Industrial Workers in the USSR* (London, 1967).

25. There are numerous studies in English dealing with STUO's. Most of them, however, have tended to focus on the organization, structure, and nature of STUO's. Virtually none of them has attempted an indepth analysis of the juridical status and the legal foundations of the functions of STUO's. The present study proposes to fill this gap in Western literature on the subject. For those who wish to do some background reading on STUO's, the following sources are recommended: M. Dewar, *Labor Policy in the USSR: 1917-1928* (London, 1956): I. Deutscher, *Soviet Trade Unions* (London, 1950); S. Schwartz, *Labor in the Soviet Union* (New York, 1952). As general sources of reference on STUO's, see Brown, *Soviet Trade Unions, supra* note 12; G. P. van den Berg, "Unions," in F. Feldbrugge (ed.), *Encyclopedia of Soviet Law* (Leyden, 1973), pp. 710-713.

26. I. Smirnov, *Profsoiuzy SSSR: 100 voprosov–100 otvetov* (STUO's: 100 Questions–100 Answers), (Moscow, 1972), pp. 22-23 (Hereafter cited as: Smirnov, *STUO's*).

27. For example, a member of the Central Committee of the CPSU could at the same time be a member of the Supreme Soviet of the USSR, as well as a member of the *VTsSPS*.

28. V. I. Lenin, *Complete Works*, Vol. 42, p. 203, as cited in Smirnov, *STUO's, supra* note 26, p. 13.

29. L. Brezhnev, *Sovetskie profsoiuzy: vliiatel'naia sila nashego obshchestva* (STUO's: An Influential Force in Our Society). A speech delivered to the delegates at the 16th Congress of STUO's on March 21, 1977. (Moscow, 1977), p. 16. (Hereafter cited as: Brezhnev, *Soviet Trade Unions*).

30. For a representative Soviet view on the harmonious relationship between the CPSU and the leadership of the STUO's, see Smirnov, *STUO's, supra* note 26, pp. 5-20.

31. The Russian TUO's were founded in the course of the Popular Democratic

Revolution of 1905-1907. Because of their close alliance with the Bolshevik Party, they were regarded as "TUO's of a new type." Unlike the Western TUO's which called for "reform" of the capitalist working relationships, the Russian TUO's called for a revolutionary transformation of the then dominant capitalist economic system. The relationship between the Russian TUO's and the Russian Communist Party has since continued, even after the victory of the Bolshevik Revolution of 1917.

32. V. I. Lenin, *Complete Works*, Vol. 16, p. 430, as cited in Smirnov, *supra* note 26, p. 14.

33. *Ustav professional'nykh soiuzov SSSR* (Charter of STUO's), (1977 Edition, Moscow, 1977), p. 5, 6. The current Charter of STUO's was adopted at the 13th Congress of STUO's and has since been amended by each of the subsequent Congresses of the STUO's—by the 14th Congress on March 4, 1968; by the 15th Congress on March 24, 1972, and by the 16th Congress on March 25, 1977. Unless otherwise stated, all references in this study to the Charter of STUO's are to the Charter as amended by the 16th Congress. (Hereafter cited as: Charter of STUO's).

34. For a general discussion of the ways in which the CPSU exercises its leadership over the STUO's, see Smirnov, *STUO's, supra* note 26, pp. 17-20.

35. For a discussion of the relevant provisions of the 1919 Resolution (of the 8th Congress) of the CPSU, see Smirnov, *id.*, p. 18.

36. The formal lifting of this obligation is documented in Smirnov, *STUO's, supra* note 26, p. 18.

37. For a discussion of the reasons for the lifting of this obligation on its members by the CPSU, see Smirnov, *STUO's, supra* note 26, p. 18.

38. Under art. 1 of the Charter of the STUO's (as amended by the 16th Congress of STUO's in March of 1977), membership in STUO's is voluntary.

39. A recent study of the Party affiliation of STUO members shows that over 50% of all *FZMK* chairmen are CPSU members. See Smirnov, *STUO's, supra* note 26, p. 19.

40. For the source of the latest statistics on STUO membership, see note 46 below.

41. A general discussion of the relationship between the STUO's and the Soviet government may be found in Smirnov, *STUO's, supra* note 26, pp. 20-22.

42. The meaning of the "production principle" as the basis for the organization of TUO's in the Soviet Union is spelled out in art. 14 of the Charter of STUO's. It may be noted that when TUO's were first organized in Russia they were organized according to professional affiliation of the workers and not on the basis of the production principle. See V. Smoliarchuk, *Prava profsoiuzov v regulirovanii trudovykh otnoshenii rabochikh i sluzhashchikh* (The Rights of TUO's in the Regulation of the Labor Relations of Workers and Civil Servants), (Moscow, 1973), p. 5 (hereafter cited as Smoliarchuk, *Rights of TUO's*).

43. The number of national TUO's in the Soviet Union tends to change from time to time in order to reflect the current changes in the organization of Soviet national economy. For a full listing of the 22 national TUO's that existed in 1960 see Brown, *Soviet Trade Unions, supra* note 12, p. 68.

44. See Livshits and Nikitinsky, *An Outline of Soviet Labor Law, supra* note 24, p. 26. This figure amounted to about 98 million members. See Smoliarchuk, *Rights of TUO's, supra* note 42, p. 3. But by 1975 the membership of STUO's had increased to 101 million persons. See A. I. Masliaev, *Pravo sobstvennosti profsoiuzov SSSR* (The Right of STUO's to Own Property), (Moscow, 1975), p. 3 (hereafter cited as: Masliaev, *Rights to Own Property*).

45. Traditionally, membership in STUO's had been open to state farm workers and to certain contractual employees of the collective farms; *i.e.* the specialists and machinists. However, the ban against the admission of collective farmers into the trade union was lifted in 1964. Accordingly, under art. 1 of the Charter of STUO's (as amended by

the 16th Congress of STUO's in 1977), collective farm workers may become members of STUO's if they so wish. Many of them have done so. See note 46 below for the latest figures on the general STUO membership.

46. Pursuant to the Preamble to the Charter of STUO's, as well as under art. 1 of the Charter, membership in the TUO's is open to all industrial and agricultural (*i.e.* state farm) workers, transport and construction workers, civil servants working in enterprises or in institutions, including the highest governmental administrators, professional personnel and managers of enterprises, as well as students in institutions of higher learning, in middle specialized schools, and in professional technical schools, without regard to race, national origin, sex or religious belief. Admission is based on application from the prospective member. Action on the application shall be taken by the general meeting of the professional group to which the application was made. The decision of the general meeting of the professional group shall be ratified by the shop committee. In those TUO's where there is no shop committee, the decision of the general meeting of the professional group shall be sent directly to the *FZMK* for ratification. Also, in those trade union cell organizations where there is no professional group, initial action on the application for membership shall be taken by the general meeting of the members of the cell organization.

Prospective applicants pay an application fee in the amount of 1% of the applicant's monthly salary or stipend. (See art. 55 of Charter of STUO's). Upon admission to the organization, the member shall pay a monthly membership due in the amount of .5% of his/her monthly earnings for those who earn less than 70 rubles per month, and 1% for those who earn over 70 rubles per month (see art. 54 of Charter of STUO's).

Membership in STUO's has progressively increased over the years as can be seen from the following table:

In 1918 the membership stood at 2.6 m.;
in 1919– 4.2 m.;   in 1920– 4.2 m.;   in 1921– 8.5 m.;   in 1922– 4.5 m.;
in 1924– 6.4 m.;   in 1926– 9.2 m.;   in 1928–11.5 m.;   in 1932–17.5 m.;
in 1949–28.5 m.;   in 1950–31.5 m.;   in 1954–40.4 m.;   in 1959–52.8 m.;
in 1960–55.2 m.;   in 1963–68.0 m.;   in 1971–98 m..

(See Brown, *Soviet Trade Unions, supra* note 12, p. 48; Smirnov, *STUO's, supra* note 26, p. 201). In 1975 the figures stood at 101 m. At the 16th Congress of the STUO's (March 26, 1977), it was reported that membership in the STUO's then stood at 113.5 m. This figure included: 74 m. workers and 5.6 m. collective farm workers. See Report of Comrade A. I. Shibaeva to the 16th Congress of the STUO's, *Pravda*, March 22, 1977, p. 5. It should be pointed out that these are Soviet official figures and should be appropriately treated as such.

47. See art. 13 of Charter of STUO's.

48. For a vivid discussion of the electoral processes inside a Soviet TUO, see Brown, *Soviet Trade Unions, supra* note 12, pp. 143-152.

49. Even though the elections are by secret ballot, the influence of the CPSU in shaping the outcome of the election of trade union officers cannot be discounted. The CPSU, acting through the local Party organization, nominates a slate of candidates, and even though all the Party nominees may not always get elected, it will be difficult to conceive of a mass rejection of the Party nominees at the polls. The Party, however, does not wish to staff the TUO offices with only members of the CPSU. A highly reliable trade union insider is reported to have told an American student of Soviet trade union movement that "the Party requires at least 40% of all union officers to be non-Party members." See Brown, *Soviet Trade Unions, supra* note 12, p. 93. Not incidentally, the chairman of the *VTsSPS* has always been a high-ranking member of the CPSU.

50. Whereas membership in the TUO's is voluntary as of today, this has not always been so. For example, between 1917-1920 membership in the TUO's was mandatory. For a general discussion of the historical development of membership policy inside STUO's see Brown, *Soviet Trade Unions, supra* note 12, pp. 48-71.

51. The Bill of Rights of union members is listed in arts. 2 and 4 of the Charter of STUO's.

52. The duties of members of STUO's are contained in art. 3 of the Charter of STUO's.

53. See art. 46 of the Charter of STUO's. As of 1977, it was estimated that there were about 700.000 trade union cell organizations throughout the USSR. See Brezhnev, *Soviet Trade Unions, supra* note 29, p. 15.

54. Arts. 16 and 46 of the Charter of STUO's.

55. See art. 48 of the Charter of STUO's. Depending on the size of the membership in the cell organization, the size of the *FZMK* may range from 5-25 members. If the cell organization has less than 15 members, an organizer and a deputy organizer shall be elected instead of an *FZMK*. See art. 48 of the Charter of STUO's. The powers of the *FZMK* are listed in art. 23 of the *KZoT*-RSFSR. For a general discussion of the rights enjoyed by the *FZMK* within the production unit, see Section 4.3. of this study.

56. The shop committees *(tsekhovye komitety)* and trade union bureaus are established by a decision of the *FZMK*. It is estimated that as of 1977 there were about half a million shop committees throughout the Soviet Union. See Brezhnev, *Soviet Trade Unions, supra* note 29, p. 15.

57. The general structure of the regional organs of the STUO's is described in greater detail in art. 38-45 of the Charter of the STUO's.

58. Regional committees with the powers of an *FZMK* are generally formed in those instances where one industrial complex of related enterprises, which employs thousands of workers, is concentrated in one locality. For the purpose of better coordination among the various units of this complex, the workers prefer to elect one umbrella (regional) committee to perform the functions which are normally reserved for the *FZMK* in a one-enterprise operation. In 1972, it was estimated that there were about 10,000 such regional committees throughout the USSR. Such regional committees generally elect their own presidia.

59. The professional group is the lowest group within the cell organization. It enables members of the same profession to group together to further their own professional interests within the framework of the cell organization. The professional group elects its own organizers. As of 1977, it was estimated that there were about 2.5 million professional groups throughout the USSR. See Brezhnev, *Soviet Trade Unions, supra* note 29, p. 15.

60. Under art. 25 of the Charter of STUO's, the Congress of STUO's is the highest organ within this federation of STUO's. It meets once every five years. Because of the large number of delegates who attend the sessions of these congresses (*e.g.* at the 1963 Congress there were 4001 delegates), the Congresses cannot act as a deliberative body. Rather, they meet to lay down policy lines which, in turn, are based on the policy directive issued by the CPSU and its Central Committee. The sessions of the Congress last from a couple of days to just over a week.

61. Between sessions of the Congress of the STUO's, the activities of the Federation of STUO's are coordinated by the *VTsSPS* (art. 28 of the Charter of STUO's). This organ consists of 370 full members and 125 alternate members. It holds its plenary sessions at least once during every six months (art. 31 of the Charter of STUO's). The *VTsSPS*, in turn, elects a Presidium and establishes a Permanent Secretariat, as well as Sections. The offices of the *VTsSPS* are located in Moscow.

62. The Congress is the highest organ within each national TUO. It meets once in 5 years.

63. The Central Committee is elected by the respective Congress of the TUO. It is responsible both to the *VTsSPS* and to the Congress which elected it. The Central Committee, in turn, elects a Presidium which directs its day-to-day operations. The offices of the Central Committees of the 25 national TUO's are located in Moscow.

64. In Soviet law, the term "social organization," *stricto sensu*, is reserved for those voluntary mass organizations which—more or less—enjoy full legal personality and engage in non-economic activities. Generally speaking, the so-called cooperative enterprises are not included among the social organizations. For an encyclopedic discussion of the legal status of the various types of social organizations in Soviet law, see G. Crespi Reghizzi, "Association," in F. Feldbrugge (ed.), *Encyclopedia of Soviet Law* (Leyden, 1973), pp. 61-65.

65. In what is perhaps the best analysis of the legal personality of STUO's under Soviet law, a group of Soviet authors in their 1973 book discussed the status of these organizations from the standpoint of constitutional law, labor law, law of property, other branches of Soviet civil law, as well as Soviet administrative law. See A. I. Tsepin, Ts. A. Iampol'skaia, A. I. Shchiglik, A. I. Masliaev, K. B. Iaroshenko, and E. V. Dodin, *Pravovye aspekty deiatel'nosti profsoiuzov SSSR: profsoiuzy—sub"ekty Sovetskogo prava* (Legal Aspects of the Functions of Trade Unions in the USSR: Trade Unions—Subjects of Soviet Law), (Moscow, 1973), (hereafter to be cited as: A. I. Tsepin *et al., Legal Aspects of the Functions of Trade Unions in the USSR*). For an encyclopedic discussion of the attributes of juridical persons under modern Soviet Law, see A. Hastrich, "Persons," in F. Feldbrugge (ed.), *Encyclopedia of Soviet Law* (Leyden, 1973), pp. 514-515; S. N. Bratus, *Iuridicheskoe litso* (Juridical Person), in S. N. Bratus' *et al., Encyclopedia of Soviet Law, supra* note 4, pp. 510-511.

65a. The liability of a TUO may be limited by law. For example, art. 14, *KZoT*-RSFSR expressly provides that no damages resulting from a violation of a collective bargaining agreement may be assessed against the property of the TUO.

66. See art. 23, RSFSR Civil Code.

67. Art. 225, *KZoT*-RSFSR. This is one of the exceptions contemplated under Soviet civil law. See art. 26 of the RSFSR Civil Code.

68. Art. 26, RSFSR Civil Code.

69. For a detailed discussion of the right of STUO's to own property see Masliaev, *Rights to own Property, supra* note 44.

70. A most comprehensive listing of the objects that trade unions may own may be found in art. 24, FPLL, as well as in art. 103 of the RSFSR Civil Code or in the corresponding article of the civil codes of the other union republics. These two lists are by no means exhaustive of the objects that STUO's may own. Not even the Charter of the individual trade union contains an exhaustive listing of such objects. Rather, the determination as to whether or not a particular TUO may own a specific object shall be made on a case-by-case basis, depending on the nature of the recognized functions of the trade union organization in question. For a detailed analysis of this question, see A. I. Tsepin *et al., Legal Aspects of the Functions of Trade Unions in the USSR, supra* note 65, pp. 297-325.

71. A special chapter in this volume of *Law in Eastern Europe* is devoted to an analysis of the administration of socialist property in the Soviet Union. See S. Pomorski, "Administration of Socialist Property: New Trends," pp. 123-138.

72. The discussion of the contemporary functions of STUO's in this study is based upon the comprehensive listing of the functions of STUO's contained in the Preamble to the Charter of STUO's. See, 1977 Edition of the Charter of STUO's, *supra* note 33, pp. 7-11.

73. For a general discussion of the classical Marxian reference to trade unions as a "school," see Smirnov, *STUO's, supra* note 26, p. 25.

74. See, generally, Smirnov, *id.*, p. 35.

75. The current *Osnovy zakonodatel'stva SSSR i soiuznykh respublik o trude* (The Fundamental Principles of Labor Legislation of the USSR and the Union Republics—FPLL) were promulgated by a Law of the USSR Supreme Soviet of July 15, 1970, and went into force on January 1, 1971. See, *Ved. V.S. SSSR*, 1970, No. 29, item 265. The right of STUO's to participate in the preparation and implementation of state economic plan is provided for in art. 96, FPLL.

76. See art. 2, FPLL. For an economic analysis of wage scales in the USSR see, Brown, *Soviet Trade Unions, supra* note 12, pp. 270-308.

77. See art. 34 of the USSR Constitution.

78. See art. 5, FPLL.

79. The production conferences *(Postoianno-deistvuiushchie proizvodstvennye soveshchaniia)* were first created in the years 1921-1922 as a revolutionary experiment by some Moscow factories. Since then, the PC's have become a regular feature of the Soviet labor scene.

80. A detailed discussion of the structure and operations of these production conferences may be found in Brown, *Soviet Trade Unions, supra* note 12, pp. 248-256.

81. The current *Kodeks zakonov o trude* (Code of Labor Legislation—*KZoT*) of RSFSR was promulgated by Law of the RSFSR Supreme Soviet of December 9, 1971, and it went into effect on April 1, 1972. An official text of the *KZoT*-RSFSR was published by the RSFSR Ministry of Justice in 1972. See *KZoT-RSFSR: Offitsial'nyi tekst* (Official Text), (Moscow, 1972).

82. See art. 27(d) of the Charter of STUO's, as amended by the 16th Congress of STUO's (March 25, 1977).

83. See Livshitz and Nikitinsky, *An Outline of Soviet Labor Law, supra* note 24, p. 26.

84. For an exhaustive listing of the many ways in which the *VTsSPS* exercises its right of legislative initiative see, art. 29, para. (d) of the Charter of STUO's. These activities of the *VTsSPS* are also discussed in Brown, *Soviet Trade Unions, supra* note 12, pp. 80-87.

85. See *Polozhenie o poriadke rassmotreniia trudovykh sporov* (Statute on the Procedure for the Settlement of Labor Disputes), as adopted by a decree of the Presidium of the USSR Supreme Soviet of May 20, 1974, in A. V. Piatkov, N. P. Kolosova, V. P. Silaev, A. M. Koftanovskaia, V. V. Glazyrin, and S. A. Goloshchapov, *Sbornik zakonodatel'nykh aktov o trude* (A Collection of Legislative Acts Relating to Labor Questions), (Moscow, 1974), pp. 942-955 (hereafter to be cited as: A. V. Piatkov *et al., A Collection of Labor Legislation*).

86. See *Polozhenie o pravakh FZMK* (Statute on the Rights of the FZMK), as adopted by a decree of the Presidium of the USSR Supreme Soviet on September 27, 1971, in A. V. Piatkov *et al., A Collection of Labor Legislation, supra* note 85, p. 177.

87. See *Polozhenie o postoianno-deistvuiushchem proizvodstvennom soveshchanii* (Statute on the Permanently Functioning Production Conferences), as adopted by a joint decree of the USSR Council of Ministers and the *VTsSPS* on June 18, 1973, in A. V. Piatkov *et al., A Collection of Labor Legislation, supra* note 85, pp. 985-990.

88. See *"O merakh po dal'neishemu uluchsheniiu okhrany truda na predpriiatiiakh i stroikakh"* (On the Measures Designed to Further Improve the Protection of Labor at Enterprises and Construction Sites), a joint decree of the USSR Council of Ministers and the VTsSPS, issued on January 23, 1962, in A. V. Piatkov *et al., A Collection of Labor Legislation, supra* note 85, pp. 746-748.

89. The trade union inspectors enjoy the same rights as the state technical inspectors, *i.e.* they have full warrantless access to all facilities within the enterprise; they may issue binding orders calling upon the management to correct or eliminate noted violations of work safety conditions at the enterprise. The trade union technical inspectors are appointed by the central and regional organs of the STUO's. In addition to the technical inspectors of the trade unions, there are also the so-called social inspectors of the trade unions. Unlike the technical inspectors who are generally persons with higher technical education, the trade union social inspectors are elected by trade union groups from within the ranks of the workers at each plant and they require no special qualifications to hold the position. These social inspectors help the *FZMK* to gather information relating to work safety at the plant. The social inspectors, after consultation with the technical inspectors, may issue orders to the management requiring the latter to eliminate or correct noted safety violations at the work place.

90. Smirnov, *STUO's, supra* note 26, p. 28.

91. Some of the methods listed here may have been alluded to in our earlier discussion of the participation of STUO's in the administration and economic management of the enterprise. Their inclusion here is intended to emphasize the critical point that STUO's may, in fact, resort to analogous methods in their exercise of ostensibly different functions.

92. Art. 226, *KZoT*-RSFSR.

93. Art. 231, *KZoT*-RSFSR.

94. The present Soviet law regulating working hours and overtime work is contained in arts. 21, 23, 27, 31, 69, and 78, FPLL.

95. The present Soviet law regulating the duration and terms of annual vacation for workers is contained in arts. 66, 67, 68, and 75, *KZoT*-RSFSR.

96. Art. 244, para. 2, *KZoT*-RSFSR.

97. Soviet law (art. 33, *KZoT*-RSFSR) allows the administration on its own initiative to fire a worker without prior consultation with the *FZMK* only in few instances specifically provided for by law. Among such permissible grounds for firing a Soviet worker are the following: liquidation of an enterprise or reduction of staff; worker's lack of the requisite qualification or his incapacity to do the required work; systematic non-fulfillment of labor obligations or violation of state or labor discipline; absence without acceptable excuse; and demand by the cell organization of the trade union to discharge a particular worker. Where discharge is not based on the fault of the worker, two weeks notice or two weeks severance payment is required.

98. Art. 35, *KZoT*-RSFSR.

99. Art. 35, para. 2, arts. 213-215, *KZoT*-RSFSR. For details, see the section of this study dealing with the procedure for the settlement of labor disputes.

100. Arts. 160-172, *KZoT*-RSFSR.

101. Arts. 173-183, *KZoT*-RSFSR.

102. The TUO's right to demand the firing or transfer of an administrator who consistently violates the norms of labor law may not be exercised by a TUO organ below the level of a regional organ. Such a demand by the TUO may be appealed by the defendant administrator or by the administration in his behalf. Such appeals shall be taken to a higher organ of the TUO. Any decision rendered by the appellate organ of the TUO in the case shall be final.

103. Livshits and Nikitinsky, *An Outline of Soviet Labor Law, supra* note 24, pp. 193-194.

104. Livshits and Nikitinsky, *id.*, p. 194.

105. *Id.*, p. 194.

106. As a matter of policy, the determination of workers' wages in the USSR is a

purely governmental function which is within the exclusive jurisdiction of the state planners and as such is placed outside the labor-management decisional processes. Workers' wages cannot be the object of negotiation between the FZMK and the management of the enterprise. Workers' input into the determination of wages is secured through other means. See Section 4.2. of this study for details.

107. Arts. 10 and 223, *KZoT*-RSFSR.

108. Art. 201, *KZoT*-RSFSR.

109. The general law governing the procedure for the settlement of labor disputes is contained in the following acts. FPLL; 1974 USSR Statute on the Procedure for the Settlement of Labor Disputes; arts. 201-224, *KZoT*-RSFSR, as well as the corresponding provisions of the respective labor codes of the other union republics. The procedure for the settlement of labor disputes by the peoples' court (district courts) is set out in the codes of civil procedure of the respective union republics, as well as in art. 210, *KZoT*-RSFSR.

110. For an overview of the procedure for the settlement of labor disputes in Soviet Law, see G. P. van den Berg, "Labor Disputes and Labor Arbitration," in F. Feldbrugge (ed.), *Encyclopedia of Soviet Law* (Leyden, 1973), pp. 369-370.

111. Art. 203, *KZoT*-RSFSR.

112. The general jurisdiction of the *KTS* is contained in art. 204, *KZoT*-RSFSR.

113. For random samples of disputes that have actually come before the *KTS*, see Brown, *Soviet Trade Unions*, *supra* note 12, pp. 207-209.

114. The detailed regulation of the contents and procedure for the conclusion of individual employment contracts may be found in arts. 15-50, *KZoT*-RSFSR. For a general discussion of the nature and contents of the individual contract of employment, see G. P. van den Berg, "Contract of Employment," in F. Feldbrugge (ed.), *Encyclopedia of Soviet Law* (Leyden, 1973), pp. 248-251. Art. 5, *KZoT*-RSFSR provides that any provision of an individual employment contract which diminishes an employee's rights as guaranteed under law shall be null and void *ab initio*.

115. Art. 204, *KZoT*-RSFSR.

116. Art. 205, *KZoT*-RSFSR.

117. Art. 206, *KZoT*-RSFSR.

118. If the initial decision was rendered by the shop *KTS*, it may be appealed by the worker to the plant (factory) *KTS*.

119. Art. 207, *KZoT*-RSFSR.

120. Art. 217, *KZoT*-RSFSR.

121. Art. 218, *KZoT*-RSFSR.

122. Art. 209, *KZoT*-RSFSR.

123. Art. 209, para. 2, *KZoT*-RSFSR.

124. Art. 211, *KZoT*-RSFSR.

125. Art. 211, *KZoT*-RSFSR.

126. Art. 212, *KZoT*-RSFSR.

127. Art. 213, *KZoT*-RSFSR.

128. Art. 214, *KZoT*-RSFSR.

129. Smirnov, *STUO's*, supra note 26, p. 35.

130. See International Labor Office, *Trade Union Rights in the USSR* (Geneva, 1959), p. 74.

131. *Id.*, 74, as cited in Brown, *Soviet Trade Unions*, *supra* note 12, p. 230.

132. For a general discussion of the right, *vel non*, of STUO's to organize labor strikes, see C. Osakwe, *Soviet Participation*, *supra* note 1, pp. 60-61.

133. Neither the Soviet government nor the officially controlled Soviet press, as a matter of policy, would report incidents of workers' strikes in the USSR. Reports of

illegal strikes, however, have filtered to the West through various secondary sources, *i.e.* observations of Western diplomats and correspondents stationed in the USSR, and eye-witness accounts by foreign exchange students studying in the USSR, etc.

134. See *"Polozhenie o pravakh FZMK"* (Statute on the Rights of the *FZMK*), the major provisions of the 1971 federal Statute of the *FZMK* have been incorporated into art. 230, *KZoT*-RSFSR of 1972 which today is the most comprehensive codification of the rights of the *FZMK*.

135. A detailed regulation of the form, contents, and procedure for the conclusion of bargaining agreements may be found in arts. 7-14, of *KZoT*-RSFSR. Other relevant rules regarding these matters are contained in the following sources: Arts. 6-7, FPLL; Arts. 1-12 of *Postanovlenie o zakliuchenii kollektivnykh dogovorov na predpriiatiiakh* (Decree on The Conclusion of Collective Bargaining Agreements at the Enterprise), adopted jointly by the USSR Council of Ministers and *VTsSPS* on March 6, 1966. See A. V. Piatkov, *et al., A Collection of Labor Legislation, supra* note 85, pp. 92-93; Arts. 1-15 of *Postanovlenie o poriadke zakliucheniia kollektivnykh dogovorov* (Decree on the Procedure for the Conclusion of Collective Bargaining Agreements), adopted jointly by the Presidium of *VTsSPS* and the State Committee on Labor and Wages on August 20, 1971, and as amended on August 31, 1973. See A. V. Piatkov, *id.*, pp. 93-97.

136. Smirnov, *STUO's, supra* note 26, p. 71.

137. Art. 7, *KZoT*-RSFSR.

138. Art. 9, *KZoT*-RSFSR.

139. Art. 7, *KZoT*-RSFSR.

140. A more detailed discussion of the provisions of a typical Soviet collective bargaining agreement may be found in Brown, *Soviet Trade Unions, supra* note 12, pp. 186-194. Art. 8, *KZoT*-RSFSR also lists those items that are generally covered by collective bargaining agreements.

141. Art. 8, *KZoT*-RSFSR.

142. Art. 7, *KZoT*-RSFSR.

143. Brown, *Soviet Trade Unions, supra* note 12, p. 186.

144. It is true, of course, that the TUO as a juridical person may sue and be sued in its own name, including suit arising from its breach of the collective bargaining agreement. But as a measure of protection of the TUO's against such suits, art. 14, *KZoT*-RSFSR expressly provides that the TUO, as an entity, is immuned from any monetary damages that may result from a violation of a collective bargaining agreement. See our general discussion of the legal personality of STUO's in Section 3.3. of this study.

145. Art. 12, *KZoT*-RSFSR.

146. Robin Knight, "Why Workers Want to Flee USSR," *US News and World Report*, May 29, 1978, 57.

147. Art. 43 of the USSR Constitution.

148. Art. 237, *KZoT*-RSFSR. The failure of the enterprise to make contributions towards the workers' social insurance and pension fund would not deprive the deserving worker of the payment of benefits to which he is otherwise entitled (art. 237, *KZoT*-RSFSR).

149. The general regulation of the state social insurance system may be found in arts. 237-243, *KZoT*-RSFSR, and in arts. 100-103, FPLL.

150. See art. 238, *KZoT*-RSFSR.

151. The conditions and terms of old age pension under present Soviet law are contained in art. 242, *KZoT*-RSFSR.

152. Art. 243, *KZoT*-RSFSR.

153. Soviet social insurance system was made applicable to the collective farm workers by a Law of 1964—*Zakon o pensiiakh i posobiiakh chlenam kolkhozov* (Law on

Pensions and Other Benefits to Members of Collective Farms). Pursuant to the decree of the 24th Congress of the CPSU "On the 9th 5-year Plan" (issued on July 1, 1971), members of the collective farms are now subject to the same system for the computation of retirement age as is used for the workers and civil servants. In 1969, the 3rd All-Union Congress of Collective Farm Workers adopted a Resolution to follow a unified social insurance system for all collective farm workers. According to this Resolution, all collective farms shall make periodic contributions to the Central Fund For the Social Insurance of Collective Farm Workers. At the request of the highest organ of the collective farm workers' organization—the Union Council of Collective Farms—the responsibility for the administration of collective farm workers social insurance system is entrusted to the STUO's.

154. Art. 100, FPLL.

155. The use of the social insurance funds for an undesignated purpose is categorically prohibited by Soviet law. See art. 238, para. 3, *KZoT*-RSFSR.

156. Smirnov, *STUO's, supra* note 26, p. 176.

157. For an overview of Soviet housing norms and their application, see, D. Barry, "Soviet Housing Law. The Norms and Their Application," in D. Barry, G. Ginsburgs, P. Maggs (eds.), *Soviet Law After Stalin, Part I, The Citizen and the State in Contemporary Soviet Law* (Leyden, 1977), pp. 1-32; B. Rudden, "Housing Law," in F. Feldbrugge (ed.), *Encyclopedia of Soviet Law* (Leyden, 1973), pp. 314-316.

158. See arts. 296, 298, RSFSR Civil Code.

159. See Smirnov, *STUO's, supra* note 18, p. 146.

160. Program of the CPSU, (1971 Russian ed.), p. 62.

161. Smirnov, *STUO's, supra* note 26, p. 47.

162. This means that there must be at least two competing parties (*i.e.* individual workers or workers' collectives) who shall enter into an agreement to compete. The competition agreement shall set out a goal for the competitors, as well as a time framework for achieving such goal. For example, two workers' collectives might agree to compete under the following slogan: "We promise to fulfill the 9th 5-Year Plan ahead of schedule."

163. See art. 131, *KZoT*-RSFSR.

164. See arts. 133, 134, *KZoT*-RSFSR.

165. As of 1972, it was estimated that there were over 21,600 trade union clubs throughout the Soviet Union. According to the provision of the Statute on Trade Union Clubs, a trade union club is "a center of cultural education among the masses. It is designed to propagate political, scientific-technical, economic, and general knowledge among the workers, as well as to ensure that their rest period is spent in a manner that is culturally enriching." The 24th Congress of the CPSU directed the trade union clubs to make the creation of the "new man" one of their major functions. (See Smirnov, *STUO's, supra* note 26, p. 158.) The decision to open a trade union club is generally taken by the *FZMK* under whose direction the clubs operate.

166. Red corners (*krasnye ugolki*) are different from trade union clubs. A red corner is a small room set aside inside an enterprise, institution, or workers' dormitory where lectures on matters of current interests are held. The decision to set up a red corner is made by the *FZMK*, but the day-to-day operation of the red corner is placed under the direction of a council which is elected by the *FZMK*. The space for the red corner, as well as the furniture inside it, is provided by the management of the enterprise or institution.

167. As of 1972, it was estimated that the STUO's were operating over 28,000 public libraries with total book holdings in excess of 272 million volumes. (See Smirnov, *STUO's, supra* note 26, p. 169.) During that same year these trade libraries had a readership of about 24 m. people, *i.e.* about 20% of all the users of Soviet libraries. (See

Smirnov, *STUO's, supra* note 26, p. 169.)

168. The purpose of any official Soviet newspaper is to propagate the idea of communism among the masses. In this regard, STUO newspapers are not different from all the other official Soviet newspapers. The STUO's publish numerous newspapers and journals, the best known of which are *Trud* (with an estimated daily circulation of 5.5 m. in 1972); *Sovetskii Profsoiuz* (a bi-monthly journal of the *VTsSPS*); *Okhrana Truda*; *Sotsial'noe Strakhovanie*; *Klub i Khudozhestvennaia Samodeiatel'nost'*; *Turist*; *Izobretatel' i Ratsionalizator;* and *Sovetskii Shakhter*; etc. STUO's also operate their own printing press — the *Profizdat* — which is located in Moscow.

169. Smirnov, *STUO's, supra* note 26, p. 190.

170. See Preamble to the Charter of STUO's.

171. As of 1972, it was estimated that the STUO's maintained working contacts with trade union organizations in about 116 different countries. In 1971 alone, the STUO's received, at their invitation, visits from 764 foreign TUO's. In 1950, the number of such visits by foreign TUO's to the USSR was 61 but in 1960 it had grown to 260. See Smirnov, *STUO's, supra* note 26, p. 219.

172. Smirnov, *STUO's, supra* note 26, p. 217.

173. This Marxist-Leninist analysis of the socio-economic foundations of trade unionism is corroborated by the vivid account of the history of unionization of American workers as given in A. Cox, D. C. Bok, and R. Gorman, *Labor Law: Cases and Materials*, (Mineola, NY, 1977), pp. 7-18.

174. In the words of Selig Perlman, the AFL is dedicated to "a philosophy of pure wage consciousness," *i.e.* it is a "labor movement reduced to an opportunistic basis, accepting the existence of capitalism and having for its object the enlarging of the bargaining power of the wage earner in the scale of his labor." In other words, it is a trade union movement which is committed to "an attitude of aloofness from all those movements which aspire to replace the wage system by cooperation, whether voluntary or subsidized by government, whether greenbackism, socialism or anarchism." S. Perlman, *History of Trade Unionism in the United States*, (1922), p. 78, as cited in Cox, Bok and Gorman, *supra* note 173, p. 11.

175. See, generally, V. Smoliarchuk, *The Rights of Trade Unions, supra* note 42, pp. 21-42.

176. The General Statute on Tariff was adopted in 1920. See *Sobr. Uzak.*, 1920, Nos. 61-62, item 276, arts. 22, 31, and 71.

177. *Sobr. Zak. SSSR*, 1933, No. 40, item 238.

178. See Decree of the *SNK-SSSR* "On The Procedure for the Issuance of Instructions, Rules, and Interpretations in Implementation of Labor Legislation", *Sobr. Zak. SSSR*, 1934, No. 43, item 342.

179. See *Spravochnik profsoiuznogo rabotnika* (A Handbook for Trade Union Activists), (Moscow, 1972), p. 46.

180. See *Sobr. Post. SSSR*, 1965, Nos. 19-20, item 153.

181. A joint Decree of the Central Committee of the CPSU and the Council of Ministers of the USSR "On The Transfer of Additional Matters Relating to Economic and Cultural Construction to the Jurisdiction of the Union Republics", *Sobr. Post. SSSR*, 1965, Nos. 19-20, item 153.

182. Adopted by the Council of Ministers of the USSR on October 4, 1965. See *Sobr. Post. SSSR*, 1965, Nos. 19-20, item 155.

183. See *Ved. V.S. SSSR* 1970, No. 29, item 265.

184. Adopted on September 27, 1971. See *Ved. V.S. SSSR*, 1971, No. 39, item 382.

185. See V. I. Nikitinskii, "Professional'nye soiuzy" (Trade Unions), in S. N. Bratus' *et al.*, *Encyclopedia of Soviet Law, supra* note 4, p. 391.

THE COMMUNIST PARTY AND THE ADMINISTRATION OF JUSTICE IN THE USSR

Robert Sharlet

The Stalinist period was marked by a heavy-handed Party and secret police domination, and even preemption, of the administration of justice. In the late 1920s and early 1930s during the forced collectivization campaign, a virtual tidal wave of political justice washed over the legal system, marooning even judicial officials themselves in the countryside.[1] In the cities and towns after 1934, the reorganized "special boards" began the mass production of the "manufacture of deviance" which bypassed the ordinary administration of justice, sweeping up many legal cadres in the process, as a wide range of conduct and non-conduct was simultaneously politicized and criminalized.[2] After Stalin's turn toward legal stabilization in the late 1930s, the floodtide of political justice slowly receded as Party supervision of and interference in the restabilized judiciary gradually became more salient. The revolutionary storm "from above" began to wane, to be replaced by a greater degree of bureaucratic institutionalization of the Soviet system, including its legal subsystem.[3]

By the time of Stalin's death in 1953, this process apparently had not yet been completed, judging by the materials of the 20th Party Congress and related legal policy statements which indicated that secret police influence still exceeded Party authority in the ordinary as well as in the extra-judicial administration of justice in the USSR.[4] Since Stalin, a major priority and administrative objective has been the Party's resumption of control over the security apparatus and its former satellite, the legal system. The main task was accomplished very early in the post-Stalin period through the reorganization and subordination of the monolithic secret police to the Party-state apparatus, but the secondary objective has proved more elusive and remains an on-going problem as the Party continues to perfect its control over the administration of justice. The purpose of this chapter is to explore the Party's *modus operandi* in theory and practice and attempt to evaluate how effective it may be. Emphasis will be on criminal justice and its derivative "political justice."

321

1. Party Control of Justice in Theory

Party control over the administration of justice in the post-Stalin period has been legitimated through an interconnecting network of doctrinal pronouncements, Party rules, constitutional clauses, legislative principles, policy statements, and learned commentary on law.

In the spirit of the Party as "the brain, the honor, and the conscience . . . of the Soviet people," the 1961 Party Program projects the "further *enhancement of the role and importance of the Communist Party* as the leading and guiding force of Soviet society."[5] In this context, the Program announces that the "Party calls for enforcing strict observance of socialist legality, for eradication of all violations of law and order, for the abolition of crime and the removal of all its causes" through the "further *strengthening* of the socialist legal order . . . ."[6]

The Rules of the CPSU echo the Party Charter, describing the CPSU as the "tried and tested militant vanguard . . ." that "directs the great creative activity of the Soviet people . . . ."[7] The Preamble adds that strict Party discipline in the ranks is an inviolable law of the CPSU.[8] With the administration of justice in mind, it should be noted that Party membership entails acceptance of the Party Program *and* Rules, participation in the activity of a Party group or organization, and the carrying out of "all Party decisions."[9]

Other rules which ensure that Party jurists, as well as all other members, give primary allegiance to political creed over occupational loyalty, include displaying vigilance (#I-1-f), resisting all actions injurious to the Party-state (#I-1-g), applying political criteria in personnel selection (*nomenklatura:* #I-1-h), and observing "Party and State discipline, which is equally binding on all Party members . . . irrespective of their past services or the positions they occupy" (#I-1-i). For those who violate Party discipline, Rule #9 prescribes a series of penalties up to expulsion from the Party. To protect the inviolability of the Party as an institution, members committing criminal offenses shall be first expelled from the Party and then prosecuted (#12).

In addition, the duties of subnational Party organizations include "guidance" of the organs of the administration of justice "through Party groups in them while taking care not to usurp their duly constituted functions" (#42-c). Finally, primary Party organizations in legal institutions are expected "to inform the appropriate Party bodies in good time about shortcomings in the work of the respective offices and individuals, regardless of what posts the latter may occupy" (#60), while the smaller "Party groups" are assigned the task of "strengthening the influence of the Party in every way . . . and verifying the fulfillment of Party and government directives" (#68).

Promulgated seventeen years after the 1961 Program and the since-amended Party Rules, the USSR Constitution of 1977 proclaims that the leading role of the Party "has grown" since the 1936 Constitution. The new Constitution, which codifies the main themes of the post-Stalin reforms, has moved the CPSU from the back of the 1936 state charter to the very front of the current document.

Although much of the "Party hegemony" clause is familiar, the constitutional emphasis and some of the language is new. After pronouncing the CPSU "the hegemonial force of Soviet society" as well as the "nucleus of its political system" and legal subsystem, the framers added the amendment "All Party organizations operate within the framework of the USSR Constitution," a promising but puzzling commitment by an essentially meta-juridical institution (Art. 6). [10] The Party clause—coupled with the Party's continued, implicit constitutional "right to nominate" candidates (Art. 100) for election to judicial office—strengthens the CPSU's position in the new Constitution in general and with regard to the administration of justice in particular.

In the second section of the 1977 Constitution, the Party and the draftsmen have given the citizen's rights and duties *vis-à-vis* the state far more prominent placement than in the 1936 document. The basic "protections" for the individual against arbitrary actions by the legal and extra-judicial organs of the state have been carried over from the preceding Constitution, but now with better prospects for compliance in most cases (Arts. 57-58). Several affirmative rights have been added, affording the citizen some constitutional leverage *vis-à-vis* the state, although not the Party apparatus (Arts. 49 and 58).

The clauses on the administration of justice are located in Part VII of the Constitution and, while they reflect the marked post-Stalin improvement in both law and practice of the citizen's status in the criminal justice system, they suggest no constitutional reduction or qualification of the Party's control over the justice process in general.

The "judicial independence" clause has been carried over from the Stalin Constitution with the single change that the people's assessors have been brought within its purview, making them "independent and subordinate only to law" as well (Art. 155). This is consistent with article 9 of the 1959 Basic Principles of Legislation on the Judicial System. [11] However, it is an axiom of Soviet jurisprudence that an independent judiciary in the Western sense of the term is not intended here. On the contrary, while political interference in particular non-political cases is generally ruled out, Party supervision over the judicial process is not, as the USSR Ministry of Justice journal *Soviet Justice* has clearly stated:

> "Guidance by the Communist Party surpasses all political and judicial means of assuring that the courts observe socialist legality in their actions. . . . The task of the local Party organization is, while not interfering in the judicial process, actively to influence courts to improve their work, to instill in officers of the court a high sense of responsibility, to take steps to strengthen discipline, [and] fulfill Party and government decisions." [12]

Several public proposals to further buffer the court from possible outside pressures were put forward during the constitutional discussion of 1977, but quietly ignored in the revision and ratification process. [13] Almost as if in a low-keyed rebuttal, the Soviet press later published a brief statement summarizing the consensual understanding of judicial independence: "The Party organs oversee the selection, placement, and ideological education of juridical cadres. But, at the same time, any kind of interference in the administration of justice in specific cases is absolutely ruled out." [14] However, this non-debate never questioned the various opportunities for Party influence over individual cases within and internal to the judicial process as expressed, for instance, in the criminal and civil procedural basic principles, as well as the corresponding republican codes. All of the relevant "judicial independence" articles echo the official formulation with an added proviso which does not appear in the new Constitution. Judges and people's assessors in both criminal and civil process are expected to decide cases on the basis of law but "in conformity with socialist legal consciousness" as well. [15] The particular admixture of Party-orientation (*partiinost'*) in any given judge's conception of "socialist legal consciousness" cannot, of course, be determined, but its presence should never be doubted.

Even though the Soviet version of "presumption of innocence" (Art. 160) has now been given constitutional authority, and the "right to defense" clause (Art. 158) has been reinforced by the constitutional recognition of the colleges of advocates (*advokatura*) (Art. 161), these changes are best understood as enhancing the defendant's position *vis-à-vis* the procurator and court rather than weakening the Party's posture with regard to the state authorities in this area.

In fact, the 1977 state charter has constitutionally strengthened Party leverage in the administration of justice through the combination of a stronger "Party hegemony" clause (Art. 6) with the new "political culture" clause (Art. 9) which implicitly encourages peer justice, as well as the introduction of a "social accuser/defender" clause which elevates to constitutional status the role of the representative of the collective (*kollektiv*) in the criminal trial process (Art. 162). In practice, both comrades' courts and social accusers permit greater, direct Party influence in the administration of Soviet justice.

The formal legitimation of Party control over the administration of justice is found not only in fundamental Party and state documents, but is periodically reaffirmed in Party statements on legal policy and regularly reiterated in learned juridical commentary. [16]

A priority task of the post-Stalin period was criticism of the "cult of personality," and the reassertion of Party control over socialist legality. The 20th Party Congress of 1956 acknowledged the problem in one resolution and addressed the remedy in another. After acknowledging the secret police's service to the Party up to the early 1930s, a resolution of the Congress continued: "The situation changed after the supervision of these organs by the Party and the government gradually came to be replaced by the personal supervision of Stalin; and his individual decisions were frequently substituted for the ordinary administration of the norm of justice." [17]

Turning to the remedy, the Party in another resolution added:

> "The Congress fully supports the measures effected by the Central Committee to strengthen Soviet legality, to ensure strict observance of the rights of citizens, as guaranteed by the Soviet Constitution, and places all party and soviet organs under the obligation of vigilantly guarding legality, of putting an end—severely and decisively—to any manifestation of lawlessness, arbitrariness, or violation of the socialist legal order." [18]

Five years later, before the 22nd Party Congress in 1961, Khrushchev summarized what had taken place in the phrase "The 20th Congress restored justice. . . ." [19] Following up on this, A. N. Shelepin, then *KGB* chairman, assured the Congress that Party control had been reestablished over the secret police which "have been reorganized, . . . cut down substantially, relieved of functions not proper to them and purged of careerist elements." He added that the Party had assigned a large number of its own personnel to the *KGB*, ensuring that the organization was "under continued supervision of the Party and the government. . . ." Signalling the demise of the Stalinist "special boards," Shelepin concluded to prolonged applause "Today no one can be adjudged guilty of committing a crime and punished other than by sentence of a court." [20]

By the time of the 24th Party Congress a decade later in 1971, socialist legality had been fully rehabilitated and Brezhnev, in his "Report," indicated that the Party was continuing to *"strengthen legality and law and order."* Towards this end, he reported that the work of the organs of the administration of justice had been improved in the preceding five year period since the 23rd Party Congress of 1966. [21] Most recently before the 25th Party Congress in 1976, Brezhnev spoke confidently of Party "control" as an accomplished fact which would be continually perfected by the CPSU's "constant attention to improving the activity of the *militia, the procurator's office, the courts and the organs of justice . . . ,*" and by providing them with "well-trained and worthy cadres." [22]

Finally, Soviet jurists have contributed to the reification of Party control over justice, by converting it from a projected policy into an *a priori* premise of contemporary post-Stalin juridical scholarship.

From Soviet political philosophy to legal theory, the subordination of law to politics, of the legal system to Party leadership, is reiterated in myriad variations on the common theme. A specialist on "scientific communism" distinguishes between the political and legal "superstructures" and subordinates the latter to the former. [23] A prominent legal philosopher writes of the internal unity of the "Soviet political-legal superstructure" with law as the expression of Party policy.[24] A juridical study of the decisions of the 22nd Party Congress describes law as "one of the most important instruments for implementing Party and state policy". [25] A similar study a decade later declares that the 24th Party Congress had reinforced the Party's "line in strengthening socialist legality and the legal order." [26] Specifically, the team of jurists authoring the volume state:

> "After the 23rd Party Congress, measures were taken to further strengthen the organs of internal affairs, the court, and the Procuracy; to create the USSR Ministry of Internal Affairs and the union-republic Ministry of Justice of the USSR; [and] to improve the working conditions of the organs leading the struggle against lawbreaking . . . . The 24th Party Congress recognized the necessity and further improved the work of the court, the Procuracy, and the militia. . . ." [27]

The latest volume, based on the 25th Party Congress, emphazises that in "developed socialism" the Party continues to exercise its control over the organs of justice as an essential component of its objective of perfecting a "system of stable legality and a durable legal order." [28] All of this juridical exegesis of the Party-justice relationship falls within the context of the important post-Stalin study by the Academy of Science's Law Institute, which was addressed to correcting and avoiding the repetition of past errors. The authors, under the aegis of the leading reform jurist Academician M. S. Strogovich, express an operative meaning of the interaction of politics and law:

> "The principle of the independence of the court and its subordination to law cannot ... be interpreted to mean that the court in its activity stands outside of politics, that in being guided in its decisions only by law, the court somehow exempts itself from participating in the resolution of those immediate political tasks which the Party and the government place before the state and all of Soviet society in each specific historical period."

The authors unequivocally concluded that "the court does not stand and cannot stand outside of politics . . . beyond the guidance of the Party."[29]

2. Party Control of Justice from Theory to Practice

Party hegemony over the administration of justice begins with the power of appointment over all key legal personnel which is vested at the highest level in the Central Committee Secretariat. Long gone is the time when the Party had to directly conscript its members for law school and eventually

326

judicial roles. [30] Today with the abundance of legally-trained and politically-reliable candidates for juridical office, the Party's role in this process is far more refined and calculated. Nomination for election or direct appointment to legal office is vested in an appropriate legally competent governmental or social authority, but subject to the power of appointment (*nomenklatura*) of the corresponding supervisory body in the parallel Party hierarchy.

This means, in effect, that prior to the formal, juristic acts of nomination or appointment, a designated Party body first must give its approval to the pre-nomination or pre-appointment before either can be officially finalized. For instance, the eventual successor to R. A. Rudenko as Procurator-General of the USSR will be legally appointed by the USSR Supreme Soviet, but only after prior approval by the Party, probably by the Politburo itself on recommendation from the Secretariat of the Central Committee because of the significance of the post. The Procuracy, in turn, is empowered to make certain subappointments, but again subject to the same political norms. For example, the USSR Procurator-General shares the power of appointment (or "patronage") over the senior positions in the All-Union Institute for the Study and Prevention of Crime, with the Chairman of the USSR Supreme Court and, as Peter Solomon reports, "Before the file of a person recommended for one of these positions reached the Procurator-General it had to include the approval of a Party organ (the level would depend on the position and the man chosen)." [31]

This process continues on down through the system with lower Party organizations carefully screening nominations for judicial election and even the candidates for election as people's assessor. [32] The result is that all those who investigate, prosecute, preside, defend, and even study the administration of justice in the USSR, first must pass through a system of political filters before they can take office or assume their responsibilities. For Lesage, *nomenklatura* is the "very symbol of the Party's directing role" as its most effective instrument of control over the Soviet system generally, and its legal subsystem in particular, because incumbent legal cadres cannot be reappointed, renominated, transferred, or even relieved of their offices except again with the prior approval of the Party organs on whose *nomenklatura* they are listed. [33]

In the Central Committee Secretariat, the Administrative Organs Department exercises the power of *nomenklatura* for the highest legal offices and, along with its hierarchy of subordinate branches down to the level of the Regional Party committee (*obkom*), supervises and carries out spot checks on the administration of justice in all of its aspects. This includes supervision over "the *KGB*, the Ministry of Justice, the *MVD*, courts, soviets, colleges of advocates, and the Procuracy." [34] Simultaneously, supervision over the support functions of legal education and research is carried out by the Central Committee's Department of Science and Educational Institutions and its local branches. [35]

327

Apparently, the Administrative Organs Department under Khrushchev played an important role not only through supervising the legal system, but also in restoring Party control over the security agencies, the courts, and the Procuracy after years of Stalinist abuses and arbitrariness. This was especially true under the leadership of N. R. Mironov, a former *KGB* official who headed the Department from 1959 until his death in 1964. [36] He died in a plane crash in October, the month that Khrushchev was ousted, and a replacement was not immediately appointed to head the Department. Instead, Shelepin assumed the duties of the post along with his other responsibilities until 1966, when M. A. Suslov began to oversee the Department's work. [37] Finally, in 1968 N. I. Savinkin, the first deputy, was appointed to head the Department of Administrative Organs.

According to Solomon's information, the Department's staff, at least between 1964 and 1968, was small. The Legal Affairs Section, which under Mironov was responsible for the courts, Procuracy, *MVD-MOOP* and, since 1970, the Ministry of Justice as well, had only five or six staff members, including one instructor for supervising the court system. [38] Generally, this Section primarily performed its supervisory duties in connection with personnel selection and questions of policy implementation, with much less time left for policy-making questions compared to the better-staffed higher legal agencies which are being "supervised." Possibly to close this supervisory gap, Savinkin or one of his deputies has made it a practice of representing the Department at nearly every top level meeting on "law and order" problems, although these meetings have tended to bear more on corrective measures rather than new policy proposals. [39]

The need to carry out supervision over a wide front is less pronounced below the national level. The subordinate work of the Administrative Organs Department at the Regional Party committee level is performed by the Department of Administrative, Trade, and Financial Organs whose main focus is ideological work and verification of decisions in the regional legal system and security apparatus within its jurisdiction. This leads to the tentative conclusion that Party supervisory control over the administration of justice may be more extensive and intensive at the republic-level of the Party where more staff and resources are available, and, presumably, below which supervision is most needed. Conversely, the power of *nomenklatura* is probably employed with greater precision and reliability at the top where the implications of nomination or appointment are greatest. [40]

3. Party Control of Justice in Practice

The line between Party "supervision" of and "interference" in the administration of justice is usually a clear one. "Supervision" is intended to mean cadre selection, placement, and ideological education, and periodic review of the implementation of Party policy and governmental directives by legal organs. [41] For example, the Party organizations of the USSR Ministry of Justice and its branches took the lead in developing a plan for improving the work of training legal cadres for the courts and other justice institutions based on a 5-10 year perspective on their cadre requirements. [42] Similarly, in recent years, the Moscow City Party Committee has devoted the greatest part of its supervisory effort to cadre work in the Procuracy organs as a way of improving their effectiveness. [43]

Cadre work, however, does not cease with personnel selection. Procurators, judges, and other justice personnel then become subject to the Party principle of "raising the ideological and political level of cadres." This includes, for instance, Party supervision over the political education of judges who are "obliged to systematically study Marxist-Leninist theory and the classics of Marxism-Leninism . . . in Party schools and universities of Marxism-Leninism, as well as the history of the Communist Party, the decisions of Party congresses and plenums, and the resolutions of the CPSU Central Committee," all of which are the most effective means for "raising the political knowledge of workers in the judicial organs." [44]

In performing their ideological function beyond the legal cadres themselves, Moscow City Party organizations have also devoted a considerable amount of time to the supervision of the legal propaganda work of municipal law enforcement agencies towards the objective of raising the level of "legal culture" among Muscovites. For instance, the Dzerzhinskii District Party Committee, which was concerned about the incidence of petty theft and violations of state and labor discipline in a local factory, oversaw the necessary law enforcement work, but also followed up by organizing a program of "lectures and talks on legal themes" in the factory by District Procuracy personnel. [45]

However, the line between Party supervision and interference in the organs of justice narrows considerably in the performance of the implementation-review function. Mironov, in his writings in the early 1960s, set the tone for what is expected of Party organizations in the post-Stalin period in terms of this review function. Party bodies should systematically check the work of the justice organs, "hear reports from the leading personnel of the Procuracy, courts, and militia in District, City, and Regional Party committees, sharply calling to account those cadres who perform poorly, mismanage a case, fail to solve crimes, or violate legality themselves." [46] And, he added, Party organs should not hesitate to relieve incompetent legal cadres of their responsibilities. [47] By way of an example of a vigorous Party review, Mironov as a Central Committee official castigated the militia and Procuracy for poor work in law enforcement, including the failure to coordinate between organs of inquiry and preliminary investigation in uncovering criminal conduct, the lack of responsiveness to citizens' "tips" so that crimes remain undiscovered, and the generally unsatisfactory performance of cadres in not apprehending, investigating, and prosecuting the many recidivists and other criminals still at large. [48]

In contrast, impermissible Party "interference" in the administration of justice clearly is intended to mean when a Party organ or official goes beyond an aggregate review of the quality and quantity of work in the justice apparatus and directly intervenes in the disposition of an individual case at one stage or another, by bringing political pressure to bear on the arresting officer or his superior, the investigator assigned to the case, the procurator charged with its prosecution, or the presiding judge or assessors. All Party organs are frequently warned against preempting the functions of the state institutions they supervise, and reminded that the Party apparatus is the "staff" in a staff-line relationship to the state. [49] Nonetheless, the problem apparently persists because general statements—such as Brezhnev's that "Party bodies must completely eliminate their petty tutelage of the government bodies and the practice of overriding them . . ."—are periodically issued by higher Party bodies. [50]

In particular, specific prohibitions against Party organizations' "petty tutelage" in the administration of justice appear with regularity in the political and legal literature, which suggests that Party interference may be a recurring problem. Shortly after Stalin's death, the CPSU Central Committee had adopted a special resolution concerning the "impermissibility of illegal interference by local Party organs in the direct work of the courts and procurators." [51] Yet, a book on the 22nd Party Congress published in 1963 was still condemning Stalinist practices, and the author found it necessary to deny in the most uncompromising terms that Party supervision of the organs of justice had anything "in common with the interference by Party committees and their officials in the resolution of specific judicial cases, [or] with exerting political or moral pressure on judges, procurators, and investigators." [52]

By 1977, the emphasis had become more affirmative than prohibitive. Declaring that the necessity of ensuring politically that the Procuracy is independent and subordinate only to law is one of the "most important principles of Party supervision" in the field of justice, a prominent legal scientist wrote that Party organs must use all of their authority to guard the Procuracy agencies from any kind of outside interference. [53] He concludes that Party interference in the justice process is not only a violation of Party discipline, but a "violation of socialist legality" as well. [54]

Nevertheless, the literature continues to suggest that Party organs do sometimes go beyond their general supervisory function and interfere in specific cases in the criminal justice process, apparently more often than not on behalf of their own officials or members who have run afoul of the law. During his incumbency as head of the Administrative Organs Department of the Cen-

330

tral Committee Secretariat, Mironov brought this problem to public notice. In a 1962 lecture at the Higher Party School, he stated:

"It must be said that not all Party organizations supervise the organs of justice correctly. It often happens that some Party workers see their role not only in systematically working with cadres, but also in dictating their opinion concerning the resolution of one or another specific case under investigation. More often than not, this occurred when the question being decided concerned the criminal reponsibility of a Party member who had committed crimes." [55]

Echoes of Mironov's criticism, as well as actual cases appearing in the legal press today, indicate a continuing gap between the theory and practice of Party control of the administration of justice, although, as will be seen, the "problem" seems to be more diverse and complex than even the candid Mironov cared to admit or criticize.

The distinction between mandated supervisory review and political interference in justice by the Party, can be seen in two studies of the Soviet-type East German and Czech legal systems of the 1950s. Otto Kirchheimer, relying on GDR legal literature, has described the formal structure of the Party-justice relationship, while Otto Ulč, a Czech judge from 1953 to 1959, drew on his experience to fill in the informal relationships as well. The GDR, absent relevant information about the informal structure, can be taken as a model of the "correct line" of Party supervision of the administration of justice, while the richly documented Czech study can serve as a case study of the "incorrect line" of Party interference in justice.

In the GDR, the judge is politically "controlled" from above by "instructors," and from below by the court's Party unit. Instructors, presumably with Party affiliation, operating out of the Ministry of Justice and the Office of the Attorney General, regularly supervise district courts and district prosecutors, while instructors from the local branches of the two agencies perform the same function at the level of the local court. In the words of a GDR Minister of Justice, an instructor is a "helper and political advisor" to the judge. [56] Or, as Kirchheimer aptly puts it, "In the person of the instructor, the job of functional and political supervision merge; he studies, compares, evaluates, and criticizes the judge's performance from both professional and political viewpoints." [57]

The instructor's task is to help the judge constantly improve on his performance both judicially and politically, in the latter sense by repeatedly sensitizing him to the political and social implications of his decisions. However, the instructor is not expected to reopen and re-try individual cases which would, in effect, mean preempting the judicial role. Nevertheless, the possibility of role conflict is built into the structure at this point since the instructor is under pressure "from above" to ensure that his judicial charges conform to the political line; hence the tendency to re-investigate cases in order to demonstrate to the judge the "political" errors he made in their adjudication. Finally, each court is subject to an annual inspection by a team of instructors supplemented by higher court officers to determine "to what extent each court's collective effort has contributed to the fulfillment of the judiciary's political and ideological obligations." [58]

From below, political supervision in the GDR is exercised over the judge by the Party unit of the court which comprises all Party members from the charwoman to the court's administrative personnel "who make the assignments and supervise the docket, and enjoy a higher party rank and corresponding influence on the cell's resolutions than does the judicial personnel." [59] At this level, the judge is subject to political criticism and must be responsive to it like any other Party member. Finally, the Party unit is sometimes called upon to deal with a judge who has been unresponsive to professional criticism at the frequent judicial conferences held by each court during which each judge's performance is constantly evaluated.

Although a clear view of the formal model of Party supervision emerges from the East German literature, this does not of course preclude the possibility of Party interference which is more difficult to discern from an external perspective. The most complete picture of the relationship between legality and *partiinost'*, or between supervision and interference in a communist system, is provided by the memoir of former Czech judge Ulč who accents the ambiguity of the problem:

"Only the insiders knew for sure whether or not the Party ran the courts. There was neither total independence nor unqualified subordination. The practice of the *apparatchiki* varied from leaving the judges entirely alone to drafting verdicts in the Party Secretariats." He goes on to add that in 90% of the cases, "there was not the slightest sign of interference in our decision-making," but the converse experience in the remaining 10 percent and "the awareness that someone might at any time inflict his 'suggestion' upon us, conditioned *all* our adjudication." [60]

The Czechs also evolved a formal model for the Party-justice relationship. Ulč mentions the regional interdepartmental conferences of legal and Party cadres where the "current Party line," as well as professional questions are discussed; the regular procedure by which lower courts report to the Regional Court about pending cases on their dockets "which might prove politically sensitive;" and the collusion between the Regional Party committees and Regional Courts to effect change of venue in order to depoliticize certain cases involving well known local personnel.[61] Each of these procedures was designed to maintain the hegemony of the Party over the justice apparatus and to reduce, wherever possible, avoidable conflicts between Party officials and justice personnel over a particular case.

332

Clearly, the formal structure shades off quickly into the informal area of "hints" and "orders" where Party interference is the norm. Generally, this is the standard in cases of anti-state crimes or political cases, and ordinary criminal cases involving the death penalty; but Ulč also records instances of Party meddling in routine criminal cases and even in civil cases as well.

The latter incidents of petty interference usually involve an individual Party official or a Party member holding state office who attempts to intercede on behalf of a friend or a relative entangled in the courts. Ulč mentions two attempts of this sort in which he happened to have sufficient political leverage to rebuff the pressure, one from a district administrative official on behalf of a friend in a divorce case and the other from a minor Regional Party official on behalf of his wife in a civil damages suit. In the latter case, judge Ulč was approached by a man who announced himself as the husband of the defendant and a Regional Party official and declared "my wife is no crook, and I am just reminding you that I am from the Party apparatus. I don't wish to threaten you but only warn, that's all." [62]

In Czechoslovakia, even institutional interference was unpredictable, going through cycles of severity and moderation which were often dependent upon the fluctuations of Party legal policy during the politically turbulent mid-1950s. There was also a personality variable affecting the degree of Party interference with "hard" and "soft" jurisdictions, dependent upon the personal inclinations of the incumbent Party secretary.

Basically, the Party conveys its wishes to the courts "informally." More often than not, Party officials would "suggest," "advise," or "plead for understanding" rather than "order," and judges quickly learned that defiance of a Party "recommendation" was extremely hazardous. [63] In this spirit charges would be dropped, indictments quashed, and even expert medical testimony set aside to accommodate a Party organization's interest in a case.

Occasionally the Party would "order," as in a simple eviction case in 1959 when a Central Committee official telephoned the local Party secretary who informed the presiding judge: "he wants and orders you to confirm the eviction, and I am held co-responsible to see that you go along." [64]

This type of tutelage, minor and major, was institutionalized in the late 1950s by the Czech Ministry of Justice which established a new procedure of weekly meetings of the judges, prosecutor, and local police chief at the District Party office "to discuss with the first secretary the 'area problematics of socialist legality.'" In effect, Party supervision was fused with Party interference with the latter now legitimated as part of the formal structure of Party supervision over the organs of justice. At these meetings, general law enforcement issues would be discussed consistent with the Party's supervisory function, but invariably pending cases would come up. Decisions would be made on which trials would be suitable for "visiting sessions," and occasionally the District Secretary "transmitted the desire of the Party on how individual cases, both criminal and civil, were to be decided." [65]

One might argue that, in the late 1950s, the East German and Czech regimes were at a lower level of political and legal development than the USSR and that there were more residual "bourgeois" influences to contend with than in the 40-year-old Soviet system. Hence, the argument would follow that the East European systems required both more formal Party supervision and more informal Party interference to ensure effective control of the administration of justice. However, this argument flounders on the fact that the Soviet system was the model for these regimes. In the post 1956 period, this was not the model of the USSR of the 1930s, but the contemporary post-Stalin model. Even allowing for some local variation in the reception of the Soviet model in East Germany and Czechoslovakia, there is no solid evidence to suggest that similar formal and informal relationships between the Party and the justice organs do not also exist in the USSR—perhaps with less efficient supervision than in the GDR and more routinized interference than in the ČSSR.

Soviet literature on formal supervision is somewhat more veiled and less explicit than GDR literature and, as yet, we have no memoirs of ex-Soviet jurists (although several are in the planning or writing stages). But we can benefit from the reports of close observers of the Soviet administration of justice. Alexander Solzhenitsyn from "inside" and George Feifer from outside the system, are diametrically opposed on the question of the existence and degree of Party interference. For Solzhenitsyn, the question is easily answered: "In his mind's eye the judge can always see the shiny black visage of truth—the telephone in his chambers. This oracle will never fail you, as long as you do what it says." [66] In contrast, for Feifer the constitutional clause "the court is independent and subordinate only to the law," which adorned a village courtroom he visited, has a particular functional meaning within the context of the Soviet system. [67] Speaking with defense lawyers, he raised the inevitable question "are there specific instructions to judges in individual cases? The lawyers doubted this; certainly if direct interference happens, it happens rarely." Instead, his informants outlined for him an indirect system of Party supervision of justice personnel, especially apparent during the periodic Party-led "campaigns" against crime. At these times "the judges get the word . . . *S verkhu*—from upstairs. From the smell of things, from the way the wind is blowing . . . the *rukovodstvo* (leadership, or brass) makes known what it wants in a thousand open ways, and the courts make decisions accordingly. Every judge is reminded every day that there is a campaign against bribery. And no one tries to fight it, believe me." [68]

Feifer himself provides another example of this variation on Party supervision as indirect interference. Asking a people's judge who had reduced the incidence of crime in his district to what he attributed his success, Feifer received the reply "the Party" which "is going all-out to eliminate crime—to root it out completely." [69] In his own words, Feifer concluded that "the third ear of Moscow judges seemed to be tuned not to the inner meaning of the case, but to those strong signals *s verkhu.*" [70]

From Solzhenitsyn's vantage point, judges are free to try on their merits "without telephoning somebody to receive instructions" only the few cases, perhaps 15%, which affect "neither the interests of the state, nor the reigning ideology, nor the personal interests or comfort of some officeholder. . . ." He continues, that in all other cases—criminal or civil—it is not merely a matter of indirect pressure from the political environment concerning various classes of cases, but direct political interference in individual cases because the great majority of them

> "inevitably affect in some important way the interests of the chairman of a *kolkhoz* [collective farm] or a village soviet, a shop foreman, a factory manager, the head of a Housing Bureau, a block sergeant, the investigating officer or commander of a police district, the medical superintendent of a hospital, a chief planning officer, the heads of administrations or ministries, special sections or personnel sections, the secretaries of district or *oblast* [regional] Party Committees—and up-ward, ever upward! In all such cases, calls are made from one discreet inner office to another; leisurely, lowered voices give friendly *advice*, steady and steer the decision to be reached in the trial of a wretched little man caught in the tangled schemes, which he would not under-stand even if he knew them, of those set in authority over him." [71]

The reality of Party control over the organs of Soviet justice is probably located somewhere between Solzhenitsyn's and Feifer's positions. Solzhenit-syn's extreme views are no doubt the result of his emphasis on Stalinism and his reluctance to acknowledge that post-Stalin changes have had any effect. Moreover, most of his informants and even many of the prisoners (*zeks*) who had written to him in the early 1960s have had their views shaped mainly by the Stalin years when, no doubt, the phone rang in the judge's chambers incessantly. But even Ulč, a jurist of the post-Stalin period under the Czech neo-Stalinist leader Novotný, concedes that the overwhelming majority of cases were decided without interference. Conversely, Feifer's position is too narrow, attributing political pressure only to the occasion of special cam-paigns.

The question of Party supervision/interference over the administration of justice in the USSR is far more complex, differentiated, and ambiguous than either Solzhenitsyn or Feifer indicate.

The following analysis of the problem will serve to explicate and evaluate the authoritative statement on the Party-justice relationships made by the current USSR Minister of Justice V. Terebilov:

"... legal guarantees apart, great importance attaches to the instructions issued on this point by the organs of the Communist Party, which exercised political guidance of the state. But Party leadership does not interfere administratively in judicial activity. Party bodies keep an eye on the state of the eradication of crime and other infringements of laws, on the measures adopted to prevent offenses, on the improvement of legal propaganda among the people; they render the courts assistance of an organizational character. Party bodies do not interfere in the adjudication of criminal and civil cases. Party directives ban any intervention by Party bodies in the administration of justice." [72]

The analysis will draw upon the available "cases" and other examples gleaned from the literature on the Soviet legal system. *Part one* examines the Party's *supervisory* role, first in its ideological function, subdivided into the (1) political education of legal cadres and (2) the legal socialization of the mass public in general and (3) youth in particular. Next, I discuss the *organizational* function of the Party in its supervisory role, which is subdivided as follows: (1) higher Party control over the legal supervisory work of regional, lower, and primary Party organizations; (2) the professional and moral qualifications of legal cadres; (3) judicial and procuratorial practice; (4) "visiting sessions" and social accusers/defenders; (5) peer controls; and (6) special "campaigns."

Part two explores the less visible realm of Party *interference* subdivided into three sections: (1) routine; (2) *ad hoc* institutional; and (3) *ad hoc* individual interference in the justice process. The *routinized* form is further broken down into (a) cases involving Party members and officials, and (b) cases of "political justice." *Ad hoc institutional interference* is subsectioned into (a) cases involving prominent offenders and victims, (b) specific cases of conspicuous crimes, and (c) political or professional rivalry. Finally, *ad hoc individual interference* concerns cases involving intercession on behalf of (a) a family member, (b) friend, or (c) associate.

It should be noted that these categories are intended only as a means of preliminary classification and not as a precisely articulated typology. In fact, as the reader will note, the categories shade into each other—supervision in "campaigns" shades off into interference, whereas *ad hoc* individual interventions in specific cases have come to our attention primarily because they have been subjected to supervisory action. Internally, as well, the categories are not meant to be analytically discrete. For instance, organizational supervision over the choice of social accusers/defenders and the designation of cases for "visiting sessions," and the more general oversight over judicial practice, tend to telescope into each other, although they are still analytically distinguishable for heuristic purposes.

336

Part One: Party Supervision—Ideological

An incessant theme of the literature on the Party and the justice organs is the need for constant Party supervision of the *political education of legal cadres*. Each Party congress is immediately followed by a wave of editorials and leading articles in the legal press, acknowledging that the legal profession has received and is prepared to directly implement the congress' message, as well as its particular resolutions relevant to the administration of justice. [73] The first duty of the Secretary of a Primary Party Organization (PPO) in the justice apparatus is to initiate discussions of these messages and themes in the PPO meetings, to guide the integration into the organization's "plan" of the directives explicitly addressed to legal matters, and, beyond that, to ensure that the PPO remains attentive to the implementation of the Party's latest requirements. [74]

A leading Party specialist on Party-justice relations advocates further enhancing the role of the Secretary of the PPO in law enforcement agencies in order to facilitate his leadership in politically supervising the justice agency personnel. Two or three-day seminars, such as one held by the Pskov Regional Party Committee in 1973, are recommended with the "justice" Secretaries temporarily relieved of their regular duties in order to better enable them to "exchange experience [and] more quickly grasp the complex art of leading a primary collective of Communists." In a short list of subjects on which "justice" secretaries exchanged ideas at the Pskov seminar, the first item was the "individual education of Communists." [75]

An even more direct route by which the Party carries out its ideological supervision of the legal system is to staff the justice organs wherever possible with Party members or Party-recommended politically and ideologically reliable types. The former head of the Latvian Central Committee's Administrative Organs Department reports that the Republican Party organization in the late 1960s assigned to law enforcement careers "a great number of Communists, Young Communists and non-Party comrades recommended by their collectives." [76] He assures his readers that those sent by the Party quickly acquired the necessary specialized skills, presumably in the service of the *MVD* and especially the militia, for which he cites several prominent career histories. [77] In the Moscow region, the City and the District Party committees regularized this procedure by setting up a special Party-led commission for the selection of *MVD*, and especially militia, personnel. All of this activity was in compliance with a November 1968 joint decree of the Central Committee and the USSR Council of Ministers on measures for "further strengthening the Soviet militia." The response to this decree by the mid-1970s had yielded 57,000 Party-recommended militia candidates, of whom 45,000 were members of the Party or Young Communist League. [78]

After politically educating the legal cadres, the Party extends its ideological supervision to *the entire population* which increasingly, since the 24th

Party Congress in 1971, *has become the object of "legal propaganda"* towards raising the general level of "legal culture." In effect, the Party organizations lead the legal cadres in the mass legal socialization of the public. In the words of a 1972 editorial in *Soviet Justice*, "a fundamental part of the ideological-educational work of the Party . . . is the legal education of the citizen." [79] In Latvia, the Party set up special subcommittees "to coordinate the work of organizations involved with the legal education of the population." The special coordinating groups comprised from 10 to 15 people, including representatives of law enforcement agencies, the local press, the local education department, the "Knowledge Society," and the District Committee of the Young Communist League, among other groups. The coordinators of mass legal socialization in the Latvian Republic drew upon "sociological research" [80] among other methods of carrying out their assignment.

From such data and with the impetus provided by the 24th Party Congress, the First Secretary of the Rostov Regional Party Committee, writing in *Pravda* in 1972, stated that the *obkom* was setting up guidelines for its lower Party organizations to ensure that legal propaganda would be less superficial and more lively. And, he added that "52 people's universities of legal knowledge are now operating in the region." In addition, he reported that personnel of the Regional Procuracy, Court, and *MVD* Department had helped "set up so-called preventive councils at many enterprises . . . for the prevention of all law violations by various means of influence, first of all educational means." [81]

Most recently, after the 25th Party Congress, the Secretary of the Party Committee of the USSR Procuracy assured the readers of *Socialist Legality* that the problems of legal socialization "are discussed regularly" in both the professional and Party meetings within the Procuracy organization. [82]

The Party's ideological supervisory attention is especially focused on *raising the legal consciousness of Soviet youth*, the group responsible for the rampant problems of juvenile delinquency and the largest percentage of adult crime as well, a fact now recognized by the Party as well as the criminologists. For instance in 1971, the newspaper of the Young Communist League reported that a public opinion survey of 28 districts "shocked the authorities" because it revealed "that the overwhelming majority of young people did not know that criminal responsibility in the USSR starts at the age of 14, and not at 18 as they thought. Likewise, the Ministry of Internal Affairs established that 76% of young offenders had not realized they were committing an offense; they only thought that they were being naughty and would be disciplined by their parents or teachers at the most." [83]

The Party's approach to the legal socialization of youth has been multi-sided, including the introduction of elementary legal education into the general educational system, the encouragement of contacts between youth and legal cadres, and the mobilization of parents. For instance, an 8-10 hour course called "The School of the Young Jurist" was set up by the Pioneer organization of Irkutsk. During the 1972-1973 academic year, a new course on "Problems of Soviet Law," taught by social studies teachers and legal personnel, was included in the curricula of middle and higher technical schools throughout the country. [84] As the Rostov Regional Party Committee First Secretary put it in 1972, "we are giving special attention to the propaganda of legal knowledge among young people." [85] In addition, members of the militia's children and youth bureaus have been sent into the schools with greater frequency with films and talks on "moral and legal themes," while meetings have been arranged between judges and procurators and the older schoolchildren. [86]

Another technique used by the Party to reach teenagers are the "parents committees" which work with school personnel and are usually led "by lower-level Party or *Komsomol* [Young Communist League] activists. . . ." Among their responsibilities is "to apply social pressure to other parents who are not bringing their children up correctly," in effect, a parent-to-parent resocialization effort. [87] Clearly, the Party's emphasis is on juvenile crime prevention through socialization, but as Peter Juviler points out, the Party has not found it easy "to get courts, law enforcement agencies and social organizations to cooperate," a problem which brings us to the boundary between the Party's ideological and organizational functions within its supervisory role.

Part One: Party Supervision-Organizational

The first priority of the *organizational function is higher Party control over lower and Primary Party organizations* involved in organizational supervision of the organs of justice at their respective level of the system. In this regard, an opportunity to establish a "leading case" arose very early in the post-Stalin period in March 1954. A people's judge in the city of Tula was formally reprimanded by name in a resolution of her District Party organization for "ignoring Party organs" by refusing to submit to District Party Committee (*raikom*) pressure to render illegal judicial decisions. Normally, the matter would probably have ended there with the judge possibly transferred from criminal to civil cases and most certainly not renominated to stand for election the next time around. Apparently, though, the first stirrings of destalinization were already in the air because the judge took her "case" to Khrushchev in the form of a complaint against the local Party officials who had attempted to preempt her judicial function. Khrushchev received her and after her complaint was verified the Central Committee used the opportunity to condemn an illegal Party practice common under Stalin by issuing a resolution warning local Party organizations against improper interference in the administration of justice. [88] So, in the spirit of the emerging concern for "socialist legality," the Party reaffirmed its organizational supervisory functions, and reinforced the line-staff distinction in the justice organs' relationship to corresponding Party organizations.

The Tula case was originally called to public attention by Procurator-General Rudenko in a 1954 *Party Life* article. Over the years, the tide of destalinization ebbed and flowed until it was again battering against Stalinist practices in the legal process and elsewhere in the wake of the 22nd Party Congress of 1961. It was in this context that the Tula case again resurfaced, on this occasion in the first issue of *Kommunist* for 1963. A year later, *Izvestiia* added its voice in support of judicial independence by citing two cases of "inadmissible petty tutelage" by Party officials. Both involved Regional Party committee instructors, one of whom had pressed for the conviction of an innocent person, while the other had obstinately insisted on the innocence of a juvenile delinquent convicted of assault. Condemning these practices, *Izvestiia* reaffirmed that the correct mode of Party organizational supervision of the administration of justice "is absolutely indispensable." [89]

In this spirit of essential organizational supervision, the Latvian Central Committee called to account a major City Party commitee (*gorkom*), in particular, to exercise supervision over how the *gorkom* had implemented the joint 1966 Party-state directive on stepping up the struggle against crime. In displaying the deficiencies of the *gorkom*, the Party inversely indicated what is intended by organizational supervision of the local administration of justice. The Party official, at that time in charge of the Latvian Central Committee's Administrative Organs Department, subsequently wrote:

> "... a number of deficiencies, especially in the style of Party work, were noted. In many of its decisions the City Party Committee merely duplicated the decisions of higher organs. An intensive analysis was not carried out of the work of the city's administrative agencies and the related social organizations or of the reasons for antisocial behavior. The City Party Committee established a plan of measures to strengthen the struggle with crime, but did not even acquaint the primary Party organizations in the enterprises or institutions with the plan. The Bureau of the City Party Committee did not receive a single report about how Communists were struggling to strengthen law and order."[90]

Similarly, an inquiry by the Novgorod Regional Party Committee about shortcomings in the work of one of its District Party committees revealed that, for a long period of time, no one in the *raikom* apparatus had been responsible for "the collection and analysis of information about the implementation of the decisions of the Party and government concerning the strengthening of discipline, the struggle with drunkenness and crime [and] the guaranteeing of the protection of socialist property." [91]

The most extreme example of the Party's failure to perform its organiza-

340

tional supervisory task over "socialist legality" is the colossal "Georgian case" of economic and political corruption, first publically revealed in 1972 and for which hundreds of Party officials from the former First Secretary on down have been demoted with the Party "transfers" continuing into early 1978.

Clearly, the Party expects its lower organs to avoid direct interference in individual cases as a general principle and instead to devote substantial organizational energy and time to the local implementation of national policies bearing on the administration of justice. This includes primary Party organizations and Party groups in the organs of the administration of justice which are often nearly interchangeable with the staff of a people's court or Procuracy office, due to the heavy Party saturation of legal cadres. [92] As a result, the regular Party functions of recruitment of new members and the supervision of the administration of the institution (which since 1971 includes PPOs in governmental agencies) are rendered somewhat superfluous. Therefore, it appears that PPOs in legal institutions tend to concentrate on the remaining function of ideological work among the legal cadres while radiating their Party control influence outside their institutions.

A case in point are the PPOs in the Procuracy which exercise "direct influence not only on the standard of the supervisory activity of the Procuracy at a given level, but also on the general status of legality in the district, region and republic." [93] In effect, Party procurators exercise self-supervision as a group, by ensuring that the Procuracy workers fulfill the laws as well as Party and state directives. This is done through the usual method of spot checks, the results of which are reported at Party meetings.

At best, this self-checking is probably *pro forma* to satisfy the requirements of the Party Rules, and, at worst, it may entail conflicts of interest. The author had the opportunity on one occasion to observe a Party group meeting of a university law school department (*kafedra*) with 100% Party membership. A department meeting had just adjourned with everyone remaining seated as the focus shifted from the department head to the Party group leader (an associate professor) who immediately convened the Party meeting. A desultory discussion of self-evaluation then occurred which took on the tone of *partiinost'* only when the subject turned to the members' "social work" outside of the *kafedra*. At that point, differentiation between the *kafedra* and a Party group became discernible as the Party *aktiv* became more active.

In the same spirit, when the target of supervision shifts to the external environment, the PPOs of the Procuracy also become more vigorous in their Party roles. Observed violations of legality in "other institutions" are duly reported to "the appropriate Party organs," thus fulfilling the procurators' Party obligation under Rule No. 60 of the Party Rules. [94]

When the PPO in a legal institution does carry out self-supervision at Party meetings, N. G. Novikov assures us that the discussion never touches on the "decisions in specific criminal, civil or administrative cases" which would constitute "Party interference" and a violation of Party discipline. [95] Instead, the Party discussion involves questions of the institution's compliance with the law and Party policy, and the PPO's "control" over compliance at the subordinate level of the institution. Finally, a PPO performs its ideological function by providing the correct political orientation to cadres of its particular institution, including even the Procurator or the Chief Judge, all of whom are equally subject to political indoctrination.

Another view of a PPO in a legal institution suggests that it may also perform an internal "mediation" function not provided for by the Party Rules. On the basis of an interview with a former Party group leader in the All-Union Procuracy Institute, Solomon reports that the

> "Party group mediated conflicts between researchers and administration and between individual researchers; it tried to maintain a sense of group commitment to the work and an awareness of the relationship between the Institute's work and societal goals; and it watched that promotions, hiring and firing were fair." [96]

The PPO's ideological function is apparent and its "mediation" function similar to the grievance procedure in Western collective bargaining contracts, but notably absent in the group leader's description is the PPO's supervisory function.

A necessary precondition for correct implementation of legal policy is *Party organizational supervision over both the professional qualifications and law-abiding conduct of legal cadres*. Fundamental to this task, one Party specialist argues, is the necessity of improving the quality of Party personnel in the *raikom* and *gorkom* charged with these and other organizational supervisory duties. Since the "legal" instructors operate out of the *obkoms*, no one at the lower levels has charge of legal supervision as a regular, full-time responsibility. Therefore, the few local instructors usually have neither legal education nor legal experience and, consequently, they are "not sufficiently qualified to bring influence to bear on law enforcement agencies and their primary Party organizations." Because of this personnel problem, S. E. Zhilinskii concludes, the work of Party supervision over legality at the district and municipal levels is "usually fraught with great difficulties and is not always carried out satisfactorily." [97]

As a result, supervision over the professional qualifications of jurists is carried out at *obkom* and higher levels of the Party apparatus. For instance, the Party-state decree of 1970 on improving the performance of the judiciary and Procuracy meant that "special attention was devoted to the improvement of the [legal] staff at the district level," including the creation of the "All-Union Institute for the Improvement of Workers of Justice, republic-wide courses for raising the qualifications of these workers, and regular, on-going higher courses for the additional training of the leading cadres of the Republic, Krai, and Regional Procuracy."[98] In addition, the lower Party organizations have exercised their influence over judicial nominations with the candidates' legal credentials in mind to the extent that as of 1975, 94% of the elected people's judges had higher legal education.[99]

The local Party organizations are less at a disadvantage in their organizational supervision over the moral-legal conduct of the justice personnel within their jurisdictions. The problem can be subdivided into one of incompetence and one of malfeasance. Mironov wrote approvingly of those Party organizations which effect the dismissal and transfer of incompetent legal personnel and cited as examples the removal, in the late 1950s and early 1960s, of the Georgian and Turkmen *MVD* ministers, the Chairman of the Turkmen Supreme Court, the Procurators of the Tadzhik and Kirgiz republics, several regional procurators, and others.[100] For judges in particular, disciplinary proceedings were conducted by panels of superior judges until 1965, when special presidia were established to deal with misconduct on the bench. One "sanction" is to enter a critical note in the judge's personnel record which may mean that the Party will drop him or her at the next election.[101]

In more flagrant cases of lapses by judges or other legal personnel which are brought to its attention by citizens' complaints, a Party organization may supersede the professional disciplinary procedures and take varying degrees of direct political action against the cadre accused of ethical misconduct. For instance, investigative reporters from *Pravda* and *Izvestiia* turned up two such cases in 1971-1972 and, in the glare of national publicity, the appropriate Party organizations swung into action. In one instance, the Archangel City Party Committee formally reprimanded a people's judge and a district procurator, both Party members, with notations in their personnel files "for carelessly and superficially examining" a citizen's complaint, and "for violating socialist legality evidenced in the pressing of unfounded criminal charges against her." In addition, the *gorkom* raised the question with the judge's *raikom* and the Regional Soviet Executive Committee's Department of Justice, "whether Comrade Skutin should be retained as a people's judge."[102] In an analogous case uncovered by *Pravda*, the Party organization of the USSR Procurator's Office reported that it had issued the offending procurator "a severe Party penalty" for "careless examination" of a citizen's complaints, and directed the attention of the procurator's superior to "the violations he permitted" by his subordinate.[103]

A far more serious problem requiring constant organizational supervision are actual violations of law by legal cadres. Mironov indicates that the number of violations involved are not insignificant.[104] The most frequent crime committed by legal personnel is the acceptance of a bribe to ignore, or "cover-up" the commission of another offense, usually an economic crime. As Mironov puts it, when militia, judicial, and procuratorial personnel fall "outside the

343

field of vision of Party organs," they sometimes fall in with "criminal elements." As an example, he cites a major economic crime ring, discovered in the early 1960s in the Kirgiz Republic, which made monthly payoffs to law enforcement officials, including the Chief of the Republican Militia's anti-economic crime unit. [105] The problem of corrupt legal cadres is not confined to the provinces. Andrei Sakharov reports that "in the 1960s, during a routine campaign against corruption, the majority of the procurators and judges in one of the boroughs (*raions*) of Moscow were removed for systematically taking bribes." [106]

The correct Party supervisory posture towards this problem is revealed in the self-criticism of the Party organization of the Kirgiz Procurator's Office which had failed in the above economic crime case on two counts—first, that it did not effectively exercise procuratorial supervision over legality in general; and secondly, that self-supervision of its own incriminated personnel was neglected. [107] Acknowledging the latter failing, the Party members of the Kirgiz Procuracy noted that "they had not manifested the necessary vigilance in relation to the improper conduct of certain procurators and investigators, had not reacted critically to their offenses, had not attached the necessary importance to the signals [*signalam*] about bribery, and had committed serious errors in the selection of cadres." [108]

Implicit in the self-criticism of the Party procurators of Kirgizia is the preoccupation with Party discipline and the idea of "control" as an end in itself. As Alexander Shtromas argues, "the control over ... [law enforcement] agencies is more important for the Party than the control over the crime situation itself." [109] In this spirit, the latest Party directives loom large in the *organizational supervision* of *judicial and procuratorial practice.* Central Committee resolutions or joint decrees with the Council of Ministers are "translated" into the juridical language of policy implementation through the instructions and orders of the Ministry of Internal Affairs and the Ministry of Justice, the Procurator-General, and finally appear in the form of Supreme Court directives. "Such instructions ... are more important than the formal laws themselves since they clarify what the authorities want to make out of the laws in that particular period of time. Through such acts, the elastic framework of the criminal law acquires a more or less practically applicable content which, to a great extent, reflects the Party line at the time. ..." [110]

The Party line on criminal law can be seen at work in the "Babysitter case." A young woman was brought to justice for robbing homes under the pretext of babysitting, and related charges which ensured her a minimum sentence of six years. Unexpectedly, the court applied a different article of the RSFSR Criminal Code which permitted lighter sanctions and she received only a two-year sentence. As Shtromas relates it, the girl's defense counsel "was astonished at such mildness and asked the judge privately for an explanation. The answer was that, the day before the trial, the courts received an instruction from the Supreme Court which said that Arts. 43 and 44 . . . (the latter providing for release on parole) should be widely applied to young offenders; thus he acted according to the new instructions." The judge added that if the trial had occurred a few days earlier, he would have given her 10 years. [111]

There is a built-in incentive for such spontaneous compliance with the changing Party line in the administration of justice. Judges, as well as other legal personnel, are required to make monthly, quarterly, and annual reports on the cases decided by them, using a standard, statistical form which is submitted to the link in the Party apparatus exercising supervision over them. A former Soviet defense lawyer (*advokat*) has observed that too many marks in the acquittal "column" are frowned upon by Party officials. As a result of this pressure, there is a tendency for people's courts to convict [112] and sentence in such a way as to minimize overturns on appeals to higher courts. This is illustrated in the private conversation between the defense attorney and judge in the "Babysitter case." Amplifying on his light sentence, the judge added "If I had given her more, you would complain and my sentence would be changed by the appellate court, thus worsening the indexes of my work." [113] Other party directives, combined with instant judicial responsiveness, produced sharp fluctuations in bail policy for minors and first offenders during late 1960s, with one directive encouraging bail decisions on a wholesale basis until the resulting recidivism elicited a countervailing Party directive which effectively meant replacing bail with "heavy sentences for the slightest offenses." [114]

Organizational supervision over the application of justice also takes place within the Primary Party organizations of the justice organs. To avoid crossing the line between general supervision and specific interference in the work of the courts, these PPOs use "a form of *a posteriori* control" by means of Party-oriented judicial conferences "at which one or another aspect of the court's performance is evaluated and appropriate conclusions formulated." [115]

However, the effectiveness of this technique of organizational supervision may depend to some extent on the size of the PPO and the interplay of personalities. No doubt, a critical mass of Communists is necessary if a review conference is not to degenerate into an informal, small-group discussion; one which could more easily be dominated by a strong-willed judge who is protective of his or her record. Possibly in consideration of these and other problems, Party jurists in a number of rural areas are grouped together in a single "combined" PPO which includes judges, procurators, legal advisors to enterprises, notaries, and *MVD* personnel. However, because *MVD* Party members are usually the most numerous in this kind of arrangement, the organizational supervision function of such a combined PPO sometimes becomes "one-sided." For instance, in one combined "justice" PPO in the Novgorod Region with *MVD* personnel making up 90% of its membership, neither Party judges nor Party procurators discussed their work in the meetings of the PPO during the period 1973-1975.[116]

The Party supervises and, in turn, relies heavily on the Procuracy, through its general supervisory role, to monitor and maintain conformity in policy execution among the other organs of the justice apparatus. Mironov, in his 1964 book reprinted in 1969, emphatically underscores that "the leaders of the Procuracy organs," in fulfillment of their obligations to the Party and state, "must undertake the organizational coordination of the methods of the Procuracy, courts, agencies of internal affairs, and organs of state security in the battle against crime and law breaking."[117] This theme is repeated in the Soviet literature with the added implication that the Party regards the Procuracy as the most politically reliable, as well as professionally competent component of its organizational supervision of the ordinary administration of justice.

However, even the procurators apparently are not immune to the practice of "false reporting" of crime data, a consequence of Party pressure on the justice organs to "produce" results combined with the penalties of demotion awaiting those juridical personnel who fail to satisfy the demand. In this atmosphere, legal cadres become preoccupied with submitting reports to the Party, regardless of their reliability, which will promote a positive image of their work and avert career dislocation.[118] As a Lt. Colonel of the militia involved in falsification of juvenile delinquency data in the Moscow area candidly put the situation, "If I were to send genuine figures about child crime in my precinct into the city militia headquarters, I would not last a day in my job. This is what they all do. I am not the only one."[119]

We have already seen that equivalent behavior for people's judges is manifested in their reluctance to acquit and their proclivity for "safe sentencing" to avoid professional criticism from above, which could result in low political "grades" and possible withdrawal of Party support for re-election. Report-padding is no less "a way of life" for the procurators who, at the very least, morally collude in the militia's statistical concealment of unsolved crimes by not effectively exercising their supervisory powers over militia agencies. This enables procurators to show in their own reports that "the crime rate is decreasing slightly every time," thereby protecting their jobs.[120]

The routine and interlocking nature of false reporting may have been a contributing factor in the appointment of a Republic Procurator so unfit for the position that he was subsequently expelled from the Party and relieved of his post. The man had apparently advanced steadily over the years due to largely *pro forma* "file checks" on his job performance by superiors. A much closer inspection of his career by higher Party bodies in the Tadzhik SSR revealed that, in the past as a regional procurator, he had violated legality by ordering illegal arrests, delaying cases illegally, evaluating investigative reports

346

improperly, and ignoring instructions from the Procurator of the Republic. [121]

Obviously, this case represented a serious failure of Party organizational supervision over procuratorial practice, as well as a failure of its ideological supervision over cadre selection. But by far the most serious breakdown of Party organizational supervision over procuratorial practice and the administration of justice in general, has been in Soviet Georgia where the process of exposing an extraordinary pattern of political and economic corruption from the top down has been underway since 1972. A spectacular economic swindler/entrepreneur managed to corrupt the former Georgian First Secretary, a candidate member of the Politburo, and through him, key personnel in the Party and state apparatus. Before his fall and arrest in 1972, the economic crime chief, O. Lazeishvili, reportedly included on his patronage list and within a wide-ranging economic conspiracy, Republican Party secretaries, government ministers, officials of the Tbilisi City Party Committee, and of course such key legal personnel as the Militia Chief of Tbilisi. [122]

Corruption, however, did not cease in Georgia with the fall of the so-called Georgian "Godfather". After two years of Party purges and criminal prosecutions under the new First Secretary, it was clear that Party discipline and law and order had still not been fully restored. The Party leader admitted as much before the Georgian Central Committee in late 1974, remarking that personnel policy was still characterized by "corruption, chummy relations, favoritism [and] nepotism," that fresh cases of bribes solicited by public officials were still turning up, and that the work of restoring socialist legality by the organs of justice was "clearly inadequate." He especially referred to "numerous instances" of the "Republic prosecutor's office and its local agencies . . . exercising feeble supervision over the execution of Soviet laws." [123] The implied message was clear—the Procuracy, which had to have been complicit in the original pattern of corruption, remained impaired and had still not fully resumed its general supervisory activities. Absent an effective Procuracy to coordinate the work of other law enforcement agencies, the Party's overall organizational supervisory position in the administration of justice remained in a weakened condition in the scandal-racked Georgian SSR.

Although the Georgian "case" is exceptional, it does illustrate that the Party's basic supervisory role is premised on a relatively sound, functioning law enforcement system. If this premise collapses, the Party's first priority is to regain control over the justice apparatus and, only then, can its secondary priority of maintaining law and order be readdressed. The Party's dependency on reliable "line" organizations in order to exercise its "staff" function can be seen in its *organizational supervision over "visiting sessions" and social accusers/defenders*, two auxiliary devices for bringing the "community" into play in the process of administering justice.

Reports indicate that during the 1960s, approximately 25% of all criminal cases in the USSR were tried by people's courts "on circuit" in the so-called "visiting sessions" at the scene of the crime or at the location of the offender's "collective".[124]

Visiting sessions, in effect, are small-scale "show trials" designed to bring the court's "parental" message to the population where it lives and works. As such, the Party plays a significant role at several levels. First, "a judge will not decide to try a case in visiting session without consulting the local procurator ... and Communist Party Committee, which has the last word, one would think." Secondly, the judge coordinates the staging of the trial by going "over the details of the coming spectacle with the management, Party organization, and trade union and *Komsomol* people in the organization on whose premises the visiting session will take place." Finally, the judge will work with the local PPO and on-site officials in helping to select lay counsel from the collective involved, who will work with professional counsel on both sides of the case.[125] The semi-visible Party presence at all stages of individual cases heard "on circuit" is justified on the grounds that a visiting session is "not only a judicial action but also an important mass political measure," an argument that is intended to have the dubious effect of not infringing upon the Soviet conception of judicial independence.[126]

In fact, though, Party organizational supervision ideally works in the direction of selecting a clearcut case which will have the maximum public "educational" impact on the audience. Thus, the Party's prestige is committed in each of these visiting sessions, implying stronger indirect pressure than usual on the court to convict. If acquittals are rare in regular sessions,[127] one can well imagine that the so-called "corporate honor" of the legal profession precludes the possibility of a judge publically embarrassing the Procuracy, not to mention the heavily engaged Party itself. In its decisive influence over the selection of individual cases to be heard in visiting sessions, we can begin to discern the problems of boundary-determination between Party supervision and Party interference.

Either way, several cases suggest that the Party's organizational supervision has its limits in terms of the outcome of any given visiting session. A clearcut hooligan trial involving a knifing, held before 700 workers at a printing plant, produced a divided audience on the appropriate length of sentence.[128] The "Perfume case" was staged before a thousand spectators, but "booing and cheering lustily on both sides, growing noisy and restless whenever the action on stage slowed down, they seemed to take it more as an entertainment than as a trial, to say nothing of a lesson."[129] A minor case of petty economic crime heard in the employees' club of the Lenin Stadium before a group of co-workers drew the audience's unanimous hostility towards the state inspector who had caught their comrade.[130]

Finally, in Juviler's meticulously reported "Bookthief case," we can see the Party working against itself at different levels. Higher Party demands for more

348

use of visiting sessions generally and a serious booktheft problem at the Lenin Library, apparently influenced local Party and legal officials of Moscow's Frunze borough to organize a visiting session for a complex case unsuited for trial in such a forum. The result was that many of the hundreds of spectators apparently went away divided about the fairness of the sentence, with some critical of the presumptive nature of the proceedings altogether. [131] In an even more explicit political sense, the trial pitted two Primary Party organizations against each other—the offender's and the victimized library staff's. The former PPO was represented by the Party organizer of the offender's institute who testified as a defense witness while the latter PPO was represented indirectly through the library's "social accuser." [132] The result was to split the sympathies of the audience along functional lines, readers *vs.* librarians, thus mitigating the educational impact of the session.

Admittedly, the Party does not come in for direct criticism for ill-conceived or poorly planned visiting sessions, but the legal organs involved do suffer a certain diminution of prestige among critical spectators and occasionally receive professional criticism from above as well.[133] Consequently, such negative feedback has to be seen as an adverse reflection on the performance of the organizational supervisory function by the responsible Party organizations which are charged with the duty of "maintaining in every possible way the authority" of the institutions of justice. [134] Probably as a result of these general considerations, as well as the inherent difficulties of effectively staging visiting sessions, the number of such trials as a percentage of all criminal trials in the RSFSR dropped perceptibly from the mid-1960s to the mid-1970s. [135]

In contrast, the auxiliary institution of social accuser or social defender is more readily susceptible to effective Party organizational supervision. These lay counsel can and do participate in many regular criminal trials as well as in most visiting sessions. They are selected by the collective of the offender and/or victim within which, of course, the PPO plays a predominant role. The "message" they bring to the proceedings represents the voice of the collective coached, as it were, by the Party *aktiv*. Generally, lay counsel fulfill the part of special character witnesses for or against the accused, but they sometimes also bring into court general or specific sentencing recommendations which can possibly influence the court's sentence one way or the other. Such lay influence on the court is possible so long as the judge feels that he or she is within the sentencing consensus for the particular crime and can therefore avoid having the sentence revised on appeal, a kind of reversal which would effect adversely the judge's indicators of statistical "success". In effect, lay counsel—selected and guided by a Party group or PPO—afford the Party an additional indirect but immediate presence in the courtroom without violation of the post-Stalin line against direct interference in the adjudication of an individual case.

Party influence, as in the visiting sessions, is again codified and institution-alized, further blurring the boundary between legal and political "space" in the Soviet administration of justice. Social counsel are commonly found in visiting sessions. For instance, the Lenin Library collective's social accuser asked that the bookthief be "severely punished" for harm done to the library and its readers, [136] while the social defender in the "Cognac case" pleaded for a symbolic sentence by extolling the accused's virtues as a co-worker and minimizing her offense. [137]

Two cases, one in regular session and the other in visiting session, will suffice to display the Party's organizational supervision over lay counsel, especially the social accuser. In the case of a brutal murder, the social accuser, a foreman and chairman of the trade union committee, gave very damaging evidence of the accused's "negative characteristics" and summed up as fol-lows, addressing the court with the familiar Party appellation:

> "The collective held a general meeting ... discussed Chernov's case thoroughly, and on the basis of these considerations instructed me to ask the court to apply to him the highest measure of punishment for his crime. Comrade Judges, we earnestly recommend that he be shot."

Some months later, all of his appeals and petitions exhausted, the convicted murderer was executed in 1962. [138]

The remaining case, which was also in the 1960s, involved a heavy-drinking and abusive housepainter and reveals most clearly the guiding hand of the Party in the social regulation process generally, and the administration of justice specifically. The Secretary of a Moscow Party organization reported that a hooligan had been unresponsive to Party residential agitation ("It became clear that our words did not reach him,"), so the Party organization decided to bring him before the residential comrades' court (which had "no influence" on the hooligan's behavior either). Finally the matter was for-warded to the people's court which decided, presumably with Party concur-rence, to try the case in visiting session. In the words of the Party Secretary,

> "The court sitting took place in the assembly hall of the school. The day before, our activists posted announcements and visited the homes of residents and invited them to attend the court. . . . The hall was overcrowded. *The public accuser from our organization* was Colonel Nikolai Nilovich Kolosov (ret.), a man of great culture and education, a former submariner and the holder of thirteen decorations and medals.
>
> His speech to the court was gripping. The hall listened with bated attention. Even the prosecutor said afterwards that he had not heard such a powerful and well-argued speech in a long time.
>
> Kuznetsov was sentenced to two-and-a-half years of strict regime [imprisonment]. He served his sentence and returned to us with a good reference." [139] (Italics added.)

350

And so, in a model of good Party work, a happy ending was achieved—a visiting session that went well, a social accuser who performed smoothly, and a social deviant who returned "re-educated," all due to successful organizational supervision by the Party.

The shadow of the Party over the administration of justice becomes even more apparent as we descend the social regulatory ladder to observe its *organizational supervision over the institutions of peer justice*. The comrades' courts, people's voluntary patrols, and anti-parasite proceedings were revived in the late 1950s as part of Khrushchev's renewed emphasis on the gradual "withering away" of the state by creating, among other things, a politically-directed social control network that "not even a gnat would be able to fly past without our noticing it." [140]

All of these "popular" institutions have been subjected to far greater professional juridical control since Khrushchev's ouster, but they still theoretically afford the Party considerable leverage over the personal lives of Soviet citizens through the peer control stratum of the administration of justice. From the outset, the Party took a strong interest in the comrades' courts, and it was estimated that one out of every three comrades' court judges in the early 1960s was a Party member. [141] Likewise, a Soviet source from that period reported "the organization and control of the [*druzhinniki*] squads and their headquarters are carried out by Party organs." [142] A Western observer added that they had "become an action arm of—the Party." [143]

The new 1974 statute on the people's voluntary patrols continues the trend towards the greater juridicization of the peer control process by placing them under the administrative control of local soviets; yet a Soviet source indicates that "a secretary of the local Party committee is, typically, chief of staff of the area's detachment." [144] For instance, in Riga where more than half of the patrollers (*druzhinniki*) are members of the Party or the *Komsomol*, the patrols are supervised by a *raikom* secretary at the district level, by the Secretary or his deputy of the PPO at the enterprise level, and by the Party organizations of the housing administrations at the subdistrict level. [145]

In the same spirit, the speeches and glosses on the new 1977 statute on the comrades' courts suggest that the earlier procedure by which the work of the comrades' courts was "regularly discussed at Party meetings," which "point out shortcomings and give the courts the right direction in the struggle for discipline and the legal order," has probably been reinvigorated as the regime tries to enlist the comrades' courts in the struggle against juvenile delinquency. [146] At the very least, it can be assumed that the Party organizations still provide "a great deal of help and full scale support" to the comrades' courts in such places for example, as Mine #35 in Karaganda. [147]

However in spite of the strong Party presence in the very operation of these peer controls, they have had a checkered record during the past two decades. From their contemporary re-introduction, the pattern has been that comrades' courts tend to "operate infrequently, lapsing into inactivity until prodded to meet in one of the periodic campaigns of the Party for grass roots prevention."[148] A recent Soviet public opinion survey indicates that the "prestige" of comrades' courts is very low among the population, suggesting a major reason for the reluctance to use this forum more often.[149]

The comrades' court of the Law School of Moscow University met only twice during the year 1963-1964, in spite of the fact that there were a number of other cases which lent themselves to this form of social pressure.[150] When comrades' courts do meet, the evidence tends to discount direct Party manipulation of the proceedings. Party input is certainly present in terms of the decision to bring the "case" before the comrades' court, in the personnel of the "court," and through participation in the proceedings from the "floor;" but Western observers have witnessed "too much confusion and uncertainty behind the desk, too much genuine debate in the auditoriums, and too little preparation on paper to suggest pre-arrangement."[151]

In the two cases at Moscow Law School, members of the audience were very reluctant to "judge" their peers, one a minor disturber of the peace, and the other a wife-beater and abusive neighbor.[152] A 1962 proceeding before an apartment house comrades' court ended indecisively after hours of mutual vituperation between angry neighbors.[153] Another housing "case," intended to be a model proceeding with cameramen present, ended in a debacle of mockery and ridicule by members of the audience, in spite of the best efforts of the District Party Committee to make "a good showing" and an excellent agitational speech from the floor by the Secretary of the apartment complex's Party organization. A mother of one of the teenagers before the "court" for taunting an elderly, prudish youth worker, summed it up by saying to the cheers of the audience: "What a ridiculous waste of time, your big deal Comradely Court. Just get rid of the incompetent social worker and my boy will be fine."[154]

The problem of backfiring Party influence was no less serious with the people's voluntary patrols, an equally unpredictable organization in spite of the Party's guiding and steadying hand. The patrols carry out a wide variety of duties in serving as a street-level peer control institution. While probably a great percentage of *druzhinniki* carry out their responsibilities with a sense of civic integrity, many others, as with poorly conducted comrades' court proceedings, undermine the law enforcement mission they are pledged to support. During their formative period in the post-Stalin years, criminal types even managed to infiltrate the patrols, using "their post as detachment commanders to terrorize the people they were supposed to protect. They abused their office, raped and humiliated women, and stole public funds. An outside prosecutor and court might have to step in to penetrate the cover provided by local Party and soviet officials."[155]

More often than not though, the patrols were usually well-intentioned but overzealous, which like a "runaway" comrades' court proceeding, tended to erode rather than strengthen respect for socialist legality among the affected public. In the abortive comrades' court proceeding discussed above, another mother had the sympathy of the audience in exculpating her teenager when she insisted that "her son learned his bad habits from the *druzhinniki*, which his Young Communist group had pressed him to join." [156] This kind of complaint of the patroller as hooligan and juvenile delinquent, as well as the generally adverse public reaction to their intrusiveness, contributed to the progressive reduction of the relative functional autonomy of the people's voluntary patrols which have been brought more and more under militia control, thus diluting, to some degree, *direct* Party organizational supervision.[157]

The anti-parasite proceedings were probably the most pernicious of the Khrushchev peer controls. The early decrees in the late 1950s ran counter to the Party's simultaneous policy of strengthening socialist legality. In their initial form, Party organizational supervision tended to manifest itself in direct involvement behind the scenes of the amorphous "general assembly" of neighbors which was empowered to banish a so-called "parasite" to a place of remote exile and compulsory work. In effect, at this stage Party orientation (*partiinost'*) expressed through a mobilized community (*obshchestvennost'*) merely bypassed legality (*zakonnost'*).

The spirit of the early phase of the anti-parasite legislation was epitomized by the First Secretary of the Kirgiz Central Committee who "reported that public (Party, trade-union, *Komsomol*, etc.) organizations in the Kirgiz Republic had been slow to expose able-bodied heads of families who had, he declared, distorted the "national tradition" of respect for elders by refusing to work and by spending their time at bazaars and tea rooms." [158] Party involvement was still strong and direct in 1963 when the Dzerzhinskii District Party Committee of Leningrad organized a "conference" of "parasites" at which a reformed former parasite gave the principal address. Predictably, the conferees adopted the resolution "To work!"[159]

However, in response to strong criticism from the legal profession in particular, anti-parasite's proceedings were progressively juridicized by new legislation of the mid 1960s and 1970s. The trend has been to reduce the spontaneous social element and to bring implementation of the legislation under the jurisdiction of the legal professionals in the courts, the local soviets, and the *MVD*. [160] The consequence of this process of institutionalization has meant that direct Party involvement has receded in favor of the more traditional oversight method of organizational supervision. This is not to say that the Party does not cross the "line" between supervision and interference in such cases. It may well do so, especially since the "line" in such cases is considerably more blurred than in a regular criminal case. The point is that anti-parasite's statutes are now administered by reliable, trained, and predictable legal cadres who are constantly subject to Party supervision. Under these

353

circumstances, the "hand" of the Party is screened off from observation, except in those instances when an anti-parasite's proceeding has been convened by the authorities against a non-conformist or dissident. In such cases, the Party's involvement is somewhat more "heavyhanded" and we find ourselves passing into the disputed border zone between Party supervision and Party interference.

The two best documented cases of the application of the anti-parasite's legislation for political, rather than the intended socio-economic reasons, are the Brodskii case of 1964 and the Amalrik case of 1965. In both cases, Party influence was manifested through its supervisory role over the *KGB*. Iosif Brodskii's prosecution was instigated by a retired *MVD* captain serving as a Leningrad *druzhinnik*, a man, who according to Efim Etkind, a defense witness at Brodskii's trial, was used by the Leningrad *KGB* "to organize the 'public indignation' around the parasite Brodskii, his trial, the press coverage and the necessary intrigues. . . ." [161]

In Etkind's opinion as well as in the opinion of another well informed Leningrader, the Regional Party Committee also apparently had an interest in the case of the non-conformist poet Brodskii. According to Etkind the judge in the case was no doubt "rung up that very morning [of the trial], whether by the Provincial [*i.e.*, Regional] Committee or the *KGB*, I don't know." [162] Another scenario has the judge taking the initiative: "In all probability, either before the hearing began or during the adjournment, Judge Savelieva made it her business to look into the case to determine just who was behind it. . . . If Brodskii had been described to her as a 'hardened case' whose punishment was a matter of particular interest to local Party organization, that would all but require of her a finding of guilty." [163] Etkind concurs on the Party's influence on the judge, adding that "her orders were to condemn Brodskii to the most severe sanction allowed in an administative court." [164]

The Party interest and probably indirect involvement through the *KGB* was confirmed after the trial when the three literary witnesses for Brodskii were reprimanded "for political shortsightedness, [and] lack of vigilance" by the Leningrad branch of the Union of Soviet Writers. The reprimands were preceded by speeches by officials of the writers' union, defending the writer Voevodin who had served as the main prosecution witness against Brodskii. Their speeches seemed to echo arguments they probably had first heard in the Regional Party Committee. One speech in particular clearly implied the Party-*KGB* presence behind the trial:

> "There you were, naively refuting the charge of parasitism against Brodskii, but do you really think that's what it was all about? He is an anti-Soviet, he slanders Marx and Lenin in his letters and diaries. . . . But would it have been better for him to have been tried not for parasitism but for anti-Soviet activities and statements? What if his trial

354

had been openly political? According to the existing law, he would not be a free man in some northern village, but a prisoner in a strict regime camp, and he wouldn't thank you for that! He was lucky, they were kind to him—the *KGB* agreed to be indulgent—and let him be tried by an administrative court, so that only an administrative sanction was applied to him. Administrative, not criminal. Surely you see the difference. *And yet there you are, the three of you, turning up at the court and upsetting everything.* You start trying to prove that Brodskii can't be tried for parasitism. That means that you want him to be tried for anti-Sovietism and sent to a camp. It's lucky for you that Voevodin came to the rescue." [165] (Italics added.)

Andrei Amalrik, a dissident historian in Moscow, was also the victim of an anti-parasite's trial manipulated by the *KGB* and, behind it, by the Party which had by the mid-1960s shifted reponsibility for monitoring dissidence from local Party organizations to the *KGB*. [166] In this case, the *KGB* officer assigned to coordinate the surveillance of Amalrik even attended his trial for parasitism. [167] The court retired to consider its verdict and Amalrik recorded:

"They deliberated for forty minutes, though usually, when a 'parasite' is being tried, it takes them no more than five, and sometimes they don't even bother to leave the courtroom. The judge and his assessors were not completely isolated from the outside world during their deliberations; several times I heard the phone ring. . . . Much depended on the attitude of the Moscow department of the *KGB*, which, through Goncharenko, had been in charge of my case from the outset." [168]

Later, while serving his exile term, Amalrik was permitted a brief furlough to visit his dying father. While in Moscow, he sought to recover his confiscated art works and paid a visit to his militia interrogator who immediately disclaimed any responsibility for Amalrik's expulsion from Moscow. Confirming the political involvement in the case, the police official told him "As you know yourself . . . it wasn't me who expelled you but the Committee [*KGB*]. They just wanted to do it through us, though we did our best to get out of it." [169] The investigator added that the head of the Moscow *KGB* had blocked the City Procuracy's attempt to seek a reversal of the exile sentence. Referring to Amalrik, the *KGB* general had said "Let him stay where he is." And that he did until many months later, when his lawyer managed to bypass the local political authorities and get his case before the RSFSR Supreme Court which overturned the verdict as unjustified. [170]

We now come to the final section of the first part on Party supervision over the administration of justice—*organizational supervision over special "campaigns"*. With this topic, we move deeper into the uncharted border region between Party supervision and Party interference. Boundary markings are no longer easily distinguishable, but we are clearly headed towards the unambiguously demarcated frontier of Party interference. When the Party leadership launches an anti-crime campaign, the Party apparatus swings into action with the intensification of its organizational supervision *or* massive, institutionalized interference in the class of cases that are the object of the particular campaign.

At such times, the usual martial spirit of Party discipline is reinforced. Under normal circumstances of the routine administration of justice, a high Soviet Party official has made the analogy between a Party organization exercising its supervisory function and a "military commander on the field of battle" who "mobilizes" and coordinates his "troops" towards the attainment of the objective. [171] The same military metaphor appears in Ulč's memoir, where he points out that a judge's disregard of Party advice on a pending case "brought retribution almost equal to the punishment inflicted upon those refusing to obey an order on the battlefield." [172] In this sense then, one can well imagine that in the heat of a special Party campaign against crime, legal cadres are left little or virtually no discretionary space in which to perform their juridical functions.

Campaign "justice" is a branch of the jurisprudence of political expediency in which the imperatives of *partiinost'* supersede the requirements of *zakonnost'*. Stanislaw Pomorski aptly characterizes the paradox of legal campaigning which involves not just "a fuller or more efficient enforcement of rules," but also "almost invariably . . . substantial *abandonment* of the rules for the sake of expediency." He continues:

> "Anti-crime campaigns, Soviet style, tend to blur the line between administration, governed by considerations of expediency, and adjudication, governed by impersonal, general rules. They represent a major retreat of the due process function in favor of the crime control function. . . . Consequently, during campaigns, *the party apparatus* and the police overshadow regular agencies of prosecution and adjudication and usurp part of their powers." [173] (Italics added.)

Shtromas confirms the above observation that during campaigns "law enforcement agencies at all levels are equally committed to producing a proper response to the Party's demands, and considerations of justice as such are equally irrelevant to all of them." He adds that the appellate process is also affected by the campaign atmosphere and it becomes

> "impossible to overrule a decision in the cases in which Party authorities at higher levels (all-union, republican) have somehow become directly involved or in which the vested interest of law enforcement agencies to get a person convicted significantly surpasses the first local level." [174]

356

The impact of campaigning on the activity of the Procuracy can be extrapolated from Gordon Smith's carefully documented study of Party control over that institution in general. He has traced the increasing trend of the Procuracy to issue "representations" as the principal means of controlling economic violations. Concomitantly, procurators issuing such representations frequently send "information notes" to local Party committees concerning either specific problems or the general status of law enforcement within the jurisdiction of that level of the Party. From 1968 through 1972, Smith reports that the issuance of these notes increased by approximately one-third in the RSFSR, and that the increase in one particular *raion* was as high as 136% in a five-year period. More than half of these information notes were sent to Regional Party committees, confirming that the *obkom* is indeed the principal locus of Party supervisory activity over the administration of justice.

However, even more interesting is Smith's comparison of the data on follow-up action (criminal, administrative, or disciplinary) on procuratorial representations. For all such representations, "subsidiary action" is undertaken in approximately one of every three instances. Although information notes to Party organs represent not quite 10% of all representations, it is interesting to learn that subsidiary action was initiated in three of every four cases of which the Party was informed. Finally, when an anti-economic crime campaign is injected into this Party-Procuracy relationship, the percentage of all cases resulting in subsidiary action rises steeply in the form of administrative punishments. [175]

The implication is clear—when the Party campaigns against crime, the Procuracy responds with sharply higher quantitative indicators of its vigilance. For the executives or individuals who get "caught" during a campaign, the probability of punishment is infinitely higher. For those offenders generally who are subjected to criminal prosecution in the course of a campaign, the judiciary's response to the Party's special demands comes into play. Since the judges are the most visible stratum of the legal system, their job security is commensurately the most vulnerable if they incur the displeasure of their local Party organization or even other legal agencies upon whose good will their incumbency, re-nomination, and "re-election" is dependent. Given the anxiety that this situation must induce, judges tend toward "excessive severity" on the grounds that it is "safer to mete out a more severe punishment than to indulge in leniency and to be censored later for excessive sympathy toward offenders." [176] Therefore, under campaign conditions, one can expect that the normally infinitesimally small percentage of acquittals will shrink to near zero, while the only slightly larger percentage of cases remanded for re-investigation will decline precipitously as the judges strive to meet their "delivery quotas" with stiffer sentences than usual.

The view from the defense table of Party supervision *qua* interference in the conduct of a campaign can be seen in an attorney's remark in the midst of an anti-bribery campaign—"If you have a bribery case these days, you might as well give up." [177] Although the view is somewhat more veiled, the same air of resignation is apparent in a murder trial of the late 1950s. In this case—let's call it the "Apples case"—a man shot and killed a boy who was stealing apples from the orchard on his private plot. Because a Party-led campaign against the "psychology of private property" was then underway, the investigator and procurator classified the act as pre-meditated murder and took the case to trial. An able defense lawyer skillfully argued in court for re-classification of the crime to the article dealing with the use of excessive force in self defense.

The hearing of the case had been announced on the bulletin board at Moscow Law School as one of special interest to future Soviet jurists, and an American exchange scholar attended the trial. During a recess, he congratulated the defense counsel and expressed optimism that the case at the very least would be remanded for re-investigation. The lawyer was generally unresponsive and ill at ease at this approach, and merely said cryptically of the outcome of the trial "You will see." Shortly afterward, the court returned with a verdict of pre-meditated murder under especially "socially dangerous" circumstances and consequently sentenced the accused to death by shooting. Although the death sentence was later commuted by higher court to 10 years imprisonment, the American observer reconstructed the probable rationale for the original sentence rather persuasively:

> "Perhaps the trial we had just witnessed had been intended not only to uphold the law but to point a broader moral.
>
> There was the fact that the Bazhenov case had been singled out for its special interest to law students. There was the whole tenor of Judge Shepilov's initial examination of the accused. There was the prosecutor's concentration on the non-juridical aspects of the case and his obvious complacency about the outcome. There was the surprise shown at the vigor of Bykovsky's defense of the accused. . . . Finally, there was Bykovsky's message to us. Retrospectively, 'You will see' seem to suggest 'no matter that you are persuaded and impressed by my defense, the key to this case lies outside my influence.' "

As for the reduction of sentence, the observer concluded that the trial judge, "aware that the case before him had special political and ideological significance, had overreacted."[178]

Two major campaigns of the post-Stalin period will serve to illustrate the fusion of Party organizational supervision over and political interference in the administration of justice. Khrushchev's anti-economic crime campaign of the early 1960s displayed this fusion most conspicuously. During 1961-1962, the Party mobilized not only the legal system, but the press and the public as well in pursuit of major ecnomic criminals. To get a sense of the prevailing atmosphere then, a Ukrainian survey conducted under more normal conditions reveals that 35% of the judges surveyed and 43% of the procurators responded that they were "subjected to external influences such as the press, the workers' collectives, and organizations of the public" which "played a significant role in their decision-making." [179] Based on a 1963 USSR Supreme Court ruling (*postanovlenie*) and a major *Kommunist* article by Mironov, it appears from Pomorski's following reconstruction that Khrushchev's campaign virtually obliterated the line between Party supervision and Party interference:

> "*Party functionaries massively interfered with prosecutorial and judicial decisions.* The practice became so pervasive that in some provinces it was officially endorsed by the court administrators. Defendants were being convicted without any evidence of guilt whatsoever, or on the ground of legally insufficient evidence. The right to a defense was brutally violated, defense counsel barred from participation, and their motions and arguments ignored. Judges oftentimes were showing unqualified and totally unreasonable severity in sentencing. Appellate and supervisory activities of higher tribunals became paralyzed to a large extent: flagrant violations of the law were widely tolerated by provincial courts and republican supreme courts."[180] (Italics added.)

The tenor of the campaign is best epitomized by the case of Ia. Rokotov and V. Faibishenko, two notorious foreign currency speculators who had managed to bribe a number of senior Moscow police officials before they were arrested. The two ringleaders were sentenced three times, twice retroactively under new legislation post-dating their arrests. On the last occasion, Khrushchev himself apparently intervened personally, demanding retroactive application of the death penalty. Since the two men had already been retroactively sentenced to a longer prison term once, Procurator-General Rudenko and Supreme Court Chairman Rubichev pointed out to the First Secretary that another retroactive sentence revision would further violate "socialist legality" and create a public scandal. Khrushchev reportedly replied to the two jurists in the strongest possible language "What is more important to you, your *zakonnost'* or your *partiinost'*?" Rokotov and Faibishenko were accordingly re-sentenced to death and executed. [181] The message is unmistakable—in major campaigns, the Party does not confine itself to supervision/interference merely in a class of cases, but—given the highly visible public commitment of its prestige—will not hesitate to intervene when necessary in individual cases as well.

Finally, Brezhnev's campaign against hooliganism, launched in the mid-1960's, was less erratic and more routinized, but equally illustrative of the migration from organizational supervision to Party interference in the administration of justice. The catalyst was the new 1966 anti-hooliganism legislation which became the topic of discussion in Party meetings and social organizations, and the object of a major media campaign. The latter culminated in a rare televised press conference of senior legal officials and major print and broadcast journalists. [182] The legal cadres responded with alacrity as the "docks suddenly became filled with hooligans whose acts would have not been considered offenses at all before the decrees were issued. Sentences passed on them were always indiscriminately heavy." [183] In effect, investigators, procurators, and judges rushed to indict, prosecute, and convict under article 206 of the RSFSR Criminal Code (and corresponding articles in other republican codes), in order to ensure their individual "statistical successes" in complying with the Party's then current campaign directives. Ivo Lapenna attended one such trial in Moscow in which a very minor assault, normally subject to no more than one year in jail under the appropriate article of the Criminal Code, was instead classified under article 206/II and the offender sentenced to three years imprisonment. [184]

In this obscure case, one can see how even a garden-variety criminal case can suddenly take on political "coloration," as compliant legal cadres readily respond to Party pressure "from above." This brings us at last into the realm of Party interference in the administration of justice.

Part Two: Party Interference

In spite of Justice Minister Terebilov's disclaimer that "Party bodies do not interfere in the adjudication of criminal" cases and his flat assertion that "Party directives ban any [such] intervention. . .," the evidence of Party interference in the administration of justice—both in "approved" and "disapproved" forms—is overwhelming. [185]

A few years ago in Yugoslavia, a provincial Party secretary asserted the Party's right to intervene in the process of justice with unusual candor for a contemporary Communist Party official. He argued that "judges must be flexible in interpreting the law in cases involving officials or others the party wants ousted," and warned that "if some judges ignore the political stands, they are assuming views in opposition to the League of Communists." [186]

Few Soviet Party officials would be so politically indiscreet in public but, nonetheless, *Party interference in the USSR routinely* occurs in criminal cases involving Party officials and even ordinary members, and, of course, in cases designated by the Party as "political". *More randomly, Party organizations as institutions intervene on an* ad hoc *basis*, in ordinary criminal proceedings where either a prominent offender or victim is involved, when a publically conspicuous crime has been committed, or less frequently, as a manifestation of political conflict between different Party organizations or professional rivalry between different law enforcement agencies.

For the above types of Party intervention, the distinction between implicitly approved and disapproved interference is often blurred. However, the final category of *ad hoc interference in the adjudication of specific cases by*

360

individual Party officials acting on their own behalf, is clearly disapproved by virtue of the fact that these cases are brought to light by the Party itself acting in its supervisory role over the administration of justice.

Party interference in Soviet justice is illuminated by Roy Medvedev's observation, in an obvious comparison with Watergate, that "interference by Party leaders in criminal prosecutions 'is not considered a crime in our country.' " [187] In fact, Party intervention via the *KGB* is actually codified in post-Stalin Soviet criminal procedural law. For instance, articles 117 and 125 of RSFSR Criminal Procedure Code list the *KGB* among the agencies of "inquiry" and "preliminary investigation" respectively, leading Christopher Osakwe to assume "that both articles merely confer discretionary jurisdiction upon the *KGB* to pick and choose those cases in which it might have an interest. A *KGB* decision to intervene in a particular case may, in many instances, be induced by a direct signal from the CPSU itself." [188]

However, more often than not, Party interference probably proceeds without benefit of formal legal sanction. Drawing upon a 1973 article in *Literary Gazette*, René Beermann observes that there are still direct complaints of "trials 'by telephone' or by 'the press,' or critical notes in the press that 'references' or 'testimonials' are sometimes issued by influential institutions or individuals in order to induce the courts to make a particular decision." [189]

In this spirit, Roy Medvedev has observed that "Party officials are investigated only with the approval of their superiors," [190] an assertion in direct contradiction to officially-prescribed practice. The *Handbook* for Secretaries of Primary Party organizations states that a Party member suspected of committing a crime is *simultaneously* subject to the evaluation of his Party status by the PPO and consideration of his criminal liability by the organs of justice. If a Communist has in fact committed a criminal offense, he is to be expelled from the Party under the Party Rules, but the "court does not have to wait for the Party's action" before proceeding. The *Handbook* declares that the "Judicial and investigative organs inform the appropriate Party committees and forward to them the file on the individual committing the crime. But the court adjudicates the case independently of the decisions of the Party organs." [191]

However, Mironov testifies to the fact that a discrepancy exists between the Party Rule "in the books" and Party practice "in action." He records that, as of the early 1960s, a number of Party organizations were "blocking the prosecution of Party members who had committed crimes but had not been expelled from the Party, and ordering the criminal cases against such lawbreakers dropped." In some of these cases when Party members and non-Party members were accomplices to the same crimes, the latter were being prosecuted while the former were protected by virtue of their Party status. Moreover, Mironov reports that Party protection is not confined to its members only, but is also sometimes extended to non-Party individuals as well. As he describes this, "sometimes a Party organization 'delays' criminal proceedings against an individual listed on its *nomenklatura* who has committed a crime."[192]

Mironov concedes that the most common type of Party intervention in the administration of justice occurs on behalf of its members.[193] Despite his sharp disapproval of such practices, the available evidence tends to suggest that *Party interference in cases concerning Party officials and members is highly routinized.* Although such interventions occur in a proportionately small number of cases in general, Shtromas, a former Soviet jurist, insists that the specific Party behavior under criticism by Mironov in 1962, is covertly sanctioned by the Party itself. He writes:

> "To the knowledge of the present writer, there exists a special secret instruction . . . saying that a Party member cannot be convicted by a court before the fate of his Party membership is decided by an appropriate Party committee; as far as members of the *nomenklatura* are concerned, law enforcement agencies cannot do anything about them before the Party authority in charge of the *nomenklatura* on an appropriate level directly, and on its own initiative, commissions a law enforcement agency to deal with a particular member of that *nomenklatura* according to given instructions (the members of *nomenklatura* enjoy in this way a status of relative immunity). The present writer has not seen this instruction personally but has heard reference to it many times; in the USSR, it is an open secret indeed."[194]

The "secret" instruction apparently prevailed in one of the few known, but certainly the most spectacular case of Party interference on behalf of one of its officials. Before he was removed from office in 1972, Vasilii Mzhavanadze, the former Republican Party First Secretary, was the fulcrum of an extraordinary system of political and economic corruption throughout Soviet Georgia. A former *New York Times* Bureau Chief in Moscow "was told by Party members and people with good Party connections, that Mzhavanadze and his wife had become millionaires several times over during his 19-year tenure as Party boss of Georgia." Yet, according to Roy Medvedev, when the new Republican Procurator had " 'more than enough evidence' " to justify searches of Mzhavanadze's apartment and country houses, the Soviet leadership "blocked the investigation."[195] When faced with the possibility of an embarrassing criminal prosecution against a former member of the Politburo, his erstwhile comrades opted in favor of a political cover-up.

Presumably, the Party exercises considerable care in selecting its executive officials, with the result that few such "cases" occur and even fewer come to light, even as cover-ups. However, the number of rank and file Party members running afoul of the law is substantially greater, necessitating a greater frequency of Party interference in such cases. Because some Party organizations are inevitably overzealous in "protecting" their members, higher Party bodies sometimes step in to penetrate lower-level cover-ups primarily on behalf of the Party's image and discipline, and, secondarily in the interest of justice. Hence, more instances of Party interference in cases involving ordinary members tend to come into public view.

As a general rule, the Party tends to obstruct justice only in selected cases concerning members who are in influential or sensitive positions, or on behalf of those Party members who are able to mobilize Party influence in their favor.

In the early 1960s, Party interference on behalf of Party members was so rampant in the Uzbek SSR that the Republican Party Central Committee issued a directive on the "incorrect practice by Regional, City, and District Party committees" of delaying legal proceedings against Party members who had committed crimes from six to eight months and longer. In one case, a *gorkom* took half a year to evaluate the Party status of a former construction executive who, along with others, had illegally misappropriated over 7,000 rubles. In the meantime, criminal proceedings were pressed against his non-Party accomplices while "he remained free." [196]

In a variation on this case which also involved a Party member who held an influential position, an Uzbek *raikom* effectively obstructed justice in the case of one Safarov. He was the head of a retail store, whose arrest for stealing 76,000 rubles the local Procurator had sought the *raikom*'s agreement on. Instead, the Party organ "suggested to the criminal that he repay the theft and gave him 10 days to do so. Safarov availed himself of the *raikom*'s 'kindness' and escaped investigation and prosecution." [197]

In a related case, a gang of thieves from the collective farm "*Pravda*" in the Turkmen Republic were convicted, but the former farm chairman, who was also implicated in the crime, avoided prosecution. By the time the crime was discovered, he had already changed jobs and held an executive position in the Regional construction trust where, as a *nomenklatura* appointee, he was protected by the *obkom* which "delayed" his case by dragging out a decision on his Party status for a year. Only after he began to abuse his official position and defraud the state in his new capacity, was he finally expelled from the Party and arrested. [198]

The Party also intervenes in the justice process to protect its members in sensitive positions. For example, a Latvian militiaman who committed assault and battery against a citizen was subjected only to "Party punishment." [199] Similarly, a District Party committee instructor, guilty of flagrant disturbance of the peace, was merely dismissed from his Party job and received a Party penalty. [200]

Finally, there are those Party members, and even non-Party members, whose positions are neither influential nor sensitive, but who can muster

Party influence to avert the imposition of justice. In an early post-Stalin case of this type, a Kazakh *raikom* blocked the execution of sentence for two convicted thieves and, instead, censured both and expelled them from the Party.[201] In a 1957 "ticket-fixing" case, a driver for the Latvian Academy of Sciences, apprehended driving while intoxicated, avoided full punishment thanks to the intervention of an "Academician Comrade" who petitioned the Riga auto-inspection agency to mitigate his penalty "because this offense will be tried in a Party meeting. . . ." [202]

Party interference in politically sensitive cases is even more predictable and more highly routinized. In fact, the Party appropriates to itself exclusive jurisdiction in matters of political justice, predetermining and scripting for the legal cadres the basic questions of guilt, innocence, and sentencing. The Stalinist "jurisprudence of terror" [203] has given way to a more insidious but less fatal jurisprudence of political expediency which is reflected in the growing body of "case law" that has been steadily accumulating during the post-Stalin years. [204]

Ulč's vivid image of the Party's routine preemption of juridical decision-making in Czechoslovakia during the late 1950s, serves to set the "stage" for Soviet political justice as well:

> "For the majority of the judiciary, political trials, staged nationally or provincially, remained a *terra incognita*. The files were kept secret from all but a handful of carefully selected, taciturn clerks. One wing of the top floor of the Plzeň court was blocked by iron bars, behind which handleless doors, a system of bells and guards guaranteed against unauthorized entry. In all my years at court I never once succeeded in penetrating this sacred realm, and there were not many who did." [205]

In the ČSSR, and no doubt in the USSR as well, the Party's "jurisdiction" comes into play in most major cases of anti-state crimes which are subject to the investigative jurisdiction of the security agencies. In fact, to underscore the politicization of these cases, Soviet defense lawyers require a special "license to defend," subject to approval of the *KGB*, in order to participate as counsel in such cases. [206]

Generally, Party involvement in political cases is modestly veiled from public view, but in the rash of dissent-related cases since the early 1960s, the Party and *KGB* have scarcely bothered even to stand in the "wings" just off the legal "stage." Countless Soviet dissidents have been "summoned" by Party and *KGB* officials, as well as by legal officials, and warned to cease their "anti-Soviet" activities or face prosecution with a predictable outcome. In an unusually candid moment, a Leningrad Party official rhetorically asked a dissident mathematician:

> "What do you want? If you think that we ever will allow somebody to speak and write anything that comes into his head, then this will

never be. We will not allow this. . . . Of course, we don't have enough power to force all people to think the same, but we still have enough power not to let people do things that will be harmful to us." [207]

In a similar "interview" with another dissident, a Moscow *KGB* officer clearly revealed the place of *partiinost'* in Soviet justice even more bluntly:

"I'm not going to argue about what *you* think about any trials conducted by a Soviet court or what *you* think the constitution says. Who do you think you are, challenging what has been decided by the responsible people in the Party? I'll tell you: a cheap little sensation-seeking subversive like the rest of them. And *our* decision is this: we are not going to put up with your dirty activities any longer. Traitors like you will never change. You just have to be dealt with so you can never be treacherous again. One more false move and I guarantee the only thing you'll teach your dirty politics to from then on is trees in a nice Siberian forest." [208]

A former Soviet defense lawyer, with considerable experience at the "political" as well as the ordinary bar, has stated that "Party and *KGB* agencies instruct judges from the center and, in advance, in major [political] cases, or by local ongoing contact during minor ones." [209] The basic types of the judicial form of political justice in the USSR are the low-profile criminal trial *qua* political trial, and the high-profile political trial itself. [210]

The manipulation of criminal justice by the Party and KGB in order to demean and criminalize the political activity of would-be Jewish emigrants and dissidents, is commonplace. False charges are pressed to inevitable conviction with the effect of portraying the victim as a common criminal. Due to *samizdat*, the "case law" in this category is abundant, but a brief sampling will suffice to make the point.

After the Kirov Ballet dancer Valerii Panov declared his desire to emigrate to Israel in 1972, he was summoned for an "ideological interview" at a Leningrad *raikom* headquarters. The Party secretary tried unsuccessfully to dissuade Panov from emigrating and concluded the conversation on the ominous note "we'll do anything we want with you anyway." A few days later, Panov was summoned by a procurator to answer a trumped-up charge of "malicious hooliganism" on the alleged complaint of his mentally unbalanced mother-in-law who opposed her daughter's emigration. Panov managed to escape prosecution on that occasion, only to be framed for petty hooliganism and sentenced to 10 days imprisonment a short time later during President Nixon's visit to Leningrad. [211]

In late 1973, a Jewish carpenter was subjected to criminal prosecution in Daghestan after applying to emigrate. On the basis of an affidavit by one of the people's assessors in his trial now living in Israel, it is clear that Pinkhas Pinkhasov was incontrovertibly framed. During a recess in the trial, the judge sent the assessor, who was Jewish and a Party member, to tell Pinkhasov that "the prosecution would be dropped" if he "were to renounce his desire to go to Israel and were to persuade his wife and children to return to the USSR." The defendant refused this "political" plea-bargain and was convicted and sentenced to five years. [212]

Just a few weeks later in late 1973, a militant "refusenik" was sentenced to a $3\frac{1}{2}$-year term in Kiev on a spurious "malicious hooliganism" charge (art. 206/II of the Ukrainian Criminal Code) of knocking a cake out of a woman's hands. Alexander Feldman had been arrested four times and sentenced to brief terms of detention three times (like Panov, he too was "detained" during Nixon's visit), in less than eighteen months for his pro-emigration activities. These included trying to hand in a petition at the USSR Supreme Soviet building in Moscow. He was clearly a thorn in the side of the authorities, and their entrapment of him in Kiev was so obvious that the prosecution's version speaks for itself:

> "On 18 October 1973, Feldman was near his home in a drunken state when he bumped into a woman carrying a large cake. Feldman then swung his briefcase at the woman and started abusing her. Three young law students of the local authority's legal department who happened to be nearby came to her aid. Feldman resisted arrest and began attacking them, too, tearing the football shirt off of one of them. At that point in time, the head of the Investigation Department of Kiev's Darnitskii Region, Khriapa, just happened to be passing by. Feldman was immediately arrested and taken in Khriapa's car to the police station." [213]

The record is replete with similar cases of the Party's illegal use of ordinary criminal proceedings for the political persecution of dissidents, but the emigration-related case of a Jewish doctor in the Ukraine best epitomizes this type of Party interference and its effect on legal personnel. The physician, the target of concocted charges in connection with his practice, was convicted and sentenced to eight years. In the course of the trial, the presiding judge walked over to the holding pen where the accused was being kept during recesses and said defensively: "Doctor Stern, you are not guilty, but I am forced to convict you. I have a family and children. *I want to live too.*" [214]

The production of political trials by the Party and KGB *is even more routinized.* The "case law" in this area is richly documented and even more abundant than for the criminal trial as surrogate political trial. Once again, the Party and *KGB* orchestrate the instruments of formal legality to achieve the desired effect—the neutralization or exclusion of a real or putative foe from the political arena. In political trials, the problem of judges who "call the district party committee or some other nonjudicial body to ask for advice or for approval of a particular verdict" during the actual trial or while the

366

verdict is being considered, does not often arise. [215] Such trials are pre-planned with the outcome foreordained in the spirit of the phrase "sentenced and tried" from Stalinist times. [216]

In political cases, the Party is involved at every phase from the prevention to the cure of political "deviancy." For instance, the main *samizdat* journal *Chronicle (Khronika)* reported that a local dissident activist was summoned by the First Secretary of the Vladimir *gorkom* who forbade him

> "on behalf of the *KGB* and the party authorities, and in the presence of ... the Secretary of the Chemical Works Party Committee, to make any political utterances whatsoever, threatened him with imprisonment in a concentration camp, and told him that the *KGB* would follow him for the rest of his life."

Failing to deter the young man who styled himself as the founder-leader of "The Union of Independent Youth," the local Party and *KGB* eventually sent him for a "cure" to a psychiatric prison hospital where he died in 1970. [217]

In cases which go to trial under the "political" articles of the criminal code, *KGB* investigators prepare the indictment under the direction of Party authorities, who determine the sentence and verdict well in advance. The procurators and judges involved are then instructed accordingly. In recognition of the role of *partiinost'* in such proceedings, a member of an Armenian separatist group reportedly refused to participate in his trial "on the ground that the judge and the two assessors were Communist Party members and could not be objective about members of another party." [218]

However, in planning a political trial, the Party leaves little to chance. Defense counsel and even the courtroom audience are subject to political screening. We have already referred to the fact that counsel in politically sensitive cases must be cleared by the *KGB*. In spite of this restriction on a Soviet defendant's right to counsel of his own choosing, several distinguished defense lawyers have been admitted to the "political" bar and have defended dissidents as effectively as possible within the narrow space left for a political defender. However, in some cases, this political restriction on choice of counsel has "meant hostile lawyers [who] refused to call witnesses, or take appeals as desired by their clients," while in many political cases it has "meant counsel who would not sharply challenge the prosecution, and generally would confine their efforts to pleas for mitigation of the sentences. . . ." [219]

Similarly, the Party even selects what Solzhenitsyn calls the "semi-public,"[220] the individuals with whom it "packs" the courtrooms at political trials. The following anonymous account describes the procedure followed for the trial of the Red Square demonstrators held in Moscow in 1968:

> "I was summoned to the Party district committee a few days before the trial, together with a few active Party members from our works.

Some thirty people assembled. We were told that a group of people who had slandered the Soviet system were to be tried and that we were to attend the hearing. We were told how to behave: make no notes, sit together, try not to answer questions from others present. If we could not avoid explaining how we got into the courtroom, we should say that it was our day off, that we had gone in by chance that morning and became interested. We were then asked to split into three groups, to decide which day we would be going. I got the second day."

The local Party committee even provided transportation and generally attended to the comforts of the "spectators," just as one would expect an American court to do for a sequestered jury. [221]

Nor does the Party neglect to follow up after the trial and conviction of dissidents. A lawyer, who conducts too spirited a defense in a political case, runs the risk of being denied permission to participate in such cases in the future, and of being subjected to political sanctions as well. In this spirit of vengeance, the advocate who vigorously defended Alexander Ginzburg in the 1968 "trial of the four" was expelled from the Party and dismissed as head of a legal consultation office "for adopting a non-Party, non-Soviet line in his defense." [222]

Finally, in those rare instances when the production of a political trial is halted, the Party is merely exercising its prerogative to terminate a proceeding which it had originally initiated. A dissident Soviet writer, who had been in the custody of the Leningrad *KGB*, was abruptly allowed to emigrate after his 1975 trial. He attributes his good fortune to the impact of Western public opinion on his case which had altered the Party's "cost-benefit ratio" in deciding to bring him to trial. He writes:

> "There is even proof of this: in the first place only a month before my trial, at the termination of the investigation, they planned quite a different denouement for my case: and in the second place, after the trial, in March, those who lecture to the Leningrad Regional Party Committee, commenting on my case at the meetings which are obligatory in such instances, said—and I quote, 'In view of the international situation it was profitable for us to show humanity.' " [223]

However, such displays of "humanity" are the exception to the norm of Party interference in political cases. Speaking in his own defense, Anatolii Shcharanskii recently summarized the norm, saying that he had "no doubt that this court will carry out the instructions given it" and "confirm a predetermined sentence." [224] Or, as Leon Lipson in his commentary on the Shcharanskii trial expressed it,

> "if it's a managed trial from political authorities way above the court, both the sentence and the fundamental determination of guilt or in-

nocence are decided well in advance and the court is moving to unheard music which the court knows very well." [225]

The *second major variation* on Party interference in the administration of justice can be characterized as *ad hoc institutional interference* or the Party's less routine and more random intrusion of its institutional authority into the justice process. When the Party chooses to opt for this mode of interference, there is no doubt that the force of its presence in a proceeding is unmistakably felt by all involved. Roy Medvedev has written that "local [Party] organs exert considerable influence on both judges and procurators at the district level, even more so at the regional level—and at the republican level it is evidently overwhelming."[226] Just as Ulč reported on Czechoslovakia,[227] the intensity and frequency of Party pressure apparently varies in the USSR as well, with "different *oblasts* [regions] and cities" having "distinct reputations for harder or softer Party lines." [228] Whether there is also variation along urban-rural lines is unclear, although a former senior investigator in the office of the Moscow Procuracy during the 1960s has reportedly stated that the Party organizations telephoned frequently in cases of economic crime. [229]

The pattern of *ad hoc* institutional interference in *cases involving prominent offenders or victims* tends to confirm the former investigator's observation. Four of the five cases or examples concerning influential lawbreakers involve economic crimes. The *leitmotif* is expressed by an "expediter" (*tolkach*) using pull (*blat*) on behalf of his enterprise while on a trip to Moscow, who explains to a foreigner why he is not afraid of being charged with an economic crime—"my director will protect me. He is in well with the local party people and has done them many favors. If they touch me, they'll have to purge many others much more important than I am." [230] The speaker is of course describing the familiar local "family circles and mutual protection associations" which dilute central control and are the source of constant irritation to the national Party leadership. [231] However, for our purposes the remark clearly implies that Soviet "collectivism" is the norm in economic crime as well, suggesting one very persuasive reason for the incidence of Party interference in such cases.

In this vein, a small-scale network of complicity among influential officeholders can be glimpsed in a Latvian case, in which a department chief of a local soviet

> "*secured an illegal decision of the District Executive Committee*, by virtue of which ten hectares [approximately 25 acres] of forest meadows were allocated to him, although he had no cattle to feed on them. Ruska thereupon turned over two hectares of the meadows to another official of the Finance Department, Finance Inspector Pigulevs. Pigulevs sold the harvested three tons of hay in the Degu rural settlement, but Ruska sent the hay from the eight hectares to Riga, 'where hay prices are higher.' " (Italics added.)

369

Before initiating prosecution of the two officials, the District Procurator forwarded the case file to the *raikom* where the proceedings terminated with the lesser official fired from his job, while Ruska "was allowed to continue in his office" without even administrative action being taken against him. According to the Latvian press, the comment of local citizens on this case was "the greater the crime, the lesser the punishment." [232]

Party interference combined with "scapegoating" can also be seen in the "Prostitutes' case" of the mid-1960s. Some dozen Moscow college students from politically prominent families staged an orgy with six young prostitutes in the apartment of one of the parents who had left for their country house (*dacha*). The boisterousness of the party grew in volume, the neighbors called the police, and the militia arrested the hosts and their "guests." "Strings" were obviously "pulled" by the students' influential fathers who included "a *KGB* colonel, a judge, an editor, a Party official, a writer and a well-known composer . . . . " The court dealt with the students leniently while the prostitutes, who could tell embarrassing tales, were "scapegoated" as "parasites" and sent out of Moscow:

> "To mitigate their own punishment, the students supplied investigator and judge with every detail of the girls' behavior. But they were not convicted of prostitution; it was established that they lacked steady employment, and they were sentenced as parasites. The older girls were exiled from Moscow for five years. ('Ways will be found to keep them out of the city for at least another five after that,' said the Muscovite who knew the details of the trial.) The younger ones were dispatched to 'the 101st kilometer', one of the best-known penal colonies, populated, it is said, largely by prostitutes from eleven to eighteen, the age of legal maturity."

However, although the Party may intervene to mitigate possible legal sanctions for members of the "new class," Party penalties or non-juridical deprivations may still be imposed on the offenders (and their families in this case) through political channels. This is probably the rule when the scandal is of such magnitude (in terms of its ruble value or public curiosity) that "news" of it leaks out. Although the "Prostitutes' case" was tried *in camera* because of the sensational details and the prominence of the families involved, accounts of the trial circulated in Moscow. Therefore the students, "although open to conviction for Depraved Actions," were administratively punished by expulsion from their institutes while their parents were "subjected to the disgrace and potential damage of personal Party reprimands." [233]

As Medvedev points out, the higher a case ascends politically, the greater the pressure on the legal process. This is certainly the prevailing rule in the remaining two cases of prominent offenders. When the "Godfather" of Georgian corruption was finally brought to justice, "his sentencing in February 1973, contained an open hint that he still wielded influence with the Georgian courts. Whereas much smaller fry elsewhere had been sentenced to death for more modest economic manipulations, Lazeishvili got only 15 years." [234] Finally, at the highest possible level, Minister of Culture Furtseva violated unwritten Party "rules" in building her third *dacha* with construction materials illegally acquired at wholesale prices by way of a political favor. Because of her stature, the possibility of criminal prosecution apparently never even arose. The Furtseva affair was treated as an intra-Party "case," and it was never more than a question of what political and administrative sanctions might be imposed. By appealing personally to Brezhnev when the scandal broke in 1974, Madame Furtseva managed to retain her ministerial post and was only mildly "punished" by the loss of her seat in the Supreme Soviet. She was also required by the Party leadership to reimburse the state for the full price of the *dacha*, a sum of about 60,000 rubles "that she managed to produce within a couple of days. . . ." [235]

The Party is also especially attentive to cases involving prominent victims and will, in such instances, bring its immense influence to bear on law enforcement agencies assigned to a particular case of special interest to the political authorities. This is true to the general axiom that compared with the average crime victim, celebrities and well-placed individuals in most countries usually find law enforcement officials more responsive to their problems generally, and receive prompter, if not better legal service. The mayor of New York is rarely indifferent when a famous actress has her jewels stolen from a midtown hotel or a former Olympic champion is brutally mugged while jogging in a city park, especially when such crimes receive maximum publicity in the local media. Neither the Party authorities nor the "mayor" of Moscow need worry about the press or fear the effect of adverse publicity on their "administration." Nevertheless, the Party apparatus from time to time will act on behalf of a prominent victim by "exerting pressure on the militia" which under the eye of the Party is "forced to find an offender at any cost." Shtromas describes a celebrated instance of this type of *ad hoc* Party interference:

> "When . . . in 1972 the flat of the famous violinist, David Oistrakh, was burgled and goods worth many thousands of rubles were stolen from it, the highest organs of the Party took a personal interest in the case and asked for day-to-day reports on the progress of the case. In response to such an interest, the whole militia force of Moscow was put to work in solving this case, and after several months these efforts brought fruit. The burglars were caught and brought to justice (almost all the stolen goods were also recovered)." [236]

In the same spirit, politicians the world over are equally sensitive to the "fallout" from especially vicious or highly visible crimes within their jurisdiction which capture public attention through the notoriety of such press labels as the "Boston strangler" or "son of Sam." However, the Soviet Party authorities are not likely to read in the morning headlines that a homicidal maniac has struck again. As Hedrick Smith has pointed out after seeing a *samizdat* summary of the basic censor's list, crime data in the Soviet Union is carefully controlled and screened from public view, especially the more dramatic, eye-catching information on dangerous offenders at large, and serious crimes which remain unsolved. [237] Yet, when a Soviet-style Jack-the-Ripper was stalking Moscow in 1974, women were being officially warned at their place of work to exercise caution. However, absent any "hard" information on the progress of the manhunt, the jittery public reacted by producing rumors more frightening than the actual situation.[238]

Hence, uncensored press or not, the Party's image as the leading stratum in society is sometimes challenged by *cases of conspicuous crime.* To such cases, it responds on an *ad hoc* basis by bringing the full weight of its institutional authority to bear on the organs of justice to find the offender(s) and thereby repair the temporary rent in the reputation of the responsible Party agencies.

Thus, the Politburo itself quickly intervened in the case of the explosion at the Minsk radio/television factory in March 1972, which probably killed and injured hundreds of workers. A special government commission was immediately appointed "to ascertain the causes and circumstances of the calamity. . . ." The commission's report was heard in early April and the Central Committee and Council of Ministers issued a joint resolution attributing the cause of the explosion to design errors and negligence in the operation of the factory. The Party-state leadership went on to inflict political and administrative retribution on the responsible executives and officials:

> "V. V. Nikitin, Director of the Leningrad State Design Institute, and L. G. Zakharenko, Director of the Minsk Radio Plant, were dismissed from their positions and expelled from the Party for criminal negligence in the performance of their duties. E. I. Saks, head of the USSR Ministry of the Radio Industry's Chief administration, was dismissed from his position and issued severe reprimand. . . .
>
> The Prosecutor's office is conducting an investigation with an eye to instituting criminal proceedings against the guilty parties." [239]

To further underscore the Party's interest in the case, the central press announced that, following the instructions of the Politburo and Central Committee, the Procurator-General had dispatched to the scene of the criminal negligence his "Senior Investigator of Especially Important Cases" who led "a brigade of twenty investigators." [240] The offenders were tried in the summer of 1972 by the Criminal Division of the USSR Supreme Court on one of the rare occasions when it has sat in original jurisdiction, a point which again adumbrated the Party's *ad hoc* involvement in the case. [241]

Given this degree of Party involvement in a specific case, law enforcement personnel find themselves under overwhelming pressure to apprehend and bring to justice the perpetrator of a crime. Failure to do so would cost the leading personnel involved their jobs. Under the circumstances, if *the* offender cannot be found, *any* offender or credible suspect will do to satisfy the Party's demand for results.

This was what occurred in the Salming case of 1956-1958. Several girls were raped and murdered in a Moscow suburb. Unofficial accounts of the crime circulated among the public and the regional and local Party organs became actively involved in the solution of the crime. Under extraordinary political pressure, the legal cadres produced a "suspect"–the boyfriend of one of the dead girls–and extracted a forced confession under conditions of threat and intimidation. There was virtually no other "evidence." Although Salming repeatedly denied committing the rape-murders and exposed the circumstances under which the confession had been obtained, he was convicted and sentenced to death. Several re-trials and numerous petitions on his behalf by prestigious legal scholars were to no avail since, as Shtromas points out, so many legal officials from the local to the all-union level were finally involved in the case, that the "corporate honor of the law enforcement agencies" had to be defended. Salming was executed in 1958, an innocent victim of the Party's *ad hoc* institutional interference in the process of justice. [242]

In effect, the initial Party pressure in a case initiates a process which gains a momentum of its own because of the political and career consequences for the militia, investigators, procurators, and judges of "reversible error" at any stage in a criminal proceeding which has engaged the Party's attention. Thus, these personnel not infrequently come to the collective defense of their "corporate honor." Shtromas reports a similar case in which two village boys in Lithuania were convicted of murder on the basis of neither evidence nor confessions. The legal cadres involved, including the judges themselves, were convinced that the boys were innocent, but as the trial judge told Shtromas privately:

> "It would be a political mistake to leave this murder un[solved] since it received prominence among the local population, and *the local Party committee* insisted that the trial should be held with whatever evidence available." [243] (Italics added.)

Clearly, it can be seen that the Party intervenes on an *ad hoc* basis in cases of vicious crimes, but it should also be noted that a Party organization will "enter" a case which is merely of high visibility in the community. This occurred in two minor cases, both of which nevertheless evoked a tremendous public outcry–the senseless killings of Zhurka, a tame crane in a small mining town, and Bor'ka, the pet swan at the Moscow zoo. In both cases, local Party committees responded to the clamor of their "constituents." Law enforcement officials were given their marching orders, and the militia swung into action with predictable results. Both "operations" were succesfully concluded with the conviction of a young hooligan gang for the killing of Zhurka and a group of drunken revelers for the destruction of Bor'ka. [244]

Finally, for that rare law enforcement officer who is unresponsive to Party signals generally and a Party command in particular, a summons to Party headquarters awaits him. Since no example of "insubordination" to direct Party command is available, we will have to infer what might lay in store for an insubordinate judge from a "case" of insufficient judicial *partiinost'* in response to unwritten Party norms and indirect pressure. In a case reported by Yuri Luryi, a judge who presided over the trial of a group of construction executives charged with "swindling" state funds and convicted all but one whom he acquitted, was summoned by the Party. When the judge explained the acquittal on the grounds of insufficient evidence, a Party official reportedly asked him: "What are you, a Communist or a formalist?" The judge was reassigned from the criminal bench to the civil bench, [245] and presumably was not re-nominated by the Party for the next judicial election.

A final aspect of the Party's *ad hoc* institutional interference in the administration of justice involves intervention as a surrogate for intra-Party conflict and, occasionally, as the result of professional rivalry between law enforcement agencies. This mode of Party interference is understandably more heavily veiled than most, thus only a few cases and situations are available for discussion. According to Hedrick Smith's sources, secret trials of Party officials are held more often than one would expect, but frequently for reasons of political maneuver rather than considerations of justice. Smith has recorded an unofficial account of one such trial held in the Ukraine in which the Republic Party boss manipulated the criminal justice process for intra-Party purposes:

> "A Soviet journalist informed me of a secret trial against four important Party officials in the Voroshilovgrad province on corruption charges in late 1973, leading ultimately to the forced retirement of the Party boss of that province, Vladimir Shevchenko. But in such cases, Soviet insiders say, *the principal motive is not usually an urge to wipe out corruption within the Party, but internal political feuding among rival Party factions.* In the Voroshilovgrad case, the journalist said, Vladimir Shcherbitsky, the Ukrainian Party chief, had long been looking for a way to remove Shevchenko, an important member of a rival faction, and corruption provided a useful pretext. Many, many other cases of corruption within the Party go unpunished, according to Party members." [246] (Italics added.)

One other more tragic case can be reconstructed from *samizdat* and emigré sources. Sakharov begins the sad tale, "a man by the name of Khudenko, who headed up a 'socio-economic' experiment under Khrushchev, died in prison a year ago [1974]." It seems that I. Khudenko until 1971 ran an experimental state farm in Kazakhstan where he succesfully carried out a number of labor- and cost-saving innovations. In Sakharov's words, "these changes were advantageous to the workers and the nation, but they ran counter to the conservatism, cowardice, and selfish interests of the *nomenklatura*."

This version is confirmed by the emigré economist Aron Katsenelinboigen, who places Khudenko's experiment in the context of the policy struggle by "opposition economists who proposed improving the economy *from below....*" However, he continues, "this position lost out and the Politburo members supporting it were evidently forced to curtail their activity as well." Katsenelinboigen concludes that other members of the Politburo were opposed to the ideas embodied in Khudenko's innovative state farm and "through the direct connivance of certain Politburo members," the experiment was terminated and Khudenko framed on "trumped-up charges." [247]

Sakharov describes the denouement of this classic account of the Party's exploitation of justice as a surrogate arena of intra-Politburo rivalry:

> "When the state farm was closed down by order of a republic ministry, Khudenko filed a petition in court demanding that the workers be paid the money they had earned. He was charged with attempting to damage the state on an especially large scale. The punishment for this kind of crime ranges up to the death penalty. But he was accorded 'clemency' (in view of his past services, his family situation, and the state of his health), and was sentenced to eight years of incarceration— which nonetheless turned out to be a death sentence for him." [248]

Political intervention in the administration of justice, as the result of intra-legal system professional rivalry, tends to straddle an ambiguous demarcation line between "approved" and "disapproved" forms of Party interference. As a general rule, legal cadres defend their "corporate honor" once a case moves upward through the legal system.

In the manner of a mutual aid society, judges rarely acquit, infrequently remand cases for re-investigation, and, at most, will sometimes send back an especially weak and poorly prepared case for "supplementary preliminary investigation" which minimizes the damage to the investigator's and procurator's work records. [249] Another manifestation of "corporate honor" is the collusion and compromise between trial judge, procurator, and appellate judges to "save" a case clearly warranting acquittal on the basis of defense arguments, by giving the defendant a light or symbolic sentence which is sustained on appeal. [250] In effect, to protect themselves individually and collectively from Party displeasure for poor performance, reversals on appeal, or even honest mistakes, the legal cadres close ranks when necessary, preferring a miscarriage of justice to acknowledgement of error.

However, there is evidence to suggest that the vested interest of a law enforcement network at one level in the system may run counter to the institutional interests of legal organs at a higher level. Occasionally, there is even feuding between otherwise complementary legal institutions, as occurred between the Lithuanian Supreme Court and Procuracy in mid-1960s.[251] More often than not, what probably happens is that the vested interests of local justice organs—working in tandem with the local Party authorities—may run contrary to the requirements of national legal policy or higher Party directives and discipline. In such instances, a superior and more powerful Party-justice combination, with its own vital interests foremost in mind, will carry out intervention *qua* supervision over the offending subordinate Party-justice organs. This brings us to the last pages of Section 3 on "Party Control of Justice in Practice."

The final variation on Party interference is *ad hoc individual intervention* in a specific case. When practiced by local Party officials in a way injurious to the Party's image and prejudicial to its interests, this type of interference is clearly disapproved of by higher Party bodies which move in to penetrate the cover-up and discipline the offending local cadres.

The distinction between condoned *ad hoc* institutional interference and uncondoned individual interference is by no means always clear in *cases of institutional/individual Party involvement on behalf of Party members, or for or against* nomenklatura *appointees.* This type of case only comes to light after a higher Party body has ordered corrective action and limited publicity is permitted for politically didactic purposes. Because the Party is naturally protective of its image, published accounts of such cases are carefully tailored to present the given situation in the least unflattering light, which often makes it difficult to discern whether the intervention is the work of a Party institution as an entity, or of an individual Party official acting on his own personal initiative. Whatever the determination, corrective action entails either effecting the rehabilitation of someone unjustly victimized, or ensuring the prosecution of a person illegally exculpated.

In 1973, *Pravda*'s investigative reporters called attention to a case, nominally of institutional victimization, which on closer inspection may have been the result of individual action, possibly a vendetta. Fedorova, director of a children's home in Latvia, "was unjustifiably arrested and criminal proceedings were instituted against her" in violation of the "norms of criminal procedural legislation." *Pravda*'s interest in the case set the Bureau of the Latvian Central Committee in motion. The case was "discussed" by the Bureau, by the *raikom* involved, and by the Collegium of the Latvian Procuracy. As a result, the following corrective actions were taken: 1) the district investigator, for his "superficial and non-objective investigation of the case," received a "reprimand" from his *Komsomol* organization and a "severe reprimand" from the Procuracy's Collegium; (2) the district procurator, for not ensuring "a fully objective investigation," received a "reprimand" from the *raikom* and was dismissed from his post; and last but not least, (3) the *raikom* First Secretary, who had to have been in collusion with the censured legal cadres for the miscarriage of justice to have come to the attention of higher authorities, was criticized by the Latvian Central Committee for failing to exercise "proper control over the activity of the Procuracy," and the *raikom* Bureau was instructed to "strengthen its work with the cadres of administrative organs." [252]

At best, this is probably an example of the absence of institutional interference in the adjudication of an individual case where the complaint of injustice was probably first addressed to the *raikom*; at worst, this is possibly an instance of a District Procurator colluding with a local Party official, or vice versa, employing legal procedure for his/their personal ends.

Similarly, Novikov refers to a number of such cases from the 1960s where the Party behavior involved was clearly not condoned, although, again, the problem of whether the offending behavior was the result of collective decision or individual discretion cannot always be precisely determined. In 1963, the Tadzhik Central Committee publically reprimanded the First Secretaries of three *raikoms* for their "violations of socialist legality." In January 1968, the Krasnodar *kraikom* exercised its supervisory intervention in the case of a schoolteacher, and the Daghestan *obkom* did likewise "in connection with the chauffeur Murzaev who was illegally fired from his job."

While the latter two cases seem to involve victimization as a result of improper local Party interference in the administration of justice, Party "oversight" in the Tadzhik cases concerned exculpation of Party members by virtue of disapproved local intervention on their behalf. The Tadzhik Central Committee decree described how the three *raikom* First Secretaries had interfered in the investigation of criminal cases involving Party members by "illegally protecting Communists who had committed crimes, and attempting to have the charges dropped against some of them." The situation was apparently so blatant that the Tadzhik leadership felt constrained to warn all *gorkoms*, *raikoms*, and lower Party organizations against interference in the process of justice on behalf of Communists, reminding them that

> "Party members possess neither advantages nor privileges apart from the rest of the working people, and are dually accountable for offenses punishable under criminal law—to the Party and to the court." [253]

The explicit reference to individual Party Secretaries in the Tadzhik Republic suggests that each may have intervened on his own initiative but under the guise of an organizational decision. Given the power of a First Secretary *vis-à-vis* the Bureau of the relatively smaller District Party committee, this is quite plausible.

This would seem to have been the situation in an earlier Latvian case in which a determined Party *satrap* intervened with exceptional persistence to shield a Party member and *nomenklatura* appointee from the criminal justice process. In this case, documented by the Latvian press, a District Procurator drew up an indictment for embezzlement against a local executive of the Grain Procurement Agency after his accomplice was caught in the act, and informed the *raikom* of the conclusive results of the preliminary investigation. The *raikom* First Secretary, Comrade Kupčs, responded by ordering the trial of Mishurin delayed until the Party examined the case against him.

As a result of the *raikom*'s independent investigation, "all testimony was found untrustworthy—all except that given by Mishurin." Comrade Kupčs pointedly told the Procurator that if the Party had not intervened, "an innocent man would have been behind bars." However, the Procurator gathered additional evidence and finally convinced the *raikom* that Mishurin was indeed an embezzler, but Comrade Kupčs continued to block a trial on the grounds that the culprit had been sufficiently punished by a "severe [Party] reprimand." Not wanting to "buck" his superior the *raikom* Secretary, the Procurator yielded to the power of *partiinost'* and closed the case.

Later, through a quirk of civil jurisprudence, the District Procurator found an opportunity to re-open the case and sent the file to the Republican Procurator in order to bypass Comrade Kupčs and the *raikom*. The Latvian Procurator then decided that Mishurin should be prosecuted, but the *raikom* again opposed the trial, arguing a novel doctrine of double jeopardy "that a Party member who has already been punished by a Party authority cannot be tried in court for the same case." [254] The final outcome of this case of *ad hoc* individual interference is not known, but we can assume that if higher Party authority exercised its supervisory power and lent its weight to the demand for a trial, then even a patron as dedicated as Kupčs could not have withstood the pressure "from above."

As we turn from cases concerning friends, associates, or subordinates of Party officials to *family cases* involving relatives of Party officials or members serving in influential *nomenklatura* positions, *ad hoc* individual interference in the administration of justice becomes far more visible. These cases almost invariably involve attempts to exculpate an offender who happens to be in the family. In the typical scenario, a ne'er-do-well member of the Soviet upper-class gets in trouble with the law until temporarily "rescued" by an obliging relative. In the final scene, higher power prevails, the "good guys" always win (at least in the published accounts), the criminal offender gets his just desserts, and the interfering relative is punished politically for abuse of influence.

The "plot" varies but this is basically the "storyline" as a "leading case" related by Mironov illustrates:

> "A scandalous incident took place in Tadzhikistan. Comrade Dzhuraev, an investigator in the Kuibyshev district, displayed firmness and

378

stood up against open pressure from the first secretary of the Party *raikom*, Suleimanov, who demanded that he discontinue the investigation of *the rape of two girls by a group of* raikom *officials, among whom was a relative of a* raikom *secretary.*

Soon after the conviction of the rapists, the investigator, Comrade Dzhuraev, was expelled from the Party on the basis of slanderous charges. It was necessary for the CC of the Communist Party of Tadzhikistan to intervene before the *raikom* reversed its decision.

Here is what Comrade Dzhuraev wrote in his statement:

'After the reversal of his decision, Comrade Suleimanov called me to his office and we had a personal conversation, where he said that he had wanted to expel me from the Party because I had not listened to him in the rape case.

Also, he told me that I was still a young man and ought not to ignore the *raikom* first secretary. If I were always to listen to the secretary, then I would become a big and a smart man. The law is the law. But the *raikom* secretary is the *raikom* secretary.' "[255] (Italics added.)

For exerting personal pressure on behalf of his relative, the *raikom* Secretary merely suffered a political reverse. Later, however, Suleimanov intervened on behalf of other offenders as well, taking a "payoff" from one, and was finally himself expelled from the Party, turned over to the courts, and convicted.[256]

The most familiar version of personal intervention involves a parent "pulling strings" to save a wayward or felonious offspring from the consequences of his criminal conduct. *Izvestiia* reported a routine case of this kind which occurred in 1964. A group of youths were arrested in Magnitogorsk on an assault charge. One of the fathers was a Party member and Vice-Chairman of the Executive Committee of the City Soviet. He brought pressure to bear on the arresting officers and managed to get his son off with a nominal fine. A "whistleblower," however, brought the case to the attention of the local press which predictably "condemned the behavior of father and son." In the final "chapter" of this basic version, the Party exercises its supervisory intervention, and "socialist legality," as well as Party discipline triumph in a classic "happy ending:"

"The intervening father received a 'strict reprimand' from the *city's Party committee* and was relieved of his vice-chairmanship, while the delinquent son was ejected from the Komsomol and from the metallurgical institute at which he had been studying." [257] (Italics added.)

The final case is an extreme version of the above. A spoiled child of the "new class" in Tashkent killed a man during a minor altercation, and was sentenced to 15 years in 1971. However, his mother, a Party member and the manager of a large factory, who had gotten him out of minor scrapes before, brought the full weight of her considerable influence to bear on behalf of her son. In *Izvestiia*'s words:

> "She saw to it that the judges were recalled, the investigators dismissed, the case retried, and the sentence reduced. She first tried to intimidate the victim's widow, then bribed her handsomely. The lawyer Razumny drove about in a government automobile to prepare the defense, broke into a hospital ward against doctors' orders to interview a witness, and forcibly broke into another witness's apartment. The witnesses recanted previous testimony and only later told *Party bodies* how they had been pressured into doing so." (Italics added.)

"Mama Abdullaeva," as *Izvestiia* dubbed her, did not stop here. She even managed to persuade her son's friend, a dropout, to take the blame for his crime, and then mobilized her friends, neighbors and employees to sign a parole request and a pardon petition. One of these appeals was signed by

> "Sh. S. Akhmadalieva, *First Secretary of the Kirov Borough Party Committee*. Akhmadalieva knew the whole story. The murder occurred in her borough. She should have told the truth, but the Iulduz firm is situated in her borough also, and she is a close friend of mama Abdullaeva. They had traversed together the difficult path from working women to executives." (Italics added.)

As the story ends, the felonious son is back in jail, and the Tashkent City Party Committee has administered a Party penalty to his mother, who was also dismissed from her prestigious managerial post.

The standard "happy ending," or is it? *Izvestiia*'s correspondent concludes with some troubling questions which go to the heart of "Party control of justice in the USSR." He asks "how all this could have happened . . . who helped protect the criminal and pressured people to evade the law?" Obviously, this was more than a case of "a mother's kisses." The newspaper account ends: "the case cannot be considered closed until all these questions are answered." [258]

4. Evaluating Party Control of Justice in the USSR

Since 1953, destalinization and the far-reaching legal reforms have been reflected in the Party's much greater reliance on law and lawyers to assist in guiding Soviet society through an orderly transition to advanced modernity. To this end, the Party continues to claim hegemony and effective control over the legal process and its personnel as the principal component of the post-Stalin social regulation process in the USSR. But this requires striking a fine balance in cadre management and crime control between the imperatives of policy and the demand for equity—both necessary conditions for effective political control of the administration of justice. The purpose of this essay has been to explore and analyze the available evidence in order to evaluate the proposition that the Party does in fact control Soviet justice. However, since the evidence is mixed, a tentative evaluation will follow:

1. *Political control of justice appears to be assured by heavy Party saturation of legal cadres, but this premise is weakened by increasing professional group self-consciousness among jurists* who have significantly begun to gain access to the Party's legal policy-making process. [259]

2. The intensive elite political socialization process has by now produced several generations of jurists who have internalized *partiinost'* in administering justice or, as Ulč aptly puts it, "The judge becomes his own *apparatchik*." [260] *But internalization is offset by the fact that false reporting has become a way of life in the Soviet legal system* as a means of avoiding the inevitably unpleasant consequences of implementation failure, since the Party does not allocate sufficient resources to fulfill the assigned law enforcement tasks. [261] In effect, "socialist legality" is not fully implemented while Party control over cadres is circumvented, with the result that crime continues to flourish in spite of its "withering away" on paper.

3. *The Party also relies on its formidable control system to check on cadre performance generally, but the apparatus lacks sufficient time and energy to conduct systematically its control mission over law.* Describing the ČSSR, Ulč points out "the means available" to the Party "were ludicrously inadequate to the enormity of the task," compelling them to make choices, with the result that "the judiciary . . . did not rate at the top of their attention." [262] The deployment of Party energies in the USSR reflects a similar downgrading of supervision of the justice process. The upper echelon of the Party's controls over justice is lightly staffed, while the lower rungs rely mainly on *raikom* instructors who are thinly spread and are at best generalists. [263] Finally, at the *obkom* level where Party control over justice is operational, a chronic shortage of qualified instructors for supervising justice exists, since the national leadership assigns legal control a decidedly lower priority than economic regulation among the myriad problems competing for Party attention and time. [264]

4. *Therefore, the Party depends upon an elaborate system of checks and balances within and among legal institutions themselves, to fashion an intra- and inter-regulatory network, but even the strongest "links" sometimes prove unreliable, or fail to fully achieve higher expectations.* Procurators have been known to succumb to the blandishments and the "safety" of local "family

circles" or mutual protection arrangements, while institutional cross-checks such as the "People's Control posts" within the Procuracy are not likely to afford the Party any significant leverage on the problem. [265] Similarly, the Party ordered the re-establishment of the Ministry of Justice in 1970, with the purpose of effecting better supervision of the judiciary and more effective crime control, but the Ministry generally occupies a low status within the state apparatus which has the effect of depressing salaries and probably morale, thus diminishing the quality of personnel and organizational efficacy in general. [266] Moreover, ministerial officials at the center are mainly preoccupied with long range planning, while at the operational levels, supervisory control is often reduced to a "numbers game" of trying to hold down the percentage of reversals and sentence revisions on appeal, or even trivialized to the point of running "socialist competitions" between different courthouses. [267]

5. *At a last resort, the Party keeps legal cadres on a "short leash," but this merely creates job insecurity with its counter-productive consequences of self-protective, compensatory behavior.* Judges are easily recallable through electoral law, while other legal personnel are expressly excluded from standard labor law protection and can be summarily demoted or dismissed for lapses—professional or political—with little difficulty. [268] However, instead of deterring undesirable types of behavior, job vulnerability combined with low salaries at the local level mainly seems to encourage more report padding, "over-implementation" during "campaigns" (which subsequently has to be corrected by higher legal bodies), and a tendency to close ranks around the banner of "corporate honor" as a way of denying error, concealing poor performance, and, of course, protecting jobs from Party retribution. [269]

6. Finally, the Party itself tends to thwart its own mission of controlling justice. The residual Bolshevik nihilism towards law and the traditionally low level of legal culture in Russia as epitomized by the remark "The law is the law, but the *raikom* secretary is the *raikom* secretary," contributes to serious role conflict for the lower Party officials. [270] They are told to "supervise," but have within their reach the power to "interfere" as well in the administration of justice. This conflict is often resolved by the neutralization of the supervisory function, due to the irresistible, temptation to intervene in a specific case under the general pressure "from above" to meet production quotas and avoid embarrassing scandals, or simply because a wayward Party secretary falls prey to the lure of corruption.

Consequently, a great deal of supervisory effort at the upper levels of the Party is expended on countervailing local Party interference which constitutes defiance of the center's legal policies and established Party procedures. The net result is that the Party works against itself with the effect that legal cadre control is diminished, the cause of "socialist legality" suffers, and crime grows like weeds in the cracks in the system.

382

In conclusion, the Party "muddles through" by dominating the "commanding heights" of the legal process through which it manages to co-opt justice but barely contain crime, a compromise which nonetheless ensures the maintenance of a relatively stable equilibrium between *partiinost'* and *zakonnost'* in the increasingly complex post-Stalin society.

NOTES

1. R. Sharlet, "Pashukanis and the Withering Away of Law in the USSR," in S. Fitzpatrick (ed.), *Cultural Revolution in Russia, 1928-1931* (Bloomington, Ind., 1978), pp. 169-188; and N.V. Krylenko's remarks at the 16th Party Congress summarized in M. Lewin, *Russian Peasants and Soviet Power* (London, 1968), pp. 504-505.

2. A. Solzhenitsyn, *The Gulag Archipelago* (New York, 1974), Vol. I.; W. Connor, "The Manufacture of Deviance: The Case of the Soviet Purge, 1936-1938," *Amer. Soc. Rev.*, 37 (1972), 403-13; and R. Sharlet, "Stalinism and Soviet Legal Culture," in R. C. Tucker (ed.), *Stalinism* (New York, 1977), esp. pp. 163-168.

3. R. Sharlet, note 2 above, pp. 168-179.

4. This became especially apparent after the process of "de-Vyshinskyization" got underway following the 22nd Party Congress. R. Sharlet, "Legal Policy Under Khrushchev and Brezhnev: Continuity and Change," in D. Barry, G. Ginsburgs, P. Maggs, (eds.), *Soviet Law After Stalin, Part II, Social Engineering Through Law* (Alphen aan den Rijn, The Netherlands, 1978), pp. 320 *ff*.

5. J. Triska (ed.), *Soviet Communism: Programs and Rules* (San Francisco, 1962), p. 125; and B. Meissner, "Party Supremacy: Some Legal Questions," *Problems of Communism*, 14 (Mar.-Apr., 1965), 28-33.

6. J. Triska, note 5 above, p. 100.

7. D. Barry and C. Barner-Barry, *Contemporary Soviet Politics* (Englewood Cliffs, NJ, 1978), Appendix B, p. 342.

8. *Ibid.*, p. 343.

9. Rule I-1. *Ibid.*

10. R. Sharlet, *The New Soviet Constitution of 1977: Analysis and Text* (Brunswick, Ohio, 1978), p. 78.

11. *Fundamentals of Legislation of the USSR and the Union Republics* (Moscow, 1974), p. 139.

12. P. Juviler, *Revolutionary Law and Order* (New York, 1976), p. 99.

13. R. Sharlet, note 10 above, p. 42.

14. *Ibid.*, p. 64 fn. 52.

15. FPCL, art. 10, and FPCivL, art. 9, note 11 above, pp. 275 and 209, respectively; RSFSR CCP, art. 16, in H. Berman (ed.), *Soviet Criminal Law and Procedure* (Cambridge, Mass., 2nd ed., 1972), p. 210; and RSFSR CivCP, art. 7, in *Grazhdanskii protsessual'nyi kodeks RSFSR* (Moscow, 1968), p. 6.

16. R. Sharlet, "Soviet Legal Policy-Making," in H. Johnson (ed.), *Social System and Legal Process* (San Francisco, 1978), pp. 209-229.

17. R. McNeal (ed.), *Resolutions and Decisions of the Communist Party of the Soviet Union* (Toronto, 1974), Vol. IV, p. 63.

18. *Ibid.*, p. 42.

19. *Current Soviet Policies* (New York, 1962), Vol. IV, p. 68.

20. *Ibid.*, p. 182.

21. *24th Congress of the CPSU* (Moscow, 1971), p. 97.

22. L. I. Brezhnev, *Report of the CPSU Central Committee and the Immediate Tasks of the Party in Home and Foreign Policy: XXV Congress of the CPSU* (Moscow, 1976), p. 98.

23. A. K. Belykh, *Politicheskaia organizatsiia obshchestva i sotsialisticheskoe upravlenie* (The Political Organization of Society and Socialist Administration), (Moscow, 1967), pp. 93-95.

24. V. M. Chkhikvadze, *Gosudarstvo, demokratiia, zakonnost'* (The State, Democracy, and Legality), (Moscow, 1967), pp. 54-55.

25. N. G. Aleksandrov (ed.), *Razvitie marksistko-leninskoi teorii gosudarstva i prava XXII s"ezdom KPSS* (The Development of the Marxist-Leninist Theory of the State and Law by the 22nd Congress of the CPSU), (Moscow, 1963), p. 97.

26. D. A. Kerimov (ed.), *XXIV s"ezd KPSS ob ukreplenii sovetskogo gosudarstva i razvitii sotsialisticheskoi demokratii* (The 24th Congress of the CPSU on the Strengthening of the Soviet State and the Development of Socialist Democracy), (Moscow, 1973), p. 171.

27. *Ibid.*, p. 186.

28. *XXV s"ezd KPSS o razvitii sotsialisticheskoi demokratii, zakonodatel'stva i upravleniia* (The 25th Congress of the CPSU on the Development of Socialist Democracy, Legislation and Administration), (Moscow, 1977), p. 247.

29. M. S. Strogovich (ed.), *Pravovye garantii zakonnosti v SSSR* (The Legal Guarantees of Legality in the USSR), (Moscow, 1962), p. 179.

30. E. Pashukanis, who already had a legal education, was conscripted by the Party to serve as a people's judge in 1918. L. Sheinin was conscripted to serve as a criminal investigator in 1923. See his *Diary of a Criminologist* (Moscow, 1956/1957), pp. 8-11. Similarly, in Communist Czechoslovakia during its formative period, Otto Ulč was routed into law school in 1949 and became a judge in 1953. See his *The Judge in a Communist State* (Athens, Ohio, 1972), ch. 1.

31. P. Solomon, *Soviet Criminologists and Criminal Policy* (New York, 1978), p. 58 and p. 183 fn. 32.

32. P. Juviler, note 12 above, pp. 99-100.

33. M. Lesage, *Les Institutions Soviétiques* (Paris, 1975), p. 13.

34. P. Juviler, note 12 above, p. 125.

35. *Ibid.*

36. F. Barghoorn, "The Security Police," in H. Skilling and F. Griffiths (eds.), *Interest Groups in Soviet Politics* (Princeton, NJ, 1971), pp. 117-118; and F. Barghoorn, *Politics in the USSR* (Boston, 1966), p. 314 fn. 3, and p. 348.

37. F. Barghoorn, *Politics in the USSR*, p. 349; and P. Solomon, note 31 above, p. 204 fn. 12.

38. P. Solomon, note 31 above, p. 204 fn. 14.

39. P. Juviler, note 12 above, p. 126, and p. 231 fn. 18.

40. P. Solomon, note 31 above, pp. 203-204 fn. 8. Generally, legally trained cadres are fairly rare at the Regional Party committee level. See J. Hough, *The Soviet Prefects* (Cambridge, Mass., 1969); P. Stewart, *Political Power in the Soviet Union: A Study of Decision-Making in Stalingrad* (Indianapolis, Ind., 1968); and J. Moses, *Regional Party Leadership and Policy-Making in the USSR* (New York, 1974).

41. N. R. Mironov, *Programma KPSS i voprosy dal'neishego ukrepleniia zakonnosti i pravoporiadka* (The Program of the CPSU and Problems of the Further Strengthening of Legality and the Legal Order), (Moscow, 1962), p. 54.

42. *Sud v SSSR* (The Court in the USSR), (Moscow, 1977), p. 320.

43. R. A. Rudenko (ed.), *Sovetskaia Prokuratura* (The Soviet Procuracy), (Moscow, 1977), p. 236.

44. I. D. Perlov (ed.), *Organizatsionnoe rukovodstvo o sudami v SSSR* (Organizational Guidance of the Courts in the USSR), (Moscow, 1966), p. 182.

45. R. A. Rudenko, note 43 above, pp. 224 and 231.

46. N. R. Mironov, note 41 above, p. 54.

47. *Ibid.* Mironov cites nine cases of senior and middle-ranking legal personnel "recently" so relieved of duties.

48. *Ibid.*, p. 53.

49. N. G. Novikov, *Prokurorskaia sistema v SSSR* (The Procuratorial System in the USSR), (Moscow, 1977), pp. 40 and 43.

50. *23rd Congress of the CPSU* (Moscow, 1966), p. 130.

51. N. G. Novikov, note 49 above, p. 45.

52. A. Ia. Berchenko, *XXII s"ezd KPSS i dal'neishee ukreplenie zakonnosti* (The 22nd Congress of the CPSU and the Further Strengthening of Legality), (Moscow, 1963), p. 60.

53. N. G. Novikov, note 49 above, p. 42.

54. *Ibid.*, p. 45.

55. N. R. Mironov, note 41 above, p. 55.

56. O. Kirchheimer, *Political Justice* (Princeton, NJ, 1961), p. 273.

57. *Ibid.*, p. 272.

58. *Ibid.*, p. 273.

59. *Ibid.*, p. 272.

60. Ulč, *The Judge in a Communist State*, p. 61.

61. *Ibid.*, pp. 66-67.

62. *Ibid.*, pp. 64-65.

63. *Ibid.*, p. 63.

64. *Ibid.*, p. 302.

65. *Ibid.*, p. 68.

66. A. Solzhenitsyn, *The Gulag Archipelago* (New York, 1978), Vol. III, p. 521.

67. Art. 112 of the 1936 Constitution then in effect. G. Feifer, *Justice in Moscow* (New York, 1964), p. 223.

68. *Ibid.*, pp. 248-249.

69. *Ibid.*, p. 328.

70. *Ibid.*, p. 252.

71. A. Solzhenitsyn, see note 66 above, p. 524.

72. V. Terebilov, *The Soviet Court* (Moscow, 1973), pp. 48-49.

73. Following the 25th Party Congress, see "Pod znamenem Leninskoi partii" (Under the Banner of the Leninist Party), *Sov. Iust.*, 1976, No. 7, 1-2; and "Peredovaia–Gluboko izuchat', aktivno propagandirovat' i pretvoriat' v zhizn' resheniia XXV s"ezda KPSS" (Editorial–Closely Study, Actively Propagandize and Implement the Decisions of the 25th Congress of the CPSU), *Sots. Zak.*, 1976, No. 4, 3-5.

74. S. E. Zhilinskii, *Rol' KPSS v ukreplenii zakonnosti na sovremennom etape* (The Role of the CPSU in the Strengthening of Legality in the Contemporary Period), (Moscow, 1977), p. 145; and V. A. Churkin, *Kommunist na strazhe zakona* (Communist on Guard of Law), (Moscow, 1974), p. 34.

75. S. E. Zhilinskii, note 74 above, p. 145.

76. V. A. Churkin, note 74 above, pp. 9-10.

77. *Ibid.*, p. 10.

78. S. E. Zhilinskii, note 74 above, p. 138, and for an example from the Novgorod Region, see p. 139 fn. 1.

79. "XXIV s"ezd KPSS o vospitanii uvazheniia k zakonu" (The 24th Congress of the CPSU on the Teaching of Respect for the Law), *Sov. Iust.*, 1972, No. 13, 1.

80. V. A. Churkin, note 74 above, p. 42.

81. *CDSP*, 24 (1972), No. 6, 9.

82. E. Trofimov, "Vliianie partiinogo komiteta na organizatsiiu pravovoi propa-

gandy" (The Influence of A Party Committee on the Organization of Legal Propaganda), *Sots. Zak.*, 1976, No. 8, 3.

83. *Komsomol'skaia Pravda*, July 28, 1971, 2.

84. N. Ia. Sokolov, *Organizatsiia pravovoi propagandy* (The Organization of Legal Propaganda)), (Moscow, 1974), pp. 30-31.

85. *CDSP*, note 81 above.

86. N. Ia. Sokolov, note 84 above, p. 31.

87. W. Connor, *Deviance in Soviet Society* (New York, 1972), p. 117.

88. N. R. Mironov, note 41 above, pp. 57-58.

89. J. Collignon, *Les Juristes en Union Soviétique* (Paris, 1977), pp. 351-352 fn. 87.

90. V. A. Churkin, note 74 above, p. 41.

91. S. E. Zhilinskii, note 74 above, p. 105.

92. D. Barry and H. Berman, "The Jurists," in H. Skilling and F. Griffiths, note 36 above, p. 311 fn. 57.

93. N. G. Novikov, note 49 above, p. 44.

94. *Ibid.*

95. *Ibid.*

96. P. Solomon, note 31 above, p. 183 fn. 33.

97. S. E. Zhilinskii, note 74 above, p. 105.

98. *Ibid.*, p. 137.

99. *Ibid.*

100. N. R. Mironov, note 41 above, p. 54.

101. J. Collignon, note 89 above, p. 320; and Y. Luryi, "The Soviet Legal Profession: Notes of an Ex-Soviet Lawyer," lecture at Union College, Schenectady, NY, Feb. 10, 1976.

102. *CDSP*, 24 (1972), No. 3, 27.

103. *Ibid.*, 23 (1972), No. 52, 20. On disciplining procurators, see N. R. Mironov, *Ukreplenie zakonnosti i pravoporiadka v obshchenarodnom gosudarstve—Programma zadacha partii* (The Strengthening of Legality and the Legal Order in the All People's State—A Programmatic Task of the Party), (Moscow, 2nd ed., 1969), pp. 222-223.

104. *Ibid.*, p. 222.

105. N. R. Mironov, note 41 above, pp. 53-54.

106. A. Sakharov, *My Country and the World* (New York, 1975), p. 44.

107. N. R. Mironov, note 103 above, p. 222.

108. *Ibid.*, p. 223.

109. A. Shtromas, "Crime, Law, and Penal Practice in the USSR," *Review of Socialist Law*, 3 (1977), No. 3, 303.

110. *Ibid.*, p. 310.

111. *Ibid.*, pp. 309-310.

112. Y. Luryi cited in P. Juviler, note 12 above, p. 119.

113. A. Shtromas, note 109 above, p. 310.

114. *Ibid.*, pp. 310-311.

115. J. Collignon, note 89 above, p. 322.

116. S. E. Zhilinskii, note 74 above, p. 143.

117. N. R. Mironov, note 103 above, p. 79.

118. A. Shtromas, note 109 above, p. 313.

119. *Ibid.*, and pp. 315-316 fn. 21.

120. *Ibid.*, pp. 320-321.

121. N. R. Mironov, note 103 above, p. 224.

122. H. Smith, *The Russians* (New York, 1976), pp. 97-98. For additional details, see Y. Brokhin, *Hustling on Gorky Street* (New York, 1975), pp. 34-37.

123. See *CDSP*, 26 (1974), No. 46, reprinted in *The USSR Today* (Columbus, Ohio, 3rd ed., 1975), pp. 6-7.

124. N. R. Mironov, note 103 above, p. 77; and P. Juviler, "Mass Education and Justice in Soviet Courts: The Visiting Sessions," *Soviet Studies*, 18 (1967), No. 4, 494, fn. 4.

125. See P. Juviler, *ibid.*, pp. 495 and 497 for his suggestion that the procurator may also initiate and coordinate a "visiting session" as well.

126. *Ibid.*, p. 509.

127. No data is available on acquittals, but A. Shtromas reports that in 1971 appellate courts "quashed 4% of all convictions" for not being based on appropriate evidence. See A. Shtromas, note 109 above, p. 315. For an account of a rare acquittal, see An Observer [pseudonym for G. Feifer], *Message from Moscow* (New York, 1971), pp. 135-137.

128. G. Feifer, note 67 above, pp. 108-110.

129. *Ibid.*, p. 110.

130. R. Sharlet, "The Trial of Ushakova," *The Milwaukee Journal*, Feb. 8, 1964, 12.

131. P. Juviler, note 124 above, especially pp. 506-508.

132. *Ibid.*, pp. 504-05.

133. P. Juviler, "Law and the Delinquent Family," in D. Barry, G. Ginsburgs, P. Maggs, note 4 above, pp. 219-220.

134. N. R. Mironov, note 41 above, p. 65.

135. P. Juviler, note 12 above, p. 76.

136. P. Juviler, note 124 above, p. 505.

137. R. Sharlet, note 130 above.

138. G. Feifer, note 67 above, pp. 278, 283, and 286.

139. He eventually fell back into his old ways and moved to Tula where he finally went "straight." See A. Unger, *The Totalitarian Party* (Cambridge, UK, 1974), pp. 137-38.

140. *Ibid.*, p. 65.

141. D. Hammer, "Law Enforcement, Social Control and the Withering Away of the State: The Recent Soviet Experience," *Soviet Studies*, 14 (1963), No. 4, 381.

142. R. Conquest (ed.), *The Soviet Police System* (New York, 1968), p. 64.

143. G. Morgan, "People's Justice," in Z. Szirmai (ed.), *Law in Eastern Europe*, Vol. 7, (Leyden, 1962), pp. 65 and 66-68.

144. P. Juviler, note 12 above, p. 79.

145. V. A. Churkin, note 74 above, pp. 44-45.

146. D. Hammer, note 141 above, p. 390; and on the rejuvenation of the comrades' courts, see "Sovershenstvovat' deiatel'nost' tovarishcheskikh sudov" (Perfect the Activity of the Comrades' Courts), *Sov. Iust.*, 1977, No. 10, 4-5. For comments on and a translation of the new 1977 Statute by W. E. Butler, see *Review of Socialist Law,* 3 (1977), No. 3, 325-343.

147. N. R. Mironov, note 103 above, p. 147.

148. P. Juviler, note 12 above, p. 82.

149. A. Targonsky, *A Research Project on Legal Consciousness Carried Out by the All-Union Institute for the Study of the Causes of Crime* (summary in English, text in Russian) Hebrew University Soviet Institutions Series, Paper No. 9 (Jerusalem, 1977), p. 78.

150. P. Juviler, note 12 above, p. 82. For an account of the two cases which were heard at the law school, see R. Sharlet, "Russia's Courts of Public Pressure," *The Nation*, Jan. 18, 1965, pp. 55-57 and 68.

151. G. Feifer, note 67 above, p. 127; and R. Sharlet, *ibid.*

152. R. Sharlet, note 150 above.

153. G. Feifer, note 67 above, pp. 115-120.

154. *Ibid.*, p. 123.

155. P. Juviler, note 12 above, p. 80.

156. G. Feifer, note 67 above, p. 123.

157. Generally, legal professionals were critical of peer justice institutions and lobbied succesfully for tighter professional control over them.

158. M. Armstrong, "The Campaign Against Parasites," in P. Juviler and H. Morton (eds.), *Soviet Policy-Making* (New York, 1967), p. 172.

159. N. R. Mironov, note 103 above, p. 189.

160. P. Juviler, note 12 above, pp. 92-94.

161. E. Etkind, *Notes of a Non-Conspirator* (New York, 1978), p. 90.

162. *Ibid.*, p. 101.

163. R. Blum, "Freeze and Thaw: The Artist in Soviet Russia-III," *The New Yorker*, Sept. 11, 1965, p. 213.

164. E. Etkind, note 161 above, pp. 100-101.

165. *Ibid.*, pp. 107-108.

166. R. Medvedev, *On Socialist Democracy* (New York, 1975), pp. 160-161.

167. A. Amalrik, *Involuntary Journey to Siberia* (New York, 1970), pp. 8 and 108.

168. *Ibid.*, p. 11.

169. *Ibid.*, pp. 207-208.

170. *Ibid.*, pp. 206, 208, and 283.

171. V. A. Churkin, note 74 above, p. 33.

172. O. Ulč, note 30 above, p. 63.

173. S. Pomorski, "Criminal Law Protection of Socialist Property in the USSR," in D. Barry, G. Ginsburgs, and P. Maggs (eds.), *Soviet Law After Stalin, Part I, The Citizen and the State in Contemporary Soviet Law* (Leyden, 1977), p. 235.

174. A. Shtromas, note 109 above, p. 314.

175. G. Smith, "Procuratorial Supervision of Economic Violations in the USSR," in D. Barry, G. Ginsburgs and P. Maggs, note 4 above, pp. 282-285.

176. R. Beermann, "The Rule of Law and Legality in the Soviet Union," *Review of Socialist Law*, 1 (1975), No. 2, 99.

177. G. Feifer, note 67 above, p. 248.

178. J. Azrael, "Murder Trial in Moscow," *Atlantic Monthly,* May 1962, 63-69, esp. 68-69.

179. R. Beermann, note 176 above, p. 102.

180. S. Pomorski, note 173 above, p. 235.

181. Y. Luryi as cited in R. Sharlet, note 2 above, p. 156 fn. 3. See also Y. Brokhin's account, note 122 above, ch. 1, esp. pp. 42-43.

182. See G. Smith, "Campaigns Against Crime in the USSR," elsewhere in this volume, p. 148.

183. A. Shtromas, note 109 above, pp. 323-324 fn. 41, and 311 where he points out a similar pattern of heavy sentences against drunken offenders in the course of recent anti-drunkenness campaigns.

184. I. Lapenna, "The Contemporary Crisis of Legality in the Soviet Union: Substantive Criminal Law," *Review of Socialist Law,* 1 (1975), No. 2, 79.

185. See page 335-336 above.

186. R. Anderson, "Yugoslav Purges of Party Step Up," *New York Times*, Sept. 24, 1973, 9.

187. H. Smith, note 122 above, p. 99.

188. C. Osakwe, "Due Process of Law and Civil Rights Cases in the Soviet Union,"

in D. Barry, G. Ginsburg, and P. Maggs, note 173 above, pp. 220-221 fn. 76.

189. R. Beermann, note 176 above, pp. 103-104.

190. H. Smith, note 122 above, p. 99.

191. *Spravochnik sekretaria pervichnoi partiinoi organizatsii* (Handbook of the Secretary of a Primary Party Organization), (Moscow, 2nd ed. rev. & supp., 1967). pp. 210-211.

192. N. R. Mironov, note 41 above, p. 55.

193. *Ibid.*

194. A. Shtromas, note 109 above, p. 322 fn. 37.

195. R. Medvedev, note 166 above, pp. 161-162; H. Smith, note 122 above, pp. 98-99.

196. N. R. Mironov, note 41 above, p. 55.

197. *Ibid.*

198. *Ibid.*, p. 56.

199. K. Grzybowski (ed.), *Highlights of Current Legislation and Activities in Mid-Europe*, 6 (1958), No. 7-8, 276.

200. *Ibid.*, pp. 276-277.

201. G. Smith, *The Soviet Procuracy and the Supervision of Administration* (Alphen aan den Rijn, The Netherlands, 1978), p. 15 and p. 32 fn. 9.

202. K. Grzybowski, note 199 above, p. 277.

203. R. Sharlet, note 2 above, pp. 163 and 164-168.

204. R. Sharlet, "*Samizdat* As a Source for the Study of Soviet Law," *Soviet Union*, 1 (1974), No. 2, 181-196; R. Sharlet, "Dissent and Repression in the Soviet Union," *Current History*, 73 (1977), No. 430, 112-117 and 130; and R. Sharlet, "Dissent and Repression in the Soviet Union and East Europe: Changing Patterns Since Khrushchev," *International Journal*, 33 (1978), No. 4, 763-795.

205. O. Ulč, note 30 above, p. 138.

206. Y. Luryi, "The Role of Defence Counsel in Political Trials in the USSR," *Manitoba Law Journal*, 7 (1977), No. 4, 307-312.

207. B. Gwertzman, "Soviet Scientist and Party Aide Clash on the Freedom of Ideas," *New York Times*, Oct. 8, 1970, 2.

208. G. Feifer (pseudonym), note 127 above, p. 63.

209. Y. Luryi paraphrased by P. Juviler, note 12 above, p. 119.

210. R. Sharlet, "Dissent and Repression in the Soviet Union and East Europe," note 204 above, 768-771.

211. V. Panov, *To Dance* (New York, 1978), pp. 311-317 and 321-326.

212. T. Taylor *et al.*, *Courts of Terror* (New York, 1976), pp. 168-169 and 56-58.

213. I. Lapenna, note 184 above, p. 81.

214. A. Stern (ed.), *The USSR vs. Dr. Mikhail Stern* (New York, 1977), p. 2.

215. R. Medvedev, note 166 above, p. 151.

216. E. Loebl, *Sentenced & Tried: The Stalinist Purges in Czechoslovakia* (London, 1969). In the USSR, both A. Amalrik in the 1960s and Iu. Orlov in the late 1970s were apparently told or given a clear indication by their investigators of what their respective sentences would be in advance of trial.

217. P. Reddaway, *Uncensored Russia* (New York, 1972), pp. 405-408, esp. 406.

218. C. Wren, "Separatist Group Tried in Armenia," *New York Times*, Nov.17, 1974, Sunday ed., Sec. 1, 9.

219. T. Taylor, "Trials and Tribulations in Soviet Courts," *New York Times*, June 26, 1975, 39.

220. A. Solzhenitsyn, note 66 above, p. 515.

221. N. Gorbanevskaya, *Red Square At Noon* (New York, 1970), pp. 76-77.

390

222. P. Reddaway, note 217 above, pp. 84-85.

223. V. Maramzin, Letter-to-the-Editor, *New York Review of Books*, Jan. 22, 1976, 50.

224. A. Shcharanskii's brother's notes on the trial as read on the NBC television special of July 20, 1978; and A. Shcharanskii's "final word" to the court before the verdict and sentencing, see *New York Times*, July 15, 1978, 1.

225. L. Lipson quoted from the NBC television special on the Shcharanskii trial, note 224 above.

226. R. Medvedev, note 166 above, pp. 161-162.

227. See page 333 above.

228. R. Kaiser, *Russia* (New York, 1976), p. 123.

229. As passed on to this author by J. Hazard on the basis of his discussion with the emigré jurist.

230. Justan, "Some Aspects of Soviet Reality," *Problems of Communism*, 11 (1962), No. 1, 55.

231. M. Fainsod, *How Russia Is Ruled* (Cambridge, Mass., Rev. ed., 1964), p. 237.

232. K. Grzybowski, note 199 above, p. 277.

233. G. Feifer, *Our Motherland and Other Ventures in Russian Reportage* (New York, 1973), pp. 168-169.

234. H. Smith, note 122 above, p. 98; and see also p. 347 above.

235. H. Smith, note 199 above, pp. 99-100.

236. A. Shtromas, note 109 above, p. 307.

237. H. Smith, "In Moscow, The Bigger the News, The Smaller the Story," *New York Times Magazine*, Dec. 1, 1975, Sun. ed., 107.

238. H. Smith, note 122 above, pp. 346-347.

239. *CDSP*, 14 (1972), No. 13, 28.

240. Y. Luryi, note 206 above, p.,311.

241. P. Juviler, note 12 above, p. 100; and L. N. Smirnov *et al.* (eds.), *Verkhovnyi sud SSSR* (The Supreme Court of the USSR), (Moscow, 1974), pp. 22-23.

242. A. Shtromas, note 109 above, pp. 308-309.

243. *Ibid.*, p. 323 fn. 40.

244. *Ibid.*, p. 308 and p. 322 fn. 39; and "Contemporary Life in Russia Reflected in Furor Over Swan," *St. Louis Post-Dispatch*, Sept. 26, 1965, 1 and 4. To satisfy the public demand for justice in the swan case, the trial was held in a "visiting session" with 1,600 people in attendance while the press ran a strident campaign against the swan "murderers."

245. Y. Luryi cited in R. Sharlet, note 2 above, p. 156 fn. 3.

246. H. Smith, note 122 above, p. 99.

247. A. Katsenelinboigen, *Studies in Soviet Economic Planning* (White Plains, NY, 1978), p. 66.

248. A. Sakharov, note 106 above, pp. 46-47.

249. A. Shtromas, note 109 above, p. 313 and p. 324 fn. 44; and R. Beermann, note 176 above, pp. 100-101.

250. Y. Luryi's lecture, note 101 above.

251. A. Shtromas, note 109 above, pp. 314-315.

252. N. G. Novikov, note 49 above, p. 46.

253. *Ibid.*, pp. 45-46.

254. K. Grzybowski, note 199 above, pp. 273-274.

255. N. R. Mironov, note 41 above, pp. 58-59 as translated in D. Hammer, *USSR: The Politics of Oligarchy* (Hinsdale, Ill., 1974), p. 360 from another publication by N. R. Mironov in which he described the case almost identically.

256. N. R. Mironov, note 41 above, p. 59.

257. W. Connor, note 87 above, pp. 96-97.

258. *CDSP*, 23 (1971), No. 37 reprinted in *The USSR Today* (Columbus, Ohio, 2nd ed., 1973), pp. 101-102.

259. See M. Lodge, *Soviet Elite Attitudes Since Stalin* (Columbus, Ohio, 1969) *passim*; see also P. Solomon, note 31 above, and D. Barry and H. Berman, note 92 above.

260. O. Ulč, note 30 above, p. 69.

261. A. Shtromas, note 109 above, pp. 302-303 and p. 324 fn. 43.

262. O. Ulč, note 30 above, p. 62.

263. *Raionnyi komitet partii* (The District Committee of the Party), (Moscow, 1972), pp. 196-197 and 204-207.

264. On the "insignificant number of men with legal training in the administrative elite," see J. A. Armstrong, "Tsarist and Soviet Elite Administrators," *Slavic Review*, 31 (1972), No. 1, 17-18.

265. See *Spravochnik narodnogo kontrolera* (Handbook of the People's Controller), (Moscow, 2nd supp. ed., 1977), pp. 273-274.

266. A. Shtromas, note 109 above, p. 322 fn. 36.

267. See A. Nikulin, "Rol' partiinoi organizatsii Ministerstva iustitsii RSFSR v sovershenstvovanii stilia i metodov raboty apparata" (The Role of the Party Organization of the Ministry of Justice of the RSFSR in Improving Style and Methods of Work of the Apparatus), *Sov. Iust.*, 1974, No. 13, 10-11; and K. Fedorenko, "Rabota otdela iustitsii s kadrami" (The Work of the Justice Section [of a Regional Soviet] With Cadres), *Sov. Iust.*, 1976, No. 8, 7-8.

268. A. Shtromas, note 109 above, pp. 320-321 fn. 21.

269. On the salaries of legal personnel, see M. Matthews, *Privilege in the Soviet Union* (London, 1978), p. 32; and on the general tendency towards "over-implementation," see M. McAuley, *Politics and the Soviet Union* (New York, 1977), pp. 278-279. On correcting for over-zealousness, see J. Azrael, note 178 above, p. 69; I. Lapenna, note 184 above, pp. 79-80; and S. Pomorski, note 173 above, p. 236.

270. On legal nihilism, see R. Sharlet, note 1 above. The "*raikom*" quotation is from pages 378-379 above.

THE RELATIONSHIP OF THE CPSU
TO THE MINISTRY OF JUSTICE

Boris Meissner

Prof. Sharlet has given in his paper a first-rate survey of the manner and methods whereby the Party exercises control over the judiciary.

As I concern myself primarily with constitutional and municipal law, I should like to supplement this exellent analysis merely with a few comments on the Ministry of Justice in relation to the new Constitution of the USSR and the new law on the Council of Ministers of the USSR. In my judgment, the significance of the Ministry for the guidance and control of the judiciary should not be underestimated.

Prof. Sharlet has justly drawn attention to the change which the Soviet Union has undergone since the death of Stalin. At the same time, there has been no alteration in principle in the relationship between the Party and the judiciary.[1] Thus, the judiciary in the Soviet Union has always been viewed as an instrument of the Party and government rule, as well as an integral part of the apparatus of political leadership.

The political function of the Soviet judiciary under the "Stalin Constitution" was very clearly expressed by N. N. Polianskii in the following words:

> "The provisions of Art. 112 of the Constitution that the judge is independent and subject only to the law, does not mean that he is also independent of the political directives of the party and the Soviet government ... the courts in our Soviet state count as a part of the apparatus of political leadership and appropriate measures are taken to insure that the courts actually do serve as instruments of the policy of the Communist Party and the Soviet government ...
>
> The essence of judicial policy consists of implementing in practice the policy of the Communist Party and the Soviet government in the forms peculiar to the judiciary and employing the means available to the judicial authorities ...
>
> The policy of the Communist Party determines the activity of the administration of justice through its directives and through the medium of the special organs of the Soviet regime. The resolutions of the party are unconditionally binding upon all officials of the State and therefore upon the judiciary."[2]

The dependence of the judiciary within the framework of the one-party system flows from the claim of the CPSU to be the sole personification of the whole people and thus in the name of society to be superordinated over the state and its organs. One-party rule, ideologically legitimated in this way, and possessing an autocratic character, finds far clearer expression in the new USSR Constitution of October 7, 1977,[3] than was the case in the old union Constitution.

It is not only that the CPSU is referred to three times (in the Preamble and Arts. 6 and 100) and not twice as previously; the decisive thing is that it is given greater prominence and dealt with at greater length. The CPSU's power monopoly, which in effect means the unlimited authority of its oligarchical topleadership, now has the whole of Article 6 devoted to it, whereas it was formerly mentioned only tucked away in Article 126, which dealt with the freedom of association.

Article 6 states:

"The Communist Party of the Soviet Union is the leading and guiding force of Soviet society, and the nucleus of its political system and of state and social organizations. The CPSU exists for the people and serves the people.

Armed with Marxist-Leninist doctrine, the Communist Party determines the general perspective of the development of society and the course of the domestic and foreign policy of the USSR, directs the great creative activity of the Soviet people, and imparts a planned and scientifically-sound character to their struggle for the victory of communism.

All party organizations function within the framework of the Constitution of the USSR."

Just as the state of the "dictatorship of the proletariat" has given way to a "state of the whole people," so the CPSU has changed from a "vanguard of the working people" to a "vanguard of the whole people." It is now termed the leading and directing power of the whole Soviet society and the kernel of the whole political system and not only as previously of all state and social organizations. It not only lays down the general perspectives of social development, but also fixes "the internal and foreign policy lines of the USSR," i.e., of the state. This characterization reveals the full totality of its power claims, for which basically only a totalitarian form of one-party rule could be fully appropriate.

The important thing that clearly emerges from the formulation of Article 6 is that the CPSU claims the directing authority with respect to the internal and foreign policy of the Soviet state. From this, it follows that limits are imposed in advance on the political operation of the particular organs of the state on various levels listed in the Constitution.

394

That applies not only to the Supreme Soviet of the USSR and its Presidium, whose power has been strengthened by the new Constitution, but also to the Council of Ministers of the USSR.

By virtue of the change that the Party Statute of 1961 underwent at the 23rd Congress of the CPSU, it is the Politburo which between the brief plenary meetings of the Central Committee takes those basic decisions on internal and foreign policy which in a parliamentary-democratic system are taken by the government. Just as the CC Secretariat stands at the summit of the party-administration, so the Council of Ministers of the USSR, though formally designated the government of the Soviet Union, is in fact merely the summit of the state administration. This also applies to its Presidium, which is named for the first time in the Constitution, and which judging by its composition is allotted the status of an economic cabinet.

In the law of July 5, 1978, on the Council of Ministers of the USSR,[4] it is expressly laid down that the Council of Ministers carries out its activity within the framework of its competence in accordance with the decisions of the Communist Party, *i.e.*, that the basic decisions taken by the supreme Party organs and thus primarily by the Politburo are binding upon it legally and not merely in practice. This applies in equal measure to the 62 ministries which belong to the Council of Ministers under the law of July 5, 1978 (arts. 23 and 24). These include the Ministry of Justice which is of especial importance as the Party's instrument for directing the administration of justice.

Presenting the draft of the new law of the USSR Council of Ministers, Kosygin paid tribute to the CPSU as "the leading and guiding force of Soviet society" and told the Supreme Soviet:

> "In all its work, the Council of Ministers is being guided by the clear-cut and well founded political line of the Party's Central Committee and the corresponding instructions from the Politburo of the Central Committee, as regards both general problems of principle and concrete questions of our Communist construction."[5]

Krushchev had contributed significantly to the greater autonomy of the organs for the administration of justice by abolishing the union Ministry of Justice in 1956 and subsequently also having the Justice Ministries in the union and autonomous republics dissolved.[6] Their tasks were taken over partly by the courts and partly by the new-formed Juridical Commissions, which on the republican level also exercised certain administrative powers.

The recentralization of administration under Khrushchev's successors led to the reestablishment of the union-republican Ministry of Justice under the decree of August 31, 1970.[7] The former dualism in the field of the administration of justice was removed. The tasks of the new Justice Ministry were laid down in their main lines under a decree of August 12, 1971.[8] The details were specified in the regulation "On the Ministry of Justice of the USSR" of March 21, 1972.[9] It is apparent from these decisions that they essentially reestablish the system of direction in the field of justice as it existed prior to Khrushchev's administrative reforms.

The competence of the Justice Ministry has been broadened as compared with the situation before 1956. It is now responsible for the following tasks:

1) The organizational guidance of the courts of the union republics, and the military tribunals in particular, with the aim of the greatest possible strengthening of "socialist legality" and a successful struggle against crime;

2) participation in the work of codification and current legislation;

3) "methodical guidance" of legal work in the national economy, *i.e.*, guidance of the *iuriskonsul'ty*;

4) guidance of the notariat and the legal expertise institutions;

5) the "general guidance" of the *kollegiia* of attorneys and the office of civil registration;

6) the training and allocation of legal cadres;

7) the propagation of legal knowledge and the explanation of legislation;

8) the promotion of legal scholarship and the evaluation of its research results;

9) the establishment of international contacts in questions of law.

With respect to the relationships of subordination, it is significant that, in para. 4 of the regulation, the Justice Ministry of the USSR, the Justice Ministries of the union and autonomous republics, the justice departments of the local soviets, the notary offices, scholarly research and teaching institutions, as well as other subordinate institutions and organizations are characterized as "a unified structure of the Ministry of Justice of the USSR."

The responsibility of the Justice Ministry *vis-à-vis* the Party is given particular prominence in the regulation.

The Party's capacity to exercise influence on the judicial organs and the administration of justice manifests itself primarily in two fields. On the one hand, alongside supervision of the employment and service of judges, which does not embrace disciplinary competence with respect to them, the Justice Ministry exercises a very far-reaching supervision over their professional activity.[10] Even if the Justice Ministry may not issue directions on the decision of a particular case, it nevertheless has extensive possibilities to interfere in questions of detail. It constantly makes use of these either through direct measures "for improving the organization of the work" of the courts or through indirect influence "for perfecting the activity of the courts."[11] This manipulation of professional activity makes it possible for the Party to influence the administration of justice through the medium of the Justice Ministry.

On the other hand, personnel policy within the framework of the *nomen-*

klatura system [12] offers the Justice Ministry the possibility of ensuring that the administration of the law will be malleable. In the field of cadre policy, the Party is able to directly enforce its wishes, insofar as important leadership positions are involved.

Within the apparatus of the Central Committee of the CPSU, responsibility for the Justice Ministry is exercised by the Department of Administrative Organs. It cannot issue directives to the Justice Ministry, but it can express recommendations. As a rule, these are supposed to be transmitted by the CC Secretariat to the Justice Ministry *via* the Administrative Office (*upravlenie delami*) of the Council of Ministers. The Head of the Administrative Office (*upravliaiushchii delami*), who now has the status of a member of the Council of Ministers, is obliged by virtue of the law of July 5, 1978 (art. 32) to ensure the carrying out of the decisions of the Party and not only of the government. Should the Justice Ministry not be prepared in a particular case to meet the recommendation emanating from the CC Secretariat, it has the possibility of bringing the matter before the Chairman of the Council of Ministers of the USSR. The Prime Minister, whose power position has been considerably strengthened by the law of July 5, 1978, might as a rule settle the matter himself, since article 29 offers him the opportunity of doing so. In disputes cases, the CC Secretariat could involve the Politburo with the matter, and the latter's decision on the matter would be final and binding upon the Justice Ministry.

In the field of personnel policy, there exists a considerably closer link with the responsible CC department. The Central Committee Department of Party Organs directly decides on appointments to important positions. Its approval is required on the filling of leadership positions of lesser importance.

Also important for the Justice Ministry is the General Department of the Central Committee, into which the Special Sector—responsible for the secret police and secret materials—was incorporated following Stalin's death.

The Minister of Justice is appointed and released by the Supreme Soviet of the USSR or its Presidium on the proposal of the Chairman of the Council of Ministers. This offers the Prime Minister the opportunity of exerting considerable influence on this personnel decision. The same applies to the appointment of the deputy ministers of justice. Should there be differences of opinion on the person to be chosen for a post, this is also a case where the final decision rests with the Politburo.

The comparative weakness of the Party political standing of the Justice Ministry is revealed by the fact that the Minister V. I. Terebilov enjoys only the status of a candidate member of the CC. The President of the Supreme Court of the USSR, L. N. Smirnov, on the other hand, has been a member of the CC since the 25th Party Congress and, as such, enjoys the same status as the Procurator General of the USSR, R. A. Rudenko. Altogether, the police has a higher percentage representation than the judiciary and the procuracy combined.

NOTES

1. Comp. R. Maurach, *Das Rechtssystem der UdSSR* (Tübingen, 1953); *idem*, "Die richterliche Unabhängigkeit in der UdSSR," in *Fragen der Gerichtsverfassung im Ostblock* (München, 1958), p. 5 *ff.*; B. Dirnecker, "Die Entwicklung des sowjetischen Strafverfahrens- und Justizverfassungsrechts seit dem Tode Stalins," *Recht in Ost und West*, 1 (1957), 225 *ff.*; L. Révész, *Justiz im Ostblock: Richter und Strafrecht* (Köln, 1967); H. T. Schmidt, "Die Gerichtsverfassung der Sowjetunion," *Recht in Ost und West*, 18 (1974), 8 *ff.*; F. C. Schroeder, "Systematische Stellung und Gegenstand des Gerichtsverfassungsrechts in der Sowjetunion," *Jahrbuch für Ostrecht*, IX (1968), No. 1, 99 *ff.*; M. Fincke, "Das Justizverfassungsrecht," *Osteuropa-Recht*, 24 (1978), 113 *ff.*

2. N. N. Polianskii, "Sovetskii ugolovnyi sud kak provodnik politiki partii i sovetskoi vlasti," in *VMU (ser. obshch. nauk.)*, 11 (1950), No. 4, 125 *ff.*, cited from B. Dirnecker, *Recht in Ost und West* (Pfaffenhofen, 1955), p. 71 *ff.*

3. For text see *Ved. V.S. SSSR* 1977, No. 41, item 617.

4. For text see *Ved. V.S. SSSR* 1978, No. 28, item 436.

5. *Izvestiia* July 7, 1978.

6. Comp. S. Kucherov, *The Organs of Soviet Administration of Justice: Their History and Operation* (Leyden, 1970); B. Meissner: *Russland unter Chruschtschow* (München, 1960), p. 17 *ff.*

7. Comp. G. Brunner, "Die Reform der sowjetischen Justizverwaltung," *Recht in Ost und West*, 15 (1971), 149 *ff.*

8. *Ved. V.S. SSSR* 1971, No. 33, item 332.

9. *Sobr. Post. SSSR*, 1972, No. 6, item 32.

10. Comp. Brunner, *op. cit.* p. 150.

11. Comp. Kucherov, *op. cit.*, p. 318 *ff.*

12. In considering the CPSU's *nomenklatura* system, one needs to distinguish between the basic *nomenklatura* (*osnovnaia nomenklatura*) and a registration-and-control *nomenklatura* (*uchetno-kontrol'naia nomenklatura*). In the former, appointments to *nomenklatura* positions are made by the Party organs and, in the case of agencies of the state, are then approved by the responsible organs of the state. In the latter, the Party organs must be consulted by the state organs in the filling of *nomenklatura* posts. Along with these, there exists the general *nomenklatura* of all leading personnel (*rukovodiashchii sostav*) which also includes posts of lesser importance, which may be directly filled by the state organs, including organs of the judiciary.

"DOES SOVIET LAW MAKE SENSE?" RATIONALITY AND FUNCTIONALITY IN SOVIET LAW: AN EPILOGUE

F. J. M. Feldbrugge

Five years of work on Soviet law and the participation of about fifty scholars from both sides of the Atlantic have resulted in three volumes, together containing forty longer and shorter studies. The complete opus of *Soviet Law After Stalin* can be said, without exaggeration, to cover developments in all major areas of Soviet law during the last quarter of a century. The editors could have stopped at that and announced to the public: if you want to know what happened and is happening in Soviet administrative, criminal, family law, etc., here it is. They felt, however, that the presentation of such a vast array of facts and views called for at least some attempt at generalization. For practical reasons, the person who was closest to final editorial arrangements appeared the most convenient candidate for the job.

It is not my task to write a book review. I do not intend critically to investigate the original frame of reference of the organizers and to compare it with the findings of the contributors. Neither do I propose to criticize the work of individual contributors. I believe that the most useful thing to be done at this stage is a collection of observations and an attempt to interpret them in their totality. It follows that this overview will strongly reflect personal choices and interests. The comparative lawyer will not be struck by the same phenomena as the sociologist, and the political scientist will notice again different things in these volumes. My perspective, for what it is worth, is that of somebody with a legal training and a keen interest in broad social and political developments in the Soviet Union, seen in connection with different but comparable developments in the West.

What is the most obvious is often not the most striking, but still it is best to begin by observing the general air of stability and institutional maturity which surrounds Soviet law sixty years after the Revolution. The legislative achievement since 1958 has been most impressive, but the innovative element is modest and has in fact been decreasing since the early stages of the reform, when the most urgent changes in the criminal law were brought about. The Fundamental Laws of the later years were basically consolidations of the *status quo*. Whether the present stability of Soviet law is more apparent than real is a question to which we shall return presently.

The student of individual branches of Soviet law has to explain changes in the law which are effected within a comparatively short time-span, and this forces him to pay attention to current events which influence such changes. The emergence of new leaders, even a new minister of justice, pronouncements of Party congresses and Central Committee meetings, the outcome of debates in the highest echelons of the legal world, international events, etc., may have their immediate effect upon specific institutions in individual branches of law. These short-wave modulations, important as they are, should not make the observer unaware of the undercurrent of longe-range developments.

In this respect, Soviet law displays another kind of stability which one might call diachronic. The foundations of Soviet society were laid in the years following the Revolution, and the structure of legal-economic relationships within this society was completed in the early 1930s. Anything that happened afterwards can be (but need not be) described as variations on the same theme. Ginsburgs, in his discussion of court reforms (Vol. I, pp. 99-100), points to the cyclical character of certain legal innovations. Smith's study of Procuracy campaigns in Vol. III shows how many of these may be regarded as recurrent manifestations of identical and temporary changes in the application of the law. A study of the secret police function may show extensions (as registered by Luryi in Vol. I, p. 108) and recessions, but such judgments should not replace the much more basic observation that the secret police function—whether somewhat larger or somewhat smaller—remains central and vital, now as ever, in the Soviet state.

However, we have spoken not only of the stability but also of the maturity of Soviet law. If the basic institutions of Soviet law have shown a great amount of permanence over at least six decades, the same cannot be said about its spirit, its attitude, its orientation. Many moods have prevailed in Soviet law since the Revolution, and none except the most recent one can be called mature. What I mean by this is not that Soviet law is at present more effective, or better, or morally more attractive than in the past, but that it reflects a more experienced and sober estimate of the actual potential of a legal system. That the Soviet leaders have come to a more realistic appraisal of what can be achieved through law, is illustrated by Juviler's studies on Family law in Vols. I and II. Smith's examination of procuratorial campaigns (Vol. II, especially pp. 285-287) shows that the real objective of the Procuracy in such cases is not to eliminate certain violations altogether, but rather to control them and keep them at acceptable levels.

Even more comprehensively, Pomorski's studies on *ochkovtiratel'stvo* (Vol. II) and the administration of socialist property (Vol. III) seem to indicate that the Soviet government has actually resigned itself to a degree of legal control of the economy that is far less than complete. In this respect, it is customary to talk of the "second economy" of the USSR, but, as has been remarked,[1] this concept is by no means precise. If it is taken to refer to the

400

non-socialized sector of the economy, it encompasses activities which are completely legal, albeit politically somewhat less respectable, such as production from private plots. It is better to distinguish first between the official and the unofficial economy. The official economy then would be the economy established and regulated by the state, *as it actually operates*. This addition is important because, as has been observed by Pomorski (Vol. II, pp. 306-308), the Soviet economy is organized according to a machine model: "One center of political and economic disposition, supplied with maximum relevant data and equipped with infallible tools for their interpretation, makes all the important decisions. The decisions, conveyed to various parts of the system, are faithfully carried out, and their implementation is quickly and exactly reported back to the center." The reality of the official economy, as is amply demonstrated by Pomorski, is quite different from this model. To quote one example, the practice of *ochkovtiratel'stvo* ("eyewash") is indicative of the lack of central control of what happens at the provincial and local level. The official economy therefore does not operate as a single and centrally controlled machine, but as a collection of only partially coordinated machines. Then there is the officially tolerated private economy, of which the private plots in agriculture are by far the most important. Finally, there is the illegal parallel economy. It is of course difficult to define the latter in quantitative terms; it certainly is quite extensive. It is present in many areas of the economy, but especially in building, the production of consumer goods, and the provision of services. If unofficial (*samizdat*) reports may be believed, certain economic activities have almost completely been taken over by the parallel economy (*e.g.*, small repairs). Even large scale economic activities may be accommodated in the parallel economy by making use of the façade of a socialist enterprise (*cf.* art. 153 of the RSFSR Criminal Code).

Although the existence of the second economy is officially recognized only as a criminal phenomenon which must be eliminated, the evidence suggests that underneath there is more tolerance, at least for certain manifestations of the second economy. Where the state considers itself unable to provide a particular product or service, it may decide that the cheapest solution (in terms of both political and economic costliness) is to let the second economy take over. In other cases indeed, when a certain activity is taken off the list of forbidden professions, it even passes from the parallel into the official economy.

Behind this increasing acceptance of the economic facts of life one might discern the leadership's final resignation in the face of the "private property mentality." In a last effort, Khrushchev lashed out against this "survival of the past," but after he had left, his work was undone (*cf.* Barry, Vol. I, p. 25). Millenarian aspirations have effectively been abandoned, and law is not any longer an instrument to bring about a metamorphosis of society. But this does not mean that law does not retain other functions and even acquire new ones. In his essay on the new Soviet Constitution of 1977, Hazard described fortress-building as one of its purposes: the Communist Party monopoly as vanguard leader, the totally-owned state economy, the state apparatus paralleling the Party, centralized economic planning and industrial management are the building blocks of a wall that will prevent, hopefully, society's drift into the "post-industrial era" (Vol. II, p. 19). If the preponderant role of Soviet law is protective and conservative, then we may expect increased appreciation of its officials. In a climate of activism, mobilization, and directed radical change, lawyers and their procedures tend rather to be seen as brakes on progress and obstacles to change. It is precisely the affirmative attitude of the government towards the legal profession which is stressed by several authors (Luryi, Vol. III, pp. 178-182; Zile, Vol. III, pp. 230-231; Butler, Vol. III, pp. 239-242). Also, as Barry points out, there is a general trend in favor of a larger role of law and the courts in public administration, especially where the state comes into contact with the individual citizen (*cf.* Barry, Vol. I, pp. 25-26; *id.*, Vol. II, pp. 253-259). The new constitutional provisions concerning this sphere of contact (especially Articles 49 and 58, the rights to criticize, make proposals and complaints to public bodies and officials) support this trend.

In this connection, it should be noticed that certainly not all indicators reflect the law's conservatism. Transformation of the collective farm structure and public participation in administration are singled out by Hazard as areas of planned social change in the view of the 1977 Constitution (Vol. II, pp. 9-11). In his discussion of the new constitutional provision on judicial review, Barry mentions its "growth potential" (Vol. II, p. 258; see also Barry, Vol. III, p. 17): regardless of the intentions of Brezhnev's Constitutional Commission, Article 58 may become the starting point of unforeseen developments. Sharlet speaks of "the Party's much greater reliance on law and lawyers to assist in guiding Soviet society through an orderly transition to advanced modernity" (Vol. III, p. 380), and this is not the same as maintenance of the *status quo*.

An understanding of the basic trends in Soviet law will, of course, be helped by relating them to the development of the Soviet political system. Both Soviet ideologists and Western observers are in agreement about what lies at the basis of this system. It is the same as Hazard's building blocks, which were mentioned above. But the political system which has been constructed—or rather which has grown on the foundation of these blocks—is not something which is candidly discussed in official Soviet literature. Nevertheless, unofficial literature from the Soviet Union, no matter what its political color is, is quite outspoken on this point.[2] According to it, the Communist Party, itself a rigidly hierarchically organized elite, has appropriated all political and economic power in the country, and uses this power, behind a façade of socialist ideology, to further its own interests.

If we look at Soviet law with this view in mind as a working hypothesis, two observations may be made. The first one is that there is little or nothing in Soviet law which contradicts it. The second one is that there is neither much positive corroboration. If the hypothesis is correct, then we must conclude that the privileged position of the Party elite is not strongly reflected in Soviet law, at least not visibly. Low visibility of privileged positions can easily be explained by the prevalence of administrative discretion. There is no need to spell out privilege publicly, as long as the rules are vague and their application is left to an administration which is not bothered by the glare of publicity. This, of course, is precisely the situation in the USSR. The possibility of administrative discretion is stressed by authors who deal with topics which provide scope for administrative privilege: housing and budgetary allocation (Barry, Vol. I, p. 27; Maggs, Vol. III, p. 101). Loeber, in his study of the position of the CPSU in Soviet financial law (Vol. III), mentions not only administrative discretion in this field, but also administrative discreetness.

If one accepts the analysis of the Soviet political system, as given by a wide variety of Soviet dissidents, many aspects of Soviet law can be explained which remain puzzling contradictions in a more simplified view of Soviet law and society. The most common example of such a simplified view, quite current outside the USSR and strongly promoted by Soviet propaganda, is that of a nation, morally united behind its political leaders—the Communist Party—which, in its turn, is motivated by its desire to build the communist society and rear the new communist man. How can the following phenomena be accommodated in such a view?

1. The proclamation of a regular system of courts, adjudicating in public and the existence of special, secret courts (Luryi, Vol. I, p. 107).

2. A marriage and family legislation which has shown little consistency over the sixty odd years of Soviet power, and which, at least at present, is hard to reconcile with the teachings of Marx and Engels (*cf.* Juviler, Vol. I, p. 121).

3. Central economic planning and management, and toleration of local practices which run counter to these (*cf.* Maggs, Vol. III, pp. 102, Pomorski, Vol. II, p. 307).

4. Prohibition of certain economic activities, and maintenance of a system of economic management which actually promotes and encourages such violations (*cf.* Smith, Vol. II, p. 286).

5. The profession of an ethical code which rejects self-interest as a guiding force for the individual, and maintenance of a labor ethic which lays great stress on material incentives (*material'naia zainteresovannost'*), but which is translated in practical terms as almost no carrot and very much stick. Notwithstanding its high-sounding talk about the exalted moral outlook of Soviet man, the Soviet system takes no chances and as no other relies on

coercion, threats, and all kinds of punitive action to make its citizens toe the line (*cf.* Pomorski, Vol. II, p. 308).

6. The awareness of the leadership that a wholesale organizational reform of the economy is inevitable (*cf.* Pomorski, Vol. III, p. 124), and the stubborn refusal to go anywhere beyond bureaucratic tinkering.

7. Most comprehensively, the unresolved dilemma between legality and political expediency, which was the central theme of the entire project, which underlies the whole of Soviet law, and about which more will have to be said.

All these points, and many other similar ones, have been noted by participants in the project and they have often been characterized as dysfunctionalities. This is indeed what they are, seen within the narrower context of a particular branch of law. It does not seem to make much sense, for instance, to reward substandard production economically, and punish it at the same time by making it into a criminal offense. The government or the legislator is apparently not acting quite rationally in such cases. It may be explained, at least in part, by adherence to what was previously called the machine model of legislation: the government, believing to be fully informed and fully in control, is under the impression that the operation of certain legislative levers will automatically bring about the desired result. Of course, this particular kind of legislative blindness is not typical for the Soviet government only.

However, the dysfunctionalities enumerated above cannot be fully explained in this way. In fact, they disappear to a great extend, *i.e.*, they can be explained as rational behavior, if we adopt a more sophisticated view of the Soviet political system.

In many of the studies of the project, the underlying dilemma of Soviet law has been defined as one between legality and arbitrariness. Indeed, this formula was articulated in the "Framework for Analysis," appended to the first volume. But arbitrariness suggests irrational behavior, the unpredictable whim of the tyrant; this is demonstrated by the editorial introduction of Vol. I which juxtaposes "law" and "force," "legality" and "terror," and "legality" and "violence." If one recognizes the existence of an hierarchically organized elite, which strives towards the acquisition of all political and economic power, legitimizing its position through ideological claims, then the dilemma can be defined as one between legality and political expediency, and much of the irrationality of official behavior disappears.

As an example, let us look at *ochkovtiratel'stvo*, as analyzed by Pomorski in Vol. II. Distorting accounts concerning plan fulfillment is penalized by criminal law, but in practical terms, encouraged and sometimes almost dictated by economic law. Probably, the practice could be eliminated easily, as Pomorski suggests, by radical changes aimed at leaving more initiative and freedom to operational entities. An alternative and opposite method would be to increase repression of "eyewash" by means of supervision and punishment to such an extent that potential delinquents would be effectively discouraged. In fact neither solution is chosen, and the motives are not difficult to guess. The radical changes in the organization of the economy, which would be required to make "eyewash" unrewarding for potential delinquents, would involve sacrificing a significant element of central control by central authorities, and, of equal importance, the ideological commitment to central economic planning. Increasing sanctions, on the other hand, would lead to economic disorganization, and what could be even more disastrous, would weaken the coherence among the various echelons of the ruling class. All of them know that certain illegal practices, provided they are kept within certain limits, are necessary to keep the economy functioning as it is. If the present leadership, which itself undoubtedly has practised *ochkovtiratel'stvo* in the past and may still be doing so now, seriously disturbs this balance, this would be experienced at lower levels as a breach of an implied agreement, an undermining of the job security which goes with dedicating oneself to the Party. In this light, the present middle course: fighting "eyewash" energetically, but ineffectively, becomes a rational policy.

In the cost-accounting between legality and expediency, ideology assumes a key role. Is it true, as Hazard says (Vol. II, p. 28), that ideology is not dead? I wonder whether the images of life and death are wholly applicable to ideology. A dead ideology can become alive again when new faithful appear; a dead ideology, which does not provide effective motivation for political behavior anymore (and I believe that Soviet ideology is dead in this sense), may still provide legitimation for a particular regime, and be alive in that sense.

The question has been asked why the Soviet regime does not abandon its ideological claims and transform itself, in the words of an irreverent Frenchman, from a USSR into an All-Russian Police and Military Empire?[3] The advantages in terms of economics and social psychology would be enormous. The country could rationalize its economy and greatly increase its wealth and economic well-being. Moreover, as numerous dissidents have pointed out, the most indigestible aspect of Soviet life is not a relative lack of freedom, nor material backwardness in comparison with the West, nor the privileged position of the Party elite, but the necessity to live with the omnipresent lie. Abandonment of the ideology would eliminate this necessity.

But of course the regime is unable to drop the ideological pretense, as Besançon remarks, because then the real state of affairs in the country would become manifest to the whole population, the regime would have lost its legitimacy, and the situation would become untenable, if only because of the exacerbation of national tensions. Incidentally, these tensions, which are so fundamental for an understanding of the present political scene in the Soviet Union, are only dimly reflected in Soviet law. In these volumes, one may find some reference to the national question in Juviler's chapter on demography (Vol. II, pp. 212-213).

Behind every system of law there is an anthropology—an explicit or implicit set of assumptions about man. Although Marxism has always been more concerned with society and social relations, the rudiments of an anthropology are certainly there. The liberation of labor should produce a society in which man would freely and selflessly contribute his labor for the common good, in a general atmosphere of mutual trust. As a lucid and little known work by Michel Heller demonstrates, exactly the opposite happened in the Soviet Union.[4] A few months after the Revolution, the first concentration camps were established; labor became forced labor, an instrument of discipline for the entire population, and of punishment and extermination for millions. With this came the ambivalence towards *material'naia zainteresovannost'*; according to the ideology, Soviet citizens would contribute to their society freely, enthusiastically, generously. In fact, they have to be motivated by the fear of sanctions and by small rewards, and the leaders know this. The elite itself is motivated by self-interest, and of course the leaders know that. But although this is clear to almost everyone, it cannot be admitted because this would be tantamount to admitting the uselessness of the system itself.

These considerations prompt the following thoughts concerning the future of Soviet law. The Soviet political system, and the legal system which is an appendix of it, have shown considerable tenacity over the years and a flexibility of response to changed circumstances, albeit within a strictly defined perimeter. As long as the present political system prevails, one may expect about the same mix of legality and political expediency as is characteristic of Soviet law at present. This means that there will be changes in favor of modernization, efficiency, foreseeability of law, and orderliness of legal procedures, provided such changes do not seriously affect the power monopoly of the Party elite. Over a longer period, when the contemporaries of Stalin have left the stage and *if* the present ideological-political system becomes unable to accommodate and digest the accumulating economic, national, and psychological stresses in the country, then and then only one may expect more fundamental systemic adaptations which will, of course, entail major legal reforms as well.

For the time being, the conclusion is that the legal system which emerged as a result of the October Revolution may not appear overly attractive to other nations, but that the political system which Soviet law reflects may appear to have its advantages to the leaders of some nations.[5]

NOTES

1. Gregory Grossman, "The 'Second Economy' of the USSR," *Problems of Communism*, 1977, No. 5, 25-40.

2. *Cf.* my *Samizdat and Political Dissent in the Soviet Union* (Leyden, 1975).

3. Alain Besançon, "L'avenir de l'URSS," *Pouvoirs* 1978, No. 6, 111-115.

4. Michel Heller, *Le monde concentrationnaire et la littérature soviétique* (Lausanne, 1974).

5. The only part of Soviet law which commends itself for imitation may be the fiscal system which, as Maggs points out (Vol. III, p. 000), works efficiently and cheaply, and causes minimal pain to the citizen. Undoubtedly, however, the successfulness of this system is a corollary of a state-owned and state-run economy. But even if Soviet tax law is not suitable to be imitated all by itself in countries with a different economic system, it may still teach the lesson that collection of taxes at points which are less visible to the ordinary citizen has enormous advantages.

INDEX

412

COLOPHON

letter: Press Roman 10/12, 8/10
setter: Pecasse-Eurozet
printer: Samsom Sijthoff Grafische Bedrijven
binder: binderij Callenbach
cover-design: J. v.d. Bijl

414

ERRATUM

To the regret of the publishers, a misprint has been discovered in:
Soviet Law After Stalin. Part III: Soviet Institutions and the Administration of Law, (D.D. Barry *et al.*, eds.), No. 20 (III) in the series *Law in Eastern Europe,* (F. J. M. Feldbrugge, ed.).

In the article by D. A. Loeber,
page 114, line 33 reads:
". . . it appears that discreetness, a characteristic feature. . ."
This sentence should read:
". . . it appears that discretion is a characteristic feature. . ."